2023
The Supreme Court Review

"Judges as persons, or courts as institutions, are entitled to no greater immunity from criticism than other persons or institutions . . . [J]udges must be kept mindful of their limitations and of their ultimate public responsibility by a vigorous stream of criticism expressed with candor however blunt."
—*Felix Frankfurter*

". . . while it is proper that people should find fault when their judges fail, it is only reasonable that they should recognize the difficulties. . . . Let them be severely brought to book, when they go wrong, but by those who will take the trouble to understand them."
—*Learned Hand*

THE LAW SCHOOL

THE UNIVERSITY OF CHICAGO

Volume 2023

The Supreme Court Review

EDITED BY

DAVID A. STRAUSS

GEOFFREY R. STONE

JUSTIN DRIVER

AND WILLIAM BAUDE

THE UNIVERSITY OF CHICAGO PRESS

CHICAGO AND LONDON

The Supreme Court Review, Volume 2023

Published annually by The University of Chicago Press.
www.journals.uchicago.edu/SCR/

© 2024 by The University of Chicago

All rights reserved. No part of this book may be reproduced in any form by any electronic or mechanical means (including photocopying, recording, or information storage and retrieval) without permission in writing from the publisher. Chapters may be copied or otherwise reused without permission only to the extent permitted by Sections 107 and 108 of the U.S. Copyright Law. Permission to copy articles for personal, internal, classroom, or library use may be obtained from the Copyright Clearance Center (www.copyright.com). For all other uses, such as copying for general distribution, for advertising or promotional purposes, for creating new collective works, or for resale, please contact Permissions Coordinator, Journals Division, University of Chicago Press, 1427 E. 60th Street, Chicago, IL 60637 USA. Fax: (773) 834-3489. E-mail: journalpermissions@press.uchicago.edu.

Subscriptions: For individual and institutional subscription rates, visit www.journals.uchicago.edu, email subscriptions@press.uchicago.edu, or call (877) 705-1878 (US) or (773) 753-3347 (international). Free or deeply discounted institutional access is available in most developing nations through the Chicago Emerging Nations Initiative (www.journals.uchicago.edu/inst/ceni).

Please direct subscription inquiries to Subscription Fulfillment, 1427 E. 60th Street, Chicago, IL 60637-2902. Telephone: (773) 753-3347 or toll free in the United States and Canada (877) 705-1878. Fax: (773) 753-0811 or toll-free (877) 705-1879. E-mail: subscriptions@press.uchicago.edu.

Standing orders: To place a standing order for this book series, please address your request to The University of Chicago Press, Chicago Distribution Center, Attn. Standing Orders/Customer Service, 11030 S. Langley Avenue, Chicago, IL 60628. Telephone toll free in the U.S. and Canada: 1-800-621-2736; or 1-773-702-7000. Fax toll free in the U.S. and Canada: 1-800-621-8476; or 1-773-702-7212.

Single-copy orders: In the U.S., Canada, and the rest of the world, order from your local bookseller or direct from The University of Chicago Press, Chicago Distribution Center, 11030 S. Langley Avenue, Chicago, IL 60628. Telephone toll free in the U.S. and Canada: 1-800-621-2736; or 1-773-702-7000. Fax toll free in the U.S. and Canada: 1-800-621-8476; or 1-773-702-7212. In the U.K. and Europe, order from your local bookseller or direct from The University of Chicago Press, c/o John Wiley Ltd. Distribution Center, 1 Oldlands Way, Bognor Regis, West Sussex PO22 9SA, UK. Telephone 01243 779777 or Fax 01243 820250. E-mail: cs-books@wiley.co.uk.

The University of Chicago Press offers bulk discounts on individual titles to Corporate, Premium, and Gift accounts. For information, please write to Sales Department—Special Sales, The University of Chicago Press, 1427 E. 60th Street, Chicago, IL 60637 USA or telephone 1-773-702-7723.

This book was printed and bound in the United States of America.

ISSN: 0081-9557
E-ISSN: 2158-2459
ISBN: 978-0-226-83563-1 (cloth)
E-ISBN: 978-0-226-83564-8 (ebook)

IN MEMORIAM

JUSTICE SANDRA DAY O'CONNOR

CONTENTS

THE CURE AS DISEASE: THE CONSERVATIVE CASE AGAINST
   SFFA v. HARVARD   1
   Justin Driver

THE INVENTION OF COLORBLINDNESS   67
   Cass R. Sunstein

FIRST AMENDMENT NEGLECT IN SUPREME COURT
   INTELLECTUAL PROPERTY CASES   85
   Mark A. Lemley and Rebecca Tushnet

THE CALIFORNIA EFFECT, PROCESS-BASED REGULATION,
   AND THE FUTURE OF PIKE BALANCING   125
   Jack Goldsmith and Alan Sykes

FROM BAD TO WORSE: STALKING, THREATS,
   AND CHILLING EFFECTS   175
   Danielle Keats Citron

DORMANT COMMERCE AND CORPORATE JURISDICTION   213
   Stephen E. Sachs

PUBLIC ACCOMMODATIONS AND THE FIRST AMENDMENT:
   303 CREATIVE AND "PURE SPEECH"   251
   Robert Post

STATE STANDING AFTER BIDEN v. NEBRASKA   303
   Ann Woolhandler and Julia D. Mahoney

CAN OUR DEMOCRACY SURVIVE THIS SUPREME COURT?   345
   Armand Derfner

JUSTIN DRIVER

THE CURE AS DISEASE: THE CONSERVATIVE CASE AGAINST SFFA v. HARVARD

Introduction

In 1979, following *Regents of the University of California v. Bakke*,[1] then-Professor Antonin Scalia published a short article with a long title excoriating the decision, *The Disease as Cure: "In Order to Get Beyond Racism, We Must First Take Account of Race."*[2] Scalia—in only eleven crisp pages—contended that *Bakke*'s validation of affirmative action marked an unwise retreat from the Fourteenth Amendment's colorblind mandate. If race-conscious student assignment plans presented an unconstitutional malady in cases like *Brown v. Board of*

Justin Driver is the Robert R. Slaughter Professor of Law at Yale Law School.

Author's note: I received valuable feedback on this project from Samantha Bensinger, Gregory Briker, William Edwards, Jonathan Entin, Owen Fiss, Pratheepan Gulasekaram, Randy Kozel, Sanford Levinson, Samuel Moyn, Kerrel Murray, Saikrishna Prakash, David Schleicher, David Strauss, and Melvin Urofsky. I received exemplary research assistance from Ella Bunnell, Kishore Chundi, Rosemary Coskrey, Emma Gray, Remington Hill, Josh Hochman, Jim Huang, Alexandra Johnson, Charlotte Lawrence, Romina Lilollari, Jamie Piltch, Sarah Shapiro, Riley Tillitt, and Henry Wu.

[1] 438 U.S. 265 (1978).

[2] Antonin Scalia, *The Disease as Cure: "In Order to Get Beyond Racism, We Must First Take Account of Race,"* 1979 Wash. U. L.Q. 147. The quotation in Scalia's subtitle is drawn from Justice Blackmun's concurring opinion in *Bakke*. See 438 U.S. at 407 (Blackmun, J., concurring).

Education,³ Scalia suggested, how could race-conscious admissions policies somehow receive a clean bill of health in *Bakke*?⁴ In other words, how could racial classifications have been the "disease" during the Jim Crow era and then suddenly somehow morph into the "cure" in the late 1970s? Scalia asserted that *Bakke* would not only fail to help America's race relations, but would significantly harm them: "From racist principles flow racist results."⁵

Scalia's article denouncing *Bakke* from more than four decades ago has now largely been forgotten.⁶ But it merits renewed attention in the wake of last Term's decision invalidating affirmative action in *Students for Fair Admissions, Inc. (SFFA) v. President and Fellows of Harvard College*,⁷ as Scalia's critique proved prescient along four dimensions. First, Scalia argued that affirmative action policies boost undeserving beneficiaries, advancing the most privileged racial minorities—including "the son of a prosperous and well-educated black doctor or lawyer."⁸ Second, articulating an early version of what has come to be known as mismatch theory, Scalia blamed affirmative action for promoting Black students with mediocre standardized test scores into elite academic environments where they are likely outgunned. "Was it really 'helping' these young men and women ... to place them in an environment where it was quite probable ... that they did not belong?" he queried.⁹ Third, Scalia contended that affirmative action balkanized American society, paving the road to racial resentment by unjustly requiring "many white ethnic groups that came to this country ... relatively late in its history" to sacrifice valuable opportunities as compensation for a racial debt that long predated their arrival.¹⁰ Making the argument in unusually personal

---

³ 347 U.S. 483 (1954).

⁴ Scalia, *supra* note 2, at 150.

⁵ *Id.* at 157.

⁶ A Westlaw search reveals that Scalia's article attacking affirmative action has been cited only 143 times. By way of comparison, Antonin Scalia, *The Rule of Law as a Law of Rules*, 56 U. CHI. L. REV. 1175 (1989), has been cited more than 2,000 times. Even one of Scalia's articles exploring an administrative law decision published prior to his judicial elevation—Antonin Scalia, Vermont Yankee: *The APA, the D.C. Circuit, and the Supreme Court*, 1978 SUP. CT. REV. 345 (1979)—has been cited nearly 300 times, or more than twice as often as *The Disease as Cure*.

⁷ 600 U.S. 181 (2023).

⁸ Scalia, *supra* note 2, at 153–54.

⁹ *Id.* at 155–56.

¹⁰ *Id.* at 152.

terms, he noted: "My father came to this country when he was a teenager. Not only had he never profited from the sweat of any black man's brow, I don't think he had ever seen a black man."[11] Finally, Scalia contended that Justice Powell's controlling opinion in *Bakke*—by embracing the nebulous diversity rationale—seemed almost designed to forestall meaningful judicial review. Due to Justice Powell's opinion, Scalia lamented, affirmative action plans "will be effectively unappealable to the courts," as "[t]here's no way to establish . . . that the diversity value of New York City oboists has not been accorded its proper weight."[12] Various Justices in the *SFFA v. Harvard* majority echoed each of these four claims as they eliminated affirmative action.

Not surprisingly, conservatives have overwhelmingly hailed *SFFA* as among the most venerable judicial decisions in modern Supreme Court history. A *Wall Street Journal* editorial, titled "A Landmark for Racial Equality," saluted *SFFA* as a "watershed declaration," and deemed it "one of [the Supreme Court's] finest hours."[13] SFFA founder Edward Blum celebrated the decision as nothing less than "the restoration of the colorblind legal covenant that binds together our multi-racial, multi-ethnic nation."[14] Writing in *National Review*, Ed Whelan praised *SFFA* as—without exception—Chief Justice Roberts's "greatest opinion in his eighteen years on the Court."[15]

The right's initial celebration of *SFFA* may, however, quickly yield to condemnation. Liberal law professors have, of course, roundly castigated *SFFA*.[16] But even as assessed from the perspective of conservatives' own principles, *SFFA* ushers in a legal regime that is markedly worse than the one it replaced. Indeed, while conservatives have long believed that a decision ending affirmative action would help to cure what they deem America's primary racial ailments, now that *SFFA* has arrived, it is becoming apparent that the decision only

---

[11] *Id.*

[12] *Id.* at 148.

[13] Editorial, *A Landmark for Racial Equality*, WALL ST. J., June 30, 2023, at A14.

[14] Michelle N. Amponsah & Emma H. Haidar, *Students for Fair Admissions, Allies Celebrate End of Affirmative Action*, HARV. CRIMSON (June 30, 2023), https://www.thecrimson.com/article/2023/6/30/sffa-decision-reaction.

[15] Ed Whelan, *The Chief Justice's Greatest Opinion*, NAT'L REV. (June 29, 2023, 3:22 PM), https://www.nationalreview.com/bench-memos/the-chief-justices-greatest-opinion.

[16] *See, e.g.*, Angela Onwuachi-Willig, *Roberts's Revisions: A Narratological Reading of the Affirmative Action Cases*, 137 HARV. L. REV. 192 (2023).

intensifies the disease. By conservatives' own professed lights, then, *SFFA* contains not an antidote, but a toxin.

Affirmative action's supporters too often pretend that the policy has no drawbacks whatsoever, portraying it as a first-best solution, rather than a second-best solution. Sophisticated backers of affirmative action have, however, acknowledged that it possesses costs as well as benefits. Reacting to *Bakke*, Professor Derrick Bell in 1979 emphasized that the program's supporters, including himself, "should not forget that the relief these programs provide is far from ideal," and encouraged all observers to "recognize the limitations of minority admissions programs."[17] Similarly, in 2013, Professor Randall Kennedy stated: "Some defenders of affirmative action, fearful of making any concessions, argue as if affirmative action poses no costs, entails no risks, involves no dangers. The reality is far different."[18]

Unrecognized in the voluminous affirmative action debates, however, is that the converse point also holds: Affirmative action's detractors have failed to recognize that their preferred approach raises dangers of its own. Those dangers are considerable, and even one who is dedicated to advancing conservative principles must grapple forthrightly with the serious risks *SFFA* poses to their ideological commitments. This point has been permitted to hide in plain sight because conservatives have been targeting affirmative action so ardently and for so long that they have dedicated insufficient attention to the particularities of the regime that will replace the old affirmative action model now that it has been destroyed. Following *SFFA*, however, these questions can no longer be evaded. Today, with its long-sought victory firmly in hand, the conservative legal movement may soon recognize that the opinion is actually a glorious defeat.[19]

---

[17] Derrick A. Bell, Jr., Bakke, *Minority Admissions, and the Usual Price of Racial Remedies*, 67 CALIF. L. REV. 3, 19 (1979).

[18] RANDALL KENNEDY, FOR DISCRIMINATION: RACE, AFFIRMATIVE ACTION, AND THE LAW 115 (2013); *see also* Randall Kennedy, *Persuasion and Distrust: A Comment on the Affirmative Action Debate*, 99 HARV. L. REV. 1327, 1327 n.1 (1986) ("On all too many occasions . . . proponents of affirmative action have hurt their own cause by evading the difficulties posed and costs incurred by the policy they advance.").

[19] *Cf.* Kenneth B. Clark, *Racial Progress and Retreat: A Personal Memoir*, *in* RACE IN AMERICA: THE STRUGGLE FOR EQUALITY 3, 18 (Herbert Hill & James E. Jones, Jr. eds., 1993) (reflecting upon his pivotal role in the *Brown v. Board* litigation psychologist Kenneth Clark wrote: "I look back and I shudder at how naïve we all were in our belief in the steady progress racial minorities would make through programs of litigation and education, . . . I am forced to recognize that my life has, in fact, been a series of glorious defeats."). I do not share Clark's grim assessment of *Brown*'s significance. For my own views of *Brown* and its legacy, see

Conservatives have over the years identified a wide array of problems stemming from affirmative action. In addition to the concerns that then-Professor Scalia identified involving mismatch, balkanization, and undeserving beneficiaries, opponents of affirmative action have blamed the policy for not only increasing the salience of race, but perpetuating a mindset that prioritizes victimization. The Court's opinion in *SFFA*, however, does not eliminate those concerns; it accentuates them. In advancing his anti-*Bakke* broadside, then-Professor Scalia argued, "There is ... a lot of pretense or self-delusion (you can take your choice) in all that pertains to affirmative action."[20] Perhaps. But *SFFA* makes undeniably clear that, as we enter the post-affirmative action era, the conservative legal movement has long been harboring copious amounts of pretense or self-delusion about what that world would entail.

The balance of this Article proceeds as follows. Part I briefly sets the scene by exploring the Supreme Court's various opinions in *SFFA v. Harvard*. It does so with an eye toward establishing how the arguments contained in those opinions amplify longstanding conservative criticisms of affirmative action, including several of those voiced by then-Professor Scalia in the 1970s.

Next, Part II—the Article's heart—analyzes four distinct ways that *SFFA* undermines conservative principles, contending that the right will grow to loathe the regime that *SFFA* created even more than the one that it destroyed. First, by eliminating racial boxes on college applications, *SFFA* encourages Black and brown students to write application essays focusing upon tales of racial aggrievement, rewarding the very victimology mindset that conservatives purport to detest. Second, *SFFA* promises to place many students of color in university social settings where they are unlikely to flourish, heightening the mismatch concerns that conservatives often emphasize—even in the face of strong evidence challenging the idea. Third, *SFFA*'s excusing military academies from its general rule threatens to balkanize American society further along racial lines, even though conservatives routinely condemn government policies that they believe promote racial resentment. Fourth, *SFFA* represents a betrayal of both Burkean conservatism and a traditional mode of judicial

---

Justin Driver, The Schoolhouse Gate: Public Education, the Supreme Court, and the Battle for the American Mind 242–314 (2018).

[20] Scalia, *supra* note 2, at 148.

conservatism, as its efforts to claim the mantle of stare decisis were strained to the point of becoming risible.

Finally, Part III steps back to examine a pair of broader implications raised by the highly destabilizing *SFFA* decision. This Part begins by demonstrating that *SFFA* recasts a dominant view that portrays Chief Justice Roberts as singularly devoted to incrementalism and institutionalism. *SFFA*, however, illuminates Roberts's radicalism involving race, marshaling evidence that shows how his opinion fails the institutionalist test that he articulated for himself at the dawn of his tenure. In addition, Part III analyzes how *SFFA* could augur ill for the future by returning to the past. In the 1960s, many universities struggled mightily to adapt to the transformed admissions landscape that affirmative action introduced. While it is thus tempting to view *SFFA* only as *ending* affirmative action, it is important to remember that the opinion marks the *beginning* of a new, highly volatile chapter in American higher education.

Before pursuing these arguments in earnest, I wish to establish at the outset that I am neither a conservative nor an opponent of affirmative action. Quite the opposite: I identify as a liberal, who has dedicated substantial effort to defending affirmative action and, indeed, attempting to forestall an outcome very much like the one the Supreme Court announced in *SFFA*.[21] In this Article, however, I do not focus upon advancing my own first-order view of this contested terrain. Instead, I aim to articulate a conservative critique of *SFFA*, demonstrating how conservative principles that the right has long championed actually undercut rather than support that opinion. I seek to make this argument in a manner that will be recognizable to conservatives of various stripes themselves, and that endeavor requires me to do so relying upon some ideas, premises, and even language that I wholeheartedly reject. To take only two of the many possible examples, I am unconvinced either that a victimology mindset ranks high on the list of what ails Black Americans, or that the supposed mismatch phenomenon presents a major problem in higher education. Rather than contesting such ideas and others that enjoy widespread adherence in conservative circles, however, this

---

[21] *See, e.g.*, Adam Chilton, Justin Driver, Jonathan S. Masur & Kyle Rozema, *Assessing Affirmative Action's Diversity Rationale*, 122 COLUM. L. REV. 331, 381–88 (2022) (offering empirical evidence supporting affirmative action); Justin Driver, *Think Affirmative Action Is Dead? Think Again.*, N.Y. TIMES, Oct. 31, 2022, at A18.

Article instead shows how accepting those conservative views should mean rejecting *SFFA*.

Although I am not a conservative, this Article nevertheless attempts to illuminate some oft-overlooked aspects of modern legal conservatism. I use the term *conservatism* here in two different senses. The primary, context-sensitive sense of *conservatism* is painfully straightforward, as I identify the right's central arguments that have been used to condemn affirmative action over the years in judicial opinions, legal journals, newspaper columns, bestselling books, and Federalist Society gatherings. Foregrounding this rough-and-ready distillation of conservatism, as found in the affirmative action setting, underscores two central points. First, many of the conservative attacks on affirmative action examined in the pages that follow sound not in originalism, but instead firmly in consequentialism.[22] The right's breathtaking array of prudential reasoning in this area demonstrates not only that it is mistaken to view conservatism as synonymous with originalism, but also that legal liberals are far from alone in centering consequentialist thought in constitutional interpretation. Second, and related, the multiplicity of conservative attacks on affirmative action do not always neatly cohere. To the contrary, conservative attacks sometimes point in diametrically opposed directions. Highlighting the internal clashes that exist within various conservative critiques of affirmative action should spark an overdue conversation regarding the actual regime that conservatives wish to create now that the old practice has been upended. The secondary, broader sense of *conservatism* focuses upon the historical commitment that many right-leaning theorists made to preserving the extant legal order. *SFFA* demonstrates how that older, time-honored sense of conservatism has receded from view, and been replaced by a far more aggressive, even totalizing constitutional vision. In this sense, then, the right's dramatic rupture with the past in *SFFA* should be understood as anything but conservative.

I. Sketching *SFFA v. Harvard*

This Part provides a brief overview of the written opinions that emerged from *SFFA v. Harvard*, aiming to tee up analysis of

---

[22] *See* Philip Bobbitt, Constitutional Interpretation 12–13 (1991) (identifying six modalities of constitutional interpretation).

how the decision promises to yield results that undermine prevalent conservative positions. Accordingly, the aim here is not to provide a comprehensive overview of *SFFA*, which is readily available elsewhere. Instead, this Part simply lays the groundwork for demonstrating how the demise of affirmative action—one of the conservative legal movement's most intensely coveted treasures[23]—reveals itself upon close inspection to be fool's gold.

Chief Justice Roberts wrote the majority opinion in *SFFA*. He framed the case in a straightforward manner as "involv[ing] whether a university may make admissions decisions that turn on an applicant's race."[24] In answering the question presented in the negative, Chief Justice Roberts spoke in the register of colorblind absolutism: "Eliminating racial discrimination means eliminating all of it."[25] Given that *SFFA* construed Harvard and UNC's affirmative action measures as forms of racial discrimination, those programs must fall.

But *SFFA* carved out two overt exceptions to its broad colorblindness decree. First, in footnote four, Chief Justice Roberts noted that the Solicitor General's brief had emphasized the importance of affirmative action policies to the nation's military academies, and that they were not parties in *SFFA*.[26] Therefore, *SFFA* concluded that those institutions were exempted from altering their race-conscious admissions programs—at least for the time being[27]—"in light of the potentially distinct interests that military academies may present."[28]

Second, Chief Justice Roberts clarified that all universities may in fact consider race during the admissions process if they received application essays exploring racial themes—at least in certain circumstances. In a highly significant passage, Chief Justice Roberts allowed: "[N]othing in this opinion should be construed as prohibiting

---

[23] OFF. OF LEGAL POL'Y, U.S. DEP'T OF JUSTICE, THE CONSTITUTION IN THE YEAR 2000: CHOICES AHEAD IN CONSTITUTIONAL INTERPRETATION 44–55 (1988) (suggesting that affirmative action should be ruled unconstitutional).

[24] Students for Fair Admissions, Inc. v. President & Fellows of Harvard Coll. (*SFFA*), 600 U.S. 181, 208 (2023).

[25] *Id.* at 206.

[26] *Id.* at 213 n.4.

[27] In early 2024, the Supreme Court rejected an additional effort to require one of the nation's military academies to comply with *SFFA*'s holding. *See* Abbie VanSickle, *Supreme Court Won't Block Use of Race in West Point Admissions for Now*, N.Y. TIMES (Feb. 2, 2024), https://www.nytimes.com/2024/02/02/us/politics/scotus-admissions-west-point.html.

[28] *SFFA*, 600 U.S. at 213 n.4.

universities from considering an applicant's discussion of how race affected his or her life, be it through discrimination, inspiration, or otherwise."[29] *SFFA* warned, however, "universities may not simply establish through application essays or other means the regime we hold unlawful today."[30] Instead, universities may provide a boost on the basis of racial application essays only if they addressed *individualized* experiences. "A benefit to a student who overcame racial discrimination, for example, must be tied to *that student's* courage and determination," *SFFA* explained.[31] "Or a benefit to a student whose heritage or culture motivated him or her to assume a leadership role or attain a particular goal must be tied to *that student's* unique ability to contribute to the university."[32] Chief Justice Roberts contended that this restricted use of race in admissions was desirable because it would prevent universities from teaching "the touchstone of an individual's identity is not challenges bested, skills built, or lessons learned but the color of their skin."[33] These universities' fixation on race, he reasoned, had baleful consequences for the nation.

Chief Justice Roberts did not expressly indicate that *SFFA* overruled *Bakke* and *Grutter v. Bollinger*.[34] To the contrary, *SFFA* at times seemed to suggest that it could be viewed as adhering to *Grutter*. The Harvard and UNC admissions programs were both driven by the wrongheaded belief that "there is an inherent benefit in race *qua* race—in race for race's sake."[35] In so doing, Chief Justice Roberts asserted that those universities "tolerate the very thing that *Grutter* foreswore: stereotyping."[36] Where Harvard embraced "the pernicious stereotype that 'a black student can usually bring something that a white person cannot offer,'"[37] he noted, UNC maintained

---

[29] *Id.* at 230.

[30] *Id.*

[31] *Id.* at 230–31 (emphasis in original).

[32] *Id.* at 231 (emphasis in original).

[33] *Id.*

[34] 438 U.S. 265 (1978); 539 U.S. 306 (2003). For an article exploring this point at length, see Bill Watson, *Did the Court in* SFFA *Overrule* Grutter?, 99 NOTRE DAME L. REV. REFLECTION 113 (2024).

[35] *SFFA*, 600 U.S. at 220.

[36] *Id.*

[37] *Id.* (quoting Regents of the Univ. of Cal. v. Bakke, 438 U.S. 265, 316 (1978) (op. of Powell, J.) (describing Harvard College's admissions program)).

"race in itself 'says [something] about who you are.'"[38] Chief Justice Roberts further suggested that *SFFA*'s holding could be reconciled with the well-known twenty-five-year sunset provision for affirmative action that *Grutter* announced in 2003—even though the sun seemed to be setting five years early. Nonetheless, Chief Justice Roberts insisted: "[T]he high school applicants that Harvard and UNC will evaluate [in] fall [2023] . . . are expected to graduate in 2028—25 years after *Grutter* was decided."[39]

SFFA's approach to the strict scrutiny framework that the Court embraced in *Grutter* nonetheless represented a sea change from the earlier era. *Grutter* waxed eloquent about how racial diversity in higher education satisfied a most important "compelling interest,"[40] even as its companion case—*Gratz v. Bollinger*—made clear that universities could run afoul of the "narrow tailoring" prong of strict scrutiny.[41] But in *SFFA*'s key jurisprudential innovation—one that has received too little attention—Chief Justice Roberts made clear that the universities had faltered on strict scrutiny's first prong by failing to identify a compelling government interest. "[T]he interests [Harvard and UNC] view as compelling cannot be subjected to meaningful judicial review," *SFFA* concluded, because "it is unclear how courts are supposed to measure [the universities'] goals."[42] This analytical move strongly resembles the concern then-Professor Scalia articulated in 1979 that *Bakke*'s rationale was "effectively unappealable to the courts" because it was impossible to ensure "diversity value[s]" received their "proper weight."[43]

Justice Thomas's uncommonly rich, expansive concurring opinion contained several significant lines of attack condemning affirmative action. Justice Thomas had disdained affirmative action since long

---

[38] *Id.* at 220 (alteration in original) (quoting Transcript of Oral Argument at 97–98, Students for Fair Admissions v. Univ. of N.C., 600 U.S. 181 (2023) (No. 21-707)).

[39] *Id.* at 224–25.

[40] Grutter v. Bollinger, 539 U.S. 306, 332–33 (2003) (finding that the University of Michigan Law School's admissions program pursued a "compelling interest," because "it is necessary that the path to leadership be visibly open to talented and qualified individuals of every race and ethnicity" "[i]n order to cultivate a set of leaders with legitimacy in the eyes of the citizenry").

[41] Gratz v. Bollinger, 539 U.S. 244, 270 (2003) (invalidating the University of Michigan's undergraduate admissions plan because its mechanical use of race was not narrowly tailored).

[42] *SFFA*, 600 U.S. at 214; *see id.* at 215 (emphasizing the "elusive nature" of the universities' asserted interests).

[43] Scalia, *supra* note 2, at 148.

before he joined the Court, and he relished this moment, when *SFFA* "rightly [made] clear that *Grutter* is, for all and intents and purposes, overruled."[44] Notably, a trio of Justice Thomas's central arguments in *SFFA* extended claims ventured in then-Professor Scalia's article from more than four decades prior. Start with Justice Thomas's contention that affirmative action often promotes undeserving beneficiaries—not racial minorities who are down on their luck, but instead those whose families have already risen. Scalia raised the specter of affirmative action boosting the children of "prosperous and well-educated black" physicians and attorneys.[45] Justice Thomas upped the ante. He observed that a hypothetical Black applicant named "Jack, ... the son of a multimillionaire industrialist," could plausibly receive a race-based admissions boost over another Black student from humble origins because "both [applicants] are black, after all."[46] This absurdity laid bare affirmative action's shameful overinclusiveness, Justice Thomas contended: "[T]hese programs ... provid[e] the same admissions bump to a wealthy black applicant given every advantage in life as to a black applicant from a poor family with seemingly insurmountable barriers to overcome[, and thus] may ... help[] the most well-off members of minority races without meaningfully assisting those who struggle with real hardship."[47]

Next, Justice Thomas highlighted the mismatch argument, i.e., the (controverted) idea that affirmative action elevates Black and brown students into settings in which they are ill-prepared to succeed.[48] It is essential to realize, Justice Thomas asserted, that affirmative action does not meaningfully expand the pool of Black and brown college students. Instead, he observed: "[T]hose racial policies simply redistribute individuals among institutions of higher learning, placing

---

[44] *SFFA*, 600 U.S. at 287 (Thomas, J., concurring).

[45] Scalia, *supra* note 2, at 153–54.

[46] *SFFA*, 600 U.S. at 282 (Thomas, J., concurring).

[47] *Id.* at 271.

[48] For prominent articulations of this idea in legal circles, see Richard H. Sander, *A Systematic Analysis of Affirmative Action in American Law Schools*, 57 STAN. L. REV. 367 (2004); and RICHARD H. SANDER & STUART TAYLOR, JR., MISMATCH: HOW AFFIRMATIVE ACTION HURTS STUDENTS IT'S INTENDED TO HELP, AND WHY UNIVERSITIES WON'T ADMIT IT (2012). Several scholars have offered powerful challenges to Professor Sander's arguments. *See, e.g.*, Ian Ayres & Richard Brooks, *Does Affirmative Action Reduce the Number of Black Lawyers?*, 57 STAN. L. REV. 1807, 1809 (2005); Daniel E. Ho, *Affirmative Action's Affirmative Actions: A Reply to Sander*, 114 YALE L.J. 2011, 2011–12 (2005); *see also SFFA*, 600 U.S. at 371 (Sotomayor, J., dissenting) (contending that mismatch theory had been "debunked long ago").

some into more competitive institutions than they otherwise would have attended. In doing so, those policies sort at least some blacks and Hispanics into environments where they are less likely to succeed academically relative to their peers."[49] While these students could well have thrived at less demanding universities, Justice Thomas asserted, "[t]he resulting mismatch places many blacks and Hispanics ... in a position where underperformance is all but inevitable because they are less academically prepared than the white and Asian students with whom they must compete."[50] While allowing that many well-intentioned people believe that affirmative action actually benefits Black students, he concluded that the question's importance demanded constitutional colorblindness. "The stakes are simply too high to gamble," Justice Thomas stated.[51]

Third, Justice Thomas emphasized that affirmative action produces racial resentment and balkanization. Where Scalia focused upon the harms he believed flowed from requiring many white immigrants to pay down a racial debt that they did not owe, Justice Thomas highlighted the racial invective that some hopeful college applicants who receive rejection letters might direct toward admitted Black and brown students. "Applicants denied admission to certain colleges may come to believe—accurately or not—that their race was responsible for their failure to attain a life-long dream," Justice Thomas wrote.[52] "These individuals, and others who wished for their success, may resent members of what they perceive to be favored races, believing that the successes of those individuals are unearned."[53] Justice Thomas contended that affirmative action policies thus yield "[n]ot racial harmony," but instead "creat[e] new prejudices," "increase[e] racial polarization and friction," and produce "*exactly* the kind of factionalism that the Constitution was meant to safeguard against."[54]

In addition, Justice Thomas's *SFFA* concurrence advanced two linked arguments that require explication. Justice Thomas—spotlighting a prominent conservative grievance with affirmative action—charged

---

[49] *SFFA*, 600 U.S. at 268–69 (2023) (Thomas, J., concurring) (internal citation omitted).

[50] *Id.* at 269 (internal quotation marks omitted).

[51] *Id.* at 268.

[52] *Id.* at 275.

[53] *Id.* at 275–76.

[54] *Id.* at 276, 275, 277, 276 (emphasis in original) (citing THE FEDERALIST No. 10 (James Madison)).

that such programs encourage Black and brown students to adopt a "self-defeating" attitude that prioritizes racial "victimization."[55] Instead of noting "the great accomplishments of black Americans, including those who succeeded despite long odds," Justice Thomas contended affirmative action's defenders incorrectly insist upon "label[ing] all blacks as victims."[56] That view was not just "irrational," but "unfathomable," according to Justice Thomas: "What matters is not the barriers [Black students] face, but how they choose to confront them. And their race is not to blame for everything—good or bad—that happens in their lives."[57] Justice Thomas called the "racial[ly] determinis[t]" mindset "an insult to individual achievement," one that is "cancerous to young minds seeking to push through barriers, rather than consign themselves to permanent victimhood."[58]

Relatedly, Justice Thomas contended that affirmative action programs heightened the salience of race on college campuses and thus marred the broader American society. "Far from advancing the cause of improved race relations in our Nation," he claimed, "affirmative action highlights our racial differences with pernicious effect."[59] He contended further: "[T]hese policies appear to be leading to a world in which everyone is defined by their skin color, demanding ever-increasing entitlements and preferences on that basis."[60] Supporting this claim, Justice Thomas stated, "[i]t has become clear that sorting by race does not stop at the admissions office," as racially identifiable clubs, centers, and even housing have proliferated on campuses in recent decades.[61] Justice Thomas suggested *Bakke* and its progeny shouldered the blame for the "stagnat[ion]" of "racial progress on campuses," as "the legacy of *Grutter* appears to be ever increasing and strident demands for *yet more* racially oriented solutions."[62]

Justice Gorsuch's concurrence in *SFFA* contended that Title VI of the 1964 Civil Rights Act required reaching the same result that the

---

[55] *Id.* at 283.
[56] *Id.* at 279.
[57] *Id.* at 279–80.
[58] *Id.* at 280.
[59] *Id.* at 274.
[60] *Id.* at 276.
[61] *Id.* at 274.
[62] *Id.* (emphasis in original).

majority reached by interpreting the Equal Protection Clause.[63] He further suggested that the college application processes at Harvard and UNC fueled racial obsession: "[T]he trial records show [that] applicants are prompted to tick one or more boxes to explain 'how you identify yourself.'"[64] For Justice Gorsuch, who has sometimes expressed libertarian inclinations,[65] this unhealthy obsession with racial identification's salience was particularly galling because the various boxes had suspect origins. "Where do these boxes come from?" he asked. "Bureaucrats. A federal interagency commission devised this scheme of [racial] classifications in the 1970s to facilitate data collection."[66] In addition, Justice Gorsuch expressed concern that "a cottage industry" of college consultants had sprung up that helped Asian American students attempt to conceal their racial identities in an effort to maximize their chances of admission to leading universities.[67] He suggested that indigent Asian Americans might be particularly harmed by being priced out of this industry: "[I]t is hard not to wonder whether those left paying the steepest price are those least able to afford it—children of families with no chance of hiring the kind of consultants who know how to play this game."[68]

Justice Kavanaugh dedicated his concurrence to amplifying the contention that *SFFA* in no sense marked an abandonment of the Court's affirmative action precedents, including *Grutter*'s twenty-five-year timeline. To the contrary, he argued that *SFFA* "is consistent with and follows from the Court's equal protection precedents, including the Court's precedents on race-based affirmative action in higher education."[69] *Grutter*'s quarter-century expiration date for affirmative action was not a haphazard aside, Justice Kavanaugh observed, but instead "an important part of [a] nuanced opinion

---

[63] *See id.* at 287–91 (Gorsuch, J., concurring) (citing 42 U.S.C. § 2000d). Justice Thomas joined Justice Gorsuch's concurrence. *Id.* at 287.

[64] *Id.* at 291 (quoting Joint App'x at 1732, Students for Fair Admissions, Inc. v. Univ. of N.C., 600 U.S. 181 (2023) (No. 21-707)).

[65] *See, e.g.*, David G. Savage, *On an Often Unpredictable Supreme Court, Justice Gorsuch Is the Latest Wild Card*, L.A. Times (July 12, 2019), https://www.latimes.com/politics/la-na-pol-gorsuch-supreme-court-conservative-20190712-story.html (calling Gorsuch "a libertarian who is quick to oppose unchecked government power").

[66] *See SFFA*, 600 U.S. at 291 (Gorsuch, J., concurring).

[67] *See id.* at 293.

[68] *Id.* at 294.

[69] *Id.* at 311 (Kavanaugh, J., concurring).

for the Court"—a notion supported by the fact that "four of the separate opinions in *Grutter* discussed the majority opinion's 25-year limit."[70] Justice Kavanaugh stated that he—and *SFFA*—"abide[d] by *Grutter*'s ... temporal limit"—because the majority opinion meant that colleges were in fact permitted to use affirmative action through the admissions cycle "for the college class of 2028."[71] Those contending that *Grutter*'s twenty-five-year timeline meant that universities should be permitted to use affirmative action through 2028, he suggested, should be understood as in effect arguing the regime extended until "the college class of 2032," which would be a full twenty-nine years post-*Grutter*.[72] Finally, Justice Kavanaugh noted "neither Harvard nor North Carolina argued that *Grutter*'s 25-year period ends with the class of 2032 rather than the class of 2028," as the universities steadfastly refused to "embrace[] *any* temporal limit on race-based affirmative action."[73]

The leitmotif of Justice Sotomayor's dissent lambasted *SFFA* for embracing constitutional colorblindness in a world that remains color conscious. "[T]he six unelected members of today's majority," Justice Sotomayor stated, "upend the status quo based on their policy preferences about what race in America should be like, but is not, and their preferences for a veneer of colorblindness in a society where race has always mattered and continues to matter in fact and in law."[74] This approach had nothing to recommend it, she believed: "Ignoring race will not equalize a society that is racially unequal.... Equality requires acknowledgement of inequality."[75] For Justice Sotomayor, *SFFA* marked a retreat not just from the Court's affirmative action decisions but from *Brown v. Board of Education* itself.[76] The affirmative action decisions, she posited, "extended *Brown*'s transformative legacy to the context of higher education," by "promot[ing] *Brown*'s

---

[70] *Id.* at 315; *see id.* at 312–13 (noting Justice Thomas referred to *Grutter*'s twenty-five-year expectation as a "holding," and Justice Kennedy referred to it as a "pronouncement").

[71] *Id.* at 316 & n.1.

[72] *Id.* at 316 n.1.

[73] *Id.* (emphasis in original).

[74] *Id.* at 353 (Sotomayor, J., dissenting). Justices Kagan and Jackson joined Justice Sotomayor's dissent. *Id.* at 317.

[75] *Id.* at 334.

[76] *Id.* at 318 (Sotomayor, J., dissenting) (citing 347 U.S. 483 (1954)).

vision of a Nation with more inclusive schools."⁷⁷ Where the majority construed itself as rooting out racial obsession from college admissions, Justice Sotomayor viewed *SFFA* as imposing an unfair tax on Black and brown students who may well conceive of themselves in racial terms: "By singling out race, the Court imposes a special burden on racial minorities for whom race is a crucial component of their identity."⁷⁸ Justice Sotomayor dismissed the majority's concession that universities may sometimes consider race in application essays as "an attempt to put lipstick on a pig."⁷⁹

Justice Jackson's dissent sounded similar dominant themes, as she, too, warned of the perils of *SFFA*'s premature embrace of colorblindness. "With let-them-eat-cake obliviousness, . . . the majority . . . announces 'colorblindness for all' by legal fiat," she wrote. "But deeming race irrelevant in law does not make it so in life."⁸⁰ Further, Justice Jackson argued: "The best that can be said of the majority's perspective is that it proceeds (ostrich-like) from the hopes that preventing consideration of race will end racism. . . . And, ultimately, ignoring race just makes it matter more."⁸¹ Justice Jackson also marshaled extensive empirical evidence chronicling the "[g]ulf-sized race-based gaps that exist [regarding] health, wealth, and well-being of American citizens."⁸² In Justice Jackson view, "the well-documented intergenerational transmission of inequality that still plagues our citizenry" rendered it ludicrous to assert "that anyone is now victimized if a college considers whether [this] legacy of discrimination has unequally advantaged its applicants."⁸³

The dissents by Justices Sotomayor and Jackson launched potent lines of liberal attack against *SFFA* and the world that it threatens to create. Largely absent from those dissents, however, were sustained arguments demonstrating that *SFFA* undermines the very principles

---

⁷⁷ *Id.* (Sotomayor, J., dissenting).

⁷⁸ *Id.* at 361.

⁷⁹ *Id.* at 363.

⁸⁰ *Id.* at 407 (Jackson, J., dissenting); *see also id.* at 385 ("Our country has never been colorblind."). Justice Jackson recused herself from participating in the Harvard litigation, so her opinion formally pertained only to the UNC case. Justices Sotomayor and Kagan joined Justice Jackson's dissent.

⁸¹ *Id.* at 407–08.

⁸² *Id.* at 384.

⁸³ *Id.* at 385 (internal quotation marks omitted).

that conservatives themselves have long championed. The next Part pursues that vital task.

II. THE CONSERVATIVE CASE AGAINST *SFFA V. HARVARD*

SFFA contravenes time-honored conservative principles in four fundamental ways. First, the opinion places a new premium on college application essays that emphasize racial victimization, a dynamic that will heighten both the salience of race and the notion that racial progress has stalled. Second, *SFFA* encourages leading universities to usher students who attended struggling high schools into alien environments where they are likely to flounder, rather than flourish, a particular version of mismatch theory that Justice Thomas himself has repeatedly articulated. Third, the opinion's carveout for military academies invites racial balkanization, as the Black and brown communities will resent that some of their brightest, most ambitious young minds are being funneled into not only an unusually hostile racial environment, but also harm's way. Finally, *SFFA* is at war with important visions of conservativism itself, as the decision rejects both Burkean conservatism and the traditional notion of constitutional conservatism that prioritizes stare decisis.

A. VICTIMIZING ESSAYS

In perhaps *SFFA*'s most arresting feature, Chief Justice Roberts allowed that colleges may award applicants an admissions boost if their personal essays "discuss[] . . . how race affected his or her life, be it through discrimination, inspiration, or otherwise."[84] This allowance, combined with *SFFA*'s prohibition of racial boxes on college applications,[85] seems virtually guaranteed to produce a state of affairs that conservatives will detest even more than the system that *SFFA* replaced. Under the old regime, Black and brown college applicants could (if they so desired) check the relevant racial box, and then write their personal statements about their passion to study Proust, Plato, differential geometry, string theory, *The Odyssey*, or anything else

---

[84] *Id.* at 230.

[85] *SFFA* has been widely interpreted to prohibit racial boxes on university applications. *See, e.g.*, Jessica Cheung, *Affirmative Action Is Over. Should Applicants Still Mention Their Race?*, N.Y. TIMES MAG. (Sept. 4, 2023), https://www.nytimes.com/2023/09/04/magazine/affirmative-action-race-college-admissions.html ("This year, in response to the court's decision, many colleges will hide the box on the Common App that indicates the applicant's race. . . .").

under the university's sun. Under the *SFFA* regime, in contrast, Black and brown applicants are strongly encouraged to produce narratives of racial woe that not only utilize the victimhood mindset that conservatives loathe, but also complicate the tale of America's racial progress that conservatives prize. College application essay writing, moreover, is a far more deliberate, constitutive act than simply checking a racial box, which can happen quickly and without much thought at many quotidian settings—including, for example, the doctor's office or the DMV. Exemplary college application essays, of course, require careful planning, sustained thought, and numerous rounds of revisions. As Black and brown college applicants spend an outsized amount of time polishing their statements of highly individualized brushes with racism in response to *SFFA*, they will not simply abandon those sentiments when they arrive at college. Instead, much to conservatives' chagrin, those students will lug their senses of racial aggrievement to campus right along with their dorm trunks. This essay-driven dynamic will surely succeed in heightening the salience of race at universities—and around the nation.

Many prominent conservatives have vehemently denounced affirmative action's penchant for requiring racial minorities to conceive of themselves as victims. While Justice Thomas's *SFFA* concurrence voiced concern that race-conscious admissions promoted a "self-defeating" belief in Black "victimhood,"[86] the undisputed urtext of racial victimization is Shelby Steele's bestselling book from 1990, *The Content of Our Character: A New Vision of Race in America*.[87] Steele contended that a major "liability of affirmative action comes from the fact that it ... encourages blacks to exploit their own past victimization as a source of power and privilege."[88] Affirmative action, Steele maintained, thus "nurtures a victim-focused identity in blacks" such that in order "to receive the benefits of preferential treatment one must, to some extent, become invested in the view of one's self as a victim."[89] Steele deemed this self-conception plainly counterproductive, as Black people "become inadvertently invested in the very condition we are trying to overcome. Racial preferences send us the

---

[86] *SFFA*, 600 U.S. at 280, 283 (Thomas, J., concurring).

[87] *See* Shelby Steele, The Content of Our Character: A New Vision of Race in America (1990).

[88] *Id.* at 118.

[89] *Id.*

message that there is more power in our past suffering than our present achievements...."[90] When suffering becomes a source of empowerment, Steele argued, "blacks are encouraged to expand the boundaries of what qualifies as racial oppression, a situation that can lead us to paint our victimization in vivid colors, even as we receive the benefits of preference."[91] In a particularly evocative turn of phrase, Steele asserted: "The power to be found in victimization, like any power, is intoxicating and can lend itself to the creation of a new class of super-victims who can feel the pea of victimization under twenty mattresses."[92]

It would be difficult to overstate how influential *The Content of Our Character*'s concern about victimization proved among conservative critics of affirmative action. Six years after Steele contended that affirmative action created hypersensitive "super-victims," Lino Graglia similarly expressed fear that the idea of Black authenticity had become synonymous with "displaying an exceptional ability to discern and protest supposed racial slights."[93] In 2000, John McWhorter's condemnation of race-conscious admissions in his own bestseller—*Losing the Race: Self Sabotage in Black America*—openly acknowledged his debt to Steele.[94] "[T]he Cult of Victimology," McWhorter asserted, "has become a keystone of cultural blackness," which wrongly "treat[s] victimhood not as a problem to be solved but as an identity to be nurtured."[95] McWhorter contended that this mindset militates against any acknowledgement of racial progress: "[T]he grip of the Cult of Victimology encourages the black American from birth to fixate upon remnants of racism and resolutely downplay all signs of its demise."[96] Further, McWhorter contended that this victimization ideology exerted power pervasively, including in African Americans' most rarefied domains: "Even black students themselves are [c]arefully [t]aught by Victimology to conceive of themselves as somehow cosmically

---

[90] *Id.*

[91] *Id.*

[92] *Id.*

[93] Lino A. Graglia, *Affirmative Action: Today and Tomorrow*, 22 OHIO N.U. L. REV. 1353, 1356 (1996).

[94] *See* JOHN MCWHORTER, LOSING THE RACE: SELF-SABOTAGE IN BLACK AMERICA 28 (2000) ("My debt . . . to Shelby Steele's *The Content of Our Character* is obvious.").

[95] *Id.* at xi.

[96] *Id.*

'disadvantaged' *regardless of their life circumstances*."[97] In 2010, Linda Chavez similarly argued: "Victimology and affirmative action go hand in hand.... But thinking you're a victim is a lousy way to get ahead.... It's a defeatist attitude that encourages failure, not success."[98]

The *SFFA* essay-based approach to racial diversity, however, seems almost perfectly designed to increase the disempowering sense of victimhood that conservatives have long lamented. That is because the new system invites applicants to fixate on their encounters with racism far more than the box-checking method that *SFFA* jettisoned. Admittedly, prior to *SFFA*, some racial minorities doubtless dedicated their application essays to recounting instances when racism knocked at their door. One former college admissions officer discerned a trend before *SFFA* that, in personal statements, "white students discussed their passions," and "Black students discussed their pain."[99]

In the new post-*SFFA* era, however, even Black and brown applicants who would prefer to avoid focusing upon their racial pain now may feel compelled to do so. The *New York Times* covered a high school senior named Rayne Rivera-Forbes, who identified as Afro-Latina, and noted that *SFFA* caused her to "'just feel a bit lost.'"[100] Rivera-Forbes's personal statement could have conceivably focused upon her time serving as a student representative on the local schoolboard or her desire to someday become an elected official. Indeed, she "didn't want to write her essay about race," the *Times* noted, but "now that the race box is gone, she feels she should at least mention it."[101] Similarly, one Black high school student who hoped to study neuroscience at a leading college noted: "It's now put onto the student to display all the struggles that they went through and relive that trauma of growing up in an underprivileged community...."[102]

---

[97] *Id.* at 169 (emphasis added).

[98] Linda Chavez, *Affirmative Action Needs to End*, COLUMBUS DISPATCH (Aug. 9, 2010, 10:43 AM ET), https://www.dispatch.com/story/opinion/cartoons/2010/08/09/linda-chavez-affirmative-action-needs/23662199007.

[99] Aya M. Waller-Bey, *The 'T' Word: Resisting Expectations To Share Trauma In College Essays*, FORBES (Dec. 10, 2021, 9:00 AM EST), https://www.forbes.com/sites/civicnation/2021/12/10/the-t-word-resisting-expectations-to-share-trauma-in-college-essays.

[100] Cheung, *supra* note 85.

[101] *Id.*; *see also id.* (noting that Rivera-Forbes feared that if she did not write her essay about race her potential would not "be properly recognized").

[102] Melissa Korn, *College Applicants Ask: Can I Mention My Race, or Not?*, WALL ST. J. (July 31, 2023, 11:00 AM ET), https://www.wsj.com/articles/college-applicants-ask-can-i-mention-my-race-or-not-833fa774; *see also* Bernard Mokam, *Highlighting Their Race In Essays*

Not surprisingly, at least some Black college students have expressed delight that they applied under the pre-*SFFA* system, and were thus able to avoid any temptation to capitalize upon their racial tribulations. On the heels of *SFFA*, a Black freshman at Duke University voiced relief that she had felt free to write her essays about her family, reality television, and recreational activities. "But if I were applying now, I think I would ... opt for writing about things that I don't really like thinking about, like my experiences with racism or racial trauma," the Duke student stated. "You're going to be having a lot of minority students basically telling a single story, and it's not fair because that takes away from the uniqueness of the applicant."[103] *SFFA* thus unwittingly requires students to cram their individual lives into a preset racial narrative, and in the process negates their individuality.

It is hardly accidental that two Black students quoted above invoked the word *trauma* in discussing the sort of material that they felt admissions offices would expect. "[T]he trauma plot," it has been argued with some force, has become the dominant narrative structure or our time, and "[t]he appetite for stories about Black trauma" seems insatiable.[104] Nowhere is that phenomenon more pronounced than in the college application essay. *SFFA*, of course, promises only to expand what one high school senior labeled "this fad of trauma dumping" in college applications.[105] Indeed, no less a legal authority than *Teen Vogue* has noted that *SFFA* "puts an even harsher burden on applicants' essays," and that students now "are ... ranking themselves against their peers in a form of trauma Olympics."[106]

For College, N.Y. TIMES, Jan. 21, 2024, at 11 (noting several college applicants who had initially drafted essays that omitted discussing race, but after *SFFA* they "decided to rethink their essays to emphasize one key element: their racial identities").

[103] Rikki Schlott, Opinion, *How Colleges Brazenly Get Around Supreme Court's Affirmative Action Ruling*, N.Y. POST (Sept. 30, 2023, 7:00 AM ET), https://nypost.com/2023/09/30/how-colleges-are-skirting-supreme-couts-affirmative-action-ruling.

[104] Parul Sehgal, *The Key to Me*, NEW YORKER, Jan. 3, 2022, at 66; *see also id.* at 64–65 (contending that trauma has become "a source of moral authority, even a kind of expertise," and that "[t]rauma trumps all other identities, evacuates personality, remakes it in its own image"); *cf.* AMERICAN FICTION (Orion Pictures 2023) (satirizing the fervent cultural market for Black trauma narratives).

[105] Anemona Hartocollis, *After the Affirmative Action Ruling, Asian Americans Ask What Happens Next*, N.Y. TIMES (July 8, 2023), https://www.nytimes.com/2023/07/08/us/affirmative-action-asian-american-students.html.

[106] Claire Hodgdon, *College Essays and Trauma: Students Are Being Pushed to Write About Their Worst Experiences*, TEEN VOGUE (Sept. 21, 2023), https://www.teenvogue.com/story/college-essays-trauma-students.

This new premium placed on racially traumatic experiences has numerous undesirable consequences. Most prominently, many college applicants will be filled with racial resentment that they feel compelled to—in the parlance—*perform their trauma* for admissions officers. Applicants who have experienced genuinely traumatic events seem likely to find reliving those events *ad nauseum*, well, traumatizing. As a *Harvard Crimson* editorial, titled "College Essays and the Trauma Sweet Spot," observed recently: "[T]his pressure to package adversity into a palatable narrative can be toxic."[107] The editorial continued: "It can make applicants, accepted or not, feel like their admissions outcomes are tied to their most vulnerable experiences. The worst thing that ever happened to you was simply not enough, or alternatively, it was more than enough, and now you get to struggle with traumatized-imposter syndrome."[108] Predictably, students who win admission to elite universities after submitting an essay sounding in racial trauma may also experience a distinct type of imposter syndrome, believing that they secured their spots only because of their brushes with misfortune.[109]

Even more insidiously, the trauma premium in college application essays encourages Black and brown students who have—mercifully—led lives largely devoid of such painful experiences both to feel that they have been robbed of the authentic racial experience and to comb through their pasts, groping for that elusive "pea of victimization" buried beneath dozens of well-insulated mattresses.[110] On this account, applicants who have ample reason to hum a few bars of the song "Happy"[111] will instead feel obligated to write essays intoning "Nobody Knows the Trouble I've Seen."[112] *Teen Vogue*'s Trauma

---

[107] Editorial, *College Essays and the Trauma Sweetspot*, Harv. Crimson (Oct. 21, 2022), https://www.thecrimson.com/article/2022/10/21/editorial-college-admissions-essay; *see* Mokam, *supra* note 102, at 11 (noting that some college applicants resented feeling compelled to write their college essays about race, as *SFFA* "made them feel like they were not writing for themselves, but for someone else").

[108] *Id.*

[109] Elijah Megginson, Opinion, *When I Applied to College, I Didn't Want to 'Sell My Pain'*, N.Y. Times (May 9, 2021), https://www.nytimes.com/2021/05/09/opinion/college-admissions-essays-trauma.html (recounting a student who felt that her slot at NYU had been illegitimately secured due to her trauma).

[110] Steele, *supra* note 87, at 118.

[111] Pharrell Williams, *Happy*, *on* Girl (Columbia Recs. 2014).

[112] Louis Armstrong, *Nobody Knows The Trouble I've Seen*, *on* I've Got the World on a String (Verve Recs. 1960).

Olympics thus may—for at least some applicants—be superseded by the Microaggression Olympics.[113] Although *SFFA* surely intended no such outcome, the opinion nevertheless effectively discharged the starter's pistol in that ungainly contest.

Encouraging applicants to write elaborate, individualized narratives of racial aggrievement to gain admission to elite universities also clashes with a foundational conservative commitment holding that America has witnessed tremendous strides toward the goal of racial equality during the last several decades. Whereas renowned critical race theorist Professor Derrick Bell once emphasized "the *permanence* of racism,"[114] conservatives endorse almost exactly the inverse proposition. For conservatives, racism in the United States is a problem that has been overwhelmingly defeated, and it makes no sense—legal or otherwise—to obsess over what McWhorter labeled the "remnants of racism."[115]

This conservative emphasis on American racial progress, of course, animated the Roberts Court's decision in *Shelby County v. Holder*,[116] which invalidated Section 5 of the Voting Rights Act of 1965's coverage formula. The VRA's preclearance approach may have been justified to combat 1960s-style southern racism, *Shelby County* reasoned, but increasing racial equality rendered that approach obsolete. "The Voting Rights Act of 1965 employed extraordinary measures to address an extraordinary problem," Chief Justice Roberts wrote for the Court in *Shelby County*.[117] But, he emphasized, "history did not end in 1965."[118] *Shelby County* noted that the 1960s witnessed horrific anti-Black violence in Philadelphia, Mississippi, and Selma, Alabama. But "[t]oday both of those towns are governed by African-American mayors," Chief Justice Roberts wrote, a racial transformation that must be acknowledged, as "there is no denying that . . . our Nation has made great strides."[119]

---

[113] *Cf.* Peggy C. Davis, *Law as Microaggression*, 98 YALE L.J. 1559 (1989).

[114] DERRICK BELL, FACES AT THE BOTTOM OF THE WELL: THE PERMANENCE OF RACISM (1992).

[115] MCWHORTER, *supra* note 94, at xi.

[116] 570 U.S. 529 (2013).

[117] *Id.* at 534.

[118] *Id.* at 552.

[119] *Id.* at 549. For an extended examination of how the Roberts Court's narrative of racial progress shapes its jurisprudence, see Khiara M. Bridges, *The Supreme Court, 2021 Term—Foreword: Race in the Roberts Court*, 136 HARV. L. REV. 23 (2022).

Chief Justice Roberts's opinion in *SFFA*, however, encourages racial minorities to minimize or even outright deny the nation's racial progress that he touted in *Shelby County*. The strongest, most powerful essays that Black and brown applicants can produce in the post-*SFFA* era will dwell upon—indeed, luxuriate in—the absence of racial progress. In response to *SFFA*, students will write essays bemoaning the police stop that seemed like a fishing expedition, the time a fellow camper hurled a racial epithet, the teacher who doubted whether Advanced Placement calculus was the right fit, the store clerk who refused to accept a polite "just browsing," and myriad other racial indignities. Instead of being attuned to ways in which the nation's racial situation has improved, Black and brown students will instead be rewarded for highlighting life experiences that reveal the nation's racial progress has stalled—or perhaps even moved in reverse.

As a theoretical matter, of course, *SFFA* permits applicants to write essays exploring how race shaped their lives "through discrimination, inspiration, or otherwise."[120] It hardly seems extravagant to maintain, though, that applicants will gorge on "discrimination," and largely abstain from "inspiration" and "otherwise." During oral argument in *SFFA*, Justice Barrett asked a question that sketched how an essay sounding in "inspiration" or "otherwise" might run. "What if ... an applicant wrote an essay about how integral their racial identity was to them as a source of pride and the cultural attributes of the racial heritage were very important? Would that be okay even if it were all intimately tied up, say, with ... the traditions of a Mexican family?"[121]

For better or for worse, this hypothetical racial essay of pride and inspiration sounds excruciatingly dull. In modern times, an excellent personal statement—like many pieces of good writing—requires at least some friction and tension, including obstacles overcome, or, as *SFFA* itself put it, "challenges bested."[122] Drawing inspiration from family gatherings—of whatever racial heritage—is the personal statement equivalent of exploring one's love for rainbows, ice-cream sundaes, or long walks on the beach. Those essays are simply not going to get the job accomplished in the ultracompetitive world of college admissions.

---

[120] Students for Fair Admissions, Inc. v. President & Fellows of Harvard Coll. (*SFFA*), 600 U.S. 181, 230 (2023).

[121] Transcript of Oral Argument at 9–10, *SFFA*, 600 U.S. 181 (No. 20-1199).

[122] *SFFA*, 600 U.S. at 231.

Although conservatives—including then-Professor Scalia,[123] Chief Justice Roberts,[124] Justice Alito,[125] and Justice Thomas[126]—have often objected that affirmative action typically benefits wealthy racial minorities, it seems quite probable that *SFFA*'s new essay-driven diversity approach will redound even more to the benefit of privileged Black and brown applicants. Here, too, *SFFA* perversely threatens to intensify the very problem that it sought to remedy. Why would *SFFA*'s newfangled essay-based regime favor Black and brown students from affluent backgrounds more than those from humble backgrounds? One might intuitively believe that the exact opposite dynamic would materialize. After all, Black and brown students from poorer backgrounds could be assumed to have more ugly encounters with overt racism than students from wealthier backgrounds, whose privilege might serve to insulate them from some of life's racial indignities. That ugliness—while searing—would nevertheless furnish poorer applicants with powerful material for personal statements that could well move the admissions needle.

The trouble with this analysis, however, is that the *SFFA* essay-based diversity approach will most reward sophisticated applicants who know how to finesse the system, as those with access to circles of affluence will have much greater success navigating the new, murkier world created by *SFFA* than those lacking such access. Conservatives vociferously maligned the box-checking approach to college admissions because the attendant boost benefitted the Black scion of a wealthy industrialist as well as the Black son of a struggling sanitation worker.[127] But it is also true that the box-checking regime virtually assured that all Black applicants—even the poorest ones—would receive the boost. All they needed to do was simply check the box, a straightforward step that democratized the racial bump.

---

[123] *See supra* text accompanying notes 8, 45.

[124] During oral argument in *SFFA*, Chief Justice Roberts expressed profound skepticism that a Black applicant who "grew up in Grosse Point . . . had a great upbringing, . . . his parents went to Harvard, he's a legacy" should be eligible to receive an admissions boost. Transcript of Oral Argument at 62, *SFFA*, 600 U.S. 181 (No. 20-1199).

[125] Fisher v. Univ. of Tex. (*Fisher II*), 579 U.S. 365, 419 (2016) (Alito, J., dissenting) (referring to a race-conscious admissions program that provided a boost to students from comparatively "fortunate" backgrounds as "affirmative action gone wild").

[126] *See supra* text accompanying notes 46–47.

[127] *See supra* text accompanying note 46.

SFFA's novel approach means that the racial boost will be reserved only for those who obtain the required knowledge to access it effectively, and poorer applicants are less likely to acquire that knowledge. Justice Gorsuch's *SFFA* concurrence made a version of this argument, though it appeared in a quite disparate context. In *SFFA*, recall, Justice Gorsuch contended that a "cottage industry" had emerged helping Asian Americans conceal their racial identities, and that this dynamic would harm students who could not pay the freight.[128] Surely, though, *SFFA* will foment a new "cottage industry"—if it has not already created one—that helps wealthy Black and brown applicants strike exactly the right tone in their personal statements to maximize their chances of winning admission.

The concern that *SFFA*'s essay-based approach to diversity will inflict outsized harms on underprivileged Black students is, alas, hardly hypothetical. Following *SFFA*, the *Washington Post* profiled Demar Goodman's shifting college-application strategy. Goodman, prior to *SFFA*, had planned his personal statement to be "about growing up Black in a poor part of Atlanta. About attending an underserved high school with a reputation for drug use. About making do with subpar materials, out-of-date technology and people's prejudices. About how he persevered, rejoicing at every academic accolade because it disproved assumptions about who he could be and what he could achieve."[129] Goodman's intended statement, in other words, seemed to be exactly the sort of writing that could materially improve his chances in the college admissions sweepstakes.

But *SFFA*'s intervention provoked Goodman to dramatically alter his plans. Not only did *SFFA* convince Goodman that it was no longer worth even applying to Harvard—his dream college—he also decided against addressing race in his personal statement because he believed doing so was now useless. Instead of chronicling his resilience in the face of racial adversity, Goodman's personal statement focused upon his extensive "collection of flag lapel pins."[130] The story of how *SFFA* almost certainly harmed Goodman—one of the very sorts of students the majority portrayed itself as helping—is as

---

[128] *SFFA*, 600 U.S. at 293–94.

[129] Hannah Natanson, *After Affirmative Action, a White Teen's Ivy Hopes Rose. A Black Teen's Sank*, Wash. Post (Nov. 18, 2023, 6:05 AM), https://www.washingtonpost.com/education/interactive/2023/affirmative-action-race-teen-college-applications.

[130] *Id.*

evocative as it is dispiriting. And early returns suggest that Goodman is far from the only racial minority growing up in challenging circumstances whose college plans suffered from the more complex admissions world created by *SFFA*.[131]

The unintended upshot of *SFFA*'s essay-based approach to racial diversity is that it will increase the salience of race on college campuses—exactly the opposite effect that conservatives hoped they would achieve by dismantling affirmative action. Justice Thomas was not the only conservative voice in *SFFA* who blamed affirmative action for elevating the significance of race in university settings.[132] During oral argument, *SFFA* counsel—Cameron Norris—stated flatly: "[R]acial preferences on college campuses in our belief . . . have increased racial consciousness."[133] Patrick Strawbridge, who represented *SFFA* in the UNC case, made a closely related remark during oral argument.[134] Chief Justice Roberts also repeatedly floated the idea at oral argument that affirmative action policies should be blamed for establishing the wrong racial climate: "I'm talking about student groups taking [their] cue from the university and saying we ought to take race into account [with] whatever we're doing."[135] Elsewhere, he stated: "I get the sense . . . that race permeates a lot of what happens at the university."[136] Chief Justice Roberts did not intend this as a compliment.

Such statements in *SFFA* are only the most recent and most prominent of the widespread conservative anxiety that contends race-conscious admissions systems have the deleterious effect of increasing race's salience. Lino Graglia pressed this point memorably in 1970: "Affirmative action is a prescription for racial conflict and animosity, and the prescription is being filled. It is the root cause of the majority of problems plaguing American campuses today."[137]

---

[131] *See* Cheung, *supra* note 85 (chronicling the college application process of Francesco Macias of the Bronx who expressed hesitation about exploring race in his college applications).

[132] *SFFA*, 600 U.S. at 274–75 (Thomas, J., concurring).

[133] Transcript of Oral Argument at 21, *SFFA*, 600 U.S. 181 (2023) (No. 20-1199).

[134] *See* Transcript of Oral Argument at 5, Students for Fair Admissions, Inc. v. Univ. of N.C., 600 U.S. 181 (2023) (No. 21-707) ("[T]here is no evidence that after two decades, *Grutter* has somehow reduced the role of race on campus.").

[135] *See id.* at 130.

[136] *See id.* at 129.

[137] Graglia, *supra* note 93, at 1358.

Similarly, Carl Cohen asserted that affirmative action delayed the day when skin color possessed no greater significance than eye color.[138] "Race preference . . . obliges everyone to think early and often about his ethnic identity," Cohen argued. "Race becomes the irritant underlying almost every public issue, the intensifying ingredient of community controversy, and the salt in social wounds."[139] Cohen contended that affirmative action promotes both a sort of racial tribalism and the lesson that race represents the core of one's humanity: "Ethnic identification begins to saturate everyday life. We must be able to prove *what* we are. You are an American, yes—but an American of *which kind?* . . . Race preference does this terrible thing to our community and ourselves; it compels us . . . to 'think with our blood.' "[140]

Yet, as should be clear by now, the Court's opinion in *SFFA*—which will lead to the proliferation of racialized personal statements—seems likely to yield even greater racial salience on university campuses than did racial box-checking. Indeed, the essay prompts many universities have devised in response to *SFFA* further instill the very lesson that conservatives wish would dissipate: the notion that racial differences define who we are. Only six weeks after the Court issued *SFFA*, a *New York Times* article—titled "Colleges Want to Know More About You and Your 'Identity'"—surveyed the new college application landscape and found: "A review of the essay prompts used this year by more than two dozen highly selective colleges reveals that schools are using words and phrases like 'identity' and 'life experience,' and are probing aspects of a student's upbringing and background that have, in the words of a Harvard prompt, 'shaped who you are.' "[141] Some new essay prompts overtly instruct applicants to write about race if they so wish.[142] But even prompts that take a subtler approach—inquiring about applicants' "identity" and what has

---

[138] *But see* TONI MORRISON, THE BLUEST EYE (1970).

[139] CARL COHEN & JAMES P. STERBA, AFFIRMATIVE ACTION AND RACIAL PREFERENCE: A DEBATE 179 (2003).

[140] *Id.* at 178 (emphasis in original).

[141] Anemona Hartocolis & Colbi Edmonds, *Colleges Want to Know More About You and Your 'Identity,'* N.Y. TIMES (Aug. 14, 2023), https://www.nytimes.com/2023/08/14/us/college-applications-admissions-essay.html.

[142] *See, e.g., id.* (noting that Johns Hopkins's post-*SFFA* application states: "Any part of your background, including but not limited to your race, may be discussed in your response to this essay if you so choose.").

"shaped who you are"—nevertheless reinforce the paramount importance of race; they are just doing so in a roundabout fashion. Some of the roundabout approaches are, moreover, awfully straightforward. Consider Dartmouth College's post-*SFFA* prompt, which will win few points for subtlety: "'It's not easy being green . . . ' was the frequent refrain of Kermit the Frog. How has difference been a part of your life, and how have you embraced it as part of your identity and outlook?"[143] Similarly, the University of Pennsylvania Law School's new application instructs aspiring students to write an essay explaining "[w]hat defines you" and how your "lived experience informs who you are today."[144]

This new state of college applications strongly resembles the mindset from which Chief Justice Roberts's *SFFA* opinion recoiled, including when he noted with evident disdain that a lawyer defending UNC's admissions program contended that race "'says [something] about who you are.'"[145] Universities now—both directly and indirectly—instruct students that race says not only *something* about who they are, but something *major*, and prompts students to write lengthy testimonials exploring the centrality of race to their identity formation. How then, from a conservative perspective, did *SFFA* not inaugurate a marked decline from the status quo?

One need not be conservative, moreover, to harbor significant reservations regarding how *SFFA* encourages Black and brown applicants to conceive of race as *the* singular, dominant aspect of their identities. In his 1994 memoir, Professor Henry Louis Gates, Jr.—a liberal, distinguished scholar of African American literature and history at Harvard—balked at the notion that Black people must subscribe to the totalizing, all-consuming vision of race that *SFFA* unintentionally promoted. "I rebel at the notion that I can't be part of other groups, that I can't construct identities through elective affinity, that race must be the most important thing about me," Gates

---

[143] Nick Anderson, *After Supreme Court Ruling, College Applicants Still Write About Race*, WASH. POST (Nov. 27, 2023, 6:00 AM EST), https://www.washingtonpost.com/education/2023/11/27/college-applications-race-affirmative-action.

[144] *See Application Instructions*, UNIV. PA. CAREY L. SCH. 8, https://www.law.upenn.edu/live/files/12752-2024-application-instructions.pdf.

[145] Students for Fair Admissions, Inc. v. President & Fellows of Harvard Coll. (*SFFA*), 600 U.S. 181, 220 (2023) (quoting Transcript of Oral Argument at 98, Students for Fair Admissions, Inc. v. Univ. of N.C., 600 U.S. 181 (2023) (No. 21-707)).

wrote.[146] "Is that what I want on my gravestone: Here lies an African American?"[147] If Gates bristled at being thrust into racially confined roles, many other liberals will doubtless chafe when they feel themselves being eased into the racial straitjacket.

Similarly, many Black liberal intellectuals may object on racial grounds to *SFFA*'s encouragement of Black applicants to showcase their racial agonies. In the 1960s, Ralph Ellison published an essay protesting the dubious notion "that unrelieved suffering is the only 'real' Negro experience."[148] Ellison insisted that "there is ... an American Negro tradition which teaches one to deflect racial provocation and to master and contain pain," and "which abhors as obscene any trading on one's own anguish for gain or sympathy."[149] Assuming Ellison's characterization is correct, *SFFA* guarantees that college admissions offices today confront a veritable torrent of racial obscenity.

B. MISMATCHING STUDENTS

Conservative critics of affirmative action—including then-Professor Scalia[150] and Justice Thomas[151]—have often lambasted the policy because they insist that it promotes racial minorities into academic settings for which they are unprepared. This critique—which has come to be labeled "mismatch"—predates the Court's validation of affirmative action in *Bakke*. In 1970, eight years prior to *Bakke*,[152] Professor Graglia advanced the mismatch criticism in one of the earliest law review articles to wrestle with the then-novel affirmative action phenomenon. "Special admission programs, almost by definition, operate to ensure that students are placed in schools for which they are not qualified," Graglia stated. "As a result, many students fully qualified for other schools, attend institutions for which they are

---

[146] HENRY LOUIS GATES, JR., COLORED PEOPLE: A MEMOIR, at xv (1994).

[147] *Id.* In a fascinating twist, when Gates applied to Yale College in the 1960s, his personal essay opened: "My grandfather was colored, my father was Negro, and I am black." *Id.* at 201.

[148] RALPH ELLISON, *The World and the Jug*, in SHADOW AND ACT 107, 111 (1964).

[149] *Id.*

[150] *See* Scalia, *supra* note 2, at 155–56.

[151] *See* Students for Fair Admissions, Inc. v. President & Fellows of Harvard Coll. (*SFFA*), 600 U.S. 181, 268–70 (2023) (Thomas, J., concurring).

[152] 438 U.S. 265 (1978).

ill-equipped."[153] Economist Thomas Sowell, who has profoundly influenced Justice Thomas's thought,[154] has articulated influential versions of the mismatch idea. In an article published shortly before *Bakke* appeared, Sowell condemned affirmative action for inflicting "a disastrous and permanently scarring experience" on young racial minorities "who would normally qualify for good, non-prestigious colleges where they could succeed, [but] are instead enrolled in famous institutions where they fail."[155] Sowell contended that the overpromotion of underqualified Black students at the nation's most revered universities produced a cascading effect, as less celebrated institutions also compromised their standards to guarantee that they enrolled an acceptable percentage of Black students. "When the top institutions reach further down to get minority students," Sowell explained, "then academic institutions at the next level are forced to reach still further down, so that they too will end up with a minority body count high enough to escape criticism and avoid trouble with the government and other donors."[156]

Though respected scholars have challenged the empirical basis for mismatch theory in recent years,[157] many conservatives nonetheless remain firmly committed to the notion's veracity—at times seeming almost to accept it as an article of faith. Justice Thomas's *SFFA* concurrence,[158] embraced over the vociferous objections of Justice Sotomayor,[159] presents only a recent illustration of mismatch theory's durability within conservative circles.

Assuming arguendo that mismatch is a real phenomenon, however, it seems almost certain that *SFFA* will exacerbate the phenomenon—placing even more students into settings for which they

---

[153] Lino A. Graglia, *Special Admission of the "Culturally Deprived" to Law School*, 119 U. Pa. L. Rev. 351, 360 (1970).

[154] *See* Bill Kauffman, *Freedom Now II: Interview with Clarence Thomas*, Reason (Nov. 1987), https://reason.com/1987/11/01/clarence-thomas (identifying Sowell's influence on Thomas's thinking).

[155] Thomas Sowell, *Are Quotas Good for Blacks?*, Commentary, June 1, 1978, at 39, 41.

[156] *Id.*

[157] *See supra* the sources cited in note 48.

[158] *SFFA*, 600 U.S. 181, 268–70 (2023) (Thomas, J., concurring); *see also* Grutter v. Bollinger, 539 U.S. 306, 372 (2003) (Thomas, J., concurring in part and dissenting in part) (arguing that affirmative action prompts "overmatched students [to] take the bait, only to find that they cannot succeed in the cauldron of competition").

[159] *SFFA*, 600 U.S. at 371–72 (Sotomayor, J., dissenting).

are ill-prepared to flourish. *SFFA* will not, of course, extinguish the desire of universities to enroll significant numbers of Black and brown students. The diversity ethos is, as several scholars have suggested, too firmly embedded in higher education to be completely eradicated by a single judicial decision.[160] But *SFFA* will likely inspire universities to admit more Black and brown students from very different high schools than those who were typically admitted under the old system of racial diversity. And these new students may be much less well prepared to succeed than the students who were typically admitted before *SFFA*.

Consider the transformation that is almost certainly now underway in many college admissions offices, and recall that standardized test scores are now largely optional, which increases the significance of grades.[161] Under the pre-*SFFA* regime, the Ivy League and its peer institutions often admitted Black and brown students who attended private schools and boarding schools where they certainly compiled strong grades, but often finished outside the top one percent of graduates. Under the post-*SFFA* regime, it will be more difficult to admit such students and to justify such admissions in a litigation context. Accordingly, leading universities may respond by admitting the valedictorians and salutatorians from large, unprivileged urban high schools. Conservatives may well be tempted to cheer this transformation, contending that if any racial minorities are receiving

---

[160] *See* KENNEDY, *supra* note 18, at 240 ("Racial affirmative action will remain a substantial presence in American life for the foreseeable future, no matter how the Supreme Court resolves [the issue]. The racial homogeneity in key institutions that was so prevalent and taken for granted prior to the 1960s ... is inconceivable today."); *id.* at 15, 239; *see also* MELVIN I. UROFSKY, THE AFFIRMATIVE ACTION PUZZLE: A COMPREHENSIVE AND HONEST EXPLORATION OF ONE OF THE MOST CONTROVERSIAL LEGAL AND SOCIAL ISSUES IN US HISTORY 485 (2022) ("While affirmative action plans may change in forthcoming years, it does not seem that, whatever the Supreme Court may say [in *SFFA*], they will go away. There may be more emphasis on economic status, but race and ethnicity will still be there."); Lauren S. Foley, *The Supreme Court May End College Affirmative Action. Then What?*, WASH. POST (Oct. 27, 2022, 2:12 PM ET), https://www.washingtonpost.com/politics/2022/10/27/harvard-supreme-court-affirmative-action ("[E]ven if the court bans college affirmative action, my research finds that the goals behind these programs may survive.").

[161] *See* David Leonhardt, *Colleges Fled SATs, Despite Their Utility*, N.Y. TIMES, Jan. 12, 2024, at A1 ("Without test scores, admissions officers sometimes have a hard time distinguishing between applicants who are likely to do well at elite colleges and those who are likely to struggle. Researchers who have studied the issue say that test scores can be particularly helpful in identifying lower-income students and underrepresented minorities who will thrive."); Raj Chetty et al., *Diversifying Society's Leaders? The Determinants and Causal Effects of Admission to Highly Selective Private Colleges* (Nat'l Bureau of Econ. Rsch., Working Paper No. 31492, 2023).

a preference in college admissions, that preference should surely go to students from modest, not wealthy backgrounds. The trouble with this approach, however, is that the racial minorities who conservatives often deem undeserving beneficiaries may well be the students who are best prepared to flourish at elite universities.

This claim is sure to stir considerable controversy; indeed, Justice Alito stridently attacked a version of this idea as an elitist delusion several years ago. At the outset, then, it may be helpful to offer a few notes of clarification. For one thing, it is not necessary to believe that students who attended large, urban, underprivileged public schools are not *academically* prepared for leading universities to believe that a version of the mismatch idea nevertheless pertains. That is because many students who graduate from such schools will be accustomed to learning and living in thoroughly monoracial environments, leaving them *socially* unprepared to flourish in their new racially diverse environments. For another, it is important to realize that Black and brown students who attend private and boarding schools need not have been raised by wealthy parents; to the contrary, the existence of scholarships at these schools means that it is overly simplistic to assume that having attended a privileged school means that one hails from an affluent household. Finally, it is important to realize that no less a conservative authority than Justice Thomas has repeatedly suggested that Black students who attended non-racially diverse, underprivileged public schools are mismatched at elite universities. Thus, according to perhaps the nation's preeminent constitutional conservative, *SFFA* itself is poised to lure many Black students into alien settings where they are set up to fail.

The notion that it would be advantageous to undertake special effort to admit some students of color who attended high school in racially diverse—rather than only monoracial—settings became hotly contested in 2016.[162] In *Fisher v. University of Texas* (*Fisher II*), the Supreme Court weighed the ability of one of the nation's foremost public universities to engage in race-conscious admissions. The overwhelming majority of UT's Black and brown students were admitted through the Top Ten Percent program, whereby graduates of Texas public high schools who ranked within the top decile received automatic admission to the state's flagship university in Austin. The

---

[162] 579 U.S. 365 (2016) (*Fisher II*).

Top Ten Percent program yielded significant racial diversity in Austin because many Texas high schools featured student bodies that were composed almost exclusively of Black and brown students. In addition to this formally race-neutral program, though, UT also admitted some students using racial classifications. When this race-conscious system was initially challenged in *Fisher I*, UT defended that program, in part, by noting that racial classifications allowed UT to ensure that it matriculated students of color who graduated not exclusively from urban, all-minority high schools, but instead included some who graduated from meaningfully integrated environments. In *Fisher I*, UT explained that students of color admitted through race-conscious means guaranteed that it could welcome, say, "[t]he African-American or Hispanic child of successful professionals in Dallas," or even "[t]he black student with high grades from Andover."[163]

The Supreme Court in 2013 issued a narrow, technical decision in *Fisher I*, clarifying the strict-scrutiny approach.[164] When the matter returned to the Court three years in *Fisher II*, UT no longer foregrounded its Andover defense.[165] But when *Fisher II* resulted in the Court upholding UT's race-conscious system, Justice Alito demonstrated that he had in no sense forgotten the discarded, unorthodox justification. Rather, Justice Alito pounced on the idea, excoriating it as an unconscionable distortion of affirmative action's true aims: "UT has ... claimed at times that the race-based component of its plan is needed because the Top Ten Percent Plan admits the *wrong kind* of African–American and Hispanic students, namely, students from poor families who attend schools in which the student body is predominantly African–American or Hispanic."[166] Evidently, Justice Alito deemed this a winning formulation, as he used almost identical language twice in other *Fisher II* passages.[167] Any notion that

---

[163] *Id.* at 391 (Alito, J., dissenting) (quoting Brief for Respondents at 34, Fisher v. Univ. of Tex. (*Fisher I*), 570 U.S. 297 (2013) (No. 11-345)); *id.* at 417–18 (quoting Brief for Respondents at 33, *Fisher II*, 579 U.S. 365 (No. 14-981)).

[164] *Fisher I*, 570 U.S. 297.

[165] *Fisher II*, 579 U.S. at 417–18 (Alito, J., dissenting).

[166] *Id.* at 391 (Alito, J., dissenting) (emphasis in original).

[167] *See id.* at 418 ("[T]he Top Ten Percent Law is faulted for admitting *the wrong kind of African–American and Hispanic students*." (emphasis in original)); *id.* at 392 (contending "UT now disowns the argument that the Top Ten Percent Plan results in the admission of the wrong kind of African–American and Hispanic students").

"African–Americans and Hispanics admitted through the Top Ten Percent Plan only got in because they did not have to compete against very many whites and Asian–Americans" was, Justice Alito insisted, a "pernicious stereotype."[168] He dismissed any race-based preferences for the children of Andover and the Dallas professional class an unjust inversion, one that "turn[ed] affirmative action on its head," as the "the programs were created to help *disadvantaged* students."[169] Summarizing his incredulity, Justice Alito concluded: "[W]e are told that a program that tends to admit poor and disadvantaged minority students is inadequate because it does not work to the advantage of those who are more fortunate. This is affirmative action gone wild."[170]

This castigation, of course, resonates with a dominant view among affirmative action's conservative critics—including then-Professor Scalia[171] and Justice Thomas in *SFFA*[172]—that the program too often rewards relatively privileged racial minorities. The objection that race-conscious programs reward undeserving beneficiaries has figured prominently in conservative commentary from the very beginning. In Graglia's foundational critique from 1970, for example, he charged: "Negroes may be specially admitted [under affirmative action] even though they are of middle class background, have professional parents, or otherwise appear to have had average or above average cultural opportunities."[173] In 1999, Stephen and Abigail Thernstrom put the point in even starker terms: "It never occurs to

---

[168] *Id.* at 419.

[169] *Id.* at 391 (emphasis in original).

[170] *Id.* at 419. For his part, Justice Alito contends that empirical evidence belies the notion that students admitted under the Top Ten Percent program suffer more academically than students admitted through the race-conscious model. *See id.* at 410–16. This empirical conclusion, like many empirical matters, is hotly disputed. For a claim that Top Ten Percent students do in fact encounter greater difficulties, see Eric Furstenberg, *Academic Outcomes and Texas's Top Ten Percent Law*, 627 AM. ACAD. POL. SOC. SCI. 167 (2010). Assuming arguendo that Justice Alito is correct about the success of Top Ten Percent students, it is important to bear in mind that this conclusion—from the University of Texas—offers limited insight for how matters might unfold at Ivy League colleges and their peer institutions. The University of Texas is, of course, an excellent, selective university in that it admits thirty-one percent of applicants, whereas most universities admit much higher percentages. But Harvard admits three percent of applicants, Yale admits four percent of applicants, and Princeton admits six percent of applicants. Those institutions are therefore quite distinct.

[171] *See supra* text accompanying notes 8, 45.

[172] *See* Students for Fair Admissions, Inc. v. President & Fellows of Harvard Coll. (*SFFA*), 600 U.S. 181, 268–70 (2023) (Thomas, J., concurring).

[173] Graglia, *supra* note 93, at 351.

[universities] that [admitting] . . . a white working-class kid from Staten Island might bring more true diversity to an Ivy League campus than adding another Exeter-educated African American who grew up in Scarsdale."[174] Five years later, Walter Benn Michaels offered perhaps the most famous version of the critique: "When students and faculty activists struggle for . . . diversity, they are in large part battling over what skin colors the rich kids have."[175]

Conservative opponents of affirmative action have thus vehemently advanced two critiques, contending that the programs promote both mismatch and undeserving beneficiaries. Conservatives have dedicated insufficient attention, however, to acknowledging that the two critiques can be viewed as existing in substantial tension with each other, and perhaps may even be irreconcilable. Those critiques are competing, that is, because the students from the least privileged backgrounds—the deserving beneficiaries—may be the very students who are most mismatched at the nation's elite campuses. One year after *Bakke*, then-Professor J. Harvie Wilkinson acknowledged this very point, when he noted that university administrators thought that "[n]othing . . . could be worse" than an admission program that targeted economic disadvantage because that approach "would . . . disqualify by definition many of the ablest minority students, those from middle-class backgrounds."[176] Candid liberal supporters of affirmative action have sometimes made this point in reverse, noting that racial minorities from the most deprived backgrounds are likely to be overmatched at ultracompetitive universities.[177]

Perhaps surprisingly, though, the preeminent advocate of the idea that students of color who attended high school in modest, monoracial circumstances may be mismatched in elite universities is Justice Thomas. But because Justice Thomas has not ventured this particular version of mismatch in his judicial writings, legal scholars have generally neglected this significant feature of his views on affirmative action. In the early 1990s, Justice Thomas read journalist Ron

---

[174] Stephen Thernstrom & Abigail Thernstrom, *Reflections on The Shape of the River*, 46 UCLA L. REV. 1583, 1627 (1999).

[175] Walter Benn Michaels, *Diversity's False Solace*, N.Y. TIMES, Apr. 11, 2004, at 12.

[176] J. HARVIE WILKINSON, FROM BROWN TO BAKKE: THE SUPREME COURT AND SCHOOL INTEGRATION: 1954–1978, at 288–89 (1979).

[177] *See, e.g.*, STEPHEN L. CARTER, REFLECTIONS OF AN AFFIRMATIVE ACTION BABY 80 (1991) (noting that "the truly disadvantaged are not likely to succeed in college").

Suskind's *Wall Street Journal* profile of Cedric Jennings, an ambitious high school student who was earning top marks at Ballou High School, "[t]he most troubled and violent school in the blighted southeast corner of Washington, D.C."[178] All too predictably, Ballou educated a student body that was almost entirely Black.[179] Justice Thomas was sufficiently impressed by the young man's efforts to achieve in the face of adversity that he extended Jennings a standing invitation to visit his Supreme Court chambers. When the momentous visit occurred several months later, Suskind accompanied Jennings and chronicled Justice Thomas remarkably warning the hopeful twelfth grader that he was about to receive an extended, harsh lesson in mismatch.

After the subject of college plans arose during the visit, Jennings excitedly informed Justice Thomas that he was headed to Brown University in the fall. But "Thomas frown[ed] and [shook] his head," informing Jennings: "Well, that's fine, but I'm not sure I would have selected an Ivy League school. . . . You're going to be up there with lots of very smart white kids, and, if you're not sure about who you are, you could get eaten alive."[180] Understandably, Jennings seemed taken aback, but Thomas continued: "It's not just at the Ivies, you understand. It can happen at any of the good colleges where a young black man, who hasn't spent much time with whites, suddenly finds himself among almost all whites. You can feel lost."[181] To make sure that Jennings understood the enormous stakes of feeling lost, Justice Thomas drew upon his own college days at Holy Cross, telling Jennings about the "smartest black kid [he] ever knew" who "got confused about who he was and ended up getting addicted to drugs and dropping out."[182] Justice Thomas's unvarnished advice

---

[178] Ron Suskind, A Hope in the Unseen: An American Odyssey from the Inner City to the Ivy League 1 (1998).

[179] *Id.* at 2.

[180] *Id.* at 120.

[181] *Id.* Justice Thomas's private advice to Jennings about the perils of attending an all-Black high school stands in stark contrast with his public opinions that have attested to the greatness of some all-Black high schools. *See* Missouri v. Jenkins, 515 U.S. 70, 114 (1995) (Thomas, J., concurring) ("It never ceases to amaze me that the courts are so willing to assume that anything that is predominantly black must be inferior."); Parents Involved in Cmty. Schs. v. Seattle Sch. Dist. No. 1, 551 U.S. 701, 763 (2007) (Thomas, J., concurring) (touting Washington, D.C.'s Dunbar as "an exemplary black school").

[182] Suskind, *supra* note 178, at 120. Surprisingly, a Westlaw search reveals that Justice Thomas's admonition to Jennings appears in legal scholarship only once. *See* Ronald Turner,

to Jennings is, of course, an unmistakable embrace of the notion that racial minorities who attend monoracial high schools are mismatched at first-rate universities.

It may be tempting to dismiss Justice Thomas's advice to Jennings as mere off-the-cuff talk that in no way reflects his considered judgment. But yielding to that temptation would be misguided. In his memoir, *My Grandfather's Son,* Justice Thomas stated in a significant passage that he had witnessed several Black college classmates at Holy Cross in the late 1960s suffer badly from the mismatch of being thrust into a racially alien environment. Black Holy Cross students who had previously attended school in all-Black environments struggled, Justice Thomas maintained, because "they lacked the social experience that would have made it easier for them to leave the comfort zone of segregation and move into the white world."[183] He explained: "Many of them ... might have done better had they gone to schools closer to home or to predominantly black colleges, which would have allowed them to grapple with the ordinary challenges of young adulthood without having to simultaneously face the additional challenge of learning how to live among whites."[184] Justice Thomas objected that Holy Cross placed these Black students in a position to fail, and allowed that he "couldn't see the point of putting them through an experience for which they were unprepared. Why, I asked, were these gifted young people being sacrificed on the altar of an abstract theory of social justice—and who profited from their failure?"[185]

Justice Thomas is far from alone in arguing that Black college students who are unfamiliar with what Langston Hughes once termed "the ways of white folks"[186] are socially mismatched at the nation's leading universities. In 2019, Professor Anthony Abraham Jack wrote an important book exploring the plight of poor students in elite universities. Jack emphasized that the varying life experiences of students who come from indigent backgrounds indelibly shape their college experiences. The "Privileged Poor," Jack noted, may have

---

On Parents Involved *and the Problematic Praise of Justice Clarence Thomas,* 37 HASTINGS CONST. L.Q. 225, 231 n.45 (2010).

[183] CLARENCE THOMAS, MY GRANDFATHER'S SON: A MEMOIR 54 (2007).

[184] *Id.*

[185] *Id.*

[186] LANGSTON HUGHES, THE WAYS OF WHITE FOLKS (1934).

attended a top-notch high school which would afford them "the privilege of an early introduction to the world they will enter in college."[187] In contrast, the "Doubly Disadvantaged," who would have attended the Ballous that exist around the nation, "are both poor and unfamiliar with this new world."[188] Whereas the Privileged Poor are prepared to navigate the Ivy League's folkways, Jack contended, the Doubly Disadvantaged often struggle to adapt. "The experiences of the Privileged Poor and the Doubly Disadvantaged differ most clearly in their disparate institutional knowledge of and familiarity with elite spaces, and these differences affect both their well-being and their strategies for navigating college," Jack noted. "The Doubly Disadvantaged are not adequately integrated into the norms that govern student life at an elite institution . . . that the Privileged Poor learned in high school. . . . [T]he Privileged Poor have the kind of cultural capital that enables them to be at ease when engaging with their peers and professors."[189]

This relatively intuitive insight renders it hardly surprising that elite universities—when admitting students of color from modest backgrounds—have often admitted students who can be categorized as the Privileged Poor. Jack himself noted that a large percentage of the indigent Latino students who attend leading universities arrived from "private high schools like the Brearley School in New York and the Thacher School in California."[190] The Prep for Prep program—which has furnished scholarships for low-income Black and brown students to attend New York's toniest schools since the 1970s—regularly sends large numbers of alumni to the Ivy League and its ilk.[191] As a normative matter, it seems deeply regrettable both that elite universities look for students of color who are in some sense

---

[187] ANTHONY ABRAHAM JACK, THE PRIVILEGED POOR: HOW ELITE COLLEGES ARE FAILING DISADVANTAGED STUDENTS 11 (2019).

[188] *Id.*

[189] *Id.* at 22. Jack did emphasize that elite colleges should do a better job of addressing the Privileged Poor's financial privations—including, say, making sure that students who lack means can access food when the dining halls close over Spring Break. *See id.* at 180. Of course, the Privileged Poor would nevertheless have greater familiarity with the financial chasm that separates them from many of their classmates than would the Doubly Disadvantaged.

[190] *Id.* at 11.

[191] *See* Vinson Cunningham, *Prep for Prep and the Fault Lines in New York's Schools*, NEW YORKER (Mar. 2, 2020), https://www.newyorker.com/magazine/2020/03/09/prep-for-prep-and-the-fault-lines-in-new-yorks-schools.

already members of the club, and that those students flourish more readily than students from racially isolated backgrounds. As a descriptive matter, however, this phenomenon packs even less astonishment than a newspaper headline declaring: "Dog Bites Man."

At first blush, *SFFA* might have been thought to quell the mismatch issue, but—upon close inspection—it instead promises only to foreground the issue. The consequences for students from marginalized backgrounds could prove catastrophic. One can easily imagine Justice Thomas, in a moment of candor, expressing deep concern for this group of guinea pigs preparing to embark on a journey into the unknown, and also wondering: Who stands to gain from any failures in this high-stakes experiment?

Perspicacious readers may object that a tension exists between two different claims about *SFFA*'s harms. On the one hand, the Article above contended that students from affluent families will more readily succeed in navigating *SFFA*'s essay-based diversity regime. On the other hand, the Article's mismatch claim now contends that *SFFA* will redound to the (short-term) benefit of students from underprivileged high schools. What gives? One way to reconcile these claims is to note that *SFFA* could plausibly increase the percentages of Black and brown students from both ultra-privileged backgrounds *and* ultra-deprived backgrounds, effectively squeezing out applicants from the middle-class. To the extent that the two claims still seem irreconcilable, though, that difficulty stems from conservatives' multifarious, kitchen-sink-style attack on affirmative action. On this view, conservatives have launched a thousand arrows against affirmative action over the years, but they have dedicated inadequate energy to examining the analytical incoherence that bedevils their varied charges.[192] In our new post-affirmative action world, though, conservatives will need to dedicate greater effort to contemplating the assorted tradeoffs, resolving firmly what values they seek to maximize and what values they wish to minimize.

C. THE BALKANIZING MILITARY CARVEOUT

One of *SFFA*'s most notable, most surprising features appeared in footnote four, which declined to require the nation's military academies

---

[192] For an extended critique of judicial incoherence in one legal domain, see generally Justin Driver & Emma Kaufman, *The Incoherence of Prison Law*, 135 HARV. L. REV. 517 (2021).

to comply with the decision.[193] This carveout was driven by the fear that, in the absence of overt affirmative action, those institutions—including the United States Military Academy at West Point and the Naval Academy in Annapolis—would be unable to produce a racially diverse officer corps to lead a racially diverse group of enlisted servicemembers. The consequences of having few Black and brown officers would pose grave national security concerns, a dynamic that infamously emerged during the Vietnam War.[194] In *Grutter*, Justice O'Connor's opinion for the Court invoked and relied upon an amicus brief filed by several esteemed former military generals, who drove home the necessity of a diverse officer corps for the military's ability to function effectively.[195] Whereas *Grutter* construed the military's racial diversity needs as applicable to the larger society of which the military is part, *SFFA* in effect concluded that the military's needs on this front could stand it apart from the larger society.

Conservatives might be thought to abhor *SFFA*'s military exemption for a few different reasons. Most intuitively, colorblindness proponents could believe that *SFFA* adopted a partial remedy to a problem demanding an absolute solution. On this account, Chief Justice Roberts's opinion failed to exhibit the courage of its own convictions, because though it broadly proclaimed "[e]liminating racial discrimination means eliminating all of it," *SFFA* in fact eliminated only some of it.[196] In addition, conservatives who believe that the military's unique position in American society means that it should in fact receive greater leeway to consider race may object that

---

[193] *See* Students for Fair Admissions, Inc. v. President & Fellows of Harvard Coll. (*SFFA*), 600 U.S. 181, 213 n.4 (2023).

[194] "In Vietnam, racial tensions reached a point where there was an inability to fight." David Maraniss, *U.S. Military Struggles to Make Equality Work*, WASH. POST (Mar. 5, 1990), https://www.washingtonpost.com/archive/politics/1990/03/06/us-military-struggles-to-make-equality-work/e43bfbf9-e170-4f3f-b6c5-ff74cade07f4 (quoting Lt. Gen. Frank Petersen, Jr.).

[195] *See* Grutter v. Bollinger, 539 U.S. 306, 331 (2003) (citing Consolidated Brief of Julius W. Becton, Jr., et al. as Amici Curiae Supporting Respondents, *Grutter*, 539 U.S. 306 (No. 02-241)).

[196] *SFFA*, 600 U.S. at 206. Edward Blum's SFFA organization follows this line, as it quickly filed a lawsuit challenging the military academies' use of race following the Supreme Court's decision. Anemona Hartocollis, *Anti-Affirmative Action Group Sues West Point Over Admissions Policy*, N.Y. TIMES (Sept. 19, 2023), https://www.nytimes.com/2023/09/19/us/affirmative-action-west-point.html.

SFFA's carveout will be spectacularly ineffective in realizing its ambitions. Conservatives in this camp would note that the military academies produce only nineteen percent of the officers, with ROTC programs producing the overwhelming majority.[197] In order for the military exemption to prove effective in ensuring a racially diverse office corps, then, *SFFA* should have afforded civilian universities with ROTC programs at least some discretion regarding racial classifications.[198]

The most significant conservative objection to *SFFA*'s military exemption, however, would note that the carveout fosters racial balkanization, promising to deepen the nation's divides. *SFFA*'s military exemption could have the effect of funneling ambitious Black and brown students—who prize the status associated with graduating from a first-rate university—into a career in the military, even though they may hold no deep desire to serve. But the persistence of race-conscious admissions at West Point and Annapolis—which provide a top-notch education that is also tuition-free—will make it easier for underrepresented minorities to gain admission to those academies than to their civilian peer institutions. Some Black and brown twelfth-graders will surely resent being forced to select between receiving an excellent education at a military academy and a weaker education at a nonmilitary college. Those feelings of resentment will only grow when they realize that the U.S. military—including the academies—continues to be plagued by an unvarnished racism that would be unfathomable on many American college campuses today.[199] More broadly, even apart from the students of color who feel coerced into entering the academies, *SFFA*'s military exemption seems likely to foster the belief in Black and brown communities that the Supreme Court offered this special dispensation intentionally to

---

[197] OFFICE OF THE UNDER SEC'Y OF DEF., PERSONNEL & READINESS, DEP'T OF DEF., ACTIVE COMPONENT COMMISSIONED OFFICER CORPS, FY18: BY SOURCE OF COMMISSION, SERVICE, GENDER, AND RACE/ETHNICITY, App. B, tbl. B-33, at 96 (2018), https://www.cna.org/pop-rep/2018/appendixb/appendixb.pdf.

[198] While it may be tempting to believe that the importance of ROTC to producing military officers amounts to so much inside baseball, this point arose during oral argument, with Solicitor General Prelogar expressly noting "more officers come from ROTC programs" than from the academies. *See* Transcript of Oral Argument at 150, Students for Fair Admissions, Inc. v. Univ. of N.C., 600 U.S. 181 (2023) (No. 21-707).

[199] *See Racism Plagues U.S. Military Academies Despite Diversity Gains*, NBC NEWS (Dec. 3, 2021), https://www.nbcnews.com/news/nbcblk/racism-plagues-us-military-academies-diversity-gains-rcna7523.

harm those communities by coopting bright young minds and placing their bodies in harm's way.[200]

Conservatives—including then-Professor Scalia[201] and Justice Thomas in *SFFA*[202]—have often contended that one of race-conscious admissions' most deleterious features is that it sows the seeds of racial discord, thereby balkanizing American society. In *Grutter*, Justice Kennedy's dissent struck this point with great force. Affirmative action's "unhappy consequence will be to perpetuate the hostilities that proper consideration of race is designed to avoid," Justice Kennedy asserted, making it harder to "bring[] about the harmony and mutual respect among all citizens that our constitutional tradition has always sought."[203]

Parents Involved in Community Schools v. Seattle School District No. 1, which invalidated racial classifications in public school placements, also prominently featured antibalkanization sentiments.[204] Chief Justice Roberts's plurality opinion, for example, contended that racial classifications "lead to a politics of racial hostility," which conceives of "a Nation divided into racial blocs, thus contributing to an escalation of racial . . . conflict."[205] For his part, Justice Thomas similarly asserted in *Parents Involved* that the governmental action under review "is precisely the sort . . . that pits the races against one another, exacerbates racial tension, and provoke[s] resentment among those who believe that they have been wronged by the government's use of race."[206] Although Justice Kennedy's *Parents Involved* controlling opinion refused to require school districts to be completely colorblind, he voted to invalidate the plans' racial classifications on antibalkanization grounds. "Governmental classifications that command

---

[200] As one college student put it, "It is very challenging not to assume that the [C]ourt ignores the benefits of affirmative action only in higher education, where the status quo and long-standing inequality are at risk, but not in settings where marginalized communities have long been exploited and taken advantage of. Only there, where people are needed to put their lives at risk for the safety of their country, is diversity needed." Aina Marzia & Lajward Zahra, *How the Affirmative Action Exemption for Military Academies Exploits Students of Color*, NATION (Sept. 8, 2023), https://www.thenation.com/article/politics/affirmative-action-exemption-military-academies-scotus.

[201] *See* Scalia, *supra* note 2, at 154–55.

[202] *See SFFA*, 600 U.S. 181, 270 (2023) (Thomas, J., concurring).

[203] Grutter v. Bollinger, 539 U.S. 306, 394–95 (2003) (Kennedy, J., dissenting).

[204] 551 U.S. 701 (2007).

[205] *Id.* at 746 (plurality opinion) (internal quotation marks and citations omitted).

[206] *Id.* at 759 (Thomas, J., concurring) (internal quotation marks and citations omitted).

people to march in different directions based on racial typologies can cause a new divisiveness," Justice Kennedy reasoned, and that "practice can lead to corrosive discourse."[207]

While it is certainly true that conservatives have overwhelmingly highlighted concerns about racial balkanization when seeking to avoid feelings of white resentment, conservatives surely would not contend that the principle turns a blind eye to the racialized resentments of nonwhite people. The overarching conservative commitment of the right's race jurisprudence holds that the law must not treat different racial groups in a racially differentiated fashion. Thus, if white racial aggrievement can merit judicial solicitude, Black and brown racial aggrievement can also merit judicial solicitude—a view that the foremost scholarly treatment of racial balkanization espouses.[208] And *SFFA*'s military exemption seems almost designed to foster Black resentment toward not just the military, but even toward the nation it serves.

---

[207] *Id.* at 797 (Kennedy, J., concurring in part and in the judgment). Judge J. Harvie Wilkinson commended *Parents Involved* for its antibalkanization commitments, as "the majority took at least a small step toward establishing a principle that what unites us overshadows what divides us by race." J. Harvie Wilkinson III, *The Seattle and Louisville School Cases: There Is No Other Way*, 121 HARV. L. REV. 158, 183 (2007); *see also* Adarand Constructors, Inc. v. Peña, 515 U.S. 200, 239 (1995) (Scalia, J., concurring in part and in the judgment) ("In the eyes of government, we are just one race here. It is American.").

[208] *See* Reva B. Siegel, *From Colorblindness to Antibalkanization: An Emerging Ground of Decision in Race Equality Cases*, 120 YALE L.J. 1278, 1359 (2011) (contending antibalkanization "should be enforced in ways that are at least as responsive to practices and conditions of concern to minority as to majority communities"). I have learned much from Professor Siegel's foundational, generative analysis of antibalkanization, and that work informs this subpart. Nonetheless, I view antibalkinzation in ways that depart significantly from Siegel's conceptualization. Whereas Siegel argues that racial *moderates* primarily embrace antibalkanization concerns, I emphasize that racial *conservatives* have often trafficked in these considerations. Indeed, though she lavishes considerable attention on Justice Kennedy's opinion from *Parents Involved*, *id.* at 1305–14, she neglects to observe that Chief Justice Roberts and Justice Thomas also emphasized antibalkanization values, and that Justice Kennedy himself offered an antibalkanzation view when he dissented with conservatives in seeking to invalidate affirmative action in *Grutter*.

On a broader level, I harbor doubts about whether antibalkanization either can be or should be operationalized as a constitutional principle. After all, even universally praised civil-rights advancements have been marked by contemporaneous claims that the advancement threatens to balkanize American society. In 1956, for example, the Southern Manifesto's condemnation of *Brown v. Board of Education*, 347 U.S. 483 (1954), asserted that: "[*Brown*] is destroying the amicable relations between the white and Negro races that have been created through 90 years of patient effort by the good people of both races. It has planted hatred and suspicion where there has heretofore been friendship and understanding." Justin Driver, *Supremacies and the Southern Manifesto*, 92 TEX. L. REV. 1053, 1065–66 (2014) (analyzing and quoting the Manifesto). In this Article, however, I, of course, set aside my doubts of antibalkanization's constitutional vitality and desirability because the notion has loomed large in conservatives' race jurisprudence.

Racism in the U.S. military has a lengthy, sordid history,[209] but events stemming from the Vietnam War era play an outsized role in shaping modern perceptions that the armed services were particularly inhospitable places for Black people. Last year, an academic study exploring why Black Americans support using military force less than white Americans observed: "Vastly disproportionate rates of Black casualties at the beginning of the Vietnam War offended many Black Americans, and they did not soon forget this unequal distribution of harm."[210] In 1966, long before the rise of mass mobilization against the Vietnam War, Huey P. Newton and Bobby Seale's Black Panther platform declared: "We want all Black men to be exempt from military service."[211] A landmark oral history chronicling Black soldiers' experiences during the Vietnam War teems with instances of racial mistreatment.[212] Not only were Black soldiers disproportionately assigned the most dangerous tasks, they also received harsher military discipline.[213] For example, one Black Marine bitterly recalled: "If I had been white, I would never have went to jail for fighting. That would have been impossible."[214] The paucity of Black officers in Vietnam—combined with a heavily Black group of enlisted soldiers—created optimal conditions for racial balkanization. As the amicus brief of retired military generals invoked in *Grutter* found, these disparities "heightened racial tension" and "the armed forces suffered increased racial polarization, pervasive disciplinary problems, and racially motivated incidents in Vietnam and on posts around the world."[215]

---

[209] Formal racial segregation existed in the U.S. military until 1948. *See* Maraniss, *supra* note 194.

[210] Naima Green-Riley & Andrew Leber, *Whose War Is It Anyway? Explaining the Black-White Gap in Support for the Use of Force Abroad*, 32 SECURITY STUD. 811, 836 (2023).

[211] *The Black Panther Party's Ten-Point Program*, UC PRESS BLOG (Feb. 7, 2017), https://www.ucpress.edu/blog/25139/the-black-panther-partys-ten-point-program. Explaining their position, the Black Panthers reasoned: "We believe that Black people should not be forced to fight in the military service to defend a racist government that does not protect us. We will not fight and kill other people of color in the world who, like Black people, are being victimized by the White racist government of America." *Id.*

[212] WALLACE TERRY, BLOODS: BLACK VETERANS OF THE VIETNAM WAR: AN ORAL HISTORY (1984).

[213] *See, e.g.*, DEP'T OF DEF., 1 REPORT OF THE TASK FORCE ON THE ADMINISTRATION OF MILITARY JUSTICE IN THE ARMED FORCES 19–20, 109 (Nov. 30, 1972) (recounting racism within the American military during the Vietnam War).

[214] TERRY, *supra* note 212, at 11.

[215] Consolidated Brief of Julius W. Becton, Jr., *supra* note 194, at 6–7.

The profound racial problems within the military are far from confined to the past. To the contrary, the modern military is marred by some of the most naked anti-Black racism that appears throughout American society. Following *SFFA*, one West Point graduate, who went on to pursue legal training at Yale, noted that the opinion "doom[s] more minority students to the discrimination that exists within the ranks of our nation's military," and that "discriminatory policies and attitudes ... stifle [the] success [of racial minorities]" in the military disproportionately.[216] Data support this assessment, as more than half of the military's racial minorities recently told the *Military Times* that "they had seen examples of white nationalism or ideologically driven racism among their fellow troops."[217]

Racial minorities make up forty-three percent of the military, moreover, but the highest rungs of leadership in no way reflect that diversity. Indeed, although the nation's top military brass included more than forty commanders in 2021, only two of those were Black.[218] In October 2020, when a photograph emerged of President Donald Trump in the Oval Office surrounded by top admirals and four-star generals, the assemblage appeared so monochromatically white that one Black retired Army official noted that judging by the photo's complexion, "You would have thought it was 1950."[219] The lack of prominent Black leaders in today's military did not occur by accident. Rather, a reputable article recently stated, "The African-Americans who do become officers are often steered to specialize in logistics and transportation rather than the marquee combat arms specialties that lead to the top jobs."[220]

---

[216] Zoe Kreitenberg, Opinion, *Affirmative Action Is Banned—Except at Military Academies? Why That Won't Help Students*, L.A. TIMES (July 17, 2023), https://www.latimes.com/opinion/story/2023-07-17/military-exception-supreme-court-affirmative-action.

[217] Helene Cooper, *African-Americans Are Highly Visible in the Military, But Almost Invisible at the Top*, N.Y. TIMES (Oct. 18, 2021), https://www.nytimes.com/2020/05/25/us/politics/military-minorities-leadership.html. For a thoughtful book contending America's military has served as an incubator of white nationalism, see KATHLEEN BELEW, BRING THE WAR HOME: THE WHITE POWER MOVEMENT AND PARAMILITARY AMERICA (2018).

[218] *See* Cooper, *supra* note 217.

[219] *Id.* Another Black retired military official stated that if "[i]t's America's military," then "[w]hy doesn't this photo look like America?" *Id.*

[220] *Id. See* Helene Cooper, *Lloyd Austin Confronts the Perils of Being a Private Man in a Public Job*, N.Y. TIMES (Jan. 13, 2024), https://www.nytimes.com/2024/01/13/us/politics/lloyd-austin-private-public.html (noting that Secretary of Defense Lloyd Austin "has spoken of getting a white officer to give his briefings back when he was the commander of the storied 82nd Airborne Division because he figured a white officer was more likely to be listened to").

The modern military's overt, everyday racism would be anathema on most college campuses.[221] As recently as three years ago, the West Point official intercollegiate football team's flag featured a white supremacist acronym that it borrowed from the Aryan Brotherhood prison gang.[222] Black servicemembers, moreover, continue to be pelted with a barrage of racial epithets: Some Marines routinely refer to their Black colleagues as "nonswimmer[s]," and some Army Rangers routinely refer to their fellow Black servicemembers as "Night Ranger[s]."[223] Black Navy pilots receive racist call signs, including "8-Ball," and their colleagues have referred to them collectively as "eggplants."[224] Receiving such odious treatment would—quite understandably—cause many Black servicemembers to resent not only their individual racist tormenters, but also the Nation that permits such abuse to be directed toward those who dedicate their lives to providing its security.

Beyond those most immediately effected by *SFFA*'s military exemption, moreover, the asymmetric policy seems likely to breed resentment within the broader African American community. Conservatives often note that racially conspiratorial thought directed toward the government exerts a powerful grip in some segments of the Black community.[225] The affirmative action controversy has not been immune to such thinking. In the wake of *Bakke*, Professor Charles Lawrence suggested: "Many members of California's minority community believe that [UC Davis] set the case up to rid itself of a program that it never wanted."[226] That suspicion strains credulity, though, because the most straightforward method for a university bent on avoiding affirmative action would call for simply not establishing such a program in the first instance. No measure *required* universities to establish affirmative action programs. So, why would

---

[221] I certainly would not contend that college campuses are racism-free zones. I do believe, however, that they evince less overt racism than occurs in many sectors of American society. *See* Randall Kennedy, *How Racist Are Universities, Really?*, Chron. Higher Educ. (Aug. 12, 2020), https://www.chronicle.com/article/how-racist-are-universities-really.

[222] *See* Cooper, *supra* note 217.

[223] *Id.*

[224] *Id.*

[225] *See* McWhorter, *supra* note 94, at 11 (noting various racial conspiracy theories, including one holding that white physicians intentionally injected Black people with the AIDS virus).

[226] Wilkinson, *supra* note 176, at 259.

any university devise such an elaborate plan, seek a time-consuming lawsuit, and then defend the program vigorously by retaining former Solicitor General Archibald Cox—all for the sake of taking a litigation dive?[227]

If the *Bakke* conspiratorial theory gained traction, the notion that Chief Justice Roberts intentionally devised *SFFA*'s military exemption to harm the Black community seems virtually guaranteed to gain wide adherence, thus increasing America's racial balkanization. After all, rather than needing to subscribe to a cloaked roundabout conspiracy, many people of color will observe that the Roberts Court has demonstrated scant regard for Black America's well-being—including not least in *Shelby County*'s evisceration of the VRA,[228] and, of course, *SFFA*'s abandonment of affirmative action in nonmilitary settings.[229] Many members of the Black community would no doubt assert: *It is hardly coincidental that the one exception the Roberts Court gave to Black folks involving affirmative action somehow made it easier for us to go into armed combat. The Supreme Court of the United States is endangering some of the best Black minds by sending us to the battlefield and exposing us to those patriotism factories that are the military academies.* This argument cannot be dismissed as some wild-eyed racial conspiracy, of course, because the reading emerges from *SFFA*'s actual text. Although the Roberts Court's military exemption may have been well-intentioned, it will not create the racial harmony that antibalkanization jurists prize. Rather, *SFFA* threatens to cause many Black Americans to feel alienated and disillusioned from their homeland, which would court even greater balkanization than now exists in our already woefully fractured country.[230]

---

[227] *See* UROFSKY, *supra* note 160, at 195–223.

[228] Shelby Cnty. v. Holder, 570 U.S. 529 (2013).

[229] Students for Fair Admissions, Inc. v. President & Fellows of Harvard Coll. (*SFFA*), 600 U.S. 181 (2023).

[230] In their dissents, Justice Sotomayor and Justice Jackson both seized upon *SFFA*'s military exemption to argue that the Court should have permitted universities more broadly to continue engaging in affirmative action. *See id.* at 355–56 (Sotomayor, J., dissenting); *id.* at 411 (Jackson, J., dissenting) (contending, memorably, that the exemption "prepare[s] Black Americans and other underrepresented minorities for success in the bunker, [but] not the boardroom"). This Article's critique differs from those advanced by *SFFA*'s dissents because it highlights how the military exemption can be construed as betraying conservatives' own principles. If anything, moreover, Justice Jackson's riposte, quoted above, can be viewed as pulling its punch. For it is not "*success* in the bunker," *id.*, that will most concern Black Americans, but failure there. That grave point drives the balkanization concern.

D. ABANDONING CONSERVATISM

While *SFFA* has been widely celebrated as a major victory for the conservative legal movement, the opinion can also be viewed as a betrayal of conservatism itself. That statement applies in at least two overlapping senses. First, a significant strand of conservative thought—most prominently associated with Edmund Burke[231]—counsels against swiftly upending systems that have worked decently for generations because those moves destabilize society. Second, a now largely forgotten brand of constitutional conservatism extols stare decisis because adhering to precedent quite literally serves to *conserve* the prevailing legal order.[232] But *SFFA*'s brisk repudiation of affirmative action—a practice in American society dating back the 1960s,[233] and validated by the Supreme Court in an extensive line of decisions dating back to the 1970s[234]—casts aside both versions of conservatism.

By the time that the Court issued *SFFA* last year, universities had been making concerted efforts to usher in underrepresented racial minorities for well over five decades. This practice had thereby become woven into the very fabric of American higher education—and of American society more broadly. In 2013, following the Court's decision in *Fisher I*, Professor Randall Kennedy observed: "The affirmative action ethos has become deeply rooted. The social forces that created it, combined with changes it has wrought, have made racial homogeneity unacceptable in most key public forums."[235]

---

[231] *See generally* EDMUND BURKE, REFLECTIONS ON THE REVOLUTION IN FRANCE (J.C.D. Clark ed., Stanford 2001) (1790). This point and, indeed, much of this subpart owe a significant intellectual debt to David Strauss's illuminating work. *See* David A. Strauss, Fisher v. University of Texas *and the Conservative Case for Affirmative Action*, 2016 SUP. CT. REV. 1 (2017). For helpful explorations of Burke's relationship to constitutional thought, see Anthony T. Kronman, *Alexander Bickel's Philosophy of Prudence*, 94 YALE L.J. 1567 (1985); Ernest Young, *Rediscovering Conservatism: Burkean Political Theory and Constitutional Interpretation*, 72 N.C. L. REV. 619 (1994).

[232] Justin Driver, *The Constitutional Conservatism of the Warren Court*, 100 CALIF. L. REV. 1101, 1105–06 (2012) (noting that "[c]onstitutional conservatives ... sought to *conserve* the prevailing legal regime" (emphasis in original)); *cf.* JAMES T. PATTERSON, CONGRESSIONAL CONSERVATISM AND THE NEW DEAL: THE GROWTH OF THE CONSERVATIVE COALITION IN CONGRESS, 1933–1939, at viii (1967) (exploring conservatism during the New Deal era though political actors who "sought to 'conserve' an America which they believed to have existed before 1933").

[233] UROFSKY, *supra* note 160, at 58.

[234] Regents of the Univ. of Cal. v. Bakke, 438 U.S. 265 (1978).

[235] KENNEDY, *supra* note 18, at 15.

Following the Court's decision in *Fisher II*, Professor David Strauss similarly observed: "At least by the time of *Fisher [II]*, and probably long before, it had become clear that affirmative action is deeply embedded in American society. Institutions throughout the nation—universities, corporations, governments—engage in [the practice]."[236]

In 2023, seven years after *Fisher II*, affirmative action had, of course, only become more firmly ensconced within the nation. A Burkean conservative would insist that the very fact that affirmative action has existed for decades cautions against its casual defenestration. In *Reflections on the Revolution in France*, Burke famously emphasized that wisdom accrued through the ages ought not be discarded by today's intelligentsia. "[I]t is with infinite caution that any man ought to venture upon pulling down an edifice which has answered in any tolerable degree for ages the common purposes of society," Burke instructed.[237] Even if modern thinkers hold significant doubts regarding longstanding practices, Burke would insist that proven, hard-won practices should usually dominate abstract principles.[238] Justice O'Connor's opinion for the Court in *Grutter* implicitly appealed to a kind of Burkean justification for refusing to invalidate affirmative action. "Since this Court's splintered decision in *Bakke*, Justice Powell's opinion . . . has served as the touchstone for constitutional analysis of race-conscious admissions policies," *Grutter* instructed. "Public and private universities across the Nation have modeled their own admissions programs on Justice Powell's views on permissible race-conscious policies."[239] In stark contrast with *Grutter*, *SFFA* exhibited precious little caution in demolishing the affirmative action edifice.

In addition to eschewing Burkean conservatism, *SFFA* betrayed a related vision of constitutional conservatism. In the 1960s, roughly contemporaneous with the rise of affirmative action, constitutional conservatism "meant embracing a few closely related concepts: venerating precedent; resisting sharp breaks with the past; [and] conceiving

---

[236] Strauss, *supra* note 231, at 3.

[237] BURKE, *supra* note 231, at 220 (cited in Strauss, *supra* note 231, at 21).

[238] BURKE, *supra* note 231, at 220; *see* Strauss, *supra* note 231, at 21 (contending that the recognition "that established practices might deserve to be maintained even if, in principle, they are questionable—is derived from an important current of conservative thought," which provides "in dealing with complex political issues, abstract principles are not as good a guide as the actual practice, over time, of people engaged day to day in operating institutions").

[239] Grutter v. Bollinger, 539 U.S. 306, 323 (2003).

of the judicial role as modest."²⁴⁰ During the Warren Court era, the constitutional conservative beau ideal was Justice John Marshall Harlan II, whose jurisprudence was defined by "a profound respect for precedent," and who exhibited "distrust[] of abrupt change, comfort[] with accustomed rules and practices, and . . . reluctan[ce] to revise the judgments of predecessors."²⁴¹ While the Supreme Court has allowed that following precedent "is not an inexorable command,"²⁴² constitutional conservatives of yesterday particularly valued stare decisis because it fosters respect for the notion that legal "principles are founded in the law rather than in the proclivities of individuals, and thereby contributes to the integrity of our constitutional system of government."²⁴³

SFFA was not, of course, wholly insensitive to how openly rejecting precedents can corrode the integrity of the nation's constitutional order. The significance of stare decisis in our legal system explains both why *SFFA* refused to declare outright that *Bakke*, *Grutter*, and *Fisher II* had been overruled, and why Chief Justice Roberts's majority opinion and Justice Kavanaugh's concurring opinion endeavored to explain how the outcome could be squared with *Grutter*'s twenty-five-year sunset for affirmative action. Courts do not, however, demonstrate fealty to stare decisis principles by simply managing to avoid intoning the magic word *overturned*.²⁴⁴

An honest appraisal of *SFFA* requires acknowledging (with Justice Thomas) that it cast aside decades of precedent, perhaps most glaringly in its assessment that the universities had failed to provide even a compelling government interest for affirmative action.²⁴⁵ That determination represented nothing less than an abrupt volte face not just from *Bakke* and *Grutter*, but from *Fisher II*, which had been decided only seven years before *SFFA*. In 2016, *Fisher II* stated: "[T]he

---

[240] Driver, *supra* note 232, at 1105.

[241] Norman Dorsen, *The Second Mr. Justice Harlan: A Constitutional Conservative*, 44 N.Y.U. L. Rev. 249, 250, 257 (1969).

[242] Vasquez v. Hillary, 474 U.S. 254, 266 (1986).

[243] *Id.* at 265.

[244] See Watson, *supra* note 34, at 131. For thoughtful scholarship exploring precedent, see generally William Baude, *Precedent and Discretion*, 2019 Sup. Ct. Rev. 313 (2020); Frederick Schauer, *Stare Decisis—Rhetoric and Reality in the Supreme Court*, 2018 Sup. Ct. Rev. 121 (2019); and Randy J. Kozel, Settled Versus Right: A Theory of Precedent (2017).

[245] Students for Fair Admissions, Inc. v. President & Fellows of Harvard Coll. (*SFFA*), 600 U.S. 181, 214 (2023); *id.* at 232 (Thomas, J., concurring).

decision to pursue the educational benefits that flow from student body diversity ... is, in substantial measure, an academic judgment to which some ... judicial deference is proper," and underscored that "deference must be given to the University's conclusion, based on its experience and expertise, that a diverse student body would serve its educational goals."[246] With *SFFA*, though, the Supreme Court broke sharply with this era of judicial deference, instead aggrandizing itself authority over admissions offices throughout the land in a manner that would make traditional constitutional conservatives wince.

The strained judicial efforts to contend that ending affirmative action in 2023 somehow honored the twenty-five-year timeline that *Grutter* issued in 2003 only highlights the Supreme Court's severe break with traditional tenets of constitutional conservatism. SFFA's brief acknowledged that *Grutter* afforded affirmative action a quarter-century "grace period" in 2003, but also requested that the Court overturn *Grutter*.[247] Chief Justice Roberts's majority opinion and Justice Kavanaugh's concurrence, though, claimed both to honor that grace period and to avoid overturning that provision of *Grutter*. The twenty-five-year timeframe in *Grutter* has generated a firestorm of criticism, and some lawyers have sought to construe it as dicta.[248] Like the *SFFA* majority and Justice Kavanaugh's concurrence, though, I advanced a claim on the eve of *SFFA*'s oral argument that *Grutter*'s twenty-five-year sunset could be construed as possessing legal authority.[249] But the way that *SFFA* and Justice Kavanaugh's concurrence in *SFFA* sought to claim that the twenty-five-year period had in effect already run in twenty years simply cannot be taken seriously. The majority and Justice Kavanaugh—recall—suggested that prohibiting admissions offices from engaging in affirmative action immediately accorded with *Grutter* because students admitted to the class of 2028 (and beyond) would have their applications reviewed in a post-affirmative action world.

---

[246] 579 U.S. 365, 376–77 (2016) (internal quotation marks and citations omitted).

[247] Brief for Petitioner at 12, 68, *SFFA*, 600 U.S. 181 (2023) (No. 20-1199).

[248] *See, e.g.*, Lee C. Bollinger & Geoffrey R. Stone, A Legacy of Discrimination: The Essential Constitutionality of Affirmative Action 70 (2023) (ridiculing *Grutter*'s "expiration date"); Transcript of Oral Argument at 99, *SFFA*, 600 U.S. 181 (2023) (No. 20-1199) (quoting Solicitor General Prelogar arguing that *Grutter*'s timeline did not provide a firm end date for affirmative action).

[249] *See* Driver, *supra* note 21.

This method of counting, however, would cause even those brazen politicians seasoned in the dark art of fuzzy math to blush with embarrassment. Upon even limited reflection, it becomes plain that if 2028 holds any significance, it matters for the timing of admissions decisions, not the timing of when one's college graduating class is admitted. Set aside for the moment the obvious point that many, many college students take longer than four years to graduate from college—if they end up graduating at all.[250] The Court's decision in *SFFA* governs—at a minimum—all of American higher education, not only undergraduate admissions. But reputable universities, of course, offer degree programs that typically take fewer than four years to complete—including a juris doctor degree (which typically takes three years to complete), and a master's of business administration (which typically takes two years to complete). Implementing the Class-of-2028 argument therefore would mean allowing law schools to use affirmative action in admitting JD candidates for one additional year, and business schools to use affirmative action in admitting MBA candidates for two additional years. That cannot be right. Or if it is, *SFFA* should have stated as much.

The fact that *SFFA* felt compelled to pull the plug on affirmative action five years before it could have claimed (with a straight face) that *Grutter*'s twenty-five-year window had in fact actually closed reveals how completely the opinion rejects old-school constitutional conservatism. Whereas constitutional conservatives once disdained repudiating the considered judgments of their predecessors and abhorred sharp breaks with the past, *SFFA* revealed that the Roberts Court has limited time for such niceties. A distinguished legal scholar once waxed eloquent about "the [judiciary's] marvelous mystery of time,"[251] but *SFFA* shows unmistakably that the Roberts Court is in a hurry.

III. IMPLICATIONS

Picking up where the previous Part ended, this Part examines two major aspects of *SFFA*'s stark destabilization of the prevailing

---

[250] *Digest of Education Statistics*, NAT'L CTR. FOR EDUC. STAT. (Feb. 2023), https://nces.ed.gov/programs/digest/d22/tables/dt22_326.10.asp (finding that less than half of the 2011–2015 college entry cohorts graduated within four years of matriculating).

[251] ALEXANDER M. BICKEL, THE LEAST DANGEROUS BRANCH: THE SUPREME COURT AT THE BAR OF POLITICS 26 (1962).

constitutional order. First, it explores how *SFFA* casts a new light on Chief Justice Roberts's reputation for prizing incrementalism and institutionalism. Even as assessed by Chief Justice Roberts's own guiding principles, *SFFA* represents a radical break with both of those ideals and the ideals of his judicial mentors. Indeed, *SFFA*'s evisceration of affirmative action managed to accomplish a seemingly impossible task: making Donald Trump's successful presidential campaign seem as though it promoted racial inclusion and egalitarianism. Second, this Part surveys how *SFFA* could spell doom for the immediate future of higher education. Over the last several decades, leading universities had honed their admissions systems—through trial and error—to produce classes of students who would be able to flourish. While conservatives deeply disliked the overt race-consciousness of these systems, they may soon find that universities adapt in ways that harm vulnerable students and even the universities themselves.

A. ROBERTS'S RADICALISM

Chief Justice Roberts enjoys a reputation as both an institutionalist and an incrementalist, a jurist who is dedicated to ensuring that the Supreme Court serves as a stabilizing force in American society.[252] That reputation has, of course, not been invented out of whole cloth. Indeed, Chief Justice Roberts is far less willing to rethink entire legal doctrines from the ground up than, say, Justice Thomas, who believes that original public meaning must be vindicated though the heavens may fall.[253] Juxtaposing the two jurists, Chief Justice Roberts's desire to preserve the existing legal order can mark him as a constitutional conservative, whereas Justice Thomas's unwillingness to follow precedent if it does not accord with his preferred methodology can mark him not as a constitutional conservative, but instead a constitutional radical.

The sharply divergent positions that Chief Justice Roberts and Justice Thomas recently adopted in *Dobbs v. Jackson Women's Health*

---

[252] *See, e.g.*, UROFSKY, *supra* note 160, at 474 (calling Chief Justice Roberts "an institutionalist").

[253] Justice Scalia can be viewed as rebuking Justice Thomas, when he noted that—unlike his fellow originalist, Justice Thomas—he nevertheless believed in at least some role for stare decisis. "I'm an originalist—I'm not a nut," Justice Scalia said. *See* DAVID A. STRAUSS, THE LIVING CONSTITUTION 17 (2010).

Organization exemplify this dichotomy.[254] For his part, Chief Justice Roberts's concurring opinion preferred to uphold Mississippi's fifteen-week ban on abortions, but nevertheless sought to avoid overruling *Roe v. Wade* and *Planned Parenthood v. Casey* "all the way down to the studs" by finding that the ban did not pose an undue burden on the right to an abortion.[255] In contrast, Justice Thomas's concurrence in *Dobbs* not only advocated gutting *Roe* and *Casey*, but insisted further that the Court should rethink other landmark opinions in that line of cases, including *Griswold v. Connecticut* and *Obergefell v. Hodges*.[256]

SFFA unmistakably reveals, however, that the dominant portrait of Chief Justice Roberts as an incremental institutionalist is overdrawn, at least when it comes to race. When push met shove in the arena of race-conscious decisionmaking—a core jurisprudential project for Chief Justice Roberts—he shed institutionalism in favor of radicalism. Seeing Chief Justice Roberts—and thus the Court that bears his name—with clarity means understanding that, if he feels sufficient passion about the underlying issue, he is all too willing to embrace his inner Justice Thomas. At first blush, this account may sound utterly intuitive. But it bears emphasizing because *SFFA*'s radicalism fails the very models that Chief Justice Roberts himself has pledged to follow. Measuring *SFFA* by his own jurisprudential standards, then, Roberts's opinion comes up short.

Following the completion of his first Term on the Court in 2006, Chief Justice Roberts gave a remarkable extended interview to *The Atlantic*'s Jeffrey Rosen. The Chief Justice articulated something like a juridical mission statement that could be used for evaluating his tenure at the Court. "I think judicial temperament is a willingness to step back from your own committed views of the correct jurisprudential approach and evaluate those views in terms of your role as a judge," he stated. "It's the difference between being a judge and being a law professor."[257] While law professors might understandably value

---

[254] 597 U.S. 215 (2022).

[255] *Id.* at 353–54 (Roberts, C.J., concurring in the judgment) (referencing *Roe*, 410 U.S. 113 (1973), and *Casey*, 505 U.S. 833 (1992)).

[256] *Dobbs*, 597 U.S. at 332 (Thomas, J., concurring) (referencing *Griswold*, 381 U.S. 479 (1965), and *Obergefell*, 576 U.S. 644 (2015)).

[257] Jeffrey Rosen, *Roberts's Rules*, ATLANTIC, Jan./Feb. 2007, at 104, 113.

holding a consistent position over time, Chief Justice Roberts suggested, jurists should instead focus upon the Court as an institution remaining consistent over time. Chief Justice Roberts expressly extolled judges who were willing to "factor in the Court's institutional role," which Rosen summed up as "a willingness ... to suppress his or her ideological agenda in the interest of achieving ... stability."[258]

Chief Justice Roberts offered an example of one of his predecessors commendably elevating the Court's institutional role above his own ideological commitments in a hotly disputed field for the purpose of promoting stability. When then-Justice Rehnquist joined the Court in the early 1970s and when Roberts clerked for him in October Term 1980, Rehnquist was perhaps the Court's foremost critic of *Miranda v. Arizona*.[259] Nevertheless, when the Court had an opportunity to overrule *Miranda* in 2000, Chief Justice Rehnquist wrote the Court's opinion fundamentally affirming the decision's continued vitality.[260] Chief Justice Roberts deemed this turnabout laudable and consistent with his vision of judging that emphasizes continuity: "[Rehnquist] appreciated that it had become part of the law—that it would do more harm to uproot it—and he wrote that opinion as chief for the good of the institution."[261] Relatedly, he acknowledged that, when new Justices join the Court, concerns heighten about long-standing precedents being jettisoned, as the institution "seem[s] to be lurching around because of changes in personnel."[262]

It is highly admirable that Chief Justice Roberts dedicated energy to contemplating and articulating his vision of judging at the outset of his time at the Court. One way to understand this gesture is that the Chief Justice sought to bind himself to the mast, publicly extolling a judicial vision that prioritizes stability and institutionalism and therefore eschews ideologically-driven careening because of the arrival of new Justices. On this theory, the public proclamation of judicial humility offered early in his tenure would inoculate him from temptations to embrace a more ideological approach down the line.

---

[258] *Id.*

[259] 384 U.S. 436 (1966); *see* Edward Walsh, *High Court Upholds* Miranda *Rights*, 7-2, WASH. POST, June 27, 2000, at A1 (noting that Rehnquist was "a frequent and vocal critic of . . . *Miranda* . . . during his earlier years on the bench").

[260] Dickerson v. United States, 530 U.S. 428 (2000) (upholding *Miranda*).

[261] Rosen, *supra* note 257, at 112.

[262] *Id.*

But Chief Justice Roberts's opinion in *SFFA* managed to violate virtually every tenet of the judicial approach that he embraced two decades ago. The opinion evinced no willingness whatsoever to relinquish his own ideological priors in order to embrace the larger institutional considerations, as Chief Justice Rehnquist had in his latter-day affirmation of *Miranda*. To the contrary, Chief Justice Roberts hastily uprooted the Court's affirmative action jurisprudence—even though *Fisher II* had validated that line of decisions only a few years prior, and *Grutter* could have been interpreted to reach his preferred jurisprudential destination in only five years' time. Indeed, it is impossible to understand *SFFA*'s swift disavowal of affirmative action as anything other than a "lurch[] . . . because of changes in personnel."[263] Between the Court's decisions in *Fisher II* and *SFFA*, Justice Kavanaugh replaced Justice Kennedy, and Justice Barrett replaced Justice Ginsburg; and it was those two replacements that effectively signed affirmative action's death warrant. If ever there were a time where institutional considerations prizing stability may have been thought to eclipse an individual Justice's ideological commitments, moreover, it would have been 2023, as the nation reeled from *Dobbs*'s recent repudiation of abortion rights. But these weighty considerations all proved insufficient to cause Chief Justice Roberts to swerve from his headlong pursuit of constitutional colorblindness.

Chief Justice Roberts's *SFFA* opinion also seems to fall short of the standard that he attributed to Judge Henry J. Friendly, the towering jurist for whom a young Roberts clerked on the U.S. Court of Appeals for the Second Circuit. Even accounting for the generous amounts of adulation that law clerks routinely shower upon their judges, Chief Justice Roberts revered Judge Friendly to an unusual degree.[264] During his time on the D.C. Circuit, then-Judge Roberts managed to cite Judge Friendly in six opinions, even though he published fewer than fifty opinions total during his two years on that court.[265] Consistent with this high esteem, then-Judge Roberts noted

---

[263] *Id.*

[264] Robert Gordon, *Friendly Fire*, SLATE (Aug. 11, 2005), https://slate.com/news-and-politics/2005/08/friendly-fire.html (noting that one of Roberts's former colleagues stated that Roberts spoke of Friendly "with 'deeper reverence' and 'a certain twinkle in his eye'").

[265] Brad Snyder, *The Judicial Genealogy (and Mythology) of John Roberts: Clerkships from Gray to Brandeis to Friendly to Roberts*, 71 OHIO ST. L.J. 1149, 1230 (2010) (noting the high frequency with which then-Judge Roberts invoked Judge Friendly). Chief Justice Roberts continues to cite Judge Friendly on the Supreme Court with some regularity, even if the earlier frenetic clip

during his Supreme Court confirmation hearings in 2005 that Friendly "ha[d] an essential humility about him. He was an absolute genius."[266] Judge Friendly's fundamental humility loomed large in then-Judge Roberts's conception of the qualities that made for a model jurist. He pressed this point in his 2005 opening statement: "Judges have to have the humility to recognize that they operate within a system of precedent shaped by other judges equally striving to live up to the judicial oath."[267] But Chief Justice Roberts's *SFFA* opinion, by effectively overturning decades of accumulated precedents, exhibited little of the judicial humility that he identified as one of Judge Friendly's primary virtues.

In addition, Chief Justice Roberts's substantive position on affirmative action clashed with Judge Friendly's vision. *SFFA* derided Justice Powell's controlling opinion in *Bakke* as being driven by the "pernicious stereotype that 'a black student can usually bring something that a white person cannot offer.'"[268] But Judge Friendly viewed Justice Powell's *Bakke* opinion in a far more flattering light, deeming it a masterwork. Indeed, Judge Friendly admired the opinion so thoroughly—not least because it avoided imposing a radical solution—that he immediately sent Justice Powell a fan letter celebrating the opinion. Friendly, a man who was notoriously stinting with praise, thanked Justice Powell "for the great service you have rendered the nation. This case had the potential of being another *Dred Scott*.... Your

---

has grown less frequent. For the Chief Justice's most recent invocation of Judge Friendly, see Dep't of Commerce v. New York, 139 S. Ct. 2551, 2575 (2019) (quoting United States v. Stanchich, 550 F.2d 1294, 1300 (2d Cir. 1977) (Friendly, J.) ("Our review is deferential, but we are 'not required to exhibit a naiveté from which ordinary citizens are free.'").

[266] Confirmation Hearing on the Nomination of John G. Roberts, Jr. to Be Chief Justice of the United States: Hearing Before the S. Comm. on the Judiciary, 109th Cong. 1, 202 (2005). Brad Snyder's scholarship examining the relationship between Roberts and Friendly deeply influenced my own thinking on this topic. *See* Snyder, *supra* note 265, at 1215–21, 1231–41. As Snyder noted, the dramatically varying levels of enthusiasm that then-Judge Roberts expressed in his Senate questionnaire for the two jurists who employed him is illuminating. "I was fortunate to have two appellate clerkships immediately after law school," Roberts stated. "Judge Henry J. Friendly is justly remembered as one of this Nation's truly outstanding federal appellate judges. The clerkship on the Supreme Court for then-Associate Justice Rehnquist the following year was an intensive immersion in the federal appellate process at the highest level." *Confirmation Hearing on the Nomination of John G. Roberts, Jr. to Be Chief Justice of the United States*, GovInfo 72 (Sept. 12–15, 2005), https://www.govinfo.gov/content/pkg/GPO-CHRG-ROBERTS/pdf/GPO-CHRG-ROBERTS.pdf (questionnaire for United States Committee on the Judiciary) (quoted in Snyder, *supra* note 265, at 1232).

[267] *Confirmation Hearing on the Nomination of John G. Roberts, Jr.*, *supra* note 266, at 55.

[268] Students for Fair Admissions, Inc. v. President & Fellows of Harvard Coll. (*SFFA*), 600 U.S. 181, 220 (2023) (quoting Regents of the Univ. of Cal. v. Bakke, 438 U.S. 265, 316 (1978) (op. of Powell, J.)).

moderation and statesmanship saved us from that. . . . It reminds one of Mark Twain's remark that God protects children, drunkards, and the United States of America."[269]

It is important to emphasize that, when Judge Friendly wrote that missive to Justice Powell extolling *Bakke*, he was a septuagenarian, a lifelong Republican (who had been nominated to the appellate court by President Eisenhower), and decidedly no one's idea of a wild-eyed left-winger. Judge Friendly and Justice Powell were among the first generation of Republican-appointed jurists who made an uneasy truce with affirmative action, but many would follow in their wake. To name only two, Justice O'Connor in *Grutter* and Justice Kennedy in *Fisher II* wrote opinions for the Court that refused to eliminate affirmative action, even though both appointees of President Reagan had previously expressed deep misgivings about racial classifications.[270] Yet, when confronted with the opportunity to eradicate affirmative action, they evidently viewed the "moderation and statesmanship" of Justice Powell's approach as preferable to the sort of radicalism that Chief Justice Roberts evinced in *SFFA*.[271]

There are few better indicators of *SFFA*'s radicalism than comparing the opinion with how Donald Trump approached affirmative action when he mounted his successful campaign for the presidency. President Trump's ascent to the Oval Office is widely—and, in my view, correctly—viewed as predicated on his ability to capitalize upon the politics of white Americans' sense of racial aggrievement. From suggesting that President Obama's supposed birth in Kenya rendered him ineligible for the presidency, to his campaign kickoff announcement that branded Mexicans "rapists," and far too many other incidents to recount here, President Trump repeatedly advanced the idea that white people must reclaim the nation from racial minorities.[272] Yet, when Chuck Todd asked Trump about the policy on *Meet the Press* in August 2015—"Affirmative action. Should we keep it? Yes or

---

[269] DAVID M. DORSEN, HENRY FRIENDLY: GREATEST JUDGE OF HIS ERA 204 (2012) (quoting Letter from Henry J. Friendly to Lewis F. Powell, Jr. (July 1, 1978) (quoted in JOHN C. JEFFRIES JR., JUSTICE LEWIS F. POWELL, JR. 498 (1994))).

[270] *See* Chilton et al., *supra* note 21, at 347–48 (detailing how Justices Powell, O'Connor, and Kennedy could all be viewed as improbable saviors of affirmative action, given their prior positions on questions of race). The list of Republican-appointed Justices who voted to uphold affirmative action programs also includes: Justices Blackmun, Souter, and Stevens.

[271] DORSEN, *supra* note 269, at 204.

[272] Liam Stack, *Donald Trump's Moments and Missteps: A Look Back*, N.Y. TIMES (Nov. 4, 2016), https://www.nytimes.com/2016/11/04/us/politics/donald-trump-presidential-race.html.

no[?]"—the candidate did not launch into a tirade about the evils of reverse racism or even tout the colorblind imperative.[273] To the contrary, Trump offered the policy a warm embrace. "I'm fine with affirmative action," he stated. "We've lived with it for a long time."[274] Trump offered affirmative action support in the heat of his presidential campaign, even though railing against the policy had been a standard part of the racial demagogues' playbook for more than a quarter century.[275]

President Trump has been called many things over the years, but the term Burkean must seldom appear on that list. Nevertheless, during his successful presidential campaign in 2015, it must be acknowledged that Trump—by emphasizing affirmative action's durability—espoused a far more Burkean approach to the policy than the supposedly incrementalist- and institutionalist-minded Chief Justice Roberts would adopt just eight years later.[276] If that stunning contrast does not mark *SFFA* as a radical intervention in American society, then what would?

B. THE DESTABILIZATION OF HIGHER EDUCATION

Affirmative action has been a pillar of elite education for the last several decades. It is certainly possible to view *SFFA*'s removal of that pillar through rose-tinted spectacles, as it may spur universities to reappraise preferences—most prominently for legacies, donors, recruited athletes, and children of faculty—that are in desperate need of reappraisal.[277] But this moment of possibility also contains

---

[273] Chris Cillizza, *Donald Trump on 'Meet the Press,' Annotated*, WASH. POST (Aug. 17, 2015, 11:28 AM EDT), https://www.washingtonpost.com/news/the-fix/wp/2015/08/17/donald-trump-on-meet-the-press-annotated.

[274] *Id.*

[275] *See* BOLLINGER & STONE, *supra* note 248, at 57 (commenting upon Senator Jesse Helms's notorious campaign advertisement lambasting affirmative action in his successful reelection bid in 1990); *cf.* ERIC A. POSNER, THE DEMAGOGUE'S PLAYBOOK: THE BATTLE FOR AMERICAN DEMOCRACY FROM THE FOUNDERS TO TRUMP (2020).

[276] Admittedly, former President Trump did praise *SFFA* after it was decided. *See* Sara Dorn, *Trump Cheers 'Amazing' Affirmative Action Ruling: 'What A Wonderful Day,'* FORBES (June 29, 2023), https://www.forbes.com/sites/saradorn/2023/06/29/trump-cheers-amazing-affirmative-action-ruling-what-a-wonderful-day. But it seems significant that Trump's initial instinct was to celebrate the program rather than to condemn it.

[277] Anemona Hartocollis & Amy Harmon, *Affirmative Action Ruling Shakes Universities Over More Than Race*, N.Y. TIMES (July 26, 2023), https://www.nytimes.com/2023/07/26/us/affirmative-action-college-admissions-harvard.html.

tremendous possibility for peril. In this spirit, conservatives—a group that often longs for the halcyon days of yore and is highly attuned to the notions that major social changes produce not growth but decay[278]—may soon appreciate that *SFFA*'s destabilization of higher education has initiated a steep decline.

The volatility created by *SFFA* could yield truly disastrous consequences, not least for Black and brown students and the leading universities who educate them. The peril of this new post-*SFFA* moment is perhaps best captured by recalling the profound difficulties that beset some universities when affirmative action was in its infancy. Before so doing, however, it is helpful to establish first that some sophisticated proponents of affirmative action acknowledge the possibility that race-conscious admissions policies can be ill-designed and, if they are, those policies ought to be roundly rejected. For example, Professor Randall Kennedy's book defending affirmative action—titled *For Discrimination*—carefully couches its backing for race-conscious policies. "I support *sensibly designed* affirmative action, which means that I eschew affirmative action programs that are ... stupid," Kennedy wrote.[279] "Hence, I disavow any initiative that knowingly or negligently over-promotes beneficiaries, placing them in settings in which they are conspicuously less prepared than nonpreferred peers, a situation rife with risks of demoralization and the creation or reinforcement of racist stereotypes."[280] Kennedy reiterated this point, contending that "it is important to be careful in selecting the beneficiaries of racial affirmative action" because "[p]oor performance on their part can be dispiriting and reinforce stereotypes."[281]

Kennedy's nuanced evaluation of affirmative action merits admiration, as too many scholars (among both critics and supporters)

---

[278] *See, e.g.*, ANTONIN SCALIA, A MATTER OF INTERPRETATION: FEDERAL COURTS AND THE LAW 3, 40–41 (1997) (emphasizing the ever-present possibility of social "rot"); *see also* Jack M. Balkin, *The Recent Unpleasantness: Understanding the Cycles of Constitutional Time*, 94 IND. L.J. 253, 254–57 (2019) (exploring the notion of constitutional rot and constitutional renewal).

[279] KENNEDY, *supra* note 18, at 145 (emphasis supplied).

[280] *Id.*

[281] *Id.* at 86. For another affirmative action supporter who nevertheless rejects ill-designed programs, see James Sterba's argument: "To be justified, [affirmative action] must be directed at candidates whose qualifications are such that when their selection or appointment is combined with a suitably designed educational enhancement program, they will normally turn out, within a reasonably short time, to be as qualified as, or even more qualified then, their peers." COHEN & STERBA, *supra* note 139, at 260–61.

depict the issue with disfiguringly broad brushes. Regrettably, Kennedy declines to identify any affirmative action programs that he would deem "[in]sensibly designed," let alone "stupid."[282] Kennedy's unwillingness to identify such programs is regrettable because doing so would have helped administrators wishing to follow his guidance. And the absence of "stupid" affirmative action programs from *For Discrimination* is not because such programs have always been flawlessly executed. Flawless execution is, of course, an impossibility in the realm of policy architecture. The earliest days of affirmative action, though, provide some particularly graphic examples of race-conscious admissions gone wrong. Consider only two examples, both from law schools. Professor Graglia's early article exploring affirmative action recalled: "At New York University Law School, . . . a special admissions program was first adopted in 1966. . . . After two years, twelve of fifteen specially admitted students were not maintaining a passing average."[283] Similarly, the class that entered Yale Law School in fall 1969 included more than thirty Black students—a much larger cohort than had ever previously matriculated. But one year later, more than half of those students had received sufficiently low marks that they were forced to withdraw.[284]

The aim here, of course, is not to rap 1960s administrators on the knuckles for having erred. They were doubtless doing their level best to adapt in a vastly transformed admissions landscape. And that, of course, is precisely the point. Enormous, life-altering mistakes are likely to occur when a policy is in its infancy, and that fledgling, treacherous state is the one that *SFFA* has now thrust admissions

---

[282] KENNEDY, *supra* note 18, at 145.

[283] Graglia, *supra* note 93, at 359.

[284] *See* KEN FOSKETT, JUDGING THOMAS: THE LIFE AND TIMES OF CLARENCE THOMAS 119–20 (2004); Macklin Fleming & Louis Pollak, *The Black Quota at Yale Law School*, 1970 PUB. INT. 44, 44–45. Justice Thomas, who entered Yale Law School in 1971, recalled many years later: "When I went to Yale Law School, they had reduced black admissions from 40 to 12. We were all there on our own merit." Joan Biskupic, *Thomas Caught Up in Conflict*, WASH. POST (June 7, 1996), https://www.washingtonpost.com/archive/politics/1996/06/07/thomas-caught-up-in-conflict/31fe2547-14e9-4679-bea7-06982f8d94b2. It is well known, of course, that Justice Thomas has vehemently rejected any notion that his application to Yale Law School benefited from affirmative action. It is far less appreciated, however, that Justice Thomas entered Yale at a time of tremendous upheaval, when the institution must have still been reeling from the mass Black exodus that occurred a few years prior. To the extent that Justice Thomas's jurisprudential hostility toward affirmative action is at all animated by his personal experiences, it is possible that his having come into close proximity with a poorly designed program may have soured his view of such programs altogether.

officers into around the nation. *SFFA* will not eliminate universities' desire to enroll significant numbers of Black and brown students, as discussed above.[285] But those universities will not have the benefit of more than five decades of pertinent trial and error as they attempt to traverse this new, rocky terrain. I fervently hope that the serious damage of the late 1960s does not portend the shape of things to come after *SFFA*. In debates about affirmative action, conservatives have often expressed concerns about ensuring that Black and brown students realize their full academic potential.[286] Taking them at their word, though, the uncertainty created by *SFFA* imperils those students' prospects.

Relatedly, conservatives might be expected to fear that *SFFA*'s volatility places elite universities themselves in jeopardy. In the current hour—when prominent Republican politicians have forged careers based on assailing universities as out-of-touch, left-wing bastions[287]—harming the Ivy League may seem more a virtue than a vice. It is important to recall, however, that widespread conservative suspicion—if not downright loathing—of higher education is a relatively novel phenomenon.[288] As recently as 2015, Gallup found that a clear majority of Republicans held either "a great deal" or "quite a lot" of confidence in higher education.[289] But in 2023, less than one in five Republicans espoused those same positive attitudes toward universities.[290]

The traditional conservative ambition to maintain universities has animated numerous critiques of affirmative action over the years. When universities had recently begun implementing affirmative action programs, Graglia in 1970, for example, pitched his opposition

---

[285] *See* KENNEDY, *supra* note 18, at 15, 239, 240.

[286] *See, e.g.*, Sander, *supra* note 48, at 442–54.

[287] *See* Nicholas Confessore, *As Fury Erupts Over Campus Antisemitism, Conservatives Seize the Moment*, N.Y. TIMES (Dec. 10, 2023), https://www.nytimes.com/2023/12/10/us/universities-antisemitism-conservatives-liberals.html (analyzing how Governor Ron DeSantis of Florida and Representative Elise Stefanik of New York have attracted national attention by condemning universities).

[288] *See* Ross Douthat, *Harvard Couldn't Save Both Claudine Gay and Itself*, N.Y. TIMES (Jan. 3, 2024), https://www.nytimes.com/2024/01/03/opinion/claudine-gay-harvard.html ("[U]ntil quite recently, the right's critique of academic bias coexisted with a surprisingly strong respect for American universities among Republicans.").

[289] *See* Megan Brenan, *Americans' Confidence in Higher Education Down Sharply*, GALLUP (July 11, 2023), https://news.gallup.com/poll/508352/americans-confidence-higher-education-down-sharply.aspx.

[290] *See id.*

as stemming importantly from society's "responsibility to preserve what is worth preserving" about higher education.[291] "[O]ur academic institutions have much to lose.... I will not be easily convinced that [progress] will be brought about by the destruction or radical disruption of [higher education]," Graglia insisted.[292]

More than five decades later, of course, *SFFA* itself has radically disrupted elite American higher education. This disruption could quite plausibly harm universities by inspiring them to make changes that weaken the overall quality of the institutions. Only eight years ago, in *Fisher II*, the Supreme Court reasoned: "A university is in large part defined by those intangible qualities which are incapable of objective measurement but which make for greatness. Considerable deference is owed to a university in defining those intangible characteristics, like student body diversity, that are central to its identity and educational mission."[293] *SFFA* can therefore be viewed as consciously inflicting a mortal blow to something that has long been central to universities' educational mission, hampering their ability to pursue that ineffable quality that produces greatness. For decades, American higher education has been the envy of the world; let us hope that *SFFA* does not spark a sequence of events that transforms it into a laughingstock.

CONCLUSION

In *Bakke*'s immediate wake, then-Professor Scalia allowed in 1979 that he held "grave doubts about the wisdom of where we are going in affirmative action," and that he found the jurisprudence involving race "an embarrassment to teach."[294] Scalia deemed it an "utterly confused field," and concluded: "[I]t is increasingly difficult to pretend to one's students that the decisions of the Supreme Court are tied together by threads of logic and analysis—as opposed to what seems to be the fact that the decisions ... are tied together by threads of social preference and predisposition."[295]

---

[291] Graglia, *supra* note 93, at 362–63.

[292] *Id.* at 362.

[293] Fisher v. Univ. of Tex. (*Fisher II*), 579 U.S. 365, 388 (2016) (internal citations and quotation marks omitted).

[294] Scalia, *supra* note 2, at 147.

[295] *Id.*

Legal conservatives have, of course, long pined for affirmative action's demise. But as *SFFA* thrusts the nation into the post-affirmative action era, conservatives may once again quickly grow to harbor deep reservations about the wisdom of where we are heading. Now that the long-sought victory has been realized, it has become apparent for several powerful reasons that they will profoundly regret the legal order that *SFFA* generates. According to conservatives' own principles, then, the edifice that *SFFA* hastily erected seems far less hospitable than the one that the Supreme Court dismantled.

CASS R. SUNSTEIN

THE INVENTION OF COLORBLINDNESS

Who controls the past controls the future. Who controls the present controls the past. (George Orwell)

I. Almost a Song

What is most extraordinary about *Students for Fair Admissions, Inc. v. President & Fellows of Harvard College*[1] is the simplicity of the Court's analysis. The core of that analysis consists of about five pages. In places, it is elegiac. It is almost a song.

The almost-a-song begins with a stunningly brief, one-paragraph account of the historical origins of the Equal Protection Clause, which, in the Court's view, had "transcendent aims."[2] The central aim was "absolute equality" in the form of a flat prohibition on "any distinctions of law based on race and color."[3] Soon after ratification of the Fourteenth Amendment, the Court itself recognized the "broad sweep" of the Clause.[4] The problem came in what might be called the Age of Segregation, when the Court (inexplicably) departed from the

---

Cass R. Sunstein is the Robert Walmsley University Professor at Harvard University.

AUTHOR'S NOTE: I am grateful to Nick Caputo, Larry Lessig, and Thomas Nielsen for valuable comments on an earlier draft and to Caputo for superb research assistance.

[1] 600 U.S. 181 (2023).

[2] *Id.* at 202.

[3] *Id.* (internal citations omitted).

[4] *Id.*

Constitution, invoking the idea of "separate but equal" in a self-evidently doomed effort "to derive equality from inequality."[5] *Plessy v. Ferguson*[6] was plainly inconsistent with the "Clause's core commitments."[7] In *Brown v. Board of Education*,[8] the Court finally returned to those "transcendent aims" of the Equal Protection Clause, recognizing once more that "the Constitution is color blind."[9] Hence, "[t]he time for making distinctions based on race had passed."[10] (It was as if *Brown* had essentially struck down affirmative action programs.)

The Court celebrated what it depicted as the Age of *Brown*, in which, it said, its rulings "continued to vindicate the Constitution's pledge of racial equality."[11] In invalidating segregation, the Court embraced "the 'core purpose' of the Equal Protection Clause," which was to eliminate racial discrimination in all its forms.[12] "Eliminating racial discrimination means eliminating all of it."[13]

---

[5] *Id.* at 203.

[6] 163 U.S. 537 (1896).

[7] *Students for Fair Admissions*, 600 U.S. at 203.

[8] 347 U.S. 483 (1954).

[9] *Students for Fair Admissions*, 600 U.S. at 204 (internal citations omitted). For a valuable discussion, see ANDREW KULL, THE COLOR-BLIND CONSTITUTION (1992). Consider by contrast this statement: "A blanket prohibition of racial classifications is impossible to locate in a literal reading of the constitutional text, and it has never been acknowledged by the Supreme Court as a requirement of the 'equal protection of the laws' guaranteed by the Fourteenth Amendment." *Id.* at 1. Of course the claim that "Our Constitution is color-blind" can be found in Justice Harlan's dissenting opinion in *Plessy v. Ferguson*, 163 U.S. 537 (1896), but it is speculative in the extreme to say that Justice Harlan would have voted against affirmative action programs on constitutional grounds. After all, his statement on colorblindness was immediately preceded by this one: "There is no caste here." *Id.* at 559. An anticaste principle might permit or even welcome affirmative action programs. *See* Bryan K. Fair, *The Acontextual Illusion of a Color-Blind Constitution*, 28 U. S.F. L. REV. 343, 361 (1994): "Justice Harlan did not simply declare that our constitution is colorblind. Rather, he wrote that in the eye of the law there is no superior class or caste, and that our constitution does not tolerate classes among citizens. If Justice Harlan's central concern was the elimination of caste and racial subordination, it is a significant stretch to interpret his dissenting opinion to prohibit racial classifications designed to eliminate such caste." Compare Martin Luther King, Jr., who famously said, "I have a dream that my four little children will one day live in a nation where they will not be judged by the color of their skin but by the content of their character." Martin Luther King, Jr., I Have a Dream, March on Washington for Jobs and Freedom (Aug. 28, 1963). With those words, King's goal was not to attack affirmative action programs, which he undoubtedly would have supported. *See generally* JONATHAN EIG, KING: A LIFE (2023); Cass R. Sunstein, *What the Civil Rights Movement Was and Wasn't*, 1995 U. ILL. L. REV. 191.

[10] *Students for Fair Admissions*, 600 U.S. at 204.

[11] *Id.* at 205.

[12] *Id.* at 206.

[13] *Id.*

That is all of it — the Court's analysis, that is. The rest is not elegiac. It is not a song. It is an anticlimax, a kind of extended footnote.

The Court explored, in some detail and with a palpable sense of struggle, the Court's affirmative action rulings, largely to emphasize that the Court applied "strict scrutiny" to the relevant programs,[14] that it had flatly forbidden the use of historical discrimination[15] to justify those programs,[16] and that it had allowed affirmative action only in the narrowest circumstances and in the interest of diversity, with a promise that the relevant permission slip would terminate by a date certain (2028, as it happens).[17] The Court's exploration of its affirmative action decisions was a labored effort to show that under the influence of Justice Powell's tie-breaking vote in *Regents of the University of California v. Bakke*,[18] the Court has maintained essential faith in the "transcendent aims" of the Equal Protection Clause (read: colorblindness), while approving some affirmative action programs under very narrow circumstances and for a limited period of time. It is impossible to read this part of the Court's opinion without reaching the conclusion that the current majority disagrees strongly with Justice Powell, and that it thinks that it would have been much better if the Court had struck down affirmative action programs from the get-go.

Bringing "the Constitution's pledge of racial equality"[19] into contact with the affirmative action programs at Harvard and the University of North Carolina, the Court went on to invalidate those programs on three independent grounds: (1) they failed "strict scrutiny," (2) they used race as a negative and a stereotype, and (3) they lacked an end date.[20] Note well: The Court's conclusion that the Harvard and North Carolina programs failed strict scrutiny would carry over intact and without even modest changes to *Bakke*[21] and *Gratz*,[22] in which the

---

[14] *Id.* at 206–13.

[15] There is an exception for remedial efforts in response to discrimination by the very institutions who create those efforts. *Id.* at 208.

[16] *Id.*

[17] *Id.* at 224 (citing Grutter v. Bollinger, 539 U.S. 306, 342 (2003)).

[18] Regents of the Univ. of Cal. v. Bakke, 438 U.S. 265 (1978).

[19] *Students for Fair Admissions*, 600 U.S. at 205.

[20] *Id.* at 230.

[21] *Bakke*, 438 U.S. 265.

[22] Gratz v. Bollinger, 539 U.S. 244 (2003).

Court had upheld similar programs. Exactly the same is true of the Court's conclusion that the two programs used race as a negative and a stereotype. Note well, once more: In the programs upheld in *Bakke* and *Gratz*, race was also used as a negative and as a stereotype according to the analysis in *Students for Fair Admissions*.

II. THE SIMPLE NARRATIVE

Everything in *Students for Fair Admissions* depends on an exceedingly simple narrative about the Equal Protection Clause, consisting of just three chapters:

(1) the ratification of the Equal Protection Clause in 1868, requiring colorblindness, and the Court's early and clear recognition of its "transcendent aims";[23]
(2) the "ignoble" era of separate-but-equal,[24] violating the Clause, and lasting from the late 1870s until 1954;
(3) the glorious Age of *Brown* and colorblindness in 1954 until the present, sullied only by the occasional validation of affirmative action programs.[25]

Of the three chapters, the most important, by far, is (1). But are things really so easy?[26] The Fourteenth Amendment was ratified in 1868.[27] *Plessy v. Ferguson* was decided in 1896. As the Court notes in a revealing footnote, the idea of strict scrutiny of racial classifications did not come until the later stages of World War II, in *Korematsu v. United States*, decided in 1944.[28] That raises a puzzle: If the Constitution banned such classifications in 1868, how can we explain the failure to

---

[23] A New Hope?

[24] The Empire Strikes Back?

[25] Return of the Jedi? It is more than a bit ridiculous, I know, to offer the first Star Wars trilogy by way of analogy, but in this particular case: close, the analogy is.

[26] KULL, *supra* note 9, demonstrates otherwise, though it also shows that the idea of colorblindness—with indeterminate implications for affirmative action programs—has been around for a very long time.

[27] For valuable clarifications on multiple levels, see generally PAMELA BRANDWEIN, RETHINKING THE JUDICIAL SETTLEMENT OF RECONSTRUCTION (2011).

[28] 323 U.S. 214, 216 (1944).

use strict scrutiny until 1944, in a case involving the Fifth Amendment's Due Process Clause no less?[29]

In any case, *Brown* was not decided until 1954. Racial segregation was taken to be constitutional in 1944, 1934, 1924, and 1914. For the Court in 1954, *Brown* was hardly an easy case. If Chief Justice Robert Vinson had not died and had not been replaced by Chief Justice Earl Warren, it is less than entirely clear that *Brown* would have come out as it did.[30] Even if the outcome was in little doubt, the rationale was elusive. No one thought that the Court should simply write an opinion like that in *Students for Fair Admissions*. No one thought that the Court should say that racial classifications are impermissible. The much-admired Justice Robert Jackson greatly struggled with the case.[31] He did not believe that *Plessy* was wrong when decided.[32] Was he negligent? Did he simply fail to understand the clear command of the Equal Protection Clause? Here is part of what Jackson wrote in a draft opinion[33]:

> It is hard to find an indication that any of the influential body of the movement that carried the Civil War Amendments had reached the point

---

[29] *Korematsu* involved the national government, not the states, which means that the Fifth Amendment's Due Process Clause, and not the Equal Protection Clause, was the operative constitutional provision. It would be difficult to say that the core purpose of the Fifth Amendment's Due Process Clause was to forbid racial classifications.

[30] It probably would have, but it is not entirely clear. For a detailed account, see RICHARD KLUGER, SIMPLE JUSTICE (2d ed. 2004). It is simply not possible to read Kluger's account and also to give a credulous reading to the brisk, confident, gaslighting treatment of racial classifications in *Students for Fair Admissions*.

[31] Consider in this regard a memorandum written by law clerk William Rehnquist, which is said to reflect what Justice Jackson was thinking at one point (though generally thought to reflect Rehnquist's own thoughts): "I realize that it is an unpopular and unhumanitarian position, for which I have been excoriated by 'liberal' colleagues, but I think *Plessy v. Ferguson* was right and should be re-affirmed. If the Fourteenth Amendment did not enact Spencer's Social Statics, it just as surely did not enact Myrdahl's American Dilemma." Memorandum from William H. Rehnquist to Justice Robert Jackson, A Random Thought on the Segregation Cases (1952), *reprinted in* 117 CONG. REC. 45, 441 (1971). Even if these words merely reflect the views of a law clerk, they are not without historical interest; they suggest that the simple narrative of the 2023 Court was wildly out of step with what many people thought in 1954. Perhaps Rehnquist was simply wrong, and perhaps Jackson himself was simply wrong. But if they were wrong, was it because the Equal Protection Clause simply required colorblindness in 1868? Recall that Justice Thomas so argued, and I have not said or shown that he was wrong. (I believe that he was.) My topic here is the majority's simple narrative, and my aim is to show that it is wildly out of step with the arc of constitutional history; it was undoubtedly written in good faith, but there is something Orwellian about it. *See* GEORGE ORWELL, 1984, at 44 (1949) ("Who controls the past ... controls the future. Who controls the present controls the past.").

[32] *See generally* DAVID O'BRIEN, JUSTICE ROBERT H. JACKSON'S UNPUBLISHED OPINION IN BROWN V. BOARD: CONFLICT, COMPROMISE, AND CONSTITUTIONAL INTERPRETATION (2017).

[33] *Id.* at 125–26.

of thinking about either segregation or education of the Negro as a current problem, and harder still to find that the Amendments were designed to be a solution. If we turn from words to deeds as evidence of purpose, we find nothing to show that the Congress which submitted these Amendments understood or intended to prohibit the practice here in question. The very Congress that proposed the Fourteenth Amendment, and every Congress from that day to this, established or maintained segregated schools in the District of Columbia, where its power over purse and policy was complete.... Turning from Congress to look to the behavior of the states, we find that equally impossible to reconcile with any understanding that the Amendment would prohibit segregation in schools.

Note that Jackson can be understood to be speaking here of intent, original public meaning, and purpose. He was insisting that Civil War Amendments do not embed a ban on racial classifications.[34] It is surely relevant that in the 1950s and 1960s, prominent legal thinkers, including Judge Learned Hand and Herbert Wechsler, prominently thought that *Brown* was wrongly decided.[35] Did they not know what happened in 1868? Did they fail to understand the "transcendent aims" of the Equal Protection Clause? We will get to the question of method in constitutional law before very long;[36] the only point here is that *Brown* was not universally regarded as easy.

Perhaps more fundamentally, the *Brown* opinion did not sound even a little bit like *Students for Fair Admissions*. The Court did not speak of "transcendent aims" or "central purposes." It did not speak of colorblindness. It did not say that racial classifications were forbidden. It is very hard to read it to condemn affirmative action programs. It did not purport to turn the clock back to 1868. Here is what the Court said:

> In approaching this problem, we cannot turn the clock back to 1868, when the Amendment was adopted, or even to 1896, when *Plessy v. Ferguson* was written. We must consider public education in the light of its full development and its present place in American life throughout the Nation.

---

[34] For a vigorous argument to this effect in the context of anti-miscegenation laws, see R. Carter Pittman, *The Fourteenth Amendment: Its Intended Effect on Anti-Miscegenation Laws*, 43 N.C. L. Rev. 92 (1964). It is important to emphasize that *Students for Fair Admissions* is emphatically not an originalist opinion, which raises the question of the source of the colorblindness principle that it endorses. *See infra* notes 50–51 and accompanying text.

[35] *See generally* Herbert Wechsler, *Toward Neutral Principles of Constitutional Law*, 73 Harv. L. Rev. 1 (1959); Learned Hand, The Bill of Rights (1958).

[36] Jackson seems to be speaking in originalist terms, as the *Students for Fair Admissions* Court was not.

Only in this way can it be determined if segregation in public schools deprives these plaintiffs of the equal protection of the laws.[37]

The Court insisted that "[t]o separate [black children] from others of similar age and qualifications solely because of their race generates a feeling of inferiority as to their status in the community that may affect their hearts and minds in a way unlikely ever to be undone."[38] At that point, the Court quoted a finding by a lower court:

> Segregation of white and colored children in public schools has a detrimental effect upon the colored children. The impact is greater when it has the sanction of the law, for the policy of separating the races is usually interpreted as denoting the inferiority of the negro group. A sense of inferiority affects the motivation of a child to learn. Segregation with the sanction of law, therefore, has a tendency to [retard] the educational and mental development of negro children and to deprive them of some of the benefits they would receive in a racial[ly] integrated school system.[39]

The Court added this: "Whatever may have been the extent of psychological knowledge at the time of *Plessy v. Ferguson*, this finding is amply supported by modern authority. Any language in *Plessy v. Ferguson* contrary to this finding is rejected."[40] It is plain that the *Brown* Court did not contend that from the jump,[41] the Equal Protection Clause flatly prohibited consideration of race and that for over eighty years, the nation and the Court had simply neglected or transgressed that command. The *Brown* Court certainly did not announce that *Plessy* had somehow overlooked an unambiguous constitutional "aim." The Court said instead that current psychological knowledge established that separate was not equal.

It is reasonable to doubt whether that was the best justification of *Brown*. In my view, the best justification would point to the fact that segregation was a central part of an effort to create a system of racial caste. Such a justification would draw on the unforgettable account of Charles Black:

> Equality, like all general concepts, has marginal areas where philosophic difficulties are encountered. But if a whole race of people finds itself

---

[37] Brown v. Bd. of Educ., 347 U.S. 483, 492–93 (1954).

[38] *Id.* at 494.

[39] *Id.* (corrections in original, citing Belton v. Gebhart, 87 A.2d 862, 865 (Del. Ch.), aff'd, 91 A.2d 137 (Del. 1952)).

[40] *Id.* at 494–95.

[41] I add this colloquialism to make sure the reader is paying attention.

confined within a system which is set up and continued for the very purpose of keeping it in an inferior station, and if the question is then solemnly propounded whether such a race is being treated "equally," I think we ought to exercise one of the sovereign prerogatives of philosophers—that of laughter. The only question remaining (after we get our laughter under control) is whether the segregation system answers to this description. Here I must confess to a tendency to start laughing all over again. I was raised in the South, in a Texas city where the pattern of segregation was firmly fixed. I am sure it never occurred to anyone, white or colored, to question its meaning.[42]

Whatever its proper justification, it is noteworthy that the *Brown* opinion operates in a different jurisprudential universe from the *Students for Fair Admissions* opinion. *Brown* found it necessary to emphasize the *consequences* of segregation; it did not purport to discover, in the Equal Protection Clause, a long-lost ban on consideration of race. Indeed, it took the Court *thirteen years after Brown* to strike down bans on racial intermarriage.[43] When the Court finally did so in *Loving v. Virginia*, it did not contend that the original public meaning of the Fourteenth Amendment was inconsistent with such bans, or that its "transcendent aims" included a flat prohibition on consideration of race. The Court did not offer a historical exegesis. It was wise not to do so, for these would have been dangerous waters; southern legislators in the years following the Civil War repeatedly used the specter of cross-race sexual relations to scare others into not voting for Reconstruction-era acts, including the Fourteenth Amendment.[44]

---

[42] Charles L. Black, Jr., *The Lawfulness of the Segregation Decisions*, 69 YALE L.J. 421, 424 (1960).

[43] *See* Loving v. Virginia, 388 U.S. 1 (1967). Part of the reason for the delay involved prudential considerations. Nonetheless, it is relevant that the colorblindness principle was not enforced, by the Court, for well over a decade after *Brown*.

[44] For instance, Republican Glenn W. Scofield, criticizing Democrat invocations of the miscegenation problem to dissuade passage of the Fourteenth Amendment, stated that "This cry has been too often raised to alarm even the most ignorant.... This is a standing argument with the Opposition, and is brought out on all occasions when any legislation is proposed touching the interest of the colored population.... Let our sensitive friends compose their nerves and try to tell us how a little enlargement of the elective franchise ... will result in marriage between the two races. It is fright that makes you mistake a ballot for a billet-doux. It cannot be possible that any man of common sense can bring himself to believe that marriages between any persons, much less between white and colored people, will take place because a colored man is allowed to drop a little bit of paper in a box .... It is too trifling for argument." CONG. GLOBE, 38th Cong., 2d Sess., pt. 1, at 484 (1865) (quoted in Alfred Avins, *Anti-Miscegenation Laws and the Fourteenth Amendment: The Original Intent*, 52 VA. L. REV. 1224, 1230 (1966)).

True, the *Loving* Court did refer to "the broader, organic purpose"[45] of the Fourteenth Amendment, but let there be no mistake; the word "organic," suggesting change and growth over time, is in a different jurisprudential universe from the tale told in *Students for Fair Admissions*. And in *Loving*, the Court emphasized that there "is patently no legitimate overriding purpose independent of *invidious* racial discrimination which justifies this classification."[46] To drive that point home, the Court said that "the racial classifications must stand on their own justification, as measures designed to maintain White Supremacy."[47]

Cards on the table: *Students for Fair Admissions* makes everything much too easy. It is a form of constitutional gaslighting.[48] The truth is that *Brown* was complicated. It was an achievement. It was a product of the twentieth century, not the nineteenth. It had something to do with World War II. It was hardly a simple act of recovering something firmly established in 1868.

III. METHOD

Turn now to a fundamental question: What is the *Students for Fair Admissions* Court's theory of constitutional interpretation? To know the source of the newly announced principle of colorblindness,[49] we need to answer that question.

The Court does not claim to be textualist. It does not contend that colorblindness can be read off the text of the Equal Protection Clause.[50] That is good, for it would be preposterous to make that claim.[51] English speakers could accept and celebrate that text without committing themselves to colorblindness. They might think: "I believe in equal protection of the laws, but I do not believe that racial preferences in higher education are inconsistent with my commitment to equality. In fact I believe that such preferences are required by my commitment."

---

[45] *Loving*, 388 U.S. at 9.

[46] *Id.* at 11 (emphasis added).

[47] *Id.*

[48] *See generally* Cass R. Sunstein, *The Problem of Extravagant Inferences* (Harv. Pub. L., Working Paper 23-33, 2023), https://papers.ssrn.com/sol3/papers.cfm?abstract_id=4369531.

[49] The genesis of the idea would require, and deserve, a book. A good one is KULL, *supra* note 9.

[50] "[N]or shall any State ... deny to any person within its jurisdiction the equal protection of the laws." U.S. CONST. amend. XIV, § 1.

[51] KULL, *supra* note 9, at 1.

Then there is the matter of "protection," an important word that the Court ignored. As a matter of simple textualism, ignoring that word is irresponsible. An English speaker might say: "I do not understand the Equal Protection Clause to set out a broad antidiscrimination principle. I understand it to say that if the law protects white people (from, say, private violence), it also protects black people."[52] And indeed, the Equal Protection Clause is best taken, as a matter of history, to be about equal protection, not about equality more generally. If asked whether the Equal Protection Clause forbids affirmative action, a conscientious textualist would have to say: *I have no idea*.[53] (Regrettably, the Court did quote, with approval, Justice Powell's statement: "If both are not accorded the same protection, then it is not equal."[54] Good luck with that.[55])

The Court does not claim to be originalist. It does not delve into history to uncover the original public meaning. It is worth underlining the point. Justice Thomas and Justice Jackson had a spirited debate about whether colorblindness was mandated by the Fourteenth Amendment. For instance, Justice Thomas writes:

> The drafters and ratifiers of the Fourteenth Amendment focused on this broad equality idea, offering surprisingly little explanation of which term was intended to accomplish which part of the Amendment's overall goal. "The available materials ... show," however, "that there were widespread expressions of a general understanding of the broad scope of the Amendment similar to that abundantly demonstrated in the Congressional debates, namely, that the first section of the Amendment would establish the full constitutional right of all persons to equality before the law and would prohibit legal distinctions based on race or color."[56]

Justice Jackson responds:

> After the war, Senator John Sherman defended the proposed Fourteenth Amendment in a manner that encapsulated our Reconstruction Framers'

---

[52] *See* Randy E. Barnett & Evan Bernick, The Original Meaning of the Fourteenth Amendment 319–71 (2021).

[53] As a matter of text and the original understanding, the Privileges or Immunities Clause would be a far better foundation of a general antidiscrimination principle. *See id.* Of course, it is true that on that question, the relevant ships have sailed.

[54] Regents of the Univ. of Cal. v. Bakke, 438 U.S. 265, 290 (1978) (Powell, J., concurring).

[55] *See generally* Peter Westen, *The Empty Idea of Equality*, 95 Harv. L. Rev. 537 (1982).

[56] Students for Fair Admissions, Inc. v. President & Fellows of Harvard Coll. 600 U.S. 181, 241 (2023) (Thomas, J., concurring) (internal citations omitted).

highest sentiments: "We are bound by every obligation, by [Black Americans'] service on the battlefield, by their heroes who are buried in our cause, by their patriotism in the hours that tried our country, we are bound to protect them and all their natural rights." To uphold that promise, the Framers repudiated this Court's holding in *Dred Scott v. Sandford*, by crafting Reconstruction Amendments (and associated legislation) that transformed our Constitution and society. Even after this Second Founding—when the need to right historical wrongs should have been clear beyond cavil—opponents insisted that vindicating equality in this manner slighted White Americans. So, when the Reconstruction Congress passed a bill to secure all citizens "the same [civil] right[s]" as "enjoyed by white citizens," President Andrew Johnson vetoed it because it "discriminat[ed] ... in favor of the negro."[57]

While Justice Jackson seems to me to get the better of the argument, it is immensely discouraging to see that history is so regularly understood in a way that fits with the hopes and goals of those who are reading it—a real challenge for the originalist project. But for present purposes, what is most important is that the Court itself does not engage with either view and rests content with a general insistence on the "aspiration" or "core principle" of the Equal Protection Clause, without showing or finding it necessary to show that its reading is historically mandatory.

To be sure, a rapid and all-important paragraph, beginning the core of the Court's analysis, does offer some quick historical references, with short quotations. But there are just three such quotations, from Representative John Bingham, soon-to-be-President James Garfield, and Senator Jacob Howard.[58] And while the three men did speak of equality, it would be extravagant to take anything in their words to forbid affirmative action programs. For example, Senator Howard said that the Amendment would give "to the humblest, the poorest, the most despised of the race the same rights and the same protection before the law as it gives to the most powerful, the most wealthy, or the most haughty."[59] What on earth does that have to do with affirmative action programs? Does it even suggest that *Brown* was right, or *Loving*?

As noted, Justice Thomas did offer a detailed discussion of the original meaning, purporting to show, in some detail, that the Fourteenth Amendment was originally understood to call for

---

[57] *Id.* at 386–87 (Jackson, J., dissenting) (internal citations omitted).

[58] *Id.* at 202–03.

[59] *Id.* at 203 (quoting Cong. Globe, 39th Cong., 1st Sess. 2766 (1866)).

colorblindness.[60] Whether or not his argument is convincing,[61] he spoke only for himself. The Court did not rely on his arguments, or summarize them, or offer its own historical account. True, one could read the Court's opinion to be consistent with the claim that colorblindness is compelled by the original public meaning of the Fourteenth Amendment. But the Court pointedly declined to defend that claim, or even to make it. In that respect, *Students for Fair Admissions* is in a different category from cases, prominently including Second Amendment cases, that are written in originalist terms.[62]

The Court speaks instead of "transcendent aims,"[63] and both of those words are worth emphasizing. What does "transcendent" mean, in this context? According to a standard account, it means "greater, better, more important, or going past or above all others."[64] Perhaps the word is a signal that the relevant aims have a defining or fundamental character. And what of "aims"? That seems to be a reference to general goals or purposes. And indeed the Court refers to the "aspirations of the framers of the Equal Protection Clause"[65] and to "the core purpose" of the Clause, which is "do[ing] away with all governmentally imposed discrimination based on race."[66]

What is an aim, an aspiration, or a purpose? It could, of course, be the same as the original public meaning—but one more time: The Court does not offer any such claim. It could be a broad principle that could have attained broad support at the time of ratification, even if people disagreed about what the principle specifically entailed. It could be a broad principle that was expected to grow over time. Compare the term "the freedom of speech." That term might have had "transcendent aims," connected with the goals of republican self-government,

---

[60] One more time, and a little more sharply, because we are here in the footnotes: It is noteworthy, and very bad, that those who seem to disapprove of affirmative action in principle seem to think that it is plainly inconsistent with the original meaning of the Fourteenth Amendment, and that those who seem to approve of affirmative action in principle seem to think that it is plainly consistent with that original meaning. It would be noteworthy, and very good, to see more people finding the original meaning to be inconsistent with their deepest convictions. *See generally* FRANK CROSS, THE FAILED PROMISE OF ORIGINALISM (2013).

[61] In my view, it is not close to convincing. *See, e.g.*, KULL, *supra* note 9.

[62] *See* District of Columbia v. Heller, 544 U.S. 570 (2008).

[63] *Students for Fair Admissions*, 600 U.S. at 202.

[64] *Transcendent*, CAMBRIDGE DICTIONARY, https://dictionary.cambridge.org/us/dictionary/english/transcendent.

[65] *Students for Fair Admissions*, 600 U.S. at 203.

[66] *Id.* at 206 (quoting Palmore v. Sidoti, 466 U.S. 429, 432 (1984)).

and perhaps we could say that in ruling in ways that depart from the original understanding of the scope of the term (by, for example, protecting certain forms of libel), the Court has maintained faith with those transcendent aims. For instance, in the famous passage in *Whitney v. California*,[67] Justice Brandeis spoke of the First Amendment in strikingly purposive, nonhistorical terms:

> Those who won our independence believed that the final end of the State was to make men free to develop their faculties, and that, in its government, the deliberative forces should prevail over the arbitrary. They valued liberty both as an end, and as a means. They believed liberty to be the secret of happiness, and courage to be the secret of liberty. They believed that freedom to think as you will and to speak as you think are means indispensable to the discovery and spread of political truth; that, without free speech and assembly, discussion would be futile; that, with them, discussion affords ordinarily adequate protection against the dissemination of noxious doctrine; that the greatest menace to freedom is an inert people; that public discussion is a political duty, and that this should be a fundamental principle of the American government . . . . Fear of serious injury cannot alone justify suppression of free speech and assembly. Men feared witches and burnt women. It is the function of speech to free men from the bondage of irrational fears.[68]

This purposivism, as Justice Thomas has noted in cases like *Counterman v. Colorado*,[69] is hardly originalist. It is hardly the "First Amendment as it was understood at the time of the Founding."[70] Discussing *New York Times v. Sullivan*,[71] Justice Thomas in *Counterman* noted that "[t]he constitutional libel rules adopted by this Court *in New York Times* and its progeny broke sharply from the common law of libel, and there are sound reasons to question whether the First and Fourteenth Amendments displaced this body of common law."[72] On this view, perhaps, *Students for Fair Admissions* is *New York Times v. Sullivan*,[73] and both of them are *Brown v. Board of Education*, and all three are *Goldberg v. Kelly*.[74]

---

[67] 274 U.S. 357 (1927).
[68] *Id.* at 375–76 (Brandeis, J., concurring).
[69] 600 U.S. 66 (2023).
[70] *Id.* at 105 (Thomas, J., dissenting).
[71] 376 U.S. 254 (1964).
[72] 600 U.S. at 105 (Thomas, J., dissenting) (internal citations omitted).
[73] 376 U.S. 254 (1964).
[74] 397 U.S. 254 (1970).

But this view raises many questions. We might say about "transcendent aims" what Gertrude Stein once said about Oakland: "There is no there there."[75] Consider this view: the "transcendent aim" of the Fourteenth Amendment was to undo a system of racial caste, in which one group is subordinated to another;[76] affirmative action programs are compatible with that aim, and so do not violate the founding document. Why is that view wrong? The Court gave no answer. It is possible that it is wrong as a matter of the original public meaning, but recall that the Court makes no argument to that effect. What, then, is the *source* of the colorblindness requirement?

It is tempting to say that it is a concoction—a creation of the Court in 2023. On that view, *Students for Fair Admissions* is *Lochner v. New York*,[77] and both of them are *Roe v. Wade*,[78] and all three of them are *Obergefell v. Hodges*.[79] That view is not exactly wrong, but it is imprecise. The colorblindness idea was not entrenched until 2023, but it was invented long before.[80] It is better to say that the colorblindness requirement is a product of interpretation in Ronald Dworkin's sense of law as "integrity."[81] In fact Dworkin gives the best account of what purposivism actually is or entails. The basic idea is that judges owe a duty of fidelity to the legal materials, or "fit," but that when fit leaves matters open, judges must make the best constructive sense of those materials by putting them in their best light—by making them the best that they can be.[82] Suppose, for example, that a court has ruled that people have a constitutional right to use contraceptives within marriage. Now the question arises: Do unmarried people have a right to use contraceptives outside of marriage? On Dworkin's view, judges have to identify the principle that underpins the initial decision, and to do that, they have to figure out what principle makes best sense of it. That is precisely the method used by the Court in *Students for Fair*

---

[75] GERTRUDE STEIN, EVERYBODY'S AUTOBIOGRAPHY 289 (1937).

[76] This is, in my view, the best reading of *Brown*. *See generally* Black, *supra* note 42; *see also* Cass R. Sunstein, *Black on* Brown, 90 VA. L. REV. 1649 (2004).

[77] 198 U.S. 45 (1905).

[78] 410 U.S. 113 (1973).

[79] 576 U.S. 644 (2015).

[80] *See generally* KULL, *supra* note 9.

[81] *See generally* RONALD DWORKIN, LAW'S EMPIRE (1985).

[82] Dworkin's own view was complicated and changed over time; I am not offering an exegesis here.

Admissions. The idea of colorblindness can be understood, most charitably, as a principle that fits and justifies an assortment of rulings, including both *Brown* and *Loving*. Those who want to engage with the Court's approach ought to argue with it along the dimensions of both fit and justification, just as those who want to engage with *New York Times v. Sullivan* or *Obergefell* must do.

A possible objection to that method is suggested by Justice Thomas's separate opinion. Some originalists would insist that fit-and-justification is the wrong way to approach constitutional law, and that the real and only question is the original public meaning. Originalism might be taken as a challenge to Dworkin's conception of interpretation, or it might be taken as an excellent example of it, seeking to fit and to justify our practices. On one view, originalism is our law (and hence fits).[83] On another view, originalism makes best sense of our law, within the constraints of fit, because it casts the existing legal materials in the best constructive light.[84]

But let us put originalism to one side. Does *Students for Fair Admissions* fit previous cases? It clearly does not. As noted, *Bakke* and *Gratz* would have had to come out the other way, given the Court's analysis of strict scrutiny, and also given the Court's analysis of the use of race as a negative or a stereotype. Both decisions are effectively overruled, which is a serious problem from the standpoint of fit.

From the standpoint of justification, things are less straightforward. Some people think that the colorblindness principle is the right one and that as a matter of constitutional morality, it is good and right for the Court to embrace it (even if it would do well to soften the claim that the Equal Protection Clause necessarily embraces it). If they are right, then *Students for Fair Admissions* is probably right, for the same reason that *Brown*, *Loving*, and *Obergefell* were right.[85] But we might instead think that the best understanding of the Clause allows race-conscious efforts, by academic institutions and others, to respond to a legacy of discrimination or to promote racial diversity in

---

[83] William Baude & Stephen Sachs, *The Law of Interpretation*, 130 HARV. L. REV. 1079 (2017).

[84] *See* Lawrence B. Solum, The Constraint Principle (Apr. 6, 2019) (unpublished manuscript), https://ssrn.com/abstract=2940215.

[85] I am bracketing some Thayerism caution, which might put a thumb on the scales in favor of deference to other institutions. *See* Cass R. Sunstein, Thayerism (Sept. 14, 2022) (unpublished manuscript), https://papers.ssrn.com/sol3/papers.cfm?abstract_id=4215816.

their institutions.[86] Return in this regard to *Brown* itself, which emphasized that separation of black children "from others of similar age and qualifications solely because of their race generates a feeling of inferiority as to their status in the community that may affect their hearts and minds in a way unlikely ever to be undone."[87] Affirmative action programs do not involve the separation of black people from white people (or others); if anything, they involve the opposite. And those who are disadvantaged by such programs do not suffer anything akin to the kind of injury that segregation imposed.

IV. Politics and Law

The central claim in *Students for Fair Admissions* is simple: The Equal Protection Clause forbids racial discrimination, period. The simplicity of that claim is similar to that of Justice Black's approach to the First Amendment: No law abridging means no law abridging, period.[88] If either claim is one about semantic meaning, the problem is one of the extravagant inference, in which a text is taken to have one necessary meaning, when it could easily have at least one other.[89] But the *Students for Fair Admissions* Court did not make a claim about semantic meaning, and it did not accept or even engage with Justice Thomas's effort to show that the original public meaning of the Fourteenth Amendment requires colorblindness.

Some constitutional principles lack clear roots in the founding document but count as reasonable implementing doctrines.[90] In the domain of free speech, consider the clear and present danger test[91] or the distinction between content-based and content-neutral restrictions. In the domain of equality, consider careful scrutiny of laws that discriminate on the basis of sex.[92] The Court rarely claims that such

---

[86] *See generally* John Hart Ely, *The Constitutionality of Reverse Racial Discrimination*, 41 U. Chi. L. Rev. 723 (1974); Lee C. Bollinger & Geoffrey R. Stone, A Legacy of Discrimination: The Essential Constitutionality of Affirmative Action (2023).

[87] 347 U.S. 483, 494 (1954).

[88] Hugo Black, *The Bill of Rights*, 35 N.Y.U. L. Rev. 865 (1960); N.Y. Times Co. v. Sullivan, 376 U.S. 254, 293–98 (1964) (Black, J., concurring).

[89] *See* Sunstein, *supra* note 48.

[90] For relevant discussion, see Lawrence Solum, *The Interpretation-Construction Distinction*, 27 Const. Comment. 95 (2010).

[91] *See* Brandenburg v. Ohio, 395 U.S. 444 (1969).

[92] *See* Mississippi v. Hogan, 458 U.S. 718 (1982).

doctrines are a direct or mandatory reflection of some judgment—or transcendent aim, commitment, aspiration, or core principle—laid down in (say) 1789 or 1868. The first problem with *Students for Fair Admissions* is the Court's insistence that the Equal Protection Clause necessarily embodies a principle of colorblindness. It does not. The second problem is that if the Court is to use the Equal Protection Clause as the launching pad for principles of its own choosing,[93] the principle of colorblindness is not the right one for the Court to choose.

---

[93] I am bracketing the possibility that (1) originalism is the right method of constitutional interpretation and that (2) on originalist grounds, colorblindness is mandatory. I do not believe either (1) or (2) to be correct, but that is not my topic here. On (1), see CASS R. SUNSTEIN, HOW TO INTERPRET THE CONSTITUTION (2023).

MARK A. LEMLEY AND
REBECCA TUSHNET

FIRST AMENDMENT NEGLECT IN SUPREME COURT INTELLECTUAL PROPERTY CASES

The Supreme Court decided two cases of central importance to free speech during the 2022 Term—in both cases without addressing the First Amendment implications. In *Andy Warhol Foundation v. Goldsmith*,[1] the Court upheld a ruling that Andy Warhol's reworkings of Lynn Goldsmith's photograph of the artist Prince into highly stylized silkscreens and drawings were not transformative, and thus were unfair, at least when images of the artworks were licensed to illustrate articles about Prince. In *Jack Daniel's v. VIP Products*,[2] the Court found that a parody dog toy in the general shape of a Jack Daniel's bottle, with the label "Bad Spaniels," deserved no special protection for its parody against Jack Daniel's trademark claim. The Court reached these results using ideas about the lesser status of profitable speech that it flatly rejected in other cases the same Term, and with

Mark A. Lemley is the William H. Neukom Professor of Law at Stanford Law School, and of counsel at Lex Lumina PLLC. Rebecca Tushnet is the Frank Stanton Professor at Harvard Law School.

AUTHORS' NOTE: We thank Justin Driver, Christine Haight Farley, Rose Hagan, Laura A. Heymann, Mark McKenna, Lisa Ramsey, Pam Samuelson, and Mark Tushnet for comments on a prior draft.

[1] 598 U.S. 508 (2023).

[2] 599 U.S. 140 (2023).

The Supreme Court Review, 2024.
© 2024 Mark A. Lemley & Rebecca Tushnet. All rights reserved. Published by The University of Chicago Press. https://doi.org/10.1086/729397

rationales that seem directly at odds with its First Amendment jurisprudence.

In this Article, we show that the Court's decisions cannot be reconciled with its approach to any other area of speech and that they are already having pernicious effects in the lower courts. We consider some possible explanations for the inconsistency: the possibility that the Court just doesn't see First Amendment issues in IP cases; the possibility that a political realignment has left conservative Justices less enchanted with speech in the marketplace; and the possibility that this is part of a broader trend away from holding courts to the same constitutional standard as the other branches of government, combined with statutes that leave room for substantial judicial discretion in individual cases. Whatever the explanation or explanations, the decisions in *Warhol* and *Jack Daniel's* to cut back dramatically on judicially-created, speech-protective rules may have the ironic effect of forcing the Court to confront directly the constitutional fragility of much modern IP law.

I. The Transformation of Transformative Use in Copyright

In *Andy Warhol Foundation v. Goldsmith*, the Court stomped the brakes on thirty years of jurisprudence involving copyright's fair-use doctrine, under which providing a new purpose, meaning, or message was held to favor fair use. The Court expressed skepticism that Andy Warhol's iconic portraits of celebrities were transformative contributions to the art world, while at the same time expressing great confidence in its own ability to judge the meaning of that art, redefined as its interchangeability with the photo on which it was based. The Court would make that judgment, it said, without the need for any input from the artist, the audience, or the artistic community about whether the photo and the Warhol works were interchangeable.[3] But it also concluded that how much of a contribution Warhol

---

[3] *Warhol*, 598 U.S. at 545 (agreeing with the court of appeals that it was unnecessary to consider what meaning the artist intended or critics perceived); *see also id.* at 546 (reasoning that, because images of faces could reasonably be perceived to have many meanings, a change in meaning brought out by the use of a later artist's style was "less likely" to constitute a favored transformation in purpose). The Court also stated that "the meaning of a secondary work, as reasonably can be perceived, should be considered to the extent necessary to determine whether the purpose of the use is distinct from the original, for instance, because the use comments on, criticizes, or provides otherwise unavailable information about the original," *id.* at 545, though in *Warhol* itself the Court found no difference in purpose because both works could be used on the cover of a magazine, albeit for different reasons.

made ultimately didn't matter: Even if the *creation* of Warhol's works and their display in museums might be permissible (a topic on which the Court purported not to opine), *licensing* copies of them to magazines was not. The Court reasoned that licensing the work Warhol had created was a commercial use, and commerciality weighed strongly against a finding of fair use. Further, that license might possibly compete with a license of the underlying photograph from which Warhol worked.[4]

Copyright has always been treated by the Court as special when it comes to the First Amendment. The Court has described copyright as "the engine of free expression" because copyright law as a whole has the goal of promoting new speech, and it has accordingly given deference to copyright laws because they are intended to encourage speech.[5] But that aphorism has always sat uneasily in First Amendment jurisprudence because copyright laws encourage new speech by restricting the repetition of speech by others. And the First Amendment does not protect only original messages; Cohen need not have come up with the phrase "fuck the draft" to be protected in communicating it.[6]

The Court has long recognized that its "engine of free expression" aphorism works only if copyright comes with limits designed to reduce the harm it does to the speech of others. In prior cases, the Court held that originality was a constitutional prerequisite for copyright protection[7] and that freedom to copy the works of others was the norm to which IP rights were an exception.[8] In *Eldred v. Ashcroft*, the case most directly addressing the relationship between the First Amendment and copyright, the Court emphasized two fundamental limits on copyright: the idea-expression dichotomy, which prevents

---

[4] It almost certainly would not have competed. In fact, as Justice Kagan's dissent pointed out, no reasonable editor would have considered them to send the same message about the content of the magazine, even for stories about Prince. *Id.* at 566–67 (Kagan, J., dissenting). But the Court seemed satisfied that the abstract *possibility* of competition was sufficient to doom Warhol's fair-use claim.

[5] Harper & Row, Publishers, Inc. v. Nation Enters., 471 U.S. 539, 558 (1985).

[6] Cohen v. California, 403 U.S. 15 (1971).

[7] Feist Publ'ns, Inc. v. Rural Tel. Serv. Co., 499 U.S. 340, 347 (1991).

[8] Bonito Boats, Inc. v. Thunder Craft Boats, Inc., 489 U.S. 141, 151 (1989) (referring specifically to patents, but using constitutional logic based on Art. I, § 8, cl. 8, which covers both patent and copyright); Sears Roebuck & Co. v. Stiffel Co., 376 U.S. 225, 232 (1964); Compco Corp. v. Day-Brite Lighting, Inc., 376 U.S. 234 (1964).

copyright owners from controlling another's expression of the same idea, and the fair-use doctrine, which (among other things) affirmatively protects uses of a copyrighted work that transform that work by adding new expression or meaning.[9]

But if fair use is a key part of what reconciles copyright and the First Amendment, substantial cutbacks in fair-use doctrine reraise First Amendment issues that fair use supposedly resolved.

Warhol cut back on the protection that fair use gave to transformative works in at least three ways. First, and most significantly, it held that fair use must be evaluated based on the particular use of speech, not based on the content of the speech itself. According to the Court, even if Warhol had created an original, transformative work that was entitled to the protection of the fair-use doctrine and the First Amendment, *creating* that work didn't necessarily give Warhol protection for other *uses* that might be made of that work. Creators relying on fair use therefore have second-class status in practice if they hope to sell their works (as nearly all do). This is new doctrine; courts had never before held that a transformative *work* somehow became non-transformative if it was used in a different way, or that a work that was lawful when created nonetheless had to be justified anew with each use.

Some kinds of fair uses—those involving pure copying—are certainly context-dependent. Private home taping was fair use, while taping in order to sell videotapes to others would not have been.[10] "Intermediate" copying of a work in order to create a new, noninfringing work such as a search engine[11] or a product that works with the copyright owner's software[12] is fair use, but selling the full copy wouldn't be. But these cases don't involve transformation of the copyrighted *work* itself. The copying is permissible because it serves a transformative *purpose*, opening up a new market or making it possible to create a new, noninfringing work.

Transformative works have not been subject to the same limit, because by creating a new thing, the defendant is the one operating the "engine of free expression." True, even transformation that

---

[9] 537 U.S. 186, 219–20 (2003).

[10] Sony Corp. of Am. v. Universal City Studios, Inc., 464 U.S. 417 (1984).

[11] Kelly v. Arriba Soft Corp., 336 F.3d 811 (9th Cir. 2003).

[12] Google LLC v. Oracle Am., Inc., 141 S. Ct. 1183, 1203 (2021); Sega of Am. v. Accolade Inc., 977 F.2d 1510 (9th Cir. 1992); Sony Comp. Ent., Inc. v. Connectix Corp., 206 F.3d 596 (9th Cir. 2000).

involved changing the content of a work, such as the use of Roy Orbison's well-known "Pretty Woman" riff as part of a parody of that song,[13] might not give the parodist unrestricted rights to create additional works that were not parodies. For example, if the parodist attempted to license a ten-second excerpt of the song containing only the riff, say, for a ringtone, we would do a new analysis, but that is because the transformative elements would have been stripped out of the riff-only recording.[14] The ringtone might fail the fair-use analysis, but that's because it wasn't a sufficient transformation of the work itself.

But the Court's new tack suggests that each new use of a fully content-transformative work requires new analysis. It was legal for 2 Live Crew to make their parodic use of Roy Orbison's song; but under *Warhol*, use of the "Pretty Woman" parody in full in a movie instead of just on the radio or licensing that song to a greatest-hits compilation cannot benefit from that holding. So, too, with a movie version of Alice Randall's novel *The Wind Done Gone*, a highly transformative critique of Margaret Mitchell's *Gone with the Wind*.[15] Quotes that were fine in a historian's book for a university press may have to be reanalyzed for adaptation into a history podcast. Perhaps the new rule also requires a new analysis when 2 Live Crew licenses its parody for streaming, not just radio, or when Alice Randall releases her novel as an e-book. A cease-and-desist letter can threaten to sue anew each time a work appears—if an artist moves from displaying her work in a local coffee shop to a New York gallery, for example. While something that starts life as a commercial fair use—a favored "parody" or commentary, for example—is probably safe, even if used in a new commercial context, the uncertainty is part of the point: The Court's new treatment, by asking whether both the original and the accused work could have appeared in a particular commercial medium and thus served the same "purpose," equates commerciality with non-transformativeness by *ipse dixit*.

That change was compounded by the second significant shift in copyright doctrine in *Warhol*—a retrenchment of thirty years of recognition in copyright cases that speech can be valuable and worth

---

[13] *See* Campbell v. Acuff-Rose Music, Inc., 510 U.S. 569 (1994).

[14] Jim Gibson offered this example in discussions; it is perhaps notable that no actual case itself has suggested this.

[15] *See* Suntrust Bank v. Houghton Mifflin Co., 268 F.3d 1257 (11th Cir. 2001).

protecting even if it is done for profit. While the Court had stated in dictum in 1984 that commercial uses were "presumptively unfair" (in the course of making the inverse point that noncommercial uses were presumptively fair),[16] it soon recognized that that presumption was unsustainable and expressly abandoned it a decade later in *Campbell v. Acuff-Rose*, which protected a commercial parody of Roy Orbison's "Oh, Pretty Woman" in the form of a mocking reconceptualization of the attractiveness of that woman.[17] And the Court had good reason to reject any presumption against profit-seeking: Much of our most valuable speech—from news media to art to literature to movies to corporate speech on matters of public concern—would be unprotected if speech done for profit didn't count.

Unfortunately, *Warhol* reversed course yet again, declaring that even if an artist like Andy Warhol is permitted to create art (and the Court was wishy-washy on that question, as we note below), licensing that work in the market for magazines, a market in which Goldsmith also participated, weighed heavily against a finding of fair use on the first factor.[18] This view not only threatens three decades of good precedent on commerciality in copyright law; it means that the fair-use doctrine goes from a strong protector of creativity to a weak and contingent one. Under *Warhol*'s new approach, many creators may be disentitled to invoke the fair-use doctrine at all, and even those who create in noncommercial settings may lose the right to those creations once they try to sell their work.

Warhol's strong thumb on the scale against profiting from creativity has already begun to have troubling effects in the lower courts. In one case about editorial speech in newspapers, a court read *Warhol* to mean that it didn't matter whether commentary was critical, as long as it was also profit-seeking. It reasoned that "[b]oth positive and negative commentary or criticism" of the plaintiff's work would "generate attention for [defendant newspapers'] webpages," and that the "ultimate goal" of such use was "to generate more revenue."[19] This holding is extreme and, we hope, unlikely to be repeated by too many courts, but the focus on "commercial" use has distracted judges

---

[16] Sony Corp. of Am. v. Universal City Studios, Inc., 464 U.S. 417, 449 (1984).

[17] 510 U.S. at 584.

[18] Andy Warhol Found. for the Visual Arts v. Goldsmith, 598 U.S. 508, 545–46 (2023).

[19] Campbell v. Gannett Co., No. 4:21-00557-CV, 2023 WL 5250959, at *5 (W.D. Mo. Aug. 15, 2023).

from the widely-accepted fact that speakers can legitimately seek to profit from their speech without sacrificing First Amendment protection.[20]

Finally, *Warhol* cast doubt on whether art like Warhol's is transformative at all—less than two years after the Court majority had cited Warhol himself as an example of transformative use entitled to protection.[21]

The transformative-use doctrine is designed to protect new creativity that, like all creativity, builds on that which came before. While parody of the sort the Court protected in *Campbell* is one way in which a work can be transformed, there are many different ways to transform a work besides making fun of it. And art is speech we protect under the First Amendment. As the Court noted in protecting the rights of parade organizers to exclude disfavored speakers, even when the parade's own "message" was rather inchoate, "a narrow, succinctly articulable message is not a condition of constitutional protection, which if confined to expressions conveying a 'particularized message' ... would never reach the unquestionably shielded painting of Jackson Pollock, music of Arnold Schoenberg, or Jabberwocky verse of Lewis Carroll."[22]

Warhol's work is well-respected in the art community precisely because it does more than just depict its subjects. Warhol used Goldsmith's photograph as a reference in creating Orange Prince, but he did not merely copy Goldsmith. Goldsmith's photo portrays Prince; Warhol's transformation *comments upon* Prince's cultural impact in the 1980s by recasting elements of the photograph in an

---

[20] Speech that is itself the expressive product being sold has routinely been held to be noncommercial, even when sold for profit. *See, e.g.*, Brown v. Ent. Merchs. Ass'n, 564 U.S. 786, 790 (2011) (analyzing video games as a form of speech); City of Lakewood v. Plain Dealer Publ'g Co., 486 U.S. 750, 756 n.5 (1988) ("Of course, the degree of First Amendment protection is not diminished merely because the newspaper or speech is sold rather than given away."); Smith v. California, 361 U.S. 147, 150 (1959) (same); Cardtoons, L.C. v. Major League Baseball Players Ass'n, 95 F.3d 959, 970 (10th Cir. 1996) ("Cardtoons' trading cards ... are not commercial speech—they do not merely advertise another unrelated product. Although the cards are sold in the marketplace, they are not transformed into commercial speech merely because they are sold for profit.").

[21] Google LLC v. Oracle Am., Inc., 141 S. Ct. 1183, 1203 (2021).

[22] Hurley v. Irish-Am. Gay, Lesbian & Bisexual Grp. of Boston, 515 U.S. 557, 569 (1995); *see also Brown*, 564 U.S. at 790 ("Like the protected books, plays, and movies that preceded them, video games communicate ideas—and even social messages—through many familiar literary devices (such as characters, dialogue, plot, and music) and through features distinctive to the medium (such as the player's interaction with the virtual world). That suffices to confer First Amendment protection.").

artistic style that conveys the subject's iconic, otherworldly status. But the *Warhol* Court was not interested in differences of meaning. If editors might, in theory, use either image on a magazine cover, they were substitutes; and if they were substitutes, the Court thought Warhol's use in that context couldn't be transformative.

There is much to criticize in this approach, starting with the fact that the Court reached the wrong outcome even according to its own cramped reading of transformativeness, as Justice Kagan's dissent pointed out.[23] Although the Court purported to allow consideration of different meaning to the extent necessary to analyze whether the two works served as substitutes for each other,[24] even that limited protection was of no avail to Warhol. The Court simply ignored differences that mattered to magazine editors, whose uncontroverted evidence was that they would not have used the two images as substitutes for one another.[25]

It is also double-counting to treat market effect—the focus of the fourth factor—as determinative of the first factor. More generally, the idea that market competition defeats a claim of transformativeness is radically overbroad. Lots of things—such as law-review articles on the same subject—compete but are not sufficiently similar even to constitute infringement; competition is a necessary but insufficient condition for copyright liability.[26] And fair use has long encouraged new expression that builds on a prior work but offers a different take on things, whether it is transformative art, satire, a critical review, or just a different spin on a rap song.[27] Those are

---

[23] *Warhol*, 598 U.S. at 567 (Kagan, J., dissenting).

[24] *Id.* at 544–45 ("[T]he meaning of a secondary work, as reasonably can be perceived, should be considered to the extent necessary to determine whether the purpose of the use is distinct from the original, for instance, because the use comments on, criticizes, or provides otherwise unavailable information about the original.").

[25] *Id.* at 567 (Kagan, J., dissenting); Andy Warhol Found. for the Visual Arts, Inc. v. Goldsmith, No. 17-cv-02532 (S.D.N.Y. Oct. 13, 2018), ECF No. 58-20, Exh. TT (showing Conde Nast emails about why the Warhol image was desirable).

[26] *See generally* Jeanne C. Fromer & Mark A. Lemley, *The Audience in IP Infringement*, 112 MICH. L. REV. 1251 (2014).

[27] *See, e.g.*, Est. of Smith v. Graham, 799 F. App'x. 36 (2d Cir. 2020) (affirming a finding of fair use where an artist changed a claim about jazz as a genre to a claim about good music in general); Blanch v. Koons, 467 F.3d 244 (2d Cir. 2006) (finding fair use of a fashion photo in artwork that was orthogonal to the purpose of the original, in the context of a critique of consumption). *But see Warhol*, 598 U.S. at 532 n.7 ("Even book reviews are not entitled to a presumption of fairness.").

things that an "engine of free expression" would want to encourage. All that is potentially in jeopardy after *Warhol*.

Contributing to the problem, *Warhol* revived the Court's previous unfortunate distinction between satire and parody; only the latter, the Court reasoned, needed special solicitude from fair use, because the former didn't need to borrow from any specific work to make its satirical point and could just be using an existing work to avoid the "drudgery" of new creation.[28] This distinction is historically ungrounded,[29] conceptually flawed,[30] and possible only by ignoring the rule the Court purported to honor: Judges shouldn't be art critics. Distinguishing between satire and parody is *definitionally* an act of literary criticism.[31] Treating the distinction as relevant to fair-use doctrine because copyright owners don't generally license parodies

---

[28] Campbell v. Acuff-Rose Music, Inc., 510 U.S. 569, 580–81 (1994) ("Parody needs to mimic an original to make its point, and so has some claim to use the creation of its victim's (or collective victims') imagination, whereas satire can stand on its own two feet and so requires justification for the very act of borrowing."); *see also Warhol*, 598 U.S. at 512 (endorsing the distinction).

[29] Bruce P. Keller & Rebecca Tushnet, *Even More Parodic Than the Real Thing: Parody Lawsuits Revisited*, 94 TRADEMARK REP. 979, 983 (2004) (explaining that, in the history of fair use, parody and satire were always treated as equally favored before *Campbell*). For example, *Berlin v. E.C. Publications, Inc.* found that Mad Magazine lyrics set to Irving Berlin's tunes were fair even though the target was not Berlin's songs, but the "idiotic world we live in today." 329 F.2d 541, 542 (2d Cir. 1964).

[30] Keller & Tushnet, *supra* note 29, at 995–98 (explaining that the market does not distinguish between parody and satire); *id.* at 998–99 (arguing that satire provides at least as much, and sometimes more, public benefit than parody of a specific work, and that First Amendment principles counsel against deciding that a speaker could have used different expression to convey her message); Alex Kozinski & Christopher M. Newman, *What's So Fair About Fair Use?*, 46 J. COPYRIGHT SOC'Y 513, 517 (1999) (noting that satire is not a particularly good way to avoid the "drudgery of working up something fresh," as the Court claimed).

[31] *See* SIMON DENTITH, PARODY 36 (2000) ("[P]arody has the paradoxical effect of preserving the very text that it seeks to destroy.... Thus the classic parody of Don Quixote ... preserves the very chivalric romances that it attacks—with the unexpected result that for much of its history the novel has been read as a celebration of misplaced idealism rather than a satire of it."); *id.* at 105–06 (discussing the persistent uncertainty over whether certain texts are parodic or respectful, including works by Alexander Pope, such as *The Rape of the Lock*); Keller & Tushnet, *supra* note 29, at 985–94 (exploring multiple litigated examples of dueling characterizations); Rebecca Tushnet, *Judges as Bad Reviewers: Fair Use and Epistemological Humility*, 25 LAW & LITERATURE 20, 26–27 (2013) (discussing cases in which copyright owners insisted that Holden Caulfield was always pathetic and thus it wasn't fair use to write a book in which he is old and pathetic, or that Humbert was always a monster and thus it wasn't fair use to write a book from "Lolita's" perspective showing his monstrousness (citing, *inter alia*, Salinger v. Colting, 641 F. Supp. 2d 250, 257–58 (S.D.N.Y. 2009), *rev'd on other grounds*, 607 F.3d 68 (2d Cir. 2010))); PIA PERA, LO'S DIARY (2001); Dmitri Nabokov, *On a Book Entitled Lo's Diary*, 103 EVERGREEN REV. (Aug. 23, 1999), https://evergreenreview.com/read/on-a-book-entitled-los-diary). The point is that to agree or disagree with those claims is to *take sides* in a dispute over meaning that is primarily literary, not legal, and thus requires artistic judgment.

also assumes—often incorrectly—that *someone* will license their work to the satirist even if the copyright owner won't. And even if they do, making an artist rewrite satire to fit a market of willing licensees involves the courts intimately in deciding what can be made fun of and how.

Justice Kagan's dissent treats this problem as a matter of statutory language: Factor one of the fair-use inquiry requires courts to consider both the "purpose" and "character" of the accused use.[32] Justice Kagan correctly points out that the majority gives short shrift to "character," though one can infer from the cases it distinguishes that parodies, at least, have a different "character" from the original, even when they appear in the same commercial medium. The difficult question avoided by the majority is, then, what other kinds of new "character" can make a work transformative for purposes of fair use, and not just an infringing derivative work? The majority simply tells us that meaning *can* influence our evaluation of whether works have the same purpose, but how? Beyond parody, there is no way to know. And the majority refuses to consider any source of evidence on the issue (though it does not outright bar future courts from doing so in other cases). It explicitly rejected reliance on what the artist themselves intended, how the market treated the work, and expert views about the new character; all three of those things unambiguously favored Warhol. It may be that the Court has in mind significant limits on the scope of its ruling, but because its analysis of Warhol's work is entirely *ipse dixit*, there is no way to predict how it will be applied.

Because of these defects, *Warhol* is already chilling speech. Artists are worried about having gallery and museum shows canceled for fear of copyright infringement.[33] And lower courts are cutting back. For

---

[32] 17 U.S.C. § 107; *Warhol*, 598 U.S. at 567 (Kagan, J., dissenting).

[33] *See, e.g.*, Blake Gopnik, *Ruling Against Warhol Shouldn't Hurt Artists. But It Might.*, N.Y TIMES (May 19, 2023), https://www.nytimes.com/2023/05/19/arts/design/warhol-prince-supreme-court-copyright.html ([Artists] "might begin to 'slide down the fear hill' of seeking licenses for every appropriation they have in mind, and not creating anything they can't license. 'We know self-censorship is real, at individual and institutional levels.'"); Amy Adler, *The Supreme Court's Warhol Decision Just Changed the Future of Art*, ART IN AM. (May 26, 2023), https://www.artnews.com/art-in-america/columns/supreme-court-andy-warhol-decision-appropriation-artists-impact-1234669718 ("[T]he Court's *Warhol* decision will significantly limit the amount of borrowing from and building on previous works that artists can engage in.... [I]t is now far riskier for an artist to borrow from previous work.").

We have spoken to industry insiders who say that appropriation artists are having shows canceled or having to rework material. Adler warns: "Any artist who works with existing

example, after *Warhol*, a court hearing a dispute about whether a tattoo infringed the photo reference on which it was based reversed its previous holding on transformativeness. Previously, it had found the tattoo transformative because the tattoo artist added "movement" and a "melancholy aesthetic," but it determined that this rationale "relies on a formal analysis of the Tattoo's aesthetic character," which was "foreclosed" by *Warhol*.[34] This conclusion, while understandable given the tone of the majority in *Warhol*, unfortunately ignores the majority's statement that meaning can at least be considered in evaluating whether a work has a different purpose from the original,[35] as a tattoo that someone chose to mark her body permanently with might well have.[36]

We acknowledge the views of Pamela Samuelson and others that the weird posture of *Warhol*—a lawsuit by a party (the Warhol Foundation) who merely licensed the alleged infringement and was therefore not properly a copyright defendant at all, hijacked by the Solicitor General to try to change the law[37]—means that it should not be applied broadly. Even after *Warhol*, cases involving putting a copyright owner's work to a transformative *purpose* in a different market, such as those engaged in what Matt Sag calls a "creativity shift" from fiction to nonfiction or the reverse,[38] or from output to

---

imagery should now reconsider her practice. Hire a lawyer, maybe try to negotiate a license and be ready to move on if you get turned away or can't afford the fee. The safest and cheapest route—a consideration particularly relevant to younger artists and those who are not rich and famous—is to just steer clear of referencing existing work." *Id.*

Xiyin Tang suggests that many "art world" artists aren't upset about the decision because they see Warhol-style appropriation art as played out and thus artistically uninteresting. Xiyin Tang, *Art After Warhol*, 71 UCLA L. REV. (forthcoming 2024), https://papers.ssrn.com/sol3/papers.cfm?abstract_id=4542784. Respectfully, we disagree that this group is representative of artists in general or of potential targets of threats from copyright owners. *See, e.g.*, Mattel Inc. v. Walking Mountain Prods., 353 F.3d 792 (9th Cir. 2003) (concerning a lawsuit against a photographer who took pictures of Barbies with various food and kitchen items). But even if it were, the fact that the decision won't bar all types of art, but instead only disfavored genres, hardly recommends it.

[34] Sedlik v. Drachenberg, No. 21-cv-01102, 2023 WL 6787447, at *4 (C.D. Cal. Oct. 10, 2023) (citing *Warhol*, 598 U.S. at 541).

[35] *Warhol*, 598 U.S. 544–45.

[36] *See* Aaron Perzanowski, *Tattoos & IP Norms*, 98 MINN. L. REV. 511, 560–64 (2013) (discussing tattoo artists' justifications for copying non-tattoo art, grounded in the special role of tattoos as individualized body modifications).

[37] *See* Pamela Samuelson, *Why Did the Solicitor General Hijack the* Warhol v. Goldsmith *Case?* (unpublished manuscript) (on file with authors).

[38] Matthew Sag, *Predicting Fair Use*, 73 OHIO ST. L.J. 47, 80 (2012) (noting that the predictive effect of such a shift is strongest when the copying is only partial).

input into a new, noninfringing work, should be secure.[39] Indeed, the Court's explicit statement that its own reproductions of images in the opinion—both the parties' and others used for comparison—were fair uses reinforces that conclusion.[40] Noncommercial uses such as fan fiction remain unshaken precisely because of their noncommerciality. And even a commercial creator should be able to explain their reasons for targeting an original in many cases.[41]

We would be delighted to look back with hindsight and see *Warhol* as a "derelict on the waters of the law."[42] But the Court's opinion, while clearly confused about what it itself was holding and not holding, contains enough broad language that we fear it will be hard to cabin. And the early interpretations in the lower courts have not been encouraging.

II. JOKING HAZARD—SPEECH IN TRADEMARKS

The federal trademark statute lacks a general, copyright-like "fair use" provision.[43] Courts have instead created special tests for situations where greater scope for unauthorized use of a trademark seems justified—such as comparative advertising, resale of used goods, and artistic references. The "*Rogers* test"—named for the case in which the Second Circuit held that claims against titles of "expressive" works had to meet a very high standard before a court could find actionable confusion[44]—generally refuses trademark liability for an expressive work, regardless of evidence of confusion, unless the

---

[39] *See, e.g., Warhol*, 598 U.S. at 529 n.5 (endorsing both Núñez v. Caribbean Int'l News Corp., 235 F.3d 18, 21–23 (1st Cir. 2000) (holding that a newspaper's reproduction, without alteration, of a photograph of a beauty pageant winner to explain a controversy over whether her title should be withdrawn had transformative purpose because "'the pictures were the story'") and Leibovitz v. Paramount Pictures Corp., 137 F.3d 109, 114–15 (2d Cir. 1998) (holding that a film advertisement's alteration of a well-known photograph by superimposing an actor's face on an actress's body had the transformative purpose of parody)); *id.* at 530 (citing with approval Authors Guild v. Google, Inc., 804 F.3d 202, 214 (2d Cir. 2015) (op. of Leval, J.), which found that the Google Books project that involved scanning entire books, but only making "snippets" available for searches, had a favored transformative purpose).

[40] *Warhol*, 598 U.S. at 550 (stating that the idea-expression distinction and fair use protect "the dissent's own copying (and the Court's, too)").

[41] *Id.* at 528 (highlighting special consideration for criticism).

[42] Ala. Pub. Serv. Comm'n v. S. Ry. Co., 341 U.S. 341, 357 (1951) (Frankfurter, J., concurring).

[43] "Descriptive fair use," such as using "apple" to describe a candy flavor, is the subject of a separate statutory provision. 15 U.S.C. § 1115(b)(4).

[44] Rogers v. Grimaldi, 875 F.2d 994, 999 (2d Cir. 1989).

defendant's reference to a trademark lacks any relevance to the underlying work or is explicitly misleading. Some version of *Rogers* has been adopted by every circuit to decide the issue, and the test has often been used in cases involving for-profit, nonadvertising speech.

In *Jack Daniel's v. VIP Products*, the Court held that it did not need to apply, or even decide the validity of, the *Rogers* test to a parodic product.[45] So long as the defendant was using a similar term as a trademark to brand its own goods (here, "Bad Spaniels" dog toys that parodied Jack Daniel's well-known whisky bottle), trademark law's ordinary multifactor test for consumer confusion was all that was required to accommodate the First Amendment. The Court did not decide whether the First Amendment ever offered any protection against trademark-infringement claims even for purely expressive, noncommercial speech, as every circuit to have considered the issue had held.[46] Instead, it said the First Amendment offered no further protection for this speech than it would give to the label on a can of peaches, because JDI's speech was in part serving as a trademark. (At oral argument, several Justices expressed skepticism that confusion was likely here, and the opinion cited with approval the claim that parodies, because they make fun of a trademark owner, are unlikely to cause confusion.[47] But it didn't engage with the question of whether noncommercial parody could be regulated merely for confusing people about whether a trademark owner is somehow involved with it—or with the fact that the district court had found confusion in this very case.)

---

[45] 599 U.S. 140 (2023).

[46] The cases are not necessarily consistent, but there has generally been some recognition of the special status of noncommercial speech. *See, e.g.*, Twentieth Century Fox T.V. v. Empire Distrib., Inc., 875 F.3d 1192, 1196 (9th Cir. 2017) (using *Rogers*, except for *Rogers*'s own exclusion of title-versus-title conflicts from its scope); Univ. of Ala. Bd. of Trustees v. New Life Art, Inc., 683 F.3d 1266, 1279 (11th Cir. 2012); Utah Lighthouse Ministry v. Found. for Apologetic Info. & Rsch., 527 F.3d 1045, 1052–53 (10th Cir. 2008); Parks v. LaFace Records, 329 F.3d 437, 449 (6th Cir. 2003) (purporting to adopt *Rogers*); Taubman Co. v. Webfeats, 319 F.3d 770, 774 (6th Cir. 2003) ("The Lanham Act is constitutional because it only regulates commercial speech, which is entitled to reduced protections under the First Amendment."); Westchester Media v. PRL USA Holdings, Inc., 214 F.3d 658, 664–65 (5th Cir. 2000) (endorsing *Rogers*).

[47] *Jack Daniel's*, 599 U.S. at 161 (stating that a "trademark's expressive message—particularly a parodic one, as VIP asserts—may properly figure in assessing the likelihood of confusion" (citing Louis Vuitton Malletier S.A. v. Haute Diggity Dog, LLC, 507 F.3d 252, 265 (4th Cir. 2007), for the proposition that parody "influences the way in which the [likelihood-of-confusion] factors are applied")).

Trademark law has long been treated under the less strict First Amendment rules governing commercial speech. But in *Jack Daniel's*, the Court bypassed the First Amendment inquiry even though the Court did not categorize the dog toy as commercial speech, and even though it would not have qualified as commercial speech under ordinary standards.[48] Three Justices (among them Justices who have been among the strongest advocates of First Amendment expansion in other circumstances) went further. They wrote separately to express their skepticism that even purely expressive noncommercial speech involving trademarks merited treatment under *Rogers*, apparently concerned that the *statute* did not specifically outline such a test.[49] Possibly they were signaling only that *Rogers*—which is not without its problems—was an imperfect version of a speech-protective test. But it is striking that they expressed no explicit concerns about trademark lawsuits' demonstrated ability to chill speech.

In *Jack Daniel's*, the Court claimed that the multifactor likelihood-of-consumer-confusion test applied in ordinary trademark cases "does enough work to account for the interest in free expression" in the context of trademark uses.[50] This language, as others have noted,[51] is very similar to its previous statement in *Eldred* that "copyright law

---

[48] The Court's only discussion of "commercial" versus "noncommercial" comes in its treatment of the dilution claim. *Id.* at 145. The analysis of trademark infringement does not even mention the question of whether VIP's use of "Bad Spaniels" constituted noncommercial or commercial speech.

[49] *Id.* at 165 (Gorsuch, J., concurring, joined by Thomas & Barrett, JJ.) ("[I]t is not entirely clear where the *Rogers* test comes from—is it commanded by the First Amendment, or is it merely gloss on the Lanham Act, perhaps inspired by constitutional-avoidance doctrine?"). Never mind the facts that the statute also doesn't compel the multifactor likelihood-of-confusion test the Court applied either, and that the First Amendment often imposes limitations on torts, whether common-law or statutory. *E.g.*, N.Y. Times Co. v. Sullivan, 376 U.S. 254 (1964); People for the Ethical Treatment of Animals, Inc. v. N.C. Farm Bureau Fed'n, Inc., 60 F.4th 815 (4th Cir. 2023) (finding that North Carolina's "ag-gag" law barring unauthorized recordings of "images or sound occurring within an employer's premises" violated the First Amendment rights of animal-rights groups to expose animal mistreatment); ERIN K. COYLE, THE PRESS & RIGHTS TO PRIVACY: FIRST AMENDMENT FREEDOMS VS. INVASION OF PRIVACY CLAIMS 23 (2012) ("[T]he press's First Amendment rights occasionally conflict with privacy rights recognized by state common law and statutory torts that protect individuals' privacy interests against invasions by individuals or private entities.").

[50] *Jack Daniel's*, 599 U.S. at 159.

[51] Graeme B. Dinwoodie, *Trademark Law as a Normative Project*, SING. J. LEGAL STUD. (forthcoming) (unpublished manuscript at 32), https://papers.ssrn.com/sol3/papers.cfm?abstract_id=4344834#:~:text=Professor%20Dinwoodie%20argues%20that%20trademark,trademark%20as%20a%20normative%20project.

contains built-in First Amendment accommodations."[52] But in *Eldred*, the Court coupled its statement with the explanation that the Copyright Clause provided a robust foundation for federal copyright, and that the contemporaneous adoption of the Bill of Rights and the first federal copyright act showed their compatibility.[53] Further, it pointed to fair use and the idea-expression distinction that disallows any copyright in facts or ideas. There, the Court identified specific limits and defenses that (at least when *Eldred* was decided)[54] imposed real limits on the scope of what could otherwise be found to be copyright infringement.[55]

There is no Trademark Clause and no Founding Era federal trademark statute; indeed, the Court invalidated Congress's first attempt to pass a trademark statute, nearly a century later, because it could not be justified under the IP clause.[56] Nor would what current courts call "likelihood of confusion" be recognizable to post-Reconstruction courts or even mid-twentieth century courts, both of which protected trademark owners in far more limited circumstances. Until recently, trademark law applied only in cases of "passing off," where the defendant's goods would substitute for purchases of the plaintiff's goods.[57] The Court's statement that the multifactor likelihood-of-confusion test provides the only necessary protection for the First Amendment thus lacks the explanatory apparatus it offered in *Eldred*: a basis in text, history, or structure, including the substantive protections of fair use.

Where, then, does the idea that likelihood of confusion is sufficient to accommodate the First Amendment come from? It has long been true that the First Amendment assigned no value to false statements of fact, justifying restrictions on deceptive commercial speech.[58]

---

[52] Eldred v. Ashcroft, 537 U.S. 186, 219 (2003).

[53] *Id.*

[54] *See supra* Part I.

[55] *Id.* at 219–20.

[56] Trade-Mark Cases, 100 U.S. 82 (1879).

[57] Mark P. McKenna, *The Normative Foundations of Trademark Law*, 82 NOTRE DAME L. REV. 1839, 1858–96 (2007) (reviewing pre-twentieth century American law); *see, e.g.*, Borden Ice Cream Co. v. Borden's Condensed Milk Co., 201 F. 510 (2d Cir. 1912) (finding no infringement between the Borden mark for ice cream and the Borden mark for sweetened condensed milk because the products were not the same, so no consumer would buy one thinking it was the other).

[58] Cent. Hudson Gas & Elec. Corp. v. Pub. Serv. Comm'n, 447 U.S. 557, 563 (1980).

But commercial speech has long been narrowly defined, roughly speaking, as speech that "does no more than propose a commercial transaction."[59] Courts had also been careful to limit who gets to declare what's false or misleading since it is possible to turn almost any objection to speech into the claim that the speech is misleading.[60] And if anything, recent trends had suggested that the Court was edging towards giving more, not less, protection to commercial speech.[61]

Jack Daniel's, by contrast, doubled down on *Warhol*'s idea that speech sold for profit gets less protection. Indeed, the Court suggested that such speech might get *no* First Amendment protection against claims labeled "trademark" beyond whatever dubious safety a multifactor likelihood-of-consumer-confusion test may provide, any time a court is willing to find a "use as a mark."[62]

The Court also revived Jack Daniel's dilution claim. The dilution cause of action was not even arguably based on any falsity or risk of confusion, but instead on the theory that being associated with dog poop would "tarnish" the consumer image of Jack Daniel's, even though consumers understood that there was no relation between the companies.[63] One of the statutory exceptions to dilution—the exception for parody and other forms of commentary—applies only to commentaries that were not also used as marks for the defendant's own goods or services.[64] Because the parody exception does not

---

[59] Va. State Bd. of Pharmacy v. Va. Citizens Consumer Council, 425 U.S. 748, 762 (1976) (Stewart, J., concurring).

[60] The most prominent recent examples involve attempts by states, encouraged by the meat and dairy industries, to suppress the use of meat/dairy-associated words for vegan alternatives on the ground that terms like "vegan sausages" or "vegan butter" are misleading because sausage and butter can't be vegan. *See, e.g.*, Miyoko's Kitchen v. Ross, No. 3:20-cv-00893, 2021 WL 4497867 (N.D. Cal. Aug. 10, 2021) (concerning "vegan butter"); *cf.* Ocheesee Creamery LLC v. Putnam, 851 F.3d 1228 (11th Cir. 2017) (rejecting the state's argument that it was misleading to use "skim milk" to describe milk from which fat had been skimmed, but which was not supplemented with Vitamin A, as required by statute).

[61] *See, e.g.*, Matal v. Tam, 582 U.S. 218, 251–52 (2017) (op. of Kennedy, J., joined by three Justices); Sorrell v. IMS Health Inc., 564 U.S. 552 (2011).

[62] On the challenges of evaluating signifiers that are both expressive and serve as trademarks, see Stacey L. Dogan & Mark A. Lemley, *Parody as Brand*, 47 U.C. Davis L. Rev. 473 (2013).

[63] 15 U.S.C. § 1125(c) (protecting famous marks against dilution by "tarnishment" or "blurring").

[64] *Id.* § 1125(c)(3)(A) (excepting "[a]ny fair use, including a nominative or descriptive fair use, or facilitation of such fair use, of a famous mark by another person other than as a designation of source for the person's own goods or services," including "identifying and

cover use as a trademark, the Court reasoned, it must also be the case that the *separate* exception for all "noncommercial" uses[65] also excluded any uses as marks, thus overturning the Ninth Circuit's reliance on the latter exception.[66]

This is nonsense as a matter of statutory interpretation. Usually, the presence of a limitation in one statutory provision and its absence in a neighboring statutory provision is taken to mean precisely the opposite: that Congress meant to limit one provision and not the other.[67] Worse, the Court's interpretation ignores the reason for the exceptions: to ensure that dilution—which, again, does not require any confusion and therefore cannot be justified as an application of commercial-speech doctrine to false statements of fact—would not interfere with even arguably protected speech.[68] Nor did the Ninth Circuit's approach render either provision redundant. Parodying a mark in a commercial for a different product, as some advertisers do,[69] would be covered by the parody exception but not the noncommercial speech exception, while a product like "Bad Spaniels"— even accepting the Court's analysis of trademark use—would have been covered by the noncommercial speech exception, even if the

---

parodying, criticizing, or commenting upon the famous mark owner or the goods or services of the famous mark owner").

[65] *Id.* § 1125(c)(3)(C) (excepting "[a]ny noncommercial use of a mark").

[66] Jack Daniel's v. VIP Prods., 599 U.S. 140, 162 (2023).

[67] The maxim is *"expressio unius est exclusio alterius." See, e.g.,* Polselli v. IRS, 598 U.S. 432, 439 (2023) ("We assume that Congress 'acts intentionally and purposely' when it 'includes particular language in one section of a statute but omits it in another section of the same Act.'" (quoting Sebelius v. Cloer, 569 U.S. 369, 378 (2013))). *Polselli* was decided one month before *Jack Daniel's. See also* Giulio Ernesto Yaquinto, *The Social Significance of Modern Trademarks: Authorizing the Appropriation of Marks as Source Identifiers for Expressive Works*, 95 Tex. L. Rev. 739, 755 (2017) ("[T]he noncommercial use exclusion's language differs from the language of the fair use provision. Whereas the exclusion for fair use does not apply to marks used 'as a designation of source,' the noncommercial use exclusion does not have the same limiting language. The absence of such language suggests that Congress did not intend for the noncommercial use exclusion to be read as narrowly as the exclusion for fair use." (internal citations omitted)).

[68] H.R. Rep. No. 104-374, at 4 (1995), *reprinted in* 1995 U.S.C.C.A.N. 1029, 1031 ("The bill will not prohibit or threaten 'noncommercial' expression, as that term has been defined by the courts. Nothing in this bill is intended to alter existing case law on the subject of what constitutes 'commercial' speech."); Yaquinto, *supra* note 67, at 755–76 (noting that the noncommercial exclusion was added back in, in addition to the parody exclusion, for "added protection" when Congress revised dilution law in 2005).

[69] *See, e.g.,* Conopco, Inc. v. 3DO Co., 53 U.S.P.Q. 3d 1146 (S.D.N.Y. 1999) (concerning a video-game ad parodying the "Snuggle" fabric softener spokesbear).

"other than a designation of source" limitation meant that it could not be covered by the parody exception.[70]

The Court's statutory misinterpretation allowed it to cover up its worse incoherence on whether the "Bad Spaniels" dog toy was itself somehow noncommercial speech, or whether regulating the non-source-indicating aspects of trademarks constitutes an acceptable regulation of commercial speech. The Court waved its hands a bit at this point, concluding that the *name* "Bad Spaniels" was used as a brand for the parody dog toy (as VIP had conceded), but not discussing whether *the toy itself* was used as a mark—that is, as a source identifier—for itself.[71] But the district court's finding of confusion was premised on the shape and design of the toy itself (trade dress), not merely on the name "Bad Spaniels," which in isolation isn't confusingly similar to "Jack Daniel's," especially when coupled with its canine logo. We think there is something to the Court's distinction between trademark uses and other uses.[72] But its failure to clarify the limited nature of trademark use as a form of commercial speech opened the door to a lot of potential mischief.

Early indications of judicial reaction to *Jack Daniel's* are discouraging. In *Vans, Inc. v. MSCHF Product Studio, Inc.*,[73] the Second Circuit crudely applied *Jack Daniel's*, ruling that art collective MSCHF's Wavy Baby shoes used Vans's trademarks as marks, particularly what the court of appeals characterized as a distorted version of Vans's red and white logo used on the shoe boxes (Fig. 1):

---

[70] Indeed, the Court implicitly concedes as much by reading a "use as a mark" limit on the noncommercial exclusion: It cannot identify any other reason the "Bad Spaniels" toy would be commercial speech.

[71] *Jack Daniel's*, 599 U.S. at 156 (discussing Tommy Hilfiger Licensing, Inc. v. Nature Labs, LLC, 221 F. Supp. 2d 410, 412 (S.D.N.Y. 2002) (holding that *Rogers* did not apply to pet perfume, though finding confusion unlikely)). The Court's handwaving was likely aided by VIP's decision, earlier in the litigation, to claim "trade dress" in its toy. Even though VIP didn't identify the relevant elements of the putative trade dress—the spaniel logo, the bottle shape, the black and white label, or the combination—this unfortunate-in-retrospect assertion allowed the Court to lump everything together.

[72] Indeed, it cited one of us for the proposition. *Id.* (citing Stacey L. Dogan & Mark A. Lemley, *Grounding Trademark Law Through Trademark Use*, 92 Iowa L. Rev. 1669 (2007)).

[73] 88 F.4th 125 (2d Cir. 2023).

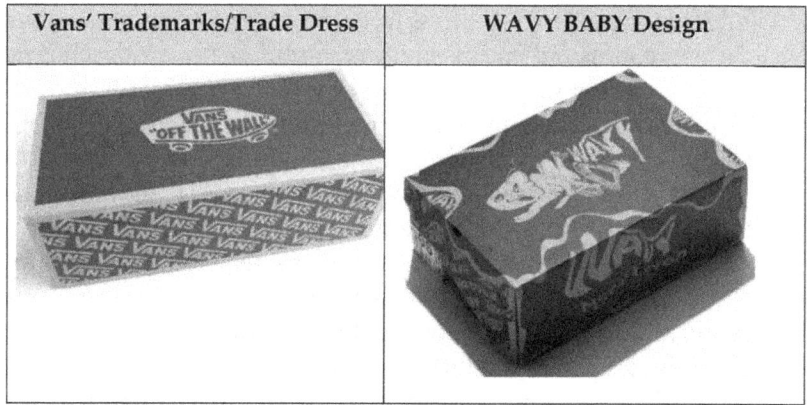

Fig. 1. Comparison of Vans and Wavy Baby packaging

The Second Circuit read *Jack Daniel's* as having held that if something was serving as a mark *even in part*, it was not entitled to the application of the *Rogers* test or any First Amendment protection.[74] Moreover, it did not limit its analysis to the logo; having found that to be use as a mark, it considered the entire shoe itself exempt from *Rogers* analysis. The Second Circuit then applied the likely-confusion factors without any consideration for the value of expression or of parody, contrary to what other courts have done, to what the *Jack Daniel's* Court encouraged lower courts to do, and to its own past practices.[75] It ruled that "if a parodic use of protected marks and trade dress leaves confusion as to the source of a product, the parody has not 'succeeded' for purposes of the Lanham Act."[76]

---

[74] *Id.* at 138 (quoting, not the Court's own language, but language from a district court case the Court cited to).

[75] The Second Circuit weighed the strength of Vans's trademarks against MSCHF, *id.* at 139–40, but prior cases recognized that parodies of strong marks are more likely to be recognized as parodies, and that parody always requires some imitation. *See, e.g.*, Louis Vuitton Malletier S.A. v. Haute Diggity Dog, LLC, 507 F.3d 252, 265 (4th Cir. 2007) (reasoning that strength of trademark weighs against likely confusion in parody cases because consumers will more easily understand the parody); *see also* Cliffs Notes, Inc. v. Bantam Doubleday Dell Publ'g. Grp., Inc., 886 F.2d 490, 494 (2d Cir. 1989) (expressive interests in parody justify construing the Lanham Act "'narrowly' ... [and] weigh[ing] the public interest in free expression against the public interest in avoiding consumer confusion").

[76] *Vans*, 88 F.4th at 142.; *cf.* Christine Haight Farley, *Hot Take on the Wavy Baby Decision*, TECH. & MKTG. L. BLOG (Dec. 11, 2023), https://blog.ericgoldman.org/archives/2023/12/hot-take-on-the-wavy-baby-decision-guest-blog-post.htm (suggesting that, under *Vans*, "within the structure of the multifactor likelihood of confusion test, it will be the burden of the parodist to prove that their joke clearly landed").

While this sounds logical on its face, it is important to understand what "leaves confusion" means in modern trademark law. Even if no purchaser is ever confused, if a nonpurchaser sees the MSCHF shoes on the street and mistakenly thinks they're authorized by Vans, that's actionable confusion ("post-sale confusion") under current law. Similarly, if a potential purchaser considers the MSCHF shoes, briefly thinks they might be a collaboration with Vans, and then learns otherwise before making any decision, that's also actionable confusion ("initial-interest confusion"). Nor does it matter whether any consumers *care* about a link between the plaintiff and the defendant; confusion on its own is actionable, even if it never changed a single purchasing decision. And that lack of a materiality requirement has feedback effects on confusion analysis: Courts consider confusion more likely when consumers aren't paying much attention, but consumers aren't careful when they don't care.[77] *Rogers* served to protect noncommercial speech from the cumulative effects of these expansive rules; it is less capable of doing so now because the Second Circuit has held that any branding taints the underlying expressive work.

This all might be manageable if courts required trademark owners to show some kind of harm from these types of "confusion,"[78] but they no longer are—indeed, as of 2020, they're entitled to a statutory presumption that the harm they suffer is *irreparable*.[79] As a result, the *Vans* court granted a preliminary injunction banning a work of art without even a final determination that it was likely to confuse anyone—a prior restraint of speech that would almost certainly be illegal in any other area of the First Amendment.[80]

---

[77] *See* Rebecca Tushnet, *Running the Gamut from A to B: Federal Trademark and False Advertising Law*, 159 U. Pa. L. Rev. 1305, 1354 (2011).

[78] *See* Mark A. Lemley & Mark P. McKenna, *Irrelevant Confusion*, 62 Stan. L. Rev. 413, 445–46 (2010) (arguing that plaintiffs in these nonstandard theories of confusion should have to show that the confusion was material to customers' purchasing decisions); Mark P. McKenna, *Testing Modern Trademark Law's Theory of Harm*, 95 Iowa L. Rev. 63 (2009) (arguing that many of trademark law's expansive concepts of confusion do not address real risks of harm to trademark owners).

[79] Trademark Modernization Act of 2020, 15 U.S.C. § 1116(a) (providing for a presumption of irreparable harm upon a showing of likely confusion, including for temporary restraining orders and preliminary injunctive relief).

[80] *See, e.g.*, Alexander v. United States, 509 U.S. 544, 550 (1993) (noting that a temporary restraining order or preliminary injunction that restricts speech before a final determination on the merits is a "classic example" of a prior restraint); Mark A. Lemley & Eugene Volokh, *Freedom of Speech and Injunctions in IP Cases*, 48 Duke L.J. 147 (1998). *See generally* Owen M. Fiss, The Civil Rights Injunction 69–74 (1978) (discussing rationales for treating injunctions as prior restraints); Vincent Blasi, *Toward a Theory of Prior Restraint: The Central*

The problem of expansive definitions of confusion is compounded by the fact that the *threshold* for what counts as likely confusion is quite low.[81] Anecdotes about people online expressing confusion or worrying that other people might be confused suffices as evidence of likely confusion to many courts, especially for purposes of granting a preliminary injunction.[82] So do consumer surveys finding that 15–20% of consumers are confused while 80–85% are not.[83] And courts do not consider whether the benefit to the nonconfused consumers of a new option outweighs those risks.[84] Again, a key function of *Rogers* has been to protect noncommercial speech from these other doctrines, mainly by insisting that actionable confusion over artworks has to come from some *explicit* falsehood about source or sponsorship by the artist.[85]

Linkage, 66 MINN. L. REV. 11, 89–92 (1981) (injunctions should be deemed prior restraints because, like licensing regimes, they are easily overused and overstate the threat of speech).

[81] Glynn S. Lunney, Jr., *Trademark's Judicial De-Evolution: Why Courts Get Trademark Cases Wrong Repeatedly*, 106 CALIF. L. REV. 1195, 1208–13 (2018); Lemley & McKenna, *supra* note 78, at 422–26.

[82] *See, e.g.*, Sara Lee Corp. v. Kayser-Roth Corp., 81 F.3d 455, 466 (4th Cir. 1996) (finding anecdotal evidence "overwhelming" based on testimony of six women who purchased wrong product and "service merchandisers" who testified about confusion of store personnel); Choice Hotels Int'l, Inc. v. Zeal, LLC, 135 F. Supp. 3d 451, 469 (D.S.C. 2015) (finding that two instances of anecdotal evidence of confusion supported a finding of actual confusion). Indeed, even anecdotes are unnecessary. Savin Corp. v. Savin Grp., 391 F.3d 439, 459 (2d Cir. 2004) ("[I]t is black letter law that actual confusion need not be shown to prevail under the Lanham Act, since actual confusion is very difficult to prove and the Act requires only a likelihood of confusion as to source." (cleaned up)).

[83] *See, e.g.*, Humble Oil & Refining Co. v. Am. Oil Co., 405 F.2d 803 (8th Cir. 1969) (ruling that 11% confusion justified injunctive relief); James Burrough, Ltd. v. Sign of Beefeater, Inc., 540 F.2d 266, 279 (7th Cir. 1976) ("We cannot agree that 15% is 'small.' Though the percentage of likely confusion required may vary from case to case, we cannot consider 15 percent, in the context of this case, involving the entire restaurant-going community, to be de minimis."); Novartis Consumer Health, Inc. v. Johnson & Johnson-Merck Consumer Pharm., Co., 290 F.3d 578, 594 (3d Cir. 2002); Eli Lilly Co. v. Arla Foods, Inc., No. 1:17-CV-00703, 2017 WL 4570547, at *9 (E.D. Wis. June 15, 2017), *aff'd*, 893 F.3d 375 (7th Cir. 2018). *See generally* MCCARTHY ON TRADEMARKS AND UNFAIR COMPETITION § 32:188 (5th ed. 2021) (discussing range of survey percentages accepted and rejected by courts as sufficient); *id.* ("Where other evidence is supportive, courts have found a likelihood of confusion when survey results are between 10% and 20%.").

[84] As Michael Grynberg has persuasively argued, the failure to consider any benefits to nonconfused consumers is a key flaw in this doctrine. Michael Grynberg, *Trademark Litigation as Consumer Conflict*, 83 N.Y.U. L. REV. 60 (2008).

[85] *Rogers* also says that uses have to be "artistically relevant" to get the benefit of this protection but instructs courts to be generous to speakers on this point. Rogers v. Grimaldi, 875 F.2d 994, 999 (2d Cir. 1989) (indicating that liability should not attach to uses of trademarks in titles "unless the title has no artistic relevance to the underlying work whatsoever, or, if it has some artistic relevance, unless the title explicitly misleads as to the source or the content of the work"). The standard is "minimal" relevance.

The general standards for actionable confusion are far, far lower than the standards for torts such as defamation. To protect free speech, courts in defamation cases carefully scrutinize accused statements to ensure that there is a clear statement of falsifiable fact;[86] courts use a normative definition of reasonability that requires some common sense and skepticism from consumers;[87] and they require at least a negligent and often a reckless state of mind.[88] As *Vans* indicates, *Jack Daniel's* may encourage lower courts to ban speech with none of those safeguards.

Even assuming the case presented only issues of commercial speech, the result in *Jack Daniel's* is questionable as a matter of First Amendment doctrine. The Court has recently struck down as unconstitutional trademark statutes that restrict speech much less directly than the injunction at issue in *Jack Daniel's*. In *Tam v. Matal*[89] and *Iancu v. Brunetti*,[90] the government's decisions not to allow a trademark registration for immoral, scandalous, or disparaging marks did not prevent the challengers from using those terms at all, or even from using them as trademarks. It merely prevented them from obtaining the additional but optional benefits of government registration.[91]

---

[86] *See, e.g.*, Levinsky's, Inc. v. Wal-Mart Stores, Inc., 127 F.3d 122, 129 (1st Cir. 1997) (requiring accused statements to have "an easily ascertainable and objectively verifiable meaning" that could render them falsifiable).

[87] Milkovich v. Lorain J. Co., 497 U.S. 1, 20 (1990); Farah v. Esquire Mag., 736 F.3d 528, 536, 537, 539 (D.C. Cir. 2013) (pointing out that the reasonable reader's perspective "is more informed by an assessment of her well-considered view than by her immediate yet transitory reaction" and that "the [defamation] test ... is not whether some actual readers were misled, but whether the hypothetical reasonable reader could be (after time for reflection)," such that even a "poorly executed" parody is ordinarily not actionable); Mink v. Knox, 613 F.3d 995, 1005 (10th Cir. 2010); Moldea v. N.Y. Times Co., 22 F.3d 310, 314 (D.C. Cir. 1994); *see also* Golb v. Att'y Gen. of N.Y., 870 F.3d 89, 102 (2d Cir. 2017) ("[A] parody enjoys First Amendment protection notwithstanding that not everybody will get the joke."). A "reasonable reader" is "'no dullard. He or she does not represent the lowest common denominator, but reasonable intelligence and learning. He or she can tell the difference between satire and sincerity.'" New Times, Inc. v. Isaacks, 146 S.W.3d 144, 157 (Tex. 2004) (quoting Patrick v. Sup. Ct., 27 Cal. Rptr. 2d 883, 887 (Ct. App. 1994)). "Nor is the reasonable person some totally humorless drudge who cannot perceive the presence of subtle invective." *Patrick*, 27 Cal. Rptr. 2d at 887.

[88] Gertz v. Robert Welch, 418 U.S. 323, 347 (1974) (requiring at least fault/negligence for defamation of private figures); N.Y. Times v. Sullivan, 376 U.S. 254, 279–80 (1964) (requiring a showing of "actual malice" for public figures).

[89] 582 U.S. 218 (2017).

[90] 139 S. Ct. 2294 (2019).

[91] No one suggested that the government could have barred the *use* of such disparaging or scandalous terms. *See* Lisa P. Ramsey, *Free Speech Challenges to Trademark Law After* Matal v. Tam, 56 Hous. L. Rev. 401 (2018). There is some doubt about whether an unregistrable

Nonetheless, the Court invalidated the bars on registration as impermissible viewpoint-based interference with speech rights. By contrast, the injunction the Ninth Circuit overturned prevented VIP Products from selling the "Bad Spaniels" dog toy at all.[92] Trademark registrations, it seems, are intangible property rights that must regularly be granted by the government *because* trademarks can express important messages, but that expression then provides rights to suppress others' speech with no First Amendment worries.[93]

Ignoring the First Amendment might have seemed harmless because *Jack Daniel's* repeatedly took pains to emphasize the narrow nature of its holding.[94] The majority cited, with approval, *Rogers* cases involving creative works that used trademarks in their titles or content—Aqua's earworm song "Barbie Girl,"[95] sports paintings that depicted recognizable university uniforms,[96] and a movie in which a character's mispronunciation of "Louis Vuitton" and use of a Vuitton-esque suitcase was a plot point.[97] Despite the Court's claim that these cases involved "solely" expressive uses and not source-indication, both *Rogers* itself and the "Barbie Girl" cases included

---

trademark is nonetheless protectable against competitors under state or federal common law, but that is a matter of exclusivity, not of freedom of *use*. See Rebecca Tushnet, *Registering Disagreement: Registration in Modern American Trademark Law*, 130 Harv. L. Rev. 867, 883 (2017) (noting that whether an unregistrable mark is protectable under common law is "a question to which, surprisingly, there is no clear answer even after nearly seven decades under the Lanham Act").

[92] In a case pending this Term, *Vidal v. Elster*, No. 22-704, the Court faces the constitutionality of another part of the same statutory section it struck down in *Tam* and *Brunetti*: the blanket prohibition on registering a mark that includes a living person's name without that person's consent. 15 U.S.C. § 1052(c). While the unconstitutionality of that provision as applied to criticism of public figures would seem a foregone conclusion under *Tam* and *Brunetti*, as the Federal Circuit concluded in *In re Elster*, 26 F.4th 1328 (Fed. Cir. 2022), indications from the oral argument are that the Court was inclined to uphold the statute.

[93] Indeed, at oral argument in *Elster*, the Court seemed receptive to the idea that the intangible "right of publicity" justified the prohibition on registering unauthorized uses of a name that were critical and nonconfusing, even though the government conceded that the right of publicity would not allow a public figure to enjoin the uses themselves. Although an intangible right to control speech, unlike a right to control who is using a specific pencil or computer, depends entirely on the government to define its boundaries, the Court nonetheless seems to consider "intangible private property" a trump. See *generally* Transcript of Oral Argument, Vidal v. Elster (2023) (No. 22-704).

[94] 599 U.S. 140, 154 (2023).

[95] Mattel, Inc. v. MCA Records, Inc., 296 F. 3d 894, 901 (9th Cir. 2002). The Court simply asserted that these were cases in which "a trademark is used not to designate a work's source, but solely to perform some other expressive function." *Jack Daniel's*, 599 U.S. at 154.

[96] Univ. of Ala. Bd. of Trustees v. New Life Art, Inc., 683 F. 3d 1266, 1279 (11th Cir. 2012).

[97] Louis Vuitton Malletier S.A. v. Warner Bros. Ent. Inc., 868 F. Supp. 2d 172 (S.D.N.Y. 2012).

survey evidence purporting to show levels of confusion that usually justify a finding of infringement. In essence, the majority seemed to think that traditional expressive works, as opposed to tchotchkes like the "Bad Spaniels" dog toy, could benefit from the *Rogers* test. Moreover, this would be perfectly consistent with the idea that *source* indication is of particular concern to consumers and to the law.

One way to resolve the tension between the Court's assertions and the facts of the cases is to say that the evidence of confusion in *Rogers* and the "Barbie Girl" case was only about confusion over whether the defendants *needed* or *had* permission from the trademark owner. That kind of confusion is not the same as anyone being confused about the actual *source* of the movie or song, which was clearly Fellini and Aqua, respectively. And it could be workable to limit *Rogers* to situations that are best described as affiliation, sponsorship, or approval confusion, and not cases in which consumers might buy one thing thinking it to be another.[98] That could also make sense of *Rogers*'s own statement that confusion over whether Jane Fonda was responsible for an unauthorized *Jane Fonda's Workout Book* would be actionable.[99]

Unfortunately, that is not how *Jack Daniel's* has been read. Among other things, while the source/affiliation divide is an attractive one intuitively, plaintiffs routinely allege both; the difference in *Rogers* cases has generally been that courts didn't accept the plaintiffs' characterizations, even for purposes of a motion to dismiss. *Vans*'s was not the only lower court to pick up on the Court's characterization of successful *Rogers* defenses as not involving *any* source-indicating functions. In *Homevestors of America v. Warner Bros. Discovery*,[100] the court held that it need not apply *Rogers* or engage in any First Amendment scrutiny in determining that the title of a TV show ("Ugliest House in America") can infringe the plaintiff's trademarks related to the sale of "ugly houses." It determined (incorrectly) that

---

[98] *See Jack Daniel's*, 599 U.S. at 157 ("The cardinal sin under [trademark] law ... is to undermine that function. It is to confuse consumers about source—to make (some of) them think that one producer's products are another's. And that kind of confusion is most likely to arise when someone uses another's trademark as a trademark—meaning, again, as a source identifier—rather than for some other expressive function." (internal citations omitted)).

[99] Rogers v. Grimaldi, 875 F.2d 994, 999 (2d Cir. 1989) (contrasting *Ginger and Fred* with "titles—such as 'Nimmer on Copyright' and 'Jane Fonda's Workout Book'—[that] explicitly state the author of the work or at least the name of the person the publisher is entitled to associate with the preparation of the work").

[100] No. 1:22-cv-01583, 2023 WL 8826729 (D. Del. Dec. 21, 2023).

because the term was the name of a TV show, it was a trademark.[101] And it then determined (incorrectly) that because it might function as a trademark, even in part, *Rogers* did not apply. This reading eliminates *Rogers* altogether. Indeed, under *Homevestors*'s view of the Court's analysis, the *Rogers* test wouldn't have been applicable to *Rogers* itself, since that case, like *Homevestors*, involved the title of an expressive work.[102]

These overreadings of *Jack Daniel's* are possible because the Court didn't give attention to the expansion of trademark law beyond source confusion in its analysis, although Justice Sotomayor's concurrence mentions the problem in her discussion of the troubling use of survey evidence in such cases. It seems clear the *Jack Daniel's* Court did not think it was abolishing *Rogers*, and much of the Court's opinion would make no sense on that view. Nonetheless, so far that seems to be the practical effect in the lower courts. At the very least, it will create drawn-out litigation requiring discovery, which itself has a chilling effect, and which *Rogers* took great pains to avoid.[103]

---

[101] In fact, titles of individual expressive works are not viewed as source-identifying in trademark law, absent exceptional circumstances, because they are not source-identifiers. Herbko Int'l, Inc. v. Kappa Books, Inc., 308 F.3d 1156, 1162 (Fed. Cir. 2002). (This rule may well be under attack in trademark law because of the relentless expansion of trademark claims, but that fact makes the threat to *Rogers* even greater, because courts may be predisposed to jump from "titles can be source-identifying" to "no First Amendment protection applies to titles.") TV-series titles also identify the expressive work the audience will see—something that seems trademark-like, but also serves core non-trademark functions and should not be treated like an ordinary commercial trademark. *Cf.* Dastar Corp. v. Twentieth Century Fox Film Corp., 539 U.S. 23, 33–34 (2003) (explaining that allowing trademark law to control ordinary uses of expressive works would conflict with copyright law).

[102] The *Rogers* court itself acknowledged that titles serve functions that seem trademark-like, insofar as they can identify a particular work (so that people know whether they are watching *Black Beauty* or *Black Mirror*). *Rogers*, 875 F.2d at 998 ("Titles, like the artistic works they identify, are of a hybrid nature, combining artistic expression and commercial promotion. The title of a movie may be both an integral element of the filmmaker's expression as well as a significant means of marketing the film to the public. The artistic and commercial elements of titles are inextricably intertwined.").

[103] MGFB Props., Inc. v. Viacom Inc, 54 F.4th 670, 688 (11th Cir. 2022) (Brasher, J., concurring) (indicating that *Rogers* avoids need for "extensive fact-finding" and that "certainty is especially important in an area like this one where even the prospect of liability has the effect of chilling constitutionally protected speech" (citing Glynn Lunney, *Trademark's Judicial De-Evolution: Why Courts Get Trademark Cases Wrong Repeatedly*, 106 CALIF. L. REV. 1195, 1201 (2018))); Mattel, Inc. v. MCA Records, Inc., 296 F.3d 894, 900–02 (9th Cir. 2002); New Kids on the Block v. News Am. Publ'g, Inc., 971 F.2d 302, 306–08 (9th Cir. 1992); Robert G. Bone, *Rights and Remedies in Trademark Law: The Curious Distinction Between Trademark Infringement and Unfair Competition*, 98 TEX. L. REV. 1187, 1213 (2020) ("[T]he open-ended nature of factual determinations in trademark cases generates uncertainty about outcome. One of the main sources of this uncertainty is the vague multifactor test for likelihood of confusion." (internal citations omitted)). For an argument for raising that threshold

III. Through a Glass, Darkly

A. THE MISSING FIRST AMENDMENT IN THE COURT'S IP CASES

Both *Warhol* and *Jack Daniel's* are in considerable tension with the Supreme Court's (explicit) First Amendment jurisprudence. The *Warhol* decision suggests that both speech that builds on someone else's work and speech for money are entitled to less protection against copyright claims. By contrast, just a month later, the Court in *303 Creative LLC v. Elenis*,[104] holding that First Amendment protections apply to the creation of a wedding website, went out of its way to emphasize that an individual's speech is protected, even if it is for profit and does not have its own standalone message.[105] It noted that "many of the world's great works of literature and art were created with an expectation of compensation,"[106] and that "the First Amendment's protections belong to all, not just to speakers whose motives the government finds worthy."[107] Indeed, over the past two decades the Court has not only given full First Amendment protection to speech with a profit motive but has arguably privileged it over other speech claims.[108]

Jack Daniel's too seems at odds with the trend in the Court's First Amendment jurisprudence. The Court's conclusion that a defendant's use as a trademark obviates the need for any further consideration of the First Amendment seems like a strong form of the rule that commercial speech receives significantly less protection than

---

to help protect speech interests, see Lisa P. Ramsey & Christine Haight Farley, *Raising the Threshold for Trademark Infringement to Protect Free Expression*, 72 Am. U. L. Rev. 1225 (2023).

[104] 600 U.S. 570 (2023).

[105] *Id.* at 588.

[106] *Id.* at 594.

[107] *Id.* at 595.

[108] Sorrell v. IMS Health Inc., 564 U.S. 552 (2011); Citizens United v. FEC, 558 U.S. 310 (2010); Lorillard Tobacco Co. v. Reilly, 533 U.S. 525, 572 (2001) (Thomas, J., concurring in part and in judgment) ("I continue to believe that when the government seeks to restrict truthful speech in order to suppress the ideas it conveys, strict scrutiny is appropriate, whether or not the speech in question may be characterized as 'commercial.'"); Nathan Cortez & William Sage, *The Disembodied First Amendment*, 100 Wash. U. L. Rev. 707, 713 (2023) (describing free speech as "the centerpiece of the Roberts Court's broadly deregulatory agenda," threatening "all kinds of regulation—from business licensing, to warning labels, to mandatory workplace disclosures, to country-of-origin labeling, to warnings of cellular phone radiofrequency exposure, to enforcement actions for unsubstantiated marketing claims, to disclosure requirements for 'conflict minerals'" (internal citations omitted)).

other forms of speech,[109] combined with an incredibly expansive definition of commercial speech.[110] But both of those things are inconsistent with existing law and with the trends in that law. Indeed, only five years ago the Supreme Court was unanimous in striking down a statute that refused registration to disparaging trademarks, with four of the eight Justices noting that even if the regulation burdened only commercial speech it was still unconstitutional.[111] The premise of that case was that the speech at issue was used as a trademark, so trademark use can't itself deprive speech of protection.

Similarly, while the Court seems happy to ignore the First Amendment in IP cases, elsewhere it has applied the First Amendment to strike down laws that impinge far less on free speech than copyright and trademark law do. The Roberts Court has, in the name of free speech, limited torts like intentional infliction of emotional distress,[112]

---

[109] Lisa Ramsey suggested to us that there may be "trademark uses" that are not "commercial uses," such as the name of a political party. But that is just to move the question around: Why would "trademark uses" that cause confusion be actionable without any requirement of intent, fault, or materiality? It happens that the most relevant political party case, *United We Stand America, Inc. v. United We Stand, America, New York, Inc.*, 128 F.3d 86 (1997), had decent evidence of materiality (i.e., people giving to the wrong group), and defendants knew the national party's objections. But nothing in trademark doctrine *required* materiality, or any fault or knowledge—or source confusion—as opposed to affiliation or sponsorship confusion. If it is acceptable to tell a political party faction to stop using its name without these things, we ought to know why. If, on the other hand, we think trademark claims against noncommercial speech should be held to a higher standard, we can't use the ordinary definition of likely confusion—whether one calls that constitutional avoidance or a direct application of the First Amendment. It's plausible that there's a compelling interest in regulating "speaker-indicating uses" even in the absence of fault, though materiality should still be required. *See* United States v. Alvarez, 567 U.S. 709, 723 (2012). Therefore, the Court wasn't relying on commercial speech concepts, but the Court's studied avoidance of any internal First Amendment concepts—compelling interest, intermediate or strict scrutiny, commercial speech—make it impossible to tell.

One could argue that, in practice, trademark claims against political speech will only succeed when there's fault and materiality, since courts will see through pretextual attempts to suppress political speech. But, even if such a thumb on the scale doesn't count as a doctrine distinguishing commercial from noncommercial speech, it only makes sense for pure source confusion; affiliation confusion is easily asserted and misused. *See, e.g.*, Browne v. McCain, 612 F. Supp. 2d 1125 (C.D. Cal. 2009).

[110] Although "commercial speech" extends beyond conventional advertising, the fact that speech is sold for profit, or ad-supported, has not been enough to make it "commercial speech" outside of IP doctrine. *See supra* note 20.

[111] Matal v. Tam, 582 U.S. 218, 244–45 (2017) (op. of Alito, J., joined in part by three other Justices) (finding that, regardless of whether trademarks are always commercial speech, the bar on registering "disparaging" marks could not stand); *id.* at 251 (Kennedy, J., concurring in part, joined by three other Justices) (same); *id.* at 254 (Thomas, J., concurring in part and in the judgment) (reiterating his argument that regulations of truthful commercial speech should be subjected to strict scrutiny).

[112] Snyder v. Phelps, 562 U.S. 443 (2011).

overruled previous doctrine to protect people who don't want to pay union dues,[113] protected deliberate lies that don't cause material harm,[114] and declined to allow Congress to expand categories of unprotected speech (at least when they couldn't be linked in some way to IP).[115]

Warhol and *Jack Daniel's* don't involve traditional political divisions. The Court's conservatives and liberals were not obviously divided in *Warhol*, with Justice Kagan joined by Chief Justice Roberts in dissent and feuding bitterly with Justice Sotomayor. And the decision in *Jack Daniel's* was unanimous, albeit with concurrences pointing in different directions. But the short shrift given to the First Amendment interests at stake suggests that the Justices see IP rights as a First Amendment-free zone, even when Congress has created—or courts have expanded—those rights far past their original scope.

B. WHY IS THE FIRST AMENDMENT MISSING?

What is going on here? At first blush one might think the answer is simply siloing: The Court simply places IP in a different category and turns its blinders on when it comes to the speech implications of preventing Andy Warhol or dog-toy companies from selling their speech. Certainly it has long been true that copyright law in particular has received an (unjustified) free pass from First Amendment strictures.[116] But the Court has deflected First Amendment worries about copyright precisely by pointing to the freedom that fair use provides to make one's own statements using copyrighted works;[117] the Court can't heavily circumscribe that freedom without resurrecting the very

---

[113] Janus v. Am. Fed'n of State, Cnty. & Mun. Emps., Council 31, 138 S. Ct. 2448 (2018).

[114] *Alvarez*, 567 U.S. at 723. Strikingly, *Alvarez* involved opinions that referred to trademark as if trademark law was unquestionably constitutional in any form. Justice Breyer even conflated dilution, which does not require consumer confusion, with infringement, which does (although it does not require materiality either). *Id.* at 735–36 (Breyer, J., concurring, joined by Kagan, J.); *see also id.* at 743–44 (Alito, J., dissenting, joined by Scalia & Thomas, JJ.) (pointing to trademark law to show that the Stolen Valor Act should be upheld as a protection against "dilution" of military honors).

[115] United States v. Stevens, 559 U.S. 460 (2010) (overturning a law banning videos that show animals being tortured and killed).

[116] *See, e.g.*, Lemley & Volokh, *supra* note 80, at 197–98; David S. Olson, *First Amendment-Based Copyright Misuse*, 52 WM. & MARY L. REV. 537, 558–63 (2010); Rebecca Tushnet, *Copy This Essay: How Fair Use Doctrine Harms Free Speech and How Copying Serves It*, 114 YALE L.J. 535 (2004); Alfred C. Yen, *Rethinking Copyright's Relationship to the First Amendment*, 100 B.U. L. REV. 1215, 1217–20 (2020).

[117] Golan v. Holder, 565 U.S. 302, 328 (2012); Eldred v. Ashcroft, 537 U.S. 186, 219–20 (2003).

First Amendment issues it sought to inter. And in any event, that First Amendment free pass has never before been true of trademark law. Indeed, twice in the last five years the Court has struck down parts of the trademark statute as First Amendment violations.[118]

Nor is it just that no one raised the First Amendment issues in these cases. To the contrary, numerous briefs in both cases discussed the free-speech implications, and Justice Kagan's dissent in *Warhol* addressed them directly,[119] while Justice Sotomayor's concurrence in *Jack Daniel's* did so indirectly by cautioning courts to scrutinize "confusion" evidence carefully in parody cases.[120] And the Ninth Circuit had applied the explicitly First Amendment-driven *Rogers* test in the opinion reversed in *Jack Daniel's*, so the Court had to affirmatively decide to ignore the First Amendment in favor of a likelihood-of-confusion and dilution inquiry. In both cases, it rejected speech-protective limiting doctrines without mentioning, much less distinguishing, the First Amendment doctrines it cast aside.

We can't, of course, read the minds of the Justices. But we believe there are three possible explanations for this loud silence.

First, perhaps the Court is indeed engaged in a form of siloing, though not with as coarse a filter as "IP is exempt from the Constitution." Rather, the Court's decisions reflect a determined focus on a particular legal issue to the exclusion of the broader framework of the law. The Court proceeds from the conclusion it wants to reach (i.e., Warhol shouldn't be able to compete with Goldsmith to sell images of Prince for magazine covers) and ignores the larger implications of its rather dramatic changes to fair-use law. This is consistent with some criticisms of the Court's decisions in patent cases: The Court reaches the result it wants to reach in the case before it and lets the

---

[118] Iancu v. Brunetti, 139 S. Ct. 2294 (2019); Matal v. Tam, 582 U.S. 218 (2017).

[119] Andy Warhol Found. for the Visual Arts, Inc. v. Goldsmith, 598 U.S. 508, 560 (2023) (Kagan, J., dissenting) ("Congress and the courts have long recognized that an overly stringent copyright regime actually stifles creativity by preventing artists from building on the work of others.... The fair-use test's first factor ... provides 'breathing space' for artists to use existing materials to make fundamentally new works, for the public's enjoyment and benefit. In now remaking that factor, ... the majority hampers creative progress and undermines creative freedom." (cleaned up)).

[120] Jack Daniel's v. VIP Prods., 599 U.S. 140, 163–64 (2023) (Sotomayor, J., concurring) ("[I]n the context of parodies and potentially other uses implicating First Amendment concerns, courts should treat the results of surveys with particular caution.... Allowing such survey results to drive the infringement analysis would risk silencing a great many parodies, even ones that by other metrics are unlikely to result in the confusion about sourcing that is the core concern of the Lanham Act.").

chips fall where they may.¹²¹ But this explanation begs the question of *why* the Court wants to reach those results, which seem somewhat at odds with its own instincts. Justice Kagan's majority opinion in *Jack Daniel's* seems quite skeptical that "Bad Spaniels" dog toys would confuse anyone,¹²² and Justice Sotomayor's concurrence even more so.¹²³ But the Court's reversal of the Ninth Circuit's ruling sets up a scenario where the district court might once again accept dubious survey evidence suggesting confusion.

Second, it is possible that trademark and copyright have become ensnared in the larger, sudden reversal of the political valence of the Free Speech Clause to conservatives, especially with respect to commercial-speech doctrine. States like Florida and Texas are increasingly attempting to dictate what private parties can say and defending their acts as ordinary regulations of commercial speech,¹²⁴ while at the same time punishing private parties for speech that is unpopular.¹²⁵ A key to this inversion is the idea that speech by

---

[121] *See* Paul R. Gugliuzza & Mark A. Lemley, *Myths and Reality of Patent Law at the Supreme Court*, 104 B.U. L. Rev. (forthcoming 2024), https://papers.ssrn.com/sol3/papers.cfm?abstract_id=4304442.

[122] *Jack Daniel's*, 599 U.S. at 161 (reaffirming cases that state that parodies are unlikely to confuse).

[123] *Id.* at 164–65 (Sotomayor, J., concurring) (explaining why well-resourced trademark owners can silence parodists).

[124] *See, e.g.*, NetChoice, L.L.C. v. Paxton, 49 F.4th 439 (5th Cir. 2022) (concerning a state law restricting the ability of private social media platforms to control speech on their platforms), *cert. granted*, 144 S. Ct. 477 (2023) (No. 22-555); NetChoice, LLC v. Att'y Gen., 34 F.4th 1196 (11th Cir. 2022), *cert. granted sub nom.* Moody v. NetChoice, LLC, 144 S. Ct. 478 (2023) (No. 22-277) (same); Media Matters for Am. v. Paxton, 23-cv-03363 (D. Md. Dec. 12, 2023) (concerning a state investigation of a nonprofit for "deceptive trade practices" in reporting on Nazi and related content found on X); Honeyfund.com, Inc. v. DeSantis, 622 F. Supp. 3d 1159 (N.D. Fla. 2022) (concerning a state law prohibiting employers from requiring any activity that promoted any of eight forbidden concepts); *Investment Policy Statement*, Ariz. State Treasurers Off. 1 (2022), https://www.aztreasury.gov/_files/ugd/8bb536_415fda871e864b9ea1fb95fce704874e.pdf (prohibiting state investment in a fund that "is branded, advertised or otherwise publicly described ... as furthering: 1. International, domestic, or industry agreements relating to environmental or social goals. 2. Corporate governance structures based on social characteristics. 3. Social or environmental goals ..."); Cora Neas, *Seattle Hospital Sues After Texas Attorney General Asks for Handover of Patient Records*, KXAN Austin (Dec. 2023), https://www.kxan.com/news/texas/seattle-hospital-sues-after-texas-attorney-general-asks-for-handover-of-patient-records/amp (reporting on how the Texas Attorney General informed an out-of-state hospital that it was investigating alleged "misrepresentations regarding Gender Transitioning and Reassignment Treatments and Procedures and Texas law" that purportedly violated the Texas Deceptive Trade Practices-Consumer Protection Act).

[125] *See, e.g.*, Wollschlaeger v. Governor, 848 F.3d 1293 (11th Cir. 2017) (concerning a law prohibiting pediatricians from asking about guns); Woodlands Pride, Inc. v. Paxton, No. H-23-2847, 2023 WL 6226113 (S.D. Tex. Sept. 26, 2023) (concerning an anti-drag law);

corporations—long a conservative *cause celebre* when they liked the content of that speech[126]—is entitled to less protection, not because it does no more than propose a commercial transaction, but simply because they *are* corporations, so what they are doing is "commercial" in a nonconstitutional sense.[127] A lower level of protection for speech that can be characterized as commercial thus seems attractive to conservative theorists who previously doubted that anything other than strict scrutiny should ever apply to any speech regulation. But the reversal is far from complete, especially among Justices.

In this shifting environment, it's hardly surprising that the Court simply declined to address either (1) the sharp divergence between what counts as "commercial" use for copyright purposes and the First Amendment definition of "commercial" speech or (2) the question of whether trademark uses are always commercial speech. It seems unlikely that the Justices could have achieved even a majority, much less a consensus, on those topics, for reasons having little to do with IP.

Imperial Sovereign Ct. v. Knudsen, No. CV 23-50, 2023 WL 4847007 (D. Mont. July 28, 2023) (same); HM Fla.-ORL, LLC v. Griffin, No. 6:23-cv-950, 2023 WL 4157542 (M.D. Fla. June 23, 2023) (same); S. Utah Drag Stars v. City of St. George, No. 4:23-cv-00044, 2023 WL 4053395 (D. Utah June 16, 2023) (same); K. C. v. Individual Members of Med. Licensing Bd. of Ind., No. 1:23-cv-00595, 2023 WL 4054086 (S.D. Ind. June 16, 2023) (concerning a state law prohibiting counseling on gender transition); Brandt v. Rutledge, 551 F. Supp. 3d 882, 892 (E.D. Ark. 2021) (same), *aff'd*, 47 F.4th 661, 671–72 (8th Cir. 2022); Amended Complaint at 73–78, Disney v. DeSantis, No. 23-cv-163 (N.D. Fla. May 8, 2023) (challenging a state law depriving Disney of previous benefits in retaliation for opposing "Don't Say Gay"). Far more bills of this type have been proposed and passed than have been litigated.

[126] *See, e.g.*, Alex Kozinski & Stuart Banner, *The Anti-History and Pre-History of Commercial Speech*, 71 TEX. L. REV. 747, 762 (1993) (criticizing the lower level of protection for commercial speech compared to political speech); *see also* John C. Coates IV, *Corporate Speech & the First Amendment: History, Data, and Implications*, 30 CONST. COMMENT. 223, 223–24, 249 (2015) (finding that "corporations have increasingly displaced individuals as direct beneficiaries of First Amendment rights" and that the Court's "docket now [is] roughly split between business and individual cases"); David A. Strauss, *Why the Burger Court Mattered*, 116 MICH. L. REV. 1067, 1067–70 (2018) (discussing the effect of the "conservative counterrevolution" on First Amendment commercial and corporate speech doctrines).

[127] *See, e.g.*, Evelyn Douek & Genevieve Lakier, *First Amendment Politics Gets Weird: Public and Private Platform Reform and the Breakdown of the Laissez-Faire Free Speech Consensus*, 2022 U. CHI. L. REV. ONLINE 1, 1, 6 (noting that conservatives now evince discomfort with corporate power, and that Republicans in 33 states have introduced anti-content moderation bills after January 2020, when multiple platforms banned Donald Trump); Amanda Shanor & Sarah E. Light, *Anti-Woke Capitalism, the First Amendment, and the Decline of Libertarianism*, 118 NW. U. L. REV. 347, 391 (2023) ("The libertarian, pro-business, and private-property-supporting strains of the conservative legal movement—which have been dominant since the Reagan Administration and flourished within First Amendment law over the last thirty years . . . — are increasingly being eclipsed by a new form of legalism [that] seeks to tie the hands of businesses and investors that express views associated with progressive politics, even if done for profit-seeking reasons." (footnotes omitted)).

This can't be a complete explanation, because this reversal of polarity is so far limited only to some conservative jurists, and they didn't write either *Warhol* or *Jack Daniel's*. But it may explain the otherwise strange bedfellows the opinions created and, in particular, the willingness of the Court's right wing to sign onto rulings that seem quite obviously inconsistent with decades of their own First Amendment jurisprudence.

This dynamic raises a question hardly limited to IP: What are speech categories—whether called strict scrutiny versus intermediate scrutiny or something else—good for? We use them to judge whether the government's articulated interest is sufficiently linked to the restrictions it has chosen or whether differing treatment is based on legally sound distinctions. Even for First Amendment theorists who don't want rigid categories of strict and intermediate scrutiny, the very different implications of confusion claims applied to movies and confusion claims applied to cans of corn deserve attention. Likewise, even if the Andy Warhol Foundation ought to pay Lynn Goldsmith, we should worry about a fair-use doctrine that tells factfinders to distinguish satire from parody—inviting them to allow only those critical reuses with which they agree. And we should worry even more about a doctrine that says that *creating* speech might be permissible but sharing it with the world will not be.

Third, the Court's First Amendment jurisprudence in IP may reflect its current preoccupation with legislative over judicial restrictions on speech. The legal realists taught us that an injunction issued by a judge and enforced by the threat of prison is every bit as much state action as an ordinance passed by a city council.[128] And that recognition made it into Supreme Court jurisprudence in the twentieth century.[129] But the Court today seems much less concerned about

---

[128] *See, e.g.*, Robert L. Hale, *Coercion and Distribution in a Supposedly Non-Coercive State*, 38 POL. SCI. Q. 470, 471 (1923); Arthur Allen Leff, *Law and*, 87 YALE L.J. 989, 997 (1978); Morris R. Cohen, *Property and Sovereignty*, 13 CORNELL L.Q. 8, 22 (1927). *See generally* LOUIS MICHAEL SEIDMAN & MARK V. TUSHNET, REMNANTS OF BELIEF: CONTEMPORARY CONSTITUTIONAL ISSUES 70–71 (1996) (discussing tensions in state-action doctrine inherited from Realists).

[129] N.Y. Times Co. v. Sullivan, 376 U.S. 254 (1964); Shelley v. Kraemer, 334 U.S. 1, 20 (1948) (holding that judicial enforcement of racially restrictive covenants was an unconstitutional exercise of state power); *see* Yochai Benkler, *Freedom in Systems*, 127 HARV. L. REV. F. 351, 351–52 (2014) ("*New York Times Co. v. Sullivan* was the first major legal realist First Amendment opinion.... [T]he great innovation in *Sullivan* was its willingness to acknowledge that an established rule of private law could become a source of constitutionally proscribed censorship." (internal citations omitted)).

courts actually ordering people not to speak than it is about the potentially chilling and distorting speech implications of ordinary regulations by other branches of government.[130] The Court's willingness to see threats to speech in the government's refusal to register trademarks, but not in a court altogether banning the sale of products bearing messages, is of a piece with this new emphasis.[131]

One factor explaining this view is the Court's (likely misplaced) epistemological confidence: Where judges are in charge of the standard, we can count on them to do the right thing, and there is no need to worry about free-speech suppression and chilling effects from expensive litigation. There are some resonances in this approach with the Court's insistence that there is an eternal, unchanging common law established at the Founding or Reconstruction against which legal innovations (at least some of them) must be measured by the Justices.[132] This approach can be seen in the Court's Takings[133] and Second Amendment jurisprudence[134] and cases like *TransUnion LLC v. Ramirez*, which held that courts must decide whether Congress had identified a harm that was common-law-like enough to allow Congress to create a private right of action in federal court.[135] Or perhaps it

---

[130] *See, e.g.*, Expressions Hair Design v. Schneiderman, 581 U.S. 37, 47 (2017) (holding that a ban on surcharges for using a credit card unconstitutionally regulated speech because it dictated how stores communicated prices).

[131] Even an expected reversal in *Elster* would not change our analysis if, as seems likely, it's based on the claim that refusing registration protects the publicity right of the named person, even in the absence of confusion. The government would then only be acting to protect private intangible property, not asserting interests of its own (notwithstanding that the right of publicity doesn't currently allow people to suppress criticism).

[132] *See* Reva B. Siegel, *How "History and Tradition" Perpetuates Inequality:* Dobbs *on Abortion's Nineteenth-Century Criminalization*, 60 Hous. L. Rev. 901, 901 (2023) (explaining that the choice of period ensures that both common and statutory law were explicitly biased against nonwhites and in favor of men); *cf.* Jones v. United States, 529 U.S. 848 (2000) (reversing federal conviction for arson, a "paradigmatic common-law state crime," on the ground that the commerce power did not reach the targeted building); United States v. Morrison, 529 U.S. 598 (2000) (invalidating portions of the Violence Against Women Act as exceeding congressional authority under the Commerce Clause and Section 5 of the Fourteenth Amendment); Reva B. Siegel, *"The Rule of Love": Wife Beating as Prerogative and Privacy*, 105 Yale L.J. 2117, 2201–02 (1996) (explaining how the federalism and commerce objections to VAWA are founded in the common-law approach to violence against women as a purely private matter).

[133] *See, e.g.*, Lucas v. S.C. Coastal Council, 505 U.S. 1003, 1029 (1992) (requiring Takings analysis to use a baseline of "common law" nuisance).

[134] *See* N.Y. State Rifle & Pistol Ass'n, Inc. v. Bruen, 597 U.S. 1 (2023); District of Columbia v. Heller, 554 U.S. 570, 635 (2008).

[135] 141 S. Ct. 2190, 2204 (2021).

reflects a power dynamic in which the Court strengthens its hand at the expense of other branches of government.[136]

We're not sure this distinction makes sense even in the abstract. The trademark statute doesn't refuse or cancel trademark registrations; individual judges and bureaucrats do. But in any event, it seems an odd line to draw in IP. Federal copyright is a creature of statutory law. There is no federal common-law copyright,[137] and statutory law displaces any state common-law copyrights for fixed works.[138] Defenses like fair use are also codified (sometimes in exhaustive detail).[139] Meanwhile, as noted above, the federal trademark statute goes far beyond what was available to trademark claimants at common law, including by providing a variety of presumptions favoring a trademark owner and protecting against "dilution."[140] So, even if the decisions reflected a newfound discomfort with the idea that judges are state actors, in both of these cases it was a statute, not merely a judicial decision, whose application presented the First Amendment questions.

A variant of this theory is that the Court disdains judicially-created speech-protective doctrines—perhaps as a general matter, or perhaps where they coexist with a statutory scheme. This is most evident in Justice Gorsuch's concurrence in *Jack Daniel's*, which casts doubt on whether the *Rogers* test or anything like it has any legitimacy because it's not in the statute.[141] But you can see echoes of it in the majority opinion's treatment of dilution, which starts and stops with (mis)reading the statute and suggests that if there is a statutory defense, nothing more need be said. And you catch hints of it in *Warhol*'s

---

[136] *Cf.* Mark A. Lemley, *The Imperial Supreme Court*, 136 HARV. L. REV. F. 97 (2021) (noting this dynamic, but also noting that the Court has been weakening lower courts as well).

[137] Wheaton v. Peters, 33 U.S. 591 (1834).

[138] 17 U.S.C. § 301.

[139] *Id.* §§ 107–122.

[140] *See, e.g.*, 15 U.S.C. § 1057(b) (creating a presumption of validity for registered marks); *id.* §§ 1065, 1115(b) (creating "incontestable" registrations whose source-indicating function cannot be challenged under most circumstances); *id.* § 1125(c) (creating the federal dilution cause of action); Lemley & McKenna, *supra* note 78 (detailing massive expansion in scope of trademark law, including what counts as actionable confusion); Jeremy N. Sheff, *Veblen Brands*, 96 MINN. L. REV. 769, 776–77 (2012) (explaining how the concept of confusion has dramatically expanded with the creation of doctrines such as post-sale confusion).

[141] Jack Daniel's v. VIP Prods., 599 U.S. 140, 165 (2023) (Gorsuch, J., concurring with two other Justices).

deemphasis of transformative works—the central focus of fair-use doctrine for the past thirty years[142]—in favor of the nonexclusive list of categories described in the fair-use statute.

Even to articulate this theory indicates that the Court has taken a wrong turn. Courts can't develop judicial doctrines that embody First Amendment safeguards? Really? Not only have they been doing so for decades in all sorts of fields, from defamation to prior restraints, but the whole point of the Constitution is that it trumps statutes that are inconsistent with it and that the courts make that determination. It is no answer to a constitutional challenge to say "well, the statute doesn't provide for that challenge." If that's true, it is the statute that is the problem, not the First Amendment. And the reason courts develop speech-protective doctrines that prevent unconstitutional applications of a statute is precisely to avoid the much harsher alternative of invalidating the statute outright.

But in any event, this statutory supremacy theory doesn't make any sense in IP, because in both copyright and trademark, the infringement standards, key defenses, and limiting doctrines are also not defined in the relevant statutes.

What constitutes copyright infringement—"substantial similarity"—is a doctrine made up and applied by courts. It is found nowhere in the statute. If we took the statute truly seriously, the reproduction right would be much narrower, covering only true "copies" (and the separate derivative-works right would also require reassessment).[143] And, although the statute lists four nonexclusive factors to consider in assessing fair use, Congress borrowed them from the fair-use doctrine as it had evolved without statutory codification for over a century and intended that courts should continue

---

[142] *See, e.g.*, Clark D. Asay et al., *Is Transformative Use Eating the World?*, 61 B.C. L. REV. 905, 944 (2020) (finding that transformativeness played an outsized role in litigated case outcomes); Barton Beebe, *An Empirical Study of U.S. Copyright Fair Use Opinions Updated, 1978–2019*, 10 NYU J. INTELL. PROP & ENT. L. 1, 25 (2020) ("[W]hen a court finds that the defendant's use is transformative, the ratio of the odds a defendant will prevail in its fair use defense to the odds it will fail is anywhere from 86 to 91 times greater. By this measure, a finding of transformativeness exerts by far the greatest impact of any finding on a court's likelihood of making an overall determination of fair use."); Neil Weinstock Netanel, *Making Sense of Fair Use*, 15 LEWIS & CLARK L. REV. 715, 734 (2011) (arguing that transformativeness "overwhelmingly drives fair use analysis in the courts today"); Sag, *supra* note 38, at 74 ("[T]he evidence from litigated cases analyzed in this Article confirms the centrality of transformative use.").

[143] Glynn S. Lunney, Jr., *Copyright, Literally*, 51 AM. INTELL. PROP. L. ASS'N. Q.J. 479, 504, 516–19 (2023).

that common-law-like process of developing fair-use doctrine.[144] The only statutory amendment to the fair-use provisions, in fact, rejected cases in the Second Circuit that seemed to read the statute to create a bright-line rule against any fair use of an unpublished work.[145]

Similarly, the trademark statute doesn't set forth a test for likely confusion.[146] Instead, courts developed increasingly expansive concepts of confusion and eventually adopted a multifactor test in most cases.[147] This test considers, among other things, the strength of the plaintiff's mark, the relatedness of the parties' goods or services, any evidence of actual confusion, the defendant's intent, and other factors. None of these factors are listed in the statute, and they reflect a remarkable broadening of historic rules.[148] So, too, does the extension of trademark infringement to new types of confusion beyond the point of sale, such as initial-interest and post-sale confusion.

Courts developed the *Rogers* test at issue in *Jack Daniel's* as a replacement for the ordinary multifactor confusion test in "artistic" uses. In such a case, among other things, the fact that the plaintiff owned a strong mark didn't really make it any more likely that people would think the art at issue came from the plaintiff; instead, (objectively) reasonable audiences would understand the use as a

---

[144] H.R. Rep. No. 94-1476, at 66 (1976) ("The bill endorses the purpose and general scope of the judicial doctrine of fair use, but there is no disposition to freeze the doctrine in the statute, especially during a period of rapid technological change. Beyond a very broad statutory explanation of what fair use is and some of the criteria applicable to it, the courts must be free to adapt the doctrine to particular situations on a case-by-case basis. Section 107 is intended to restate the present judicial doctrine of fair use, not to change, narrow, or enlarge it in any way."); Harper & Row Publishers, Inc. v. Nation Enters., 471 U.S. 539, 549–54 (1985) (holding that § 107 reflected the "intent of Congress to codify the common-law doctrine").

[145] Pub. L. No. 102-492, 106 Stat. 3145 (1992) (codified at 17 U.S.C. § 107) ("The fact that a work is unpublished shall not itself bar a finding of fair use if such finding is made upon consideration of all the above factors."); H.R. Rep. No. 836, at 9 (1992) (explaining Congress's disagreement with Second Circuit precedents, such as *Salinger v. Random House, Inc.*, 811 F.2d 90 (2d Cir. 1987), which found that limited quotation and paraphrase of unpublished letters for purposes of scholarly analysis was not fair use).

[146] 15 U.S.C. § 1114 (barring uses of registered marks "likely to cause confusion, or to cause mistake, or to deceive"); *id.* § 1125(a)(1)(A) (barring "any false designation of origin, false or misleading description of fact, or false or misleading representation of fact" that is "likely to cause confusion, or to cause mistake, or to deceive as to the affiliation, connection, or association of such person with another person, or as to the origin, sponsorship, or approval of his or her goods, services, or commercial activities by another person").

[147] *Polaroid Corp. v. Polarad Elecs. Corp.*, 287 F.2d 492 (2d Cir. 1961), is widely cited for its formulation of the test, but every circuit has its own, somewhat different, variant.

[148] *See* McKenna, *supra* note 57.

reference.[149] That test didn't exist when the Lanham Act was passed in 1946 for the simple reason that it was inconceivable to a trademark lawyer in 1946 that anyone would even think to file, much less win, a suit against the mention of a mark in an expressive work. *Rogers* is a test developed in response to the fact that courts were applying trademark law to restrict speech in a way the drafters of the statute didn't envision.

But even outside the *Rogers* context, the statute does not dictate how likelihood of confusion should be assessed or what factors a court should consider. Instead, courts have settled on a set of factors that varies somewhat across circuits for use in the average case. Although the factors are roughly the same across circuits, different circuits treat them differently. The Second Circuit rigidly insists that a district court must always (in non-*Rogers* cases) evaluate every factor,[150] while other circuits instruct with equal intensity that courts are to focus on the relevant factors for their particular case.[151] And

---

[149] Rogers v. Grimaldi, 875 F.2d 994, 998 (2d Cir. 1989) ("The title of a movie may be both an integral element of the filmmaker's expression as well as a significant means of marketing the film to the public. The artistic and commercial elements of titles are inextricably intertwined. Filmmakers and authors frequently rely on wordplay, ambiguity, irony, and allusion in titling their works. Furthermore, their interest in freedom of artistic expression is shared by their audience. The subtleties of a title can enrich a reader's or a viewer's understanding of a work.").

[150] *See, e.g.*, Arrow Fastener Co., Inc. v. Stanley Works, 59 F.3d 384, 400 (2d Cir. 1995) ("[I]t is incumbent upon the district judge to engage in a deliberate review of each factor, and, if a factor is inapplicable to a case, to explain why."); Centaur Commc'ns, Ltd. v. A/S/M Commc'ns, Inc., 830 F.2d 1217, 1219 (2d Cir. 1987) ("[O]ur precedents establish a long list of factors that must be considered before a determination may be reached. Unfortunately, there is no shortcut. To reach a principled conclusion in a trademark case, it is just as essential to recite the right formulas as it was for Ali Baba to say 'Open Sesame' in order to open the door to the treasure cave of the Forty Thieves."); *see also* FCOA LLC v. Foremost Title & Escrow Servs. LLC, 57 F.4th 939, 957 (11th Cir. 2023) (holding that courts must consider seven factors and may consider more); Insty*Bit, Inc. v. Poly-Tech Indus., Inc., 95 F.3d 663, 670 (8th Cir. 1996) ("[A]lthough no one factor is determinative, each must be analyzed."); *cf.* Homeowners Grp., Inc. v. Home Mktg. Specialists, Inc., 931 F.2d 1100, 1104 (6th Cir. 1991) ("These factors imply no mathematical precision, but are simply a guide to help determine whether confusion is likely.... Each case presents its own complex set of circumstances and not all of these factors may be particularly helpful in any given case. But a thorough and analytical treatment must nevertheless be attempted."). *But see* Orient Exp. Trading Co. v. Federated Dep't Stores, Inc., 842 F.2d 650, 654 (2d Cir. 1988) ("[W]e do not mean to suggest that district courts must slavishly recite the litany of all eight *Polaroid* factors in each and every case. A district court need only consider sufficient factors to reach the ultimate conclusion as to whether or not there is a likelihood of confusion."). As this and the next footnote indicate, there is hardly consensus or consistency on this point.

[151] *See, e.g.*, Ironhawk Techs., Inc. v. Dropbox, Inc., 2 F.4th 1150, 1160 (9th Cir. 2021) ("These factors are neither exhaustive nor dispositive; it is the totality of facts in a given case that is dispositive." (cleaned up)); Savannah Coll. of Art & Design, Inc. v. Sportswear, Inc.,

many circuits have a different test (different from their normal test and also often different from each other's) for a subset of infringement claims that concern "nominative use"—a reference to the trademark owner for the purposes of comparing products or explaining what the defendant has to offer.[152]

The point here is that the central question in a trademark or copyright case—what does it take to infringe a plaintiff's right?—is largely a matter of judicial discretion, despite the present statutory foundation of both rights. This makes copyright and trademark cases seem more like common-law cases and triggers the Court's confidence in its own judgments. The result is an indifference to things like the risks of error and chilling effects. The answer in any given case, the Court thinks, is obvious.

This judicial centrality also links trademark and copyright, despite their statutory apparatus, to the Court's approval of judicial power over legislative power. Thus, while the Court is deeply worried about administrators—trademark examiners—as censors, noting their inconsistencies in which registrations they refuse and allow, it apparently has no such qualms about judges. Although no other Justice to date has signed on to Justice Thomas's call to repudiate *New York Times Co. v. Sullivan*,[153] *Jack Daniel's* and *Warhol* are consistent with the argument that judicial enforcement of private causes of action need not trigger any First Amendment scrutiny, even when those causes of action are created by statute. On this view, judges simply aren't censors, whether they are evaluating the meaning of Andy Warhol's art or the effects of "Bad Spaniels" toys on consumers. They're just calling

---

983 F.3d 1273, 1281 (11th Cir. 2020) (stating that "[t]he district court need not consider all factors in every case," *contra FCOA*, 57 F.4th 939); Sterling Jewelers, Inc. v. Artistry Ltd., 896 F.3d 752, 756 (6th Cir. 2018); Swatch AG v. Beehive Wholesale, LLC, 739 F.3d 150, 158–59 (4th Cir. 2014) (stating that the factors are "non-exclusive and non-mandatory," "serve as a guide rather than 'a rigid formula'" and "are not all of equal importance" or "relevant in every case" (internal citations omitted)).

[152] *See, e.g.*, Int'l Info. Sys. Sec. Certification Consortium, Inc. v. Sec. Univ., LLC, 823 F.3d 153 (2d Cir. 2016) (holding that the Third Circuit's three factors must be added to ordinary multifactor test in cases of referential use); Century 21 Real Est. Corp. v. Lendingtree, Inc., 425 F.3d 211, 220–22 (3d Cir. 2005) (modifying the Ninth Circuit's test to make it more limited); New Kids on the Block v. News Am. Publ'g, Inc., 971 F.2d 302, 308 (9th Cir. 1992) (creating a new three-factor test); *cf.* Universal Commc'n Sys., Inc. v. Lycos, Inc., 478 F.3d 413, 424 (1st Cir. 2007) (declining to accept or reject nominative fair use but holding that the circuit has "recognized the underlying principle" behind it).

[153] McKee v. Cosby, 139 S. Ct. 675, 681–82 (2019) (Thomas, J., concurring in denial of cert).

balls and strikes. Because the Court just asserts its conclusions, it doesn't need to defend this position outright, but that does not seem to us to be a strength.

IV. ENDGAME

IP has long been its own discipline, one that has coexisted uneasily with the mainstream of constitutional law. But the Court's 2023 IP decisions bring the tension to a head. It is no longer possible to sweep under the rug the conflict between the ever-expanding scope of copyright and trademark infringement and a First Amendment that would in any other discipline give full-throated protection to the very things courts enjoin in IP cases without a second thought.

Courts in recent decades have carved out some space for free speech despite the expansion of infringement doctrine. Judicially created doctrines like transformative use and the *Rogers* test stop the expansion at the point where the tension with the First Amendment becomes too great. *Warhol* and *Jack Daniel's* could hobble those doctrines unless they are effectively limited to their facts—something lower courts have not yet shown an inclination to do.[154] The tensions between the Court's treatment of profit-seeking speech in IP cases and its treatment of such speech elsewhere may someday force the Court to confront what it has long been able to avoid—the fact that the current bloated trademark and copyright laws cannot, without significant modification, coexist with the non-IP version of the First Amendment.

---

[154] *Warhol* says we needn't worry about its evisceration of fair use because "copyright law is replete with escape valves: the idea-expression distinction; the general rule that facts may not receive protection; the requirement of originality; the legal standard for actionable copying; the limited duration of copyright," and, it grudgingly admits, even the now-narrowed doctrine of fair use. 598 U.S. 508, 550 (2023). We are not comforted. Cutting back substantially on the single doctrine that has provided the most direct protection to free speech can't be justified on the grounds that people will be free to publish telephone white pages or books written before 1928 without fear of legal liability.

JACK GOLDSMITH AND
ALAN SYKES

THE CALIFORNIA EFFECT, PROCESS-
BASED REGULATION, AND THE
FUTURE OF PIKE BALANCING

State regulations that govern cross-border transactions invariably impose costs on consumers and firms in other states. The Supreme Court has long struggled to craft doctrines that specify when such regulations violate the Dormant Commerce Clause (DCC).[1] In the modern era the Court has settled on two main tests for analyzing DCC problems: A state law cannot "discriminate against interstate commerce"; and it also cannot burden interstate commerce in a way that

---

Jack Goldsmith is the Learned Hand Professor at Harvard Law School. Alan Sykes is the Professor of Law and Warren Christopher Professor in the Practice of International Law and Diplomacy at Stanford Law School.

AUTHORS' NOTE: We thank Louis Kaplow, Mitch Polinsky, Hayley Ryerson, Maggie Yellen, and workshop participants at Harvard and Stanford Law Schools for generous and helpful comments. We also thank Gabriel Blacklock, Danny Bushacra, John Czubek, Christopher Gorman, Hayley Isenberg, Benjamin Pontz, Ben Rolsma, Andrew Sparkman, and John Weed for outstanding research and related assistance.

[1] On the various doctrines the Court has employed in the DCC over almost two centuries, see Daniel Francis, *The Decline of the Dormant Commerce Clause*, 94 DENV. L. REV. 255 (2017); James M. McGoldrick, Jr., *The Dormant Commerce Clause: The Endgame—From Southern Pacific to Tennessee* [sic] *Wine & Spirits—1945 to 2019*, 40 PACE L. REV. 44 (2020); James M. McGoldrick, Jr., *The Dormant Commerce Clause: The Origin Story and the "Considerable Uncertainties"—1824 to 1945*, 52 CREIGHTON L. REV. 243 (2019).

The Supreme Court Review, 2024.
© 2024 The University of Chicago. All rights reserved. Published by The University of Chicago Press. https://doi.org/10.1086/730768

is "clearly excessive in relation to the putative local benefits."[2] It has also appeared to invalidate under the DCC state laws that "control conduct beyond the boundaries of the State"—the so-called "extraterritoriality" test.[3]

An important case decided last Term, *National Pork Producers Council v. Ross*,[4] highlights the extraordinary uncertainties that persist in the proper application of these DCC principles. The basic question in *Ross* was whether California could, consistent with the DCC, ban the sale of pork meat in the state that is not sourced from a pig raised humanely by California standards. The petitioners in *Ross* claimed that the California animal welfare law violated the extraterritoriality prong of the DCC because it had a huge impact on the pork-production processes, it imposed other costs in other states, and it was in any event an excessive burden on interstate commerce.

This simple-sounding argument raised four hard questions. The first was whether "extraterritoriality" was a standalone DCC test at all, or instead simply a discrete application of the antidiscrimination or excessive-burden tests. A second question was how the Court should determine whether a state regulation excessively burdens interstate commerce—in the famous words of *Pike v. Bruce Church, Inc.*, whether "the burden imposed on such commerce is clearly excessive in relation to the putative local benefits."[5] The Court in recent decades has shied away from *Pike* balancing, in large part because it has questioned its competence to identify, assess, and balance the state law's benefits and burdens on interstate commerce. But *Ross* was the first DCC case ever decided by Justices Jackson, Barrett, and Kavanaugh, and the first by Justice Gorsuch to address *Pike* balancing, so the answer to these two central DCC issues for the current Court was unknown.

A third question raised by *Ross* was whether and how the so-called "California effect" implicates the DCC. The California effect occurs when a large state's relatively strict regulation becomes the de facto standard in other states because it is cheaper for producers serving other markets to comply with a large-state regulation than it is to withdraw from the large market or devise multiple production lines. The

---

[2] South Dakota v. Wayfair, Inc., 138 S. Ct. 2080, 2091 (2018) (quoting in part Pike v. Bruce Church, Inc., 397 U.S. 137, 142 (1970)).

[3] *See* Healy v. Beer Inst., 491 U.S. 324, 343 (1989).

[4] 598 U.S. 356 (2023).

[5] 397 U.S. at 142.

result can be that consumers in other states pay more for products due to the large-state regulation.⁶ The validity of laws challenged on this basis has never been directly addressed in Supreme Court DCC jurisprudence.

The fourth and most far-reaching question raised by *Ross* was whether California could regulate the sale of a product (pork) not based on its characteristics or quality, but rather on how it is produced in other jurisdictions. Such "process-based regulation" of goods produced in another jurisdiction raises concerns that have been much litigated in international trade law,⁷ but not in the Court's DCC jurisprudence.⁸ The answer to this question has enormous implications. For if California can prohibit importation of pork meat based on the process of pork production, it might also be able to ban products produced under other conditions with which its citizens disagree. At oral argument in *Ross*, for example, Justices asked whether a state could ban products made by undocumented immigrants, or in factories that don't comply with California environmental standards, or by firms that do not require vaccines or provide certain forms of healthcare.⁹ And commentators noted the various ways that, in a post-*Dobbs* world, a ruling for California might empower states to engage in trade wars centered on production processes tied to abortion.¹⁰

---

⁶ *See generally* DAVID VOGEL, TRADING UP: CONSUMER AND ENVIRONMENTAL REGULATION IN A GLOBAL ECONOMY (1995).

⁷ For an overview of the relevant cases in the context of the *Tuna-Dolphin* disputes, see generally David Sifonios & Andreas R. Ziegler, *"Tuna-Dolphin Forever"? The Development of the PPM Debate Related to Trade and Environment in the WTO*, 12 INDIAN J. INT'L ECON. L. 106 (2020). That dispute centered on the U.S. Marine Mammal Protection Act, which prohibited imports of tuna caught by fishing methods that pose an undue danger to dolphins in the view of the United States. Mexico challenged the law as discriminatory, claiming that Mexican tuna products were a target of discrimination because physically identical tuna produced by U.S. tuna fleets could lawfully be sold.

⁸ The closest the Court has come to addressing this issue appears to be two cases in the 1930s. *See* Kentucky Whip & Collar Co. v. Illinois Cent. R. Co., 299 U.S. 334 (1937); Whitfield v. Ohio, 297 U.S. 431 (1936). The Court in these cases held that federal statutes that authorized states to ban the import of prison-made goods from other states (*Kentucky Whip*) or in-state sale of goods made in prisons in other states (*Whitfield*) fell within Congress's power to regulate interstate commerce. The Court in both cases was unclear in its dicta whether the states could have regulated goods made from prison labor in other states via nondiscriminatory sales and import bans in the absence of the federal statutes.

⁹ Transcript of Oral Argument at 43–44, 97, 98, 99, Nat'l Pork Producers Council v. Ross, 598 U.S. 356 (2023) (No. 21-468).

¹⁰ *See, e.g.*, Mary Anne Pazanowski, *Top Court's Pork-Producer Ruling Could Affect Abortion-Pill Suit*, BLOOMBERG L. (May 22, 2023, 3:01 PM), https://news.bloomberglaw.com/health-law-and-business/genbiopro-west-virginia-address-top-court-commerce-clause-case.

The Supreme Court in *Ross* upheld the California animal welfare law but in so doing answered only the first of these questions, ruling unanimously that extraterritoriality was not a standalone DCC test. On the second question the Court fractured. There was no majority opinion on how to conceptualize *Pike* balancing or on the Court's competence to do the balancing. And on the important third and fourth questions, the Justices said very little, and nothing in a majority voice.

One explanation for the Court's confusion and reticence on these latter three questions is that it still lacks a settled normative vision of what the DCC is supposed to accomplish. The Court has long suggested that a primary justification for the DCC is an efficiency criterion: to ensure free trade and associated benefits in interstate transactions.[11] But it has never consistently or deeply operationalized the efficiency criterion. In this Article, building on earlier work,[12] we seek to do just that. We use the efficiency criterion as a normative account of the DCC that helps to conceptualize, clarify, and (in some respects) resolve the hard questions left open by *Ross*.[13] The efficiency rationale, we maintain, animates the two primary DCC tests (antidiscrimination and *Pike* balancing). We interpret *Pike* as calling for a variant of cost-benefit analysis that asks whether out-of-state costs clearly outweigh in-state benefits, and we contend that the antidiscrimination rule is a doctrinal "shortcut" for identifying cases that fail the *Pike* balancing test, so conceived.

From this point of departure, our major conclusions are as follows. First, the Court correctly ruled that a nondiscriminatory state law with extraterritorial effects violates the DCC only when it runs afoul of *Pike* balancing (effectively extinguishing "extraterritoriality" as a separate test under the DCC). Second, the extraterritorial effects of the California law due to California's large market raises potential efficiency concerns under *Pike*. These concerns can in theory be sorted

---

[11] *See, e.g.*, Dep't of Revenue v. Davis, 553 U.S. 328, 337–38 (2008); Bos. Stock Exch. v. State Tax Comm'n, 429 U.S. 318, 336 (1977); H.P. Hood & Sons, Inc. v. Du Mond, 336 U.S. 525, 532–33 (1949).

[12] Jack L. Goldsmith & Alan O. Sykes, *The Internet and the Dormant Commerce Clause*, 110 YALE L.J. 785 (2001) (cited in *Ross*, 598 U.S. at 374).

[13] We do not claim that efficiency is the only normative rationale for the DCC. *See infra* Part II. For other analyses of *Ross*, see Bradley W. Joondeph, *The 'Horizontal Separation of Powers' After* National Pork Producers Council v. Ross, 61 SAN DIEGO L. REV. (forthcoming 2024); Douglas A. Kysar, *State Public Morality Regulation and the Dormant Commerce Clause*, Yale Law School, Public Law Research Paper (forthcoming).

out by cost-benefit analysis, even in cases, like *Ross*, that involve process-based regulations. But whether the law actually fails the *Pike* test is a complicated empirical question. Third, and closely related, cost-benefit analysis under *Pike* is much more demanding than current judicial practice contemplates, and it cannot be done by federal courts with any rigor absent a sea change in the way they assess DCC problems. Fourth, due to the many complexities in *Pike* cost-benefit analysis, the Court should develop more targeted and less-demanding efficiency-based doctrinal tools to address the hard DCC issues left open in *Ross*. We suggest some options in this regard that draw on the law of international trade to flesh out some neglected corners of DCC jurisprudence.

Part I provides background about *Ross* and describes the Court's ruling. Part II sets forth an economic framework to help understand the hard issues raised in *Ross*. Part III uses this framework to analyze and critique *Ross*, and to seek to clarify and make progress on issues going forward that the Court did not resolve. A brief conclusion follows.

I. *Ross*

Ross came to the Court at a time of uncertainty in its DCC jurisprudence. The Court has settled on the antidiscrimination and "excessive burden" tests as the "two primary principles that mark the boundaries of a State's authority to regulate interstate commerce" under the DCC.[14] But it has seemed to narrow the antidiscrimination test in recent decades.[15] And it has grown skeptical, especially in tax cases, of its ability to identify, assess, and balance state-law burdens on interstate commerce.[16] There was also a question about the validity of the so-called extraterritoriality "prong" of the DCC. The Court decades ago had stated in dicta that state laws must fall under the DCC if the "practical effect ... is to control conduct beyond the boundaries of the State."[17] But it seemed to cast some doubt on this

---

[14] South Dakota v. Wayfair, Inc., 138 S. Ct. 2080, 2090 (2018).

[15] *See* Francis, *supra* note 1.

[16] *See, e.g.*, Dep't of Revenue v. Davis, 553 U.S. 328, 353, 355 (2008); United Haulers Ass'n v. Oneida-Herkimer Solid Waste Mgmt. Auth., 550 U.S. 330, 337 (2007) (plurality op.); Gen. Motors Corp. v. Tracy, 519 U.S. 278, 308 (1997).

[17] Healy v. Beer Inst., 491 U.S. 324, 336 (1989) (citations omitted); *see also id.* ("[T]he Commerce Clause ... precludes the application of a state statute to commerce that takes place wholly outside of the State's borders, whether or not the commerce has effects within

idea in 2003.[18] And many lower courts and commentators had claimed that there should be no "extraterritoriality" doctrine independent of the antidiscrimination or excessive-burden tests.[19]

Compounding this uncertainty was the fact that the Court's three newest Justices—Justices Kavanaugh, Barrett, and Jackson—had not ruled on a DCC issue in the lower courts and had not, prior to *Ross*, cast a meaningful vote in a DCC case at the Supreme Court. The public thus had little sense of their views on the DCC. And Justice Gorsuch, a notable DCC skeptic in the lower courts and in two prior Supreme Court DCC cases, had not yet weighed in with his views on *Pike* balancing.[20]

This was the context in which the Court considered the validity of Proposition 12, the law at issue in *Ross*, which passed by ballot initiative in 2018. Proposition 12 prohibits the sale in California of "[w]hole pork meat" by a business owner or operator who knows or should know that the meat came from breeding pigs that were confined "with less than 24 square feet of usable floorspace per pig," preventing them "from lying down, standing up, fully extending [their] limbs, or turning around freely."[21] Violations of Proposition 12 are punishable with fines up to $1,000, as many as 180 days in jail, or both, as well as civil penalties.[22] The proponents of Proposition 12 offered two main justifications for these rules: (1) eliminating animal

---

the State.") (also dicta) (citations omitted); Brown-Forman Distillers Corp. v. N.Y. State Liquor Auth., 476 U.S. 573 (1986); Edgar v. MITE Corp., 457 U.S. 624 (1982).

[18] *See* Pharm. Rsch. & Mfrs. of Am. v. Walsh, 538 U.S. 644, 669 (2003) (rejecting extraterritorial argument and seemingly limiting the doctrine to laws that "regulate the price of any out-of-state transaction, either by its express terms or by its inevitable effect").

[19] *See* Energy & Env't Legal Inst. v. Epel, 793 F.3d 1169, 1173–74 (10th Cir. 2015) (Gorsuch, J., majority op.); State v. Heckel, 24 P.3d 404, 411 (Wash. 2001); Nat'l Elec. Mfrs. Ass'n v. Sorrell, 272 F.3d 104, 108, 110 (2d Cir. 2001); Am. Beverage Ass'n v. Snyder, 735 F.3d 362, 379–81 (6th Cir. 2013) (Sutton, J., concurring); *see also* Jack Goldsmith & Eugene Volokh, *State Regulation of Online Behavior: The Dormant Commerce Clause and Geolocation*, 101 TEX. L. REV. 1083, 1090–93 (2023); Brannon P. Denning, *Extraterritoriality and the Dormant Commerce Clause: A Doctrinal Post-Mortem*, 73 LA. L. REV. 979, 979–80 (2013); Goldsmith & Sykes, *supra* note 12, at 804, 806.

[20] *See* Tenn. Wine & Spirits Retailers Ass'n v. Thomas, 139 S. Ct. 2449, 2478 (2019) (Gorsuch, J., dissenting); South Dakota v. Wayfair, Inc., 138 S. Ct. 2080, 2100–01 (2018); Direct Mktg. Ass'n v. Brohl, 814 F.3d 1129, 1148, 1150–51 (10th Cir. 2016) (Gorsuch, J., concurring); *Epel*, 793 F.3d at 1171.

[21] *See* Cal. Prop. 12, § 3(b), (e) (2018) (codified at CAL. HEALTH & SAFETY CODE §§ 25990(b), 25991(e) (2018)).

[22] CAL. HEALTH & SAFETY CODE § 25993(b) (2018).

products produced inhumanely from the California marketplace, and (2) protecting Californians from unsafe animal products.[23]

The National Pork Producers Council and the American Farm Bureau Federation sued various California officials on the ground that Proposition 12 violates the DCC.[24] They argued that Proposition 12 impermissibly regulated extraterritorial conduct because it "compel[ed] out-of-state producers to change their operations to meet California standards."[25] They also argued that the law failed *Pike* because it excessively burdened interstate commerce and served no local interest because it advanced no legitimate animal-welfare interest and addressed no legitimate health concern.[26] The district court rejected these claims, as did the court of appeals.[27] The court of appeals held that Proposition 12 did not run afoul of the extraterritoriality prong of the DCC because it did not dictate the price of out-of-state products or tie in-state prices to out-of-state ones.[28] It further held that any indirect "practical effect" on out-of-state practices and prices was not impermissibly extraterritorial.[29] And it rejected the argument that the alleged "cost increases to market participants and customers" by Proposition 12 amounted to "a substantial burden to interstate commerce."[30]

The Supreme Court affirmed.[31] In an opinion by Justice Gorsuch, the Court agreed on two major points. First, it stated that the "very core" of the DCC was the antidiscrimination principle that prohibits the enforcement of state laws "driven by ... 'economic protectionism—that is, regulatory measures designed to benefit in-state economic interests by burdening out-of-state competitors.'"[32] And second, it rejected

---

[23] *California General Election, November 6, 2018: Official Voter Information Guide, Proposition 12*, CAL. SEC'Y OF STATE, https://vigarchive.sos.ca.gov/2018/general/propositions/12/arguments-rebuttals.htm#top.

[24] Nat'l Pork Producers Council v. Ross, 6 F.4th 1021, 1025 (9th Cir. 2021), *cert. granted*, 142 S. Ct. 1413 (2022).

[25] *Id.*

[26] *Id.* at 1025–26.

[27] Nat'l Pork Producers Council v. Ross, 456 F. Supp. 3d 1201, 1210 (S.D. Cal. 2020); *Ross*, 6 F.4th at 1032 (affirming the district court's judgment).

[28] *Ross*, 6 F.4th at 1028.

[29] *Id.* at 1029.

[30] *Id.* at 1033.

[31] Nat'l Pork Producers Council v. Ross, 598 U.S. 356 (2023).

[32] *Id.* at 369 (internal quotations omitted).

petitioners' extraterritoriality argument by banishing a standalone "extraterritoriality doctrine" from DCC jurisprudence.[33] The Court noted that "in our interconnected national marketplace, many (maybe most) state laws have the 'practical effect of controlling' extraterritorial behavior."[34] It added that petitioners' extraterritoriality argument, if accepted, "would cast a shadow over laws long understood to represent valid exercises of the States' constitutionally reserved powers" and "would provide neither courts nor litigants with meaningful guidance in how to resolve disputes over them."[35] The Court distinguished the cases supposedly embracing the extraterritoriality doctrine as at bottom relying on the antidiscrimination principle, and not establishing an independent test.[36]

This left the Court to address petitioners' argument under *Pike* that the burdens on interstate commerce from the California law were excessive compared to its benefits. The Court explained that *Pike*'s core concern in assessing a state law's impact on interstate commerce was to smoke out a law's discriminatory purpose or impact—in other words, that many balancing cases were at bottom instances of the DCC's concern with discriminatory state laws.[37] Since petitioners had not alleged discrimination, their claim fell "well outside *Pike*'s heartland."[38] The Court acknowledged, however, that the *Pike* analysis is not limited to discriminatory burdens.[39] On this remaining component of *Pike* balancing—how to assess "excessive burdens" when, as in *Ross*, the state law does not discriminate—the Court sharply splintered.

The plurality opinion by Justice Gorsuch, joined by Justices Thomas, Sotomayor, and Kagan, maintained that petitioners had failed to state a successful claim under *Pike* because they had failed "to plead facts plausibly showing that" the California law "imposes 'substantial burdens' on interstate commerce."[40] The plurality compared Proposition 12 to the Maryland law at issue in *Exxon Corp. v. Governor*

---

[33] *Id.* at 371.
[34] *Id.* at 374.
[35] *Id.* at 375.
[36] *Id.* at 371.
[37] *Id.* at 377–80.
[38] *Id.* at 380.
[39] *Id.* at 379.
[40] *Id.* at 383 (plurality op.). The plurality opinion was Part IV.C.

of Maryland,⁴¹ which barred oil producers from operating retail gas stations in the state. Drawing on language in *Exxon* that the DCC doesn't protect "particular ... firms" or "particular structure[s] or methods of operation," the plurality suggested that the costs to out-of-state producers of complying with California law (either fully, or through production segregation), or of withdrawing from the California market, were not cognizable harms under *Pike*.⁴² The plurality additionally suggested that the petitioners' claim failed under *Pike* because it did not adequately allege that out-of-state consumers will face increased prices for pork products.⁴³

The four-Justice plurality opinion almost certainly represents the Court's holding regarding the *Pike* issue in *Ross* because it is the "position taken by those Members who concurred in the judgments on the narrowest grounds...."⁴⁴ The other opinion in support of the judgment—also by Justice Gorsuch, joined by Justices Thomas and Barrett—concluded that the DCC did not authorize judges to invalidate state laws based on an assessment of their costs and benefits, and that the Court lacks competence to do so in any event.⁴⁵ This is a much broader ground for the judgment—as Justice Kavanaugh noted in dissent, it "would essentially overrule the *Pike* balancing test"—and thus is not controlling.⁴⁶

And yet the plurality opinion in *Ross* left open many of the most important questions going forward about *Pike* balancing and the DCC more generally. Although the Court affirmed the Ninth Circuit's judgment that petitioners had not stated a claim under *Pike*,

---

⁴¹ 437 U.S. 117 (1978).

⁴² 598 U.S. at 383–85.

⁴³ *Id.* at 385–86.

⁴⁴ Marks v. United States, 430 U.S. 188, 193 (1977); *see also* 598 U.S. at 356 (Kavanaugh, J., concurring in part and dissenting in part) (concluding that "Part IV–C of Justice GORSUCH's opinion is controlling precedent for purposes of the Court's judgment as to the plaintiffs' *Pike* claim"). The Court has been inconsistent in adhering to the *Marks* rule, Richard M. Re, *Beyond the* Marks *Rule*, 132 Harv. L. Rev. 1942, 1952 (2019), and sometimes declines to apply it. *See* Grutter v. Bollinger, 539 U.S. 306 (2003); Nichols v. United States, 511 U.S. 738 (1994).

⁴⁵ 598 U.S. at 380–83. Justice Gorsuch's opinion for three Justices noted that the California law was particularly hard to assess under petitioners' conception of *Pike* balancing because the competing (economic) costs and (moral) benefits were "incommensurable." *Id.* at 382. In her concurrence, Justice Barrett took a softer line on *Pike* than the three-judge opinion she joined. She accepted that *Pike* balancing was possible to flesh out discrimination but stated that none of the *Pike* precedents require balancing of incommensurable goods. *Id.* at 393–94.

⁴⁶ *See* 598 U.S. at 403 (Kavanaugh, J., concurring in part and dissenting in part).

the Justices disagreed among themselves about why the claim was deficient, and at least six Justices did not question the general viability of *Pike* balancing.[47] It is unclear how these Justices will apply *Pike* in a future case.[48] And while the plurality's discussion of *Exxon* was noteworthy, as we explain below, the plurality ultimately decided very little in *Ross* even about the ultimate validity of Proposition 12. The Court disposed of the case on the pleadings and acknowledged that "[f]urther experience may yield further facts" related to the impact of Proposition 12 that could lead to a valid *Pike* claim.[49]

More broadly, the Justices disagreed sharply on their competence to do *Pike* balancing without resolving when and how such balancing is appropriate.[50] Justice Gorsuch's three-judge opinion in support of the judgment ruled out the notion—alluded to in Justice Kavanaugh's sole dissent and central to the California effect—that California's large market share might invite special scrutiny under the DCC.[51] But the other Justices declined to weigh in on the California effect. Similarly, Justice Kavanaugh's dissent raised the process-based regulation problem squarely, but none of the other Justices addressed the point, even though it was prominent at oral argument.[52]

---

[47] Chief Justice Roberts, writing for four Justices, disagreed with the plurality's reasoning and argued that petitioners stated a *Pike* claim. *Id.* at 398–402 (Roberts, C.J., concurring in part and dissenting in part). Justice Sotomayor, joined by Justice Kagan, accepted the validity of *Pike* but concluded that petitioners had not stated a *Pike* claim. *Id.* at 392–93. The views of a seventh Justice, Justice Barrett, are hard to tally since she joined the part of Justice Gorsuch's opinion that argued for the elimination of *Pike* balancing but indicated in her own concurring opinion that she would continue to apply *Pike* balancing in cases involving commensurable goods. *Id.* at 394 (Barrett, J., concurring in part) ("If the burdens and benefits were capable of judicial balancing, I would permit petitioners to proceed with their *Pike* claim.").

[48] *See supra* note 44.

[49] 598 U.S. at 386–87 (plurality op.).

[50] While the three-judge opinion by Justice Gorsuch seemed to deny judicial competence (and legal authority) to do *Pike* balancing, six Justices disagreed, though they took different attitudes on the competence question. Chief Justice Roberts, for four Justices, stated that "a freewheeling judicial weighing of benefits and burdens" was inappropriate but denied that calculating benefits and burdens was "an impossible judicial task" and asserted that "sometimes there is no avoiding the need to weigh seemingly incommensurable values." *Id.* at 394–96 (Roberts, C.J., concurring in part and dissenting in part). Justice Sotomayor, in an opinion joined by Justice Kagan, took a similar view. *Id.* at 392–93 (Sotomayor, J., concurring in part).

[51] *See id.* at 388 (op. of Gorsuch, J.) (resisting the notion that "States with smaller markets are constitutionally entitled to greater authority to regulate in-state sales than voters in States with larger markets"); *id.* at 404–06 (Kavanaugh, J., concurring in part and dissenting in part) (acknowledging the California effect).

[52] Justice Kavanaugh noted that California was seeking to regulate based on its "moral and policy" preferences for pig farming and pork production, and asked: "[W]hat if a state law

In sum, the Court's unanimous rejection of a standalone extraterritoriality test was important, but despite many pages of analysis, the Court ultimately disposed of the case on a narrow fact-bound issue that leaves all of the hard DCC issues raised by the case—except for the now-rejected independent extraterritoriality test—for another day.

II. An Economic Primer: Protectionism, the California Effect, Process-Based Regulations, and Cost-Benefit Balancing

One reason why the Supreme Court failed to answer many of the questions raised by *Ross* is that it lacks a settled theory about how to resolve them. The Court has long suggested that the DCC should be seen through the lens of multi-jurisdictional economic efficiency, and it has long acknowledged that this efficiency rationale sometimes requires courts to balance the economic costs and benefits of state regulations. But the Court has not been clear on what types of costs generated by state regulation are of concern under the DCC. And while it has been skeptical at times about its capacity to balance costs and benefits, it has continued to insist that it can do so in theory, as *Ross* confirms, albeit without saying anything concrete about how balancing is supposed to work. These uncertainties left the Court with few normative tools to analyze the subtler questions raised in *Ross* about how to think about the California effect or the validity of process-based regulations.

This Part sets out an economic framework to help clarify the hard issues raised in *Ross*. In focusing on the economics, we do not claim that multi-jurisdictional economic efficiency is the sole normative concern of the DCC. The case law and the literature discuss virtual representation and correcting dysfunctions in the state legislative process, among others, as DCC rationales. But economic efficiency is clearly a central DCC concern, and the one we seek to elucidate. This Part and the remainder of the Article thus use the efficiency criterion to analyze *Ross*, to explain why the issues it raised are so hard, to clarify those issues, and to suggest how courts might resolve them.

---

prohibits the sale of fruit picked by noncitizens who are unlawfully in the country? ... What if a state law prohibits the sale of goods produced by workers paid less than $20 per hour? [And] what if a state law prohibits the retail sale of goods from producers that do not pay for employees' birth control or abortions?" *Id.* at 407.

A. SOURCES OF INEFFICIENCY

We posit that an important objective of the DCC is to promote efficiency on a multi-jurisdictional basis by constraining state policies that impose out-of-state costs that exceed the in-state benefits. But why would such inefficiencies arise in the first place? The answer follows from the "public choice" literature, which observes that government policies are the result of a political process in which affected interest groups are not equally well represented.[53] Policies that favor well-organized interest groups at the expense of poorly-organized or underrepresented interest groups can become politically viable even if the aggregate harm to the latter group exceeds the aggregate benefit to the former group.

A familiar example is the standard economic account of protectionist trade policy. Firms and workers may have high stakes in addressing import competition in their industry and may organize to influence policy by delivering votes and campaign contributions. Consumers in the industry may also have substantial aggregate stakes in the outcome of trade policy, but the effects of policy on individual consumers may be small and they may fail to organize. Protectionism that benefits firms and workers may thus emerge even if it is typically inefficient in the aggregate.

A second example—and one more directly pertinent to the DCC—arises because political actors tend to be responsive primarily to their own constituents, and will often exclude consideration of the effects of policy on outsiders. Thus, policymakers in jurisdiction A may be happy to permit activity within the jurisdiction that imposes considerable harm on citizens in jurisdiction B (perhaps firms in jurisdiction A emit pollution that causes harm in jurisdiction B, for example, or firms in jurisdiction A form a cartel that extracts exorbitant profits from consumers in jurisdiction B). In economic parlance, the policies in the first jurisdiction have important "externalities" for other jurisdictions. When policymakers ignore these harms to outsiders, they may embrace policies that are inefficient in a multi-jurisdictional sense even if they are efficient from the narrower perspective of their own citizens.

---

[53] The classic references are JAMES M. BUCHANAN & GORDON TULLOCK, THE CALCULUS OF CONSENT: LOGICAL FOUNDATIONS OF CONSTITUTIONAL DEMOCRACY (1962); MANCUR OLSON, THE LOGIC OF COLLECTIVE ACTION: PUBLIC GOODS AND THE THEORY OF GROUPS (Harvard Univ. Press 1971) (1965).

For these reasons, policies chosen by an individual U.S. state may be inefficient, either from the perspective of citizens in the state making policy or the broader perspective of the nation as a whole. To a degree, DCC doctrine addresses both versions of inefficiency, as we explain below. But we believe that the primary function of the DCC is to address the inefficiencies that arise when states ignore the harm done by their policies to outsiders. Indeed, in the absence of such outside harm, no outside party would have any reason to challenge state policy. And the overwhelming bulk of DCC cases involve challenges to state policies brought by out-of-state interests.

B. DISCRIMINATION/PROTECTIONISM

As noted, *Ross* confirms that a primary function of the DCC is to condemn state policies that discriminate against interstate commerce and insulate in-state firms from competition with out-of-state firms—classic "protectionism."[54] The centrality of protectionism in the DCC case law makes sense within an economic framework, as protectionism is generally inefficient for a state that employs it and almost invariably inefficient from a multi-jurisdictional perspective. Protectionism induces resources to move into local production when goods or services could be obtained from outside sources more cheaply, thus creating economic waste in the production process. It also causes increased prices for consumers that induce some of them to exit the market when they would benefit from participating in the market at lower prices. Protectionism thereby leads to a reduction in overall economic welfare in states that engage in it most of the time because the costs to in-state consumers are greater than the benefits to the protected in-state producers.[55] It represents a paradigm example of a policy that is nevertheless politically viable in many settings because the beneficiaries (local firms and workers) tend to be well organized and the losers (local consumers) tend to be poorly organized.

If all efficiency costs due to protectionism were borne in the protectionist state, however, other jurisdictions would be indifferent to

---

[54] This is also well accepted in the literature. *See* Donald H. Regan, *The Supreme Court and State Protectionism: Making Sense of the Dormant Commerce Clause*, 84 MICH. L. REV. 1091 (1986).

[55] There are a few caveats to this proposition depending on the way that protection is applied and the industries that benefit from it. *See, e.g.*, PAUL R. KRUGMAN ET AL., INTERNATIONAL TRADE: THEORY AND POLICY 269–76 (12th ed. 2022).

it. Indeed, protectionism does not always harm outsiders. When an economically "small' jurisdiction imposes a tariff, for example, such that the tariff passes through in full to its own consumers, prices elsewhere will be unaffected. Producers in other jurisdictions can replace lost sales at the same price elsewhere, and outsiders suffer no harm. In this limited case, the inefficiency of protectionism is borne entirely by the protectionist jurisdiction.[56]

But quite commonly, protectionism also imposes harm on outsiders. When the protectionist jurisdiction is "large"—in the sense that outside sellers cannot easily replace the resulting lost sales or revenues by redirecting sales elsewhere—protectionism reduces the profits of outside sellers (or more precisely, their "producer surplus," which may be shared with other entities, such as their workers). This phenomenon explains why, for example, foreign sellers reacted to the tariffs imposed by the Trump administration on steel and aluminum by persuading their governments to retaliate and encouraging them to file dispute proceedings at the World Trade Organization ("WTO"). This harm borne by outsiders when a "large" country engages in protectionism is an example of the "terms-of-trade externality" that we discuss further below. Because of this harm to outsiders, protectionism is almost always inefficient in a multi-jurisdictional sense even if it might benefit the jurisdiction that imposes it.[57]

The DCC prohibition on discrimination/protectionism can thus be viewed as a doctrinal "shortcut" for identifying cases that fail the *Pike* balancing test. It avoids the challenge of directly measuring the local and out-of-state costs and benefits of state policies by identifying an important class of cases that theory suggests will fail the balancing test almost always. In later sections, we will suggest some additional doctrinal "shortcuts" that avoid the need for full-scale *Pike* balancing.

C. INEFFICIENCY IN THE ABSENCE OF DISCRIMINATION/
PROTECTIONISM: THE BROADER PROBLEM OF INTERSTATE
EXTERNALITIES

Although concerns with protectionism and discrimination are central to DCC jurisprudence, they do not exhaust it. *Ross* itself is a case in which the plaintiffs did not allege discrimination or protectionism.

---

[56] *See id.* at 269–70.
[57] See the discussion of the "optimum tariff" in *id.* at 272–73.

The standards contained in California Proposition 12 apply equally to pork producers inside and outside California. Moreover, pork production in California is negligible and there is virtually no local pork industry to protect.[58]

Such cases are hard cases under the DCC. They span a broad range of tax and regulatory policies in many different settings, and we cannot hope in this Article to offer a comprehensive treatment of all the scenarios that can arise. Instead, our focus is narrower and tailored to the class of cases typified by *Ross*, where a large and important market for out-of-state producers imposes a regulation providing that all goods of a certain class sold within the jurisdiction must meet a particular regulatory standard regardless of where they are produced (thus, the regulation is nondiscriminatory by assumption). The fact that the market is large and important to out-of-state sellers captures the "California effect" which, as shall be seen, has important implications for the impact of regulation on outsiders.

In addition, because the U.S. pork market is an agricultural market with many producers scattered around the country, we will focus on issues that arise in competitive industries and leave aside economic complications that arise when the regulated industry exhibits imperfect competition.[59] Further, because the issues in *Ross* concern the burden on out-of-state pork producers who export to California and their customers, rather than restrictions on California pork producers who export to other states, we focus on the economic issues associated with the regulation of imports rather than those involving the regulation of exports.[60] Toward the end of our analysis, we add some additional

---

[58] No party made the argument that the objective of the law was to promote a nascent California pork industry. Likewise, no party argued that the purpose of the law was to promote the business interests of in-state producers of substitute products such as beef.

[59] In imperfectly competitive industries, several types of externalities that we do not address in the text can result from government intervention affecting trade flows. These include "profit-shifting" externalities, local knowledge spillovers, and delocation externalities. *See, e.g.*, KRUGMAN ET AL., *supra* note 55, at ch. 12; Anthony Venables, *Trade and Trade Policy with Imperfect Competition: The Case of Identical Products and Free Entry*, 19 J. INT'L ECON. 1, 16–17 (1985); Gene M. Grossman et al., *The "New" Economics of Trade Agreements: From Trade Liberalization to Regulatory Convergence?*, 89 ECONOMETRICA 215, 247 (2021).

[60] Regulatory intervention with respect to exports can also produce important externalities that we do not address in the text. A state with a large share of the supply of some important product (such as low sulfur coal) can restrict the volume of exports to jack up the price, and thereby earn monopoly profits. *See* Saul Levmore, *Interstate Exploitation and Judicial Intervention*, 69 VA. L. REV. 563, 571 (1983). Likewise, if a state controls a substantial share of the input product into some downstream processing industry, restrictions on export of that input

thoughts on cases where the regulatory standard concerns the process by which the good is produced, as opposed to physical characteristics of the final good itself.

Our starting point is the observation that regulatory heterogeneity is not tantamount to regulatory inefficiency. When different jurisdictions have differing regulatory standards and sellers serve multiple jurisdictions, compliance costs for sellers will often be greater than they would be if all jurisdictions had the same standard. But heterogeneous standards are often efficient.[61] Efficiency depends in part on the preferences and incomes of citizens in each jurisdiction, which are themselves heterogeneous across jurisdictions. The benefits that the citizens of a jurisdiction gain from a regulation, and the regulatory costs they are willing to absorb, will often be different, and so too will optimal regulatory standards from their perspective. This observation suggests why optimal regulatory policies often differ geographically, and why regulatory uniformity is not necessarily desirable.[62]

Nevertheless, the policies chosen by a regulating jurisdiction may be inefficient for the reasons given earlier; affected interest groups may be poorly organized or underrepresented in policy formulation. In the remainder of this section, we will put aside the attendant possibility that regulation actually harms the state that enacts it and assume that the DCC is not concerned with such cases. No one argued in *Ross*, for example, that California's regulation should be overturned because it is harmful on balance to Californians. Instead, we limit ourselves to the issue that lies at the center of *Pike* balancing: When is the harm to outsiders so great as to warrant invalidating a regulation despite its putative benefit to the regulating state?

With the analysis cabined in this fashion, we suggest that two potentially important channels of injury to outsiders are in play in cases such as *Ross*, both of which lead to the possibility of multi-jurisdictional

---

can lower prices locally and increase prices abroad, thereby favoring the growth of the local downstream industry at the expense of the foreign downstream industry.

[61] *See* ALAN O. SYKES, PRODUCT STANDARDS FOR INTERNATIONALLY INTEGRATED GOODS MARKETS (1995).

[62] Goldsmith & Sykes, *supra* note 12, at 796–97; *see also* WALLACE E. OATES, FISCAL FEDERALISM, 11–13, 54–63 (1972) (providing a theoretical treatment); Michael W. McConnell, *Federalism: Evaluating the Founders' Design*, 54 U. CHI. L. REV. 1484, 1504 (1987) (applying the theory to the American federal context); Alan O. Sykes, *The (Limited) Role of Regulatory Harmonization in International Goods and Services Markets*, 2 J. INT'L ECON. L. 49 (1999) (applying the theory to the international context).

inefficiency. The two channels involve a price effect known as the "terms-of-trade"[63] externality, mentioned earlier in our discussion of protectionism, and a "production-cost" externality affecting the cost and price of goods sold in outside markets. It bears emphasis that these externalities do *not* depend on the existence of regulatory discrimination or protectionism. After discussing the two externalities, we further explain why the existence of such negative externalities does not necessarily establish multi-jurisdictional inefficiency. That depends on the overall balance of costs and benefits associated with regulation, measured against some appropriate counterfactual benchmark (such as no regulation, previous levels of regulation, or incrementally different levels of regulation).

1. *The Terms-of-Trade Externality.* To understand the terms-of-trade externality, it is essential to distinguish between a "small" jurisdiction and a "large" jurisdiction. A "small" jurisdiction is defined as a jurisdiction that supplies a small component of the overall demand for a product produced by outside sellers, such that fluctuations in its total purchases do not materially impact the price of the product received by outsiders. It is essentially a "price taker," much as a firm in a perfectly competitive industry is assumed to lack the ability to influence market price. When a small jurisdiction imposes a regulation that requires outside sellers to incur some compliance cost, that compliance cost is passed along in full to its consumers in the form of higher prices, and outside sellers suffer no harm.

By contrast, in a "large" jurisdiction, the collective purchases of its consumers have an impact on the prices that outside sellers can command for their goods.[64] When demand for those goods declines in a large market, outside sellers cannot replace lost sales with sales elsewhere at the same price. Consequently, those sellers will reduce their prices to cushion the loss of revenue from a drop in demand and suffer a loss of profits (which may harm the suppliers of their input products as well, such as workers).

---

[63] The terms of trade in international economics refers to the ratio of the price of the goods that a jurisdiction imports to the price of the goods that it exports. If import prices decrease in relative terms, or if export prices increase, the "terms of trade" improve and the nation benefits. Opposite movements reduce the terms of trade and harm the trading nation.

[64] More formally, a "large" market is a market that faces an upward sloping supply curve from outside sellers. One may also say that in a "large" market, its consumers collectively have a degree of monopsony power.

In such markets, government policies that cause a reduction in demand for outside goods create the "terms-of-trade externality." If the government imposes a tariff on outside goods, for example, sellers will lower their prices and absorb some of the tariff; only part of the tariff passes through to consumers. Similarly, if the government imposes a regulation that requires costly expenditures on compliance, an attempt by sellers to pass those costs along to consumers will cause a reduction in sales, and prices will decline in response to the drop in demand. Outside sellers thus absorb some of the regulatory compliance cost by reducing their prices (net of regulatory compliance costs) and do not pass the higher costs on to consumers in full.[65]

When this type of externality arises, the associated direction of policy distortion is intuitive. Just as a polluter who need not pay the cost of pollution will tend to pollute excessively from a social standpoint, a regulating jurisdiction that does not bear the full costs of the regulation it imposes may tend to over-regulate. This problem will arise when the regulating jurisdiction captures the benefits associated with regulation, but the costs are borne in part by others.[66]

The magnitude of any over-regulation, of course, will depend on the degree to which compliance costs can be externalized. The larger is the share of outside goods in the regulated market, the greater will be the magnitude of the externality. If domestic firms produce most of the goods in question, for example, they will bear the bulk of regulatory compliance costs. Conversely, the potential for externalization of those costs is greater when outsiders supply most of the market.

The extent of cost externalization will also depend on the "elasticity of supply" from foreign producers, as well as the ability of other markets to absorb additional sales from those sellers.[67] The latter factor is plainly affected by the size of the regulating jurisdiction in

---

[65] With reference to the definition of the terms of trade given earlier, regulation lowers the price of imports (net of compliance costs), and in that sense results in an improvement of the terms of trade relative to its pre-regulation level.

[66] Robert W. Staiger & Alan O. Sykes, *International Trade, National Treatment, and Domestic Regulation*, 40 J. Legal Stud. 149, 201–02 (2011).

[67] In a simple supply and demand diagram, the elasticity of supply in a competitive industry captures the steepness of the supply curve—how much production increases as price increases. If supply is relatively "inelastic," the curve is steep and a decline in demand will cause a large drop in price because production does not decline much. The drop in price following regulation also depends on the ability of sellers to turn to other markets to absorb additional sales when demand declines in the regulating jurisdiction. The ability of sellers to redirect sales to other markets is captured by the elasticity of demand in those markets. Collectively,

relation to the size of other potential markets for the goods in question. The bigger the market of the regulating jurisdiction in relation to the markets elsewhere, the greater the terms-of-trade externality is likely to be, and the greater the tendency toward over-regulation. This observation suggests a clear connection between the terms-of-trade externality and the "California effect."

Finally, the degree of any over-regulation will depend on the nature of the regulation. If the level of regulation varies continuously, such as the level of a residue standard in a foodstuff stated in parts per million, even a small externality can induce somewhat excessive regulation "at the margin." If the nature of regulation requires a discrete choice between, say, substantial regulation or no regulation—such as a decision to admit unlimited beef imports or ban them altogether from a jurisdiction in which mad cow disease has been detected—then even though a terms-of-trade externality alters the parochial calculus regarding optimal regulation, it may not alter the (discrete) regulatory policy choice and thus need not cause inefficiency.

2. *The Production-Cost Externality.* The terms-of-trade externality flows through the prices that foreign sellers receive for the goods that they sell in the regulating jurisdiction. Another type of externality arises when regulation affects the production costs for goods that are sold in other jurisdictions, thus affecting their prices. It can be felt by foreign sellers whose costs increase and who, as a result, earn smaller profits from their sales in other jurisdictions. Or it may be felt by foreign consumers who must pay higher prices for goods that they purchase, even if they do not value the product characteristic that results in higher costs and prices. Input suppliers, such as workers, may also suffer losses due to a decline in demand for inputs to produce goods for sale in other jurisdictions.

To elaborate, many products can be made in different "varieties," having somewhat different characteristics that appeal to different segments of consumer demand. And each variety of a product may have its own cost structure. In such markets, cost and demand considerations will determine how many varieties an industry produces when left to its own devices. A tradeoff can arise between producing more

---

these factors determine the elasticity of the "import supply curve" for the regulating jurisdiction. A highly elastic (flat) import supply curve is associated with minimal terms-of-trade externality, while steeper curves lead to greater levels of externality.

varieties to satisfy different consumer segments, which may entail higher unit costs and prices, or fewer varieties, with less ability to satisfy different consumer segments but lower unit costs and prices. The tradeoff may result from the fact that each variety has a substantial fixed cost associated with it that needs to be recouped, so that unit costs (and breakeven prices) decline as the output of each variety increases. Or the tradeoff may result from increasing variable costs associated with the production of more varieties.

Against this backdrop, consider a market consisting of producers spread across multiple jurisdictions and suppose that one jurisdiction enacts a regulation prohibiting the sale of an existing variety and requiring a new variety to be produced for sale in that jurisdiction. How will the market react? We suggest three general possibilities.

One possibility is that some producers will begin producing the new variety, while the old variety continues to be produced for other jurisdictions. For example, some jurisdiction might decree that a certain type of genetically modified corn may not be sold or imported, and corn growers may then shift to other varieties for sale in that jurisdiction while continuing to sell the genetically modified variety elsewhere. In this scenario, the effect of regulation on the costs of production for goods sold outside the regulating jurisdiction is likely to be small.

A second possibility is that producers find it uneconomical to produce the new variety because of higher production cost and insufficient demand, so that the insistence of the regulating jurisdiction on a new variety leads outside firms to withdraw from its market.[68] Such an outcome is illustrated by the initial situation in the celebrated *Beef Hormones* dispute in the WTO between European Community on the one hand and the United States and Canada on the other. The European Communities introduced a regulation prohibiting the sale of beef from animals raised with certain growth hormones that were widely used by North American producers. When the European regulation was introduced, it was too costly for U.S. and Canadian producers to maintain segregated herds of animals, keep the meat from

---

[68] Notice that in this case, foreign producers are not absorbing a portion of the regulatory compliance cost (because they are not selling the new variety at all), so the terms-of-trade externality is absent. Likewise, their costs are not affected by the need to produce the new variety. This case thus appears to be one in which both externalities are absent, and the outcome is efficient, assuming that the regulation yields efficiencies within the regulating jurisdiction.

hormone-free animals segregated at packing facilities, and prove that the beef was hormone-free to the satisfaction of EC regulators. Consequently, most U.S. and Canadian ranchers were unable to comply with the EC regulation at reasonable cost and they stopped exporting to Europe. Here, too, although the North American producers were upset at the loss of the European market, their costs of production for beef produced for sale elsewhere were largely unaffected. If anything, the loss of European demand might have led to lower beef prices in North American markets accompanied by a lower cost of inputs into beef production.

A third possibility, related to the notion of the "large" jurisdiction developed above, is that the regulating jurisdiction is so important to the overall market that producers cannot economically withdraw from its market. Yet, the costs associated with producing multiple varieties may be so high that only one variety can be economically produced.[69] The result may be that many or even all producers switch to the new variety required by the regulating jurisdiction, and consumers in other jurisdictions lose the opportunity to purchase the variety(ies) that they had been purchasing before. This scenario has been labeled the "California effect" by other commentators to explain how some of that State's pollution abatement regulations became the *de facto* standard for cars sold in other states.[70] It also reflects the core idea behind Anu

---

[69] Equivalently, it may be uneconomical to produce multiple versions of any variety. It may not make economic sense, for example, to produce one type of low-polluting Chevrolet Impala for the California market and another version of the Chevrolet Impala for other states. And given the importance of California consumers to General Motors, the company may find that it maximizes its profit producing a single version that complies with California regulations to be sold everywhere, rather than to abandon efforts to sell the Chevrolet Impala in California and produce the car exclusively for other markets. As a result, consumers in other states may lose the opportunity to purchase a less expensive version of the Impala.

Implicit in this story is a suggestion that the production-cost externality increases nonlinearly with the size of the regulating jurisdiction. If a small state wishes to regulate more stringently than others, it will typically have to bear the full incremental cost of regulatory compliance as some producers create a custom variety for that state and pass along the costs to its consumers. The products sold elsewhere continue to be produced by firms operating at a scale sufficient to achieve the minimum production cost, or close to it, so that prices elsewhere are little affected. But as the regulating jurisdiction becomes larger and larger, unit production costs for the varieties sold elsewhere rise considerably as the amount of production for other markets declines. Fixed costs are spread over a significantly smaller level of output and important scale economies may be lost. At a certain point, producers find that they can do better by producing one variety to be sold everywhere rather than incur the additional fixed costs and loss of scale economies associated with producing multiple varieties.

[70] *See* VOGEL, *supra* note 6.

Bradford's suggestion that product standards enacted in Europe will often be universally adopted.[71]

To the degree that regulation creates a production-cost externality, the possible direction of policy distortion is again intuitive. If the regulating jurisdiction does not bear the cost of its regulation on out-of-state actors, it may tend to overregulate, adopting regulation that yields a net benefit in state but conceivably reducing overall economic welfare once all out-of-state costs and benefits are considered.

3. *"Trade" Versus "Investment" Externalities.* Our focus above is on the externalities that regulation in one jurisdiction may impose on producers in other jurisdictions who sell goods in the regulating jurisdiction. But there is another type of potential "externality" that befalls *citizens* from other jurisdictions who have economic interests in the regulating jurisdiction. To take the facts of *Ross* as an illustration, suppose that California Proposition 12 causes an increase in pork prices in California. As a result, in-state California distributors of wholesale pork products lose sales and profits. Suppose further that those distributors are owned primarily by out-of-state investors. It is certainly possible that regulators in a jurisdiction may ignore the costs of their policies to out-of-state investors just as they ignore that harm to out-of-state producers, resulting in a further reason why regulation may impose harm on outsiders that exceeds the local benefit.

The distinction here can be framed as one between "trade" externalities and "investment" externalities. Although both are potentially important, we suggest that trade externalities should be the primary concern of the DCC. Even when in-state firms are owned by out-of-state investors, their workers are typically local, they generally pay local taxes of various sorts, and they are in a better position to participate in the local political process than firms with no local presence. For this reason, we suspect that externalities relating to investment are less important and less likely to distort local policy.

Our intuition is confirmed to a degree by the contrast between international trade agreements and international investment agreements. International trade agreements have evolved to place numerous constraints on the regulatory policies of importing countries that are nondiscriminatory but nonetheless burden international commerce

---

[71] ANU BRADFORD, THE BRUSSELS EFFECT: HOW THE EUROPEAN UNION RULES THE WORLD (2020).

unnecessarily.[72] The constraints on regulatory policy in investment agreements are considerably more limited and do not often extend much beyond a commitment to nondiscrimination against foreign investors ("national treatment"). Similarly, we would expect DCC jurisprudence to exhibit greater concern for policies that burden outside producers than for policies that burden in-state firms that happen to be owned by outside investors. Indeed, it would seem peculiar if the strength of a DCC claim were to turn on the geographic ownership structure of in-state regulated entities.

D. THE ROLE OF COST-BENEFIT BALANCING AND ITS CHALLENGES

As noted, the existence of terms-of-trade or production-cost externalities does *not* establish that the regulation that caused the externalities is inefficient in the aggregate relative to the absence of regulation. Such externalities may lead to systematic over-regulation in economic models where regulatory standards are continuous variables set at parochially optimal levels using careful optimization methods,[73] but real-world regulation is often lumpy and chosen by political actors that are not engaged in mathematical optimization. In such settings, therefore, the in-state benefits of regulation may be greater than the out-of-state costs even in the presence of important externalities.[74] The efficiency determination thus requires empirical scrutiny of the costs and benefits of the state regulation to all affected parties, in-state and out-of-state, before any definitive efficiency judgment can be made.

Cost-benefit analysis is widely used to aid decisions in government and the private sector and is the subject of an enormous literature that we will not review here. It seeks to identify and quantify the costs and benefits of some change in behavior, such as a new public policy, usually relative to the status quo ante, and thereafter to ascertain

---

[72] Beyond the nondiscrimination principles associated with the national treatment obligation, these other principles may be found in agreements on regulatory or "technical barriers" to trade, such as the WTO Agreement on Technical Barriers to Trade and the Agreement on Sanitary and Phytosanitary Measures. Some of these principles might be viewed as aimed at *de facto* discrimination not adequately policed by the national treatment obligation alone. Others may be viewed as targeting nondiscriminatory measures that impose unnecessary compliance costs in relation to the regulatory goal. We touch on some of these principles below.

[73] *See* Staiger & Sykes, *supra* note 66.

[74] *See* Goldsmith & Sykes, *supra* note 12.

whether the benefits exceed the costs or vice-versa. To make the costs and benefits comparable, the analysis generally undertakes to place a monetary value on all costs and benefits. This exercise is straightforward when all relevant costs and benefits are monetary at the outset, but it is often extended to issues that are not normally valued in money or directly priced in a market, such as the statistical risk of death or injury from some type of accident, the value to society of clean water, or the harm due to carbon emissions.[75] Notwithstanding the challenges and uncertainties with placing monetary values on such concerns, cost-benefit analysis is extensively utilized and in fact legally required in many policy settings.[76]

When cost-benefit analysis is undertaken by a government, the usual goal is to encompass all relevant costs and benefits to society—that is, as an empirical effort to identify efficient policies. It is thus of obvious relevance to the multi-jurisdictional efficiency objective of the DCC. Indeed, *Pike*'s requirement that courts assess whether "the burden imposed on [interstate] commerce [by a state regulation] is clearly excessive in relation to the putative local benefits" is best interpreted as a call for cost-benefit analysis in DCC cases that cannot be resolved through simpler rules such as a blanket prohibition on protectionism or discrimination.[77]

One distinction between the analysis called for by *Pike* and a conventional cost-benefit inquiry is that *Pike* favors the defendant in close cases. The defendant should prevail if the burdens of regulation are not "clearly excessive" in relation to the benefits. This principle might be seen as an implicit acknowledgement that cost-benefit balancing can be difficult and inconclusive at times, coupled with a preference for state regulatory autonomy under such circumstances.

A second distinction lies in the fact that *Pike* does not explicitly call for society-wide cost-benefit balancing, but a balancing of "local benefits" with the "burden on interstate commerce." Is multi-jurisdictional cost-benefit analysis the same thing? We submit that the answer should be yes in part. We interpret *Pike* as asking whether the

---

[75] *See, e.g.*, Matthew D. Adler & Eric A. Posner, *Rethinking Cost-Benefit Analysis*, 109 YALE L.J. 165 (1999); Cass R. Sunstein, *The Real World of Cost-Benefit Analysis: Thirty-Six Questions (and Almost as Many Answers)*, 114 COLUM. L. REV. 167 (2014).

[76] *See* Sunstein, *supra* note 75, at 172–75, for the discussion of requirements imposed by the U.S. Office of Management and Budget.

[77] Pike v. Bruce Church, Inc., 397 U.S. 137, 142 (1970).

net benefits of regulation to the regulating state are clearly outweighed by the net costs to outsiders because of externalities. But note here a difference between a conventional cost-benefit analysis, such as the analysis that would typically be undertaken by a federal agency, and the analysis required by *Pike*. The former analysis would not worry about the locus of costs and benefits and would simply undertake to compute the value of all the costs incurred nationwide to comply with a state regulation and weigh them against all the benefits of the regulation nationwide. It would not be necessary to separate in-state benefits from out-of-state costs. The requirement to separate them complicates matters significantly.

To take *Ross* as an example, a conventional cost-benefit analysis would compare the costs to pork producers of complying with Proposition 12 nationwide with the benefits of improved animal welfare and (purportedly) animal health nationwide. It would make no difference whether the costs of compliance were borne by producers or passed along to consumers and no difference whether benefits arose in state or out of state. In contrast, *Pike* seems to require (for simplicity, assume no pork producers in California) a net calculation of benefits to California residents (benefits from compliance less increased cost of pork sold in state) and a net calculation of costs to out-of-state citizens (benefits of compliance less lost profits to out-of-state producers and increased pork prices to out-of-state consumers). Only then can one assess whether the out-of-state net costs are "clearly excessive."[78]

Another potential distinction between *Pike* and cost-benefit analysis by a government agency is that the agency will often be asked to identify the most cost-effective regulation from a menu of possible choices. Again with reference to *Ross*, there are perhaps many ways in which pork producers might enhance the animal welfare of pigs, of which the space requirements in Proposition 12 are but one option. *Pike* seems to envision a comparison between the chosen regulation and its absence, other things being equal, and thus seemingly foregoes any inquiry into the possibility of more cost-effective alternatives (although we touch below on the possible utility of attention to less restrictive alternatives).

---

[78] The reader may object that we have omitted to mention certain costs and benefits of a "general equilibrium" nature. For example, if pork prices increase, how does that affect producers of substitutes such as beef and chicken, and are those effects in state or out of state? A complete accounting of all possible effects of regulatory policy would often be a Herculean undertaking, and in practice the analysis is often limited to the most directly affected entities.

Finally, whether or not one undertakes the separation of in-state and out-of-state effects seemingly required by *Pike*, the analysis will confront measurement problems of the sort routinely encountered in cost-benefit assessments. The monetary costs of compliance with regulation will often be uncertain and subject to dispute, and some process must be devised to gather evidence of the issue and to resolve conflicts in the evidence.

The challenges are greater yet when the benefits or costs of regulation involve matters, such as in *Ross*, that are not immediately measurable in money, including health, safety, environmental quality, and so on. Various techniques have been devised to overcome the challenges of monetization. Inferences about the value of human safety may be drawn, for example, from labor-market evidence about the wage premium for risky jobs or how much the legislature is willing to spend to improve highway safety.[79] The value of moral or aesthetic benefits might be assessed by asking a sample of citizens about their willingness to pay for such things (or the amount they would demand to give them up).[80] These valuation methods are often controversial. It is often questionable, for example, whether survey respondents are motivated to think carefully about their answers or to tell the truth about their views.

In short, *Pike* appears to demand a form of cost-benefit analysis, yet such analysis is challenging, and its accuracy often in doubt to a greater or lesser degree depending on the complexity of the measurement problems. In principle, a court confronted with a DCC challenge could do something approaching what agencies do. It could take expert testimony addressing the cost-benefit balance, drawing on industry insiders and economists to develop a thorough record and forecast of in-state and out-of-state effects. We can imagine both sides presenting extensive economic evidence, and courts then assessing the strength of the evidence on each side much as it does in other contexts involving hard economic questions (such as rule of reason cases under the antitrust laws).

But such an approach is time-consuming, expensive, and has a high risk of error. Perhaps this is why courts invoking *Pike* balancing do not take seriously the demand to analyze and balance the benefits

---

[79] *See, e.g.*, W. Kip Viscusi, *How to Value a Life*, 32 J. ECON. & FIN. 311 (2008).

[80] For a survey, *see* Francisco Guijarro & Prodromos Tsinaslanidis, *Analysis of Academic Literature on Environmental Valuation*, 17 INT'L J. ENV'T RSCH. & PUB. HEALTH 2386 (2020).

and burdens of laws challenged under the DCC. We reach this conclusion based on observation of the major Supreme Court *Pike* balancing cases, and on a more thorough look at 105 district court DCC decisions involving *Pike* balancing over a five-year period.[81] With a handful of exceptions, district courts in these cases engage in, at best, a casual qualitative analysis of the parties' claims about the benefits and burdens of the state laws. Many district court judges elide the problem of balancing by placing a heavy (and often insurmountable) onus on the plaintiff to show a clear burden on interstate commerce.[82] Only seven of the 105 decisions mentioned expert witnesses related to *Pike* balancing, and in only one case did a court mention an economist who submitted a cost-benefit analysis report.[83] Not a single decision engaged in a serious quantitative assessment of expert testimony of the costs and benefits of the challenged law.

---

[81] The search was conducted by viewing every district court case in the Westlaw database that referenced *Pike* from September 1, 2018, through November 20, 2023, and then examining closely the seventy-nine decisions that purported to address or resolve a *Pike* balancing claim. A spreadsheet of the cases analyzed is on file with the authors.

[82] A typical example is *Fontenot v. Hunter*, where the court noted: "Any balancing approach, of which *Pike* is an example, requires evidence. It is impossible to tell whether a burden on interstate commerce is clearly excessive in relation to the putative local benefits without understanding the magnitude of both burdens and benefits. Exact figures are not essential (no more than estimates may be possible) and the evidence need not be in the record if it is subject to judicial notice, but it takes more than lawyers' talk to condemn a statute under *Pike*." 378 F. Supp. 3d 1075, 1092 n.20 (W.D. Okla. 2019) (quoting Kleinsmith v. Shurtleff, 571 F.3d 1033, 1043–44 (10th Cir. 2009)); *see also, e.g.*, Rocky Mountain Ass'n of Recruiters v. Moss, 541 F. Supp. 3d 1247, 1257 (D. Colo. 2021) ("[W]hile the court will not require precise figures or statistics ... the notable lack of specificity in Plaintiff's evidence makes it difficult for the Court to conclude that the operational costs of Plaintiff's members are indeed suggestive of the burdens on the interstate market writ large.").

[83] In *Air Transportation Association of America, Inc. v. Washington Department of Labor and Industries*, 410 F. Supp. 3d 1162 (W.D. Wash. 2019), the court on a summary judgment motion in a case involving a DCC challenge to the Washington Paid Sick Leave Act considered the affidavits of four economist expert witnesses, at least one of which produced a CBA report. The court concluded that the law did not place a substantial burden on interstate commerce without reference to these quantitative analyses. *Compare, e.g.*, Energy Mich., Inc. v. Scripps, No. 20-12521, 2023 WL 2207998, at *4 (E.D. Mich. Feb. 24, 2023) (in a *Pike* challenge to a Michigan regulation requiring energy providers to "produc[e] or purchas[e] a certain amount of locally-generated energy," weighing conflicting expert testimony and upholding the regulation because plaintiffs failed to quantify their burden in a bench trial (alterations added)), *with* Portland Pipe Line Corp. v. City of South Portland, 332 F. Supp. 3d 264, 313 (D. Me. 2018) (in a bench trial for a DCC challenge to a city ban on loading crude oil in the city harbor, considering conflicting expert witness testimony about the ordinance's in-state benefits and out-of-state burdens and upholding the statute, explaining that "[i]n light of copious conflicting evidence and scientific uncertainty ... it is not the Court's place to second-guess the findings of South Portland's political process").

E. SPECIAL ISSUES RELATING TO PROCESS REGULATION

As noted in the introduction, the regulation at issue in *Ross* concerns the process by which goods are produced in other jurisdictions rather than the characteristics of the finished goods themselves. Such cases raise special concerns relating to the assessment of regulatory benefits as well as worries about a "slippery slope" that could lead to abuses. These considerations have led some commentators, focused on the law of international trade, to worry that associated externalities are particularly likely to lead to multi-jurisdictional inefficiency.[84]

In theory, *bona fide* consumer preferences based on characteristics of the production process for goods should be treated as any other preference in an assessment of regulatory costs and benefits. And clearly some people harbor genuine concerns about matters involving production processes in other jurisdictions. We suspect that most citizens in the Western democracies would support (and be willing to bear the costs of) a prohibition on the importation of products produced with slave labor, for example, and indeed the United States recently enacted legislation limiting Chinese imports from Uyghur regions where forced labor is thought to be common.[85] Many observers place prison labor and child labor in the same category, along with production processes that kill or jeopardize endangered species. Concerns of this sort appear increasingly to be reflected in domestic law as well. Worries about animal cruelty in particular (as in *Ross*) are on the rise.[86] Proposition 12, for example, also established new process-based restrictions on the in-state sale of eggs and of veal products.

Genuine preferences on such matters are no less worthy of regulatory protection than preferences for measures that reduce cancer risk, promote environmental quality, or mitigate climate change.[87] The concept of efficiency encompasses all matters for which citizens have a genuine willingness to pay—health, safety, cleanliness, peace and quiet, a pretty view, a happy dog, and so on. When citizens' willingness to pay to promote these values exceeds the costs of regulation

---

[84] *See, e.g.*, 1 FAIR TRADE AND HARMONIZATION: PREREQUISITES FOR FREE TRADE? (Jagdish N. Bhagwati & Robert E. Hudec eds., 1996).

[85] *See* Uyghur Forced Labor Prevention Act, Pub. L. No. 117-78, 135 Stat. 1525 (2021).

[86] *See* Marta E. Alonso et al., *Consumers' Concerns and Perceptions of Farm Animal Welfare*, 10 ANIMALS MDPI 385 (2020).

[87] *See* Eric A. Posner & Cass R. Sunstein, *Moral Commitments in Cost-Benefit Analysis*, 103 VA. L. REV. 1809 (2017).

(accounting for all costs to all affected individuals, in and out of the jurisdiction), the regulation is efficient.

Nevertheless, regulations restricting the sale of goods based on their production process raise some notable concerns, especially when most of the production occurs in other jurisdictions. First, citizen preferences over such matters can be harder to observe and verify than other sorts of preferences, particularly as regulation moves farther away from deeply shared norms about subjects like slave labor. True, the issues are subject to public-opinion polling (or a plebiscite), and we can observe the results of such polling exercises. But they provide limited information at best. Polls do not measure the intensity of preferences. Many respondents are poorly informed, and answers often depend on how questions are phrased. Further, polls do not facilitate an assessment of costs and benefits unless they seek information from respondents about their willingness to pay for possible outcomes. And as noted, it is well known that respondents have little incentive to be accurate or truthful in response to questions about willingness to pay.

Second, preferences for goods made by a particular process raise a slippery slope issue. If real or purported preferences over production processes are routinely credited, then all manner of novel regulatory restrictions may be on the table. For example, California voters could enact a ban on the sale of goods produced by workers who are not guaranteed an "adequate" minimum wage by California standards. Or they could ban goods produced by firms abroad with a production process that does not comply with California's climate-protection standards. Or they could ban goods from firms that do not provide their workers with healthcare coverage that ensures they can obtain abortions (including the funds to travel if abortions are not available locally). And so on.

No doubt some citizens have genuine preferences on these issues and may be willing to pay some amount to vindicate them in the marketplace, but casual acceptance of regulations premised on the morality of the foreign production process creates a potentially large loophole for inefficient regulations. Once the production process abroad becomes a legitimate target for regulation, there are no obvious limits on process-based regulation in the name of environmental quality, human or animal health, resource conservation, or public morals. A major worry is that these facially laudatory goals may be captured by interest groups seeking to protect themselves from foreign competition, a concern often expressed with special vigor by developing countries in the international-trade context, where lower production costs contribute importantly to their perceived competitive advantage. Likewise, even where protectionist motivation is absent, other interest groups may have greater capacity to capture the regulatory process to promote their agendas based on exaggerated claims about preference intensity that are difficult or impossible to refute.

Non-discrimination norms alone are not adequate to police this slippery-slope problem. Jurisdictions can simply target imported goods for non-compliance with norms that their domestic producers already observe. To return to the examples above, California's minimum wage, environmental quality, or health-insurance coverage requirements can simply be imposed on all producers that hope to participate in the California market.

III. *Ross* and Beyond

This Part uses the economic framework and tools sketched above to analyze and critique *Ross* and seeks to clarify and make progress on issues going forward that the Court in *Ross* did not resolve.

A. EXTRATERRITORIALITY

The analysis in the previous Part showed that the extraterritorial impact of local regulation on prices, costs, and profits in other states is not a reliable marker for inefficient regulation but instead merely raises the possibility of inefficiency that requires empirical scrutiny about costs and benefits before any definitive welfare judgment can be made. Translated into DCC doctrine, this would mean, as we argued long ago, that the DCC does not impose a general prohibition on state laws with extraterritorial effects.[88] Instead, a state law with extraterritorial effects violates the DCC only when such effects run afoul of *Pike* balancing, properly conceived.

Ross unanimously adopted part of this conclusion, and at least six Justices are on board for the other part, at least at a high level of generality. The Court unanimously rejected the notion that the extraterritoriality cases establish an "almost per se" rule against state

---

[88] Goldsmith & Sykes, *supra* note 12.

laws with "extraterritorial effects."[89] It did not reject the potential relevance of extraterritorial effects for DCC analysis, however. It held that these effects could be relevant to the extent that they indicate "purposeful discrimination against out-of-state economic interests" or an impact on the "instrumentalities of commerce."[90]

More significantly for present purposes, at least six Justices made clear that certain types of extraterritorial effects beyond those that indicated discrimination or instrumentalities regulation could state a *Pike* claim. The Chief Justice in his concurring and dissenting opinion for three others stated that the California law's alleged "sweeping extraterritorial effects, even if not considered as a per se invalidation, [were] pertinent in applying *Pike*." While Justice Sotomayor, joined by Justice Kagan, disagreed on the facts alleged that petitioners had made a *Pike* claim (because of their reading of *Exxon*, more on which below), they referenced the pertinent pages of the Chief Justice's opinion in claiming that "the Court today does not shut the door" on *Pike* claims alleging extraterritorial impact.[91] Justice Barrett was skeptical of the Court's ability to do *Pike* balancing on the facts of *Ross* but appeared to be on board for using *Pike* balancing to measure extraterritorial effects in cases not involving incommensurable values.[92]

Viewing the DCC through the lens of economic efficiency, therefore, most of the Justices got it right in thinking that the extraterritorial costs of Proposition 12 were not *per se* violative of the DCC but potentially mattered within the framework of *Pike* balancing. Of course, this consensus on the relevance of *Pike* balancing to measure extraterritorial effects under the DCC belies the confusion and disagreement among the Justices on how to perform *Pike* balancing, an issue to which we now turn.

---

[89] Nat'l Pork Producers Council v. Ross, 598 U.S. 356, 373 (2023).

[90] *Id.* at 380, 392 (Sotomayor, J., concurring in part).

[91] *Id.* at 400 (Roberts, C.J., concurring in part and dissenting in part); *id.* at 392 (Sotomayor, J., concurring in part) ("[P]etitioners' failure to allege discrimination or an impact on the instrumentalities of commerce does not doom their *Pike* claim.").

[92] *Id.* at 394 (Barrett, J., concurring in part) (noting that if the burdens and benefits alleged by petitioners were "capable of judicial balancing," petitioners would have alleged a "substantial burden on interstate commerce" under *Pike* because "complaint plausibly alleges that Proposition 12's costs are pervasive, burdensome, and will be felt primarily (but not exclusively) *outside California*" (emphasis added)). Another reason Justice Barrett's vote is hard to assess is that she appears to believe that *Pike* balancing is only relevant to the extent that it reveals purposeful discrimination. *Id.*; *see also supra* notes 45, 47.

B. PIKE BALANCING

The Court sharply disagreed about when and how *Pike* balancing is appropriate. Justices Gorsuch and Thomas were skeptical that the Court could ever strike down state laws based on *Pike* balancing, and Justice Barrett was skeptical about *Pike* balancing when incommensurable goods are balanced, even though she did not reject *Pike* in all circumstances.[93] The other six Justices reiterated that *Pike* balancing remains a central component of DCC analysis.[94] And while they acknowledged, as Justice Sotomayor put it, that the balancing "inquiry is difficult and delicate, and federal courts are well advised to approach the matter with caution," they insisted that "courts generally are able to weigh disparate burdens and benefits against each other, and that they are called on to do so in other areas of the law with some frequency."[95]

From an economic perspective, all of these positions have elements of truth, but none is entirely satisfactory. As we explained above, one must balance out-of-state costs against in-state benefits when assessing aggregate efficiency. But the Justices who advocated balancing never explained how courts could or should do it. The only examples they gave of "weigh[ing] disparate burdens and benefits" (as Justice Sotomayor put it) were examples in Chief Justice Roberts's dissent of weighing competing values in non-economic contexts, such as weighing individual interests in privacy against society's interest in intrusion in assessing Fourth Amendment reasonableness.[96] The Court's success in value-balancing outside the DCC does not exactly inspire confidence.[97] But in any event, that effort is also not like balancing economic costs and benefits.

---

[93] *Ross*, 598 U.S. at 393–94 (Barrett, J., concurring in part). On the complexities in assessing Justice Barrett's view, see *supra* notes 45, 47, and 92.

[94] *Ross*, 598 U.S. at 392 (Sotomayor, J., with whom Kagan, J., joined, concurring in part); *id.* at 396 (Roberts, C.J., with whom Alito, J., Kavanaugh, J., and Jackson, J., joined, concurring in part and dissenting in part).

[95] *Id.* at 392–93 (Sotomayor, J., concurring in part). Justice Sotomayor made these points in the context of agreeing with the identical points made by Chief Justice Roberts in his four-Justice dissent. *See id.* at 396–97 (Roberts, C.J., concurring in part and dissenting in part).

[96] *Id.* at 396 (Roberts, C.J., concurring in part and dissenting in part) (citing Winston v. Lee, 470 U.S. 753, 760 (1985)).

[97] *See, e.g.*, Nadine Strossen, *The Fourth Amendment in the Balance: Accurately Setting the Scales Through the Least Intrusive Alternative Analysis*, 63 N.Y.U. L. REV. 1173 (1988); Paul W. Kahn, *The Court, the Community and the Judicial Balance: The Jurisprudence of Justice Powell*, 97 YALE L.J. 1 (1987); Alexander T. Aleinikoff, *Constitutional Law in the Age of Balancing*, 96 YALE L.J. 943 (1987).

As noted earlier, balancing out-of-state costs against in-state benefits can be done in theory, and government agencies perform similar tasks every day. It is even doable in theory for seeming incommensurables like economic costs and moral values, contrary to the suggestion of the three-Justice plurality. The key move, which administrative agencies sometimes make, is to translate the value into a monetary metric by assessing consumers' willingness to pay to protect it, and then performing traditional cost-benefit analysis based on that assessment.[98] To be sure, this technique is controversial, difficult, and sometimes speculative.

Consider some of the challenges that would arise in a case like *Ross*. To compare the California regulation to a counterfactual world with no regulation, it would be necessary to forecast the effect of California's regulation on the costs of pork production in California and elsewhere. An analyst would have to assess the accuracy of claims by the plaintiffs in *Ross* that the regulation will force them to follow the California rules in all their operations or to incur substantial costs to segregate animals and track the meat products through the packing and distribution process to ensure compliance with California rules. All the added costs would have to be quantified and aggregated.

The benefits of California's regulation would be measured by the increment in consumer willingness to pay for humanely raised pork[99] and by the value of any associated consumer health benefits, assuming that some exist. Consumer willingness to pay is not directly observable, and it would likely have to be assessed based on survey evidence that is notoriously unreliable because, *inter alia*, of a lack of incentive on the part of survey respondents to provide thoughtful and honest answers.[100] Further, consumer willingness to pay in California is not the only issue. At least some consumers in other states would likely derive some utility from knowing that animals are more humanely raised, if indeed the effect of the California regulation is to raise

---

[98] For a defense of the need to include moral commitments in cost-benefit analysis, and a full engagement with the critics of the practice, see Posner & Sunstein, *supra* note 87.

[99] This measure gives no weight to animal welfare *per se*, only to consumer willingness to pay for animal welfare.

[100] Complex mechanisms to induce survey respondents to reveal their true preferences for public goods have long been a subject of study in economics. A classic paper is Jerry Green & Jean-Jacques Laffont, *On the Revelation of Preferences for Public Goods*, 8 J. PUB. ECON. 79 (1997).

animal welfare standards for meat sold elsewhere. The financial and decision costs of carefully conducting such analyses seem likely to be extensive, and the likelihood of accuracy unclear at best.

One can imagine that *Pike* balancing might evolve into a careful cost-benefit analysis of this sort, drawing on industry and economic expertise, akin to what is undertaken by federal regulatory agencies and by some courts in cases such as those involving monopolization claims under Section 2 of the Sherman Act. This approach would turn *Pike* balancing into an expensive and complex exercise—different in kind from how it is currently performed by courts. Even if courts went down this path, one might question whether courts possess the competence to do these tasks well. Agencies typically perform cost-benefit analysis in areas where they have specialized expertise in the markets examined and regulated. Courts lack any specialized expertise in the markets implicated by the DCC, they do not have staff economists, and they have little experience in willingness-to-pay assessments that would be required to do a cost-benefit analysis with integrity on the facts of *Ross*. One can imagine courts getting up to speed in rare cases, but the task would be monumental. If these concerns undergird Justice Gorsuch's claim that courts are "not institutionally suited to draw reliable conclusions of the kind that would be necessary … to satisfy [the] *Pike*" test, then we agree.

The Court is at a crossroads on its competence to do *Pike* balancing. It has for a while now questioned its competence, and it has not invalidated a state law under *Pike* in over forty years.[101] Justice Gorsuch, joined by one colleague, made a gambit to banish *Pike* balancing from DCC jurisprudence altogether.[102] At least six Justices rejected this absolutist position even as they agreed that *Pike* balancing is hard to apply in practice. But the six offered no concrete vision about how exactly courts are supposed to do *Pike* balancing with integrity. For *Pike* balancing to be meaningful, as opposed to a ruse for eyeballing state laws and striking down the ones that "look" bad to a majority of Justices, the Court needs to take the realities of cost-benefit analysis much more seriously, as described above. What they are doing now doesn't even rise to a simulacrum of cost-benefit analysis.

---

[101] *See* Edgar v. MITE Corp., 457 U.S. 624 (1982).

[102] *Ross*, 598 U.S. at 380. Again, Justice Barrett is hard to read. *See supra* notes 45, 47, and 92.

C. *EXXON*

As noted above, the technical holding in *Ross* is the four-Justice plurality's conclusion that the *Ross* plaintiffs failed "to plead facts plausibly showing that [Proposition 12] imposes 'substantial burdens' on interstate commerce" under *Pike*.[103] As we explain, this analysis is flawed.

The Court reached this conclusion primarily in reliance on *Exxon Corp. v. Governor of Maryland*.[104] *Exxon* rejected a DCC challenge to a Maryland law that barred oil refiners from operating retail service stations in Maryland. The Court first ruled that the law did not "discriminat[e] against interstate commerce," even though it affected only interstate firms, because it "creates no barriers whatsoever against interstate independent dealers" and did not "prohibit the flow of interstate goods, place added costs upon them, or distinguish between instate and out-of-state companies in the retail market."[105] It then concluded that the law did not unduly burden interstate commerce even if some refiners would stop selling in Maryland, which in turn would "deprive the consumer of certain special services."[106] The Court also acknowledged that "the source of the consumers' supply may switch from company-operated stations to independent dealers."[107] The Court held, however, that the pre-existing interstate market structure for the retail marketing of gas was irrelevant to the DCC analysis.[108] It explained that it "may be true that the [Maryland] consuming public will be injured by the loss of the high-volume, low-priced stations operated by the independent refiners, ... that argument relates to the wisdom of the statute, not to its burden on commerce."[109]

The *Ross* plurality reasoned that "[i]f Maryland's law did not impose a sufficient burden on interstate commerce to warrant further scrutiny, the same must be said for Proposition 12."[110] Just as the "vertically

---

[103] *Ross*, 598 U.S. at 383.

[104] 437 U.S. 117 (1978).

[105] *Id.* at 126.

[106] *Id.* at 127.

[107] *Id.*

[108] *Id.* (explaining that DCC does not "protect[] the particular structure or methods of operation in a retail market"; it "protects the interstate market, not particular interstate firms, from prohibitive or burdensome regulations").

[109] *Id.* at 128.

[110] *Ross*, 598 U.S. at 384.

integrated businesses" in *Exxon* faced a choice between divesting their production capacities or withdrawing from the Maryland retail market, the Court reasoned, the "farmers and vertically integrated processors" in *Ross* had "at least as much choice: They may provide all their pigs the space the law requires; they may segregate their operations to ensure pork products entering California meet its standards; or they may withdraw from that State's market."[111] The Court suggested that the costs associated with these business decisions in the face of the Maryland and California laws were irrelevant to DCC analysis.

On this issue, the Court both misses a key point and conflates the effects of regulation on the operations of out-of-state firms with its effects on in-state firms with out-of-state investors. First, the Maryland regulation in *Exxon* altered the way that out-of-state refiners delivered retail services in Maryland, which may have affected the profitability of their participation in the Maryland market by depriving them of the advantages of vertically-integrated retailing. But nothing in the Maryland law affected the costs of doing business in other jurisdictions or the costs of producing gasoline for other jurisdictions. Thus, in contrast to the alleged facts in *Ross*, there were no production-cost externalities in *Exxon*.

Second, although the Maryland regulation may have had an effect on the consolidated bottom line profit of out-of-state companies, that effect was entirely due to its effect on the profitability of their retailing business in Maryland. Put differently, any effect on profitability was due to the effect on out-of-state investors who had invested in Maryland-based retailing. As we argued earlier in Part II, we would not expect DCC doctrine to protect out-of-state investors in local firms. Perhaps Proposition 12 will reduce the profitability of California-based pork wholesalers or retailers, for example, and perhaps shares in those firms are owned in part by investors from other states. But we are not aware of DCC cases in which a diminution in the profitability of local firms served as a predicate for invalidating state regulation simply because some of those firms were owned by outsiders.

Third, the Court also discussed the costs to consumers, and here its analysis was slipperier. It stated that the laws in both *Exxon* and *Ross* "may lead to higher consumer prices," glossing over the fact that

---

[111] *Id.*

the *Ross* plaintiffs alleged higher consumer prices for *out-of-state consumers* while only *in-state* Maryland residents faced possibly higher prices as a result of the Maryland law. Later, the Court acknowledged that "no one thinks that costs ultimately borne by in-state consumers thanks to a law they adopted counts as a cognizable harm" under the DCC.[112] But it then bafflingly stated that "the complaint [does not] allege facts plausibly suggesting that out-of-state consumers indifferent to pork production methods will have to pick up the tab" for the California law. This statement is baffling because it cannot be squared with the plaintiffs' controlling pleadings, which clearly alleged that the increase in production costs outside of California will raise the price of pork to consumers outside of California.[113]

D. THE CALIFORNIA EFFECT

The Court did not mention the California effect by name, but it was present in the back and forth between the three-Justice opinion by Justice Gorsuch and the concurring and dissenting opinions by Chief Justice Roberts and Justice Kavanaugh. Kavanaugh was clearest in identifying the California effect as he discussed the substantial burden that Proposition 12 imposed on interstate commerce:

> Yet American pig farmers and pork producers have little choice but to comply with California's regulatory dictates. It would be prohibitively expensive and practically all but impossible for pig farmers and pork producers to segregate individual pigs based on their ultimate marketplace destination in California or elsewhere. And California's 13-percent share of the consumer pork market makes it economically infeasible for many pig farmers and pork producers to exit the California market.
>
> California's required changes to pig-farming and pork-production practices throughout the United States will cost American farmers and pork producers hundreds of millions (if not billions) of dollars. And those costs for pig farmers and pork producers will be passed on, in many cases, to American consumers of pork via higher pork prices nationwide. The increased costs may also result in lower wages and reduced benefits (or layoffs) for the American workers who work on pig farms and in meatpacking plants.

---

[112] *Id.* at 386.

[113] *Id.*; *see also* Brief for the Petitioner at 15–16, Nat'l Pork Producers Council v. Ross, 598 U.S. 356 (2023) (No. 21-468); Complaint, Nat'l Pork Producers Council v. Ross, 456 F. Supp. 3d. 1201 (S.D. Cal. 2020) (No. 19CV2324W).

In short, through Proposition 12, California is forcing massive changes to pig-farming and pork-production practices throughout the United States.[114]

Justice Gorsuch says this argument claims that "California's market is so lucrative that almost any in-state measure will influence how out-of-state profit-maximizing firms choose to operate." He responded:

> But if that makes all the difference, it means voters in States with smaller markets are constitutionally entitled to greater authority to regulate instate sales than voters in States with larger markets. So much for the Constitution's "fundamental principle of equal sovereignty among the States." *Shelby County v. Holder*, 570 U. S. 529, 544 (2013) (internal quotation marks omitted).

This is an insufficient response for several reasons. First, Roberts and Kavanaugh did not maintain that the California effect "made all the difference." They only argued that petitioners had alleged a substantial burden and argued for a remand "for the court below to decide whether petitioners have stated a claim under *Pike*."[115] Second, from an economic perspective, Roberts and Kavanaugh are right: California's large size means that California can, through a mere in-state sales restriction, have an outsized influence on the behavior of firms and the prices of goods outside of California through the mechanisms described in the last Part. This is what petitioners alleged, and it is a standard consequence of large-jurisdiction regulation. These costs matter from an economic perspective in assessing aggregate inter-jurisdictional efficiency. The simple fact is that "large" jurisdictions have considerably greater capacity to cause externalities through regulation.

Third, it does not follow from this position, as Justice Gorsuch maintained, that smaller states would be "constitutionally entitled to greater authority to regulate in-state sales than voters in States with larger markets."[116] Yes, California's Proposition 12 warrants greater scrutiny under the *Pike* test than if Proposition 12 had been enacted by Vermont, due to the large impact of regulation on account of California's market size. But California is only hobbled in its ability to regulate under *Pike* when the out-of-state costs of the regulation clearly outweigh the local benefits. Depending on how the cost-benefit analysis cashes out, the DCC may in some circumstances allow

---

[114] *Ross*, 598 U.S. at 405–06 (Kavanaugh, J., concurring in part). The Chief Justice identified the California effect as well. *See id.* at 400 (Roberts, C.J., concurring in part and dissenting in part).

[115] *Id.* at 395; *see also id.* at 403 (Kavanaugh, J., concurring in part) (same).

[116] *Id.* at 388 (op. of Gorsuch, J.).

Vermont, but not California, to limit the sale of in-state pork in accord with certain humane standards. But it may also be true, again depending on the outcome of the *Pike* test, that California's Proposition 12 is allowed to affect the price and availability of pork products in Vermont, even if Vermont permits in-state sale of pork sourced without humane-condition requirements. The DCC, informed by economic principles, seeks a principled way to sort out the extent to which states are permitted to impose costs beyond their borders. To ignore the California effect altogether, as Justice Gorsuch would, is to privilege the ability of large states to impose socially excessive costs on others.

This reasoning also explains why Justice Gorsuch's principle of "equal sovereignty among the States," and related ideas of federalism and self-governance, cannot easily resolve the DCC issues raised in *Ross*.[117] People in Vermont might insist that Vermont's decisions about how animals in Vermont are treated should not be overridden by the preferences of people in California that only humanely raised pork be sold in the state. But people in California can make a parallel self-governance and federalism point: Californians' decisions about in-state pork sales should not be overridden by the preferences of people in Vermont about how pigs in Vermont should be treated. The equal sovereignty of states, and a principle of self-governance within states, have difficulty resolving DCC problems because, as the Court in *Ross* stated, "[i]n our interconnected national marketplace, many (maybe most) state laws have the 'practical effect of controlling' extraterritorial behavior"—at least to some small degree. The hard issue is figuring out when these out-of-state effects become excessive. Economic analysis can afford an answer in principle, though the empirical dimensions of that analysis, as we have emphasized, are not always straightforward.

E. THE FUTURE OF PROCESS-BASED REGULATIONS

Ross left open whether and how the Supreme Court should think about process-based regulations under the DCC. In *Ross*, only

---

[117] The quotation from *Shelby County* is about a "pertinent," but not controlling, limitation on Congress's power to impose certain voting-rights requirements on a subset of states. Shelby County v. Holder, 570 U.S. 529, 544 (2013). It has nothing to do, doctrinally or theoretically, with the Dormant Commerce Clause, or even, more broadly, with constitutional principles related to interstate harmony. *See generally* Douglas Laycock, *Equal Citizens of Equal and Territorial States: The Constitutional Foundations of Choice of Law*, 92 COLUM. L. REV. 249 (1992).

Justice Kavanaugh identified the slippery-slope concern with process-based regulations when he speculated that copycat laws might regulate the sale of fruit picked by noncitizens unlawfully in the country, or "the sale of goods produced by workers paid less than $20 per hour," or the "sale of goods from producers that do not pay for employees' birth control or abortions (or alternatively, that do pay for employees' birth control or abortions)."[118] But several other Justices expressed slippery slope concerns at oral argument[119] and fretted about how California process-based regulations combined with the California effect could permit large states to impose their moral (and policy) views nationwide.[120] Justice Kagan worried about an endless stream of such regulations, including retaliatory regulations, and the resultant economic balkanization that the DCC aims to prevent.[121]

These are plausible concerns. To recount our top-line conclusions about the economics of process-based regulations: First, they can rest on genuine consumer preferences tied to characteristics of the production process for goods, which in theory should be treated like any other preference in assessing regulatory costs and benefits. Second, however, process-based regulations raise special concerns because: (i) citizen preferences in this context are harder to verify, which gives rise to heightened concerns about pretext or interest-group capture; and (ii) such preferences place one on a long and slippery slope toward a plethora of possibly inefficient regulations since concerns about process can be leveraged into all manner of morality-based regulations. And third, a rigorous cost-benefit analysis of process-based regulations is even more challenging than the typical cost-benefit analysis because the moral concern underlying the demand for process-based regulation can be especially difficult to translate into a monetary metric.

In short, process-based regulations are worrisome but also potentially efficient in the aggregate (and thus, in our view, potentially

---

[118] 598 U.S. at 407 (Kavanaugh, J., concurring in part).

[119] The Justices asked about state bans on products because they are produced by union labor (or by non-union labor), or by people paid a too-low minimum wage, or by unlawful immigrants, or by companies that do not require their employees to be vaccinated, or that don't provide gender-affirming and other forms of health care. Transcript of Oral Argument at 83, 95, 97, 98, *Ross*, 598 U.S. 356 (No. 21-468).

[120] *Id.* at 131 ("California's view of morality [would] prevail[] over the views of people in other states because of [its] market power.") (Roberts, C.J.); *see also id.* at 116 ("Is California unconcerned about all this because it is such a giant, you can wield this power, Wyoming couldn't do it, most other states couldn't do it, but you can do it?") (Alito, J.).

[121] *Id.* at 95 (Kagan, J.).

valid under the DCC), depending on the details. But courts are even less suited in this context than usual to do *Pike* balancing and sort out the valid from the invalid state laws.

This raises the question whether the Supreme Court might have or develop other doctrinal tools to assess the difficult problem of process-based regulations. Some process-based regulations might, of course, be invalidated under a DCC-disguised protectionism rationale. And several Justices hinted at, but did not develop, the possibility that other doctrines—"the Import-Export Clause, the Privileges and Immunities Clause, and the Full Faith and Credit Clause,"[122] or perhaps the principles of "sovereignty and comity" embraced "by original and historical understandings of the Constitution's structure"[123]— might get at issues like the ones raised by Proposition 12.[124] These doctrines are beyond our scope. But there are doctrines developed in international trade law, inspired by economic theory, and present (though understated) in DCC jurisprudence, that could address some of the concerns presented by process-based regulations without open-ended *Pike*-style balancing.[125]

To elaborate, international trade law has wrestled with the effects on international commerce of national regulation for decades. Like the DCC, its initial focus was on discrimination, and the principal constraint on regulatory policy was a nondiscrimination ("national treatment") commitment subject to several exceptions.[126] But the national treatment obligation alone was found over time inadequate to police trade-distorting regulation, and the formation of the WTO introduced two new treaties on "technical barriers to trade."[127] These new treaties supplemented the national treatment principle with additional disciplines but did *not* open the door to open-ended balancing

---

[122] 598 U.S. at 408 (Kavanaugh, J., concurring in part).

[123] *Id.* at 376 (majority op.).

[124] *See* Proposition 12 (Cal. 2018).

[125] These doctrines also have important implications for cases that do not entail process regulation.

[126] *See* General Agreement on Tariffs and Trade arts. III, XX, XXII, Oct. 30, 1947, 61 Stat. A-11, 55 U.N.T.S. 194.

[127] *See* Agreement on Technical Barriers to Trade, Apr. 15, 1994, Marrakesh Agreement Establishing the World Trade Organization, 1868 U.N.T.S. 120; Agreement on Sanitary and Phytosanitary Measures, Apr. 15, 1994, Marrakesh Agreement Establishing the World Trade Organization, 1867 U.N.T.S. 493. Both Agreements are discussed at length in ALAN O. SYKES, PRODUCT STANDARDS FOR INTERNATIONALLY INTEGRATED GOODS MARKETS (1995); and ALAN O. SYKES, THE LAW AND ECONOMICS OF INTERNATIONAL TRADE AGREEMENTS, at ch. 10 (2023).

as in *Pike*. These new principles include, among many others, requirements that regulation rest on scientific evidence in certain settings and a searching inquiry into the possibility that the goals of regulation can be achieved with reasonably available, less trade-restrictive alternatives.

We argue below that such doctrinal innovations have potential utility for DCC analysis as well. Like the existing DCC prohibition on discriminatory/protectionist measures, these additional principles can serve as proxies or "shortcuts" to identify classes of cases that are likely to fail the *Pike* balancing test, thereby avoiding the challenges and complexities of full-scale cost-benefit balancing.

To elaborate, international trade law has also been forced to confront the problem of process-based regulations affecting imported goods. An early prominent decision, *Tuna-Dolphin*, ruled that the General Agreement on Tariffs and Trade (GATT) barred import restrictions based on the production process abroad on the ground that otherwise members such as the United States "could unilaterally determine the life or health protection policies from which other contracting parties could not deviate without jeopardizing their rights."[128] This reasoning, akin to petitioners' position in *Ross*, was controversial and never supported by the GATT membership.[129] Subsequent adjudications under the successor World Trade Organization (WTO) were more accepting of national regulation based on production processes in foreign jurisdictions, although the jurisprudence remains unsettled. The cumulative result of these developments is that process-based regulations on imported goods are not altogether prohibited by international trade law, but they are subject to considerably more discipline than just a non-discrimination requirement. That discipline does not include open-ended cost-benefit balancing as in *Pike*, however, but instead relies on more easily administrable principles found in GATT and the technical

---

[128] Panel Report, *United States—Restrictions on Imports of Tuna*, WTO Doc. WT/DS21/R at 5.27 (adopted Sept. 3, 1991), https://www.wto.org/english/tratop_e/dispu_e/gatt_e/91tuna.pdf. As in *Ross*, the preferences at issue pertained to animal welfare and, in particular, to concern about fishing methods that endangered dolphins.

[129] The decision was also roundly criticized by environmental groups, and numerous legal commentators argued that it was a misinterpretation of the relevant GATT provisions. *See, e.g.*, Robert E. Hudec, *The Product-Process Doctrine in GATT/WTO Jurisprudence*, in NEW DIRECTIONS IN INTERNATIONAL ECONOMIC LAW: ESSAYS IN HONOUR OF JOHN H. JACKSON 187 (Marco Bronckers & Reinhard Quick eds., 2000); Robert L. Howse & Donald H. Regan, *The Product/Process Distinction—An Illusory Basis for Disciplining 'Unilateralism' in Trade Policy*, 11 EUR. J. INT'L L. 249 (2000).

barriers agreements. To conclude this Part, we discuss the implications of two of the principles found in the technical barriers agreements because of their relevance to the issues in *Ross* and to process regulation cases more broadly.

1. *Scientific Evidence Requirements.* One of the putative justifications for the regulation in *Ross* is a claim that inhumane conditions in the pork industry enhance the risk of food-borne disease to consumers of pork. The main arguments, which come from amici and not the state itself, appear to be that (1) breeding pigs in California that are confined in gestation crates while pregnant increases the likelihood that the pigs and their offspring will develop diseases transmissible to humans in California; and (2) pork products from pigs raised in these conditions anywhere are more likely to pose food safety risks for Californians.[130] The scientific evidence in support of these claims, as we explain below, is at best scant.

Were this issue in *Ross* to arise under WTO law, it would be subject to the scientific evidence requirements found in the Sanitary and Phytosanitary Measures Agreement.[131] These provisions require that regulation be based on scientific principles and that it be preceded by a scientific risk assessment by regulators. In effect, the regulating jurisdiction is asked to provide a credible quantum of scientific evidence to support the existence of the risk in question and to show that such evidence was considered and evaluated prior to the promulgation of the regulation. Adjudicators then engage in a reasonably deferential review, asking whether respectable scientific opinion offers some support for the existence of the purported risk and the efficacy of the regulatory measure to address it. Latitude can be granted on a temporary basis in cases of genuine scientific uncertainty on the basis of a "precautionary principle."[132] This review allows regulators flexibility to address genuine issues of risk but

---

[130] *See, e.g.*, Brief for Intervenor Respondents at 37-38, Nat'l Pork Producers Council v. Ross, 598 U.S. 356 (2023) (No. 21-468); Brief of Am. Pub. Health Ass'n, et al. as Amici Curiae Supporting Respondents at 31-33, *Ross*, 598 U.S. 356 (No. 21-468); Brief of Worker Safety Advocs. as Amici Curiae Supporting Respondents at 6-12, *Ross*, 598 U.S. 356 (No. 21-468); Brief of Jim Keen, DVM, Ph.D. & Thomas Pool, MPH, DVM as Amici Curiae Supporting Respondents at 11, *Ross*, 598 U.S. 356 (No. 21-468). It is noteworthy that California itself does not make this argument.

[131] In particular, Articles 2 and 5 of the Agreement on Sanitary and Phytosanitary Measures would apply. *See* Agreement on Sanitary and Phytosanitary Measures, *supra* note 127, at arts. 2, 5.

[132] *See* Agreement on Sanitary and Phytosanitary Measures, *supra* note 127, at art. 5(7).

identifies cases in which the regulatory basis is pretext or conjecture, and where the regulatory solution is ineffective. This approach avoids the pitfalls of asking adjudicators to undertake a thorough cost-benefit analysis of regulation while retaining some discipline over facially nondiscriminatory regulations that lack a credible efficiency justification.

The Supreme Court's *Pike* jurisprudence on the relevance of in-state health and safety rationales, and any scientific evidence requirement, is inchoate. The Court has said that the trial court must examine the scientific and other evidence in support of the health or safety rationale both to ensure that it is not pretextual and to assess its strength before balancing the in-state benefits against out-of-state burdens.[133] It has said that the state law must make more than a "speculative contribution" to in-state health and safety.[134] But it has also said that a State need not "'sit idly by and wait ... until the scientific community agrees'" about risks "'before it acts to avoid such consequences.'"[135] These principles leave the Court plenty of room for a searching inquiry into the science or related evidence in support of the health or safety rationale in cases where process-based regulations are in issue.[136]

The health claim in *Ross* was too undeveloped to determine whether or how it should be credited for purposes of *Pike* balancing. The issue is complicated by the fact that the case has not proceeded beyond the pleadings. It is further complicated by the fact that Proposition 12 was enacted by referendum, not legislation, and even more so by the fact that the law had two independent justifications—the health justification and the animal-welfare justification.

---

[133] *See, e.g.*, Raymond Motor Transp., Inc. v. Rice, 434 U.S. 429, 443 (1978) (insisting that under *Pike* balancing the Court must "weigh[]the asserted safety purpose against the degree of interference with interstate commerce," and then examine the factual basis for the safety rationale closely).

[134] *Id.* at 447; *see also* Kassel v. Consol. Freightways Corp., 450 U.S. 662 (1981) (plurality op.) (conducting a searching inquiry of the scientific evidence behind the state's alleged safety rationale). The Court in purposeful-discrimination cases requires "concrete evidence" of a purported local health or safety benefit. Tenn. Wine & Spirits Retailers Ass'n v. Thomas, 139 S. Ct. 2449, 2474 (2019); Granholm v. Heald, 544 U.S. 460, 490 (2005).

[135] Maine v. Taylor, 477 U.S. 131, 140, 148 (1986).

[136] The utility of scientific evidence requirements is by no means limited to process-based cases. Any time the motivation for a nondiscriminatory regulation that burdens outside sellers concerns a scientifically observable or measurable risk, DCC analysis could require regulators to adduce a plausible scientific foundation for their claims about the existence of risk and the plausible efficacy of the regulatory solution.

That said, it is worth noting that the health justification as articulated by respondents in *Ross*, considered in isolation from the animal-welfare justification, would fail the WTO test. Separating out *amici*, and focusing on the parties' positions, respondents argue that the most that can be said for the scientific rationale is that it is uncertain but not "unreasonable" as a prophylactic.[137] California does not point to *any* scientific study or assessment of the health risk to humans from pork raised in violation of Proposition 12. It therefore fails to identify any "risk assessment" at all, let alone one that rationally supports the pork-related provisions in Proposition 12 as a health measure. And although the "precautionary principle" in WTO law allows temporary provisional measures in the face of genuine scientific uncertainty about risks, an unsupported assertion about such risk is insufficient. Provisional measures are only permissible under WTO law if based on the "available pertinent information" and where the regulating jurisdiction is actively seeking to obtain additional scientific information to resolve the scientific uncertainty.

2. *Less Restrictive Alternatives.* The other justification for the regulation in *Ross* relates to the protection of animal welfare. Unlike the health claim, this justification is not open to conventional scientific investigation, and it is not the type of justification that would be subject to the requirement of a scientific risk assessment in the WTO. But it would be subject to another type of obligation found in the technical barriers agreements and to some degree in the original GATT—an obligation to regulate using the least trade-restrictive approach that is reasonably available to achieve the regulatory objective.[138] This principle is also sometimes phrased as a "necessity" test: Is the regulatory policy in question, and its implementation, reasonably "necessary" to the attainment of the regulatory goal?

This principle, too, offers useful discipline over facially neutral regulations while stopping short of a full-blown cost-benefit inquiry.

---

[137] Brief for Intervenor Respondents, *supra* note 130, at 39; *see also* Brief for State Respondents, Nat'l Pork Producers Council v. Ross, 598 U.S. 356 (2023) (No. 21-468).

[138] *See* Agreement on Technical Barriers to Trade, *supra* note 127, at arts. 2.2, 2.8; Agreement on Sanitary and Phytosanitary Measures, *supra* note 127, at arts. 2(2), 5(6). A requirement to use the least trade-restrictive alternative also emerged in earlier GATT jurisprudence concerning exceptions for measures "necessary" to promote certain domestic objectives, such as the exception in GATT Article XX(b) for measures "necessary to protect human, animal or plant life or health." *See* General Agreements on Tariffs and Trade 1994, art. XX(b), Apr. 15, 1994, Marrakesh Agreement Establishing the World Trade Organization, 1867 U.N.T.S. 187.

In broad brush, it takes the objective of the regulating jurisdiction as a given, and it simply asks whether it can be attained more cheaply with less burden on inter-jurisdictional commerce. If the answer to that question is yes, then the existing regulation by definition imposes unnecessary costs on outsiders that can be reduced without impairing the "putative local benefits."

The possible existence of less trade-restrictive alternatives has been raised in numerous WTO/GATT disputes.[139] The resulting jurisprudence offers several guidelines for the assessment of these claims. First, it is generally up to the complainant to propose a less restrictive alternative. The respondent is not required to prove that none exists. Second, the requirement that the less restrictive alternative be "reasonably available" implies that the added cost to the respondent must be considered. An alternative that is substantially more expensive to implement is unlikely to be deemed "reasonably available." Third, the proposed alternative must suffice to meet the regulatory objective. If it falls significantly short, it does not qualify as a less restrictive alternative. In cases where the complainant and the respondent dispute the adequacy of the proposed alternative in that respect, the amount of deference afforded to the respondent's position will depend on the importance of the values at stake. Doubts about the efficacy of the proposed alternative are likely to be resolved in favor of the respondent when the measure at issue concerns the protection of human life or health, for example. In a case where the regulation is aimed at protecting consumers against deceptive advertising of safe goods, by contrast, the respondent's arguments concerning the efficacy of a proposed alternative receive less deference.[140]

The less-restrictive-alternative analysis in international trade law is potentially quite searching. It asks not only whether the regulatory objective can be obtained more cheaply with a different type of measure, but whether the adopted measure itself imposes unnecessary costs in the way that it is applied or administered. Undue burden or delay associated with establishing conformity to regulation, for example, can invalidate a measure even if the measure itself is acceptable.

DCC balancing jurisprudence contains an element akin to the less-trade-restrictive-alternative principle. *Pike* stated that the extent

---

[139] *See* John H. Jackson, William J. Davey & Alan O. Sykes, Legal Problems of International Economic Relations, chs. 12–13 (7th ed. 2021).

[140] *See* Alan O. Sykes, *The Least Restrictive Means*, 70 U. Chi. L. Rev. 403, 415–19 (2003).

of the interstate burden that the Court will tolerate will depend in part on whether the regulating States' interest "could be promoted as well *with a lesser impact on interstate activities.*"[141] The Supreme Court has alluded to the principle in a few decisions involving DCC balancing without relying on it in any detail.[142] Some lower courts have taken the "lesser impact" principle more seriously as a component of *Pike* balancing.[143] The Supreme Court thus has doctrinal space to adopt something akin to the least restrictive means test, if it so chooses.

A less-restrictive-alternative analysis in a case like *Ross* could play out in a variety of ways.[144] One potentially useful approach would be to ask whether California's objectives might be achieved through a labeling regulation regarding the treatment of breeding animals related to the product that would have a much smaller impact on interstate commerce than Proposition 12. This approach was prominently mentioned at oral argument in *Ross.*[145] And the *Tuna-Dolphin* dispute in the WTO, noted earlier, was ultimately resolved when the United States shifted from a ban on imported tuna harvested using certain fishing

---

[141] Pike v. Bruce Church, Inc., 397 U.S. 137, 142 (1970) (emphasis added).

[142] *See* Minnesota v. Clover Leaf Creamery Co., 449 U.S. 456, 473 (1981) (concluding with little analysis that "no approach" beyond Minnesota's ban on the sale of milk in plastic nonreturnable, nonrefillable containers had "a lesser impact on interstate activities"); Great Atl. & Pac. Tea Co. v. Cottrell, 424 U.S. 366, 376–77 (1976) (rejecting Mississippi's claim that its requirements for the sale of out-of-state milk justified its need to maintain its health standards because "there are means adequate to serve this interest that are substantially less burdensome on commerce"). The Court has taken nondiscriminatory alternatives seriously as part of the test for assessing overt state discrimination. *See, e.g.*, Dean Milk Co. v. City of Madison, 340 U.S. 349, 354–56 (1951).

[143] *See, e.g.*, Norwegian Cruise Line Holdings Ltd v. State Surgeon Gen., 50 F.4th 1126, 1144–52 (11th Cir. 2022); R & M Oil & Supply, Inc. v. Saunders, 307 F.3d 731, 736–37 (8th Cir. 2002); U&I Sanitation v. City of Columbus, 205 F.3d 1063, 1070–71 (8th Cir. 2000); Blue Circle Cement, Inc. v. Bd. of Cnty. Comm'rs of Cnty. of Rogers, 27 F.3d 1499, 1512 (10th Cir. 1994).

[144] One might ask, for example, whether California could attain a comparable level of animal welfare with more flexible pig-housing requirements than Proposition 12. WTO law applies the least-restrictive-alternative principle to issues such as this. *See* Agreement on Technical Barriers to Trade, *supra* note 127, at art. 5; Agreement on Sanitary and Phytosanitary Measures, *supra* note 127, art. 8, Annex C.

[145] *See, e.g.*, Transcript of Oral Argument at 49, Nat'l Pork Producers Council v. Ross, 598 U.S. 356 (2023) (No. 21-468) ("[W]ould there be a problem under *Pike* if, instead of banning sales based on morality concerns or whatever else, California allowed the sales but required the pork to be labeled?") (Jackson, J.); *id.* at 59–60 ("*Pike*, as has been pointed out, contains a sort of less restrictive means sort of standard or—or—or safety valve. And labeling allows those citizens of California who—who want to avoid purchasing pork because they believe they would be morally complicit in conduct that they think is improper in another state, enables them to do so.") (Deputy Solicitor General Kneedler).

methods that endangered dolphins to a "dolphin-safe" label that could only be displayed by sellers employing dolphin-safe methods.[146] The argument for labeling rests on the intuition that it is much less expensive for producers to implement than Proposition 12 and yet might achieve the law's main aims. Labeling allows consumers to "put their money where their mouth is." If California consumers truly care about animal welfare and are willing to pay for it, they will buy the "humanely-produced" product at a premium price. Other California consumers can buy the less expensive alternative. In that fashion, the added costs of animal welfare are borne by the consumers who are willing to bear them, and other consumers (inside and outside California) need not bear the "externality" that arises when those who care less about animal welfare impose their preferences on others.

A possible objection to labeling as a less restrictive alternative is that the regulatory goal of Proposition 12 is not simply to protect the interests of California consumers who place a high value on animal welfare, but to force all California consumers, including those who do not value animal welfare, to buy humanely-raised products. To the extent that this is true, the former group of consumers in effect seeks to impose its view of marketplace morality on everyone within California, and labeling would not suffice to that end. It might also be argued that consumers do not pay adequate attention to labels, and so "mandatory" product standards are necessary to protect them from their own inattention.

Despite these concerns, the slippery slope issues raised by process regulations, and the enormous challenges of *Pike* balancing in this context, might argue for labeling as a reasonable compromise, especially on issues that lack something approaching a national moral consensus. Labeling might be an imperfect option from an economic perspective, but the alternatives—a blank check for large jurisdictions to do what they want as long as it is "nondiscriminatory" or open-ended *Pike* balancing—may be worse. And of course, this approach would still require a prior showing that the regulation at issue creates substantial interstate externalities.

---

[146] *See* Rodrigo F. Cezar, *The Politics of 'Dolphin-Safe' Tuna in the United States: Policy Change and Reversal, Lock-in and Adjustment to International Constraints (1984–2017)*, 17 WORLD TRADE REV. 635 (2018).

CONCLUSION

Ross revealed the importance of economic analysis to the DCC as well as the challenges of applying that analysis to resolve concrete DCC cases. This Article has endeavored to explain how economic analysis would apply to the hard DCC issues raised and mostly ducked in *Ross*. In particular, the Court needs to acknowledge that balancing analysis under *Pike* must, to be coherent, engage in a much more searching and rigorous assessment of the nationwide costs and benefits of the challenged state regulation. Every Justice in *Ross* recognized the difficulty of this analysis, with some calling for its abandonment. We have argued that courts can in theory conduct the analysis, but not perfectly, and not without a dramatic alteration of how *Pike* balancing is assessed at the trial level. Absent such a sea change in the judicial approach to *Pike*, the best way forward is to search for substitutes to *Pike* balancing—like the scientific evidence and less-restrictive-means tests—that capture economic concerns at least partially and in a more manageable fashion.

DANIELLE KEATS CITRON

FROM BAD TO WORSE: STALKING, THREATS, AND CHILLING EFFECTS

INTRODUCTION

Cyberstalking laws criminalize the targeting of a specific person with a "course of conduct" that causes serious emotional distress.[1] Cyberstalking does not involve a one-time attack, but rather multiple instances of abuse that show a "continuity of purpose."[2] The mental-state requirement varies. Some laws require proof that the defendant intended to harass or intimidate the victim.[3] Other laws require proof that the

---

Danielle Keats Citron is the Jefferson Scholars Foundation Schenck Distinguished Professor in Law and the Caddell & Chapman Professor of Law at the University of Virginia School of Law, Vice President of the Cyber Civil Rights Initiative, and a 2019 MacArthur Fellow.

AUTHOR'S NOTE: My deep gratitude to Geoffrey Stone for inestimable wisdom and encouragement; to Mary Anne Franks, Helen Norton, and Phil Weiser for invaluable advice; to Eleanor Citron, Io Jones, Jeff Stautberg, and Taylor Stenberg for astute feedback; and to Leslie Ashbrook, who is a librarian extraordinaire. Special thanks to Kate Boudouris, Leslie Kendrick, Frederick Schauer, and Richard Schragger for helping me work through ideas and for Kate's (always) exceptional research. There is nothing like having wonderful and generous colleagues. All mistakes, of course, are my own.

[1] DANIELLE KEATS CITRON, HATE CRIMES IN CYBERSPACE 123–24 (2014).

[2] *Id.* at 139.

[3] *Id.* The federal cyberstalking law, 18 U.S.C. § 2261(A)(2)(B), requires an intent to cause harm, described as purposefulness under the Model Penal Code. The Model Penal Code includes four types of culpable mental states: purpose, knowledge, recklessness, and negligence. Mary Anne Franks, *How Stalking Became Free Speech*, GEO. WASH. L. REV. DOCKET (JULY 28, 2023), https://www.gwlr.org/how-stalking-became-free-speech-counterman-v-colorado-and-the-supreme-courts-continuing-war-on-women. As Mary Anne Franks explains: "Purpose means intent in the

The Supreme Court Review, 2024.
© 2024 The University of Chicago. All rights reserved. Published by The University of Chicago Press. https://doi.org/10.1086/728912

defendant knowingly targeted the victim with an abusive course of conduct in a context where it would be reasonably foreseeable that the victim would suffer serious emotional distress.[4]

Death and rape threats are included in online attacks, but not always.[5] Unwanted communications, intimate privacy violations, and defamation are other weapons.[6] Perpetrators incessantly text, email, or call victims despite no response, efforts to block communications, or even clear rejection.[7] They post victims' nude images on social media or email them to victims' supervisors and coworkers.[8] They spread defamatory falsehoods about victims' health and imagined criminality.[9] They impersonate victims, suggesting their availability for sex.[10] Victims are "doxxed"—their addresses, phone numbers, and Social Security numbers are posted online.[11]

Cyberstalking is destructive and pervasive.[12] Victims describe cyberstalking as a never-ending nightmare or an "incurable

---

commonly understood sense of an express and conscious desire for a certain result. Knowledge means conscious awareness that a certain result is almost certain to occur. Recklessness means the conscious disregard of a substantial and unjustified risk that a certain result will occur. Negligence differs from recklessness only in the sense that a reasonable person would be aware of the risk even if the actor was not. Accordingly, the negligence standard is sometimes referred to as the 'reasonable person' standard or the 'objective' standard, with 'objective' distinguishing between what a person objectively should have known from what a person in fact did subjectively know. Rarely, criminal law allows punishment for harmful acts even if a reasonable person would not have not have known that harm would result. This is the case with so-called 'strict liability' offenses, which require no demonstration of any mental state at all, objective or subjective." *Id.*

[4] CITRON, *supra* note 1, at 124.

[5] Will Carless, *They Were Flooded by Online Harassment and Hatred. They Didn't Know a Targeted Campaign Caused It*, USA TODAY (May 11, 2023, 7:13 PM), https://www.usatoday.com/story/news/nation/2023/05/03/telegram-channel-project-mayhem-paul-nicholas-miller/70171241007.

[6] CITRON, *supra* note 1, at 1–15.

[7] *Id.*

[8] Nina Jankowicz, *I Shouldn't Have to Accept Being in Deepfake Porn,*" ATLANTIC (June 25, 2023), https://www.theatlantic.com/ideas/archive/2023/06/deepfake-porn-ai-misinformation/674475.

[9] Mattathias Schwartz, *The Trolls Among Us*, N.Y. TIMES (Aug. 3, 2008), https://www.nytimes.com/2008/08/03/magazine/03trolls-t.html.

[10] Chad Pradelli, *High School Senior Cyberstalked by Friend's Dad*, ABC NEWS (May 9, 2017), https://6abc.com/teen-cyberstalked-by-friends-father-social-media/1967685; Edecio Martinez, *Alleged 'Craiglist Rapist' Ty McDowell: Ex-Marine Tricked Me into Raping Former Girlfriend*, CBS NEWS (Mar. 8, 2010, 8:15 AM), https://www.cbsnews.com/news/alleged-craigslist-rapist-ty-mcdowell-ex-marine-tricked-me-into-raping-former-girlfriend.

[11] Keith Stuart, *Brianna Wu and the Human Cost of Gamergate: 'Every Woman I Know in the Industry Is Scared,'* GUARDIAN (Oct. 17, 2014, 2:02 PM), https://www.theguardian.com/technology/2014/oct/17/brianna-wu-gamergate-human-cost.

[12] Emily A. Vogels, *The State of Online Harassment*, PEW RSCH. CTR. (Jan. 13, 2021), https://www.pewresearch.org/internet/2021/01/13/the-state-of-online-harassment (finding that in

disease."[13] They suffer severe and lasting anxiety.[14] They make themselves invisible, as best they can, in the hopes that perpetrators might forget them (alas no).[15] They close their social media profiles, withdraw from relationships, and stop socializing.[16] They are filled with dread when checking their inboxes and searching their names because they know that more abuse awaits them.[17] They drop out of school and change jobs.[18] They move to prevent physical attacks.[19] They change their names because their online reputations have been decimated.[20] Victims are more often female, and perpetrators are more often male.[21]

Law has done far too little to combat cyberstalking. Victims often do not report the abuse for fear that their complaints will not be taken seriously.[22] As expected, police officers often do nothing when victims seek help.[23] In the rare case that complaints are investigated,

---

2020, 25% of Americans reportedly experienced such abuse); Asia A. Eaton et al., *2017 Nationwide Online Study of Nonconsensual Porn Victimization and Perpetration: A Summary Report*, CYBER C.R. INITIATIVE 11–12, 15 (June 2017), https://www.cybercivilrights.org/wp-content/uploads/2017/06/CCRI-2017-Research-Report.pdf (finding that one in eight adult social media users have been threatened with or faced nonconsensual sharing of sexually explicit images or videos).

[13] DANIELLE KEATS CITRON, THE FIGHT FOR PRIVACY: PROTECTING DIGNITY, IDENTITY, AND LOVE IN THE DIGITAL AGE 41–47 (2022).

[14] *See, e.g.*, Francesca Stevens et al., *Cyber Stalking, Cyber Harassment, and Adult Mental Health: A Systematic Review*, 24 CYBERPSYCHOLOGY BEHAV. & SOC. NETWORKING REV. 367, 372 (2021); Nicola Henry & Anastasia Powell, *Beyond the 'Sext': Technology-facilitated Sexual Violence and Harassment Against Adult Women*, 48 AUSTL. & N.Z. J. CRIMINOLOGY 104, 113–14 (2015).

[15] Shannon Bond, *She Joined DHS to Fight Disinformation. She Says She Was Halted … by Disinformation*, NAT'L PUB. RADIO (May 21, 2022, 5:00 AM), https://www.npr.org/2022/05/21/1100438703/dhs-disinformation-board-nina-jankowicz.

[16] Louis Casiano, *White House 'Disinformation Czar' Nina Jankowicz Makes TikTok Account Private*, FOX NEWS (May 3, 2022, 7:07 PM), https://www.foxnews.com/politics/white-house-disinformation-nina-jankowicz-tiktok.

[17] *See generally* NINA JANKOWICZ, HOW TO BE A WOMAN ONLINE: SURVIVING ABUSE AND HARASSMENT, AND HOW TO FIGHT BACK (2022).

[18] Stevens et al., *supra* note 14, at 371–72.

[19] CITRON, *supra* note 1, at 104.

[20] *Id.*

[21] *Id.* at 1–28; JANKOWICZ, *supra* note 17 at xii–xviii.

[22] *See generally* Joanne D. Worsley et al., *Victims' Voices: Understanding the Emotional Impact of Cyberstalking and Individuals' Coping Mechanisms*, 7 SAGE J. 1 (2017).

[23] Stevens et al., *supra* note 14, at 372 (discussing several studies showing that local police refused to help, made fun of victims, suggested they were to blame, and said that they were overreacting); Billea Ahlgrim & Cheryl Terrance, *Perceptions of Cyberstalking: Impact of Perpetrator Gender and Cyberstalker/Victim Relationship*, 36 J. OF INTERPERSONAL VIOLENCE 4074 (2021).

prosecutors may drop charges for no clear reason.[24] For instance, a woman's ex-boyfriend promised to "ruin her life" after they broke up.[25] He emailed her nude photographs to her law school classmates. He impersonated her on online dating sites, posting a request for sex next to her sexually explicit photograph and home address. He posted a sexually explicit video of the woman on adult and revenge porn sites.[26] Strangers contacted her online and at home.[27] The man was indicted for cyberstalking, aggravated identity theft, and unauthorized access to the woman's computer, but prosecutors asked the court to dismiss the indictment after two years without *any* real explanation.[28] On the civil side, victims have difficulty finding low-cost counsel to obtain protective orders against perpetrators and to seek damages in civil suits. Perpetrators have few resources to recover,[29] and content platforms are shielded from liability for user-generated abuse.[30] Victims internalize the notion that law is not on their side.[31]

The U.S. Supreme Court's ruling in *Counterman v. Colorado*[32] makes it even more difficult for cyberstalking victims to achieve justice and for law to deter destructive online abuse. In *Counterman*, the defendant sent *hundreds* of unwanted text messages to singer-songwriter Coles Whalen. Some texts suggested the defendant's physical proximity; some implied their romantic involvement; some threatened violence. The defendant's messages filled Whalen's inbox. The texts terrified Whalen. They wrecked her sense of safety because she had no idea

---

[24] Matthew Goldstein, *In 'Revenge Porn' Case, a Criminal Court Decision May Impact Lawsuit*, N.Y. Times (Apr. 1, 2016), https://www.nytimes.com/2016/04/02/business/dealbook/in-revenge-porn-case-criminal-court-decision-may-affect-lawsuit.html.

[25] *Civil Lawsuit on Revenge Porn*, N.Y. Times (Jan. 29, 2015), https://www.nytimes.com/interactive/2015/01/29/business/dealbook/document-civil-lawsuit-on-revenge-porn.html.

[26] *Id.*

[27] *Id.*

[28] Goldstein, *supra* note 24. The court granted the government's request and dismissed the indictment. *Id.* A representative for the U.S. Attorney in Los Angeles, which had brought the case, "offered no explanation for dropping the case except to say that the office had decided it could not meet its burden of proof at trial." *Id.*

[29] Citron, *supra* note 13, at 82–90.

[30] *See generally* Danielle Keats Citron, *How to Fix Section 230*, 103 B.U. L. Rev. 713 (2023).

[31] *See generally* Samantha Alexis Gallagher, You Should Be Flattered: An Examination of the Non-Reporting of Stalking Victimization (2022) (M.A. Thesis, Queen's University, Kingston, Ontario, Canada); Rachel E. Morgan & Jennifer L. Truman, Stalking Victimization, 2019, Bureau of Just. Stats. (2022), https://bjs.ojp.gov/content/pub/pdf/sv19.pdf.

[32] 600 U.S. 66 (2023).

who the stalker was. She was afraid to walk outside by herself and canceled concerts for fear the stalker would confront her.[33]

Eventually, Whalen brought this situation to the attention of the state authorities and the stalker, Billy Counterman, was arrested, prosecuted and convicted of cyberstalking under Colorado law, which prohibits knowingly and "repeatedly ... follow[ing], approach[ing], contact[ing], plac[ing] under surveillance, or mak[ing] any form of communication with another person" in a "manner that would cause a reasonable person to suffer serious emotional distress and that does cause that person ... to suffer serious emotional distress."[34] The emotional-distress cyberstalking statute did not require proof of a threat.

As framed by the lower courts and the Supreme Court, the conviction's constitutionality rested on whether the defendant's cyberstalking involved unprotected "true threats." The *Counterman* decision analyzed the question under the First Amendment's chilling-effects doctrine. The Court maintained that a heightened mental state of recklessness was required by the First Amendment because it would provide prophylactic protection against the risk that potential speakers would swallow their words for fear of approaching the line or getting caught in expensive, time-consuming, and reputation-risking investigation.[35] In the Court's view, allowing objectively terrifying cyberstalking to flourish was an acceptable cost of securing breathing room for protected speech.[36] The Colorado cyberstalking law's "objective standard"—requiring proof that it was reasonably foreseeable that the online assaults would be taken as a serious threat of violence—was insufficient, the Court held, to prevent the chilling of protected speech.[37]

The *Counterman* decision made several missteps in its chilling-effects analysis. The Court's treatment of all threats as the same overprotects speech that has little affirmative free speech value.[38] A

---

[33] *Id.* at 70; Brief of Coles Whalen as Amicus Curiae in Support of Respondent at 1, 5, *Counterman*, 600 U.S. 66 (No. 22-138).

[34] COLO. REV. STAT. § 18-3-602(1)(c) (2022).

[35] 600 U.S. at 69. In a threats case, a reckless defendant is one who was aware of and consciously disregarded the substantial and unjustified risk that his statement would be taken as a threat of physical violence. *Id.*

[36] *Id.* at 78.

[37] *Id.*

[38] *See* Michael Pierce, *Protecting Online Threats After* Elonis, 110 Nw. U. L. REV. ONLINE 51, 54 (2015).

recklessness standard should not apply to threats made in private communications to private or public figures, such as Whalen in *Counterman*, or threats targeting private individuals about personal matters. Statements close to the border of such threats have scant political, cultural, social, or other normative value. They do not contribute to the search for truth, the criticism of government, or the exchange of information in public discourse.[39] By contrast, a recklessness requirement may be appropriate for borderline threats targeting public officials and public figures. Harsh criticism of political, cultural, or religious leaders in public discourse may be chilled, warranting the strategic protection provided by a heightened mental state of recklessness. But that was not the case in *Counterman*.

Moreover, the Court's chilling-effects calculus was incomplete because it failed to account for the chilling effect that such speech has on its victims. As the Court noted, the chilling-effects doctrine has "always recognized—and insisted upon 'accomodat[ing]'—the competing value[]' in regulating historically unprotected expression."[40] Besides a cursory mention of the harm suffered by victims and society, the Court did not consider potential accommodations for the "competing value" in regulating threats that destroy victims' ability to express themselves without fear.[41] The majority of cyberstalking victims withdraw from on- and offline expressive activities, just as Whalen stopped performing concerts and moved, abandoning her music career. The Court should have carefully parsed the value of borderline threats being strategically protected and considered the competing value in cyberstalking and threats laws that enable the targets of such speech to speak themselves.[42] The Court should not have imposed a recklessness requirement for threats *made in private communications* to public figures like Whalen[43] or private individuals

---

[39] *See* Frederick Schauer, *Intentions, Conventions, and the First Amendment: The Case of Cross-Burning*, 2003 Sup. Ct. Rev. 197, 211, 218.

[40] *Counterman*, 600 U.S. at 80.

[41] Mary Anne Franks will be exploring all aspects of what she calls "fearless speech" in an upcoming book. *See* Mary Anne Franks, Fearless Speech (forthcoming) (on file with author).

[42] *See* Danielle Keats Citron & Jonathon W. Penney, *When Law Frees Us to Speak*, 87 Fordham L. Rev. 2317, 2320 (2019).

[43] The Colorado court of appeals described Whalen as a "local public figure" whose band had a following and who had performed in concerts with major artists. People v. Counterman, 497 P.3d 1039, 1048 (Colo. Ct. App. 2021).

or to *private targets about personal matters*, common in domestic abuse cases.[44]

The Court's ruling will make matters worse for cyberstalking victims. In *Counterman*, the defendant was convicted of emotional-distress cyberstalking without threats. The decision could be read to apply to *all* cyberstalking cases, even ones that do not involve threats. Emotionally distressing cyberstalking can be accomplished by threats, but it also can be accomplished by other categories of unprotected speech, such as the defamation of private figures about personal matters or public matters (with proof of negligence), and by the nonconsensual disclosure of a private figure's nude image, which can be regulated consistent with the First Amendment. Even though defendants in such situations made no threats, their cyberstalking convictions would comport with the First Amendment. Nonetheless, law enforcers might decline to charge defendants. Inattention to such a distinction will exacerbate the problem of legal underenforcement.

Regrettably, the *Counterman* decision gives law enforcers a reason to follow their inclination to take the path of least resistance and ignore complaints. Recklessness is never easy to prove, but gender norms add a destructive twist. Stalkers, who are mostly male, will insist that they never meant to terrorize victims, who are more often female (and ex-partners). Officers may decline to investigate because they believe (consciously or unconsciously) the gender stereotype that women make men do crazy things. Police have been known to tell female victims that stalkers' attention is flattering. The horrific truth is that too many stalkers end up killing victims, especially in domestic abuse cases. In the wake of the *Counterman* ruling, victims and their advocates bear a far too heavy burden.

I. TRUE THREATS: THE PATH TO *COUNTERMAN*

This Part lays out the path to *Counterman*. The Court's First Amendment true-threats doctrine is a modern intervention. The regulation of threats, however, is centuries old.[45]

---

[44] *See, e.g.*, Planned Parenthood of Columbia/Willamette v. Am. Coal. of Life Activists, 290 F.3d 1058, 1075 n.7 (9th Cir. 2002) (en banc) (citing cases imposing an objective standard to assess whether threat amounts to unprotected true threat under the First Amendment).

[45] Virginia v. Black, 538 U.S. 343, 358–60 (2003).

A. THE FIRST AMENDMENT'S ROLE IN THREAT REGULATION

Under First Amendment doctrine, content-based restrictions on speech are permitted in a few limited and narrowly drawn areas, including true threats.[46] True threats are "'serious expressions'" that convey that a speaker means to "commit an act of unlawful violence."[47] True threats fall outside the First Amendment's protection because they have minimal expressive value and inflict considerable costs by instilling fear of violence, disrupting individuals and communities, and increasing the potential for violence.[48] Threats of violence cause people to withdraw from crucial life activities, including self-expression.[49] Threats are "among the most favored weapons of domestic abusers."[50] Whether described as intimidation, harassment, or threats, "the typical case in which *one person by his words makes another fear for his physical safety* is one that has traditionally coexisted comfortably with even a strong First Amendment."[51]

The Supreme Court first addressed the constitutionality of a threat conviction in its 1969 per curiam decision in *Watts v. United States*.[52] The Court took up the case because it involved a "threat that would not reasonably have been taken seriously."[53] At a Vietnam War protest held at the Washington monument, eighteen-year-old Robert Watts told a group of students: "If they ever make me carry a rifle the first man I want to get in my sights is L.B.J."[54] Watts and the students laughed.[55] Watts was convicted under a federal law that prohibited "knowingly and willfully ... (making) any threat to take the life of or to inflict bodily harm upon the President."[56]

---

[46] Chaplinsky v. New Hampshire, 315 U.S. 568, 571 (1942). Categories of unprotected speech include "advocacy intended, and likely, to incite imminent lawless action; obscenity; defamation; speech integral to criminal conduct; so-called 'fighting words'; child pornography; fraud; true threats; and speech presenting some grave and imminent threat the government has the power to prevent." United States v. Alvarez, 567 U.S. 709, 717 (2019).

[47] *Black*, 538 U.S. at 359.

[48] R.A.V. v. City of St. Paul, 505 U.S. 377, 388 (1992).

[49] CITRON, *supra* note 1, at 193–202.

[50] Elonis v. United States, 757 U.S. 723, 748 (2015) (Alito, J., concurring and dissenting in part).

[51] Schauer, *supra* note 39, at 211, 218 (emphasis added).

[52] 394 U.S. 705 (1969) (per curiam).

[53] Schauer, *supra* note 39, at 211.

[54] *Watts*, 394 U.S. at 705–706.

[55] *Id.* at 706.

[56] *Id.* at 705 (quoting 18 U.S.C. § 871(a) (1964)).

The Court reversed the conviction because Watts's statement was protected "political hyperbole."[57] The defendant's remarks were "'a kind of crude offensive method of stating a political opposition to the President.'"[58] They were characteristic of "debate on public issues" given its "unpleasantly sharp attacks on government and public officials."[59] The Court explained that, based on its "context" (a political rally where speech is often "vituperative"), the listeners' reaction (laughter), and the content (the "conditional nature of the statement"), the defendant's remarks did not amount to a true threat of violence.[60]

The Court has distinguished expressive acts that constitute unprotected threats from those that amount to political expression. In *Virginia v. Black*, two men burned a cross on an African American family's lawn in the middle of the night.[61] The men were convicted of violating a statute that banned cross burning with the "intent to intimidate." The Court affirmed that the "First Amendment permits a State to ban a 'true threat'" that involves a "serious expression of an intent to commit an act of unlawful violence to a particular individual or group of individuals."[62] The Court described the cross burning on the Black family's lawn as a "virulent form of intimidation," a type of unprotected true threat, due to the close tie between cross burnings and Ku Klux Klan violence against African Americans, the absence of permission to enter the property, and the targeting of a Black family.[63]

Since the advent of the internet, state and lower federal courts have been addressing the constitutionality of convictions for threats of violence made online. Most courts have found that First Amendment concerns are sufficiently addressed by an "objective" assessment that it was reasonably foreseeable to the speaker (or the listener) that the statement would be understood as a serious threat of violence; the objective assessment involves a negligence standard.[64] A small number of courts found that the First Amendment required proof that the

---

[57] *Id.* at 708.

[58] *Id.*

[59] *Id.*

[60] *Id.* In dicta, the Court noted that the threats statute at issue was valid. *Id.* at 707.

[61] 538 U.S. 343 (2003).

[62] *Black*, 538 U.S. at 359.

[63] *Id.* at 359, 363.

[64] Planned Parenthood of Columbia/Willamette v. Am. Coal. of Life Activists, 290 F.3d 1058, 1075 n.7 (9th Cir. 2002) (en banc) (citing cases).

defendant subjectively intended to threaten the victim to constitute a true threat.[65]

In 2014, in *United States v. Elonis*, the Supreme Court considered the constitutionality of a conviction for online threats. The defendant, Anthony Elonis, challenged his conviction under 18 U.S.C. § 875(c), which bans "any threat to injure the person of another" in interstate commerce.[66] The defendant was convicted for posting "graphically violent" rap lyrics on a Facebook page, first under his own name and then a pen name. His posts included "crude, degrading, and violent material" about his ex-wife, former female co-worker, and a female FBI agent, which caused them to fear for their safety.[67] Posts included: "Did you know that it's illegal for me to say I want to kill my wife?" Of the female FBI agent who visited his home, the defendant wrote: "Little Agent lady stood so close, Took all the strength I had not to turn the b**** a ghost, Pull my knife, fick my rist, and slit her throat." Another post read: "I've got enough explosives/to take care of the State Police and the Sherriff's Department."[68] The defendant's ex-wife sought a restraining order after his first threatening post. The defendant continued to post similar messages even after the restraining order was issued against him.

The defendant argued that the First Amendment required proof of his subjective intent to terrorize and that he never intended to terrorize anyone with his "rap lyric" posts.[69] The government argued that subjective intent was not constitutionally required to criminalize true threats. The trial judge instructed the jury that a statement is a true threat when a defendant intentionally makes a statement in a context where a reasonable person would foresee that the statements would be interpreted as a serious expression to inflict bodily injury.[70] On that basis, the jury found the defendant guilty of violating Section 875(c).

The Supreme Court explained that a true threat "speaks to what the statement conveys—not the mental state of the author."[71] An "anonymous letter that says 'I'm going to kill you' is an 'expression of an

---

[65] United States v. Twine, 853 F.2d 676, 680 (9th Cir. 1988).
[66] United State v. Elonis, 575 U.S. 723, 732 (2015).
[67] *Id.* at 731.
[68] *Id.* at 726–27.
[69] *Id.*
[70] *Id.*
[71] *Id.*

intention to inflict loss or harm' regardless of the author's intent." The Court decided the case on statutory grounds, finding that when Congress is silent as to the required mental state in a criminal statute, as it was in Section 875(c), the law should be understood as requiring a mental state that would separate wrongful conduct from innocent conduct.[72] As the Court explained, the jury was charged with "negligence"—whether a reasonable person would have understood the statement as threatening.[73] The Court explained that it has "long been reluctant to infer that a negligence standard was intended in criminal statutes."[74] Given congressional silence, the Court ruled that the lower court should not have inferred negligence as the law's *mens rea*. The Court remanded the proceedings to the appellate court to assess the proper mental state.[75] The Court declined to address whether the First Amendment required a showing of defendant's subjective intent vis-à-vis the threatening statement.[76] The Court determined that it was "not necessary to consider any First Amendment issues." Nearly a decade later, the Court granted certiorari in *Counterman v. Colorado* to consider that question.

B. COUNTERMAN V. COLORADO

Coles Whalen was a professional singer-songwriter living in Denver, Colorado.[77] In ten years, she had released six albums; her music had appeared in films and television shows.[78] Whalen had played in thousands of venues.[79] She had headlined her own shows and served as the opening act for well-known artists like Joan Jett, Pat Benatar, and Kellie Pickler.[80]

In early 2014, a stranger, Billy Raymond Counterman, began sending Whalen unwanted Facebook messages. Every day brought new messages. The defendant's texts suggested that he thought he

---

[72] *Id*. at 737, 740.

[73] *Id*. at 740.

[74] *Id*.

[75] *Id*. at 741.

[76] *Id*.

[77] Brief of Coles Whalen as Amicus Curiae in Support of Respondent, Counterman v. Colorado, 600 U.S. 66 (2023) (No. 22-138), at 1, 5.

[78] *Id*. at 2, 6–7.

[79] *Id*. at 2.

[80] *Id*.

was in a relationship with Whalen.[81] They implied he was physically following her.[82] The defendant said that he saw Whalen driving a white Jeep (a car she once owned) and that he attended her shows.[83] He commented on her outfits and travels, including her visits to her mother.[84]

Over the next two years, Whalen received dozens of texts a day. She never responded to his messages and tried to block him on multiple occasions.[85] Each time, the defendant set up a new profile and resumed contact.[86] Because Whalen was seeking to build her following, she used an auto-accept feature for new friend requests.[87] The defendant also sent her messages via her website. His messages grew increasingly hostile: "Fuck off permanently"; "You're not being good for human relations. Die"; "Your arrogance offends anyone in my position"; and "[s]taying in cyber life is going to kill you."[88]

By the time Whalen sought local law enforcement's help, Counterman had sent *hundreds* of unwanted messages. Officers took the complaint seriously.[89] Counterman had previously been incarcerated for making threatening interstate phone calls to four women in violation of 18 U.S.C. § 875(c).[90] He began sending messages to Whalen during his supervised release from prison. Officers advised Whalen to carry a gun.[91] With counsel's help, she obtained a civil protective order against Counterman,[92] who was thereafter arrested for violating Colorado's emotional-distress stalking (without a threat), harassment (with a threat), and cyberstalking (with a threat) laws. Both the harassment

---

[81] *Counterman*, 600 U.S. at 70.

[82] *Id.*

[83] *Id.*

[84] *Id.*; *see also* Allison Sherry, *One Colorado Stalking Victim Never Wanted to Become the Center of a First Amendment Case at the Supreme Court*, CPR NEWS (Apr. 18, 2023, 4:00 AM), https://www.cpr.org/2023/04/18/supreme-court-free-speech-colorado-stalking-case.

[85] People v. Counterman, 497 P.3d 1039, 1048 (Colo. Ct. App. 2021).

[86] *Id.* at 1043.

[87] *Id.*

[88] *Id.* at 1044.

[89] *Id.* at 1043. Law enforcement's rapid response and help was a rarity. CITRON, *supra* note 1, at 83–89.

[90] *Counterman*, 497 P.3d at 1042.

[91] *Id.*

[92] *Id.*

(with a threat) and cyberstalking (with a threat) charges were dropped before trial.[93]

The trial addressed Counterman's culpability under Colorado's emotional-distress stalking law, which prohibited knowingly and "repeatedly ... [making] any form of communication with another person" in a "manner that would cause a reasonable person to suffer serious emotional distress and [w]hich did cause that person to suffer serious emotional distress."[94] Whalen testified that Counterman's messages put her "in fear and upended her daily existence."[95] Her bandmate explained that she was "too frightened to book shows because it meant that we had to post online where we would be and at what time. We did not know what Bill Counterman looked like—he could be anyone at any show. [Whalen] became afraid to talk to people; she was anxious, unhappy, and constantly checking in with security."[96] Whalen "stopped walking alone, declined social engagements, and canceled some of her performances, though doing so caused her financial strain."[97]

Counterman moved to dismiss the charge before jury deliberations began. He argued that because his messages did not amount to an unprotected "true threat," any conviction would violate the First Amendment.[98] The trial court ruled that given the circumstances, the jury could find that the defendant's statements amounted to a true threat.[99] The court observed that "if something is found not to be a true threat, it's subject to First Amendment protection and it will not support a charge or a conviction of stalking or ... harassment."[100] Counterman was found guilty of emotional-distress stalking (without a threat) and sentenced to four-and-a-half years in prison.[101]

Counterman then sought to vacate his emotional-distress stalking conviction on First Amendment grounds.[102] Colorado's court of

---

[93] *Id.*

[94] *Id.* at 1052 (citing Colo. Rev. Stat. § 18-3-602(1)(c) (2022)).

[95] Counterman v. Colorado, 600 U.S. 66, 70 (2023).

[96] *Counterman*, 497 P.3d at 1042.

[97] *Counterman*, 600 U.S. at 70.

[98] *Id.* at 71.

[99] *Id.*

[100] *Counterman*, 497 P.3d at 1045.

[101] *Id.* at 1044.

[102] *Id.* at 1042.

appeals held that his messages constituted unprotected true threats because they implied a desire to see the victim dead, claimed he was physically surveilling her, and were sent directly to the victim.[103] The appellate court explained that in sending threats to Whalen via "instant messages through Facebook," such "direct targeting" is "indicative of a specific pursuit of one person and Counterman's specific intent was to have an emotional effect on [Whalen] alone."[104] The appellate court underscored that Counterman's messages were not part of a broader exchange, but were unwanted and uninvited; Counterman ignored Whalen's repeated efforts to block him—"action that communicated that [Whalen] didn't wish to be contacted by him"—creating new accounts to message her.[105] The appellate court maintained that for First Amendment purposes, a specific intent to threaten was not necessary and that the "objective standard for true threats" was sufficient.[106]

The Supreme Court granted certiorari to address "whether the First Amendment requires proof of a defendant's subjective mindset in true-threats cases" and "if so, what *mens rea* standard is sufficient."[107] Justice Elena Kagan wrote for a 7-2 majority upholding the First Amendment claim, with Justices Sotomayor and Gorsuch writing a concurring opinion, Justices Barrett and Thomas writing a dissent, and Justice Thomas writing a dissent on his own behalf. The Court's ruling began by noting that "true threats" involve "'serious expressions' conveying that a speaker means to 'commit an act of unlawful violence.'"[108] The Court explained that "[w]hether the speaker is aware of, and intends to convey, the threatening aspect of the message is not part of what makes a statement a threat."[109] The Court noted that true threats lack First Amendment protection because they "subject individuals to 'fear of violence' and to the many kinds of 'disruption that fear engenders.'"[110]

The rest of the Court's ruling makes the case for why the First Amendment's chilling-effects doctrine requires some "subjective mental-state requirement" to punish unprotected threats, even though

---

[103] *Id.* at 1048.
[104] *Id.*
[105] *Id.*
[106] *Id.*
[107] Counterman v. Colorado, 600 U.S. 66, 72 (2023).
[108] *Id.* at 74.
[109] *Id.*
[110] *Id.* at 75.

it will "shield[] some true threats from liability."[111] The Court declared that a heightened mental-state requirement was essential to prevent people from censoring their own protected expression because of a concern that their expression might cross the line or get them caught up in the legal system.[112] The chilling-effects doctrine assesses whether a legitimate regulation poses the risk of incidentally deterring protected speech. If so, an important tool to prevent the chilling of protected speech is to "condition liability on the State's showing of a culpable mental state."[113] The Court pointed to its history of imposing heightened mental states to provide "strategic protection" against self-censorship.[114] Although the Court noted that defamation was the "best known and best theorized example," it focused on the actual malice requirement for public officials and figures concerning matters of public import.[115]

The Court announced that a subjective-intent requirement was necessary to ensure that the ordinary citizen would not "swallow words that are in fact not true threats" out of "fear of mistaking whether a statement is a threat."[116] The Court expressed concern that a speaker may be "unsure about the side of a line on which his speech falls," "worry that the legal system will err, and count speech that is permissible as instead not," or "simply be concerned about the expense of becoming entangled in the legal system."[117] The Court analogized the "hazard of self-censorship" presented by threat liability to the chilling concerns raised by defamation claims brought by public officials and public figures in matters of public importance as well as a threat case involving political hyperbole.[118] According to the Court, an "objective standard, turning only on how reasonable observers would construe a statement in context," would discourage "'uninhibited, robust, and wide-open debate that the First Amendment is intended to protect.'"[119] The Court rejected an objective

---

[111] *Id.* at 75.
[112] *Id.*
[113] *Id.*
[114] *Id.* at 76–78.
[115] *Id.* at 76.
[116] *Id.* at 78.
[117] *Id.* at 75.
[118] *Id.* at 78.
[119] *Id.*

standard, "lest true-threats prosecutions chill too much protected, non-threatening expression."[120]

The Court explained that the law of *mens rea* offered different subjective standards, including purpose, knowledge, and recklessness.[121] The Court pronounced the mental state of recklessness as "the right path forward" because it "offers 'enough "breathing space" for protected speech,' without sacrificing too many of the benefits of enforcing laws against true threats."[122] Recklessness required proof that the defendant "consciously disregard[s] a substantial [and unjustifiable] risk that the conduct will cause harm to another."[123]

The Court noted that the chilling-effects doctrine has "always recognized—and insisted on accomodat[ing]—the 'competing value[]' in regulating historically unprotected expression," noting that true threats inflict harms to individuals and society.[124] The Court then concluded that recklessness was required even though it would "impede some true-threat prosecutions."[125] The Court was clear about the tradeoffs: A recklessness requirement "will shield some otherwise proscribable (here, threatening) speech because the State cannot prove what the defendant thought."[126] In other words, victims must endure objectively terrifying threats to prevent the chilling of speech at the borderline of threats.[127]

Justice Amy Coney Barrett, joined by Justice Clarence Thomas, dissented.[128] In her view, First Amendment precedent "does more than allow an objective test for true threats; on balance, it affirmatively supports one."[129] Pointing to the *Watts* decision, Justice Barrett noted that true threats can be "reliably distinguished from protected speech" like political hyperbole when context is properly considered.[130] Indeed, the objective test has been applied to distinguish protected statements

---

[120] *Id.*
[121] *Id.* at 78–79.
[122] *Id.* at 79, 82.
[123] *Id.* at 79.
[124] *Id.* at 80.
[125] *Id.*
[126] *Id.* at 81–82.
[127] *Id.*
[128] *Id.* at 105.
[129] *Id.*
[130] *Id.* at 113.

made in connection with matters of public concern, including criticism of the fitness of political or religious figures.[131] Justice Barrett argued that the Colorado stalking law protects against the chilling of protected speech by limiting liability to cases where the "entire factual context" shows an intent to commit unlawful violence against an individual or group.[132]

Justice Barrett took the Court to task for heavily relying on defamation doctrine but then "depend[ing] on a single, cherry-picked strand of the doctrine."[133] Justice Barrett argued that the Court's decisions in the defamation area "do[] not justify a heightened mens rea for true threats."[134] Justice Barrett underscored that a private person "need only satisfy an objective standard to recover actual damages for defamation" and if defamatory speech involves purely private matters, then punitive damages can be recovered on the same showing.[135] Justice Barrett explained that true threats "rarely are proximate to matters of public concern" and even "public figures cannot use counterspeech in the public square to protect themselves from serious threats of physical violence."[136] Threats are similar to defamation of private figures: They have little social value, the potential for harm is high, and counter speech cannot offset the harm.[137] She criticized the Court for according threats with a "'pride of place among unprotected speech.'"[138]

Justice Barrett underscored the significance of the Court's ruling: "Perversely, private individuals now have less protection from true threats than from defamation—even though they presumably value their lives more than their reputations."[139] It is not only that cyberstalking can be low value and as damaging as defamation of private individuals or purely private matters, but it can and is a predicate of violence that can be prevented by taking it seriously. For this

---

[131] United States v. Cassidy, 814 F. Supp. 2d 574 (D. Md. 2011).
[132] *Counterman*, 600 U.S. at 113–14.
[133] *Id.* at 111.
[134] *Id.*
[135] *Id.*
[136] *Id.* at 112.
[137] *Id.*
[138] *Id.* at 108.
[139] *Id.* at 113.

reason, stalking is known as "slow motion murder."[140] Justice Barrett noted that because the heightened mental-state requirement will apply to all matters involving true threats, victims will have difficulty obtaining protective orders, a dangerous and deadly proposition for domestic abuse victims.

Justice Barrett warned that a recklessness requirement will be used to shield the "delusional" or "devious" stalker from liability.[141] Of course, any criminal defendant can (or pretend to) be untethered from reality. But delusional assertions may be more persuasive in cyberstalking cases than other criminal matters. Take a home invasion burglary case. Jurors are unlikely to credit a burglar's belief that homeowners wanted their possessions stolen. But jurors might believe delusional cyberstalkers who say they thought victims welcomed their abuse, especially when the prosecution or plaintiff has the burden of proving otherwise.[142] Psychologists and popular culture say that love drives us crazy.[143] Gender norms and stereotypes blame women when men go to extremes for love.[144] Defendants will avail themselves of that argument, even if they are more devious than delusional. Given how gender norms and stereotypes operate, when men make those arguments, regrettably, they may prevail.

Concerns about the possibility of a delusional stalker have been raised in the aftermath of *Counterman*. On September 21, 2023, a

---

[140] *Quick Guide to Stalking: 16 Important Statistics and What You Can Do About It*, NCADV BLOG (Jan. 30, 2017), https://ncadv.org/blog/posts/quick-guide-to-stalking-16-important-statistics-and-what-you-can-do-about-it ("76% of women murdered by an intimate partner were stalked first while 85% of women who survived murder attempts were stalked."); Susanna S. Gibson, *Stalking Is Referred to as Slow Motion Murder Which I Can Personally Attest Is True*, DAILY KOS (Jan. 26, 2023), https://www.dailykos.com/stories/2023/1/26/2149406/-Stalking-Has-Been-Referred-to-as-Murder-in-Slow-Motion-Which-I-Can-Personally-Attest-Is-True.

[141] *Counterman*, 600 U.S. at 120. Justice Barrett was echoing the concerns raised by Colorado Attorney General Phil Weiser at oral argument. Transcript of Oral Argument, *Counterman*, 600 U.S. 66 (No. 22-138), at 69.

[142] I deliberately use the gender pronoun "she" to describe victims and "he" to describe perpetrators because more often victims of cyberstalking are female and perpetrators are male. CITRON, *supra* note 1, at 13–15; JANKOWICZ, *supra* note 17, at xii–xviii.

[143] Dena Domenicali-Rochelle, *Why Love Can Make You Crazy: And Why It Can Be Dangerous*, PSYCH. TODAY (Apr. 11, 2016), https://www.psychologytoday.com/us/blog/contemporary-psychoanalysis-in-action/201604/why-love-can-make-you-crazy; *see, e.g.*, CRAZY, STUPID, LOVE (Warner Bros. Pictures 2011); CRAZY LOVE (Magnolia Pictures 2007); DRIVE ME CRAZY (20th Century Fox 1999).

[144] *See generally* KATE MANNE, DOWN GIRL: THE LOGIC OF MISOGYNY (2017) (introducing the concept "himpathy" as the excessive sympathy shown toward male perpetrators of sexual violence).

Washington appellate court reversed a harassment conviction in light of *Counterman* so the defendant could be allowed to show that she was not "lucid" (subjectively aware) when she threatened to kill her fifteen-year-old daughter.[145] During a fight, the defendant grabbed her daughter by the hair and hit her.[146] After taking away her daughter's phone, the defendant ripped an air conditioner out of their home's wall, saying there were "cameras inside it" and her daughter was involved in the "set up."[147] The defendant threatened to bash in her daughter's head and kill her.[148] A jury found the defendant guilty of misdemeanor harassment based on a threat of physical violence. The court held that while the evidence supported the harassment conviction under a pre-*Counterman* objective standard, the conviction could not be sustained under the recklessness requirement.[149] The court explained that the defendant "was not lucid and was upset her daughter was recording her. One does not kill a person, much less a daughter, for secretly recording them."[150] The court remanded the case for a retrial because a "rational trier of fact could find that [the defendant's] statements were not literal and that she was subjectively unaware of their threatening nature."[151] Although the court did not exonerate the defendant but rather sent the case for retrial with revised jury instructions, *Counterman* is impacting cases in precisely the way that Justice Barrett and Colorado Attorney General Phil Weiser warned.

II. THE COURT'S FLAWED CHILLING-EFFECTS CALCULUS

The *Counterman* decision erred in requiring a heightened mental state of recklessness for *all* threat liability. It should have considered the vastly different free speech values at stake in regulating threats sent in private communications, threats targeting private figures about personal matters, and threats aimed at public officials and figures

---

[145] State v. Beal, No. 39022-5-III (Wash. Ct. App. Sept. 21, 2023).

[146] *Id.* at 2.

[147] *Id.* at 3.

[148] *Id.*

[149] *Id.* at 14–15.

[150] *Id.* at 14.

[151] *Id.* at 14–15. Eugene Volokh helpfully highlighted this case. Eugene Volokh, *A Rare Case Where the Court's New Threats Case (Counterman) May Make a Difference*," REASON (Sept. 23, 2023, 10:54 AM), https://reason.com/volokh/2023/09/23/a-rare-case-where-the-courts-new-threats-case-counterman-may-make-a-difference.

in public discourse. The chilling-effects doctrine creates a "buffer zone, a margin of error" to guard against mistakenly deterring protected speech.[152] It does so on the premise that protected expression that might be chilled is a "particularly valuable activity, toward which legal rules must show special solicitude."[153] The chilling-effects doctrine is "based on the assumption, perhaps unprovable, that the uninhibited exchange of information, the active search for truth, and the open criticism of government are positive virtues."[154]

Under the chilling-effects doctrine, the Court has imposed intent requirements as a "prophylactic shield around some speech in order to safeguard other truly protected speech."[155] Intent requirements are meant to provide "buffer zones" for speech that advances "the features that give protected expression affirmative value."[156] Consider the Court's treatment of defamation. False statements of fact that defame a person's reputation fall outside the range of speech intended to be protected by the First Amendment. The Court's decisions explicitly link the imposition of heightened mental states to the prophylatic protection of free speech values. The Court required public official and public figure plaintiffs to show *actual malice*—knowledge or recklessness as to the falsity of the statement—to ensure broad latitude for debate on matters of public concern.[157] False and defamatory statements about private figures on matters of public concern require *negligence* for compensatory damages.[158] False and defamatory statements about purely private matters may be governed by more permissive common-law standards.[159] In *Dun & Bradstreet v. Greenmoss*

---

[152] Frederick Schauer, *Fear, Risk and the First Amendment: Unraveling the Chilling Effect*, 58 B.U. L. Rev. 685, 710–11 (1978).

[153] Leslie Kendrick, *Speech, Intent, and the Chilling Effect*, 54 William & Mary L. Rev. 1633 (2013).

[154] Schauer, *supra* note 152, at 694.

[155] *See generally* Kendrick, *supra* note 153 (challenging whether intent requirements serve the purpose of strategic protection of free speech values).

[156] *Id.*

[157] N.Y. Times Co. v. Sullivan, 376 U.S. 254, 280 (1964); Garrison v. Louisiana, 379 U.S. 64, 74 (1964) (extending actual malice standard to criminal defamation action involving falsehoods alleged about a public figure where the alleged defamatory statements did not involve purely private matters).

[158] Gertz v. Robert Welch, Inc., 418 U.S. 323, 339–40 (1974).

[159] Dun & Bradstreet v. Greenmoss Builders, 472 U.S. 749, 763 (1985) (plurality op.). The Court ruled that the petitioner's credit report did not concern a matter of public import because it was solely in the speaker's interest and directed at a specific business audience. Also, because the credit report was made available to only five subscribers, it could not be said to involve any "strong interest in the free flow of commercial information." *Id.*

Builders, the Court held that defamation about private matters is not afforded strategic protection against self-censorship because borderline defamation would not impact the "unfettered interchange of ideas for bringing about political and social change" or risk self-censorship by the press.[160]

Had *Counterman* involved a threat made *in public discourse* to a *public official or figure*, the Court's adoption of the recklessness requirement would have been justified. Speakers might refrain from expressing harsh criticism of cultural, political, or religious leaders for fear of crossing the line into threats or attracting the attention of law enforcement. Time has shown that there is an especially significant risk of wrongful prosecution of protected speech when the "speech at issue is critical of government."[161] Borderline threats involving public figures or officials made in public warrant the strategic protection provided by a recklessness requirement to address the risk that speakers might otherwise refrain from engaging in protected expression.

The Court took a wrong turn in requiring a heightened mental state of recklessness for threats made in private communications (as in *Counterman*) and threats targeting private figures about purely private matters, such as personal grudges and domestic abuse. Speech at the borderline of those types of threats have "few of the features that give protected speech affirmative value."[162] Such borderline threats "do not constitute ideas that can be refuted unless responding that someone should not be [killed or] raped is a meaningful counterpoint."[163]

Threats made in private communications have no bearing on the "uninhibited exchange of information, the active search for truth, and the open criticism of government."[164] A threatening direct message, "even one directed at a public figure, does not merit protection even if an identically worded one in a publicly viewable [post] would."[165] Take Counterman's threatening messages. They were not made in a public discussion; only Whalen saw them. True, she was a public figure, but Counterman's texts had no political, cultural, or social value.[166] And in

---

[160] *Id.*

[161] Schauer, *supra* note 152, at 696 n.54.

[162] Kendrick, *supra* note 153, at 1663.

[163] *Id.*

[164] Schauer, *supra* note 152, at 693.

[165] Pierce, *supra* note 38, at 56.

[166] CITRON, *supra* note 1, at 198.

addition to the low value of direct threats, responding to stalkers like Counterman is dangerous—responses may be viewed as encouragement or a provocation to violence.

Threats targeting private figures about personal matters do not warrant strategic protection under the principles of the chilling-effects doctrine. Consider *United States v. Grob*, a domestic abuse case where the defendant, Jeffrey Grob, sent twenty-two threatening emails and fifty text messages to his ex-girlfriend after she suffered a miscarriage.[167] The defendant's emails and texts included statements like "I am going to slit your throat. I am not even kidding. It would make be fill [sic] so good to see you bleed as you gasp for air. I hope your are [sic] ready for retribution, because it is coming. You are going down bitch."[168] Messages included photos of dead and dismembered women.[169] The defendant attached a photograph of a dead infant in an email entitled "OMG our baby."[170] Grob pled guilty to one count of cyberstalking under federal law, 18 U.S.C. § 2261A(2)(B).[171]

Threats aimed at private individuals about personal matters like *Grob* have no political, cultural, or ideological value. When speakers "target private individuals against whom they have personal grudges ... there is no threat to the free and robust debate of *public issues*; there is no potential interference with a meaningful dialogue of *ideas*; and the threat of liability does not pose the risk of a reaction of self-censorship on *matters of public import*."[172] The Court in *Counterman* should have recognized that borderline threats involving private targets about personal matters do not deserve special solicitude that a required mental state of recklessness secures.

It is fruitful to compare the First Amendment restrictions on incitement to threats with private targets or threats conveyed in private messages. In *Brandenberg v. Ohio*, the Court declared that while incitement falls outside the First Amendment, the regulation of incitement requires not only proof of subjective intent, but also proof that the defendant's utterances were likely to produce imminent

---

[167] United States v. Grob, 625 F.3d 1209 (9th Cir. 2010).
[168] *Id.* at 1212.
[169] *Id.*
[170] *Id.*
[171] *Id.*
[172] Pierce, *supra* note 38, at 54.

lawless action.[173] The Court's adoption of a wide buffer zone for incitement is essential to protect against self-censorship because the "distinction between [political] advocacy and incitement is indeed too subtle, and the mistaken punishment of lawful political discourse too harmful to allow the placing of the legal line where it ideally should be drawn."[174] As Frederick Schauer has argued, the "heated discussion of political doctrine often blends imperceptibly into the forceful advocacy of illegal action. And as the likelihood for error is great, so is the harm generated by such error. The lawful advocacy of ideas is often most effective when it approaches incitement.... [T]he margin for error must be drawn in favor of speech."[175] As Geoffrey Stone has powerfully shown, the government has, time and again, overestimated the danger associated with calls for violence or illegal activity, especially in times of war or perceived national threats, because it cannot know if unknown third parties will respond to those calls and because it will be prone to overreact to calls for violence in connection with political ideas.[176]

By contrast, true threats of violence are targeted at specific individuals, not unknown third parties. Victims experience harm upon learning that someone has threatened to assault, rape, or kill them. Their fear prevents them from leaving home, interacting with friends, speaking online, and engaging with the world.[177] Threats targeting private figures or sent in private messages do not come anywhere near the realm of political advocacy or debate. Such borderline threats are not a "hair's breadth away from 'political advocacy'—and in particular from strong protests against the government and prevailing social order," as is true for incitement.[178] This comparison shows the profoundly different free speech values at stake, from the most protective realm of

---

[173] Brandenburg v. Ohio, 395 U.S. 444, 447 (1969) (per curiam).

[174] Schauer, *supra* note 152, at 725.

[175] *Id.*

[176] GEOFFREY R. STONE, PERILOUS TIMES: FREE SPEECH IN WARTIME FROM THE SEDITION ACT OF 1798 TO THE WAR ON TERRORISM 182–98 (2004) (laying out the federal government's aggressive prosecution of political dissent during World War I).

[177] In connection with my work over the years, I have interviewed more than a hundred individuals who faced threatening cyberstalking. Every single person described being afraid of physical violence and further attacks by perpetrators, which led them to shut down their social media profiles and withdraw from relationships.

[178] Counterman v. Colorado, 600 U.S. 66, 81 (2023). The dissent also distinguished incitement from threats for similar reasons. *Id.* at 112–13 (Barrett, J., dissenting, joined by Thomas, J.).

incitement to the low value of speech concerning certain threats that warrant the least protection under the chilling-effects analysis.[179]

The Court's overprotective "one-size-fits-all" approach was paired with its failure to complete the chilling-effects analysis. The Court explained that precedent has "always recognized—and insisted on 'accommodat[ing]'—the 'competing value[]' in regulating historically unprotected expression."[180] And yet the Court said nothing beyond that threat regulation "protects against profound harms, to both individuals and society, that attend true threats of violence—as evidenced in this case." Left unexplored was the "competing value" of threat regulations: the protection of victims' speech and other expressive activities. Threat and cyberstalking laws protect victims from fear that impedes their ability to speak and engage in public discourse. They enable individuals to participate in expressive activities.[181]

The Court did not consider possibilities that might accommodate the government's interest in deterring threats that inculcate fear and silencing. Empirical evidence was before the Court.[182] Studies show that cyberstalking victims close their social media accounts; some "quit the internet totally."[183] They stop using their phones.[184] Victims change how they express themselves; they are less controversial, more muted, and connect with fewer people.[185] Their withdrawal from

---

[179] Threats of violence aimed at a private person about a personal matter and threats made in private messages differ from private efforts at incitement—like X urges Y to kill Z. Threats of violence impact the listener target immediately, causing fear that disrupts their lives and silences them. There is nothing conveyed except essentially "I will kill, rape, or maim you." Threats of that type have no normative value. By contrast, the private incitement of violence is contingent. True, it may have nothing to do with politics, culture, or any ideas at all. But it raises concerns about overreaction because, once law enforcers find out, they won't know with any certainty if the listener to the private incitement will do anything at all.

[180] *Counterman*, 600 U.S. at 80.

[181] *See generally* Citron & Penney, *supra* note 42.

[182] *See generally* Brief of First Amendment Scholars Erwin Chemerinsky et al. as Amici Curiae in Support of Respondent, *Counterman*, 600 U.S. 66 (2023) (No. 22-138). On the Court's reliance on empirical research presented to it and identified by the Justices themselves, see Frederick Schauer, *The Dilemma of Ignorance: PGA Tours v. Casey Martin*, 2001 SUP. CT. REV. 267; Frederick Schauer & Virginia J. Wise, *Non-Legal Information and the Delegalization of Law*, 29 J. LEG. STUD. 495 (2000).

[183] Stevens et al., *supra* note 14, at 372.

[184] *Id.*

[185] CITRON, *supra* note 1, at 26; NICOLA HENRY, CLARE MCGLYNN, ASHER FLYNN, KELLY JOHNSON, ANASTASIA POWELL & ADRIAN J. SCOTT, IMAGE-BASED SEXUAL ABUSE: A STUDY ON THE CAUSES AND CONSEQUENCES OF NON-CONSENSUAL NUDE OR SEXUAL IMAGERY 59 (2020).

online engagement isolates them from friends and family.[186] When victims change their phone numbers to prevent stalkers from calling them, they become unreachable.[187] To return to *Counterman*, the defendant's threatening texts made Whalen so afraid that the defendant would confront and hurt her that she canceled concerts and stopped meeting fans. Whalen stopped contributing to what Jack Balkin describes as "democratic culture," a loss for her fans, audiences, and society.[188]

The "competing value" at stake—the role that cyberstalking and threat laws play in protecting victims' expressive autonomy—implicates structural disadvantages facing women and girls. In the context of workplace sexual harassment, Catharine MacKinnon has argued that the abuse "works to exclude and segregate and denigrate and subordinate and dehumanize, violating human dignity and denying equality of opportunity."[189] Time and time again, we have seen how some expression denies others' "full and equal opportunity to engage in public debate."[190] Silencing is especially likely when women and girls are stalked online.[191] As Jonathon Penney has found, women are statistically more chilled in their speech and engagement when targeted with online abuse.[192] A report issued by Data and Society in 2016 explained that "younger women are most likely to self-censor to avoid potential online harassment: 41% of women ages 15 to 29 self-censor, compared with 33% of men of the same age group and 24% of internet users ages 30 and older (men and women)."[193] In a

---

[186] Delanie Woodlock, *The Abuse of Technology in Domestic Violence and Stalking*, 23 VIOLENCE AGAINST WOMEN 584, 594–95 (2017); Soheila Pashang et al., *The Mental Health Impact of Cyber Sexual Violence on Youth Identity*, 17 INT'L J. MENTAL HEALTH & ADDICTION 1119 (2019).

[187] Woodlock, *supra* note 186, at 595; Tatiana Begotti & Daniela Acquadro Maran, *Characteristics of Cyberstalking Behavior, Consequences, and Coping Strategies: A Cross-Sectional Study in a Sample of Italian University Students*, 11 FUTURE INTERNET 1, 2 (2019).

[188] *See generally* Jack M. Balkin, *Digital Speech and Democratic Culture: A Theory of Freedom of Expression for the Information Society*, 79 N.Y.U. L. REV. 1 (2004)

[189] CATHARINE A. MACKINNON, ONLY WORDS 46 (1993).

[190] OWEN M. FISS, THE IRONY OF FREE SPEECH 15 (1996).

[191] As Jennifer Rothman aptly put it, laws combating threats deter and punish speech that "coerce[s]" people into "acting against their will." Jennifer E. Rothman, *Freedom of Speech and True Threats*, 25 HARV. J.L. & PUB. POL'Y 283, 290–91 (2001).

[192] Jonathon W. Penney, *Internet Surveillance, Regulation, and Chilling Effects Online: A Comparative Case Study*, 6 INTERNET POL'Y REV. 1, 19 (2017).

[193] Amanda Lenhart et al., *Online Harassment, Digital Abuse, and Cyberstalking in America*, DATA & SOC'Y RSCH. INST. & CTR. FOR INNOVATIVE PUB. HEALTH RSCH. 4 (Nov. 21, 2016), https://www.datasociety.net/pubs/oh/Online_Harassment_2016.pdf.

2018 global survey, the International Women's Media Foundation found that forty percent of respondents "avoided reporting certain stories as a result of online harassment."[194] The National Democratic Institute found that in 2019, politically active women sent fewer tweets in the aftermath of online attacks.[195] In 2020, Plan International conducted a study of 14,000 girls from thirty-one countries and found that nineteen percent of girls who were harassed frequently online said that they use social media platforms less and twelve percent said that they stopped using them altogether.[196] The authors argued that girls "pay a high price [to their expression] for other people's, largely men's, 'right' to free speech."[197] Cyberstalking deprives listeners of the political, cultural, and social expression of women and girls.

As the disparate impact of cyberstalking on the expressive opportunities of women and girls shows, the competing value of cyberstalking and threat laws involved speech and equality interests. The Court failed to recognize, let alone consider, ways to accommodate those profoundly important interests. This is not to suggest that a competing interest in equality demands that a different First Amendment standard apply to threats made to women and girls and those made to men and boys. Instead, it is to highlight that the Court ignored weighty competing values—the chilling of the victim/listeners' speech and the equality of opportunity—in its chilling-effects analysis.

In short, the *Counterman* decision insisted that objectively terrifying threats must be tolerated to protect potential speakers, but failed to consider how the borderline threats in private messages or targeting private figures about personal matters do not involve speech worthy of strategic protection. The Court failed to acknowledge and recognize the fact that regulating threats protects victims' expressive autonomy and equal opportunity. These considerations should have led the Court to find that the threats sent to victims in private messages and threats with private targets about personal matters require no more than what the Colorado cyberstalking statute provided—proof that a

---

[194] Michelle P. Ferrier, *Attacks and Harassment: The Impact on Female Journalists and Their Reporting*, INT'L WOMEN'S MEDIA FOUND. 7 (2019), https://www.iwmf.org/wp-content/uploads/2018/09/Attacks-and-Harassment.pdf.

[195] Kirsten Zeiter et al., *Tweets That Chill: Analyzing Online Violence Against Women in Politics*, NAT'L DEMOCRATIC INST. (June 14, 2019), https://www.ndi.org/sites/default/files/NDI%20Tweets%20That%20Chill%20Report.pdf.

[196] SHARON GOULDS ET AL., PLAN INT'L, FREE TO BE ONLINE? GIRLS' AND YOUNG WOMEN'S EXPERIENCES OF ONLINE HARASSMENT 31 (2020).

[197] *Id.*

reasonable person would have understood the threats as serious expressions to cause physical harm.

Oral argument in *Counterman* suggested that certain Justices did not take seriously the way that threats can undermine victims' expressive autonomy. The discussion highlighted the speech risks that members of the Court believed deserved recognition and other speech risks that lacked importance.[198]

Recapping the oral argument, Mary Anne Franks explained that "Chief Justice Roberts used actual examples of Counterman's threatening messages as punchlines, challenging Colorado's attorney to say them in a threatening way, while Justices Gorsuch and Thomas could barely stop laughing long enough to agree that sensitivity was surely a far graver threat to society than stalking."[199] Justice Gorsuch suggested that cyberstalking victims might be overreacting. He remarked to Colorado Attorney General Phil Weiser, who previously served as the Dean of the University of Colorado Law School: "We live in a world in which people are sensitive and—and maybe increasingly sensitive. As a professor, you might have issued a trigger warning from time to time when you discuss a bit of history that is difficult or a case that's difficult. What do we do—in—in a world in which reasonable people may deem things harmful, hurtful, threatening? And we're going to hold people liable willy-nilly for that? ... What do we—how do we talk about history?"[200] Justice Gorsuch was implying that victims of online assaults may be overly sensitive. Comparing tough classroom conversations with the death threats sent to individuals was preposterous. These attitudes make it difficult for the Court to recognize, let alone assess, the damage to cyberstalking victims' speech.

The Court has acknowledged the importance of laws that protect speech interests, even as their enforcement would undermine free speech—the sort of competing value that the *Counterman* decision failed to recognize or accomodate. In *Bartnicki v. Vopper*, the Court considered competing free speech interests in assessing the constitutionality of civil penalties under the federal Wiretap Act.[201] A person recorded a cellphone call between the president of a local teacher's

---

[198] CITRON, *supra* note 13, at 106–10 (emphasizing that law serves as a mirror into our values).

[199] Franks, *supra* note 3.

[200] Transcript of Oral Argument at 65–66, Counterman v. Colorado, 600 U.S. 66 (2023) (No. 22-138).

[201] 532 U.S. 514, 518 (2010).

union and the union's chief negotiator about salary negotiations.[202] During the call, one of parties mentioned "blow[ing] off [the] porches" of school board members' homes.[203] A radio commentator, who received a copy of the recording in his mailbox, incurred civil penalties for broadcasting the conversation.

The Court struck down the money judgment because the private conversation played on the radio involved a "matter of public concern."[204] In arriving at that decision, the Court underscored that free speech interests appeared on both sides of the calculus. The Court characterized the penalties under the Wiretap Act as "present[ing] a conflict between interests of the highest order—on the one hand, the interest in the full and free dissemination of information concerning public issues, and, on the other hand, the interest in individual privacy and, more specifically, in fostering private speech."[205] The Court recognized that concerns about self-censorship animated the Wiretap Act. The "fear of public disclosure of private conversations might well have a chilling effect on private speech."[206] The Court maintained that the privacy and private speech concerns protected by the Wiretap Act had to "give way" to "the interest in publishing matters of public importance"—a heated discussion about salary negotiations between a union's chief negotiator and the president of the teacher's union.[207] In dicta, the Court noted that the state interest in protecting the privacy of communications may be "strong enough to justify" regulation if the communications involved "purely private concerns" like domestic gossip or trade secrets.[208]

Relying on that language, appellate courts have affirmed the constitutionality of civil penalties under the wiretapping statute for the unwanted disclosures of private communiations involving "purely private matters."[209] Much like the federal Wiretap Act, Colorado's cyberstalking law protects free speech interests in the way that the federal wiretapping law fostered private speech. The Court in

---

[202] *Id.*

[203] *Id.* at 519.

[204] *Id.* at 525, 533.

[205] *Id.* at 518.

[206] *Id.* at 533.

[207] *Id.* at 534.

[208] *Id.*

[209] *See, e.g.*, Quigley v. Rosenthal, 327 F.3d 1044, 1067–68 (10th Cir. 2003).

Counterman should have at the least considered the state stalking law's competing value in combating abuse that makes it difficult for many victims to express themselves.[210]

More broadly, to "understand the risks to expression inherent in efforts to regulate online abuse, we need to account for the full breadth of expression imperiled."[211] Affirmative free speech values warrant consideration of the harm to victims' free speech and law's role protecting free expression.[212] As I wrote in *Hate Crimes in Cyberspace*, "[r]obust democratic discourse cannot be achieved if cyber mobs and individual harassers drive victims from it."[213] The silencing impact of cyberstalking "endangers deliberative democracy, which depends upon contributions from diverse voices and perspectives—particularly groups historically excluded from the 'marketplace of ideas.'"[214] The quality of communicative discourse is undermined when some listeners are intimidated into silence while others cannot receive their ideas.[215] Helen Norton explains that a "listener-centered approach permits the government to forbid speakers from coercing listeners' choices through threats."[216]

On a final note, it is important to recognize that the First Amendment's chilling-effects doctrine animates Court-imposed heightened mental-state requirements that create a buffer zone to advance free speech values. Features of the criminal law—including mental state

---

[210] Kenneth L. Karst, *Threats and Meanings: How the Facts Govern First Amendment Doctrine*, 58 STAN. L. REV. 1337, 1340 (2006); *see also* Danielle Keats Citron, *Online Engagement on Equal Terms*, B.U. L. REV. ANNEX 97, 99 (2015) (observing that our understanding of cyber harassment has evolved to recognize the speech interests of victims).

[211] CITRON, *supra* note 1, at 196; Danielle Keats Citron, *Law's Expressive Value in Combating Cyber Gender Harassment*, 108 MICH. L. REV. 373, 406 (2009) ("Although cyber harassers express themselves through their assaults, their actions directly implicate their targets' self-determination and ability to participate in social and political discourse."); Danielle Keats Citron, *Cyber Civil Rights*, 89 B.U. L. REV. 61, 101 (2009) [hereinafter Citron, *Cyber Civil Rights*] (arguing that online attacks "deprive vulnerable individuals of their right to engage in political discourse. The threats, lies, and damaging photographs generate a fear of physical violence, exclusion, and subordination that may propel victims offline").

[212] *See* Citron, *Law's Expressive Value*, *supra* note 210, at 391 (2009) (arguing that society loses when cyber gender harassment victims withdraw from online discourse and can longer engage with their commentary on issues, raising the silencing of computer scientist Kathy Sierra as an illustration).

[213] CITRON, *supra* note 1, at 195.

[214] Citron & Penney, *supra* note 42, at 2320.

[215] Helen Norton, *Powerful Speakers and Their Listeners*, 90 U. COLO. L. REV. 441, 442–43 (2019).

[216] *Id.* at 455.

requirements drafted by lawmakers—help ensure that innocent people are not prosecuted.[217] First Amendment mental-state requirements are "imposed in addition to the due process safeguards that the criminal law already requires, such as proof beyond a reasonable doubt."[218] It is important to recognize when intent requirements are serving free speech values and when they are serving other values, including protecting innocent people from investigation, prosecution, and conviction.

III. Implications for Law's Underenforcement

The *Counterman* ruling landed at a difficult time. It is a truism that when victims report cyberstalking, law enforcers do nothing, even though criminal laws ban cyberstalking, harassment, and threats. Law's underenforcement—already at alarming levels—is sure to worsen. If the opinion is given an overbroad reading to require proof of threats in *all* cyberstalking cases (regardless of whether threats are involved), then law enforcers will have unwarranted reasons to ignore complaints. In cases involving threats, the *Counterman* decision gave law enforcers an easy explanation for their decision not to investigate and prosecute complaints.

A. RISK OF OVERBROAD READING

Let's return to *Counterman*. The Court's failure to say anything about the fact that the defendant was convicted of emotional-distress stalking (not stalking with threats) may confuse law enforcers about the ruling's application. *Counterman* could be read to require proof of recklessness in *all* cyberstalking cases, even when a perpetrator's stalking did not involve express or implied threats.[219] *Counterman* did not rule that unprotected true threats are necessary for cyberstalking convictions to comport with the First Amendment. But law enforcers could get the impression that now there must be proof of recklessly made threats in any cyberstalking case.

---

[217] *See* Kendrick, *supra* note 153, at 1653–54; Larry Alexander, *Free Speech and Speaker's Intent*, 12 Const. Comment. 21, 25 (1995); Schauer, *supra* note 39, at 217–18.

[218] Schauer, *supra* note 39, at 218.

[219] Recall that the trial court in *Counterman* observed that "if something is found not to be a true threat, it's subject to First Amendment protection and it will not support a charge or a conviction of stalking or . . . harassment." People v. Counterman, 497 P.3d 1039, 1045 (Colo. Ct. App. 2021) (quoting the trial court).

If law enforcers fail to appreciate that distinction, achieving justice might be impossible in the following emotional-distress cyberstalking cases:

- A college senior photographed his girlfriend while she was partially nude. He assured his girlfriend that he would destroy the photographs. Two years after graduating, the couple broke up. The man never destroyed the photographs. He posted them on sites devoted to nonconsensual intimate images, dating sites, and advertising hubs. He emailed the woman's partially nude photograph to her supervisor, co-workers, and family members. His emails also falsely claimed that the woman had secretly been a sex worker.[220]
- A woman began posting defamatory falsehoods on social media sites about her former college professor. She accused her former professor, a novelist, of arranging for someone to rape her, sleeping with students, and stealing her work. Over months, she posted the false accusations in different online outlets. She emailed the falsehoods to the professor's publisher, literary agency, school where he taught creative writing, and various magazines where he had published, including the *London Review of Books*. The woman defaced the professor's Wikipedia page and posted Amazon reviews accusing him of plagiarism and sexually inappropriate behavior. The storm of posts and emails involved totally fabricated claims and continued for years. The professor considered suing the student for defamation, but she had no money to recover; all he wanted was for the cyberstalking campaign to stop and getting law enforcement involved seemed to offer the best chance of stopping it.[221]
- During a work trip, a woman stayed in a hotel room where a video camera was secretly recording activity in the bathroom. When she

---

[220] In that case, law enforcement initially refused to help and urged the victim to buy a gun. After a U.S. Senator pressured the state attorney general to act, law enforcement started an investigation but then dropped the case because, as officers told the victim, the man said his computer was hacked. Officers told the victim that they could not get a warrant for the man's computer because cyber harassment was a misdemeanor. That was not true—state courts issue warrants based on probable cause for misdemeanors. Despite the terrorizing nature of the abuse, officers, time and again, disappointed the victim. CITRON, *supra* note 1, at 45–50.

[221] JAMES LASDUN, GIVE ME EVERYTHING: ON BEING STALKED 53, 110–115, 134 (2013) (recounting how his former student stalked him online for years, jeopardizing his work, personal relationships, and engagement with others; local law enforcement refused to pursue charges against the former student because she had not attacked or threatened to kill him and eventually she would stop).

returned home, she received an email with a video of her showering and urinating. The sender said that he would reconsider posting the video online if she sent nude photographs. The woman refused, and the sender posted the video on hundreds of adult sites like PornHub and adult finder sites, with her name embedded in the file and postings. On the rare occasion when a site took down the video after the woman requested that they do so, the video was reposted on the site and other sites. The cyberstalking campaign spanned several months; hundreds of posts with her video remain online.[222]

Law enforcers should have pursued these cases, but social attitudes got in the way. As troubling social attitudes recede, law enforcement might point to *Counterman* and say they cannot help because no reckless threats were involved.

State and lower federal court decisions have upheld cyberstalking convictions because defendants' abuse involved non-threatening speech that enjoyed no or less rigorous protection. In *United States v. Gonzalez*,[223] the defendant posted YouTube videos that falsely accused the victim of sexually molesting her children and emailed the defamatory statements to her friends and acquaintances.[224] The defendant created a false polygraph report that suggested the victim was guilty of child sex abuse. The Third Circuit held that the defendant's harassing course of conduct could be proscribed because it involved unprotected defamation of a private person about a personal matter.[225] Cyberstalking cases involving a pattern of defamation of private figures

---

[222] CITRON, *supra* note 13, at 31–32 (discussing a case where the victim was brushed off by local law enforcement and met with FBI and Secret Service agents who first asked her if she took the video herself and posted it to get attention, but then ultimately told her that they could not figure out the identity of the perpetrator).

[223] 904 F.3d 165 (3d Cir. 2018).

[224] *Id*. at 176; *see also* United States v. Shrader, 675 F.3d 300, 312 (4th Cir. 2012) (affirming constitutionality of stalking conviction where defendant, after being released from prison for killing the victim's mother, repeatedly called the victim's unlisted phone number and sent her a 32-page letter that falsely accused her of killing her mother and aborting his child). As a statutory matter, under 18 U.S.C. § 2261A(2), the government has to show that the defendant intended to harass or intimate the targeted individual, but that is dictated by the statute and not the First Amendment.

[225] *Gonzales*, 904 F.3d at 192; *see also* Thomas v. United States, 2012 WL 1714746, at *13 (D. Me. May 15, 2012), *aff'd*, 748 F.3d 425 (1st Cir. 2014) (upholding constitutionality of cyberstalking conviction where the defendant Thomas sent letters to the victim, a former neighbor, and five other people, including a local police department, falsely claiming the victim was a serial rapist, child molester, and child pornographer and included defamatory statements and implied threats in a letter to victim).

about private matters should be understood as consistent with the First Amendment, as the court held in *Gonzalez*. But I worry that law enforcers will read *Counterman* as requiring recklessly made threats, even when the cyberstalking involves defamation at the heart of the course of conduct.

I am equally concerned that this logic will apply to cyberstalking cases involving intimate privacy violations that can be regulated consistent with the First Amendment. Although the Supreme Court has not yet ruled on the issue, criminal laws banning the nonconsensual public disclosure of someone's nude images have faced constitutional challenge and withstood the crucible of strict-scrutiny review.[226] The Vermont Supreme Court, for instance, upheld the state's nonconsensual intimate imagery law, emphasizing that "from a constitutional perspective, it is hard to see a distinction between laws prohibiting nonconsensual disclosure of personal information comprising images of nudity and those prohibiting the disclosure of other categories of nonpublic personal information" like health data.[227]

Lower federal and state courts have upheld cyberstalking convictions where the defendant's course of conduct involved the posting or sharing of a private person's nude images. In *United States v. Osinger*,[228] the defendant tormented his ex-girlfriend by emailing her nude and sexually explicit photographs to colleagues and family members.[229] He created a fake Facebook profile that featured the victim's name and nude photo and invited her co-workers to connect with the fake profile.[230] The court held that the defendant's conviction comported with the First Amendment because his cyberstalking campaign involved the disclosure and sharing of a private woman's sexually explicit photographs that she never agreed to be made public.[231] The court noted that the victim was a private person whose

---

[226] CITRON, *supra* note 13, at 145 (discussing the laws that the Cyber Civil Rights Initiative helped craft that have been upheld by states' highest courts in the face of constitutional challenges, including Illinois, Minnesota, Indiana, and Vermont).

[227] State v. VanBuren, 214 A.3d 791 (Vt. 2019).

[228] 753 F.3d 939 (9th Cir. 2014).

[229] *Id.* at 947.

[230] *Id.*

[231] *Id.* at 948.

nude images had never been disclosed publicly and the public had "no legitimate interest" in her "private sexual activities."[232]

Law enforcers must be taught that reckless threats may not be necessary for a cyberstalking conviction. Law enforcers should investigate harassing courses of conduct that involve defamatory lies about private individuals about personal matters. They should investigate harassing courses of conduct that involve private individuals about matters of public concern if negligence as to the falsehood can be shown. The same is true of cyberstalking achieved via intimate privacy violations.

B. UNDERENFORCEMENT OF THREAT CASES

The *Counterman* ruling may exacerbate the already woeful underenforcement of cyberstalking laws in cases involving threats. Long before the *Counterman* decision increased the mental state of true threats to recklessness, police officers routinely refused to investigate cyberstalking complaints.[233] To give you a sense of the underenforcement problem, consider a study of eight years (2005–2013) of official data from the Houston Police Department.[234] Researchers found that of the 3,756 stalking reports, officers followed up with sixty-six incident reports and made twelve arrests for stalking.[235] The police department made *no* stalking arrests from 2009–2013.[236]

---

[232] *Id.* The court held, on separate analytical grounds, that the defendant's "expressive" acts lacked First Amendment protection because they were "'integral to criminal conduct' in intentionally harassing, intimidating, and causing substantial emotional distress" to the victim. *Id.* at 947. In *United States v. Petrovic*, 701 F.3d 849 (8th Cir. 2012), the defendant secretly recorded himself and the victim having sex. After they broke up, the defendant texted her to say that he had videos of them having sex and would post them online unless she agreed to get back together with him. *Id.* at 853. After she refused, the defendant mailed dozens of postcards showing the victim undressed to her family members and local businesses; he created a website with links to her nude and sexually explicit images and her phone number and the Social Security numbers of her children. *Id.* The defendant repeatedly called the victim at her workplace. *Id.* The court upheld the constitutionality of the conviction for cyberstalking because First Amendment protections are less rigorous for speech about purely private matters like "intimately private facts and photographs" that had never been made public before and where the public has no legitimate interest in private sexual activities. *Id.* at 855–56.

[233] *See generally* Joanne D. Worsley et al., *Victims' Voices: Understanding the Emotional Impact of Cyberstalking and Individuals' Coping Responses*, 7 SAGE OPEN 1 (2017).

[234] Patrick Q. Brady & Matt R. Nobles, *The Dark Figure of Stalking: Examining Law Enforcement Response*, 32 J. INTERPERSONAL VIOLENCE 3149, 3165 (2017).

[235] *Id.*

[236] *Id.*

The underenforcement of law grows out of intersecting, thorny problems. State and local law enforcement "lack training that would help them understand the seriousness of the attacks, the technologies used to perpetrate them, and the usefulness of existing laws."[237] Added to the lack of training are troubling social attitudes.[238] Officers refuse to help victims because, they explain, the abuse is just "boys being boys" or harmless flirting that should be taken as flattering, not frightening.[239] Another variation on this theme is that victims are to blame for their predicaments.[240]

For victims of stalking, this is chilling. Domestic violence victims (many of whom are subject to stalking) routinely report that emotional abuse of the kind that results from physical stalking is worse than physical abuse. The wounds of emotional abuse persist in searches of victims' names, in emails, and in the fear that perpetrators are not finished attacking them. And too often stalking in domestic abuse cases leads to physical violence and death.

From a cynical perspective, the *Counterman* ruling provides a gloss of legitimacy to officers whose inadequate training or attitudes incline them to ignore victims' complaints. Officers will justify their nonresponse by invoking the concern that defendants did not know that their words were terrifying.[241] The ruling may discourage well-intentioned law enforcers from pursuing cases where defendants claim to believe the victims welcomed their attention, even when that assertion is unbelievable. There is some reason to think that the recklessness standard will deter investigators. Studies have shown that stalking charges are often reduced to lower-level offenses because they do not require proof that "the offender intend[ed] or knowingly instill[ed] fear of death or serious bodily injury."[242] A case against a serial cyberstalker who repeatedly spread nude photos of several women online was dropped because, the prosecutor explained, a key element

---

[237] CITRON, *supra* note 1, at 85.

[238] *Id.*

[239] *Id.* at 85–86; CITRON, *supra* note 13, at 77.

[240] *Id.*

[241] Mary Anne Franks, *The Supreme Court Just Legalized Stalking*, SLATE (July 6, 2023, 5:50 AM), https://slate.com/news-and-politics/2023/07/supreme-court-legalized-stalking-counterman-colorado.html.

[242] Brady & Nobles, *supra* note 234, at 3167.

was missing from the case—the defendant's intent to threaten, harass, or torment the women involved.[243]

Victims will be even more likely to under-report threatening cyberstalking. Before the *Counterman* decision, cyberstalking victims often refrained from contacting law enforcement because they worried that officers would trivialize their suffering.[244]

Consider journalist Julia Ioffe's experience with cyberstalking. Ioffe has been stalked online for five years by a man who sent threatening messages like, "They should put your ass to sleep."[245] A detective told Ioffe that, "if you never said 'no' to this guy, how is he supposed to know that you don't want him contacting you?" The detective advised Ioffe to tell the man to stop contacting her, but to do it in a "nice way" so she did not "make him mad."[246] Note the officer recognizing the danger involved in writing back to stalkers yet still suggesting that she had to tell him no "in a nice way." After the *Counterman* decision, the stalker continued to message her. Ioffe wrote to the man to ask him to stop contacting her. Although the man stopped for a short period of time, he messaged Ioffe to say that her message was "confusing." Her stalker seemed to take her reply as an invitation, as she feared.

Victims should not have to respond to their stalkers to show that they are on notice that their messages are unwelcome. Not writing their stalkers back or blocking them should be enough. And, as the officer implied, saying no to a stalker might make them angry and instigate violence—this is especially likely in domestic abuse cases. Officers can warn stalkers that their communications are frightening and unwelcome. If cyberstalkers continue sending threatening messages after such a warning, prosecutors can point to that fact to show that defendants understood the threatening nature of their statements. If victims like Whalen block stalkers and stalkers create

---

[243] Ari Schneider, *Ignored by Police, Twin Sisters Took Down Their Cyberstalker Themselves*, WASH. POST (Aug. 26, 2023, 2:41 PM), https://www.washingtonpost.com/technology/2023/08/26/revenge-porn-leaked-nudes-police.

[244] CITRON, *supra* note 1, at 75. National studies suggest that up to 80 percent of stalking victims do not contact the police because they worry that officers will think the incident is minor, fear retaliation from the offender, or believe the police will not help them. Brady & Nobles, *supra* note 234, at 3154.

[245] @juliaioffe, X (Sept. 1, 2023, 12:12 PM), https://twitter.com/juliaioffe/status/1697643717438386274.

[246] *Id.* The officer's advice shows the impossible position that victims find themselves in. The officer is effectively asking Ioffe to treat the stalker with kid gloves, as if she, not the police, are best positioned to deal with someone who has said that she should die.

new accounts to overcome those efforts, then prosecutors can argue that the defendant's actions show he knew that his messages were not welcome.[247] At the very least, more training is needed for law enforcement in the face of *Counterman*.

CONCLUSION

The Court's chilling-effects analysis was flawed. In *Counterman*, the Court should have carefully parsed the affirmative value of borderline threats being strategically protected rather than adopting a one-size-fits-all approach. The Court should have recognized that the threats made in private communications or at private targets about personal matters do not warrant strategic protection because borderline speech would have little to no value. The Court also failed to consider the competing values advanced by threat laws, including the protection of victims' expression and equal opportunity. Regrettably, the decision will likely exacerbate the underenforcement of cyberstalking laws. More and better training of law enforcement officers might provide some help in preventing officers from misconstruing the case.[248]

Perhaps, in a future case, the Court will address the argument that cyberstalking involves unprotected conduct.[249] When perpetrators call victims at all hours, day in and day out for years, the abuse is treated as unprotected conduct.[250] The content of unwanted calls and texts is not being regulated, but rather the unrelenting intrusion into private

---

[247] *Understanding the* Counterman v. Colorado *Supreme Court Decision*, STALKING PREVENTION & AWARENESS RES. CTR. (Aug. 2023), https://www.stalkingawareness.org/wp-content/uploads/2023/08/Understanding-the-Counterman-v.-Colorado-Supreme-Court-Decision.pdf.

[248] From 2015–2016, I worked closely with then-California Attorney General Kamala Harris to tackle cyberstalking involving nonconsensual intimate imagery. Our cyber exploitation task force created education tools for law enforcement so officers could see the available legal resources to assist in investigations. *Cyber Exploitation*, CAL. ATT'Y GEN., https://oag.ca.gov/cyberexploitation (providing resources for victims, law enforcement, and industry best practices); Danielle K. Citron, *Attorney General Kamala Harris to Help Law Enforcement in Investigations of Criminal Invasions of Sexual Privacy*, INT'L ASS'N OF CHIEFS OF POLICE L. ENF'T CYBER CTR. (Oct. 20, 2015), https://www.iacpcybercenter.org/the-ground breaking-work-of-attorney-general-kamala-harris-to-help-law-enforcement-in-investigations-of-criminal-invasions-of-sexual-privacy.

[249] *See* Brief of First Amendment Scholars, Evelyn Douek et al. as Amici Curiae in Support of Respondent, Counterman v. Colorado, 600 U.S. 66 (2023) (No. 22-138), at 2.

[250] *See, e.g.*, United States v. Eckhardt, 466 F.3d 938, 944 (11th Cir. 2006) (upholding conviction under federal telephone harassment statute given that the "overarching purpose" of defendant's more than 200 "sexually laced calls was to harass and frighten" his victim, which is not protected speech).

affairs.[251] When supervisors engage in workplace sexual harassment by constantly making lewd sexual propositions to employees, the harassment is viewed as unprotected conduct. Defendants hijack victims' attention and privacy via networked tools, yet the result is different.[252] First Amendment doctrine has endeavored to draw a line between speech and conduct, though that line is inevitably contested.[253] Digital technologies complicate the distinction between speech and conduct because "they make more actions achievable through 'mere' words."[254] The Court may have to reckon with the fact that the internet is not a "magical speech conversion machine."[255]

---

[251] Hence, rulings upholding telephone harassment laws and the CAN-SPAM Act.

[252] CITRON, *supra* note 1; Citron, *Cyber Civil Rights*, *supra* note 210, at 66 (contending that the legal community firmly rooted in the analog world must appreciate that the internet's aggregative character turns expressions into actions and that hundreds of destructive posts and unwanted communications amount to online harassment that should be treated as unprotected conduct).

[253] As Richard Schragger explains, acts and speech cannot be easily distinguished when it comes to the symbolic realm, like wearing an armband, burning a flag, or holding up a sign. Richard C. Schragger, *What is "Government" "Speech"? The Case of Confederate Monuments*, 108 KY. L.J. 665, 675 (2022).

[254] Citron, *Cyber Civil Rights*, *supra* note 211, at 99. *See generally* Frederick Schauer, *On the Distinction Between Speech and Action*, 65 EMORY L.J. 427, 427–28 (2015); Frederick Schauer, *Must Speech Be Special?*, 78 NW. U. L. REV. 1284 (1983); John Hart Ely, *Flag Desecration: A Case Study in the Roles of Categorization and Balancing in First Amendment Analysis*, 88 HARV. L. REV. 1482 (1975).

[255] Danielle Keats Citron & Mary Anne Franks, *The Internet as a Speech Machine and Other Myths Confounding Section 230 Reform*, 2020 U. CHI. L. REV. FORUM 45, 61.

STEPHEN E. SACHS

DORMANT COMMERCE AND CORPORATE JURISDICTION

Mallory v. Norfolk Southern Railway Co.[1] heralds the return of some very old doctrines of personal jurisdiction. Since 1945, the Court has sought substantive rules of jurisdiction in the depths of the Fourteenth Amendment, forgoing old "fiction[s]" of "mystical 'presence'"[2] for new fictions about the mystic overtones of "due process of law."[3] The result has been a complex and contradictory body of case law, less concerned with enforcing the actual Fourteenth Amendment than with preserving the legacy of *International Shoe Co. v. Washington*.[4] Recently some Justices have come to a new understanding of their task, as finding the "most appropriate home" for real jurisdictional principles

---

Stephen E. Sachs is the Antonin Scalia Professor of Law at Harvard Law School.

AUTHOR'S NOTE: I am grateful to William Baude, Richard Fallon, Richard Re, Martin Redish, and Amanda Schwoerke for advice and comments, and to Nate Bartholomew, Alexis Ciambotti, and Bill Mo for excellent research assistance.

[1] 600 U.S. 122 (2023).

[2] Int'l Shoe Co. v. Washington, 326 U.S. 310, 318 (1945); *id.* at 323 (op. of Black, J.).

[3] *Id.* at 316 (op. of the Court) (holding that "due process requires . . . minimum contacts . . . such that the maintenance of the suit does not offend 'traditional notions of fair play and substantial justice'" (quoting Miliken v. Meyer, 311 U.S. 457, 463 (1940))).

[4] 326 U.S. 310; *cf.* Ford Motor Co. v. Mont. 8th Jud. Dist. Ct., 592 U.S. 351, 360–361 n.2 (2021) (rejecting any "replacement of our current doctrine with the Fourteenth Amendment's original meaning" in favor of "proceeding as the Court has done for the last 75 years—applying the standards set out in *International Shoe* and its progeny, with attention to their underlying values of ensuring fairness and protecting interstate federalism").

The Supreme Court Review, 2024.
© 2024 The University of Chicago. All rights reserved. Published by The University of Chicago Press. https://doi.org/10.1086/729532

made "homeless" by changing doctrines.[5] Under *Mallory*, the Court may find shelter in "the so-called dormant Commerce Clause"[6]—for a little while. But before too long, it will be time for these principles to go home again.

On its surface, *Mallory* is a case about consent. Reaffirming decisions that predate *International Shoe*, it held that a Virginia corporation can subject itself to Pennsylvania's general jurisdiction in exchange for the right to do business there.[7] Despite trenchant criticism,[8] the Court seems to have gotten this one right. Consent is a valid ground for jurisdiction, even after *International Shoe*, so the consent cases remained good law.[9] Had Pennsylvania offered a crisp new $5 bill to anyone willing to consent to jurisdiction, it'd be hard to say that this violated the Due Process Clause—and "[a]t this point we are haggling over the price."[10]

Yet the real question posed by *Mallory* is one the Court properly declined to decide, namely whether Pennsylvania may *ask* for this sort of consent as a condition of doing business in the state.[11] As noted in Justice Alito's concurrence-in-judgment, today that question is typically answered under dormant commerce doctrine.[12] So the most immediate result of *Mallory* is the return of dormant commerce to the field of personal jurisdiction—a place it occupied for several decades in the early twentieth century,[13] before being swept away and then

---

[5] *Mallory*, 600 U.S. at 155 (Alito, J., concurring in part and concurring in the judgment); *see also Ford*, 592 U.S. at 372 (Alito, J., concurring in the judgment) (noting "grounds for questioning" *International Shoe*); *id.* at 384 (Gorsuch, J., concurring in the judgment) (describing aspects of *International Shoe* as "increasingly doubtful").

[6] *Mallory*, 600 U.S. at 157 (Alito, J., concurring in part and concurring in the judgment).

[7] *Id.* at 128 (plurality op.) (declining to disturb Pa. Fire Ins. Co. of Phila. v. Gold Issue Mining & Milling Co., 243 U.S. 93 (1917)); *id.* at 152–54 (Alito, J., concurring in part and concurring in the judgment).

[8] *See id.* at 163 (Barrett, J., dissenting); *see also, e.g.*, Linda S. Mullenix, *Railroading Personal Jurisdiction*, 43 REV. LITIG. (forthcoming 2024), http://ssrn.com/id=4588838.

[9] *Mallory*, 600 U.S. at 137–38 (plurality op.); *id.* at 148 (Jackson, J., concurring).

[10] *See* Brief of Professor Stephen E. Sachs as Amicus Curiae in Support of Neither Party at 11, *Mallory*, 600 U.S. 122 (No. 21-1168), 2022 WL 2783878 [hereinafter Sachs Brief]; *see also id.* at 18–22 (on unconstitutional conditions).

[11] *Mallory*, 600 U.S. at 127 n.3 (op. of the Court); *id.* at 157 (Alito, J., concurring in part and concurring in the judgment).

[12] *Id.* at 160–63 (Alito, J., concurring in part and concurring in the judgment); *accord* Sachs Brief, *supra* note 10, at 22–26.

[13] *See, e.g.*, Davis v. Farmers' Co-Op. Equity Co., 262 U.S. 312 (1923); Denver & Rio Grande W. R.R. Co. v. Terte, 284 U.S. 284 (1932); Miles v. Ill. Cent. R.R. Co., 315 U.S. 698 (1942);

largely forgotten after *International Shoe*.¹⁴ (Indeed, only a few years ago the Court treated the two fields as entirely unconnected, describing one of the exemplary cases as a dispute "over the Dormant Commerce Clause, not personal jurisdiction."¹⁵)

Rather than relitigate *Mallory*, this Article assesses the impact of dormant commerce's return, as more states consider Pennsylvania-like policies and more tribunals wrestle with the questions the Court left open. Under today's doctrines, plaintiffs like Robert Mallory may face an uphill battle.¹⁶ Yet he also has some good cases and arguments on his side, and other plaintiffs may have more luck.

Stepping back from today's doctrines, the story becomes far more complex. As indicated by Justice Alito's use of "so-called," there remain persistent worries that the dormant Commerce Clause doesn't really exist.¹⁷ And even if the textual Commerce Clause has a dormant side, it's far from clear that it has anything to say about the powers of state-created corporations in other states.

The intuition here is a simple one: "*states don't have to have corporate law*."¹⁸ If six Pennsylvanians at the Founding wanted to incorporate their backyard wheatfields, buying supplies and holding property under a common name, they'd have needed a Pennsylvania charter to do it; a permission slip from Virginia's legislature wouldn't have helped. Pennsylvania's refusal to recognize Virginia's corporate charter wouldn't prefer its own *goods and services* over Virginia's (a potential dormant-commerce problem) or its own *citizens* over Virginia's (a potential privileges-and-immunities problem); at most, it'd prefer its

---

John F. Preis, *The Dormant Commerce Clause as a Limit on Personal Jurisdiction*, 102 IOWA L. REV. 121, 132 (2016).

¹⁴ *See* Int'l Shoe Co. v. Washington, 326 U.S. 310, 315 (1945) (rejecting the corporation's dormant-commerce argument because Congress had legislated on the subject).

¹⁵ BNSF Ry. Co. v. Tyrrell, 581 U.S. 402, 412 (2017). For full disclosure, this author made a similar mistake. Brief of Professor Stephen E. Sachs as Amicus Curiae in Support of Petitioner at 11–12, *BNSF*, 581 U.S. 402 (2017) (No. 16-405), 2017 WL 950855 (describing the doctrine as a version of *forum non conveniens*). Dormant commerce has played a greater role in related doctrines of state jurisdiction to tax. *See, e.g.*, N.C. Dep't of Revenue v. Kimberley Rice Kaestner 1992 Family Trust, 139 S. Ct. 2213, 2219 n.4 (2019); South Dakota v. Wayfair, Inc., 585 U.S. 162, 171–75 (2018); Comptroller of the Treasury v. Wynne, 575 U.S. 542 (2015).

¹⁶ *See Mallory*, 600 U.S. at 160–63 (Alito, J., concurring in part and concurring in the judgment).

¹⁷ *See, e.g.*, Camps Newfound/Owatonna, Inc. v. Town of Harrison, 520 U.S. 564, 610–20 (1997) (Thomas, J., dissenting).

¹⁸ Stephen E. Sachs, *"Dormant Commerce" and Corporate Powers*, VOLOKH CONSPIRACY (June 28, 2023), https://reason.com/volokh/2023/06/28/dormant-commerce-and-corporate-powers.

own *law* over Virginia's for governing affairs inside its borders, something Pennsylvania has every right to do (and not a full-faith-and-credit problem).[19] Nor would it treat these six citizens unfairly or arbitrarily (an equal-protection problem); they could ask Pennsylvania to incorporate them on the same terms that anyone else can.

Of course, in the real world, out-of-state corporations probably do have out-of-state shareholders, trade in out-of-state goods or services, and so on. And over the last century or so, the Court developed a set of dormant-commerce limits on state corporate law, which by the early 1900s treated recognition of out-of-state corporations as something of a constitutional requirement, and which eventually extended to all aspects of a foreign corporation's internal affairs. As a matter of economic policy, maybe this wasn't so bad; if the Court's job in dormant-commerce cases is to act as a "junior-varsity Congress,"[20] maybe it succeeded in doing what Congress would have wanted done.[21]

But policy decisions like these still need a basis in law—and not just in mistakes preserved as precedents, especially ones that depart demonstrably from the original rules.[22] If a state's regulations turn out to discriminate against out-of-state traffic or goods or people, or if they turn out to be arbitrary or unequal in some other way, the original Constitution can deal with those problems directly, rather than looking at them through the distorted mirror of the corporate form. Nor is Congress powerless: It can require states to recognize each other's corporate charters, using powers under the Full Faith and Credit

---

[19] *See* Stephen E. Sachs, *Full Faith and Credit in the Early Congress*, 95 VA. L. REV. 1201, 1202 (2009) (arguing that the Full Faith and Clause didn't mandate *any* effect for state laws or records in other states, but left that determination to Congress); *see also* David E. Engdahl, *The Classic Rule of Faith and Credit*, 118 YALE L.J. 1584, 1589, 1632 (2009) (same); *cf.* Allstate Ins. Co. v. Hague, 449 U.S. 302, 313 (1981) (plurality op.) (allowing a state to choose its own law whenever it has "a significant contact or significant aggregation of contacts, creating state interests, such that choice of its law is neither arbitrary nor fundamentally unfair"); Phillips Petrol. Co. v. Shutts, 472 U.S. 797, 818, 821–22 (1985) (adopting *Allstate*'s standard as current doctrine).

[20] Mistretta v. United States, 488 U.S. 361, 427 (1989) (Scalia, J., dissenting) (discussing the U.S. Sentencing Commission).

[21] *Cf.* Prudential Ins. Co. v. Benjamin, 328 U.S. 408, 426 & n.33 (1946) (describing the Court in dormant commerce cases as looking for "policy" in "Congress's prior legislation"); *id.* at 426 (suggesting that the Court would follow Congress's lead "when it repudiates, just as when its silence is thought to support, the inference that it has forbidden state action").

[22] *See* Caleb Nelson, Stare Decisis *and Demonstrably Erroneous Precedents*, 87 VA. L. REV. 1, 1 (2001); *cf.* Ramos v. Lousiana, 140 S. Ct. 1390, 1405 (2020) ("[S]*tare decisis* isn't supposed to be the art of methodically ignoring what everyone knows to be true.").

Clause,[23] or it can license corporations to operate across state lines, using powers under the "wakeful" Commerce Clause.[24] And *maybe*, in the meantime, a corporation that wants to engage in commerce across state lines can claim some kind of dormant-commerce right to use corporate privileges along the way. But that kind of right wouldn't extend to *intra*state commerce (in which Norfolk Southern is concededly engaged),[25] as to which each state would remain free to impose conditions (as Pennsylvania does).[26]

Below the surface, *Mallory* is a case about how to reconcile twentieth-century doctrinal extrapolations with their actual sources in older law. Just as the balancing test of *Pike v. Bruce Church, Inc.*[27] wasn't hidden inside the text of the Commerce Clause all along, the modern rules of personal jurisdiction didn't spring full-grown from the Due Process Clause. As is argued elsewhere, cases like *Pennoyer v. Neff* didn't derive their principles from the Fourteenth Amendment, but instead applied principles that were already in place: principles of general and international law, which the Fourteenth Amendment secured but didn't impose.[28] Viewed broadly, *Mallory* supports the proposition that these older principles retain some of their validity,[29] homeless though they may be, until altered by Congress or other competent authority.[30]

---

[23] *See* U.S. CONST. art. IV, § 1 ("[T]he Congress may by general Laws prescribe the Manner in which such Acts, Records and Proceedings shall be proved, and the Effect thereof."); 28 U.S.C. § 1738C(a)(1) (2018 & Supp. IV) (forbidding certain grounds for non-recognition of marriages); *cf.* Sachs Brief, *supra* note 10, at 30 n.3 (suggesting this approach).

[24] Nat'l Pork Producers Council v. Ross, 598 U.S. 356, 382 (2023) (op. of Gorsuch, J.); *see* M'Culloch v. Maryland, 17 U.S. (4 Wheat.) 316 (1819).

[25] Mallory v. Norfolk S. Ry. Co., 266 A.3d 542, 560 (Pa. 2021), *vacated and remanded*, 600 U.S. 122 (2023).

[26] *See* 42 PA. CONS. STAT. § 5301(a)(2)(i) (2024) (listing qualification as a foreign corporation as a ground for general jurisdiction); 15 *id.* §§ 401(a), 411(a) (requiring registration for foreign entities doing business in Pennsylvania); *id.* § 403(a)(11) (exempting "business in interstate or foreign commerce" from this requirement).

[27] 397 U.S. 137, 142 (1970).

[28] 95 U.S 714, 729–33 (1878); *see* Burnham v. Super. Ct., 495 U.S. 604, 608–11, 616–17 (1990) (op. of Scalia, J.); Stephen E. Sachs, Pennoyer *Was Right*, 95 TEX. L. REV. 1249 (2017); Stephen E. Sachs, *The Unlimited Jurisdiction of the Federal Courts*, 106 VA. L. REV. 1703 (2020); *cf.* William Baude, Jud Campbell & Stephen E. Sachs, *General Law and the Fourteenth Amendment*, 76 STAN. L. REV. (forthcoming 2024), http://ssrn.com/id=4604902 (manuscript at 23–24).

[29] *See* Mallory v. Norfolk Southern Railway Co., 137 HARV. L. REV. 360, 369 (2023).

[30] *See* Sachs, Pennoyer *Was Right*, *supra* note 28, at 1316–18.

If the jurisdictional rules the twentieth-century Court came up with were uniquely sensible as a matter of policy, maybe their shaky origins wouldn't matter so much. But what we've been given is a system in which jurisdiction over a distant drug company turns on whether (unbeknownst to the defendant) a tourist *ingested* the defective pill in State *A* or State *B*;[31] in which the forum for a local car accident turns on whether (unbeknownst to the plaintiff) the Ford Explorer XLT is marketed there or only the base model;[32] and in which all these rules are ostensibly derived from the Fourteenth Amendment. The law may not have to make sense, but if our personal jurisdiction doctrines aren't going to make sense anyway, they may as well actually be law. *Mallory* doesn't quite get us there, but at least it points us in the right direction.

1. DORMANT COMMERCE UNDER CURRENT DOCTRINE

The Court needn't confront the dormant-commerce questions right away. *Mallory* itself is now back in a Pennsylvania trial court.[33] Only a handful of states have consent-by-registration statutes (New York's governor recently vetoed one),[34] and since *Mallory* only a handful of courts have applied them.[35] But the few decisions reaching the dormant-commerce issue have decided it in the plaintiffs' favor,[36]

---

[31] *See* Bristol-Myers Squibb Co. v. Super. Ct., 582 U.S. 255, 264 (2017) (finding it significant that certain nonresident plaintiffs "did not ingest Plavix in California"); Ford Motor Co. v. Mont. 8th. Jud. Dist. Ct., 592 U.S. 351, 369 (2021) (same).

[32] *See Ford*, 592 U.S. at 365 (declining to address a case "in which Ford marketed the models in only a different State or region"); *id*. at 367 n.5 (extending the Court's holding to a case in which a new arrival "had not considered any of Ford's activities in his new home State").

[33] Mallory v. Norfolk S. Ry. Co., 300 A.3d 1013 (Pa.) (remanding the case), *on remand from* 600 U.S. 122 (2023); Case Management Order, Mallory v. Norfolk S. Ry. Co., No. 01961 (Pa. Ct. Com. Pl. Phila. Cnty. Trial Div.—Civ. Nov. 20, 2023).

[34] *See* Gov. Kathy Hochul, Veto Message—No. 147 (Dec. 22, 2023), https://public.leginfo.state.ny.us (search for "Veto No." "147" "2023" "Text").

[35] *See, e.g.*, Sloan v. Burist, No. 2:22-cv-76, 2023 WL 7309476 (S.D. Ga. Nov. 6, 2023) (considering a Georgia statute); Skyline Trucking, Inc. v. Freightliner Truck Ctr. Cos., No. 22-4052-DDC-TJJ, 2023 WL 4846618, at *6 (D. Kan. July 28, 2023) (considering a Kansas statute); Espin v. Citibank, N.A., No. 5:22-CV-383-BO-RN, 2023 WL 6447231, at *4 (E.D.N.C. Sept. 29, 2023) (considering a North Carolina statute); Harris Teeter Supermarkets, Inc. v. ACE Am. Ins. Co., No. 22 CVS 5279, 2023 WL 6568766, at *14 (N.C. Super. Ct. Oct. 10, 2023) (same); *cf.* Cooper Tire & Rubber Co. v. McCall, 863 S.E.2d 81, 90 (Ga. 2021), *cert. denied*, 143 S. Ct. 2689 (2023) (applying Georgia's statute pre-*Mallory*).

[36] *See Sloan*, 2023 WL 7309476, at *1, *5–6 (approving jurisdiction against a dormant-commerce challenge because the accident in question occurred in Georgia, reducing the

and more statutes may be on the way. (And not only from states: Local law permitting, any plaintiff-friendly city, county, or municipal water district could make consent to general jurisdiction a condition of some license or other.)

When the issue does return, other plaintiffs may find more luck than Robert Mallory. *Mallory* is a "foreign-cubed" case—a Virginia plaintiff suing a Virginia defendant for a Virginia tort—in which the dormant-commerce objections to a Pennsylvania forum are at their height. Plaintiffs in other kinds of cases, who still might have been tossed out of court under the Court's previous decisions, might nonetheless succeed with a consent-by-registration statute in hand. And there are even some decent arguments on Mallory's own behalf.

Under today's dormant commerce doctrine, a consent-by-registration statute has to run two gauntlets. The first is that "state regulations may not discriminate against interstate commerce," on pain of "'a virtually *per se* rule of invalidity.'"[37] Justice Alito speculated that a consent-by-registration statute might discriminate in just this way, as it expands jurisdiction only for foreign (that is, out-of-state) corporations and not domestic ones.[38] On the other hand, domestic corporations are already subject to general jurisdiction,[39] so these laws might be said merely to impose an even playing field.

More dangerous to plaintiffs is the second gauntlet, that "even-handed[]" laws still mustn't "impose undue burdens on interstate commerce"; that is, that they must pursue "'a legitimate local public interest'" and not impose a "'burden'" on interstate commerce that's "'clearly excessive in relation to the putative local benefits.'"[40] As the plaintiff in a foreign-cubed case, Mallory would have a difficult time making this argument before today's Court. The opinions in *Mallory* show as many as five votes against hearing these foreign-cubed cases: Justice Alito, who found himself "hard-pressed to identify any legitimate

---

burden of litigating there, and because the defendant "is licensed to [do] business in Georgia and transacts business within the state"); *Espin*, 2023 WL 6447231, at *4 ("[T]his statute . . . neither offends against the commerce clause . . . nor runs counter to the Fourteenth Amendment." (quoting Steele v. W. Union Tel. Co., 173 S.E. 583, 587 (N.C. 1934))).

[37] South Dakota v. Wayfair, 585 U.S. 162, 173 (2018) (quoting Granholm v. Heald, 544 U.S. 460, 476 (2005)).

[38] *Mallory*, 600 U.S. at 161 & n.7 (Alito, J., concurring in part and concurring in the judgment).

[39] *See* Daimler AG v. Baumann, 571 U.S. 117, 137 (2014).

[40] *Wayfair*, 585 U.S. at 173 (quoting Pike v. Bruce Church, Inc., 397 U.S. 137, 142 (1970)).

local interest" in deciding them,[41] and Justice Barrett and the other dissenters, who likewise saw Pennsylvania as having "no legitimate interest in [such] a controversy."[42] If there's no real benefit to Pennsylvania's deciding cases without local connections, then any burden seems too great. At least some mid-sized companies might restrict their Pennsylvania operations to avoid being forum-shopped into its courts; larger ones might have to construct costly and complicated networks of subsidiaries. A single state that can impose its jurisdiction on nationwide companies might capture all the benefits of extra litigation and lobbying business while making out-of-state shareholders bear most of the extra costs.[43]

That said, other plaintiffs may have more luck. Consider a "foreign-squared" case in which either the plaintiff, the defendant, or the cause of action is local to the forum. If the defendant is local, there's general jurisdiction; if the cause of action is local, there's specific jurisdiction, or at least (according to Justice Alito) a state interest in "providing a forum to redress harms" suffered there.[44] And if the plaintiff is local—usually not enough for jurisdiction under *Walden v. Fiore*[45]—a state might nonetheless have a legitimate interest "in providing its residents with a convenient forum for redressing injuries inflicted by out-of-state actors."[46] A case that fits none of these categories might still qualify under a "retaliatory" registration statute, modeled after laws from other countries, which would subject a foreign corporation to Pennsylvania's jurisdiction whenever its home court would hear a similar case against a Pennsylvania corporation.[47] (As the Court has noted in other contexts, this kind of statute reflects a legitimate interest in *dissuading* attempts at exorbitant jurisdiction by other states, so it removes barriers to interstate commerce instead of creating

---

[41] *Mallory*, 600 U.S. at 162 (Alito, J., concurring in part and concurring in the judgment) (emphasis omitted).

[42] *Id.* at 169 n.1 (Barrett, J., dissenting) (quoting Mallory v. Norfolk S. Ry. Co., 266 A.3d 543, 567 (Pa. 2021)).

[43] *See* Stephen F. Williams, *Preemption: First Principles*, 103 Nw. U. L. Rev. 323, 328 (2009).

[44] *Mallory*, 600 U.S. at 162 (Alito, J., concurring in part and concurring in the judgment).

[45] 571 U.S. 277, 285 (2014) ("[T]he plaintiff cannot be the only link between the defendant and the forum.").

[46] *Mallory*, 600 U.S. at 163 (Alito, J., concurring in part and concurring in the judgment) (quoting Burger King Corp. v. Rudzewicz, 471 U.S. 462, 473 (1985)).

[47] *See* Gary B. Born, *Reflections on Judicial Jurisdiction in International Cases*, 17 Ga. J. Int'l & Compar. L. 1, 15 (1987).

them.⁴⁸) Of course, all these various interests are on only one side of the ledger; there's still the burden on interstate commerce to consider. But interests like these do suggest that, even under modern dormant-commerce doctrine, a consent-by-registration statute really can expand a state's jurisdiction beyond what it'd have enjoyed under *International Shoe* alone.

And these aren't the only state interests involved. Set aside any illegitimate protectionist interest in attracting judicial business from other fora; set aside also any *de minimis* interest in using registration to avoid complicated jurisdictional fights. In straightforward terms, a state has a real, legitimate, and substantial interest in *seeing justice done*, providing remedies to injured suitors who find within the state those who injured them. If the State of New York is *offended* by Radovan Karadžić's lounging at the Inter-Continental while evading liability for his war crimes, it can issue a summons and make him answer his accusers.⁴⁹ Or if Pennsylvania thinks it *unfair* that Robert Nicastro was never compensated for his injuries, and if J. McIntyre Machinery builds a giant factory in downtown Scranton (though making a different *model* of machine, to avoid "related to" jurisdiction, than the one that cut off Nicastro's fingers in New Jersey),⁵⁰ then the Commonwealth can let Nicastro sue there and force the company to appear. It's *wrong* to have scofflaws swaggering about town while injured plaintiffs are forced to wait for justice, and correcting wrongs by defendants is as legitimate a state interest as obtaining compensation for plaintiffs. Excluding this interest from the list of legitimate state interests either makes unrealistic claims about the interests states actually have, or else makes unfounded claims about the interests states are *allowed* to have—to wit, selfish ones.⁵¹

---

⁴⁸ *Cf.* W. & S. Life Ins. Co. v. State Bd. of Equalization, 451 U.S. 648, 671 (1981) (analyzing retaliatory taxes).

⁴⁹ *See* Doe v. Karadzic, No. 93 CIV 0878 (PKL), 1996 WL 194298, at *1–2 (S.D.N.Y. Apr. 22, 1996).

⁵⁰ *See* J. McIntyre Mach., Ltd. v. Nicastro, 564 U.S. 873, 894–95 (2011) (Ginsberg, J., dissenting); Ford Motor Co. v. Mont. 8th Jud. Dist. Ct., 592 U.S. 351, 365 (2021) ("Contrast a case, which we do not address, in which Ford marketed the models in only a different State or region.").

⁵¹ *Cf.* Lea Brilmayer, *Governmental Interest Analysis: A House Without Foundations*, 46 OHIO ST. L.J. 459, 479 (1985) (doubting the "empirical substantiation" of claims of state interest); *id.* at 475 (noting that "there are problems other than irrational intermeddling," and that "self-interest is not necessarily the touchstone of constitutional legitimacy"); John Hart Ely, *Choice of Law and the State's Interest in Protecting Its Own*, 23 WM. & MARY L. REV. 173, 194 (1981) (doubting such claims of "intermeddling").

This interest in seeing justice done is an ill fit for *Pike* balancing, which would stack this moral interest against the burden it imposes on interstate commerce. To some Justices, the two might be incommensurable, such that no court could hold the moral interest outweighed: comparing them would be like asking, as Justice Scalia once put it, "whether a particular line is longer than a particular rock is heavy."[52] Even if *Pike*'s point is to smoke out "the presence of a discriminatory purpose" in a facially equal law,[53] and even if this sort of investigation can't help comparing different interests (or, at least, how much we think the state *cares* about different interests),[54] the point remains. While the forbidden lure of judicial business will always be with us, as will the lobbying of the organized bar, the state's interest in seeing justice done seems real enough, and not just a cover for protectionism. If a state can be sincerely interested in pursuing Karadžić, it can be sincerely interested in pursuing J. McIntyre Machinery, too.

That's why consent-by-registration statutes are often paired with similar arguments about "tag" jurisdiction by personal service: The two stand or fall together. If Dennis Burnham has to let California "decree the ownership of all [his] worldly goods" and "custody over his children," just because he was served with a summons while spending three days there on a business trip,[55] then why—as Justice Gorsuch asked—should the Norfolk Southern Railway Company be immune to similar jurisdiction, if it's taken out a Pennsylvania business license and operates two thousand miles of Pennsylvania tracks?[56] Had Burnham considered the risk of service, he might have avoided traveling to California in interstate commerce, just as Norfolk Southern might avoid doing business in certain states. One possible conclusion is that the dormant commerce doctrine has always barred "tag" jurisdiction over

---

[52] Nat'l Pork Producers Council, Inc. v. Ross, 598 U.S. 356, 381 (2023) (op. of Gorsuch, J., joined by Thomas and Barrett, JJ.) (quoting Bendix Autolite Corp. v. Midwesco Enters., 486 U.S. 888, 897 (1988) (Scalia, J., concurring in the judgment)).

[53] *Id.* at 1157 (op. of the Court).

[54] JOHN HART ELY, DEMOCRACY AND DISTRUST: A THEORY OF JUDICIAL REVIEW 148 (1980) (noting that, if a school principal segregated a class for "aesthetic" reasons, those reasons would be in some sense facially equal and incommensurable with the harms of segregation, but also "so trivial in context that you have to believe it's a rationalization for a racially motivated choice").

[55] Burnham v. Super. Ct., 495 U.S. 604, 623 (1990) (op. of Scalia, J.).

[56] Mallory v. Norfolk S. Ry. Co., 600 U.S. 122, 142–43 (2023) (plurality op.); *accord* Transcript of Oral Argument at 63–64, *Mallory*, 600 U.S. 122 (No. 21-1168).

individuals;[57] another is that it fails to bar similar jurisdiction over corporations, as such interest-balancing has no business upsetting one of "the most firmly established principles of personal jurisdiction."[58]

Indeed, suits like Mallory's might well have gone forward even in the heyday of dormant-commerce jurisdictional limits. The leading case, *Davis v. Farmers Co-operative Equity Co.*, held in 1923 that a state had "impose[d] upon interstate commerce a serious and unreasonable burden" by making a distant railroad face a foreign-cubed suit solely because it had an agent in the forum to solicit traffic.[59] But a decade later, *Denver & Rio Grande Western Railroad Co. v. Terte* distinguished *Davis*-like facts from the case of a defendant which "owns and operates railroad lines" in the forum and is "licensed to do business there"—grounds the Court saw as sufficient for local-plaintiff jurisdiction.[60] And a decade after that, *Miles v. Illinois Central Railroad Co.* let a Tennessee plaintiff with a Tennessee claim sue an Illinois railroad in the Missouri courts, reasoning that this foreign-cubed case couldn't place any real "burden on interstate commerce" when the railroad ran daily trains into St. Louis and otherwise did "substantial business in Missouri" (just as Norfolk Southern does in Pennsylvania).[61] In other words, just as *Mallory* recognized older cases as still valid amid the new regime of *International Shoe*, a dormant-commerce "*Mallory II*" might have to consider the strength of *Terte* and *Miles* amid a new regime of *Pike* balancing—and might well conclude, as did "*Mallory I*," that these never-overruled cases remain good law.

---

[57] *See* Preis, *supra* note 13, at 159–61.

[58] *Burnham*, 495 U.S. at 610 (op. of Scalia, J.). *Compare* Preis, *supra* note 13, at 161–63 (questioning the historical basis of tag jurisdiction), *with* James Weinstein, *The Federal Common Law Origins of Judicial Jurisdiction: Implications for Modern Doctrine*, 90 VA. L. REV. 169, 189–90 (2004) (arguing that such jurisdiction is historically well-established).

[59] 262 U.S. 312, 315, 317 (1923).

[60] 284 U.S. 284, 286 (1932) (discussing the Atchison, Topeka, and Santa Fe Railway Company); *id.* at 286–87; *see also* Sloan v. Burist, No. 2:22-cv-76, 2023 WL 7309476, at *6 (S.D. Ga. Nov. 6, 2023) (applying *Terte* to uphold jurisdiction). *Compare* Mich. Cent. R.R. Co. v. Mix, 278 U.S. 492, 493 (1929) (refusing jurisdiction in Missouri partly because the defendant railroad "has never been admitted to do business there" and "no part of its line runs [there]"), *with* Balt. & Ohio R.R. Co. v. Kepner, 314 U.S. 44, 48, 51 (1941) (reading *Terte* to permit "litigation in a district where the lines of the carrier run," even when that district is "far from the scene of the accident").

[61] 315 U.S. 698, 699–701 (1942); *id.* at 701.

II. Dormant Commerce on Original Grounds

So suppose we look further back, to cases and doctrines older still. On original grounds, are consent-by-registration statutes "repugnant to the power to regulate commerce in its dormant state"?[62] Or does that question just pit the state powers preserved by the Tenth Amendment, "which appears in the Constitution, against the 'dormant commerce clause,' which does not"?[63]

What follows isn't an exhaustive history, but a brief retelling of where we started and how we got here: a picture of what corporate jurisdiction looked like at the Founding and a few data points on how the Supreme Court changed its tune.

In short, the Founding-era picture was that corporations had no right of their own to operate in other states. To exercise corporate privileges across state lines, they needed permission from those other states, which might come with conditions (such as consent to jurisdiction). But as corporations took a greater role in interstate commerce, they began to claim an entitlement to do so by constitutional right. States couldn't interfere with cross-border commerce, the argument went, so they couldn't stop a foreign corporation from engaging in commerce either—even though corporations lacked the privileges guaranteed to citizens under Article IV, and even though a state's corporate laws weren't themselves regulations of commerce. By the turn of the twentieth century, this dormant-commerce argument had carried the day, rendering incoherent both the theory and the practice of corporate jurisdiction; the ground was thus ready for *International Shoe*.

A. CORPORATE JURISDICTION AT THE FOUNDING

1. *Corporate Privileges at the Founding.* To understand the rules for corporate jurisdiction at the Founding, we have to understand how Founding-era lawyers understood corporations. Start with the basic point noted above, that states don't have to have corporations *at all*. In the modern world, general corporation laws let pretty much anyone create a corporation—sometimes in minutes, by filling out a

---

[62] Willson v. Black Bird Creek Marsh Co., 27 U.S. (2 Pet.) 245, 252 (1829).

[63] Bridenbaugh v. Freeman-Wilson, 227 F.3d 848, 849 (7th Cir. 2000) (Easterbrook, J.) (discussing the Twenty-First Amendment).

form. But at the Founding, chartering a corporation was an extraordinary event, often requiring express permission from the legislature. So while Delaware formed 313,650 new business entities in 2022 alone,[64] legal scholars once expressed shock that the 1823 New York legislative session had created as many as "*thirty-nine* new private temporal corporations" in a single year.[65]

When states did create corporations, they were understood to have given a group of natural persons the special legal power to act together under an artificial name, "bestow[ing] the character and properties of individuality on a collective and changing body of men."[66] In 1805, Chief Justice Marshall described "our ideas of a corporation" as "derived entirely from the English books," which treated the corporation as "a mere creature of the law, invisible, intangible, and incorporeal."[67] One of these books described the "*essence* of a corporation" in English law as conferring three capacities:

> 1. To have perpetual succession under a *special* denomination, and under an *artificial* form. 2. To take and grant property, to contract obligations, and to sue and be sued by its corporate name, in the same manner as an individual. 3. To receive grants of privileges and immunities, and to enjoy them in *common*.[68]

Chancellor Kent offered a similar description: Unlike common-law partners or contractually associated natural persons, members of a corporation could together enjoy the rights to "perpetual succession," letting their group stay in existence even as the individual members changed; to "sue and be sued, and to grant and to receive, by their corporate name"; to "purchase and hold lands and chattels" as a single entity, and not as tenants in common; to "a common seal" that

---

[64] Del. Div. of Corps, 2022 Annual Report 1, https://corpfiles.delaware.gov/Annual-Reports/Division-of-Corporations-2022-Annual-Report-cy.pdf.

[65] JOSEPH K. ANGELL & SAMUEL AMES, A TREATISE ON THE LAW OF PRIVATE CORPORATIONS AGGREGATE 35 (Boston, Hilliard, Gray, Little & Wilkins 1832).

[66] Providence Bank v. Billings, 29 U.S. (4 Pet.) 514, 562 (1830) (Marshall, C.J.); *accord* Trs. of Dartmouth Coll. v. Woodward, 17 U.S. (4 Wheat.) 518, 636 (1819) (Marshall, C.J.) ("It is chiefly for the purpose of clothing bodies of men, in succession, with these qualities and capacities, that corporations were invented, and are in use.").

[67] Bank of the U.S. v. Deveaux, 9 U.S. (5 Cranch) 61, 88 (1809).

[68] 1 STEWART KYD, A TREATISE ON THE LAW OF CORPORATIONS 70 (London, J. Butterworth 1793); *accord* ANGELL & AMES, *supra* note 65, at 59; 2 JAMES KENT, COMMENTARIES ON AMERICAN LAW 278 (New York, O. Halsted 2d ed. 1832).

authenticated their official actions; to "make by-laws for the government of the corporation"; and to remove other members via "amotion."[69]

Of course, we needn't view corporations today through the same lens that the Founders did. The Constitution has no corporate law: it imposes no particular theory of the corporation one way or another. But a Constitution that says nothing about corporations was nonetheless read to apply to them indirectly. As Marshall reasoned, this "artificial being" and "mere legal entity" was "certainly not a citizen" with rights of its own; yet "the rights of the members," including their constitutional rights, could in certain circumstances "be exercised in their corporate name."[70]

2. *Corporate Privileges in Other States.* This Founding-era understanding had real consequences for the rights of one state's corporations in another. One special privilege of incorporation was that it let the members' rights be exercised in their corporate name: Six Pennsylvanians might own farmland and grow wheat as "The Amalgamated Wheatfield Corporation" instead. But this special privilege had to be specially conferred by law, and by a law that applied in the place where it was invoked.

Early court decisions repeatedly reaffirmed that a corporation was "the mere creature of the act to which it owes its existence," only "what the incorporating act has made it."[71] By this logic, a Virginia charter couldn't possibly give our six Pennsylvanians a right to hold Pennsylvania property in a corporate name, any more than a Virginia fishing license could grant them a right to fish in the Susquehanna River. In this respect the states stood toward one another much like foreign countries; as one oft-cited opinion put it, "though they form a

---

[69] 2 KENT, *supra* note 68, at 277–78; *accord* 1 KYD, *supra* note 68, at 69 (providing a similar list); *cf.* ANGELL & AMES, *supra* note 65, at 58–59 (comparing Kyd and Kent).

[70] *Deveaux*, 9 U.S. at 86; *cf.* Citizens United v. FEC, 558 U.S. 310, 391–92 (Scalia, J., concurring) ("All the provisions of the Bill of Rights set forth the rights of individual men and women.... But the individual person's right to speak includes the right to speak *in association with other individual persons*."); *id.* at 390 ("Their activities were not stripped of First Amendment protection simply because they were carried out under the banner of an artificial legal entity.").

[71] Head v. Providence Ins. Co., 6 U.S. (2 Cranch) 127, 167 (1804); *see Dartmouth Coll.*, 17 U.S. at 636 (describing the corporation as "existing only in contemplation of law," and as "the mere creature of law," possessing "only those properties which the charter of its creation confers upon it, either expressly, or as incidental to its very existence"); Bank of Augusta v. Earle, 38 U.S. (13 Pet.) 519, 587 (1839) (noting that, as an "artificial being," a corporation's only rights "are the rights which are given to it in that character"); *accord* Vincent S.J. Buccola, *States' Rights Against Corporate Rights*, 2016 COLUM. BUS. L. REV. 595, 604–05.

confederated government," they nonetheless "retain their individual sovereignties, and with respect to their municipal laws are to each other foreign."[72] Thus in *Bank of Augusta v. Earle*, a group of cases about whether out-of-state corporations could make contracts in Alabama, Chief Justice Taney concluded that

> a corporation can have no legal existence out of the boundaries of the sovereignty by which it is created. It exists only in contemplation of law, and by force of the law; and where that law ceases to operate, and is no longer obligatory, the corporation can have no existence. It must dwell in the place of its creation, and cannot migrate to another sovereignty.[73]

Yet this comparison to foreign countries also created a narrow avenue for corporate rights abroad. Just as domestic courts hearing foreign contract cases usually recognized foreign contract laws, they also recognized foreign laws granting corporate privileges. An 1813 Massachusetts case drew this analogy explicitly; it treated the "existence and rights" of foreign "artificial persons" as ordinary questions of foreign law, on par with the validity of contracts formed abroad.[74] As Justice Story put it in his famous *Commentaries*, this sort of recognition was a matter of comity: so long as the state had no "positive rule" on the subject, and so long as the foreign law wasn't "repugnant to its policy, or prejudicial to its interests," courts would "presume" that law's "tacit adoption" in cases where it applied.[75]

In *Bank of Augusta*, Taney applied this analogy to support a Georgia corporation's ability to form contracts in Alabama. "In making such

---

[72] Warder v. Arell, 2 Va. (2 Wash.) 282, 298 (1796) (op. of Pendleton, P.); *accord* Rhode Island v. Massachusetts, 37 U.S. (12 Pet.) 657, 720 (1838) (describing the state parties as "foreign to each other for all but federal purposes"); Buckner v. Finley, 27 U.S. (2 Pet.) 586, 590 (1829) ("For all national purposes embraced by the federal constitution, the states and the citizens thereof are one, united under the same sovereign authority, and governed by the same laws. In all other respects, the states are necessarily foreign to, and independent of each other."); *id.* at 591 (citing *Arell*); Bromley v. Hutchins, 8 Vt. 194, 196 (1836) (describing "each state," except for federal purposes, as "hold[ing] the same relation to the other states which it holds to other nations"); State v. Knight, 1 N.C. 143, 144 (1799) (considering the states, "with respect to each other, as independent sovereignties"); Ryan C. Williams, *Federalism, the Law of Nations, and the Excluded Middle*, 1 J. AM. CONST. HIST. 721, 740–41 n.84 (2023).

[73] 38 U.S. at 588.

[74] Portsmouth Livery Co. v. Watson, 10 Mass. 91, 92 (1813) (per curiam); *see also id.* at 92 n.1 (citing Pearsall v. Dwight, 2 Mass. (1 Tyng) 84, 88–89 (1806)); *cf. Pearsall*, 2 Mass. at 89 (treating the recognition of foreign contracts as "founded on the tacit consent of civilized nations" and as "part of the law of nations adopted by the common law").

[75] JOSEPH STORY, COMMENTARIES ON THE CONFLICT OF LAWS § 38, at 37 (Boston, Hilliard, Gray & Co. 1834).

contracts," he noted, "a corporation no doubt exercises its corporate franchise."[76] But while a corporation might "live and have its being in [one] state only," the grant of its power to contract might still "be recognised in other places,"[77] through "the comity of nations and between these states"[78]—a comity which would be "presumed according to the usages of nations," just as in the case of foreign contracts.[79] Admitting the existence and powers of a foreign corporation was "but the usual comity of recognising the law of another state," which the states of the Union owed to each other no less than they did to foreign nations.[80]

This theory not only explained how corporations might operate in other states; it also explained that power's limits. If Alabama *didn't* want other corporations operating on its soil, all it had to do was say so. As in the case of foreign contracts against public policy, whenever "the interest or policy of any state requires it to restrict the rule, it has but to declare its will, and the legal presumption is at once at an end."[81] Only because there was "no law of [Alabama] which attempts to define the rights of foreign corporations"[82] would the Court apply the general default, namely that "corporations of one state" were freely "permitted to make contracts in another."[83]

In other words, corporate recognition was a matter of permission and not of right, a default rule that states could easily set aside. Individual citizens may have had Article IV privileges of trade and commerce in other states: privileges, in the famous formulation of *Corfield v. Coryell*, "to pass through, or to reside in any other state, for purposes of trade, agriculture, professional pursuits, or otherwise."[84] But these were general privileges to act in one's *own* name, not local privileges to

---

[76] *Bank of Augusta*, 38 U.S. at 596.

[77] *Id.* at 588.

[78] *Id.* at 589; *see also id.* (citing STORY, *supra* note 75).

[79] *Id.* at 596; *see also id.* at 590–91 (arguing that "[t]hese usages of commerce and trade have been so general and public, and have been practised for so long a period of time, . . . that the Court cannot overlook them").

[80] *Id.* at 590.

[81] *Id.*

[82] *Id.* at 597.

[83] *Id.* at 589; *accord* Buccola, *supra* note 71, at 645–46.

[84] 6 F. Cas. 546, 552 (C.C.E.D. Pa. 1825) (No. 3230) (op. of Washington, Circuit Justice); *cf.* Gerard N. Magliocca, *Rediscovering* Corfield v. Coryell, 95 NOTRE DAME L. REV. 701, 701 n.2 (2019) (providing the correct date of *Corfield*).

act under an artificial name. To force each state to duplicate the special privileges given out by others, Taney wrote, would "give the citizens of other states far higher and greater privileges than are enjoyed by the citizens of the state itself," and would "deprive every State of all control over the extent of corporate franchises" within its borders.[85]

This view was resoundingly reaffirmed by Justice Field in *Paul v. Virginia*. Field agreed that corporations, as "artificial persons created by the legislature," weren't "citizens" protected by Article IV's Privileges and Immunities Clause.[86] He distinguished general privileges "common to the citizens," protected under Article IV, from "special privileges" a state legislature had specifically granted "to the corporators." As "the mere creation of local law," the latter had to be "enjoyed at home" and could "have no operation" in other states "except by [their] permission, express or implied."[87] And if a foreign corporation had "no absolute right of recognition in other States," then those other states could provide their "assent . . . upon such terms and conditions as [they] may think proper to impose."[88]

3. *Corporate Privileges and Jurisdiction.* Understanding corporate privileges as specially granted, by some legislatures and not by others, had important consequences for personal jurisdiction. A corporation was in some sense a legal fiction, existing only according to the law of the state that created it. If you wanted to serve process on a corporation anywhere else, you had to find an agent authorized to receive that process, which the corporation might not have. So consent statutes, like the one in *Mallory*, became crucial devices for dragging foreign corporations before local courts.

Personal jurisdiction at the Founding wasn't based on the Fourteenth Amendment (which didn't yet exist), but on rules of general and international law, rules that governed whether a court's decision would be given effect by other courts.[89] Under these rules, nonresident defendants, whom state statutes couldn't simply order to appear, had to be properly "served with process" or to have "voluntarily made

---

[85] *Bank of Augusta*, 38 U.S. at 586–87.

[86] 75 U.S. (7 Wall.) 168, 177 (1869) (construing U.S. CONST. art. IV, § 2, cl. 1).

[87] *Id.* at 180–81. *See generally* Jud Campbell, *General Citizenship Rights*, 132 YALE L.J. 611 (2023) (distinguishing these categories).

[88] *Paul*, 75 U.S. at 181.

[89] *See* Sachs, Pennoyer *Was Right*, *supra* note 28, at 1269–87.

defence."⁹⁰ And these rules implicitly limited Congress's full-faith-and-credit statute,⁹¹ which was read to leave intact in these respects "the international law as it existed among the states in 1790."⁹²

After the Civil War, the Fourteenth Amendment again kept these rules intact. Because a jurisdictionless judgment was void—and thus inadequate support for a deprivation of "life, liberty, or property"⁹³—the Due Process Clause gave federal courts a way of testing state courts' compliance with applicable rules of jurisdiction. A state judgment could thus be reviewed by the Supreme Court by means of federal-question jurisdiction, applying the same rules of general and international law that were applied to the judgments of lower federal courts.⁹⁴

Some early American courts concluded from this that "all foreign corporations are without the jurisdiction of the process of the courts of this Commonwealth."⁹⁵ One might issue a summons against a corporation and serve process on its officer, but only in "the sovereignty where this artificial body exists"⁹⁶: an officer who just happened to be in the forum would be there in an individual capacity only, as "his functions and his character would not accompany him" outside the state "under whose laws he derived this character."⁹⁷ Maybe a corporation could voluntarily appear in another state's court by attorney, under the comity rule discussed in *Bank of Augusta*; maybe it could be compelled to appear to answer for seized property.⁹⁸ But some more general solution was needed.

---

⁹⁰ D'Arcy v. Ketchum, 52 U.S. (11 How.) 165, 176 (1851); *see id.* at 174; *accord* Sachs, Pennoyer *Was Right*, *supra* note 28, at 1273–78.

⁹¹ Act of May 26, 1790, ch. 11, 1 Stat. 122 (codified as amended at 28 U.S.C. § 1738 (2018)).

⁹² *D'Arcy*, 52 U.S. at 176.

⁹³ U.S. Const. amend. XIV, § 1.

⁹⁴ *See* Pennoyer v. Neff, 95 U.S. 714, 729–734 (1878); *accord* Sachs, Pennoyer *Was Right*, *supra* note 28, at 1287–1313.

⁹⁵ Peckham v. Inhabitants of N. Par., 33 Mass. (16 Pick.) 274, 286 (1834).

⁹⁶ M'Queen v. Middletown Mfg. Co., 16 Johns. 5, 7 (N.Y. Sup. Ct. 1819); *accord* Nash v. Rector of the Evangelical Lutheran Church, 1 Miles 78, 79 (Pa. Phila. Dist. Ct. 1835).

⁹⁷ *M'Queen*, 16 Johns. at 7; *accord* St. Clair v. Cox, 106 U.S. 350, 357 (1882).

⁹⁸ *M'Queen*, 16 Johns. at 7; *accord* Angell & Ames, supra note 65, at 228. *Compare* Bushel v. Commonwealth Ins. Co., 15 Serg. & Rawle 173, 178 (Pa. 1827) (interpreting a Pennsylvania statute to hold that state courts could "compel an appearance" of foreign corporations "by attachment of their effects within the state"), *with* President of the Union Turnpike Road v. Jenkins, 2 Mass. (1 Tyng) 37, 39 & n.a (1806) (interpreting a Massachusetts statute not to allow

States found this solution in their power to deny recognition. As Chief Justice Taney noted in *Bank of Augusta*, Maryland had passed a law in 1834 providing that any foreign corporation "'which shall transact or shall have transacted business' in the state, may be sued in its Courts upon contracts made in the state."[99] Maryland could reject the corporation's existence altogether, so the state could also recognize it with conditions, such as a requirement that it consent to jurisdiction.

This approach was expressly approved by the Court in *Lafayette Insurance Co. v. French*.[100] An Indiana corporation had had the temerity to open an office in Ohio and make fire insurance contracts there; when sued on one of those contracts, it refused to appear, and the insured tried to collect the default judgment in Indiana federal court.[101] The corporation argued that it "was created by a law of the State of Indiana" and so "could have no existence out of that State, and, consequently, could not be sued in Ohio."[102] But an Ohio statute had explicitly provided for such jurisdiction, through service of process on the Ohio agent who'd made Ohio contracts in the corporation's name.[103]

The Supreme Court gave full effect to Ohio's judgment, finding it wholly consistent with "those rules of public law which protect persons and property within one State from the exercise of jurisdiction over them by another."[104] Though the corporation itself couldn't "pass personally beyond the limits" of Indiana, it could make contracts and "transact business in Ohio," but "only with [Ohio's] consent."[105] That consent was subject to "such conditions as Ohio may think fit to impose," so long as they complied with international law on "the jurisdiction and authority of each State," and with the "principle of natural justice which forbids condemnation without opportunity

---

for attachment of corporate assets by trustee process, but noting that the state revised this statute in 1832).

[99] Bank of Augusta v. Earle, 38 U.S. (13 Pet.) 519, 592 (1839).

[100] 59 U.S. (18 How.) 404 (1856).

[101] *Id.* at 404.

[102] *Id.* at 405.

[103] *Id.* at 406.

[104] *Id.*

[105] *Id.* at 407.

for defence."[106] Here, Ohio let the foreign corporation make contracts within its borders on condition that the agent who made those contracts "should also be deemed its agent to receive service" for related lawsuits—a requirement the Court found neither "unreasonable in itself," nor "in conflict with any principle of public law."[107] Only by a fiction of Ohio law could this natural person sign contracts that bound the *corporation*; if Lafayette wanted to affirm that the agent really had authority to exercise the corporation's privileges and to "make contracts of insurance" on its behalf, then it could hardly deny "the condition upon which alone such business could be there transacted by them," namely his authority to receive service of process.[108]

Crucial to the Court's reasoning was the fact that the Lafayette Insurance Company couldn't exist or exercise privileges in Ohio without Ohio's consent. By contrast, the Court reserved the question as to "natural persons,"[109] who might have the privileges of citizens in Ohio and so needed no special permission to make contracts there by agent. As was explained in another case, "[t]he chief point of difference between the natural and the artificial person is that the former may do whatever is not forbidden by law; the latter can do only what is authorized by its charter," and so could "exercise its authority in a foreign territory" only "upon such conditions as may be prescribed by the law of the place."[110] If the condition were that the corporation "shall consent to be sued there," then even if it failed to comply with a formal registration requirement, "[i]f it do business there it will be presumed to have assented and will be bound accordingly."[111] The Lafayette Insurance Company couldn't claim to exist in Ohio when making contracts and then claim *not* to exist in Ohio when sued on those contracts; as the Court later put it, such a corporation would be "estopped to say that it had not done what it should have done in order that it might lawfully enter that Commonwealth and there exert its corporate powers."[112]

---

[106] *Id.*

[107] *Id.*

[108] *Id.* at 408.

[109] *Id.* at 409.

[110] R.R. Co. v. Harris, 79 U.S. (12 Wall.) 65, 81 (1871).

[111] *Id.* (citing *Lafayette*, 59 U.S. 404); *accord* St. Clair v. Cox, 106 U.S. 350, 356–57 (1882).

[112] Old Wayne Mut. Life Ass'n of Indianapolis v. McDonough, 204 U.S. 8, 21–22 (1907).

This consent theory didn't have a ready answer to every jurisdictional question. For example, courts disagreed on what should happen if a foreign corporation, obliged to register and submit to general jurisdiction in Pennsylvania, simply started operating and exercising privileges there without registering. To some courts, the corporation's consent could be inferred, so that it couldn't profit from its unlawful failure to register.[113] But to others, without a signed registration form, Pennsylvania could take only what we'd now call specific jurisdiction: Cases from outside its borders (say, on contracts "executed in Indiana") didn't involve the exercise of *Pennsylvania* corporate privileges, and so didn't warrant applying the statutory condition.[114] But courts tended to agree that a corporation which *did* formally register, as in *Mallory*, would be held to the terms of its bargain.[115]

B. THE EMERGENCE OF DORMANT COMMERCE

What changed all this was the growth of a new line of case law under dormant commerce. If a Virginia corporation wanted to engage in cross-border commerce—say, carrying wheat from Pennsylvania to Maine—it needed to use its corporate privileges in every state along the way: claiming property rights in its trucks and inventory, making contracts of purchase and sale, filing and responding to lawsuits about roadway accidents, and so on. The earlier case law supports the view that these privileges weren't guaranteed to corporations under the Commerce Clause, even if they were guaranteed to citizens under Article IV. Yet *Bank of Augusta* had held open a narrow window for "some rights under the Constitution of the United States, which a corporation might claim under peculiar circumstances, in a state other than that in which it was chartered."[116] Over time, the Court used that opening to tear down the entire edifice. As the dormant commerce doctrine grew in strength, courts began to limit state powers to limit corporate privileges—first as to corporations engaged in interstate commerce, and then as to their intrastate business too.

---

[113] *See, e.g.*, Tauza v. Susquehanna Coal Co., 220 N.Y. 259, 268–69 (1917).

[114] *See, e.g., Old Wayne*, 204 U.S. at 22–23.

[115] *See* Pa. Fire Ins. Co. of Phila. v. Gold Issue Mining & Milling Co., 243 U.S. 93 (1917); Edward Quinton Keasbey, *Jurisdiction over Foreign Corporations*, 12 HARV. L. REV. 1, 5–6, 18–19 (1898); Sachs Brief, *supra* note 10, at 4–5, 16–17.

[116] Bank of Augusta v. Earle, 38 U.S. (13 Pet.) 519, 597 (1839).

1. *Early Caselaw.* On first principles, it's hardly obvious that dormant commerce doctrine has anything to do with corporate privileges. Part of the argument depends on whether, and why, a "dormant" Commerce Clause exists at all. On one theory, the textual Commerce Clause gives Congress an exclusive power; states simply can't regulate commerce that's interstate in nature, and so the Clause restricts state action even "in its dormant state."[117] In dicta in *Gibbons v. Ogden*, Chief Justice Marshall found "great force in this argument," namely that "the word 'to regulate' implies . . . full power over the thing to be regulated" and thus "excludes, necessarily, the action of all others that would perform the same operation on the same thing."[118] On another theory, Congress's "dormant" choice not to exercise its regulatory power is really an active choice that interstate commerce shall in certain respects be free;[119] as Marshall described the argument, the textual commerce power "produces a uniform whole," which may be "as much disturbed and deranged by changing what the regulating power designs to leave untouched, as that on which it has operated."[120]

Either theory, though, has narrow limits. "Inspection laws, quarantine laws, health laws of every description, as well as laws for regulating the internal commerce of a State, and those which respect turnpike roads, ferries, &c.," were all thought by Marshall to be outside the scope of the textual commerce power (and *a fortiori* outside of dormant commerce too).[121] They might "have a remote and

---

[117] Willson v. Black Bird Creek Marsh Co. 27 U.S. (2 Pet.) 245, 252 (1829); *see, e.g.*, Barry Friedman & Daniel T. Deacon, *A Course Unbroken: The Constitutional Legitimacy of the Dormant Commerce Clause*, 97 VA. L. REV. 1877, 1882 (2011); Ilan Wurman, *The Origins of Substantive Due Process*, 87 U. CHI. L. REV. 815, 837–45 (2020).

[118] 22 U.S. (9 Wheat.) 1, 209 (1824); *cf.* City of New York v. Miln, 36 U.S. (11 Pet.) 102, 158 (1837) (Story, J., dissenting) ("Full power to regulate a particular subject implies the whole power, and leaves no residuum; and a grant of the whole to one, is incompatible with a grant to another of a part."). Note that this theory makes it hard for Congress to *license* a state's exercise of the exclusively federal power over interstate commerce, any more than it could license a state to coin money or grant letters of marque. *See* U.S. CONST. art. I, § 8, cl. 5, 11; *id.* § 10, cl. 1; *cf. Gibbons*, 22 U.S. at 207 (denying any "concurrent power in the States to regulate the conduct of pilots," and reasoning that "Congress cannot enable a State to legislate" over interstate commerce, though it "may adopt the provisions of a State" as a federal regulation).

[119] Welton v. Missouri, 91 U.S. 275, 282 (1876) (suggesting that congressional "inaction on this subject . . . is equivalent to a declaration that inter-State commerce shall be free and untrammelled").

[120] *Gibbons*, 22 U.S. at 209.

[121] *Id.* at 203.

considerable influence on commerce,"[122] and so they might be subject to statutory preemption, if necessary and proper to a federal regulation of commerce.[123] But they weren't automatically invalidated or preempted, as "a power to regulate commerce" was in no way "the source from which the right to pass them is derived."[124] Rather, they were "component parts" of "that immense mass of legislation, which embraces everything within the territory of a State, not surrendered to the general government."[125]

If all this is right, then corporate privileges would have been outside the limits of dormant commerce too. The power to regulate commerce wasn't in any way "the source from which the right" to charter corporations (or, more importantly, the right *not* to charter corporations) was "derived."[126] States chartered corporations for a wide variety of purposes—manufacturing, dealing in land, selling insurance, managing religious congregations, and so on—many of which were outside the scope of "commerce" to Founding-era eyes.[127] While a refusal to recognize the Amalgamated Wheatfield Corporation as owning trucks in Pennsylvania might pose a barrier to its cross-border commerce in wheat, so would a Pennsylvania health law limiting the acceptable volume of mouse droppings per bushel. And the same would be true if Pennsylvania's refusal were grounded on objections to the corporation's circular control structure, its use of dual-class shares, or any other feature nowadays ascribed to its "internal affairs."[128] Congress might choose to preempt such a law, but the Constitution wouldn't override it by default.

By contrast, taking the Commerce Clause itself to guarantee the *Corfield* privileges "to pass through, or to reside in any other state, for purposes of trade, agriculture, professional pursuits, or otherwise,"

---

[122] *Id.*

[123] *Id.* at 203–04.

[124] *Id.* at 203.

[125] *Id.*

[126] *Id.*

[127] *Compare, e.g., id.* (distinguishing commerce from activities that "act upon the subject before it becomes an article of foreign commerce"), Corfield v. Coryell, 6 F. Cas. 546, 551 (C.C.E.D. Pa. 1825) (No. 3230) (concerning harvesting oysters), *and* Paul v. Virginia, 75 U.S. (7 Wall.) 168, 183 (1869) (concerning insurance), *with* Wickard v. Filburn, 317 U.S. 111 (1942) (concerning growing wheat for home consumption).

[128] *See, e.g.,* McDermott Inc. v. Lewis, 531 A.2d 206, 215 (Del. 1987) (discussing "the relationships *inter se* of the corporation, its directors, officers and shareholders").

would render superfluous their specific guarantee *to citizens* under Article IV.[129] Indeed, those privileges might have been quite central to Marshall's reasoning in *Gibbons*. That case pitted Aaron Ogden, the holder of a state monopoly in steam travel through a portion of New York's waters, against Thomas Gibbons, who held a federal coasting license. According to Ogden, the license didn't confer on Gibbons any affirmative right to engage in interstate trade; it merely freed him from certain restrictions otherwise superadded by federal law, which could *regulate* such a right but not *confer* it. On this picture, the "rights to *trade*, to *enter*, or to *navigate*" are "portions of the *jus commune*," and they "rest on the common law, independent of any *gift* from or *right conferred* by Congress; which, in truth, has no power . . . to make such gift, its authority being only to *regulate* commerce."[130] As it turns out, Chief Justice Marshall partly agreed: He acknowledged as "true" Ogden's contentions "that the constitution does not confer the right of intercourse between State and State"; that this right "derives its source from those laws whose authority is acknowledged by civilized man throughout the world"; and that "[t]he constitution found it an existing right, and gave to Congress the power to regulate it."[131] Marshall merely reasoned that, once Congress had granted a license, "the law must imply a power to exercise the right," something frustrated by the state monopoly.[132]

The notion that a legislature might regulate preexisting rights was fundamental to Founding-era law.[133] Yet if the rights to trade, enter, and navigate were all preexisting common-law rights and privileges, as *Corfield* suggests,[134] then it's far from clear that they belonged as of right to *corporations*—which, unlike common-law partnerships, obtained their privileges by affirmative acts of legislation. It may have

---

[129] *Corfield*, 6 F. Cas. at 552.

[130] *Gibbons*, 22 U.S. at 131–32 (restating the argument of counsel); *accord id.* at 137–38.

[131] *Id.* at 211 (op. of the Court).

[132] *Id.* at 212.

[133] *See* Baude, Campbell & Sachs, *supra* note 28 (manuscript at 12); *cf.* United States v. Cruikshank, 92 U.S. 542, 552–53 (1875) (citing this passage from *Gibbons* in discussing "[t]he right of the people peaceably to assemble for lawful purposes," which it saw "not . . . [as] a right granted to the people by the Constitution," but rather as "one of the attributes of citizenship under a free government," which Congress in the First Amendment was merely prohibited "from abridging").

[134] 6 F. Cas. at 551 (discussing "those privileges and immunities which are, in their nature, fundamental; which belong, of right, to the citizens of all free governments, and which have, at all times, been enjoyed by" American citizens since Independence).

been standard practice for one state to recognize the corporations of another, but this recognition was a matter of comity, not of right.[135] So even if some dormant aspect of the Commerce Clause would stop a state from *taking away* a corporation's preexisting rights to engage in interstate commerce within its borders, it's not clear that a foreign corporation *had* such preexisting rights to begin with. Virginia couldn't confer on Amalgamated Wheatfield a right to enter and trade in Pennsylvania, and any federal right would have to be granted by Congress.

Indeed, through the Civil War, the Court seemed convinced that no dormant-commerce rule barred discrimination against foreign corporations *per se*. In *Paul*, the claim of corporate privileges and immunities was the defendant's alternative argument; his main challenge was that the Commerce Clause doesn't "exclude the commerce carried on by corporations," and that Virginia couldn't "discriminat[e]" among insurance companies "in favor of their own citizens," with "[e]ach State . . . prevent[ing] every other from trading by their agencies."[136] The Court swatted away this argument, holding that "[i]ssuing a policy of insurance" was merely a "personal contract[]" and "not a transaction of commerce."[137] Yet the *Paul* Court *didn't* say what the modern Court later would—namely that *any* regulation, even a statute of limitations, that "subject[s] the activities of foreign and domestic corporations to inconsistent regulations" and "imposes a greater burden on out-of-state companies" than on domestic companies "must fall under the Commerce Clause."[138]

The Court's position in *Paul* made sense on its terms. If a foreign corporation were a physical *thing*, which had to *move* across a border, then that movement might be a matter of interstate commerce, which a state couldn't restrict. But if a corporation is just a group of people with special legal powers (say, six Pennsylvanians growing wheat), then we care about whether those people have a right to *do* what they're *doing* (say, holding land in Pennsylvania), a right which another state

---

[135] *See* Bank of Augusta v. Earle, 38 U.S. (13 Pet.) 519, 590 (1839); *cf.* STORY, *supra* note 75, § 645, at 532 (distinguishing international law from international comity, and expressing the hope that "the comity of nations" would one day become "the justice of nations").

[136] Paul v. Virginia, 75 U.S. (7 Wall.) 168, 171, 173–74 (1869) (restating the argument of counsel).

[137] *Id.* at 183 (op. of the Court).

[138] Bendix Autolite Corp. v. Midwesco Enters., Inc., 486 U.S. 888, 894 (1988).

can't confer. Thus, into the 1870s we find the Court letting states place "more onerous" taxes on corporations created by other states, finding no general barrier to a state's "discriminat[ing] between her own domestic corporations and those of other states, desirous of transacting business within her jurisdiction."[139]

Nor would it matter that Congress's power to regulate commerce includes commerce by corporations. In the dormant-commerce context, that argument proves too much: The commerce power also includes commerce in spoiled food, but *Gibbons* clearly thought that state inspection laws could bar such commerce, at least until Congress preempted them.[140] So, too, for corporate law: Congress *could* give the Amalgamated Wheatfield Corporation a coasting license, or indeed a USDOT Number,[141] which might entail a right to exercise corporate privileges (like owning trucks and inventory) when carrying wheat from state to state. But until Congress acts, a state could still limit the sorts of foreign corporations it would recognize within its borders.

2. *Turn-of-the-Century Doctrine.* The *fin-de-siècle* change in the Court's position grew out of a second line of doctrine, that states couldn't impose a licensing requirement on people engaged in interstate commerce. On its own, this doctrine didn't do much for corporate privileges; it applied equally to corporations and to individuals. But as more and more commerce was conducted under the corporate form, it seemed more and more natural for the Court to view restrictions on that form as restrictions of commerce itself.

The Court had always had to police the line between lawful domestic regulations and forbidden restrictions on interstate trade. For example, in *Brown v. Maryland*, the Court applied both the Import/Export and Commerce Clauses to invalidate a state law forcing importers to take out a license and pay a tax before selling imported goods.[142] Chief Justice Marshall reasoned that an act of Congress had

---

[139] Ducat v. Chicago, 77 U.S. (10 Wall.) 410, 415 (1871); *accord* Doyle v. Cont'l Ins. Co., 94 U.S. 535, 540 (1876), *overruled by* Terral v. Burke Constr. Co., 257 U.S. 529 (1922); Liverpool Ins. Co. v. Mass, 77 U.S. (10 Wall.) 566, 576 (1870) (showing "no hesitation in holding" that "the law of Massachusetts, which only permits [the defendant] to exercise its corporate function in that State on the condition of payment of a specific tax, is no violation of the Federal Constitution").

[140] Gibbons v. Ogden, 22 U.S. (9 Wheat.) 1, 204 (1824).

[141] *See* 49 U.S.C. §§ 13902, 31134 (2018 & Supp. III).

[142] 25 U.S. (12 Wheat.) 419, 445, 448 (1827).

established a right to import goods, and that selling them was "an inseparable incident" of this right.[143] But in language that was easily extended to dormant-commerce cases, he wrote that a tax "on the person of the importer" and "on the thing imported . . . interfere equally with the power to regulate commerce," and that a state's tax power couldn't "obstruct the free course of a power given to Congress."[144] Otherwise, "what should restrain a State from taxing any article passing through it from one State to another, for the purpose of traffic?"[145]

Nearly fifty years later, the Court in 1873 applied a similar doctrine to corporations in the *Case of the State Freight Tax*.[146] Pennsylvania had taxed transportation companies, foreign or domestic, based on how much freight they carried.[147] The Court recognized that the state could "tax the franchises of its corporations,"[148] which (as the state argued) "owe[d] their existence to her dominion."[149] But here the burden fell on the freight itself, whether the companies were "incorporated by the State or not, and whether exercising privileges granted by the State or not," even if they "derive[d] no rights from grants of Pennsylvania" and were merely "passing up and down the Delaware."[150] So the Court invalidated the tax insofar as it applied to freight carried across the border;[151] a state could tax "its own internal commerce, and the franchises, property, or business of its own corporations," but only so long as "interstate intercourse, trade, or commerce, be not embarrassed or restricted."[152]

Even this line of doctrine didn't *necessarily* require recognition of out-of-state corporations, so long as the states made sure not to put special burdens on cross-border commerce. For example, states could apply new tort statutes to interstate shippers, which the Court distinguished from "exact[ing] a license fee from parties engaged in

---

[143] *Id.* at 448.

[144] *Id.*

[145] *Id.* at 449.

[146] 82 U.S. (15 Wall.) 232 (1873).

[147] *Id.* at 232–33 (syllabus).

[148] *Id.* at 277 (op. of the Court).

[149] *Id.* at 260 (stating the argument of counsel).

[150] *Id.* at 278 (op. of the Court).

[151] *Id.* at 275–82.

[152] *Id.* at 282.

commercial pursuits";[153] the tort statutes might "*affect* commerce" without "constituting a *regulation* of it, within the meaning of the Constitution."[154] Likewise, a state could tax property "belonging to a foreign corporation engaged in foreign or inter-State commerce," so long as it didn't tax such property "*because* it is used to carry on that commerce."[155] Interstate commerce by corporations would enjoy "the same protection against state exactions which is given to such commerce when carried on by individuals."[156]

But when a foreign corporation wanted to conduct interstate commerce, it was easy to argue that a state law requiring a license for recognition had the same effect as one requiring a license for commerce. When Florida tried to give a local company an exclusive telegraph franchise, and an interstate railroad invited Western Union to build a line along its tracks, the Court struck down the exclusive franchise as a restriction on interstate commerce.[157] The local company argued that Western Union "is a New York corporation," and that Florida had never "empower[ed] it to exercise its corporate franchises" there; it thus had "no existence or rights beyond the limits of the State which created it, except by the comity or the enabling acts of other States."[158] But the Court distinguished *Paul*, which had allowed Virginia to "exclude a corporation of another State from its jurisdiction," on the ground that *Paul* "was not . . . the case of a corporation engaged in inter-state commerce," and that "if it had been, very different questions would have been presented."[159] Because Congress had given telegraph companies a statutory right to operate along railroads, Florida's "prohibitory legislation" was "inoperative"; but the Court treated as an open question whether a foreign corporation *always* had the right to engage in interstate commerce within a state, even without special sanction from Congress.[160]

---

[153] Sherlock v. Alling, 93 U.S. 99, 102 (1876).

[154] *Id.* at 103 (emphasis added).

[155] Gloucester Ferry Co. v. Pennsylvania, 114 U.S. 196, 211 (1885) (Field, J.) (emphasis added).

[156] Phila. & S. Mail S.S. Co. v. Pennsylvania, 122 U.S. 326, 342 (1887) (describing the holding of *Gloucester Ferry*).

[157] Pensacola Tel. Co. v. W. Union Tel. Co., 96 U.S. 1, 3–5 (1878) (syllabus).

[158] *Id.* at 6–7 (stating the argument of counsel).

[159] *Id.* at 12–13 (op. of the Court).

[160] *Id.* at 13.

Justice Field, the author of *Paul*, recognized in dissent how the Court had implicitly expanded the rights of out-of-state corporations. He read the federal statute more narrowly, doubting whether Congress could permit "foreign corporations [to] exist in the State of Florida" for purposes of "local business."[161] But he also rejected as "novel and startling," and indeed as "utterly subversive of our system of local State government," the notion "that if a corporation be in any way engaged in commerce it can enter and do business in another State without the latter's consent."[162] "Let this doctrine be once established," he wrote, "and the greater part of the trade and commerce of every State will soon be carried on by corporations created without it."[163]

That doctrine was "once established" less than a decade later. In *Cooper Manufacturing Co. v. Ferguson*, decided in 1885, an Ohio corporation made a contract in Colorado for the sale and interstate delivery of a steam engine, without filing the certificate that Colorado required before a foreign corporation could "do any business."[164] When the corporation later sued, the buyers argued that the contract was invalid, citing the standard rule from *Bank of Augusta*.[165] The Court agreed that "the people of a State" could, in general, decide "the terms upon which a foreign corporation shall be allowed to carry on its business in the State."[166] But because the seller's contract "was the only business ever done by it, or that it ever purposed to do, in that State," the Court strained the Colorado statute to allow a "single and isolated act of business" without registration,[167] for fear that a contrary reading might limit the corporation's right "to make contracts in the State for carrying on commerce between the States," and so might invade "the exclusive right of Congress to regulate commerce among the several States."[168] Instead, the Court read the statute only to forbid "the *carrying on* of business," which the Court nebulously

---

[161] *Id.* at 20 (Field, J., dissenting).

[162] *Id.* at 21, 23.

[163] *Id.* at 22.

[164] 113 U.S. 727, 728 (1885) (syllabus) (internal citation omitted).

[165] *Id.* at 728–29; *id.* at 730–31 (op. of the Court) (stating the argument of counsel).

[166] *Id.* at 732 (citing Bank of Augusta v. Earle, 38 U.S. (13 Pet.) 519 (1839)).

[167] *Id.* at 733.

[168] *Id.* at 734.

defined as involving something more than "a single act of business."[169] But still it reserved the question whether, if Colorado really wanted to forbid even a single act of business, the dormant Commerce Clause would get in the way.[170]

From there, the Court's language became more general, even in cases upholding state restrictions. In 1888, for example, the Court (per Justice Field) upheld a requirement that a foreign mining corporation with a local office take out an "office license" and pay a substantial tax.[171] But Field accepted that the state's power "to exclude a foreign corporation" didn't extend "where its business is strictly commerce, interstate or foreign," as "[t]he control of such commerce, being in the federal government, is not to be restricted by state authority."[172]

Soon the Court openly held that foreign corporations, repeatedly engaged in interstate commerce, had a constitutional right to use their corporate privileges abroad. In 1891, *Crutcher v. Kentucky* rejected a state license requirement for foreign corporations carrying goods and packages, at least as applied to carriage across borders.[173] If a state couldn't forbid interstate carriage by "a partnership firm of individuals," the Court reasoned, it also couldn't forbid such carriage by a corporation, based only on the latter's need for "mere corporate facilities, as a matter of convenience in carrying on their business."[174] Of course this reasoning elided the Article IV difference between the individuals who compose a common-law partnership and a corporation without privileges in Kentucky. But to the Court, even "a foreign corporation,—an English or a French transportation company, for example," had a constitutionally guaranteed right of "coming into [a state's] borders and landing goods and passengers at its wharves."[175] By the time of *International Textbook Co. v. Pigg* in 1910, the Court no

---

[169] *Id.* (emphasis added); *id.* at 735.

[170] *Compare id.* at 736, *with id.* at 737 (Matthews, J., joined by Blatchford, J., concurring in the judgment) (arguing that the state could forbid the corporation from "manufacturing machinery" in Colorado, but not from "selling in Colorado, by contracts made there, its machinery manufactured elsewhere," for to do so was "to regulate commerce between Colorado and Ohio, which is in the exclusive province of Congress"). Notably, Justice Field did not dissent.

[171] Pembina Consol. Silver Mining & Milling Co. v. Pennsylvania, 125 U.S. 181, 182–84 (1888).

[172] *Id.* at 190.

[173] 141 U.S. 47, 47–48 (1891) (syllabus); *id.* at 57 (op. of the Court).

[174] *Id.* at 57; *see id.* at 58–59.

[175] *Id.* at 57.

longer looked to make exceptions for "single or casual transactions," but endorsed a general dormant-commerce right of corporations to carry on "regular business" in other states, so long as that business "was, in its essential characteristics, commerce among the States."[176]

These rights were then extended to a foreign corporation's in-state business too. The early-twentieth-century Court wrote glowingly of the "intimate connection which, at this day, exists between the interstate business done by interstate companies" and their "local business" in a state—"which, for the convenience of the people, must be done or can generally be better and more economically done by such interstate companies rather than by domestic companies organized to conduct only local business."[177] The Court still grudgingly admitted "the *general* rule . . . that a State may . . . exclude foreign corporations from its limits" or place "terms and conditions on their doing business."[178] But it reconceived those cases as involving exclusively intrastate enterprises, "not directly or regularly [engaged] in interstate or foreign commerce" at all.[179] Once a foreign corporation "had the right to enter and remain in the State for *interstate* business," the state couldn't impose extra fees for "doing domestic business,"[180] as "the freedom of interstate commerce shall not be trammelled or burdened by local regulations," even "under the guise of regulating local affairs."[181]

As dormant commerce doctrine evolved over the twentieth century, from "separate spheres" of state and federal regulation to *Pike* balancing of benefits and burdens,[182] the Court rephrased these rules in terms of state interests, leaving aside consideration of the firm's in-state or interstate activities. For example, in constitutionalizing the "internal affairs" doctrine as a matter of dormant commerce, the Court announced that a state "has no interest in regulating the

---

[176] 217 U.S. 91, 104, 106 (1910).

[177] W. Union Tel. Co. v. Kansas *ex rel.* Coleman, 216 U.S. 1, 37 (1910).

[178] *Id.* at 33.

[179] *Id.*

[180] *Id.* at 34–35 (emphasis added).

[181] *Id.* at 37–38. *But see id.* at 52–53 (Holmes, J., dissenting) (arguing that interstate and intrastate commerce could be regulated separately, as "the corporation has the right to enter for one purpose and the State has a right to exclude its entry for another").

[182] *See* Am. Beverage Ass'n v. Snyder, 735 F.3d 362, 377, 379 (6th Cir. 2013) (Sutton, J., concurring) (citing Pike v. Bruce Church, Inc., 397 U.S. 137 (1970)); Ernest A. Young, *"The Ordinary Diet of the Law": The Presumption Against Preemption in the Roberts Court*, 2011 Sup. Ct. Rev. 253, 257–61.

internal affairs of foreign corporations,"[183] even those with substantial local operations.[184] And without such an interest, the state had nothing that could outweigh any burden imposed on "out-of-state transactions," even just transactions in shares.[185] The result is that a foreign corporation might have a federal right to do in-state business under a forbidden internal structure: a far cry from the world in which a state had "but to declare its will, and the legal presumption" of corporate privileges was "at once at an end."[186]

3. *Dormant Commerce and Jurisdiction.* The growth of these corporate dormant-commerce rights didn't affect doctrines of jurisdiction right away. To the contrary, the Court preserved the bottom-line rules on corporate jurisdiction long after their theoretical foundations had decayed. But because these intellectual foundations *had* decayed, the Court entered the twentieth century with an unclear and self-contradictory approach to corporate jurisdiction, making it easier for *International Shoe* to clear the field.

As noted above, the consent theory used in *Lafayette* had stayed in force under *Pennoyer* and its progeny.[187] States continued to assert jurisdiction by serving corporate agents within their borders; the Court continued to distinguish agents present in their individual capacities, or those who avoided exercising corporate privileges within the state (say, by merely soliciting offers for contracts made elsewhere), from

---

[183] Edgar v. MITE Corp., 457 U.S. 624, 645–46 (1982).

[184] *See id.* at 627 (describing a statute's potential application to corporations headquartered in the state and with ten percent of their capital there).

[185] *Id*. at 644; *see id*. at 643 (discussing a "nationwide tender offer").

[186] Bank of Augusta v. Earle, 38 U.S. (13 Pet.) 519, 590 (1839). The internal affairs doctrine has also been defended on the ground that a corporation shouldn't have to "be faced with conflicting demands" as to its internal structure, *MITE*, 457 U.S. at 645; *accord* CTS Corp. v. Dynamics Corp. of Am., 481 U.S. 69, 89 (1987) (emphasizing that "each corporation will be subject to the law of only one State")—whether as a matter of due process and surprise, *see* McDermott Inc. v. Lewis, 531 A.2d 206, 216 (Del. 1987) ("[D]irectors and officers have a significant right, under the fourteenth amendment's due process clause, to know what law will be applied to their actions."), or full faith and credit and consistency, *see* Ord. of United Com. Travelers of Am. v. Wolfe, 331 U.S. 586, 624 (1947) (demanding, under the Full Faith and Credit Clause, "the same terms of membership for members of fraternal benefit societies wherever their beneficiaries may be"). But these charges of inconsistency already assume corporate operations within the state; a corporation can hardly be surprised by the different regulatory regime of a state which it may not enter.

[187] *See* Pennoyer v. Neff, 95 U.S. 714, 735 (1878) (citing Lafayette Ins. Co. v. French, 59 U.S. (18 How.) 404 (1856)); *see, e.g.*, Conn. Mut. Life Ins. Co. v. Spratley, 172 U.S. 602, 610, 614–15 (1899); Goldey v. Morning News, 156 U.S. 518, 521–22 (1895); St. Clair v. Cox, 106 U.S. 350, 356–59 (1882).

those agents who actually made contracts or compromised claims on a corporation's behalf.[188]

This consent doctrine was scrambled by the developments in dormant commerce. If a state can't exclude a foreign corporation, it can't demand consent to jurisdiction as the price of entry. Instead the Court began to phrase its theory in terms of "presence" or "doing business" rather than "consent." But these latter terms lacked the same common-law roots, and so they were difficult to define without circularity: What does it mean for an intangible corporation to be "present" in a state? In one 1913 case, for example, the Court unhelpfully explained that "in order to render a corporation amenable to service of process in a foreign jurisdiction[,] it must appear that the corporation is transacting business in that district to such an extent as to subject it to the jurisdiction and laws thereof"[189]—the kind of vacuity famously belittled by Felix Cohen, who compared it to the discovery "that opium puts men to sleep because it contains a dormitive principle."[190]

Sometimes the criteria for "doing business" would have been perfectly comprehensible under the old regime. For example, in *International Harvester Co. of America v. Kentucky*, decided in 1914, the Court noted that the corporate agents served weren't mere solicitors; they'd been authorized to take customers' promissory notes and to "collect[]" on these notes at "bank[s] in Kentucky."[191] That is, they possessed in Kentucky what they held out to be the corporation's property, and they enforced certain contracts there on its behalf. That required the exercise of corporate privileges in Kentucky, which triggered the consent rule in *Lafayette*.

---

[188] *Compare St. Clair*, 106 U.S. at 360 (concerning an agent's personal or individual capacity), *Goldey*, 156 U.S. at 521–22 (same), *and* Green v. Chi., Burlington & Quincy Ry. Co., 205 U.S. 530, 533–34 (1907) (concerning solicitation), *with Spratley*, 172 U.S. at 611–12, 616 (discussing compromising claims). *See also supra* text accompanying notes 95–115 (describing the pre-*Pennoyer* and *Pennoyer*-era doctrine).

[189] St. Louis Sw. Ry. Co. v. Alexander, 227 U.S. 218, 226 (1913); *see also id.* at 227.

[190] Felix S. Cohen, *Transcendental Nonsense and the Functional Approach*, 35 COLUM. L. REV. 809, 820 (1935); *see id.* at 809–12. *But cf.* Jeremy Waldron, *"Transcendental Nonsense" and System in the Law*, 100 COLUM. L. REV. 16, 20–24 (2000) (noting that not all circularities are vicious, and that many illuminating scientific terms are interdefined).

[191] 234 U.S. 579, 586 (1914); *see also id.* at 587; *cf.* People's Tobacco Co. v. Am. Tobacco Co., 246 U.S. 79, 86–87 (1918) (distinguishing *Green*, 205 U.S. 530, from *Int'l Harvester*, 234 U.S. 579, on this ground).

But *International Harvester* also looked to criteria that made no sense under the old regime: for example, that the company's business included "a continuous course of shipment of machines into Kentucky,"[192] which under dormant-commerce case law Kentucky had no power to prevent. Indeed, the Court explicitly rejected the company's consent-based claim that restricting its activities to "interstate business" exempted it from being "made amenable to judicial process"; the Justices distinguished "the ordinary process of the courts" from state laws that might "burden interstate commerce" or "amount to the regulation of such commerce."[193] When the former would be permitted, or when the burden would be too great, the Court did not say. It again retreated to circularity, concluding that "the presence of a corporation within a State" for jurisdictional purposes depended on whether "the corporation is there carrying on business in such sense as to manifest its presence within the State."[194]

This led to decades of confusion in jurisdictional doctrine. In 1923, for example, the Court heard a case quite similar to *Lafayette* and reached an almost precisely contrary result. An Oklahoma clothier repeatedly sent its president to New York to buy clothing; he made a contract there on the company's behalf, which it allegedly breached, and he was served with process on a subsequent trip.[195] Yet the New York seller wasn't allowed to sue the defendant in a New York federal court, the sale and service of process there notwithstanding: "Visits on such business, even if occurring at regular intervals, would not warrant the inference that the corporation was present within the jurisdiction of the state."[196]

From there the Court bounced back and forth between restrictive and permissive dormant-commerce rulings, from *Davis* to *Terte* to *Miles*,[197] until it formally abandoned categories like "presence" in *International Shoe*.[198] There, the Delaware corporation had tried to restrict its Washington State activities to mere solicitation: Its salesmen

---

[192] *Int'l Harvester*, 234 U.S. at 587.

[193] *Id.* at 587–88.

[194] *Id.* at 589.

[195] *See* Rosenberg Bros. & Co. v. Curtis Brown Co., 285 F. 879, 880–81 (W.D.N.Y. 1921), aff'd, 260 U.S. 516 (1923).

[196] *Rosenberg Bros.*, 260 U.S. at 518.

[197] *See supra* notes 59–61.

[198] *See* Int'l Shoe Co. v. Washington, 326 U.S. 310, 316–17 (1945).

operated from salesrooms they themselves had rented, with their authority limited to "exhibiting their samples and soliciting orders," and with no capacity "to enter into contracts or to make collections" in the forum.[199] As the defendant saw things, the "mere solicitation of orders," which were "accepted without the state" and filled by interstate shipments, couldn't render it "amenable to suit" in Washington.[200] But because Congress had explicitly blessed unemployment assessments on businesses in interstate commerce, the Court reasoned that this statute quieted all interstate commerce concerns,[201] leaving only the vague due process considerations of "fair play and substantial justice."[202] And because "no consent to be sued ... ha[d] been given,"[203] considerations of the state's power to demand such consent were put to one side—until *Mallory*.

CONCLUSION

In the modern world, incorporation is easy, and out-of-state corporate recognition is routine. In this world, it's hard to understand why a state might *ever* refuse recognition to a foreign corporation, except as a form of rent-seeking. Of *course* corporations may operate nationwide. What reason would a state have to say no? And if it can't say no, how could it extract an unwilling consent-by-registration?

To some, such as Justice Brennan, these social and legal differences from the Founding demand different constitutional rules. As he wrote for the Court in 1981, "the very nature of the corporation" had been transformed—from a "special privilege" given at the state's discretion to "a right generally available to all on equal terms," a right that couldn't be denied on arbitrary or self-serving grounds.[204] And

---

[199] *Id.* at 314.

[200] *Id.* at 315.

[201] *Id.*

[202] *Id.* at 316.

[203] *Id.* at 317.

[204] W. & S. Life Ins. Co. v. State Bd. of Equalization, 451 U.S. 648, 659–60 (1981) (Brennan, J.). Prior courts had gone back and forth on whether the Equal Protection Clause guarantees equal treatment to out-of-state corporations. *Compare, e.g.*, Phila. Fire Ass'n v. New York, 119 U.S. 110, 116, 118–19 (1886) (viewing a foreign corporation's "existence" as "depend[ing] purely on the comity of [other] states," so that it might be a "person" but not a "person within its jurisdiction" in the language of the Clause), Pembina Consol. Silver Mining & Milling Co. v. Pennsylvania, 125 U.S. 181, 189 (1888) (holding as a matter of equal protection that a "State [was] not prohibited from discriminating in the privileges it may grant to foreign corporations as a condition of their doing business or hiring offices within its limits"), *and* Lincoln Nat'l Life

there's no doubt that a corporation today, as compared to one in the Founding era, might find massively greater economies of scale in acting across state lines. Letting states impose differential taxes or regulations on foreign corporations would let them eat up all this added value, while shifting the costs to customers or shareholders outside their borders.

But that very real concern might not be a good reason to read the Constitution differently. It might just be a good reason for Congress to intervene. As is typical in dormant commerce cases, everything depends on the baseline: Which state interests are "legitimate" depends on what we think the state has the right to do by default. If Pennsylvania wants to limit the types of corporations it recognizes, or if it prefers different sorts of corporate-governance or internal-affairs regulations than Virginia does—or if Pennsylvania just wants to use its own apparatus to enforce these rules, rather than relying on Virginia's courts and bureaucrats—then it might rationally ask Virginia corporations to form a local subsidiary, or even to incorporate in multiple states at once.[205] And if those corporations find such options too costly to pursue, but still find Pennsylvania corporate privileges too valuable to do without, then the Commonwealth might legitimately fund its public services partly by selling those valuable privileges to the highest bidder, or might legitimately make consent to jurisdiction part of its price.

The Court's modern doctrine on corporate powers arguably resulted from a "new property"-esque one-way ratchet: having begun handing out incorporations like candy, the states are now forbidden

---

Ins. Co. v. Read, 325 US 673, 677 (1945) (discussing "the long-established rule that a State may discriminate against foreign corporations"), *with* S. Ry. Co. v. Greene, 216 U.S. 400, 418 (1910) (treating a "more onerous" state tax on licensed foreign corporations as "a denial of the equal protection of the laws"), Hanover Fire Ins. Co. v. Harding, 272 U.S. 494, 514 (1926) (expanding this rule to corporations renewing their licenses and demanding "equal application of the laws of the State to foreign and domestic corporations properly engaged in business"), *and* Wheeling Steel Corp. v. Glander, 337 U.S. 562, 572 (1949) (forbidding different tax treatment for an out-of-state corporation "solely because of the different residence of the owner"). The Court concluded in *Western & Southern* that any difference in treatment must "bear[] a rational relation to a legitimate state purpose," 451 U.S. at 668, but later cases have emphasized that "[o]nly a rational basis" is required. G.D. Searle & Co. v. Cohn, 455 U.S. 404, 408–09 n.6 (1982) (allowing different statutes of limitations under the Equal Protection Clause); *cf.* Bendix Autolite Corp. v. Midwesco Enters., 486 U.S. 888, 889 (1988) (forbidding different statutes of limitations, but this time under a dormant-commerce theory).

[205] *See, e.g.*, R.R. Co. v. Harris, 79 U.S. (12 Wall.) 65, 82 (1871) ("We see no reason why several States cannot, by competent legislation, unite in creating the same corporation or in combining several pre-existing corporations into a single one.").

to stop.[206] But at the risk of repetition, *the Constitution has no corporate law*. It takes no view on any of this: states can create corporations, or limited liability companies, or limited partnerships, or yet more exotic entities, or no artificial entities at all; they can treat incorporation as a special grant, or as a general entitlement, or as anything they like in between.[207] "The Fourteenth Amendment does not enact the Delaware General Corporation Law," and neither does the Commerce Clause.[208]

The modern doctrine also arguably resulted from a series of doctrinal errors. Key rules of law, in Justice Alito's words, were "exiled from the provisions in which they may have originally been intended to reside," finding "refuge" in due process or an "appropriate home" in dormant commerce.[209] These included not only the general-law rules governing personal jurisdiction,[210] but also those governing corporate recognition[211] and especially the privileges of citizens.[212] None of these fields was wholly settled in the Constitution's text, but none was left wholly in doubt either: Each was to be governed by rules of law that the Constitution enforced without supplying.[213] In some ways,

---

[206] *Cf.* Charles Reich, *The New Property*, 73 YALE L.J. 733, 785 (1964) ("Eventually those forms of largess which are closely linked to status must be deemed to be held as of right. . . . The presumption should be that the professional man will keep his license, and the welfare recipient his pension. These interests should be 'vested.'").

[207] *See* Buccola, *supra* note 71, at 610 ("The states never lost their plenary authority, whether through constitutional change or federal statute; they simply ceased to exercise it.").

[208] *See* Sachs, *supra* note 18. Note that in some areas of law, such as the First Amendment, doctrines of "underbreadth" may indeed lock in government benefits that have been withdrawn for a prohibited end. *Cf.* R.A.V. v. City of St. Paul, 505 U.S. 377, 402 (White, J., concurring in the judgment) (introducing but criticizing the term). Just as a city may forbid obscenity generally but may not single out obscenity critical of the Mayor, *see id.* at 384 (op. of the Court), so a state might restrict corporate privileges generally but perhaps not single out privileges used to praise or criticize a political candidate. *See* Citizens United v. FEC, 558 U.S. 310 (2010) (concerning a corporate-produced film that "would be understood by most viewers as an extended criticism of Senator Clinton's character and her fitness for the office of the Presidency"). *Compare* Buccola, *supra* note 71, at 600 ("[A]lthough the First Amendment protects speech the corporation is empowered to make, it has nothing to say about speech that is *ultra vires*."), *with Citizens United*, 558 U.S. at 386 (Scalia, J., concurring) ("To be sure, in 1791 (as now) corporations could pursue only the objectives set forth in their charters; but the dissent provides no evidence that their speech in the pursuit of those objectives could be censored.").

[209] Mallory v. Norfolk S. Ry. Co., 600 U.S. 122, 155 (2023) (Alito, J., concurring in part and concurring in the judgment); *id.* at 150.

[210] *See supra* notes 28, 89–94 and accompanying text.

[211] *See supra* notes 71–81 and accompanying text.

[212] *See supra* notes 84–88 and accompanying text.

[213] *Cf.* Sachs, Pennoyer *Was Right*, *supra* note 28, at 1260–69 (describing this technique); Baude, Campbell & Sachs, *supra* note 28 (manuscript at 6) (same).

the long history of corporate recognition under the dormant commerce doctrine may be a history of efforts to smuggle into Article I the privileges reserved for citizens under Article IV.[214]

Or perhaps the modern doctrine has simply been bewitched by metaphor—seeing the foreign corporation as an existing *thing* in another state, which can't be treated differently "solely because of [its] different residence,"[215] just as Article IV citizens can't be treated differently because of their different residence. Yet this metaphor isn't the only one available. At the Founding, the foreign corporation was seen as a collection of particular individuals given particular privileges by a particular sovereign, whose sovereign powers ran out at the state line. We might not have to use that metaphor; for our own purposes, we can design corporate law however we wish. But it's hard to argue that the textual Commerce Clause mandates a different metaphor instead, or that it gives corporations the power to act in other states without consenting to their jurisdiction. Until Congress gives such a right, or until it mandates mutual recognition of corporate privileges, these powers are still "reserved to the States respectively"[216]—right where the Constitution left them.

---

[214] *Cf.* Julian N. Eule, *Laying the Dormant Commerce Clause to Rest*, 91 YALE L.J. 425, 446–54 (1982) (arguing explicitly for overturning *Paul* and extending Article IV privileges to corporations); Stewart Jay, *The Curious Exclusion of Corporations from the Privileges and Immunities Clause of Article IV*, 44 HOFSTRA L. REV. 79 (2015) (same).

[215] Wheeling Steel Corp. v. Glander, 337 U.S. 562, 572 (1949).

[216] U.S. CONST. amend. X.

ROBERT POST

PUBLIC ACCOMMODATIONS AND THE FIRST AMENDMENT: 303 CREATIVE AND "PURE SPEECH"

The Roberts Court has repeatedly aspired to compress the complex universe of First Amendment jurisprudence into a few comprehensive rules. The ambition is impossible because, as the wise Michel de Montaigne once counseled us, "We are men, and we have relations with one another only by speech."[1] To lay down simple rules for all speech is to lay down simple rules for all human relationships. Society is far too various to fit in such a narrow, procrustean bed.[2]

On the last day of the 2022 Term, the Roberts Court yielded once again to the temptation to address difficult First Amendment problems with simple rules. In *303 Creative LLC v. Elenis*,[3] the Court confronted

---

Robert Post is the Sterling Professor of Law at Yale Law School.

AUTHOR'S NOTE: I am grateful for the advice and counsel of Ian Ayres, Jack Balkin, Vince Blasi, Guido Calabresi, Sherif Girgis, Linda Greenhouse, David Hasen, Doug NeJaime, Catherine O'Regan, Elizabeth Sepper, Amanda Shanor, Reva Siegel, Brian Soucek, Geoffrey Stone, and James Weinstein. I am also indebted to Nada Al-Jassar, Jared Hirschfield, Pablo Moraga, Federico Roitman, Victoria Suarez-Palomo, and Rachel Vogel for their superb research assistance.

[1] Michel de Montaigne, *On Liars*, *in* ESSAYS 31 (J.M. Cohen, trans., 1958).

[2] The Roberts Court's tendency toward impossible abstraction is exemplified by *Reed v. Town of Gilbert*, 576 U.S. 155 (2015), which created such terrible confusion in the lower courts that seven years later it had to be revised by the Roberts Court itself in *City of Austin v. Reagan National Advertising of Austin, LLC*, 596 U.S. 61 (2022).

[3] 600 U.S. 570 (2023).

the challenging problem of reconciling First Amendment speech rights with laws that forbid discrimination in public accommodations. The case involved a graphic designer named Lorie Smith who wanted to create wedding websites, but who had faith-based objections to serving clients involved in same-sex weddings. She feared that her reservations would violate the Colorado Anti-Discrimination Act ("CADA"),[4] which prohibits public accommodations—businesses "engaged in any sales to the public" or "offering services . . . to the public"[5]—from discriminating on the basis of "sexual orientation."[6]

Sixty years ago, Title II of the Civil Rights Act of 1964[7] extended to the entire nation a public accommodations statute forbidding discrimination on the basis of race. Title II was prompted by incidents like the 1960 Greensboro sit-in, when four Black students sought service at an all-white lunch counter. "'We don't serve Negroes here,' a waitress behind the counter said."[8] Although southern segregation involved *acts* of discrimination, it was nevertheless an institution thoroughly imbricated with *speech*. For decades it has been clear that commercial speech in the service of illegal acts is not protected by the First Amendment.[9]

This history did not inhibit Smith from invoking the First Amendment to enjoin CADA's application to her proposed websites. The Supreme Court granted her petition for certiorari to answer the question: "Whether applying a public-accommodation law to compel an artist to speak or stay silent violates the Free Speech Clause of the First Amendment."[10] Justice Gorsuch authored an opinion for six Justices, holding that Smith's First Amendment rights of free speech would be violated were Colorado to insist that she comply with CADA's requirements.

Over the past forty years, the Court has decided several cases seeking to reconcile First Amendment rights of free speech with

---

[4] COLO. REV. STAT. § 24-34-601 (2023).

[5] *Id.* § 601(1).

[6] *Id.* § 601(2)(a).

[7] Pub. L. No. 88-352, 78 Stat. 241 (1964) (codified as amended at 42 U.S.C. § 2000).

[8] Sam Roberts & Joe Bubar, *Sitting Down to Take a Stand*, UPFRONT (Jan. 6, 2020), https://upfront.scholastic.com/issues/2019-20/010620/sitting-down-to-take-a-stand.html?language=english#1210L.

[9] Cent. Hudson Gas & Elec. Corp. v. Pub. Serv. Comm'n, 447 U.S. 557, 563–64 (1980); Pittsburgh Press Co. v. Pittsburgh Comm'n on Hum. Rels., 413 U.S. 376, 385–88, 390–91 (1973).

[10] 303 Creative LLC v. Elenis, 142 S. Ct. 1106 (2022).

public accommodations laws prohibiting discrimination.[11] These decisions have been uniformly cautious. The Court has sought to negotiate a respectful path between the two fundamental values of nondiscrimination and freedom of speech. Its decisions have been restrained, careful, and narrow.

Not so *303 Creative*. In elegant, condescending prose, Gorsuch announced that the case was without "complication"[12] because it involved "pure speech."[13] The Court needn't engage in strict scrutiny, or balancing, or any attempt to reconcile the fundamental values in play. Government, proclaimed Gorsuch, is categorically forbidden to "force an individual to 'utter what is not in [her] mind' about a question of political and religious significance."[14] In dissent, Justice Sotomayor, speaking for Justices Kagan and Jackson, characterized the controversy as involving a statute that "targets conduct, not speech, ... and the *act* of discrimination has never constituted protected expression under the First Amendment."[15] In unusually strong language, she condemned the Court's opinion as "[p]rofoundly wrong."[16]

Gorsuch professed himself bewildered, as if the Court and the dissent were not "looking at the same case."[17] But instead of taking that ominous disjunction as a counsel of caution, Gorsuch displayed no second thoughts, cavalierly dismissing the dissent's concerns as "[p]ure fiction."[18] He produced an opinion turning on the wobbly, innovative abstraction of "pure speech." The reasoning of the opinion is so obscure that it effectively gives lower courts a free hand to use First Amendment doctrine to mutilate antidiscrimination laws of all kinds.

It is important, therefore, carefully to parse what *303 Creative* does and does not hold and to consider how it may be integrated into a coherent First Amendment jurisprudence. The corrosive uncertainty

---

[11] *See, e.g.,* Roberts v. U.S. Jaycees, 468 U.S. 609 (1984); Bd. of Dirs. of Rotary Int'l v. Rotary Club of Duarte, 481 U.S. 537 (1987); N.Y. State Club Ass'n, Inc. v. City of New York, 487 U.S. 1 (1988); Hurley v. Irish-Am. Gay, Lesbian and Bisexual Grp. of Boston, 515 U.S. 557 (1995); Boy Scouts of Am. v. Dale, 530 U.S. 640 (2000); Masterpiece Cakeshop, Ltd. v. Colo. C.R. Comm'n, 138 S. Ct. 1719 (2018).

[12] 303 Creative LLC v. Elenis, 600 U.S. 570, 599 (2023).

[13] *Id.*

[14] *Id.* at 602.

[15] *Id.* at 604 (Sotomayor, J., dissenting).

[16] *Id.*

[17] *Id.* at 597.

[18] *Id.* at 598.

of the opinion does honor neither to this nation's commitment to equality nor to a principled explication of the First Amendment. Justice Sotomayor's dissent is eloquent in its evocation of the former. In this brief essay, I shall attempt to explicate the latter.

I.

CADA contains two provisions pertinent to Lorie Smith. The first is the "Accommodation Clause," which states:

> It is a discriminatory practice and unlawful for a person, directly or indirectly, to refuse, withhold from, or deny to an individual or a group, because of disability, race, creed, color, sex, sexual orientation, gender identity, gender expression, marital status, national origin, or ancestry, the full and equal enjoyment of the goods, services, facilities, privileges, advantages, or accommodations of a place of public accommodation.[19]

As is the case with many other public accommodations laws,[20] the Accommodation Clause in CADA basically provides that if a commercial entity holds itself out to the public, it cannot withhold the "full and equal enjoyment" of its goods and services to customers based upon status categories that in the past have been used to justify systematic exclusion from the commercial marketplace.

The second provision in CADA pertinent to Smith is the Communication Clause, which states:

> It is a discriminatory practice and unlawful for a person ... directly or indirectly, to publish, circulate, issue, display, post, or mail any written, electronic, or printed communication, notice, or advertisement that indicates that the full and equal enjoyment of the goods, services, facilities, privileges, advantages, or accommodations of a place of public accommodation will be refused, withheld from, or denied an individual or that an individual's patronage or presence at a place of public accommodation is unwelcome, objectionable, unacceptable, or undesirable because of disability, race, creed, color, sex, sexual orientation, gender identity, gender expression, marital status, national origin, or ancestry.[21]

When Lorie Smith contemplated going into the business of designing websites for weddings, she intended to offer her for-profit services to the general public. She was willing to work with all persons,

---

[19] COLO. REV. STAT. § 24-34-601(2)(a) (2023).

[20] A survey of public accommodations laws may be found in Elizabeth Sepper, *The Role of Religion in State Public Accommodations Laws*, 60 ST. LOUIS L.J. 631 (2016).

[21] COLO. REV. STAT. § 24-34-601(2)(a) (2023).

regardless of their race, religion, gender, or sexual orientation. But she was also certain that as a Christian whose beliefs were central to her identity, she could not violate her religious commitments by creating websites promoting any conception of marriage other than that of marriage between a man and a woman. To make her stance explicit, she prepared an unambiguous statement that she intended to publish on her website.[22]

Most persons in Smith's position would seek a ruling that their proposed business model was not forbidden by CADA. Smith could have argued, for example, that her business was not a public accommodation because it was explicitly selective and so did not offer "services ... to the public."[23] Or she might have argued that CADA did

---

[22] Smith alleged that she had prepared this statement to be published on her website:

> I love weddings.
> Each wedding is a story in itself, the story of a couple and their special love for each other.
> I have the privilege of telling the story of your love and commitment by designing a stunning website that promotes your special day and communicates a unique story about your wedding—from the tale of the engagement, to the excitement of the wedding day, to the beautiful life you are building together.
> I firmly believe that God is calling me to this work. Why? I am personally convicted that He wants me—during these uncertain times for those who believe in biblical marriage—to shine His light and not stay silent. He is calling me to stand up for my faith, to explain His true story about marriage, and to use the talents and business He gave me to publicly proclaim and celebrate His design for marriage as a life-long union between one man and one woman.
> These same religious convictions that motivate me also prevent me from creating websites promoting and celebrating ideas or messages that violate my beliefs. So I will not be able to create websites for same-sex marriages or any other marriage that is not between one man and one woman. Doing that would compromise my Christian witness and tell a story about marriage that contradicts God's true story of marriage—the very story He is calling me to promote.

Order Granting in Part and Denying in Part Motion to Dismiss and Denying Motion for Preliminary Injunction and Motion for Summary Judgment, *in* Petition for Writ of Certiorari, *303 Creative LLC*, 600 U.S. 570 (No. 21-476), at 159a–160a (hereinafter, "District Court Order").

[23] COLO. REV. STAT. § 24-34-601(1) (2023). *See* Downtown Soup Kitchen v. Anchorage, 576 F. Supp. 3d 636 (D. Alaska 2021) (holding that a religious organization providing services to homeless persons was not a public accommodation because of its selectivity). On selectivity as a criterion for the determination of whether a service is a public accommodation, see, *e.g.*, Sepper, *supra* note 20, at 650 (listing "selectivity" alongside "profit status," "commercial nature," "exclusivity," and "intimacy of an entity" as factors included in the "multi-factor analysis" employed to "police" the "public-private divide"); Vejo v. Portland Pub. Schs., 204 F. Supp. 3d 1149, 1168 (D. Or. 2016), *rev'd on other grounds*, 737 F. App'x 309 (9th Cir. 2018) (holding that a private university was not a public accommodation under Oregon's antidiscrimination statute because it maintained a selective admissions process); Barnett v. E:Space Labs LLC, 2018 WL 3364660 (D. Or. July 10, 2018); and Emilee Carpenter, LLC

not apply to virtual, online services.[24] But Smith was no ordinary plaintiff. Conceding at the outset that her proposed website and statement

---

v. James, 575 F. Supp. 3d 353, 378 n.13 (W.D.N.Y. 2021). In *Fulton v. City of Philadelphia*, 141 S. Ct. 1868, 1880 (2021), the Court itself held that Catholic Social Services was not a public accommodation, in part because the provision of foster care "involves a customized and selective assessment."

In *303 Creative*, the parties stipulated that Smith intended her business to be highly selective. Her "Contract for Services" included the provision: "Consultant has determined that the artwork, graphics, and textual content Client has requested Consultant to produce either express messages that promote aspects of the Consultant's religious beliefs, or at least are not inconsistent with those beliefs. Consultant reserves the right to terminate this Agreement if Consultant subsequently determines, in her sole discretion, that Client desires Consultant to create artwork, graphics, or textual content that communicates ideas or messages, or promotes events, services, products, or organizations, that are inconsistent with Consultant's religious beliefs." Joint Statement of Stipulated Facts, *in* Petition for Writ of Certiorari, *303 Creative LLC*, 600 U.S. 570 (No. 21-476), at 184a (hereinafter, "Joint Statement of Stipulated Facts"). In dissent, Sotomayor wrote that "Even if Smith believes God is calling her to do so through her for-profit company, the company need not hold out its goods or services to the public at large. Many filmmakers, visual artists, and writers never do. . . . That is why the law does not require Steven Spielberg or Banksy to make films or art for anyone who asks." *303 Creative LLC*, 600 U.S. at 629 (Sotomayor, J., dissenting).

It is not clear how a for-profit company can fail to hold itself out to the public *except* by being highly selective. Yet of course the whole purpose of a public accommodations statute would be undermined if entities could exempt themselves from its coverage by "selectively" refusing to deal with the very categories of persons that the statute is designed to protect.

Underlying Gorsuch's opinion is a vague sense that public accommodations statutes have in recent years overreached. Gorsuch notes that whereas such statutes once applied to only "common carriers and places of traditional public accommodation, like hotels and restaurants," they have now "expanded . . . to cover virtually every place of business engaged in any sales to the public." *Id.* at 591. Whereas public accommodations laws used to forbid discrimination on the basis of core categories like race or sex, Gorsuch notes that "Importantly, States have also expanded their laws to prohibit more forms of discrimination. Today, for example, approximately half the States have laws like Colorado's that expressly prohibit discrimination on the basis of sexual orientation." *Id.* In an odd usage, Gorsuch characterizes this expansion as "entirely 'unexceptional.'" *Id.*

[24] CADA refers to a "place" of accommodation, and it is highly contested whether online websites are "places" within the meaning of public accommodations statutes. *See* David Brody & Sean Bickford, *Discriminatory Denial of Service: Applying State Public Accommodations Laws to Online Commerce*, Laws.' Comm. for C.R. Under L. (Jan. 2020), https://lawyerscommittee.org/wp-content/uploads/2019/12/Online-Public-Accommodations-Report.pdf. The district court opinion in *303 Creative* was apparently the first reported judicial decision to apply CADA to an online service. *Id.* at 11–12. The circuits are presently divided on the question of whether online services are "place[s] of public accommodation" for purposes of Title III of the Americans with Disability Act ("ADA"), 42 U.S.C. § 12182(a). *Compare* Carparts Distrib. Ctr., Inc. v. Auto. Wholesaler's Ass'n of New England, Inc., 37 F.3d 12, 19 (1st Cir. 1994) (holding that a website can constitute a place of public accommodation irrespective of its connection to a physical space), *and* Morgan v. Joint Admin. Bd., Ret. Plan of Pillsbury Co., 268 F.3d 456, 459 (7th Cir. 2001) (same), *with* Robles v. Domino's Pizza, LLC, 913 F.3d 898, 905 (9th Cir. 2019) (holding that a website can constitute a place of public accommodation only where there is "some connection between the good or service complained of and an actual physical space"), *and* Parker v. Metro. Life Ins. Co., 121 F.3d 1006, 1010–11 (6th Cir. 1997) (same), *and* Ford v. Schering-Plough Corp., 145 F.3d 601, 614 (3d Cir. 1998) (same). *See generally Title III of the Americans with Disabilities Act and Website Compliance*, Am. Bar Ass'n. (Feb. 22, 2022), https://www.americanbar.org/groups

violated CADA,[25] she was evidently more determined to provoke a broad constitutional ruling than she was to begin her wedding website business. CADA, Smith argued, violated her constitutional rights of freedom of speech and free exercise, inhibiting her ability to initiate an online business that would serve only opposite-sex marriages.

The district court held that Smith did not have standing to attack the Accommodation Clause. There was no evidence, the court said, "that anyone, much less a same-sex couple, will request Plaintiff's services.... Because the possibility of enforcement based on a refusal of services is attenuated and rests on the satisfaction of multiple conditions precedent, the Court finds that the likelihood of enforcement is not credible."[26] The court ruled that Smith did have

/gpsolo/publications/gpsolo_ereport/2022/february-2022/title-iii-americans-disabilities-act-website-compliance (surveying precedents on Title III's applicability to websites).

[25] In her complaint Smith states: "Colorado law ... provides that if Lorie and 303 Creative design, create, and publish wedding websites celebrating and promoting marriages between one man and one woman, they must also willingly design, create, and publish wedding websites celebrating and promoting same-sex marriages." Complaint ¶ 10, 303 Creative LLC v. Elenis, 405 F. Supp. 3d 907 (D. Colo. 2019) (No. 16-cv-02372).

[26] District Court Order, *supra* note 22, at 166a-67a. *See* Updegrove v. Herring, 2021 WL 1206805 (E.D. Va. 2021). An extremely strange event happened during the course of litigation over standing. After Smith filed her complaint, but before the district court ruled on standing, Smith represented to the court that she had received an email. "Ostensibly in response to a prompt from 303's website asking 'If your inquiry relates to a specific event, please describe the nature of the event and its purpose', the email states: 'My wedding. My name is Stewart and my fiancée is Mike. We are getting married early next year and would love some design work done for our invites (sic.), place-names (sic.), etc. We might also stretch to a website.'" District Court Order, *supra* note 22, at 166a; Affidavit of Lorie Smith in Support of Plaintiffs' Motion for Summary Judgment, in Joint Appendix, 2022 WL 3215065, at *16. Almost seven years later, after the Supreme Court had decided the case, it was discovered by an enterprising journalist that this email was fraudulent because "Stewart," in whose name the email had purportedly been sent, was in fact a straight, married web designer. He had never sent the email. Victoria Bisset & Jaclyn Peiser, *Man Cited in Supreme Court LGBTQ Rights Case Says He Was Never Involved*, WASH. POST (July 1, 2023), https://www.washingtonpost.com/politics/2023/07/01/supreme-court-colorado-website. The Alliance Defending Freedom ("ADF"), the "conservative legal organization" which represented Smith in the litigation, immediately issued a carefully phrased response: "Whether Lorie received a legitimate request or whether someone lied to her is irrelevant. No one should have to wait to be punished by the government to challenge an unjust law." *Id. See also* Alanna Durkin Richer & Colleen Slevin, *Legitimacy of "Customer" in Supreme Court Gay Rights Case Raises Ethical and Legal Flags*, AP NEWS (July 3, 2023), https://apnews.com/article/supreme-court-gay-rights-lgbtq-website-9c058addfdd581ce0ead81eb59660130; Kristen Waggoner & Erin Hawley, *The Smearing of Lorie Smith*, WALL ST. J. (July 11, 2023), https://www.wsj.com/articles/the-smearing-of-lorie-smith-new-republic-free-speech-fake-case-pre-enforcement-2b1f362c; Mark Joseph Stern, *The Supreme Court's Fake Praying Coach Case Just Got Faker*, SLATE (Sept. 7, 2023), https://slate.com/news-and-politics/2023/09/supreme-court-praying-coach-joe-kennedy-fake.html; Jon Swaine & Beth Reinhard, *Inside the Tactics That Won Christian Vendors the Right to Reject Gay Weddings*, WASH. POST (Sept. 28, 2023), https://www.washingtonpost.com/investigations/2023/09/24/alliance-defending-freedom-wedding-lawsuit. For a good

standing to contest the Communication Clause, for the Clause deterred her from including a planned statement on her proposed website.[27] But because Smith's statement merely proposed "to undertake an action that is made illegal by the Accommodation Clause,"[28] and because Smith lacked standing to attack the constitutionality of the Accommodation Clause,[29] the district court awarded summary judgment to Colorado.

Smith appealed, and the Tenth Circuit, "reviewing the issue de novo," found that Smith had "sufficiently demonstrated both an intent to provide graphic and web design services to the public in a manner that exposes them to CADA liability, and a credible threat that Colorado will prosecute them under that statute."[30] The court of appeals rejected Smith's claim of religious freedom because CADA was a rule of general applicability which, under the holding of *Employment Division, Department of Human Resources of Oregon v. Smith*,[31] did not violate the Free Exercise Clause. Although the court acknowledged that CADA regulated "pure speech,"[32] it nevertheless rejected Smith's free speech claim because CADA survived strict scrutiny.[33]

---

discussion of ADF, see David D. Kirkpatrick, *The Group That Overturned* Roe, NEW YORKER, Oct. 9, 2023, at 28.

The district court itself presciently discounted the Stewart email: "This evidence is too imprecise.... Assuming that it indicates a market for Plaintiffs' services, it is not clear that Stewart and Mike are a same-sex couple (as such names can be used by members of both sexes) and it does not explicitly request website services, without which there can be no refusal by Plaintiffs." District Court Order, *supra* note 22, at 166a. Although ADF emphasized the importance of the Stewart email in its brief before the Tenth Circuit in favor of standing, the Tenth Circuit held in favor of standing without explicitly mentioning the email. 303 Creative LLC v. Elenis, 6 F.4th 1160, 1171–75 (10th Cir. 2021). Strong arguments have been made that the existence of the email affected the finding of standing in both the Tenth Circuit and the Supreme Court. *See* Adam Unikowsky, *Contrived Cases Make Bad Law*, ADAM'S LEGAL NEWSL. (July 6, 2023), https://adamunikowsky.substack.com/p/contrived-cases-make-bad-law. *But see* Richard Re, *Did Factual Revelations Undermine* 303 *Creative?*, VOLOKH CONSPIRACY (Sept. 7, 2023), https://reason.com/volokh/2023/09/07/from-prof-richard-re-did-factual-revelations-undermine-303-creative.

[27] District Court Order, *supra* note 22, at 165a. Smith's proposed statement may be found in *supra* note 22.

[28] 303 Creative LLC v. Elenis, 405 F. Supp. 3d 907, 910 (D. Colo. 2019).

[29] *Id.* at 911.

[30] *303 Creative LLC*, 6 F.4th at 1172.

[31] 494 U.S. 872, 878–82 (1990).

[32] "Appellants' creation of wedding websites is pure speech." *303 Creative LLC*, 6 F.4th at 1176.

[33] *Id.* at 1178–82. "[E]nforcing CADA as to Appellants' unique services is narrowly tailored to Colorado's interest in ensuring equal access to the commercial marketplace." *Id.* at 1182.

When the case arrived at the Supreme Court, there was no independent analysis of the question of standing. The Court was content to observe that "[b]efore us, no party challenges" Smith's standing.[34] This was odd, given that standing is an independent Article III precondition for jurisdiction that cannot be waived by the parties. But the Court was apparently determined to take the case, even in the absence of a well-developed record. If the function of standing doctrine is to assure "that concrete adverseness which sharpens the presentation of issues upon which the court so largely depends for illumination of difficult constitutional questions,"[35] that function was ill-served in this case.

It was, for example, entirely unclear how Colorado interpreted CADA's Communication Clause, which was of considerable importance to the question of whether Smith might actually have standing to challenge the Accommodation Clause. At oral argument, Colorado's Solicitor General, Eric R. Olson, affirmed that Smith could publish all of her proposed statement, except the explicit refusal to provide service to customers seeking support for same sex weddings:[36]

> JUSTICE ALITO: Let me see if I understand your argument. I understand you to be arguing that a website designer can put anything it wants on a standardized website, even if that includes a denunciation of same-sex marriage. Is that correct?
> MR. OLSON: Yes.
> JUSTICE ALITO: So,... if the standard announcement is ... that a valid marriage is a union between one man and one woman, that's okay?
> MR. OLSON: If that's on every website, yes....
> JUSTICE ALITO: [T]hat website designer is not going to be serving a same-sex couple if the website designer puts that on the website. They're turning away same-sex couples by doing that, are they not?
> MR. OLSON: No, ... they're not turning away same-sex couples. They are defining their—they are able to choose what services they offer, and that is the service they are choosing to offer. The state does not regulate that at all.[37]

---

[34] 303 Creative LLC v. Elenis, 600 U.S. 570, 583 (2023).

[35] Baker v. Carr, 369 U.S. 186, 204 (1962).

[36] For Smith's statement, see *supra* note 22. In its brief to the Court, Colorado explicitly stated: "What a business chooses to sell remains entirely up to the business. The Company can define its service however it wants—including offering only websites that include biblical quotes describing marriage as the union of one man and one woman." Brief for Respondents, *303 Creative LLC*, 600 U.S. 570 (No. 21-476), 2022 WL 3597176, at *9.

[37] Transcript of Oral Argument, *303 Creative LLC*, 600 U.S. 570 (No. 21-476), 2022 WL 17980103, at *67–*68.

If CADA's Communication Clause were in fact as lenient as represented by Olson, the likelihood that Smith would ever have to refuse to provide services to a same-sex wedding is vanishingly small. In such circumstances, as Alito appears to concede in the oral argument, her standing to bring a lawsuit to attack the Accommodation Clause should have been very doubtful indeed.

Of particular importance to the Court's ultimate holding in the case is the extremely limited record with regard to the precise kind of speech that CADA would allegedly compel Smith to make. Because this issue was not actually litigated, the "facts" of the case come entirely from stipulations to which the parties agreed.[38] These stipulations are highly unusual. They contain formulations that are extremely tendentious and favorable to Smith. With regard to the question of Smith's websites, the relevant stipulations include:

46. All of Plaintiffs' graphic designs are expressive in nature, as they contain images, words, symbols, and other modes of expression that Plaintiffs use to communicate a particular message....

50. Each website 303 Creative designs and creates is an original, customized creation for each client....

57. When designing and creating graphics or websites, Ms. Smith is typically in close contact with her clients as they each share their ideas and collaborate to develop graphics or websites that express a message in a way that is pleasing to both Ms. Smith and her clients.

58. Ms. Smith ultimately has final say over what she does and does not create and over what designs she does and does not use for each website....

60. For each website 303 Creative makes, Ms. Smith typically creates and designs original text and graphics for that website and then combines that original artwork with text and graphics that Ms. Smith receives from the client or from other sources. Ms. Smith then combines the original text and graphics she created with the already existing text and graphics to create an original website that is unique for each client....

68. When considering a potential project, Ms. Smith will view the prospective client's website (if applicable) and ask questions of the prospective client to assist in the vetting process of determining whether the requested project conflicts with Plaintiffs' religious beliefs and whether it is a good fit given Plaintiffs' skills, schedule, preferences, and workload....

79. By creating wedding websites, Ms. Smith and 303 Creative will collaborate with prospective brides and grooms in order to use their unique stories as source material to express Ms. Smith's and 303 Creative's message celebrating

---

[38] Joint Statement of Stipulated Facts, *supra* note 23, at 173a–93a.

and promoting God's design for marriage as the lifelong union of one man and one woman....
81. Plaintiffs' custom wedding websites will be expressive in nature, using text, graphics, and in some cases videos to celebrate and promote the couple's wedding and unique love story.
82. All of these expressive elements will be customized and tailored to the individual couple and their unique love story.
83. Viewers of the wedding websites will know that the websites are Plaintiffs' original artwork because all of the wedding websites will say "Designed by 303Creative.com."[39]

Each of these stipulated "facts" is lifted virtually verbatim from Smith's complaint, which is long and argumentative.[40] It is fair to say that Gorsuch's entire theory of the case rests on the conclusory character of these stipulations.

Gorsuch reads the parties' stipulations as conceding that Smith's proposed websites would constitute "pure speech," which he claims is precisely the kind of communication that the First Amendment prohibits the state from compelling. Gorsuch writes:

> The Tenth Circuit held that the wedding websites Ms. Smith seeks to create qualify as "pure speech" under this Court's precedents. We agree. It is a conclusion that flows directly from the parties' stipulations. They have stipulated that Ms. Smith's websites promise to contain "images, words, symbols, and other modes of expression." They have stipulated that every website will be her "original, customized" creation. And they have stipulated that Ms. Smith will create these websites to communicate ideas—namely, to "celebrate and promote the couple's wedding and unique love story" and to "celebrat[e] and promot[e]" what Ms. Smith understands to be a true marriage....
>
> We further agree with the Tenth Circuit that the wedding websites Ms. Smith seeks to create involve *her* speech. Again, the parties' stipulations

---

[39] *Id.* at 181a–83a, 187a. It is noteworthy, however, that the stipulations do *not* include allegations in the Complaint like "Each website Plaintiffs create is their own speech." Complaint ¶ 212, 303 Creative LLC v. Elenis, 405 F. Supp. 3d 907 (D. Colo. 2019) (No. 16-cv-02372).

[40] *Compare* Complaint ¶¶ 124, 132, 129, 130, 131, 116, 147, 140, 149, 150, and 152, *303 Creative LLC*, 405 F. Supp. 3d 907 (D. Colo. 2019) (No. 16-cv-02372). After the Court's decision in *303 Creative*, Phil Weiser, Colorado's Attorney General, "sought to distance himself from his office's early strategy in defending CADA. 'This case has spanned multiple administrations,' he said, alluding to his predecessor, Attorney General Cynthia Coffman," who was a Republican. Michael Karlik, *Colorado Leaders Cautious About Altering Anti-Discrimination Law Following SCOTUS Decision*, Colo. Pol. (Aug. 4, 2023), https://www.coloradopolitics.com/courts/colorado-leaders-cautious-about-altering-anti-discrimination-law-following-scotus-decision/article_01104cf4-1788-11ee-b860-27536ba79787.html.

lead the way to that conclusion. As the parties have described it, Ms. Smith intends to "ve[t]" each prospective project to determine whether it is one she is willing to endorse. She will consult with clients to discuss "their unique stories as source material." And she will produce a final story for each couple using her own words and her own "original artwork." Of course, Ms. Smith's speech may combine with the couple's in the final product. But for purposes of the First Amendment that changes nothing. An individual "does not forfeit constitutional protection simply by combining multifarious voices" in a single communication.

As surely as Ms. Smith seeks to engage in protected First Amendment speech, Colorado seeks to compel speech Ms. Smith does not wish to provide. As the Tenth Circuit observed, if Ms. Smith offers wedding websites celebrating marriages she endorses, the State intends to "forc[e her] to create custom websites" celebrating other marriages she does not.[41]

Gorsuch explicitly rejects Colorado's theory that "this case involves only the sale of an ordinary commercial product and any burden on Ms. Smith's speech is purely 'incidental'" on the ground that it is "difficult to square with the parties' stipulations."[42]

> As we have seen, the State has stipulated that Ms. Smith does *not* seek to sell an ordinary commercial good but intends to create "customized and tailored" speech for each couple. The State has stipulated that "[e]ach website 303 Creative designs and creates is an original, customized creation for each client." The State has stipulated, too, that Ms. Smith's wedding websites "will be expressive in nature, using text, graphics, and in some cases videos to celebrate and promote the couple's wedding and unique love story." As the case comes to us, then, Colorado seeks to compel just the sort of speech that it tacitly concedes lies beyond the reach of its powers.[43]

Gorsuch concedes that at times complicated questions may arise about whether commercial vendors "provide expressive services covered by the First Amendment," but he insists that "those cases are not *this* case. Doubtless, determining what qualifies as expressive activity protected by the First Amendment can sometimes raise difficult questions. But this case presents no complication of that kind. The parties have *stipulated* that Ms. Smith seeks to engage in expressive activity."[44]

---

[41] *303 Creative LLC*, 600 U.S. at 587–88 (internal citations omitted).
[42] *Id.* at 593.
[43] *Id* at 593–94.
[44] *Id.* at 599.

Gorsuch implicitly distinguishes paradigmatic cases of public accommodations law, like the Greensboro sit-in, by drawing a distinction between prohibiting speech that facilitates an illegal act (like discrimination) and mandating pure speech to comply with the requirements of a public accommodations law, which is what he believes CADA would demand of Smith.

With respect to the latter, the logic of *303 Creative* follows the form of a simple syllogism. The major premise is that the First Amendment categorically precludes the state from compelling persons to engage in pure speech. No statute can "be 'applied to expressive activity' to compel speech."[45] A court need not balance or engage in strict scrutiny or assess the strength of a compelling state interest. The government simply cannot mandate pure speech. The minor premise is that, as established by the parties' stipulations, Smith's proposed websites would constitute "pure speech" or—what apparently is to Gorsuch the same thing—"expressive activity."[46] It follows from these two premises that CADA is unconstitutional as applied to Smith.[47]

II.

To evaluate the holding of *303 Creative*, it is necessary to begin by carefully parsing the minor premise of the syllogism that structures Gorsuch's opinion. We need to know the nature of the "pure speech" that CADA cannot compel. "Pure speech" is not a technical or

---

[45] 600 U.S. at 592 (internal citations omitted).

[46] This phrase is particularly infelicitous. It virtually invites misappropriation in ways that would vastly and improperly expand the scope of First Amendment coverage. The phrase will almost certainly cause mischief in the lower courts.

[47] At one point Gorsuch, parroting Smith's brief, Brief for Petitioners, *303 Creative LLC*, 600 U.S. 570 (No. 21-476), 2022 WL 1786990, at *13, *30, implies that the application of CADA to Smith is unconstitutional because "Colorado seeks to compel speech *in order* to 'excis[e] certain ideas or viewpoints from the public dialogue.' Indeed, the Tenth Circuit recognized that the coercive '[e]liminati[on]' of dissenting 'ideas' about marriage constitutes Colorado's 'very purpose' in seeking to apply its law to Ms. Smith." *Id.* at 588 (emphasis added). It is indeed true that statutes enacted for improper purposes are more or less automatically unconstitutional under the First Amendment. *See* Robert Post, *Recuperating First Amendment Doctrine*, 47 STAN. L. REV. 1249, 1255–60 (1995). But Gorsuch flatly mischaracterizes both the purpose of CADA and the holding of the Tenth Circuit. The Tenth Circuit was explicit that "Colorado has a compelling interest in protecting both the dignitary interests of members of marginalized groups and their material interests in accessing the commercial marketplace.... Nor do we construe Appellants' arguments as challenging Colorado's interest in combating discrimination generally.... Appellants' argument more appropriately address whether CADA is narrowly tailored—not whether CADA furthers a compelling interest." 303 Creative LLC v. Elenis, 6 F.4th 1160, 1178–79 (10th Cir. 2021).

well-defined term of First Amendment jurisprudence. Gorsuch apparently means by it roughly "speech" in the ordinary sense of the word. He believes that the parties' stipulations demonstrate that Smith's websites consist of this kind of "pure speech."

Gorsuch extracts four distinct propositions from the parties' stipulations that he regards as defining the essence of "pure speech":

1. Smith's websites will contain "images, words, symbols, and other modes of expression."[48]
2. Smith's websites will be "original, customized' creation[s]."[49]
3. Smith's websites will be created "to communicate ideas."[50]
4. Smith's websites will "involve *her* speech."[51]

Gorsuch is clear that "there are no doubt innumerable goods and services that no one could argue implicate the First Amendment."[52] The four criteria of "pure speech" that Gorsuch extracts from the parties' stipulations are meant in part to ensure that the holding of *303 Creative* will not uncontrollably expand to include all such goods and services.

The first criterion identified by Gorsuch is that pure speech must consist of "images, words, symbols" (or other modes of expression). This criterion immediately rules out the Greensboro waitress since serving food does not consist of images, words, or symbols. CADA can thus compel waitresses to serve food to Black customers without infringing on the First Amendment rights of waitresses or restaurants. This first criterion is so powerful that it might be thought that it should by itself be sufficient to trigger First Amendment protections against compelled speech. But Gorsuch is correct to reject this possibility.

Consider, for example, the owner of a bookstore who in violation of a public accommodations law refuses to sell books to customers who are Black. Although the owner distributes goods consisting of words and symbols, the communication at issue is not the owner's own expression. The owner is not himself "speaking" but is instead

---

[48] *303 Creative LLC*, 600 U.S. at 587.

[49] *Id.*

[50] *Id.*

[51] *Id.* at 588.

[52] *Id.* at 591 (quoting Masterpiece Cakeshop, Ltd. v. Colo. C.R. Comm'n, 138 S. Ct. 1719, 1728 (2018)).

transmitting the thoughts and messages of others. So far as the owner is concerned, he is selling objects that happen to consist of words and symbols. The First Amendment would thus not prohibit CADA from compelling the owner to sell books to customers who are Black in the same way that he sells books to other customers.[53]

For this reason, *303 Creative* adds three further conditions that must be met before a communication can count as the kind of pure speech that is immune from the compulsions of a public accommodations law. The second condition is that a communication must be "original" and "customized." A vendor who sells prepackaged forms of communication, like a bookstore owner, will not be immunized by the First Amendment from CADA. First Amendment immunity will not be triggered unless the government compels a vendor to communicate in a way that expresses her own unique labor or personality.[54] The mandated communication must be bespoke; it cannot be off-the-shelf and fungible.[55]

The third criterion articulated by Gorsuch is that a vendor's product must be designed "to communicate ideas." This condition might seem to articulate an elementary point, but when taken in conjunction with the preceding two criteria, it actually adds a subtle and important qualification to the definition of pure speech. Virtually every human action can communicate an idea. I effectively communicate an idea when I throw a rock through my neighbor's window because I do not want his kind in my neighborhood. But *303 Creative* holds that this kind of communication will not trigger the protection of the First

---

[53] It is important to be clear that *303 Creative* defines "pure speech" for the purpose of analyzing the constitutionality of government compulsions of speech. It does not follow from the analysis in text that a bookstore owner could not invoke the First Amendment to resist different forms of government regulation, as for example a statute prohibiting the sale of indecent books. The same qualification must be made for each of the conditions adduced by Gorsuch.

[54] Smith's attorney essentially conceded this point in oral argument. She stated: "[I]f it's a plug-and-play website ... then you don't have compelled speech because you don't have a speech creator." Transcript of Oral Argument, *303 Creative LLC*, 600 U.S. 570 (No. 21-476), 2022 WL 17980103, at *15.

[55] "Think of a store that sells paintings or sheet music or books. Lots of protected expression goes into these products, but they're not created according to the demands or preferences of the particular customer. Since the artist or composer or writer has already created the product, *the state* has not compelled their creation. Refusing to sell these expressive products to protected classes of customers amounts to illegal status- or identity-based discrimination, which is not protected by the First Amendment." Dale Carpenter, *How to Read* 303 Creative v. Elenis, VOLOKH CONSPIRACY (July 3, 2023), https://reason.com/volokh/2023/07/03/how-to-read-303-creative-v-elenis.

Amendment in the context of public accommodations laws. The First Amendment will only kick in when a vendor's product is *designed* to communicate through "images, words, or symbols."

It is for this reason that Smith's attorney, Kristen Waggoner, President and General Counsel of Alliance Defending Freedom ("ADF"), conceded in oral argument that she would not make a First Amendment free speech claim on behalf of a caterer.[56] Although caterers may through their cuisine communicate messages of care and appreciation, compelling a caterer to serve food that she would not otherwise serve does not count as compelling her to use pure speech to communicate.

It is easy to become confused about this point. Caterers can and have claimed that the very act of serving a same-sex marriage communicates a message—namely, their support for marriages that are not heterosexual.[57] But this kind of communication fails the third condition of *303 Creative*. Preparing food is not a practice designed to communicate ideas.[58] If it were accepted that the relevant communication of messages can occur through simple practices like cooking food, curating flowers,

---

[56] Transcript of Oral Argument, *303 Creative LLC*, 600 U.S. 570 (No. 21-476), 2022 WL 17980103, at *43–*46. *See id.* at *53–*54 ("[T]he caterer is not engaging in speech.... That would simply be service."); *id.* at *40 ("The person providing the chairs isn't providing speech."). In ADF's reply brief, Waggoner states: "Generally speaking, bartenders, hairstylists, landscapers, plumbers, caterers, tailors, jewelers, and restaurants do not create speech.... The question is whether a work is intended to communicate a message and is reasonably understood to do so." Reply Brief for Petitioners, *303 Creative LLC*, 600 U.S. 570 (No. 21-476), 2022 WL 4279671, at *15. *See In re* Gifford v. McCarthy, 137 A.D.3d 30, 42 (N.Y. Sup. Ct. 2016) (declining to accept a caterer's First Amendment defense against the application of New York's public accommodations law in the context of a same-sex wedding, on the ground that "the conduct allegedly compelled is not sufficiently expressive as to trigger First Amendment protections"). In oral argument, however, Waggoner did maintain that calligraphers created speech. Transcript of Oral Argument, *supra*, at *153.

Three years before the oral argument in *303 Creative*, ADF had argued that a florist could claim First Amendment immunity from the application of Washington's public accommodations statute in the context of a same-sex wedding. Washington v. Arlene's Flowers, Inc., 193 Wash. 2d 469 (2019). The Washington Supreme Court rejected the argument on the very ground properly conceded by ADF in *303 Creative*: "[T]he regulated activity at issue in this case—Stutzman's sale of wedding floral arrangements—is not 'speech' in a literal sense and is thus properly classified as conduct." *Id.* at 512. The plaintiff in the case had in effect argued that her floral arrangements met the second condition articulated by Gorsuch in *303 Creative*—that each arrangement "encompasses her 'unique expression,' crafter in 'petal, leaf, and loam.'" *Id.* at 512. But flower arrangements plainly fail the first condition articulated in *303 Creative*. Flowers are neither words nor images. If it is argued that they are "symbols," then the appellation can apply to almost anything, including the food that an "artistic" caterer might lovingly and beautifully prepare. *See infra* note 170.

[57] *In re Gifford*, 137 A.D.3d at 41–42.

[58] "[T]he fact that a nonsymbolic act is the product of deeply held personal belief—even if the actor would like it to *convey* his deeply held personal belief—does not transform action into First Amendment speech." Nev. Comm'n on Ethics v. Carrigan, 564 U.S. 117, 127 (2011).

or serving food at a lunch counter, all antidiscrimination laws would instantly be eclipsed by the First Amendment.

303 Creative explicitly repudiates this possibility because it would reach too broadly. Gorsuch states, as we have noted, that "there are no doubt innumerable goods and services that no one could argue implicate the First Amendment."[59] That is why *303 Creative* focuses instead on whether a state may "force someone *who provides her own expressive services* to abandon her conscience and speak *its* preferred message instead."[60] In this focus, *303 Creative* builds on the precedent of *Hurley v. Irish-American Gay, Lesbian and Bisexual Group*,[61] which holds that First Amendment immunity against compelled speech is applicable only when a public accommodations law effectively declares an actor's "speech itself to be the public accommodation."[62]

The first three criteria articulated by Gorsuch are by themselves insufficient to establish that a vendor's products are "pure speech." It is not enough that a vendor sell products that consist of bespoke words or symbols or images, even if those products are designed to communicate ideas. Gorsuch is explicit that a fourth condition must be added: the vendor's products must also express the vendor's own speech.

Consider the case of a commercial sign painter. The painter composes signs that consist of "images, words, symbols" and that are produced in an original and customized way for each customer. The signs are designed to communicate specific ideas. For the church, the painter produces a unique sign that reads, "Sunday brunch served after

---

[59] 600 U.S. at 591 (quoting Masterpiece Cakeshop, Ltd. v. Colo. C.R. Comm'n, 138 S. Ct. 1719, 1728 (2018)).

[60] *Id.* at 597 (emphasis added).

[61] 515 U.S. 557 (1995).

[62] *Id.* at 573. To hold otherwise would be to embrace Robert Bork's early objection to the 1964 Civil Rights Act, which was that antidiscrimination law "means a loss in a vital area of personal liberty"—that is, a loss in the right to freedom of association. Robert Bork, *Civil Rights—A Challenge*, NEW REPUBLIC, Aug. 31, 1963, at 22. If the very act of selling goods or services to a particular person communicates a message that cannot be compelled, the objection is to antidiscrimination laws *per se*, which is essentially to claim a right of association. *See, e.g.*, Richard A. Epstein, *Public Accommodations Under the Civil Rights Act of 1964: Why Freedom of Association Counts as a Human Right*, 66 STAN. L. REV. 1241 (2014). On the right of association in commercial contexts, see *infra* text at notes 123–126. The Court has explicitly repudiated the claim that a right of association should trump the application of an antidiscrimination law in the context of a commercial relationships. *See* Hishon v. King & Spaulding, 467 U.S. 69, 78 (1984); Masterpiece Cakeshop, Ltd. v. Colo. C.R. Comm'n, 138 S. Ct. 1719, 1728 (2018).

the Service." For the homeowner, the painter produces a bespoke sign that reads, "578 Main Street." Each sign is different; each reflects the painter's labor; each uses words and symbols; and each is meant successfully to communicate an idea. The painter's signs satisfy the first three criteria of *303 Creative*.

Would *303 Creative* prevent a public accommodations law from requiring that the sign painter serve Black customers in the same way that he serves other customers? Gorsuch's fourth condition indicates that it would not. This is because the words and images produced by the painter do not express the painter's *own* messages. They merely transmit the messages of his customers. The painter can no more claim immunity from public accommodations laws than can a telegraph operator who transcribes and transmits the unique message of each customer. The fourth condition laid down by *303 Creative* is thus that vendors can be compelled to comply with a public accommodations law unless the law would require them to use bespoke words and images to express *their own* messages. That is why Gorsuch emphasizes in his fourth criterion that Smith's websites "involve *her* speech."[63]

It is worth noting that the Court is not clear about why Smith's websites involve *her* speech. It might be because, unlike the sign painter, Smith will in part control the content and substance of the words she sets down.[64] Or it might be because Smith herself subjectively regards the websites as expressing her own views. Or it might be because, unlike a sign painter, a reasonable observer would understand Smith's websites to be communicating ideas that Smith herself wishes to share, as distinct from the ideas that only her clients desire to communicate.[65]

Of these three alternatives, only the last corresponds to the usual criterion of compelled speech in First Amendment jurisprudence.[66] If I pay a telegraph operator to summarize and condense my message so that it can be effectively transmitted over the wires, the resulting

---

[63] *303 Creative LLC*, 600 U.S. at 588.

[64] *See* Stipulation 58, *supra* note 39 and accompanying text.

[65] On the ambiguities of what it might mean to interpret the actions of a commercial service provider like Smith as expressing personal views, see Elizabeth Sepper, *Free Speech and the "Unique Evils" of Public Accommodations Discrimination*, 2020 U. CHI. LEGAL F. 273, 286–93.

[66] *See, e.g.*, Cressman v. Thompson, 798 F.3d 938, 954 (10th Cir. 2015); Christopher S. Yoo, *The First Amendment, Common Carriers, and Public Accommodations: Net Neutrality, Digital Platforms, and Privacy*, 1 J. FREE SPEECH L. 463, 495 (2021).

telegram does not become the operator's own speech simply because the operator will partly control the words being disseminated. There would be no First Amendment problem applying CADA to the operator. This would be true even if the operator subjectively regards himself as an artist of condensation who takes pride in translating ordinary English into telegraphic abbreviations.

ADF argued to the Court that the ambiguity of the fourth criterion is resolved by the stipulation of the parties. The parties agreed that "[v]iewers of the wedding websites will know that the websites are Plaintiffs' original artwork because all of the wedding websites will say 'Designed by 303Creative.com.'"[67] On close examination, however, this stipulation establishes only that a reasonable third party would know that the websites were *made* by Smith, not that the words on the website express Smith's own ideas. If a commercial sign painter or a telegraph operator were to sign his work product, it would not follow that reasonable observers would understand them to express the sign painter's or the telegraph operator's own views. The First Amendment would not immunize the sign painter or the telegraph operator from the application of CADA simply because they sign their work. They can be required to serve Black clients in the same way as they serve other clients.

It is not clear, then, why Gorsuch believes that the parties' stipulations establish that Smith's websites would reflect *her* speech.[68] As a matter of general social practice, wedding websites are typically understood to express the views of the marrying couple, not those of the website designer. My strong intuition is that if the record were to have been more fully developed, it would have established that the vast majority of those encountering Smith's websites would interpret them as expressing the views of Smith's clients, rather than those of Smith herself. If this were true, the minor premise of *303 Creative*—that Smith's websites constituted "pure speech"—would fail.

If one had to speculate why the Court was so receptive to the implausible claim that CADA compelled Smith's own speech, it is probably because Smith pressed urgent claims of conscience. According to her

---

[67] *See* Stipulation 83, *supra* note 39. In its brief to the Court, ADF argued that this stipulation established that "observers" would know "that Smith is speaking" and "endorsing the messages in her websites." Brief for Petitioners, *303 Creative LLC*, 600 U.S. 570 (No. 21-476), 2022 WL 1786990, at *29.

[68] *See, e.g., supra* note 39.

complaint, she regarded involvement in same-sex weddings as a profound violation of her religious convictions. Yet this claim, however true it may be, is relevant only to potential violations of Smith's Free Exercise rights, not to potential violations of her free speech rights.

Highly sympathetic to Smith's claims of conscientious objection, and apparently unwilling to overrule the holding of *Employment Division, Department of Human Resources of Oregon v. Smith*[69] that Free Exercise rights cannot be violated by laws of general application like CADA, the Court may well have unconsciously transposed the authenticity of Smith's Free Exercise claim into the jurisprudence of freedom of speech.[70] Gorsuch in fact frames the case as Colorado forcing Smith "to abandon her conscience and speak its preferred message instead."[71]

Because Smith's conscience was at stake, the Court may have recklessly leapt to the conclusion that her speech was also at stake. But, as we shall see, confusing free speech and Free Exercise doctrine in this way makes hash of basic First Amendment principles. Within the logic of a Free Exercise right, claims of conscience can be lodged against any compelled action. Claims of free speech, by contrast, can be asserted only against mandated speech, as speech is defined by relevant First Amendment doctrine.

III.

303 Creative is written in the form of a syllogism. The minor premise of the opinion is that the parties' stipulations establish that

---

[69] 494 U.S. 872, 878–82 (1990). *See supra* note 31 and accompanying text.

[70] It is surely noteworthy that the Court deliberately rewrote the question presented for decision in Smith's petition for certiorari. Smith had originally formulated the question as "[w]hether applying a public-accommodation law to compel an artist to speak or stay silent, contrary to the artist's sincerely held religious beliefs, violates the Free Speech or Free Exercise Clauses of the First Amendment." Petition for Writ of Certiorari at i, *303 Creative LLC*, 600 U.S. 570 (No. 21-476). *Compare supra* note 10 and accompanying text. The Court also refused to grant *certiorari* to decide the second question presented in Smith's certiorari petition: "Whether a public-accommodation law that authorizes secular but not religious exemptions is generally applicable under *Smith*, and if so, whether this Court should overrule *Smith*." *Id.* Although the Court sought formally to exclude Free Exercise issues from its disposition of the case, its handling of free speech questions seems very much under their influence.

[71] *303 Creative LLC*, 600 U.S. at 597. Gorsuch also writes: "In this case, Colorado seeks to force an individual to speak in ways that align with its views but defy her conscience about a matter of major significance." *Id.* at 602.

Smith's proposed websites would be "pure speech," as defined by the four conditions articulated in the opinion. Gorsuch writes as if the parties agree that Smith's proposed websites would use bespoke words and images to communicate her own messages. The major premise of *303 Creative* is that the First Amendment categorically prohibits government from compelling persons to engage in pure speech. Taken together, the major and minor premises of *303 Creative* require the conclusion that CADA cannot compel Smith to make websites that she would rather not design.

303 Creative confidently asserts that its major premise is a fundamental principle of First Amendment free speech jurisprudence. But this is flatly false. Although the categorical quality of the major premise may express protections Gorsuch believes are due conscientious objectors under the Free Exercise Clause,[72] they are descriptively and normatively indefensible in the context of free speech doctrine. Government routinely requires persons to engage in pure speech in ways that the First Amendment has never been thought to prohibit. Every year virtually every adult American is required by law to file a tax return, which is a bespoke document containing a person's own speech in words and numbers. There are countless analogous contexts in which most would agree that government *ought* to be able to compel pure speech.

The descriptive point can be illustrated by a straightforward example. Imagine that you go to your lawyer to seek her advice. She provides you with an opinion letter, upon which you rely. The opinion letter passes each of the four criteria set forth in *303 Creative*. It uses words to convey the lawyer's own bespoke ideas. The letter is an example of the lawyer's pure speech. Yet the letter turns out to be professionally incompetent because it fails to consider relevant legal standards or to disclose relevant facts.[73] Can your attorney be sued for malpractice for this failure, or does your attorney have a First Amendment defense? Can your attorney successfully argue that the First Amendment prevents the state from sanctioning her for failing to include pure speech that would change the messages conveyed by her letter?

---

[72] For Gorsuch's tendency to blend Free Exercise and free speech analysis, see Kennedy v. Bremerton Sch. Dist., 142 S. Ct. 2407 (2022).

[73] *See, e.g.*, Est. of Spencer v. Gavin, 947 A.2d 1051 (N.J. Super. Ct. App. Div. 2008).

As a matter of plain descriptive fact, government routinely imposes affirmative duties to publish pure speech on attorneys,[74] doctors,[75] and accountants.[76] These duties can even include the obligation to speak about matters of significant public controversy in ways that a professional might find wrong or offensive.[77] Consider, for example, the case of Stella Immanuel, who is a licensed physician in Texas and who passionately believes that hydroxychloroquine cures COVID-19.[78] Although the effectiveness of hydroxychloroquine is a matter of intense public controversy, if a patient with COVID-19 were to come to Immanuel's office, and if Immanuel were to recommend treatment with hydroxychloroquine, or if she were to fail to correct a patient who

---

[74] Shapero v. Ky. Bar Ass'n, 486 U.S. 466, 478–79 (1988); United States v. Greebel, 782 F. App'x. 72 (2d Cir. 2019); SEC v. Hui Feng, 935 F.3d 721 (9th Cir. 2019); Dixon Ticonderoga Co. v. Est. of O'Connor, 248 F.3d 151, 173 (3d Cir. 2001); First Nat'l Bank of LaGrange v. Lowrey, 375 Ill. App. 3d 181 (App. Ct. 2007).

[75] *See, e.g.,* EMW Women's Surgical Ctr., P.S.C v. Beshear, 920 F.3d 421 (6th Cir. 2019); Carter v. Inslee, No. C16-0809, 2016 U.S. Dist. LEXIS 187207 (W.D. Wash. Aug. 25, 2016); Guinn v. N.Y. Methodist Hospital, 183 N.Y.S.3d 431 (App. Div. 2023); Volk v. DeMeerleer, 187 Wash. 2d 241 (2016); Reisner v. Regents of Univ. of Cal., 31 Cal. App. 4th 1195 (Ct. App. 1995); Malone v. La. Dep't of Health & Hum. Res., 569 So.2d 1098 (La. Ct. App. 1990). On compelled speech of pharmacists, see Beeman v. Anthem Prescription Mgmt., LLC, 165 Cal. Rptr. 3d 800 (2013).

[76] *See, e.g.,* Rudolph v. Arthur Andersen & Co., 800 F.2d 1040 (11th Cir. 1986); Robert Wooler Co. v. Fidelity Bank, 479 A.2d 1027 (Pa. Super. Ct. 1984); 1136 Tenants' Corp. v. Max Rothenberg & Co., 36 A.D.2d 804 (N.Y. App. Div. 1971), *aff'd*, 30 N.Y.2d 585 (1972). For analogous requirements imposed on architects, see Gruppo v. London, 25 A.D.3d 486 (N.Y. App. Div. 2006). For engineers, see Alfred Conhagen, Inc. v. Ruhrpumpen, Inc., 338 So.3d 55 (La. Ct. App. 2022).

[77] It might perhaps be objected that the speech of professionals like doctors, lawyers, or accountants is unique because they must be licensed by the government. But this objection merely defers the question of why government can constitutionally impose a license as a precondition for professional speech. We are beginning to see arguments that such licensing is unconstitutional under the First Amendment. *See, e.g.,* Edwards v. District of Columbia, 755 F.3d 996 (D.C. Cir. 2014); Paul Sherman, *Occupational Speech and the First Amendment*, 128 Harv. L. Rev. F. 183 (2015); Robert Post & Amanda Shanor, *Adam Smith's First Amendment*, 128 Harv. L. Rev. F. 165 (2015). A sharp focus on speech abstracted from its social context can easily produce this result, as for example when the Third Circuit said, in the context of regulations applicable to the professional speech of physicians, "Simply put, speech is speech, and it must be analyzed as such for the purposes of the First Amendment." King v. Governor of N.J., 767 F.3d 216, 228–29 (3d Cir. 2014). This is basically the same position that Thomas intimated for the Court in *National Institute of Family and Life Advocates v. Becerra*, 138 S. Ct. 2361, 2371 (2018), when he questioned whether there was any "separate category of speech" that corresponds to "professional speech." The basic point is that whatever constitutional interest justifies professional licensing must also justify compelling the "pure speech" of professionals. The question to be explored is the nature of this justification.

[78] Dickens Olewe, *Stella Immanuel—The Doctor Behind Unproven Coronavirus Cure Claim*, BBC News (July 29, 2020), https://www.bbc.com/news/world-africa-53579773. Dr. Immanuel also believes that certain medical conditions are caused by "witches and demons." *Id.*

was self-medicating with hydroxychloroquine, Immanuel would be liable in malpractice. The First Amendment would not immunize her from the requirement that she use pure speech to offer her patients relevant competent medical advice.

Most would agree that malpractice actions *should* function in this way. If government could not compel professionals to speak in ways that ensured the provision of competent service, clients and patients would suffer. So far from being normatively questionable whether the state can compel pure speech on matters of political significance like COVID-19, most would regard it as a necessary and good thing, so long as the content of the compelled speech is strictly determined by the criterion of competent professional service.[79] Most would regard it as normatively desirable to construct law so that clients and patients can rely on the competent provision of legal and medical advice, even in areas that are beset by public controversy.

Although Gorsuch seems to imagine that the major premise of *303 Creative* is an unassailable and universally applicable truth, the example of professional speech illustrates that it is not. If we just open our eyes, we can see that American society is full of examples of compelled pure speech, ranging from required product disclosures,[80] to disclosures in real estate transactions,[81] to the required testimony of witnesses in a trial, to a raft of statutory obligations to report various events and circumstances,[82] to the myriad miscellaneous disclosure requirements imposed on commercial transactions.[83] *303 Creative*

---

[79] For a discussion, see generally ROBERT POST, DEMOCRACY, EXPERTISE, ACADEMIC FREEDOM: A FIRST AMENDMENT JURISPRUDENCE FOR THE MODERN STATE (2012).

[80] *See, e.g.*, Reyes v. Wyeth Lab'ys, 498 F.2d 1264 (5th Cir. 1974); Davis v. Wyeth Lab'ys, Inc., 399 F.2d 121 (9th Cir. 1968); Simpson v. Gen. Dynamics Ordnance and Tactical Sys.–Simunition Operations, Inc., 429 F. Supp. 3d 566 (N.D. Ind. 2019); Stephens v. G.D. Searle & Co., 602 F. Supp. 379 (E.D. Mich. 1985); Liriano v Hobart Corp., 700 N.E.2d 303 (N.Y. 1998).

[81] *See, e.g.*, 15 U.S.C. § 1667a; Ernestine v. Baker, 515 So.2d 826 (La. Ct. App. 1987).

[82] *See, e.g.*, Hiibel v. Sixth Judicial Dist. Ct., 542 U.S. 177 (2004); SEC v. AT&T, Inc., 626 F. Supp. 3d 703 (S.D.N.Y. 2022); Roe v. Hesperia Unified Sch. Dist., 85 Cal. App. 5th 13, 31–32 (2022) (mandating reporting of child abuse or neglect); N.Y. PUB. HEALTH LAW §§ 2130–2133 (mandating reporting of diagnoses of HIV or AIDS); 29 C.F.R. § 1904.2(a) (2000) (mandating reporting of workplace injuries and illnesses); N.Y. VEH. & TRAF. Law § 601 (mandating reporting of certain traffic-related incidents); 20 U.S.C.A. § 1092(f) (mandating reporting of campus crimes); CAL. HEALTH & SAFETY CODE § 25249.6 (requiring disclosure of toxic or carcinogenic chemicals).

[83] *See, e.g.*, Spirit Airlines, Inc. v. U.S. Dep't of Transp., 687 F.3d 403 (D.C. Cir. 2012); United States v. Wenger, 427 F.3d 840 (10th Cir. 2005); Nat'l Elec. Mfrs. Ass'n v. Sorrell, 272 F.3d 104 (2d Cir. 2001); Mass. Ass'n of Priv. Career Sch. v. Healey, 159 F. Supp. 3d 173

ignores all this because it is enthralled by the abstraction of an untouchable "pure speech."

This abstraction distorts Gorsuch's vision. *303 Creative* asserts, for example, that CADA puts Smith to the same unconstitutional choice as that imposed upon school children in the canonical case of *West Virginia Board of Education v. Barnette*.[84] The Jehovah's Witnesses in *Barnette* were compelled to pledge allegiance to the flag. They were required "to communicate by word and sign" an "affirmation of a belief."[85] This is far different than being required simply to speak. Every day throughout the country students are required simply to speak. They are compelled to recite multiplication tables or the Gettysburg Address; they are required to explain their opinions about controversial matters in mandatory examinations. If *Barnette* stood for the proposition that Gorsuch purports to extract from it, that persons cannot compelled to "speak as the State demands or face sanctions,"[86] education in the United States would grind to a halt.

In contrast to the students in *Barnette*, Smith was never required to sign a pledge or affirm a belief. She was merely required to publish a website. But for Gorsuch that is enough. "The United States is a rich and complex place," Gorsuch tells us, "where all persons are free to ... speak as they wish, not as the government demands."[87] The United States is a place where the state can never "force an individual to 'utter what is not in [her] mind' about a question of political and religious significance."[88] This is "because the freedom to ... speak is among our inalienable human rights."[89]

Gorsuch's rhetoric is undoubtedly true with regard to some forms of speech. But there are plainly circumstances in which it has no application at all. It turns out that communication is as various as the social landscape is complex. That is why the syllogism advanced by *303 Creative* is fatally flawed. It does not follow from the fact that communication is "pure speech" that it cannot be compelled. Some

---

(D. Mass. 2016); Boone Cnty. Cmty. Credit Union v. Masel, 665 N.W.2d 440 (Iowa Ct. App. 2003). For a general discussion, see Robert Post, NIFLA *and the Construction of Compelled Speech Doctrine*, 97 IND. L. J. 1071 (2022).

[84] 319 U.S. 624 (1943).

[85] *Id.* at 633.

[86] 303 Creative LLC v. Elenis, 600 U.S. 570, 589 (2023).

[87] *Id.* at 603.

[88] *Id.* at 596 (internal citations omitted).

[89] *Id.* at 584.

pure speech may be routinely and constitutionally compelled, and some may not. The real question is how we can tell the difference.

IV.

We can begin to construct an answer to this question by taking seriously the First Amendment value that *303 Creative* seeks to defend. The Court tells us that "the State [can] not use its public accommodations statute to deny speakers the right 'to choose the content of [their] own message[s].'"[90] The Court seeks to uphold, in other words, the value of *autonomy*—the right of persons to speak as they choose to speak. Since virtually all human relationships are constituted by speech, the First Amendment doctrine propounded by the Court makes sense in settings where we wish to endow persons with the right to speak autonomously. But by the same token the doctrine makes little sense wherever the law privileges other values over the autonomy of speakers. No society could function were persons deemed constitutionally autonomous wherever and however they choose to open their mouths to engage in "pure speech."

It is for this reason that the doctrine of *303 Creative* is inapplicable to the malpractice law by which we govern professional speech. In such contexts, law privileges the provision of competent medical or legal services over the autonomy of doctors or lawyers. The doctrine of *303 Creative* is also not applicable to schools, where law privileges student education over any simple assertion of student autonomy. Education could not occur if the First Amendment were to confer blanket immunity on students from mandatory speech.[91]

At the outset of the twentieth century, in the era of *Lochner*,[92] American constitutional jurisprudence was very much under the sway of the "free labor" ideology that had dominated the Republican party since the days of the Civil War.[93] Freedom to participate autonomously

---

[90] *Id.* at 592.

[91] *See, e.g.*, Post, *supra* note 83, at 1086–88; Robert Post, *The Classic First Amendment Tradition Under Stress: Freedom of Speech and the University*, in THE FREE SPEECH CENTURY (Lee C. Bollinger & Geoffrey R. Stone eds., 2019).

[92] Lochner v. New York, 198 U.S. 45 (1905).

[93] ERIC FONER, FREE SOIL, FREE LABOR, FREE MEN: THE IDEOLOGY OF THE REPUBLICAN PARTY BEFORE THE CIVIL WAR (1995); William E. Forbath, *The Ambiguities of Free Labor: Labor and the Law in the Gilded Age*, 1985 WIS. L. REV. 767.

in the market was regarded as essential for the independence required of American citizens. As one prominent court put it:

> It should be remembered that of the three fundamental principles which underlie government, and for which government exists, the protection of life, liberty, and property, the chief of these is property[.] ... Take from the citizen the right to freely contract and sell his labor for the highest wage which his individual skill and efficiency will command, and the laborer would be reduced to an automaton—a mere creature of the state. It is paternalism in the highest degree, and the struggle of the centuries to establish the principle that the state exists for the citizen, and not the citizen for the state, would be lost.[94]

This conception of the relationship of the citizen to the state underlies what we now call the substantive due process of *Lochner*. The Court summarized the essence of that doctrine in the proposition that "Freedom of contract is ... the general rule and restraint the exception; and the exercise of legislative authority to abridge it can be justified only by the existence of exceptional circumstances."[95]

The paradigm of Lochnerian substantive due process was upended in the great constitutional transformation of the New Deal. By extending a strong "presumption of constitutionality"[96] to social and economic regulations, the Court signaled that it no longer believed that the Constitution should be interpreted to protect the autonomy of commercial actors.[97] The reasons for this altered view of property and contract are complex, but for our purposes it is enough to observe that the Court came to believe that it was necessary instead to protect the autonomy of persons who through speech participated in the "political processes" by which public opinion was formed.[98]

The New Deal transformation signified the Court's acceptance of Brandeis's view that the United States was, most fundamentally, a democracy in which the people should be able to engage in public discussion to decide what their government ought to do.[99] Brandeis's great

---

[94] Children's Hosp. v. Adkins, 284 F. 613, 617, 621–23 (D.C. Ct. App. 1922), *aff'd*, 261 U.S. 525 (1923).

[95] *Adkins*, 261 U.S. at 545–46.

[96] United States v. Carolene Prods. Co., 304 U.S. 144, 152 (1938).

[97] *See* ROBERT POST, 2 THE TAFT COURT: MAKING LAW FOR A DIVIDED NATION, 1921–1930, at 822–78 (2024).

[98] *Carolene Prods. Co.*, 304 U.S. at 152 n.4.

[99] On Brandeis's view, see ROBERT POST, 1 THE TAFT COURT: MAKING LAW FOR A DIVIDED NATION, 1921–1930, at 311–21 (2024).

contribution to American constitutional law was the thought that Americans were more dedicated to the political project of democracy than they were to the economic project of marketplace expansion, which had sustained the Court's previous commitment to the substantive due process of *Lochner*. Reflecting this priority, the Court in the 1930s withdrew the constitutional value of autonomy from commercial actors and attributed it instead to participants in public discussion. The former were explicitly understood as subject to the governance of the latter.

This arrangement corresponded to a fundamental insight of Alexander Meiklejohn, who famously wrote that in a democracy "the governors and the governed are not two distinct groups of persons. There is only one group — the self-governing people. Rulers and ruled are the same individuals. We, the People, are our own masters, our own subjects."[100] When participating in "the arena of public discussion,"[101] citizens are rulers charged with deciding what government ought to do. Participants in public dialogue are accordingly entitled to the autonomy that constitutes sovereignty. When participating in the market, by contrast, persons are the "ruled." Their autonomy is properly limited by laws implementing the will of a sovereign democratic people.

For decades the Court constructed its First Amendment doctrine according to this paradigm. It interpreted the Constitution to ensure that the United States was a nation in which "authority" was "controlled by public opinion, not public opinion by authority."[102] The Court explicitly held that First Amendment rights were necessary for "[t]he maintenance of the opportunity for free political discussion to the end that government may be responsive to the will of the people and that changes may be obtained by lawful means, an opportunity essential to the security of the Republic," which, the Court proclaimed, "is a fundamental principle of our constitutional system."[103] "The freedom of speech and of the press guaranteed by the Constitution," the Court said, "embraces at the least the liberty to discuss publicly and truthfully all matters of public concern without previous restraint or fear of subsequent punishment. . . . Freedom of discussion, if it would

---

[100] ALEXANDER MEIKLEJOHN, POLITICAL FREEDOM 12 (1960).
[101] Cohen v. California, 403 U.S. 15, 24 (1971).
[102] W. Va. State Bd. of Educ. v. Barnette, 319 U.S. 624, 641 (1943).
[103] Stromberg v. California, 283 U.S. 539, 369 (1931).

fulfill its historic function in this nation, must embrace all issues about which information is needed or appropriate to enable the members of society to cope with the exigencies of their period."[104]

The Court did not interpret the First Amendment to protect speech *per se*. It explicitly interpreted the First Amendment to protect participation in the formation of public opinion. The First Amendment protected communications vying "for acceptance in the market of public opinion."[105] Following the Court's usage, I shall use the term "public discourse" to refer to speech categorized as essential for participating in the formation of public opinion.[106] Because public opinion ultimately determines the agenda of government action, the category of public discourse is far broader than the narrowly "political" speech famously identified by Robert Bork.[107]

Public discourse encompasses all the various forms of participation necessary to produce "that public opinion which is the final source of government in a democratic state."[108] It includes the many media for communication of ideas, like newspapers, magazines, art, or movies, that create the "public sphere" within which public opinion emerges.[109] By contrast, the Court did not extend any constitutional protection at all to speech that it did not classify as public discourse. In 1942, for example, the Court flatly held that "the Constitution imposes no ... restraint on government" regulations of "purely commercial advertising."[110]

---

[104] Thornhill v. Alabama, 310 U.S. 88, 101–02 (1940).

[105] *Id.* at 105.

[106] Snyder v. Phelps, 562 U.S. 443, 460 (2011); *see* Citizens United v. FEC, 558 U.S. 310, 373 (2010) (Roberts, C.J., concurring); Metromedia, Inc. v. San Diego, 453 U.S. 490, 515 (1981).

[107] Bork argued that "the category of protected speech should consist of speech concerned with governmental behavior, policy or personnel, whether the governmental unit involved is executive, legislative, judicial or administrative. Explicitly political speech is speech about how we are governed...." Robert Bork, *Neutral Principles and Some First Amendment Problems*, 47 IND. L.J. 1, 27–28 (1971). Bork is mistaken because public discussion determines which issues shall become "political" in the narrow sense defined by Bork. Public discourse encompasses all the various forms of speech that we regard as essential for forming public opinion. The governmental decision-making processes described by Bork are meant to implement public opinion. If public discourse were narrowly defined as speech about discrete government action, the people would be prevented from setting the agenda for government decision-making.

[108] Masses Publ'g Co. v. Patten, 244 F. 535, 540 (S.D.N.Y.), *rev'd*, 246 F. 24 (2d Cir. 1917).

[109] Robert Post, *Data Privacy and Dignitary Privacy:* Google Spain, *The Right to be Forgotten, and the Construction of the Public Sphere*, 67 DUKE L.J. 981, 1002–46 (2018); Post, *supra* note 47, at 1275–77.

[110] Valentine v. Chrestensen, 316 U.S. 52, 54 (1942).

When in the 1970s the Court revisited the question of whether commercial advertising ought to be protected by the First Amendment, it was exceedingly careful to distinguish public discourse from commercial speech. The Court went out of its way to stress that commercial actors were not to be accorded the autonomy of participants in public discourse. Commercial actors were not rulers; they were instead the ruled. Hence, "[t]he First Amendment's concern for commercial speech is based on the informational function of advertising ... [T]here can be no constitutional objection to the suppression of commercial messages that do not accurately inform the public about lawful activity."[111]

Commercial speech was protected because it provided information to listeners, not because it expressed the autonomy of commercial actors.[112] Extending constitutional protections to the latter would diminish the authority of the very democratic government the First Amendment was designed to establish. The Court was not about to repeat the mistakes of the *Lochner* era by ascribing autonomy to commercial actors and thereby constitutionally elevating the requirements of the market over the political deliberations of democracy.

Although it has become commonplace to observe that the contemporary Court has blurred the distinction between public discourse and commercial speech,[113] it nevertheless remains true that there are fundamental constitutional differences between the two forms of speech. So, for example, commercial speech can be suppressed if it is merely misleading,[114] but public discourse cannot be regulated because it is merely misleading.[115] Our entire institutional apparatus of

---

[111] Cent. Hudson Gas & Elec. Corp. v. Pub. Serv. Comm'n, 447 U.S. 557, 563 (1980).

[112] Robert Post, *The Constitutional Status of Commercial Speech*, 48 UCLA L. Rev. 1 (2000).

[113] *See, e.g.*, Amanda Shanor, *The New* Lochner, 2016 Wis. L. Rev. 133. For a good example of the current Court's confusion on this question, see Sorrell v. IMS Health Inc., 564 U.S. 552 (2011).

[114] "The government may ban forms of communication more likely to deceive the public than to inform it, or commercial speech related to illegal activity. If the communication is neither misleading nor related to unlawful activity, the government's power is more circumscribed." *Cent. Hudson Gas*, 447 U.S. at 563–64.

[115] *See* United States v. Alvarez, 567 U.S. 709 (2012). As Rehnquist pointed out:

[I]n the world of political advocacy and *its* marketplace of ideas, there is no such thing as a "fraudulent" idea: there may be useless proposals, totally unworkable schemes, as well as very sound proposals that will receive the imprimatur of the "marketplace of ideas" through our majoritarian system of election and representative government. The free flow of information is important in this context not

consumer protection, which includes essential agencies like the Federal Trade Commission, depends upon this basic distinction.

Most pertinent for our consideration of *303 Creative*, mandated factual, non-controversial disclosures are commonplace within the realm of commercial speech,[116] but are strictly forbidden within public discourse.[117] Compelled speech is prohibited within public discourse because it would compromise the autonomy necessary for persons to exercise their role as democratic sovereigns.[118] But mandatory disclosures are allowed within the domain of commercial speech because the autonomy of commercial actors is not deemed inviolable.[119] It follows that insofar as commercial speech is included in the "pure speech" that *303 Creative* identifies in its minor premise, the major premise of the opinion fails.[120] The state can indeed, under specified circumstances, compel pure speech that happens to be commercial speech.

Underlying the simple syllogism of *303 Creative* thus lies a rather large question of constitutional policy. Should Smith's proposed websites be deemed public discourse, like the work of the movie directors or artists whom the opinion twice evokes,[121] or should those websites be classified as ordinary commercial communications? If the

---

because it will lead to the discovery of any objective "truth," but because it is essential to our system of self-government.

The notion that more speech is the remedy to expose falsehood and fallacies is wholly out of place in the commercial bazaar, where if applied logically the remedy of one who was defrauded would be merely a statement, available upon request, reciting the Latin maxim "*caveat emptor*." But since "fraudulent speech" in this area is to be remediable under *Virginia Pharmacy Board*, the remedy of one defrauded is a lawsuit or an agency proceeding based on common-law notions of fraud that are separated by a world of difference from the realm of politics and government. What time, legal decisions, and common sense have so widely severed, I declined to join in *Virginia Pharmacy Board*, and regret now to see the Court reaping the seeds that it there sowed. For in a democracy, the economic is subordinate to the political, a lesson that our ancestors learned long ago, and that our descendants will undoubtedly have to relearn many years hence.

Cent. Hudson Gas, 447 U.S. at 598–99 (Rehnquist, J., dissenting).

[116] *See generally* Zauderer v. Off. of Disciplinary Couns., 471 U.S. 626 (1985); Robert Post, *Compelled Commercial Speech*, 117 W. Va. L. Rev. 867 (2015).

[117] Riley v. Nat'l Fed'n of the Blind, 487 U.S. 781 (1988).

[118] Post, *supra* note 83, at 1088–89.

[119] For a discussion of the role of autonomy in commercial speech, see Post, *supra* note 116, at 876–79.

[120] *See supra* note 45 and accompanying text.

[121] 600 U.S. 570, 589, 601 (2023); *see also infra* note 160 and accompanying text.

former, received doctrine would flatly prohibit compelled speech. But if Smith's proposed websites should instead have been deemed commercial speech, the preemptory evocation of Smith's autonomy, exemplified by the major premise of *303 Creative*, is out of order.

Notice that this constitutional question cannot be resolved simply by ascertaining whether Smith's websites are pure speech. It follows that the stipulations, which Gorsuch imagines are so decisive, do not in fact determine the outcome of the case. The validity of the syllogism that drives *303 Creative* depends in part on the social role that we wish to attribute to website designers like Smith: Should we characterize them as akin to movie directors or instead to ordinary commercial actors?

In the past, the Court has negotiated the tension between public accommodations statutes and the First Amendment by making distinctions of this kind. The First Amendment right of freedom of association protects neither intimacy, which is addressed by the Due Process Clause,[122] nor the right to associate for purely commercial purposes.[123] Instead the First Amendment right of association attaches only to associations formed "for the purpose of engaging in protected speech."[124] The right can be asserted by an organization only if it is an "expressive association."[125] As Justice Scalia has written, "The robust First Amendment freedom to associate belongs only to groups 'engage[d] in "expressive association."' The Campbell Soup Company does not exist to promote a message, and 'there is only minimal constitutional protection of the freedom of *commercial* association.'"[126] Were it otherwise, every regulation of corporate governance would be subject to strict First Amendment review.

---

[122] Roberts v. U.S. Jaycees, 468 U.S. 609, 618–19 (1984).

[123] *Id.* at 620; *see id.* at 634 (O'Connor, J., concurring) ("[T]here is only minimal constitutional protection of the freedom of commercial association.... [T]he State is free to impose any rational regulation on the commercial transaction itself. The Constitution does not guarantee a right to choose employees, customers, suppliers, or those with whom one engages in simple commercial transactions, without any restraint from the State. A shopkeeper has no constitutional right to deal only with persons of one sex.").

[124] Bd. of Dirs. of Rotary Int'l v. Rotary Club of Duarte, 481 U.S. 537, 544 (1987). "[T]he Court has recognized a right to associate for the purpose of engaging in those activities protected by the First Amendment—speech, assembly, petition for the redress of grievances, and the exercise of religion. The Constitution guarantees freedom of association of this kind as an indispensable means of preserving other individual liberties." *Roberts*, 468 U.S. at 618.

[125] *Rotary Club*, 481 U.S. at 545.

[126] Wash. State Grange v. Wash. State Republican Party, 552 U.S. 442, 467 (2008) (Scalia, J., dissenting); *see* FCC v. Beaumont, 539 U.S. 146, 162 (2003).

To determine whether an organization might assert First Amendment immunity from the application of public accommodations laws, therefore, the Court has been forced to determine whether it is an organization "engage[d] in 'expressive association.'"[127] Groups formed for commercial purposes can be prohibited from discriminating, but groups formed to participate in the formation of public opinion cannot, at least to the extent that the application of public accommodations laws would alter the messages such groups wish to convey in public discourse.[128] The Court's precedents establish that the constitutional application of public accommodations laws does not turn on the fact of association, but instead on the *kind* of association at issue.[129]

This same distinction should be applied to the syllogism that structures the reasoning of *303 Creative*. The issue is not whether Smith would have engaged in "pure speech." The issue is instead the *kind* of speech Smith was proposing to fashion. Would that speech have been public discourse, or would it instead have been merely commercial speech?

V.

The single most important thing to notice about *303 Creative* is that it does not even ask this question. In the simple syllogism that drives Gorsuch's opinion, the fact that Smith's websites would be composed of pure speech is enough to invalidate the application of CADA. This is an extraordinarily crude and imprecise way to resolve the longstanding tension between First Amendment rights and public accommodations laws.

The values at stake in public accommodations laws are of fundamental importance in a democratic society. The Court has long recognized that "public accommodations laws 'plainly serv[e] compelling state interests of the highest order.'"[130] Such laws express the Nation's commitment "to eliminating discrimination and assuring

---

[127] Boy Scouts of Am. v. Dale, 530 U.S. 640, 648 (2000). *Compare Roberts*, 468 U.S. 609, *with Rotary Club*, 481 U.S. 537.

[128] *See* Dale Carpenter, *Expressive Association and Anti-Discrimination Law After* Dale: *A Tripartite Approach*, 85 MINN. L. REV. 1515 (2001).

[129] Ascertaining the kind of association at issue "requires a careful inquiry into the objective characteristics of the particular relationships at issue." *Rotary Club*, 481 U.S. at 547 n.6.

[130] *Id.* at 549.

its citizens equal access to publicly available goods and services."[131] Public accommodations laws developed to counter the systematic exclusion of groups, like Blacks and women, from ordinary business establishments.[132] They developed because virtually all States came to believe that every person should enjoy an equality of "civil rights"— the "rights exercised by economic man, such as the capacity to hold property and enter into contracts."[133]

These rights were guaranteed as against state violations by the Fourteenth Amendment, and they were guaranteed as against private violations by public accommodations laws. Public accommodations laws effectively mandate that commercial actors who hold themselves out to the public respect the equal civil rights of all members of the public. Vendors are forbidden from exercising the unfettered "autonomy" to exclude that Lochnerian substantive due process attributed to private property. It is for this reason that the Civil Rights Act of 1964 could compel Greensboro waitresses to serve Black customers, despite their deeply held ideological and religious objections.[134]

Although Gorsuch is aware of this history,[135] he insists that the essential values served by public accommodations laws must nevertheless

---

[131] *Roberts*, 468 U.S. at 624.

[132] The classic account is by Joseph William Singer, *No Right to Exclude: Public Accommodations and Private Property*, 90 Nw. U.L. Rev. 1283 (1996). Singer argues that many of the requirements of public accommodations laws were already contained within antebellum common law, which later evolved to validate Jim Crow exclusions in the years after the Civil War. Public accommodations laws became necessary to override these exclusions. Colorado was the first state to amend a public accommodations law to prohibit sex discrimination in 1969. See Elizabeth Sepper & Deborah Dinner, *Sex in Public*, 129 Yale L.J. 78, 104 (2019); *see also* 303 Creative LLC v. Elenis, 600 U.S. 570, 613–14 (2023) (Sotomayor, J., dissenting). Recent empirical research suggests that state antidiscrimination laws have proved effective means of opening public accommodations to previously marginalized minorities. *See* Lisa D. Cook et al., *The Evolution of Access to Public Accommodations in the United States*, 138 Q.J. Econ. 37, 56–59 (2023) (finding a positive correlation between cumulative number of state antidiscrimination laws and number of nondiscriminatory public-facing businesses).

[133] Reva Siegel, *Why Equal Protection No Longer Protects: The Evolving Forms of Status-Enforcing State Action*, 49 Stan. L. Rev. 1111, 1120 (1997). Consumer rights became especially important after World War II when the nation's investment in a Keynesian mass consumption economy led to the "integration of citizenship and consumership," which in turn sparked a redoubled effort to force "open the doors of public accommodations." Lizbeth Cohen, A Consumers' Republic: The Politics of Mass Consumption in Postwar America 9, 166 (2004). After World War II, America invested in "an elaborate, integrated ideal of economic abundance and democratic political freedom, both equitably distributed, that became almost a national civil religion." *Id.* at 127.

[134] *See* Newman v. Piggie Park Enters., 390 U.S. 400 (1968).

[135] *303 Creative LLC*, 600 U.S. at 590–91. Gorsuch writes "that public accommodations laws 'vindicate the deprivation of personal dignity that surely accompanies denials of equal

be subordinated to "the demands of the Constitution," meaning that public accommodations laws cannot "be 'applied to expressive activity' to compel speech."[136] And by "expressive activity" Gorsuch apparently means any communicative activity that meets the four conditions established by the parties' stipulations.

The difficulty with Gorsuch's simple syllogism is that almost every application of public accommodations laws will mandate pure speech. If I am a real estate broker who sells homes to white clients but not to Black clients, I have committed *acts* of discrimination. My discriminatory acts can be avoided, however, only if I show to Black clients the same homes in the same way as I show them to white clients. CADA, like many public accommodations laws, requires that I extend to protected classes of consumers the "full and equal enjoyment" of my services.[137] CADA therefore requires me to *speak* to Black clients in the same way as I speak to white clients. CADA requires brokers to engage in the kind of pure speech that inevitably accompanies selling real estate.

In authoring *303 Creative*, Gorsuch apparently imagined that he could preserve the application of public accommodations statutes to classic cases of discrimination, like those provoking the Greensboro sit-in, by distinguishing between prohibitions of speech and compulsions to speak. This distinction, however, is a mirage. Discrimination has both positive and negative dimensions, and they each transpire through the medium of speech. The waitress in Greensboro may be prevented from saying that she does not serve Black customers, but unless she can be compelled to speak to Black customers in the roughly same way that she speaks to white customers, discrimination will persist. Title II of the Civil Rights Act of 1964 therefore inevitably compels waitresses to express themselves in ways that will meet the criteria of the "pure speech" that Gorsuch in *303 Creative* is so concerned absolutely to protect.

---

access to public establishments.'" *Id.* at 590. *See* Hila Keren, *The Alarming Legal Strategy Behind a SCOTUS Case That Could Undo Decades of Civil Rights Protections*, SLATE (Mar. 9, 2022), https://slate.com/news-and-politics/2022/03/supreme-court-303-creative-coordinated-anti-lgbt-legal-strategy.html.

[136] *303 Creative LLC*, 600 U.S. at 592.

[137] *See supra* note 19 and accompanying text. *See, e.g.*, Elizabeth Sepper, *The Original Meaning of "Full and Equal Enjoyment" of Public Accommodations*, 11 CALIF. L. REV. ONLINE 572 (2021).

For this reason, Gorsuch's expansive formulation of free speech rights threatens to gut public accommodations laws altogether.[138] The category of "pure speech" is such a blunt doctrinal instrument that it contradicts Gorsuch's stated ambition to leave most public accommodations laws in place. *303 Creative* is in this sense at war with itself. The ambiguity gives ample room for lower courts to pick at the bones of all public accommodations laws. One can safely predict that *303 Creative* will be erratically applied to produce arbitrary and politically slanted outcomes. The Court itself offers an instructive example of this danger.

The same six conservative Justices who formed the majority in *303 Creative* had on the previous day issued an opinion in *Students for Fair Admissions, Inc. ("SFFA") v. President & Fellows of Harvard College*,[139] which applied Title VI of the Civil Rights Act of 1964 to Harvard College. Although the Court has acknowledged for almost the past half-century that colleges are expressive associations whose regulation implicates the First Amendment, and acknowledged also that the selection of students deeply affects the educational messages colleges are able to convey,[140] the Court nevertheless held that Title VI prohibits Harvard from using race-based criteria to select its own students.[141] The Court did not so much as mention the First Amendment.

What is most arresting, however, is that the next day in *303 Creative* Gorsuch forcefully proclaimed that *Boy Scouts of America v. Dale*[142] stands for the proposition that the First Amendment precludes government from intruding on the speech rights of an expressive association by requiring "the group to 'propound a point of view contrary to its beliefs' by directing its membership choices."[143] If we were to ask the

---

[138] Consider, for example, the application to a standard real estate discrimination case this formulation in *303 Creative*: "[T]his Court [has] held that the State could not use its public accommodations statute to deny speakers the right 'to choose the content of [their] own message[s].'" 600 U.S. at 592. In authoring sentences like this, the Court has apparently lost track of the simple fact that almost all discrimination occurs through the communication of messages.

[139] 600 U.S. 181 (2023).

[140] *See, e.g.,* Grutter v. Bollinger, 539 U.S. 306, 329 (2003); Regents of Univ. of Cal. v. Bakke, 438 U.S. 265, 312–14 (1978) (op. of Powell, J.).

[141] *SFFA*, 600 U.S. at 230.

[142] 530 U.S. 640 (2000).

[143] 600 U.S. at 589; *see* Green v. Miss U.S. of Am., LLC, 52 F.4th 773, 780–81 (9th Cir. 2022).

man in the street whether Harvard College or the Boy Scouts is the more expressive association, there is little doubt that the former would be selected. By interpreting Title VI to compel Harvard to choose its students in a particular way, the Court in *SFFA* forced Harvard College to propound a point of view with which it disagreed.[144]

It is unsettling that the obvious tension between *303 Creative* and the Court's own decision the day before in *SFFA* does not seem even to have crossed the Court's mind.[145] *303 Creative* and *SFFA* offer deeply incompatible visions of how to draw the boundary between the First Amendment and antidiscrimination statutes. It is striking that the two cases are consistent only insofar as each clearly expresses a conservative perspective. The First Amendment claims of religious speakers who wish to discriminate on the basis of sexual orientation are noticed and supported; the First Amendment claims of secular speakers who wish to aid racial minorities do not enter the Court's consciousness. The abstraction and ambiguity of *303 Creative* is an open invitation to lower courts to follow the Court's own blinkered lead.[146]

---

[144] On the implications of *SFFA* for student speech, see Jessica Cheung, *Affirmative Action Is Over. Should Applicants Still Mention Their Race?*, N.Y. Times (Sept. 4, 2023), https://www.nytimes.com/2023/09/04/magazine/affirmative-action-race-college-admissions.html?smid\kern-1pt=nytcore-ios-share&referringSource=articleShare.

[145] I do not mention this tension because I endorse one or another application of the First Amendment to the problem of affirmative action in private universities. I mention it only to emphasize the extreme carelessness of the Court's construction of doctrine. The Court is so oblivious that it fails even to try to explain away the obvious apparent inconsistency. *See, e.g.*, Adam Unikowsky, *Contrived Cases Make Bad Law, Part 2*, Adam's Legal Newsl. (July 15, 2023), https://adamunikowsky.substack.com/p/contrived-cases-make-bad-law-part?subscribe_prompt=free.

[146] Particularly distressing in this regard is the Court's casual repudiation of the claim that Smith's discrimination based upon same-sex marriage is equivalent to discrimination based upon sexual orientation. The stipulated facts of the case include:

> 64. Plaintiffs are willing to work with all people regardless of classifications such as race, creed, sexual orientation, and gender.
> 65. Plaintiffs do not object to and will gladly create custom graphics and websites for gay, lesbian, or bisexual clients ... so long as the custom graphics and websites do not violate their religious beliefs, as is true for all customers.

Joint Statement of Stipulated Facts, *supra* note 23, at 184a. In dissent, Sotomayor charged that "Today, the Court, for the first time in its history, grants a business open to the public a constitutional right to refuse to serve members of a protected class. Specifically, the Court holds that the First Amendment exempts a website-design company from a state law that prohibits the company from denying wedding websites to same-sex couples if the company chooses to sell those websites to the public." 600 U.S. at 603–04 (Sotomayor, J., dissenting). Gorsuch responded that Sotomayor was simply imagining things, since "we do no such thing and Colorado *itself* has stipulated Ms. Smith will (as CADA requires) 'work with all people regardless of ... sexual orientation.'" *Id.* at 598. Most courts to have considered this question have concluded, contra *303 Creative*, that discrimination based upon the sex of marriage

It is true that *303 Creative* contains casual language that might be thought to limit the reach of its holding. At one point, Gorsuch writes that CADA cannot force "an individual to 'utter what is not in [her] mind' about a question of political and religious significance."[147] This may perhaps be interpreted to imply that the speech at issue in *303 Creative* is public discourse, not mere commercial speech. But, if so, Gorsuch's language does not achieve its objective. Consider again the case of Dr. Immanuel, who passionately believes that hydroxychloroquine cures COVID-19. Although curing COVID-19 is a matter of high political significance, it is plain that Dr. Immanuel would be guilty of malpractice if she were to fail to advise a patient against using hydroxychloroquine to self-medicate for COVID-19.

The example illustrates that the state can indeed compel physicians to utter what is not in their minds about controversial subjects.[148] This is because what makes speech public discourse is not merely its subject matter—although that is certainly relevant to its constitutional characterization—but the entire context of its utterance.[149] To characterize speech as public discourse is to classify a speech *act*, not merely the semantic content of an utterance. What is determinative is whether an utterance should be understood as directed to the

---

partners is equivalent to discrimination based upon sexual orientation. *See, e.g.*, Klein v. Or. Bureau of Lab. and Indus., 289 Or. App. 507, 517–24 (2017); *In re* Gifford v. McCarthy, 137 A.D.3d 30, 37–38 (N.Y. App. Div. 2016); Washington v. Arlene's Flowers, Inc., 193 Wash. 2d 469, 503–05 (2019); Elane Photography, LLC v. Willock, 309 P.3d 53, 61–63 (N.M. 2013); Chelsey Nelson Photography LLC v. Louisville/Jefferson Cnty. Metro Gov't, 479 F. Supp. 3d 543, 550–51 (W.D. Ky. 2020); *cf.* Christian Legal Soc. Chapter of the Univ. of Cal. v. Martinez, 561 U.S. 661, 689 (2010) ("Our decisions have declined to distinguish between status and conduct in this context."). As Justice Scalia once remarked in *Bray v. Alexandria Women's Health Clinic*, 506 U.S. 263, 271 (1993): "A tax on wearing yarmulkes is a tax on Jews." *See* Douglas NeJaime, *Marriage Inequality: Same-Sex Relationships, Religious Exemptions, and the Production of Sexual Orientation Discrimination*, 100 Calif. L. Rev. 1169 (2012). Gorsuch's insouciant dismissal of the gravity of Colorado's interest in LGBTQ persons may be a disturbing indication of the Court's larger political agenda. *See* Transcript of Oral Argument, *303 Creative LLC*, 600 U.S. 570 (No. 21-476), 2022 WL 17980103, at *118–20, *123–24, *139–44.

What is especially odd about Gorsuch's casual rejection of the claim that the Court was sanctioning explicit discrimination on the basis of sexual orientation is that, on Gorsuch's theory of the case, it is pure dicta. The logic of *303 Creative* implies that the value of free speech trumps the value of equality.

[147] *303 Creative LLC*, 600 U.S. at 596.

[148] *See, e.g.*, Planned Parenthood Minn., N.D., S.D. v. Rounds, 530 F.3d 724 (8th Cir. 2008). For a discussion, see Robert Post, *Informed Consent to Abortion: A First Amendment Analysis of Compelled Physician Speech*, 2007 Ill. L. Rev. 939.

[149] Snyder v. Phelps, 562 U.S. 443, 453 (2011).

formation of public opinion. Because we do not interpret the professional speech of doctors in this way,[150] their professional speech can be regulated or compelled as necessary to ensure the competent practice of medicine.

VI.

In *Hurley v. Irish-American Gay, Lesbian and Bisexual Group of Boston*,[151] the Court held that the application of a Massachusetts public accommodations statute to the producers of a private St. Patrick's Day parade in Boston violated the First Amendment. The key premise of the Court's opinion was that "[r]eal '[p]arades are public dramas of social relations, and in them performers define who can be a social actor and what subjects and ideas are available for communication and consideration."[152] In the Court's words, parades are a "medium[] of expression,"[153] just like newspapers or movies.[154]

Media of expression are constituted by shared conventions that facilitate communication among strangers. In the same way that the implicit understandings shared by a movie's director and her audience enable the genre of film to communicate, so implicitly shared conventions unite a parade's participants and its spectators. These conventions enable bystanders to recognize a parade as a parade. They establish parades as a medium through which ideas can be communicated.

What we now call the "public sphere" emerged with the invention of printing. What the Court has labeled "media for the communication of ideas,"[155] like newspapers and magazines, created the structural skeleton of the public sphere, which consisted of "the circulation of texts among strangers who become, by virtue of their

---

[150] On the definition of professional speech, see Claudia E. Haupt, *Professional Speech*, 125 YALE L. J. 1238, 1247–48 (2016).

[151] 515 U.S. 557 (1995).

[152] *Id.* at 568.

[153] *Id.* at 569.

[154] In *Joseph Burstyn, Inc. v. Wilson*, the Court held that movies were protected by the First Amendment because they were "a significant medium for the communication of ideas." 343 U.S. 495, 501 (1952). *See* Brown v. Ent. Merchs. Ass'n, 564 U.S. 786, 790 (2011) (holding that video games were a "medium for communication").

[155] *See supra* note 154.

reflexively circulating discourse, a social entity."[156] Without media for the communication of ideas, the multitude of strangers who comprise the public could not join together in common conversation. They could not coalesce into a "public"[157] capable of forming the "public opinion" that is the lifeblood of our democracy.[158]

Because public opinion is largely formed through communicative exchanges that transpire through media for the communication of ideas, the Court has long classified speech within such media as presumptively public discourse.[159] It need not be shown that a particular film merits constitutional protection; it need only be shown that it is a film. The essential holding of *Hurley* is that parade organizers speak to the public through the medium of parades, and that the message conveyed by any particular parade is in part determined by the identity of those who march in the parade. What is crucial about *Hurley*, therefore, is not that Massachusetts sought to compel *speech*, but rather that Massachusetts sought to compel *public discourse*. Because speakers

---

[156] MICHAEL WARNER, PUBLICS AND COUNTERPUBLICS 11–12 (2002). "The central conceptual feature of the public sphere is its openness to strangers. As opposed to private communication, public communication emerges wherever a speaker cannot control the boundaries of his or her audience. Public communication is communication to an anonymous audience, potentially engaging everyone." Andreas Koller, *The Public Sphere and Comparative Historical Research: An Introduction*, 34 Soc. Sci. Hist. 261, 263 (2010). On the public sphere, see JÜRGEN HABERMAS, THE STRUCTURAL TRANSFORMATION OF THE PUBLIC SPHERE: AN INQUIRY INTO A CATEGORY OF BOURGEOIS SOCIETY (Thomas Burger trans., 1989); CHARLES TAYLOR, PHILOSOPHICAL ARGUMENTS 257–87 (1995).

[157] JOHN B. THOMPSON, THE MEDIA AND MODERNITY: A SOCIAL THEORY OF THE MEDIA 126 (1995). "The public consists of those people who act together with an understanding of their relationship to each other.... There can be no vital political life, no viable institutions of government, no sense of mastery over our shared fate, no effective common endeavors of any kind without there being a foundation of public awareness and spirit." David Matthews, *The Public in Practice and Theory*, 44 PUB. ADMIN. REV. 120, 123 (1984). On the relationship between the development of printing and the creation of the nation state, see BENEDICT ANDERSON, IMAGINED COMMUNITIES: REFLECTIONS ON THE ORIGIN AND SPREAD OF NATIONALISM (1991).

[158] Pioneering American social psychologist Charles Horton Cooley writes that democracy is "the organized sway of public opinion." CHARLES HORTON COOLEY, SOCIAL ORGANIZATION: A STUDY OF THE LARGER MIND 118 (1909). For a discussion, see Post, *supra* note 47, at 1276; and Post, *supra* note 109, at 1016–25. "While the adjective *public* has ... a long trajectory, 'public opinion' as a political concept is an invention of the eighteenth century. Neither the term *öffentlichkeit* nor the sphere it denotes existed before the eighteenth century." Koller, *supra* note 156, at 267.

[159] The presumption, of course, is defeasible. Content within a magazine, for example, may be commercial speech or obscene. But in the absence of special circumstances, the content of a magazine will be deemed public discourse. An equivalent presumption would not, for example, extend to a private letter sent from one person to another.

within public discourse are presumed to be autonomous, compelling their speech is presumptively unconstitutional. That is why the Massachusetts public accommodations law that sought to dictate who must be included in the St. Patrick's Day parade crossed a First Amendment line.

It is no accident that Gorsuch's efforts in *303 Creative* to offer examples of obviously unconstitutional applications of public accommodations laws involve public discourse. The dissent's reasoning, writes Gorsuch, would lead to a world in which "governments could force 'an unwilling Muslim movie director to make a film with a Zionist message,'" or in which "they could compel 'an atheist muralist to accept a commission celebrating Evangelical zeal.'"[160] Although Gorsuch's examples are outlandish, because it is wildly implausible to imagine that directors or muralists would actually be subject to public accommodations laws,[161] they nevertheless underscore the First Amendment point that artists and film directors are engaged in public discourse, just like the parade organizers in *Hurley*, and hence that their speech cannot be compelled.

The difficulty is that Gorsuch omits the essential First Amendment distinction between compelling public discourse and compelling speech that is not public discourse, as for example mandating the professional speech of doctors or the speech of commercial actors. Much of the architecture of contemporary speech regulation depends upon this distinction. If the distinction is denied, the administrative apparatus of consumer protection and professional malpractice, upon which most of us rely, must also collapse. But if the distinction is accepted, we must face the hard question of where to fix the boundary of public discourse. This is precisely the question that Gorsuch fails to confront.

To adequately analyze *303 Creative*, we must determine whether Lorie Smith's proposed websites should be classified as public discourse, in which case the logic of *303 Creative* can be sustained, or instead whether the websites should be categorized as commercial speech, in which case the major premise of *303 Creative* fails. This question turns on whether we should understand Smith's proposed

---

[160] 303 Creative LLC v. Elenis, 600 U.S. 570, 589 (2023).

[161] *See supra* note 23.

websites as efforts to influence public opinion or instead as efforts to sell products to a client.[162]

We might sharpen this distinction by asking whether Smith is more like a museum-quality portrait artist or more like someone whom we might label a housepainter. Both museum-quality portrait artists and housepainters exert their labor and exercise their aesthetic judgment to communicate in bespoke ways through color and light. But we nevertheless classify the latter as commercial actors selling a service to particular customers, whereas we classify the former as participants in public discourse.[163] This is because portrait artists who seek to hang their work in museums address their communications to the general public.[164] If it is clear that the state cannot

---

[162] *See* Lowe v. SEC, 472 U.S. 181 (1985).

[163] I realize that there are distinctions among different kinds of portrait painters that might be relevant to issues of constitutional characterization. It should be noted that the law already makes analogous distinctions in the context of enforcing the right of publicity with respect to photography and photographers. A photographer who is classified as participating in public discourse may take a candid picture of someone on the street; she may hang the picture in a gallery; and she may even sell that picture for a profit. The First Amendment will prevent the subject of the picture from asserting a right of publicity that would circumscribe the photographer's art. Nussenzweig v. DiCorcia, No. 50171(U), 2006 WL 871191 (N.Y. Sup. Ct. Feb. 8, 2006), *aff'd*, 878 N.E.2d 589 (N.Y. 2007). But if a photographer takes a picture of a person without her consent and turns it into a commercial product that will be mass-produced and distributed, like a poster, the law will constitutionally hold the photographer liable for a violation of the person's right of publicity. *See* Brinkley v. Casablancas, 438 N.Y.S.2d 1004 (App. Div. 1981). This is because the photographer will be understood as engaging only in commercial speech. For a discussion, see Robert Post & Jennifer Rothman, *The First Amendment and the Right(s) of Publicity*, 130 Yale L.J. 85, 157–58 (2020). *Compare* Young v. Grenerker Studios, Inc, 26 N.Y.S.2d 357, 357–58 (Sup. Ct. 1941) (allowing liability when an image of a model made by an anonymous artist was used without consent by a defendant manufacturer to produce mass-distributed "manikins"), *with* Simeonov v. Tiegs, 602 N.Y.S.2d 1014, 1016–18 (Civ. Ct. 1993) (holding that the First Amendment bars liability when an internationally known sculptor made an unauthorized bust of a famous model, even though he had sold multiple copies of the bust for profit).

This same distinction between photography as public discourse and photography as producing merely commercial products should be relevant to a proper analysis of the many cases that seek to determine whether the First Amendment prevents the application of public accommodations laws to wedding photographers. *See, e.g.*, Updegrove v. Herring, No. 20-cv-1141, 2021 WL 1206805 (E.D. Va. Mar. 30, 2021); Telescope Media Grp. v. Lucero, 936 F.3d 740 (8th Cir. 2019); Chelsey Nelson Photography LLC v. Louisville/Jefferson Cnty. Metro Gov't, 479 F. Supp. 3d 543, 550–51 (W.D. Ky. 2020); Elane Photography, LLC v. Willock, 309 P.3d 53, 61–63 (N.M. 2013); Hila Keren, *Homophobic Business Owners Are Having a Field Day Since Last Month's Supreme Court Decision*, Slate (July 25, 2023), https://slate.com/news-and-politics/2023/07/homophobic-business-owners-supreme-court-decision.html.

Considerations of this kind imply that there may be constitutional distinctions among kinds of "portrait artists." I have tried in the text to make clear that I am referring to the kind of portrait artist who would unambiguously be classified as participating in public discourse.

[164] *See, e.g.*, White v. City of Sparks, 500 F.3d 953, 956 (9th Cir. 2007) ("Any artist's original painting holds potential to 'affect public attitudes,' by spurring thoughtful reflection in and discussion among its viewers.").

compel such portrait artists to speak, it is equally clear that house painting is the kind of a commercial service to which public accommodations laws must apply if they are to have any application at all.

The difference between the museum-quality portrait artist and the housepainter does not turn on whether the portrait artist seeks to profit from her work. Those who participate in public discourse typically do so for remuneration. As Samuel Johnson once remarked, "No man but a blockhead ever wrote, except for money."[165] The difference turns instead on how the law categorizes the communicative acts respectively produced by museum-quality portrait artists and housepainters.[166] Just as we must determine whether to classify any given association as "expressive," so we must determine whether any given communicative act is included in public discourse. On pain of incoherence, First Amendment jurisprudence cannot get off the ground until it first makes preliminary judgments of this kind.[167]

VII.

The facts stipulated in the record of *303 Creative* are relevant to the question of how constitutionally to characterize Smith's websites. Colorado agreed that each of Smith's websites is an "original artwork with text and graphics" that Smith uses "to communicate a particular message."[168] When we classify an expressive act as art, we implicitly categorize it as public discourse. From this point of view, the Court virtually prejudged the case when it granted Smith's petition for certiorari to decide "[w]hether applying a public-accommodation law to compel an *artist* to speak or stay silent violates the Free Speech Clause

---

[165] Quoted in BOSWELL'S LIFE OF JOHNSON 292 (Charles Grosvenor Osgood, ed. 1917).

[166] *See supra* note 163.

[167] For a raft of examples involving the determination of whether a given communication is "art," see, *e.g.*, Brian Soucek, *The Constitutional Irrelevance of Art*, 99 N.C. L. REV. 685, 687–88 (2021). The boundary between public discourse and other forms of speech is also important for the enforcement of dignitary torts, which are virtually forbidden within public discourse. *See, e.g.*, Robert Post, *The Constitutional Concept of Public Discourse: Outrageous Opinion, Democratic Deliberation, and* Hustler Magazine v. Falwell, 103 HARV. L. REV. 601, 667–83 (1990). If persons were treated as autonomous outside of public discourse, the law would be constitutionally disabled from protecting their dignity. *See* Robert Post, *Between Democracy and Community: The Legal Constitution of Social Form, in* NOMOS XXXV: DEMOCRATIC COMMUNITY 163 (1993). For this reason, the boundaries of public discourse are in part determined by a normative balance that I do not consider in this article.

[168] *See* Stipulations 46 & 60, *supra* note 39.

of the First Amendment."[169] We apply the appellation "artist" to those whose audience, explicitly or implicitly, is the public sphere, and therefore to those whom we imagine seek to influence the mind of the public.

On closer inspection, however, the stipulated facts do not establish that Smith is an "artist" in this sense of the word. The use of terms like "art" and "artwork" in the stipulated facts instead refer to the fact that Smith would have had to exercise aesthetic and practical judgment to construct her websites.[170] What the stipulated facts actually establish is that Smith's websites would be bespoke creations requiring individualized aesthetic judgments to complete. But when described in this way, Smith's websites seem no different than ordinary house painting.

Smith's websites are different from house painting, of course, because Smith's websites use explicit words to convey a message, whereas housepainters only manipulate color and texture. We might say, therefore, that housepainters are not in the business of selling pure speech, as that is defined in the parties' stipulations.[171] Consider, therefore, the example of traditional advertising agencies who produce old-fashioned commercials. These agencies, like Smith, are in the business of selling bespoke communicative acts that use words and images to convey particular messages. They exercise aesthetic judgments to create their own commercials. The stipulations in *303 Creative* do not distinguish Smith's proposed websites from traditional commercials.[172] According to the logic of *303 Creative*, then, such advertising agencies engage in "pure speech."

Yet traditional advertising agencies sell communications that are paradigmatic examples of commercial speech.[173] We should ask,

---

[169] 142 S. Ct. 1106 (2022) (emphasis added).

[170] This is the sense of "art" invoked by the fast food restaurant Subway when it uses the phrase "The Sandwich Artist" to refer to employees who respond to customers' bespoke orders for Subway products. *See Career Path*, Subway, https://apply.mysubwaycareer.com/us/en/career-path; Brief on the Merits for Respondents, 303 Creative LLC v. Elenis, 600 U.S. 570 (2023) (No. 21-476), 2022 WL 3597176, at *30.

[171] *See supra* text at note 48.

[172] Although traditional advertising agencies do not typically sign their commercials, there is nevertheless little doubt that if Smith's websites constitute her own speech, so also would the commercials of an advertising agency constitute the agency's *own* speech.

[173] Va. State Bd. of Pharmacy v. Va. Citizens Consumer Council, Inc., 425 U.S. 748 (1976). Traditional commercials consist of "speech proposing a commercial transaction." Zauderer v. Off. of Disciplinary Couns., 471 U.S. 626, 637 (1985). Commercial speech has been more

therefore, whether *303 Creative* would permit the application of CADA to a traditional advertising agency. The logic of Gorsuch's opinion is that Colorado cannot prohibit such an agency from discriminating against clients, if remedying the discrimination would require compelling the agency to publish commercials containing views with which it disagrees. Consider a case in which the owners of a traditional advertising agency firmly believe in white supremacy and so refuse to accept Black clients if advertising their products might convey messages of racial equality. So far as the reasoning of *303 Creative* is concerned, the First Amendment should protect that agency from the application of CADA in exactly the same way as it protects Lorie Smith.

The difficulty with this conclusion is that the commercial speech produced by traditional advertising agencies is routinely compelled.[174] The demise of *Lochner* signified that the Constitution was no longer to be interpreted as attributing unfettered autonomy to commercial actors. It would be quite striking, then, if concern for the autonomy of traditional advertising agencies were to exempt them from antidiscrimination ordinances prohibiting discrimination among clients based upon specific status categories. The autonomy of commercial speakers is not a core constitutional value,[175] whereas the protection of civil rights in the marketplace is explicitly a compelling interest.[176]

It is true that traditional advertising agencies are in the business of selling speech. In this regard, they are different from the real estate broker whose circumstances we earlier considered. The business of the broker is selling real property, not speech.[177] We might be tempted to say, therefore, that applying antidiscrimination laws to brokers is constitutional because it compels speech that is merely "incidental" to the "regulation of conduct,"[178] which is the sale of

---

expansively defined as "expression related solely to the economic interests of the speaker and its audience." Cent. Hudson Gas & Elec. Corp. v. Pub. Serv. Comm'n, 447 U.S. 557, 561 (1980).

[174] *See* Post, *supra* note 116.

[175] *Compare* Riley v. Nat'l Fed'n of the Blind, 487 U.S. 781 (1988), *with Zauderer*, 471 U.S. 626.

[176] *See supra* text at note 130.

[177] For a discussion of the example of the real estate broker, see *supra* notes 137–138 and accompanying text.

[178] Rumsfeld v. F. for Acad. and Institutional Rts., Inc., 547 U.S. 47, 62 (2006).

real estate.¹⁷⁹ By contrast, it might be argued that the application of a public accommodations law to traditional advertising agencies is unconstitutional because it would regulate the business of selling speech itself.

But this distinction is merely playing with words. CADA equally compels the "pure speech" of both the broker and the agency. The First Amendment issue is the constitutionality of the speech that CADA in fact compels, not the antecedent business of the broker or the agency.¹⁸⁰ The decisive question is what kind of speech the state is able to mandate, not whether an entity is in the business of selling speech.

The application of CADA to a traditional advertising agency will compel it to produce "pure speech" that is commercial speech. The application of CADA to a real estate broker will compel him to produce "pure speech" that is also commercial speech. If we wish the broker's Black clients to enjoy the "full and equal enjoyment" of the broker's services, this commercial speech must be compelled.

The two cases are constitutionally indistinguishable. If we were to exempt advertising agencies, we would also have to exempt the broker, in which case it would be difficult to determine when public accommodations laws would have any bite at all. This outcome is so radical that it contradicts the Court's stated premise of leaving "innumerable goods and services" untouched by its holding.

It follows that if Smith's proposed websites were classified as commercial speech, CADA could constitutionally apply to them, just as they could apply to the real estate broker and the advertising agency. It might be argued, however, that even if Smith's proposed websites were categorized as classic commercial speech, Colorado could not require Smith to publish opinions, but only uncontroversial factual statements.¹⁸¹ Were this argument accepted, public accommodations laws

---

¹⁷⁹ *See, e.g.*, Telescope Media Grp. v. Lucero, 936 F.3d 740, 757 (8th Cir. 2019) ("[A] public accommodation law requiring a restaurant to serve people of all races, genders, and sexual orientations will have the incidental effect of requiring servers to speak to customers to take their orders. But these consequences are incidental because the relevant laws target the *activities* of hiring employees and providing food, neither of which typically constitutes speech.").

¹⁸⁰ *See, e.g.*, Holder v. Humanitarian L. Project, 561 U.S. 1, 27–28 (2010) (statute "directed at conduct" will nevertheless receive "a more demanding" review if it is applied to speech).

¹⁸¹ "To be sure, our cases have held that the government may sometimes 'requir[e] the dissemination of purely factual and uncontroversial information,' particularly in the context of 'commercial advertising.' But this case involves nothing like that." 303 Creative LLC v.

would become toothless. Take the prosaic example of the bigoted real estate broker who does not wish to sell to Black clients. When this broker speaks to white clients, he offers an ordinary salesman's pitch, which consists of a fluent succession of opinions. The broker assures his clients that the house on view "is a real gem"; that the clients would "really enjoy" the neighborhood; that the house will provide "perfect space" for their growing family; and so on.

If the First Amendment were interpreted to prohibit Colorado from requiring this bigoted broker to offer the same opinions to Black clients as he offers to white clients, CADA's mandate that the broker offer "the full and equal" enjoyment of his services to Black clients would become meaningless. The broker need only disclose to Black clients unvarnished and uncontroversial factual information. Because the recital of dry objective facts is hardly the stuff of successful salesmanship, the broker's communication to white clients would be so different from his communication to Black clients that the potential for discrimination is obvious. The point of public accommodations laws is to enforce equality of treatment, which includes a rough equality of speech.

It is important to stress, therefore, that outside of public discourse there is no hard and fast First Amendment rule against compelling persons to disclose opinions. If there were such a rule, the state could not draft citizens to serve as jurors to render verdicts in criminal and civil cases.[182] The state could not impose malpractice liability on professionals like doctors and lawyers for failing to disclose relevant diagnoses and legal judgments.[183] The state could not require school children to compose examinations and papers explaining their views about various matters of political and social significance.[184] The state

---

Elenis, 600 U.S. 570, 596 (2023). *See* United States v. United Foods, Inc., 533 U.S. 405 (2001); Post, *supra* note 116, at 901–06.

[182] United States v. Haynes, 729 F.3d 178, 192–93 (2d Cir. 2013); *In re* Punishing James Pringle for a Crim. Contempt, 800 N.Y.S.2d 355 (Sup. Ct. 2005); Butler v. Perry, 240 U.S. 328, 333 (1916). *See* ANDREW GUTHRIE FERGUSON, WHY JURY DUTY MATTERS: A CITIZEN'S GUIDE TO CONSTITUTIONAL ACTION 11 (2013).

[183] 4 AMERICAN LAW OF TORTS *Diagnosis* § 15:23 (Supp. 2023). *See, e.g.*, Kline v. First W. Gov't Sec., 24 F.3d 480 (3d Cir. 1994); Ackerman v. Schwartz, 947 F.2d 841 (7th Cir. 1991); Grubbs v. Barbourville Fam. Health Ctr., P.S.C., 120 S.W.3d 682, 687 (Ky. 2003); Togstad v. Vesely, Otto, Miller & Keefe, 291 N.W.2d 686, 693 (Minn. 1980). On accountants, see Overton v. Todman & Co., 478 F.3d 479 (2d Cir. 2007).

[184] *See* JUSTIN DRIVER, THE SCHOOLHOUSE GATE: PUBLIC EDUCATION, THE SUPREME COURT, AND THE BATTLE FOR THE AMERICAN MIND 19 (2018) ("[S]tudents assigned to write a paper about the American Revolution—who would prefer to tackle the Cuban Revolution—[do

could not compel citizens to file tax returns that contain endless judgments about how to classify financial transactions.

We permit this kind of compulsory speech because we count it more important that justice be made accountable to the people than that jurors be immunized from having to render judgments. We conclude that it is more important that clients and patients be protected than that lawyers or doctors be excused from having to offer competent opinions. We believe that it is more important that students be educated than that students be able to opt out of the mandatory rigors of ordinary educational assignments. We regard the financial security of the state as more important than the right of citizens to be free from the obligations of tax self-reporting.

Nothing prevents our making a similar judgement about the importance of preventing discrimination in the commercial marketplace. It is open to us to conclude that it is more important that customers be treated equally than that commercial vendors who hold themselves out to the public be excused from the requirements of equal treatment. Just as we define the role of doctors and lawyers to be the provision of competent medical and legal treatment, so we can define the role of commercial vendors to be the provision of equal treatment.[185] Enforcing that role, including the communicative prerequisites of that role, would no more compromise the constitutional autonomy of commercial vendors than it does the constitutional autonomy of lawyers and doctors. If we do not choose to enforce that role, the goal of equal treatment must dwindle into a mere bait and switch.

We should also note that, in contrast to existing compelled commercial speech precedents, public accommodations laws do not compel the expression of specific substantive opinions.[186] They do not

---

not] have a legitimate claim to their preferred topic under the First Amendment's right to free expression.").

[185] *See, e.g.*, Douglas NeJaime & Reva Siegel, *Religious Exemptions and Antidiscrimination Law in* Masterpiece Cakeshop, 128 YALE L.J. F. 201, 219–20 (2018). On the relationship between public accommodations laws and equal treatment, see, for example, Sepper & Dinner, *supra* note 132, at 114; Elizabeth Sepper, *A Missing Piece of the Puzzle of the Dignitary Torts*, 104 CORNELL L. REV. ONLINE 70, 74 (2019); Steven J. Heyman, *A Struggle for Recognition: The Controversy over Religious Liberty, Civil Rights, and Same-Sex Marriage*, 14 FIRST AMEND. L. REV. 1, 18 (2015); and Andrew M. Perlman, *Public Accommodation Laws and the Dual Nature of the Freedom of Association*, GEO. MASON U. C.R. L.J. 111, 119–20 (1997). Being treated equally is typically understood as a prerequisite of dignity, in the sense that vendors who discriminate are said to strip their victims of dignity.

[186] *Cf.* United States v. United Foods, 533 U.S. 405 (2001).

compel vendors to assert one view or another. Vendors are at liberty to say whatever they wish. Public accommodations laws mandate only that whatever opinions a vendor chooses to communicate to one group of customers should not be withheld from other customers on the basis of identified status categories.[187] Requiring Smith to comply with CADA would be analogous to the remedy that would be applied to a state university were it to violate the Equal Protection Clause: Members of the university's faculty would be obligated to offer the same lectures—the same *opinions*—to Black students as they do to white students. No First Amendment precedent forecloses this requirement.

VIII.

Whether Smith's proposed websites should be categorized as commercial speech or as public discourse is a complex question, difficult to resolve given the inchoate state of the record in *303 Creative* and the undeveloped state of contemporary First Amendment doctrine.

There are important differences between Smith's proposed websites and the advertisements produced by traditional advertising agencies. Such agencies produce commercials that are specifically designed to sell particular goods. Smith's proposed websites would not analogously sell weddings; they would more nearly announce them. They would attempt to shape the attitudes of Smith's audience toward the weddings of her clients. In this respect Smith's proposed speech may perhaps be closer to that of a modern public relations firm than to that of a traditional advertising agency. Public relations firms are not hired to sell particular products, but to shape public opinion itself.

We might ask whether the First Amendment would preclude the application of CADA to modern public relations firms. To prohibit such firms from discriminating would in effect compel them to attempt to influence public opinion on behalf of clients whom they would otherwise reject. This seems to me to be a difficult, liminal case. To resolve it, we would need to determine whether public

---

[187] At most, some vendors might feel restrained from expressing to some customers opinions that they wouldn't feel comfortable expressing to other customers. This would not constitute a question of compelled speech, but of restrictions on commercial speech. Given the importance of preventing discrimination in the market, such restrictions should easily pass the *Central Hudson* test.

relations firms are constitutionally analogous to the muralists evoked by Gorsuch or instead to traditional advertising agencies.

Fortunately we need not settle this question, because even if we were to assume that public relations firms were like museum-quality artists, and so immune from the application of CADA, we would nevertheless need to determine whether 303 Creative is constitutionally analogous to a public relations firm. We would still need to know, for example, whether Smith aspired to create websites directed to the general public or instead to the guests of a specific client.

Public relations firms are typically hired by persons who have *public* reputations to defend. But private wedding websites are not ordinarily written to influence how the general public might think about a wedding. They instead express how a couple wishes to present their wedding to particular guests and friends. It is difficult even to imagine what it might mean to seek to influence *public* opinion about a wedding between otherwise *private* persons.

The Court's rush to judgment in *303 Creative* produced an impoverished record that makes it impossible to resolve this question.[188] The problem is compounded because the Internet has deeply and pervasively confused our sense of the distinction between public and private speech. A wedding website may technically be accessible by anyone in the public, but it may nevertheless be understood to be designed for, and directed at, particular invitees.[189] We do not yet have a reliable theoretical grasp of how constitutionally to classify speech acts that the Internet broadcasts to the general public and yet that in analogue form would clearly be categorized as private.[190]

---

[188] *See* Brief for the United States as Amicus Curiae Supporting Respondents, 303 Creative LLC v. Elenis, 600 U.S. 570 (2023) (No. 21-476), 2022 WL 3648194, at *9 (*"Masterpiece* also recognized that a business's entitlement to a First Amendment exception from a public accommodations law like CADA may depend on the 'details' of its 'refusal to provide service.' But those details are absent here because this case does not arise from any concrete application of the Accommodation Clause.").

[189] In *Dun & Bradstreet, Inc. v. Greenmoss Builders, Inc.*, 472 U.S. 749, 762 (1985), the Court held that a credit report issued by Dun & Bradstreet did not involve a matter of public concern, and hence was not protected as public discourse, in part because its distribution was limited to specific subscribers, and in part because the speech was "solely in the individual interest of the speaker and its specific business audience."

[190] On the implications of this feature of the Internet for the protection of human dignity, see *supra* note 167.

IX.

It has been universally accepted that the Civil Rights Act of 1964 can constitutionally prohibit discrimination at lunch counters and hence can bar commercial speech facilitating this illegal discrimination. All agree that the federal government can ban signs saying "No Blacks Allowed." But prior to *303 Creative* insufficient attention was given to the relationship between the First Amendment and the positive requirement of equal treatment. Public accommodations laws do not merely bar discrimination; they also require that persons be treated equally. Equal treatment cannot be achieved without mandating precisely the kind of "pure speech" whose compulsion so horrifies Gorsuch in *303 Creative*.

303 Creative may have wrongfooted the Court because relevant precedents did not address the requirement of equal treatment, whose achievement inevitably demands the compulsion of pure speech. Perhaps Gorsuch imagined that he could invalidate the requirement of equal treatment without simultaneously negating the underlying prohibition against discrimination. But banning discrimination and requiring equal treatment are two sides of the same coin. It is impossible to separate them. It is for this reason that the logic of *303 Creative* has such enormous and unacceptable implications. It would apply to ordinary advertising agencies, to housepainters, to real estate brokers, to lunch counter waitresses, and indeed to every commercial actor who must use pure speech to offer the "full and equal enjoyment" of her services to customers who might otherwise be improperly excluded.

Buried in the inflated rhetoric of *303 Creative* is nevertheless a valid constitutional point. It is correct to assert that public accommodations laws cannot be applied to public discourse to alter the message of a speaker, which is the precise holding of *Hurley*. But what *303 Creative* misses is that no public accommodations law can be effective unless authorized by the First Amendment to apply to commercial speech in the context of *both* prohibiting discrimination *and* requiring equal treatment. The fundamental constitutional distinction, therefore, is not between "pure speech" and conduct, but between commercial speech and public discourse. The former can be mandated; the latter cannot. The simple logic of *303 Creative*, if taken literally, is lethal. It would cripple requirements of equal treatment and hence sweep the board of public accommodations laws.

The vast and careless overreach of the concept of "pure speech" likely derives from the Court's urgent need to protect what it regarded as Smith's genuine conscientious objection to publishing websites announcing same-sex marriages.[191] But while claims of conscience may be relevant to Free Exercise jurisprudence, they have no natural home in free speech doctrine. That the waitress in Greensboro may have had genuine conscientious objections to serving Black customers does not endow her with a free speech right to refuse Black patrons equivalent service to white patrons. That Dr. Immanuel may have a genuine conscientious commitment to hydroxychloroquine does not endow her with a free speech right to override a malpractice action for failing to advise against taking the drug. By improperly transposing intuitions about religious freedom into the quite different context of freedom of speech, the Court in *303 Creative* creates doctrinal chaos.

When set against the Court's consequential decision in *SFFA* on the previous day, this chaos has especially troubling implications. It might be construed to suggest that the Court cares only for forms of speech or equality that embody the conservative values of a white and religious constituency.[192] Gorsuch's eloquent conclusion rings distressingly hollow in light of the unexplained contrast between *303 Creative* and *SFFA*: "The First Amendment envisions the United States as a rich and complex place where all persons are free to think and speak as they wish, not as the government demands."[193]

I am confident that the Court does not wish to be tarred with the brush of hypocrisy. But if it aspires to be appreciated as a court of law, rather than as a court intent on becoming the supple servant of conservative ideology,[194] the lesson of *303 Creative* is clear. The Court needs radically to improve its First Amendment game.

---

[191] I owe to my colleague Justin Driver the insight that in the past First Amendment doctrine has also been badly deformed by the conjunction of claims of conscience and claims of compelled speech. For a discussion of the consequences of this conjunction in *West Virginia Board of Education v. Barnette*, 319 U.S. 624 (1943), and *Wooley v. Maynard*, 430 U.S. 705 (1977), see Post, *supra* note 83, at 1074–75, 1086–89.

[192] On this point, see Khiara M. Bridges, *Foreword: Race in the Roberts Court*, 136 HARV. L. REV. 23 (2022); Leah M. Litman, *Disparate Discrimination*, 121 MICH. L. REV. 1 (2022); Caroline Mala Corbin, *The Supreme Court's Facilitation of White Christian Nationalism*, 71 ALA. L. REV. 833 (2020); and Reva B. Siegel, *Foreword: Equality Divided*, 127 HARV. L. REV. 1 (2012).

[193] 600 U.S. at 603.

[194] Oliver Wendell Holmes half-jokingly insisted that his tombstone contain the epitaph: "Here lies the supple tool of power." CHARLES EVANS HUGHES, THE AUTOBIOGRAPHICAL NOTES OF CHARLES EVANS HUGHES 175 (David J. Danelski & Joseph S. Tulchin eds., 1973).

ANN WOOLHANDLER AND
JULIA D. MAHONEY

STATE STANDING AFTER
BIDEN v. NEBRASKA

In recent years, the federal courts have seen a plethora of lawsuits originated by states challenging federal government actions.[1] This increase in state-initiated litigation,[2] facilitated by the federal courts' expansive conception of state standing,[3] has sparked concerns that the states are claiming the role of omniplaintiffs.[4] As a result, some disputes

---

Ann Woolhandler is the William Minor Lile Professor of Law at the University of Virginia School of Law. Julia D. Mahoney is the John S. Battle Professor of Law and the Joseph C. Carter, Jr. Professor of Law at the University of Virginia School of Law.

AUTHORS' NOTE: We thank Payvand Ahdout, Aditya Bamzai, Rachel Bayefsky, Michael Collins, John Harrison, Caleb Nelson, Richard Re, and participants in the Article III Standing Conference held at the University of Chicago Law School in September 2023 for helpful comments. We also thank Ann Kreuscher, Nimrita Singh, and Rajan Vasisht for outstanding research assistance.

[1] *See* William Baude & Samuel L. Bray, Comment, *Proper Parties, Proper Relief*, 137 HARV. L. REV. 153, 154 (2023) ("States—often large coalitions of states, all represented by attorneys general from the opposite political party of the President—now file suits challenging any important action taken by the executive branch."); Ann Woolhandler & Michael G. Collins, *Reining in State Standing*, 94 NOTRE DAME L. REV. 2015 (2019); Ernest A. Young, *State Standing and Cooperative Federalism*, 94 NOTRE DAME L. REV. 1893, 1893 (2019) ("States increasingly litigate before the federal courts in lawsuits challenging national policy.").

[2] *See* State Lawsuits Database, STATE LITIGATION AND AG ACTIVITY DATABASE (Sept. 2, 2023), https://attorneysgeneral.org/list-of-lawsuits-1980-present.

[3] *See* Note, *An Abdication Approach to State Standing*, 132 HARV. L. REV. 1301, 1302 (2019) (recommending state standing to challenge federal nonenforcement of federal law).

[4] *See* Tara Leigh Grove, *Foreword: Some Puzzles of State Standing*, 94 NOTRE DAME L. REV. 1883, 1887–88 (2019).

The Supreme Court Review, 2024.
© 2024 The University of Chicago. All rights reserved. Published by The University of Chicago Press. https://doi.org/10.1086/729615

that arguably belong in the political arena are instead becoming the province of the courts.

Biden v. Nebraska,[5] handed down on the final day of the Court's October 2022 Term, has intensified these concerns.[6] In *Biden v. Nebraska*, the Court held that a far-reaching student loan forgiveness program under which the federal government stood to forego an estimated $400 billion of revenue[7] was not authorized by the Higher Education Relief Opportunities for Students Act of 2003 (HEROES Act).[8] In a 6-3 decision, the Court, per Chief Justice Roberts, ruled that "using the ordinary tools of statutory interpretation" the HEROES Act "provides no authorization" for the student loan forgiveness plan.[9] The Court also invoked the "major questions doctrine" to justify its decision,[10] concluding there was no clear congressional authority for the executive branch to adopt a plan of such "staggering" political and economic significance.[11]

To reach the merits, of course, the Court had to find that at least one plaintiff had standing.[12] The Court did so, ruling that the state of Missouri could proceed because it could assert as its own injury the economic impact of student debt forgiveness on the Missouri Higher Education Loan Authority (MOHELA), a nonprofit government corporation created by the state to contract with the federal government to service federal student loans.[13]

---

[5] 143 S. Ct. 2355 (2023).

[6] *See, e.g.*, Stephen I. Vladeck, *The Lawlessness of Missouri's Standing in* Biden v. Nebraska, ONE FIRST (July 13, 2023), https://stevevladeck.substack.com/p/bonus-35-the-lawlessness-of-missouris (concluding that the Court's standing analysis in *Biden v. Nebraska* "exacerbates the perception, if not the reality, that the current Court is willing to expand its formal power in order to reach issues that would (and, arguably, should) otherwise be left to the democratic process").

[7] CONG. BUDGET OFF., COSTS OF SUSPENDING STUDENT LOAN PAYMENTS AND CANCELING DEBT (2022).

[8] 20 U.S.C. § 1070 *et seq.*

[9] *Biden*, 143 S. Ct. at 2375.

[10] *See* Daniel Deacon & Leah Litman, *The New Major Questions Doctrine*, 109 VA. L. REV. 1009 (2023); Ilan Wurman, *Importance and Interpretive Questions*, 110 VA. L. REV. (forthcoming 2024); Elysa Dishman, West Virginia v. EPA: *Major Questions for the Future of the Administrative State and American Federalism*, 53 PUBLIUS: J. FEDERALISM 435 (2023) (discussing states' raising major questions issues).

[11] *Biden*, 143 S. Ct. at 2373.

[12] *See* Rumsfeld v. F. for Acad. and Institutional Rts., Inc., 547 U.S. 47, 52 n.2 (2006).

[13] Debtors came from a variety of states. *Cf.* Joint Appendix at 66, *Biden*, 143 S. Ct. 2355 (Nos. 22-506, 22-535) (providing geographical location of loans for a bond issuance secured by certain loans).

The Court's determination that MOHELA's injuries should be imputed to Missouri was not a foregone conclusion.[14] While MOHELA is a state entity whose board is politically appointed and has reporting duties to the state,[15] its operational and financial separation from Missouri made the attribution of injury to the state highly questionable. The Court's willingness to allow Missouri to claim harms to MOHELA as its own was all the more striking given that MOHELA never claimed to be aggrieved by the student loan forgiveness program.[16]

By contrast, as the Term came to a close there were also indications that the Court might be poised to revisit its expansive approach to state standing, for in two other late-Term decisions the Court had declined to recognize standing for certain claims by state litigants. In *United States v. Texas*, the Court disallowed the states' challenge to immigration enforcement guidance,[17] and in *Haaland v. Brackeen*, the Court disallowed a state equal protection challenge to child-placement priorities under the Indian Child Welfare Act.[18]

This Article will assess state standing in the wake of *Biden v. Nebraska* and will argue that going forward the Court should limit states to the traditional roles of government parties in lawsuits. We explain why the injury-in-fact test is better suited to private parties than to government entities. We also explain how standing categories that are more grounded in governmental status—standing based on *parens patriae*[19] and sovereignty interests—have added to the increase in state suits. Because states typically allege standing based not only on injury-in-fact,

---

[14] *See, e.g.*, Brief for Samuel L. Bray and William Baude as Amici Curiae in Support of Petitioners, *Biden*, 143 S. Ct. 2355 (Nos. 22-506, 22-535).

[15] *Biden*, 143 S. Ct. at 2366.

[16] *See infra* notes 68–69 and accompanying text.

[17] 599 U.S. 670 (2023). Justice Kavanaugh's majority opinion indicated that history and tradition help decide whether a state with an injury-in-fact might nevertheless lack a legally cognizable injury, *id.* at 675 (citing Raines v. Byrd, 521 U.S. 811, 819 (1997)), emphasizing that plaintiffs generally cannot challenge government decisions not to arrest or bring enforcement proceedings against third parties. *Id.*

[18] 599 U.S. 255 (2023). The Court reiterated the traditional limitation that states could not sue as parens patriae against the United States. *See infra* notes 94–95 and accompanying text.

[19] *Parens patriae* refers to state suits based on the interests of their citizens. In addition, the courts have sometimes referred to *parens patriae* as encompassing a broad and difficult to define category of quasi-sovereign interests. *See* Alfred L. Snapp & Son v. Puerto Rico, 458 U.S. 592, 602 (1981); *infra* notes 92–99 and accompanying text.

but also *parens patriae* and sovereignty interests,[20] retrenchment under all of these categories will be necessary to return state litigation to its more traditional forms.

Part I provides an overview of the historical limitations on state standing.[21] Part II details the problems of applying the injury-in-fact test to states and analyzes the Court's use of the injury-in-fact test in *Biden v. Nebraska*. We suggest that the Court limit the ability of states to use injury-in-fact standing so that government entities will ordinarily have such standing only when they are the intended objects of government regulation.[22] Part III addresses expansive uses of the notion of *parens patriae* (or quasi-sovereign) standing and suggests that the Court reinforce the disallowance of state *parens patriae* standing against the federal government. Part IV turns to claims of sovereignty-interest standing, particularly under the rubric of a state's interest in making and enforcing its laws. We recommend that formula be retired, and that sovereignty interests should no longer be a basis for state standing except in a limited number of traditionally recognized instances.[23] Part V addresses how the expansive view of governmental interests that suffice for state standing has led the Court to allow state legislatures a larger role in defending state laws and recommends halting this trend.

---

[20] *See, e.g.*, Complaint at 5 ¶ 18, Firearms Reg. Accountability Coal. v. Garland, Case 1:23-cv-00024-DLH-CRH (D. N.D. 2023) ("Plaintiff State of West Virginia is a sovereign state of the United States of America. West Virginia sues to vindicate its sovereign, quasi-sovereign, and proprietary interests in protecting is citizens, businesses, employees, public fisc, and tax revenue."); *id.* at 5–11 ¶¶ 19–42 (making the same allegation as to twenty-four other state plaintiffs). The suit contested the government's requirement of licensing for pistol-stabilizing braces. *See also* Order Denying Motion for Preliminary Injunction, Morehouse Enters. v. Bureau of Alcohol, Tobacco, Firearms and Explosives, 3:22-cv-00116-PDW-ARS (D. N.D. 2022) (No. 22-116), 2022 WL 3597299, at *3 ("Each Plaintiff State is a sovereign state of the United States of America and alleges that it is suing 'to vindicates its sovereign, quasi-sovereign, and proprietary interest, including its interests in protecting it citizens, businesses, and tax revenue.'"), *aff'd*, 78 F.4th 1011, 1017 n.5 (8th Cir. 2023) (affirming the denial of a preliminary injunction and indicating that the states lacked standing). The case questioned ATF regulations that would require privately made firearms to be serialized when they reached the stream of commerce. *Cf.* Garland v. Blackhawk Manuf. Grp., No. 23A302, 2023 WL 6531047 (U.S. Oct. 6, 2023) (granting a temporary stay of relief for the plaintiffs in a related case).

[21] A more complete version of the history may be found in Ann Woolhandler & Michael G. Collins, *State Standing*, 81 Va. L. Rev. 387 (1995).

[22] *See* Woolhandler & Collins, *supra* note 1, at 2028; *cf.* United States v. Texas, 599 U.S. 678 n.2 (2023) (stating that regulatory objects have an easier time obtaining standing).

[23] For example, the traditional allowance of state v. state suits over border disputes would be an exception. *See* Woolhandler & Collins, *supra* note 21, at 415–16.

I. Historical Limitations on State Standing

The courts and scholars have generally divided possible bases for state standing as follows[24]:

(1) Interests similar to those of private parties. Traditionally, states could sue both in state or federal court to vindicate their common-law interests such as interests in state-owned property.
(2) Enforcement interests. State suits to enforce their own laws represent the paradigmatic way that a state appears as a party in litigation. For states, such prosecutions and enforcement ordinarily must originate in the state courts.
(3) Parens patriae interests, also called quasi-sovereign interests. In such cases, states attempt to vindicate the interests of their citizens.
(4) Sovereignty interests, in which a state sues to vindicate its power to govern a particular territory or as to a particular subject matter area.

Interests similar to those of private parties. States could sue in the original jurisdiction of the Supreme Court under the state-as-party provisions in the Constitution and the 1789 Judiciary Act.[25] But in such suits, the states were primarily limited to asserting their common-law interests, such as interests in collecting on a contract[26] or in claiming a specific property.[27]

Enforcement interests. The paradigmatic way for a state to appear as a litigant was to enforce its own laws in its own courts.[28] Such cases

---

[24] *See* Ann Woolhandler, *Governmental Sovereignty Actions*, 23 Wm. & Mary Bill of Rts. L.J. 209, 213–14 (2014) (providing a list of categories); *see also* Katherine Mims Crocker, Note, *Securing Sovereign State Standing*, 97 Va. L. Rev. 2051, 2053 (2011) (same).

[25] U.S. Const. art. III, § 2 provides, *inter alia*, that the judicial power shall extend "to Controversies between two or more States;—between a State and Citizens of another State; ... and between a State ... and foreign States, Citizens or Subjects." The Judiciary Act of 1789 § 13, 1 Stat. 73, 80–81 provided, "That the Supreme Court shall have exclusive jurisdiction of all controversies of a civil nature, where a state is a party, except between a state and its citizens; and except also between a state and citizens of other state, or aliens, in which latter case it shall have original but not exclusive jurisdiction."

[26] *See, e.g.*, South Dakota v. North Carolina, 192 U.S. 286 (1904) (involving the collection on bonds to which the state held title).

[27] *See, e.g.*, Georgia v. Brailsford, 3 U.S. (3 Dall.) 1 (1794) (involving a state suit against a rival creditor claiming ownership of debts that a Georgia citizen had incurred to loyalists during the Revolution).

[28] State enforcement actions were not generally cognizable in the federal courts and were not considered part of the state as party jurisdiction of the Supreme Court. *See* Woolhandler

wherein the state asserted its enforcement interests might come to the Supreme Court by direct review. Before 1914, such appellate review was only available at the instance of individuals arguing that their federal rights had been denied in the state courts.[29] After 1914, parties including states could seek certiorari in the Supreme Court when a state court had held a state law unconstitutional as a matter of federal law.[30]

Parens patriae interests. States also could not generally appear in the federal courts as *parens patriae*—that is, to represent the interests of either particular citizens or its citizens more generally. Thus, states were not allowed to take on the interests of private parties suing on another state's bonded indebtedness.[31] Nor were they allowed to sue on a public nuisance theory without alleging a particularized interest such as would have allowed a private party to sue.[32]

& Collins, *supra* note 21, at 401, 422–23; *id.* at 429–31 (discussing removal provisions, but concluding that removal of state civil and criminal enforcement proceedings was exceptional).

[29] *See* Cohens v. Virginia, 19 U.S. (6 Wheat.) 264, 398–99, 409 (1821) (suggesting that state prosecutions could not ordinarily begin in federal courts, although they might be reviewed under § 25). The Judiciary Act of 1789, 1 Stat. 73, 85, § 25 provided in part:

> And be it further enacted, That a final judgment or decree in any suit, in the highest court of law or equity of a State in which a decision in the suit could be had, where is drawn in question the validity of a treaty or statute of, or an authority exercised under the United States, and the decision is against their validity; or where is drawn in question the validity of a statute of, or an authority exercised under any State, on the ground of their being repugnant to the constitution, treaties or laws of the United States, and the decision is in favour of such their validity, or where is drawn in question the construction of any clause of the constitution, or of a treaty, or statute of, or commission held under the United States, and the decision is against the title, right, privilege or exemption specially set up or claimed by either party, under such clause of the said Constitution, treaty, statute or commission, may be re-examined and reversed or affirmed in the Supreme Court of the United States upon a writ of error....

The above-quoted provisions were revised in minor ways by the Act of Feb. 5, 1867, 12 Stat. 385, 386. The revision also eliminated the following from the 1789 statute: "But no other error shall be assigned or regarded as a ground of reversal in any such case as aforesaid, than such as appears on the face of the record, and immediately respects the before mentioned questions of validity or construction of the said constitution, treaties, statutes, commissions, or authorities in dispute." The textual differences in the two acts are provided in HART AND WECHSLER'S THE FEDERAL COURTS AND THE FEDERAL SYSTEM 439 (Paul M. Bator, Paul J. Mishkin & David L. Shapiro eds., 2d ed. 1973).

[30] Act of Dec. 23, 1914, ch. 2, 38 Stat. 790.

[31] *See* New Hampshire v. Louisiana, 108 U.S. 76, 91 (1883).

[32] *See* Pennsylvania v. Wheeling & Belmont Bridge Co, 54 U.S. (13 How.) 518, 561–62 (1851) (allowing the state to sue to seek to enjoin building of a bridge that obstructed navigation on the Ohio River because the state had shown a private interest similar to that an individual or corporation would have).

Sovereignty interests. States generally could not litigate their interests in exercising power to the exclusion of another sovereign in the federal courts.[33] For example, the Court in *Georgia v. Stanton* disallowed a suit by the state claiming that Reconstruction legislation infringed on the state's power to govern its inhabitants.[34] Such conflicting claims to sovereignty between the state and federal government could come before the courts when a government sought to enforce its laws against a private party who could contest them on the grounds of lack of governmental power.[35]

* * *

There were multiple benefits of the narrow role of state-initiated suits. Competing claims of power as between sovereigns could be decided indirectly in enforcement suits, in which a private party could claim an immunity from the power of the enforcing government.[36] Thus, individuals were treated as the rightsholders even in structural claims.[37] Also reinforcing individuals' status as rightsholders was the requirement that individuals were to bring their own rights claims, rather than having the state espouse their interests as *parens patriae*.

Limitations on state standing thus increased the legitimacy of the courts by linking their decisions as to the legality of government

---

[33] *See* Cherokee Nation v. Georgia, 30 U.S. (5 Pet.) 1, 28 (1831) (Johnson, J., concurring) (indicating that the Cherokees' attempt to vindicate their sovereign interests against Georgia's encroachments were nonjusticiable). States could litigate border disputes with one another in the Supreme Court's original jurisdiction. *See supra* note 23. This involved a form of sovereignty interest—states' claim to govern to the exclusion of another state. But these suits were apparently close to traditional property claims and had been contemplated by the framers. *See* Woolhandler & Collins, *supra* note 21, at 415–16 (discussing boundary disputes).

[34] 73 U.S. (6 Wall.) 50 (1868); *see also* Mississippi v. Johnson, 71 U.S. (4 Wall.) 475, 476–77 (1867) (holding that the Court lacked jurisdiction to enjoin the discretionary acts of the President in enforcing federal law). For discussion of similar questions that can arise when the United States litigates on behalf of its own sovereignty interests or the interests of its citizens, see Aditya Bamzai & Samuel L. Bray, Debs *and the Federal Equity Jurisdiction*, 98 Notre Dame L. Rev. 699 (2022).

[35] *See, e.g.*, Worcester v. Georgia, 31 U.S. (6 Pet.) 515, 561–62 (1832) (holding that the state prosecution trenched on exclusive federal power over Indian commerce on direct review).

[36] Competing claims of government power could arise not only in suits when the government enforced law against private parties, but also when individuals brought claims against government officers as individuals for common law injuries. Suits could also arise between two private parties. *See* Ann Woolhandler & Michael G. Collins, *Causes of Action to Enforce the Constitution*, *in* The Cambridge Companion to the United States Constitution (Karen Orren & John Compton eds., 2018).

[37] *See* Woolhandler & Collins, *supra* note 21, at 439, 444.

action to the necessity of deciding cases.[38] The federal courts generally were limited to pronouncing on the legality of government action only as part of their role in deciding traditional cases as between individuals and government or as between individuals.[39] As Alexis de Tocqueville stated:

> It will be seen ... that by leaving it to private interest to censure the law, and by intimately uniting the trial of the law with the trial of an individual, legislation is protected from wanton assaults and from the daily aggressions of party spirit....
>
> I am inclined to believe that this practice of American courts to be at once most favorable to liberty and to public order. If the judge could attack the legislator only openly and directly, he would sometimes be afraid to oppose him; and at other times party spirit would encourage him to brave it at every turn.... But the American judge is brought into the political arena independently of his own will. He judges the law only because he is obliged to judge a case....[40]

And as Alexander Bickel noted in a similar vein, "the 'standing' and 'case' requirement creates a time lag between legislation and adjudication, as well as shifting the line of vision. Hence, it cushions the clash between the Court and any given legislative majority."[41]

II. Standing Resembling That of Individuals: Injury-in-Fact Standing

States in the past had been limited in seeking federal jurisdiction by requirements that their injuries resemble the common-law

---

[38] *See* ALEXANDER M. BICKEL, THE LEAST DANGEROUS BRANCH 116 (1962) (stating that standing and case limitation "strengthens the Court's hand in gaining acceptance of its principles"); *see also* Alexander M. Bickel, *The Voting Rights Cases*, 1966 SUP. CT. REV. 79, 89 (1967) (disfavoring state challenges to federal laws and arguing that the independence of the state and federal governments is thereby enhanced).

[39] *See* Ariz. State Legislature v. Ariz. Indep. Redistricting Comm'n, 576 U.S. 787, 854 (2015) (Scalia, J., dissenting) ("I do not believe that the question the Court answers is properly before us. Disputes between governmental branches or departments regarding the allocation of political power do not in my view constitute 'cases' or 'controversies' committed to our resolution by Art. III, § 2, of the Constitution.... The job of the courts was, in Chief Justice Marshall's words, 'solely, to decide on the rights of individuals.'" (quoting Marbury v. Madison, 5 U.S. (1 Cranch) 137, 170 (1803))).

[40] 1 ALEXIS DE TOCQUEVILLE, DEMOCRACY IN AMERICA 102–03 (Phillips Bradley ed., 1945).

[41] BICKEL, *supra* note 38, at 116; *cf.* Antonin Scalia, *The Doctrine of Standing as an Essential Element of Separation of Powers*, 17 SUFFOLK U. L. REV. 881, 893 (1983) ("[T]he *sine qua non* for emergence of the courts as an equal partner with the executive and legislative branches in the formulation of public policy was the assurance of prompt access to the courts by those interested in conducting the debate.").

injuries of private parties. Indeed, the Supreme Court's standing doctrine early appeared in the Court's limitation of states' attempts to invoke the Court's original state-as-party jurisdiction.[42] The public status of states did not allow them to sue outside of the bounds of ordinary cases.[43] Rather, the Court required states suing as plaintiffs to have interests in property and contract like those of individuals.[44] States were to implement their interests in protecting their citizens generally by passing and enforcing their own laws in their own courts (with possibilities of Supreme Court appellate review), rather than by bringing original actions in federal courts.

In the twentieth century, however, the Court greatly expanded individuals' standing, particularly in the 1970 decision in *Association of Data Processing Service Organizations, Inc. v. Camp*.[45] *Data Processing*'s injury-in-fact test had the incidental effect of also expanding state standing, given that state standing had been based on states' interests similar to those of private individuals.

Many have noted the problems of the *Data Processing* test as applied to individuals.[46] Given the difficulty of defining injury-in-fact,[47] one problem is potentially vast standing that threatens traditional notions of limited judicial power.[48] For individuals, the courts have reined in standing by judicial applications—limitations that those favoring broad standing have criticized as illogical and inconsistent.[49]

---

[42] *See supra* notes 25–27 and accompanying text.

[43] *See* Ann Woolhandler & Caleb Nelson, *Does History Defeat Standing Doctrine?*, 102 MICH. L. REV. 689, 714–18 (2004).

[44] *See, e.g.*, Pennsylvania v. Wheeling & Belmont Bridge Co., 54 U.S. (13 How.) 518, 563 (1852) (allowing the state to sue for public nuisance, but only because it had suffered a private injury similar to that which would allow a private party to sue for public nuisance). This case is discussed in Woolhandler & Nelson, *supra* note 43, at 703–04.

[45] 397 U.S. 150 (1970).

[46] *See, e.g.*, Scalia, *supra* note 41, at 890, 895–96 (1983) (favoring a concrete injury requirement with limitations such as particularity, and focusing on *Data Processing*'s interpretation of "parties aggrieved" as providing overly broad standing); *cf.* Caleb Nelson, *Intervention*, 106 VA. L. REV. 271, 285 (2020) (noting that even trivial harms can count as injuries in fact).

[47] *See, e.g.*, Cass R. Sunstein, *Injury in Fact, Transformed*, 2021 SUP. CT. REV. 349, 349–50, 360–61 (2022) (indicating that there is not an objective way to determine injury-in-fact, and that standing should be based on legal not factual injury).

[48] *See* Scalia, *supra* note 41, at 893, 895 (positing that standing limitations are necessary to restrict courts to their proper role).

[49] *See, e.g.*, Sunstein, *supra* note 47, at 349–50 (criticizing the Court's efforts to restrict standing as "lawless"); *see also id.* at 366 (criticizing the Court's characterization of certain plaintiffs as "uninjured").

The problem of the injury-in-fact test's potential breadth, however, is increased for states claiming standing, because states' claims of injury-in-fact are more difficult to contain. At least individuals and private organizations do not have near limitless interests that may suffice to give them standing.[50] States, however, have no comparable limitations on their interests. "Their range of potential interests results from states being sovereigns that govern, that are concerned for the well-being of individuals and businesses within their borders, that provide infrastructure, social services, and schools, and that act as employers."[51] There is very little federal regulation that cannot plausibly be alleged to inflict some injury-in-fact on the individual states.[52]

Recent examples illustrate the ease with which a state can claim injury to its own economic or other interests from federal regulations. In a state suit challenging the Food and Drug Administration's [FDA's] proposed reintroduction of restrictions on mifepristone distribution, the state alleged that it would incur unrecoverable Medicaid costs for surgical abortions and pregnancy care.[53] In another case, the FDA's allowing greater sodium in school lunches would increase states' health care costs.[54] Exceptions to a federal program for reimbursing employers' payment of COVID-based leave would lead to states' loss of

---

[50] Woolhandler & Collins, *supra* note 1, at 2024.

[51] *Id.*; *see also* Seth Davis, *The Private Rights of Public Governments*, 94 NOTRE DAME L. REV. 2091, 2093 (2019) ("It is not apparent how the private rights model of standing maps onto state standing, particularly in suits against the federal government.").

[52] Baude & Bray, *supra* note 1, at 173 (indicating that states will "point to downstream costs they may suffer from federal policy, which is easy to do because every important federal policy will lead to costs *somewhere*" (emphasis in original)).

[53] Washington v. U.S. Food & Drug Admin., No. 1:23-CV-3026-TOR, 2023 WL 2825861 (E.D. Wash. Apr. 7, 2023), *op. clarified*, 2023 WL 2941567 (E.D. Wash. Apr. 14, 2023); *see also* California v. Azar, 911 F.3d 558, 571–72 (9th Cir. 2018) (allowing states to contest private employer exemptions from contraceptive coverage under the ACA by relying on states' claims that they would have to pick up costs where employers did not provide coverage); Louisiana v. Becerra, 629 F. Supp. 3d 477, 487 (W.D. La. 2022) (allowing the state to challenge a vaccine mandate for the Head Start program and stating, "The Plaintiff States also have individual standing and injury based upon the alleged loss of jobs, businesses, tax revenue, unemployment benefits, reliance interest by Plaintiff States on the Head Start program, and other damages allegedly resulting from employees being fired for refusing the vaccine, and/or providers being terminated."). *But cf.* Maryland v. U.S. Dep't of Educ., 474 F. Supp. 3d 13, 32–34 (D.D.C. 2020) (holding that states had not shown loss of tuition revenue to their own schools from the agency's rescission of rules requiring for-profit schools to reveal gainful employment data); AFT v. Cardona, No. 5:20-CV-00455, 2021 WL 4461187, at *4–5 (N.D. Cal. Sept. 29, 2021) (reaching a similar result).

[54] New York v. U.S. Dep't of Agric., 454 F. Supp. 3d 297, 305 (S.D.N.Y. 2020).

tax revenue.⁵⁵ So, too, state revenue would decline if residents quit their jobs to avoid vaccine requirements.⁵⁶ A rule narrowing joint employer liability for Fair Labor Standards Act violations would cause the state to incur costs by "requiring [it] to review new regulations," and by leading the state to increase enforcement of its own wage and hour rules.⁵⁷

Biden v. Nebraska presented a rare instance in which state plaintiffs were hard pressed to assert any injury-in-fact as the result of a federal government initiative. That the states, along with the other challengers of the student loan forgiveness plan, struggled to explain why they deserved their day in court was no accident, for the Biden administration had taken care to tailor the program to defeat standing.⁵⁸

Ultimately, the state plaintiffs—and only the state plaintiffs—were successful in persuading the Court to rule in their favor with respect to standing.⁵⁹ But the route the Court took to find that the states could sue left the Court open to charges of having finessed the standing question in order to reach the merits of the case,⁶⁰ for Missouri's argument that MOHELA's anticipated loss of $44 million dollars of revenue per year

---

⁵⁵ New York v. U.S. Dep't of Lab., 477 F. Supp. 3d 1, 8 (S.D.N.Y. 2020).

⁵⁶ Kentucky v. Biden, 23 F.4th 585, 600–01 (6th Cir. 2022) (treating this as a quasi-sovereign interest), *followed by* 57 F.4th 545 (6th Cir. 2023) (affirming as modified a preliminary injunction).

⁵⁷ New York v. Scalia, 490 F. Supp. 3d 748, 767, 769–70 (S.D.N.Y. 2020). While the state injuries in these cases are questionable, the point is not so much a lack of injury but rather the ease by which states can claim some injury-in-fact.

⁵⁸ *See* Brief for Jed Handelsman Shugerman as Amicus Curiae in Support of Respondents, Biden v. Nebraska, 143 S. Ct. 2355 (2023) (No. 22-506, 22-535); Katherine Knott, *How Student Loan Forgiveness Could Win at the Supreme Court*, INSIDE HIGHER ED (Feb. 2, 2023), https://www.insidehighered.com/news/government/2023/02/02/how-debt-relief-could-win-supreme-court (reporting that "[i]n an effort to shield the debt-relief program from legal challenges, the administration has worked to weaken the standing arguments rather than change the program or the legal justification for it" and characterizing the administration's "focus on standing" as "essentially an effort to cut the lawsuits off at the knees"); Cory Turner, *In a Reversal, the Education Dept. Is Excluding Many from Student Loan Relief*, NAT'L PUB. RADIO (Sept. 30, 2022), https://www.npr.org/2022/09/29/1125923528/biden-student-loans-debt-cancellation-ffel-perkins (reporting that "multiple legal experts" informed NPR that a change in the administration's student loan forgiveness policy that rendered an estimated 800,000 borrowers ineligible for debt relief was "likely" motivated by standing concerns).

⁵⁹ In *Department of Education v. Brown*, 600 U.S. 551 (2023), the companion case to *Biden v. Nebraska*, a unanimous Court determined that two individual borrowers who did not qualify for the maximum debt relief under the student loan forgiveness plan had failed "to establish that any injury they suffer from not having their loans forgiven is fairly traceable to the" plan and thus lacked standing. *Id.* at 561.

⁶⁰ *See e.g.*, Erwin Chemerinsky, Opinion, *The Court Rewrote the Law So It Could Stop Student Loan Forgiveness*, L.A. TIMES (June 30, 2023), https://www.latimes.com/opinion/story/2023-06-30/supreme-court-student-loans-forgiveness-biden-heroes-act; Vladeck, *supra* note 6.

from having fewer loans to service should be imputed to the state itself was questionable. While MOHELA is in some sense part of the state—it was created by the state, its board is politically appointed, and it has reporting duties to the state[61]—it is separately incorporated and has an independent legal status. MOHELA can sue and be sued, and its debts and revenues are not considered to be those of the state.[62] Particularly given Missouri's claim of financial injury, it is significant that Missouri law provides that "[n]o asset of [MOHELA] shall be required to be deposited in the state treasury, and no asset of [MOHELA] shall be subject to appropriation by the general assembly."[63]

In finding that the state could effectively bring a complaint based on MOHELA's injuries, Chief Justice Roberts relied heavily on a 1953 Justice Douglas opinion in *Arkansas v. Texas*, holding that the State of Arkansas could bring a suit within the Court's original jurisdiction.[64] Arkansas brought suit on a claim that Texas was interfering with a contract of the University of Arkansas by attempting to stop a Texas-based foundation from paying on a promise to fund a hospital wing at the university. The university had some similarities with MOHELA such as state creation and a duty to report to the state.[65] On the other hand, all property of the university was considered state property, and a suit against the university was one against the state.[66] By contrast, MOHELA's assets are not state assets,[67] and a suit against MOHELA is not a suit against the state.

---

[61] *See* 143 S. Ct. at 2366; Mo. Rev. Stat. §§ 173.360, 173.445 (1995); *cf.* Dep't. of Transp. v. Ass'n. of Am. R.Rs., 575 U.S. 43, 51–53 (2015) (declining to treat Amtrak as a private party forbidden from setting standards affecting other railroads, given the government's control of Amtrak's stock and board of directors, the government's substantial supervision of its operations, and the government's substantial financial support).

[62] *Biden*, 143 S. Ct. at 2387 (Kagan, J., dissenting) (citing Mo. Rev. Stat. § 173.385.1(3) (1995)); *see also* Baude & Bray, *supra* note 1, at 185 n.201 (suggesting that the test of whether an entity should be considered an arm of the state for litigation purposes should be "simply whether the entity has the power to sue and be sued on its own") (citations omitted); Jed Handelsman Shugerman, Biden v. Nebraska: *The New Standing and the (Old) Purposive Major Questions Doctrine*, 2022–23 Cato Sup. Ct. Rev. 209, 221 (2023) (questioning whether the state had shown harm from the debt forgiveness program).

[63] Mo. Rev. Stat. § 173.425 (1995).

[64] 346 U.S. 368 (1953).

[65] The Board of Trustees was a body corporate with power to issue bonds that did not pledge the credit of the state. *See id.* at 370.

[66] *Cf. id.* at 369.

[67] *Biden*, 143 S. Ct. at 2387 (Kagan, J., dissenting); *cf.* Z. Payvand Ahdout & Bridget Fahey, *Layered Constitutionalism and Structural Interdependency*, 123 Colum. L. Rev. (forthcoming 2024) (draft of Sept. 22, 2023) (manuscript at 29) (suggesting that the Court should have

It was evident, moreover, that the University of Arkansas was on board with the State's attempt to assure that the University received the promised funds that Texas was trying to block. By contrast, MOHELA distanced itself from the student loan forgiveness litigation, underscoring its independent operation and financing.[68] While common sense suggests that a reduction in direct loans would lead to fewer servicing fees, MOHELA apparently did not consider itself aggrieved.[69] Federal loan servicers operate in an environment of fluctuating federal policies,[70] some increasing and some decreasing the number of loans they service. For example, the Department of Education in 2021 transferred to MOHELA the servicing of the Public Service Loan Forgiveness program, bringing millions of additional loans for servicing.[71] While growth in one area of revenue does not prevent a party's

---

afforded less attention to the state's claim to represent MOHELA given its structuring MOHELA as a separate corporation); Richard M. Re, *Relative Standing*, 102 GEO. L. J. 1191, 1196 (2014) (stating that when those with the greatest interest in obtaining a remedy decline to seek it, the courts learn that resolving the dispute outside the court system may be more effective).

[68] *See* Annelise Hanshaw, *Missouri Company Plays Central Role in the Downfall of Biden Loan Forgiveness Program*, MO. INDEP. (June 30, 2023), https://missouriindependent.com/2023/06/30/missouri-company-plays-central-role-in-downfall-of-biden-loan-forgiveness-program (indicating that MOHELA's apparent lack of interest in the suit and its statement that "MOHELA has not had, and does not have, a contractual relationship or agreement with the Missouri Attorney General's Office on any topic including as to student debt relief").

[69] MOHELA's contract with the federal government required the federal government to provide a certain amount of business, but there was no violation of that term. *See* Joint Appendix at 76 ex. B, *Biden*, 143 S. Ct. 2355 (Nos. 22-506, 22-535) ("During the contract period, the Government shall place orders totaling a minimum of $1,500,000."); *see also id.* ("This is an Indefinite Delivery/Indefinite Quantity (IDIQ) contract that will be used to provide commercial services for the U.S. Department of Education (ED), Office of Federal Student Aid."); *id.* at 92 ("Base Ordering period, June 23, 2020 through June 22, 2023."); *cf.* Thomas Gokey et al., *The Suit Against Student Debt Relief Doesn't Add Up: Flawed Claims of Legal Standing in* Biden v. Nebraska, ROOSEVELT INST. (May 2, 2023), https://rooseveltinstitute.org/publications/the-suit-against-student-debt-relief-doesnt-add-up (indicating that the contracts state that the government FSA can remove and reallocate loans).

[70] There is a question, moreover, of whether a loan servicer has a legally cognizable interest in the federal government's continuing a particular volume of business, aside from what is assured in the contract. *See supra* note 69; *cf.* Air Courier Conf. of Am. v. Am. Postal Workers Union, 498 U.S. 517 (1991) (holding that the postal workers' union had no standing to contest the Postal Service's allowance of an exception to the postal monopoly statute because there were no postal workers at the time of the statutes' promulgation and thus they were outside of the zone of interest). On the other hand, the government's contracting with loan servicers is provided for in the federal student loan statute, *see* 20 U.S.C. § 1087(a), and loan servicers are included among those who can participate in certain negotiated rulemakings. 20 U.S.C § 1098a(a)(1). *But cf.* Dep't of Educ. v. Brown, 600 U.S. 551, 557 (2023) (indicating that rulemaking was not required under the HEROES Act, citing 20 U.S.C. § 1098bb(d)).

[71] *See* Gokey et al., *supra* note 69, at 9 (stating that "[m]illions of PSLF (Public Service Loan Forgiveness) accounts" were transferred to MOHELA).

complaining about reduction in another, it may shed light on why MOHELA was insufficiently troubled about loss of business to sue.[72]

Standing law gives parties who suffer injury control of the decision whether to pursue judicial redress. Even a party with a close preexisting legal relationship to an allegedly injured individual has no general license to bring suit for the injured party who declines to do so.[73] MOHELA did not want to file suit. But it was enough for the Court that Missouri's attorney general did.

* * *

While the majority decision in *Biden v. Nebraska* allows for a broad view of what injuries the state can claim as its own, the Court's decision in *United States v. Texas* suggests that some Justices may be open to restraining unlimited state standing under the injury-in-fact test. In *United States v. Texas*, Texas and Louisiana challenged federal enforcement guidance prioritizing certain immigrants for arrest and removal proceedings. The states alleged monetary injury because of the reduction in federal arrests. The Court, however, stated, "Monetary costs are of course an injury. But this Court has 'also stressed that the alleged injury must be legally and judicially cognizable.'"[74] "History and tradition" guided what was legally cognizable and did not support suits challenging federal enforcement priorities.[75] The Court noted, however, that there normally was standing where "the plaintiff is himself an object of the action (or forgone action) at issue."[76]

The Court's reasoning in *United States v. Texas* provides at least some support for emphasizing the state's role as an enforcement object in the state standing calculus. We have previously suggested that given the limitless set of potential state injuries in fact, states generally should only have standing under that rubric when they are direct regulatory

---

[72] *Cf. id.* at 9–10 (indicating that MOHELA anticipated a growth in income even from its direct loans and also that loan cancellation fees would provide revenue). While the federal government attempted to design its policies to evade judicial challenges, no suggestion has surfaced that it attempted to influence MOHELA's decision not to pursue litigation or support the state's position.

[73] *See* Elk Grove Unified Sch. Dist. v. Newdow, 542 U.S. 1 (2004) (disallowing a father's attempt to pursue an Establishment Clause claim based on the Pledge of Allegiance recitation at public school as the next friend of his daughter, and to vindicate his own parental interests, when the custodial parent did not wish the suit to proceed on behalf of the child).

[74] 599 U.S. 670, 676 (2023).

[75] *Id.*

[76] *Id.* at 678 n.2 (internal citations omitted).

objects of the federal initiative.[77] This category is not a *de minimis* set, given the interactions of the state and federal governments.[78] States, for example, were among the objects of a federal statute that conditioned their receipt of certain federal COVID funds on states' not using those funds to finance state tax cuts.[79] So, too, states as federal contractors were among the regulatory objects of a federal vaccine mandate for federal contractors.[80] States, moreover, could continue to challenge alleged commandeering legislation.[81] For example, in *Haaland v. Brackeen*, the Court allowed an anti-commandeering challenge to the Indian Child Welfare Act, even though the Court disallowed the state's raising an equal protection challenge on behalf of its citizens.[82] The state attorneys general will still have plenty to complain about even under the more restrictive state standing regime here recommended, but the injuries will more centrally be those of the state.

III. PARENS PATRIAE STANDING

A. TRADITIONAL LIMITATIONS

As noted above, states generally could not seek standing that was merely derivative of their citizens' standing. The lack of a history

---

[77] *See* Woolhandler & Collins, *supra* note 1, at 2028–29. Some might argue that state standing is a second-best solution to counteract the growth of federal executive power. *Cf.* Shugerman, *supra* note 62, at 228 ("allowing slightly more latitude for states to raise constitutional questions and to challenge the abuse of executive power strikes an appropriate balance through federalism"). The Court seems ready, however, to provide more direct limitations on executive power. *See* West Virginia v. EPA, 587 U.S. 697 (2022) (applying a major-questions limitation on administrative interpretations of statutes); Loper Bright Enters. v. Raimondo, 45 F. 4th 359 (D.C. Cir. 2022), *cert. granted*, 143 S. Ct. 2429 (2023) (granting review on the question whether to overrule Chevron U.S.A. v. Nat. Res. Def. Council, Inc., 467 U.S. 837 (1984)); *see also* Relentless, Inc. v. Dep't of Com., 62 F.4th 621 (1st Cir.), *cert. granted*, 144 S. Ct. 325 (2023) (raising the same issues).

[78] *Cf. West Virginia*, 597 U.S. at 719 ("[T]here can be 'little question' that the rule does injury to the States, since they are 'the object of' its requirement that they more stringently regulate power plant emissions within their borders." (citing Lujan v. Defenders of Wildlife, 504 U.S. 555, 561–62 (1992))).

[79] *Cf.* West Virginia v. U.S. Dep't of the Treasury, 59 F.4th 1124, 1136 (11th Cir. 2023) (holding the claim justiciable); Missouri v. Yellen, 39 F.4th 1063, 1069–70 (8th Cir. 2022) (determining that the claimed injury was unlikely to occur given the federal government's interpretation of the statute), *cert. denied*, 143 S. Ct. 734 (2023).

[80] Brnovich v. Biden, 562 F. Supp. 3d 123, 142–45 (D. Ariz. 2022) (holding that the state had its own interest as a government contractor covered by vaccine the mandates), *rev'd*, 67 F.4th 921 (9th Cir. 2023).

[81] *See, e.g.*, New York v. United States, 505 U.S. 144 (1992) (allowing states to challenge federal legislation that required them to legislate by a certain date as to certain toxic waste or take title to it); Nat'l Fed'n of Indep. Bus. v. Sebelius, 567 U.S. 519, 580–81 (2012) (upholding anti-commandeering challenges to certain provisions of the Affordable Care Act).

[82] 599 U.S. 255, 278–95 (2023).

of such suits in the federal courts is largely shown by their absence. A few cases in the Court's original jurisdiction, however, illustrated the point—such as when the Court held that states could not sue sister states to collect debts owed to their citizens.[83]

Additional historical support for a lack of *parens patriae* standing comes from cases in which state officials sought to vindicate individual rights of citizens on direct review from state courts.[84] Under Section 25 of the 1789 Judiciary Act and its 1867 successor, the Supreme Court had appellate review "where is drawn in question the validity of a statute of, or an authority exercised under any State, on the ground of their being repugnant to the constitution, treaties or laws of the United States, and the decision is in favour of such their validity" and also where a "decision is against the title, right, privilege or exemption ["exemption" changed to "immunity" in 1867] specially set up or claimed by either party" under the Constitution or federal law.[85]

The Court rejected appellate review at the instance of state officials complaining that the decision below was against a federal right, even where the state courts had allowed the officials to raise the federal rights claims. For example, in *Smith v. Indiana*, property owners brought a state court mandamus suit against a tax assessor seeking a tax exemption under a state statute that the assessor claimed violated the Fourteenth Amendment's Equal Protection Clause.[86] The Indiana Supreme Court rejected the assessor's equal protection argument on the merits, after which the assessor sought review in the United States Supreme Court. The United States Supreme Court held that the assessor lacked a sufficient personal interest to raise the denial of the equal protection claim in the United States Supreme Court. It was of no moment that the state court had allowed the assessor to raise the claim nor that he had duties with respect to tax collection as a public officer.[87]

---

[83] New Hampshire v. Louisiana, 108 U.S. 76, 91 (1883).

[84] These cases also illustrate the non-primacy of state law as to officials' taking on representative status.

[85] The 1789 Judiciary Act § 25, 1 Stat. 73; The Habeas Corpus Act of Feb. 5, 1867, ch. 28, 14 Stat. 385.

[86] 191 U.S. 138 (1903).

[87] *Id.* at 148–49 (indicating this was a matter of state law); *id.* at 148 ("Different considerations [from the state law issues] ... apply to the jurisdiction of this court, which we have recently held can only be invoked by a party having a personal interest in the litigation. It follows that he cannot sue out a writ of error in behalf of third persons." (citations omitted)). The decision did not seem to rely on anything in the text of Section 25 as opposed to concerns as to whose rights were at issue. *See id.*

The Supreme Court rebuffed other attempts to invoke the Court's appellate jurisdiction where officials had duties with respect to state laws that the officials alleged were unconstitutional.[88] For example, in *Braxton v. County Court*, the state auditor had secured a mandamus in the West Virginia court requiring the county government to limit property taxes in accordance with a state law.[89] The county government argued that the lowered tax would be insufficient to cover its interest and sinking fund obligations on municipal bonds, thereby violating the Contract Clause. The Court, however, found their interest insufficient, stating:

> Again, that the act of the State is charged to be in violation of the National Constitution, and that the charge is not frivolous, does not always give this court jurisdiction to review the judgment of a state court. The party raising the question of constitutionality and invoking our jurisdiction must be interested in and affected adversely by the decision of the state court sustaining the act, and the interest must be of a personal and not of an official nature.[90]

In short, individuals were the rights claimants against government, and state law could not necessarily give state officials a right to take on the rights of individuals in the federal courts.

B. EXPANSION OF *PARENS PATRIAE*

The Court in the twentieth century allowed expansion of state *parens patriae* standing.[91] The critical case was *Alfred L. Snapp & Son*

---

[88] *See* Marshall v. Dye, 231 U.S. 250 (1913) (refusing to hear an appeal from a state court decision forbidding certain state officials from holding an election that the officials claimed was necessary under the Guarantee Clause); Caffery v. Okla. Territory, 177 U.S. 346, 348–49 (1900) (refusing to hear an appeal by a taxing official who had been compelled in a mandamus action by the territorial board of equalization to raise assessments; the official could not meet the $5,000 amount in controversy because the appellant had neither gained nor lost any money by the judgment of the Supreme Court of the territory); *cf.* Lampasas v. Bell, 180 U.S. 276 (1901) (holding that a city seeking to avoid payment on bonds issued under a previous government could not espouse the due process rights of their inhabitants as to the constituting of the prior government in a case originating in a lower federal court).

[89] 208 U.S. 192 (1908). The state court did not necessarily treat the county as a proper party.

[90] *Id.* at 197.

[91] *See, e.g.*, Pennsylvania v. West Virginia, 262 U.S. 553 (1923) (allowing the states to challenge another state's restriction on distribution of natural gas, partly as a representative of the consuming public); Georgia v. Pa. R.R., 324 U.S. 439, 444, 450 (1945) (allowing the state to sue alleging a conspiracy among railroads that was keeping Georgia in a "state of arrested development").

v. Puerto Rico.[92] The Commonwealth brought a suit against mainland agricultural employers that were allegedly discriminating against Puerto Ricans in violation of federal law. Despite the Commonwealth's essentially suing on behalf of its residents, the Court allowed the government to proceed, using language that states and courts have used ever since in supporting broad versions of *parens patriae* standing:

> In order to maintain such an action, the State must articulate an interest apart from the interests of particular private parties.... These characteristics [of quasi-sovereign interests] fall into two general categories. First, a State has a quasi-sovereign interest in the health and well-being—both physical and economic—of its residents in general. Second, a State has a quasi-sovereign interest in not being discriminatorily denied its rightful status within the federal system.
>
> Although more must be alleged than injury to an identifiable group of individual residents, the indirect effects of the injury must be considered as well in determining whether the State has alleged injury to a sufficiently substantial segment of its population. One helpful indication in determining whether an alleged injury to the health and welfare of its citizens suffices to give the State standing to sue as *parens patriae* is whether the injury is one that the State, if it could, would likely attempt to address through its sovereign lawmaking powers.[93]

Snapp's indicating that state standing could be based on any matter that might potentially be the subject of legislation conflicted with the traditional notion that state interests in legislating should be manifested by the state's doing just that. The Court's prior holding in *Massachusetts v. Mellon* that states could not assert *parens patriae* against the federal government, however, apparently limited *Snapp*'s reach.[94] *Snapp* itself was not a suit against the federal government and the *Snapp* decision stated, "A State does not have standing as *parens patriae* to bring an action against the Federal Government."[95]

---

[92] 458 U.S. 592, 607 (1981).

[93] *Id.* at 607. Even more expansive elaborations of *parens patriae* interests can be found in recent lower court decisions. *See, e.g.*, Louisiana v. Becerra, 629 F. Supp. 3d 477, 486–88 (W.D. La. 2022) (entertaining states' challenge to the federal government's vaccine mandate for Head Start participants).

[94] Massachusetts v. Mellon, 262 U.S. 447 (1923); *see also* Florida v. Mellon, 273 U.S. 12, 18 (1927) (holding that the state could not assert a challenge to the federal inheritance tax based on injury to its citizens).

[95] 458 U.S. at 610 n.16. For some decisions applying the limitation, see, for example, Nevada v. Buford, 918 F.2d 854, 858 (9th Cir. 1990); and State *ex rel.* Sullivan v. Lujan, 969 F.2d 877, 883 (10th Cir. 1992).

But language in *Massachusetts v. EPA* undermined this apparent restriction. The Court allowed the state to sue for the EPA's declining a petition to engage in rulemaking to limit greenhouse gas emissions for new motor vehicles.[96] While Massachusetts's standing to a large extent seemed to be based on its alleged individualized injury of loss of coastal property it owned,[97] the opinion also discussed *parens patriae* standing.[98] The opinion suggested that state *parens patriae* standing against the United States was more available when the state was alleging an agency acted contrary to federal statute, than when a state attempted to protect its citizens from the operation of federal statutes that the state alleged were unconstitutional.[99] Combined with the Court's reasoning that states were entitled to "special solicitude"[100] in the standing inquiry, *Massachusetts v. EPA* seemed to encourage *parens patriae* standing against the federal government.[101]

Some lower courts nevertheless continued to disallow *parens patriae* suits against the United States. The District of Columbia Circuit construed *Massachusetts v. EPA* as basing state standing on the state's loss of coastline and declined to read the decision as generally allowing *parens patriae* standing under the Administrative Procedure Act (APA).[102] The Seventh Circuit reached a similar conclusion.[103] Some

---

[96] 549 U.S. 497, 519 (2007).

[97] *Id.* at 522 ("Because the Commonwealth 'owns a substantial portion of the state's coastal property' ... it has alleged a particularized injury in its capacity as a landowner."). This was in the section of the opinion that, after generalizations about state standing, focused on "The Injury" in the particular case. *Id.* at 521–22; *see also* Gov't of Manitoba v. Bernhardt, 923 F.3d 173, 182 (D.C. Cir. 2019) (discussing that standing in *Massachusetts v. EPA* was primarily based on loss of coastline); Jonathan Remy Nash, *Sovereign Preemption State Standing*, 112 Nw. U. L. Rev. 201, 203–04 (2017) (noting that "the actual role that sovereignty played" in the Court's determination that Massachusetts had standing "remains murky" and that "[d]espite the Court's recitation of sovereignty as a factor in its analysis, the Court, in the end, emphasized Massachusetts's ownership of coastal property—property that would disappear if the predicted effects of climate change came to pass").

[98] 549 U.S. at 519 (citing *Snapp's* language); *cf. id.* at 520 (also treating the rejection of the states' rulemaking petition as a procedural right).

[99] *Id.* at 520 n.17.

[100] *Id.* at 520; *see also id.* at 518 ("States are not normal litigants for the purposes of invoking federal jurisdiction.").

[101] Baude & Bray, *supra* note 1, at 167 (discussing the opinion's undermining *Mellon*).

[102] *See Gov't of Manitoba*, 923 F.3d at 179–83 (holding that the state could not rely on *parens patriae* and had not preserved a claim of its own interests).

[103] Michigan v. EPA, 581 F.3d 524, 529 (7th Cir. 2009) (not allowing *parens patriae* standing against the federal government when the state challenged an Indian Tribe's designation of its lands as in a more sensitive category that would impose stricter air quality standards on some emitting sources in Michigan); Am. Fed'n of Teachers v. Cardona, No. 5:20-CV-00455, 2021

cases have avoided reliance on *parens patriae* when the suit is against the federal government, although sometimes finding other grounds for state standing.[104]

Other courts, however, have taken the encouragement from *Massachusetts v. EPA* to embrace state *parens patriae* standing against federal defendants.[105] The Sixth Circuit, for example, distinguished a state's *parens patriae* standing to represent only the interests of particular citizens (not allowed) versus the states' assertion of its own quasi-sovereign interests (allowed).[106] Given expansive versions of the states' "own" quasi-sovereign interests in *Snapp*, including in the "health and welfare of its citizens,"[107] the distinction between the

---

WL 4461187, at *5 (N.D. Cal. Sept. 29, 2021) (holding that California could not assert *parens patriae* standing based on its citizens' loss of information due to the rescission of certain regulations of for-profit colleges, and that the APA provided no statutory override); Maryland v. U.S. Dep't of Educ., 474 F. Supp. 3d 13 (D.D.C. 2020) (reaching a similar result).

[104] Washington v. U.S. Food & Drug Admin., No. 1:23-CV-3026, 2023 WL 2825861, at *5 (E.D. Wash. Apr. 7, 2023) (relying on the state's own interest rather than *parens patriae*, given questions about *parens patriae* against the United States); New York v. U.S. Dep't of Labor, 477 F. Supp. 3d 1, 8 (S.D.N.Y. 2020) (not addressing the alleged quasi-sovereign interest and finding that threatened injury to New York tax revenue sufficed); *cf.* Brnovich v. Biden, 562 F. Supp. 3d 123, 142–45 (D. Ariz. 2022) (holding that the state could not use parens patriae but could rely on its own interest as a government contractor subject to vaccine mandates), *followed by* 2022 WL 19560411 (D. Ariz. Feb. 10, 2022) (entering injunction), *rev'd*, 67 F.4th 921 (9th Cir. 2023) (reversing the grant of the injunction on the merits).

[105] For example, some courts state that for alleged violations of the APA "states have *parens patriae* standing where the state is bringing an action on behalf of citizens to enforce rights guaranteed by a federal statute." *See* Louisiana v. Becerra, 629 F. Supp. 3d 477, 487 (W.D. La. 2022) (citing Massachusetts v. EPA, 549 U.S. 497 (2007)).

[106] Kentucky v. Biden, 23 F.4th 585 (6th Cir. 2022) (holding that claims challenging the government contractor vaccine mandate could not be brought on a third-party *parens patriae* theory but could be brought based on the states' own sovereign or quasi-sovereign interests). *But cf. Gov't of Manitoba*, 923 F.3d 173 at 182–83 ("The distinction is not ... between two types of *parens patriae* lawsuits, one permissible and one not. It is between a *parens patriae* lawsuit (what *Mellon* prohibits) and a State suing based on 'its rights under federal law' (not a *parens patriae* lawsuit at all).").

[107] Lower court cases are often expansive as to the states' own quasi-sovereign interests. *See Kentucky*, 23 F.4th at 598–99 (concluding that states had such interests because the federal regulation would preempt state law, and that there were sovereign interests where the federal government regulated matters in which the states believed they had control to promote the economic well-being of their populace); *id.* at 599–601 (concluding that states had standing because the federal policies would override state policies and threatened to damage state economies by resulting in workforce reductions). The Fifth Circuit has also held that the states could assert a quasi-sovereign interest in challenging federal immigration policies in that in joining the Union, the states "'surrendered some of their sovereign prerogatives over immigration' including their power to 'establish their own classifications of aliens.'" Texas v. United States, 50 F.4th 498, 571 (5th Cir. 2022) (footnote omitted); *see also* United States v. Texas, 599 U.S. 670, 723 (2023) (Alito, J., dissenting) (stating, with respect to a challenge to immigration arrest policies: "Texas's entry into the Union stripped it of the power that it

interests of citizens and states may be hard to specify. Thus, states were allowed to protect participants in the Head Start program from vaccine mandates[108] and to protect their citizens from alleged federal government suppression of free expression on the internet.[109]

The Supreme Court in *Haaland v. Brackeen*[110] moved toward restoring limitations on state *parens patriae* standing. Texas sought to challenge on equal protection grounds the Indian Child Welfare Act's priorities for Indian families in adoption and foster care proceedings.[111] The Court stated that Texas "has not equal protection rights of its own ... and it cannot assert equal protection claims on behalf of its citizens" because "[a] State does not have standing as *parens patriae* to bring an action against the Federal Government."[112] If the Court is disinclined to overrule *Snapp* outright with its unbounded definition of state quasi-sovereign interests, it can take the easier step of reinforcing *Haaland*'s apparent blanket disallowance of state *parens patriae* suits against the United States.[113] If residents of a state have claims, they can bring them themselves.

IV. STATE SOVEREIGNTY INTERESTS

The state's general interest in governing traditionally did not confer standing to bring a suit in the federal courts. The Supreme Court, however, gradually made way for sovereignty interests to ground state claims. For example, *Missouri v. Holland* allowed a state to contest the constitutionality of federal legislation and regulations implementing a treaty protecting migratory birds. The Court declined

---

undoubtedly enjoyed as a sovereign nation to ... regulate the entry of aliens."). *See generally* Nash, *supra* note 97 (arguing that states should have standing where the agency is not following federal law that takes the place of preempted state law).

[108] Louisiana v. Becerra, 629 F. Supp. 3d 477, 487 (W.D. La. 2022) (relying on *parens patriae* standing as well as individual state interests).

[109] Missouri v. Biden, 662 F. Supp. 3d 626 (W.D. La. 2023), *modified by* 83 F.4th 350 (5th Cir. 2023), *cert. granted sub nom.* Murthy v. Missouri, 144 S. Ct. 7 (2023) (also granting a stay of the preliminary injunction entered by the district court and modified by the Fifth Circuit).

[110] 599 U.S. 255 (2023).

[111] 25 U.S.C. §§ 1915(a)–(b).

[112] *Haaland*, 599 U.S. at 295; *see also* Biden v. Nebraska, 143 S. Ct. 2355, 2390 (2023) (Kagan, J., dissenting) (quoting this language). The *Haaland* Court also found wanting the state's claim of economic injuries from recordkeeping requirements and its claim that the preferences injured Texas "by requiring it to break its promise to its citizens that it will be colorblind in child-custody proceedings." *Haaland*, 599 U.S. at 295.

[113] The Court, moreover, should discard the term "quasi-sovereign" interests.

to base standing on the state's ownership of the birds, instead stating "that but for the treaty the State would be free to regulate this subject itself."[114] This holding, however, was undermined by *Massachusetts v. Mellon*, in which the Court held the state lacked standing to challenge federal legislation that addressed an area the state claimed was exclusively one of state power.[115]

Still, sovereignty interests continued to make headway.[116] For example, courts countenanced state challenges to administrative action that preempted state law—particularly beginning under statutes in which Congress contemplated an ongoing role for the state regulation that dovetailed with federal regulation.[117] And preemption-based claims became increasingly common over time.[118]

Aiding the states' ability to challenge federal action has been the formula that states have an interest in their power "to create and enforce a legal code."[119] While this states a truism as to state interests, it is historically inaccurate as a statement of a standalone interest that allowed the state to sue in a federal court outside of traditional forms.[120]

---

[114] 252 U.S. 416, 431, 434 (1920).

[115] 262 U.S. 447, 485 (1923) ("If an alleged attempt by congressional action to annul and abolish an existing state government 'with all its constitutional powers and privileges,' presents no justiciable issue, as was ruled in *Georgia v. Stanton* ... no reason can be suggested why it should be otherwise where the attempt goes no farther, as it is here alleged, than to propose to share with the State the field of state power."). The *Mellon* court seemed to treat *Missouri v. Holland* as distinguishable because "there was an invasion ... of the quasi-sovereign right of the State to regulate the taking of wild game within its borders." *Id.* at 482.

[116] *See, e.g.*, Colorado v. Toll, 268 U.S. 228, 229 (1925) (reversing dismissal by a lower federal court and allowing the state to seek an injunction to enjoin a federal park superintendent from enforcing certain regulations that the state alleged were beyond the authority conferred by statute and interfered with the sovereign rights of the state). For more discussion of this case, see Tara Leigh Grove, *When Can a State Sue the United States?*, 101 CORNELL L. REV. 851, 866 (2016). *See also* Oregon v. Mitchell, 400 U.S. 112, 117 (1970) (allowing the state to sue the United States Attorney General to challenge federal legislation providing for eighteen-year olds to vote in state elections, arguing that the legislation took away powers reserved for the states).

[117] *See* Gov't of Manitoba v. Bernhardt, 923 F.3d 173, 180–81 (D.C. Cir. 2019) (reasoning that some federal statutes had special provisions allowing for *parens patriae*-type causes of action by states, but the APA did not); Woolhandler, *supra* note 24, at 219 ("For example, the Transportation Act of 1920 provided that the Interstate Commerce Commission (ICC) could order changes in intrastate rates that were set by state agencies if the ICC found that such rates discriminated against interstate commerce. The ICC was required to notify affected states, which could then participate in the proceedings...." (footnotes omitted)).

[118] *See* Woolhandler, *supra* note 24, at 218–21 (discussing state challenges of administrative action and scholarship as to them).

[119] Alfred L. Snapp & Son v. Puerto Rico, 458 U.S. 592, 601 (1981).

[120] *See* Bickel, *supra* note 38, at 88 (indicating that state standing should be unavailable when a state asserts "nothing more than her interest in the execution of her own laws rather

Rather, states could litigate their interests in making and enforcing law primarily through traditional enforcement actions in their own courts, with Supreme Court review a possibility. In addition, individual state enforcement officials could be named as defendants in *Ex parte Young*-type[121] suits to enjoin enforcement of state law, in which case they could defend the state law they were charged with enforcing.

The create-and-enforce rubric appeared as dicta in several cases. In *Alfred I. Snapp & Son v. Puerto Rico*, a case relying on *parens patriae* standing, the Court identified a state's sovereign interest (as distinguished from a *parens patriae* or quasi-sovereign interest) in the power "to create and enforce a legal code."[122] And in *Diamond v. Charles* the Court quoted the *Snapp* language in explaining why a private doctor could not appeal a decision invalidating certain abortion restrictions that the state itself had declined to appeal.[123]

The phrase, however, was not mere dicta in *Maine v. Taylor*, where it helped to expand standing. The federal government had prosecuted Taylor for violation of a federal statute criminalizing the importation into a state of wildlife—in this instance, live baitfish—in violation of state law.[124] The federal prosecutor declined to seek Supreme Court review of the First Circuit's decision that Maine's ban on importation of live baitfish violated the Commerce Clause. When Maine sought review in the Supreme Court, the United States plausibly argued that because the federal government had the sole power to prosecute federal crimes, only it was allowed to seek Supreme Court review.[125] The Supreme Court, however, held that Maine could seek United States Supreme Court review, stating that "a State clearly has a legitimate interest in the continued enforceability of its own statutes," citing *Snapp* and *Diamond*.[126]

---

than those of Congress, and her interest in having Congress enact only constitutional laws for application to her citizens. A state is said to have no standing in such circumstances, not because the interests asserted are unreal or inadequately particular to the state, but because by hypothesis they should not ... suffice to invoke judicial action.").

[121] 209 U.S. 123 (1908).

[122] 458 U.S. at 601.

[123] 476 U.S. 54, 65 (1986).

[124] 477 U.S. 131, 132 (1986).

[125] *Id.* at 136.

[126] *Id.* The Court said, *inter alia*, that the state's prior intervention gave it full party status. The Court relied on the language of 28 U.S.C. § 2403, authorizing state attorneys general to intervene with full rights as a party in cases in which the constitutionality of state law was at issue, and the language of the then-current version § 1254(2) allowing appeal as of right by a

Courts and scholars have generally approved the create-and-enforce-laws basis for state standing.[127] For example, Professor Grove has argued that states should be able to assert this special standing when "federal statutes or regulations ... preempt or otherwise undermine the continued enforceability of state law."[128]

The favorable reception may be questionable, however, in light of the ease with which states may allege that federal law trenches on state regulatory authority. Lower courts have been amenable to finding some aspect of state law and federal regulation out of sync, thus impairing the state's interests in making and enforcing its laws. For example, Texas could challenge the Deferred Action for Childhood Arrivals (DACA) program because of its interference with the "sovereign interest in 'the power to create and enforce a legal code.' DACA is a program for alien classification, and it relates to preemption."[129] Federal guidance as to the treatment of gay and transgender employees in the wake of *Bostock v. Clayton County*[130] conflicted with state law, said a district court: "Defendants argue Plaintiff 'does not point to any actual employment policies or practices of the TDA [Texas Department of Agriculture] regarding transgender persons.' ... But the TDA does have such policies, even if Defendants consider them 'unwritten and contingent.'"[131] And in another case, a federal district court held

---

party in some cases. *Id.* at 134 n.2 (authorizing an appeal as of right to the Supreme Court "by a party relying on a State statute held by a court of appeals to be invalid as repugnant to the Constitution, treaties or laws of the United States"); *cf.* Tara Leigh Grove, *Standing Outside of Article III*, 162 U. Pa. L. Rev. 1311, 1330–31 (2014) (stating that while states may defend laws they are not enforcing—as under § 2403—that does not mean Congress can defend federal laws).

[127] *See, e.g.*, Berger v. N.C. Conf. of the NAACP, 597 U.S. 179 (2022) (holding that the state legislature should have been allowed to intervene to defend state laws and noting the state's interest in the continuing enforceability of its laws); *id.* at 206 (Sotomayor, J., dissenting) (agreeing that the state had an interest in the continued enforceability of its laws); *cf.* Woolhandler, *supra* note 24, at 220–21 (citing authority favoring state challenges when agencies preempt their law).

[128] Grove, *supra* note 116, at 857. Professor Grove would, however, disallow state standing "to challenge federal agencies' implementation of federal law." *Id.* at 873.

[129] *See, e.g.*, Texas v. United States, 50 F.4th 498, 517 (5th Cir. 2022); *see also* Louisiana v. Becerra, 629 F. Supp. 3d 777, 487 (W.D. La. 2022) (finding a conflict with state law in the federal Head Start vaccine requirements, which did not involve state employees, because Louisiana law apparently had more lenient opt-out provisions).

[130] 140 S. Ct. 1731 (2020). *Bostock* held that discrimination based on sexual orientation is sex discrimination under Title VII, 42 U.S.C. § 2000e-2(a)(1).

[131] Texas v. EEOC, No. 2:21-CV-194, 2022 U.S. Dist. LEXIS 129163, at *27 (N.D. Tex. May 26, 2022) (characterizing preemption as involving quasi-sovereign interests), *followed by*

states could challenge alleged federal government coercion of private media company speech as contrary to state law:

> Defendants argue that the Complaint points to no federal law that interferes with the States' ability to regulate behavior or provide for the administration of a state program. However, both Louisiana and Missouri have adopted fundamental policies favoring the freedom of speech. *See* Mo. Const. art. I, § 8 *and* La. Const. Ann. art. I, § 7.[132]

The interest in making and enforcing a legal code has been used as well to allow states to challenge guidance documents rather than awaiting rules or actual applications of a new policy.[133] Courts reason that even if nonbinding, the guidance may "pressure" the states to change their laws[134]—inflicting an immediate harm.[135]

---

633 F. Supp. 3d 824 (W.D. Tex. 2022) (granting and denying summary judgment motions on the merits).

[132] Missouri v. Biden, 662 F. Supp. 3d 626, 653 (W.D. La. 2023). For subsequent proceedings, see *supra* note 109.

[133] Texas v. EEOC, 933 F.3d 433, 446–47 (5th Cir. 2019) (holding that Texas could challenge EEOC guidance as to arrest records of employment applicants, and stating, "'[B]eing pressured to change state law constitutes an injury' because 'states have a sovereign interest in the power to create and enforce a legal code.'" (citation omitted)); Tennessee v. U.S. Dep't of Educ., 615 F. Supp. 3d 807, 821–22 (E.D. Tenn. 2022) (allowing immediate challenge to guidance as to discrimination against gay and transgender persons due to, *inter alia*, immediate pressure to change law).

[134] The challenges are aided by the notion of special solicitude for the states and reduced requirements for causation and redressability as to procedural injuries. *See, e.g.*, Texas v. United States, 50 F.4th 498, 514 (5th Cir. 2022) (discussing reduced causation and redressability requirements in a DACA challenge, particularly if the state asserts quasi-sovereign interests and a procedural injury); California v. Azar, 911 F.3d 558, 570–71 (9th Cir. 2018) (treating the lack of notice-and-comment rulemaking as a procedural injury that relaxed traceability and redressability requirements and affirming a grant of a preliminary injunction but limiting it to the plaintiff states); *cf. id.* at 569 (holding the case was not moot despite the fact that a notice-and-comment rule would be effective in one month); *see generally* Samuel L. Bray, *All Is Not Well with the Preliminary Injunction* (unpublished draft) (on file with authors) (arguing that courts too easily grant preliminary injunctions based on overemphasizing likelihood of success on the merits).

[135] The lightening of finality requirements for individuals has also aided states. *Cf.* U.S. Army Corps of Eng'rs v. Hawkes Co., 578 U.S. 590 (2016). For example, the Fifth Circuit allowed an immediate challenge to EEOC guidance restricting the use of arrest records in hiring, despite the fact that the EEOC could not bring court actions against states and had no substantive rulemaking authority as to the matters at issue. *Texas v. EEOC*, 933 F.3d at 444. The court treated the fact that federal agency officials would be bound by the guidance in evaluating claims as providing the legal consequences for finality. *Id.* at 443, 445. The rush to early decisions is all the more questionable given that states do not generally encounter hard choice problems of the magnitude of those faced by individuals—which led the Court to lighten finality and ripeness requirements in cases such as *Hawkes*. *See Hawkes*, 578 U.S. at 597–600 (discussing the burdens of seeking a permit or facing large daily fines).

The Courts should retire as a basis for standing the state's interest in creating and enforcing law. The states can exercise their undoubted interests in making and enforcing law by making and enforcing law.[136] More generally, the Court should reduce the role of sovereignty interests as a basis for party status in federal courts. The states exercise their power to govern by governing, not by bringing actions as plaintiffs in the federal courts. Of course, traditional cases such as for interstate boundary disputes should continue to be allowed.[137] So, too, states should have standing under statutes prescribing their participation in decisions as to specific allocations of regulatory power between the federal and state governments, as under certain FCC procedures for "jurisdictional separation."[138] But the Administrative Procedure Act itself should not be seen as providing an authorization for state claims based on the ubiquitous phenomenon of some difference between federal regulations and state law.[139] Nor should equity actions under the general federal-questions statute, 28 U.S.C. § 1331, regularly allow state sovereign interests to provide the basis for suit.[140]

V. State Legislative Standing to Defend State Law

While the focus of this Article thus far has been on states' suing as plaintiffs, the expansion of standing based on sovereignty interests has also reinforced greater allowance of state legislatures' appearing as parties in federal courts. Legislatures traditionally did not appear as federal court parties,[141] and with good reason. It is the role of the executive, not the legislature, to enforce and defend the law. This is partly reflected in the Constitution's prohibitions on bills of attainder and ex post facto laws, which apply to state legislatures as well as

---

[136] *See*. Franchise Tax Bd. v Const. Laborers' Vacation Tr., 463 U.S. 1, 20–21 (1983) (reasoning that states could not use declaratory judgment actions to test their statutes, given their ability to use enforcement actions); *see also* Woolhandler & Collins, *supra* note 21, at 420–21 (discussing state vindication of their sovereignty interests by enforcement suits and by officers' defenses of trespass suits).

[137] *See supra* note 33.

[138] *See* Woolhandler, *supra* note 24, at 219–20.

[139] *Cf.* Gov't of Manitoba v. Bernhardt, 923 F.3d 173, 180–81 (D.C. Cir. 2019) (reasoning that the APA did not provide a general authorization for *parens patriae* suits).

[140] *See* Woolhandler, *supra* note 24, at 212, 232, 234–36.

[141] *See* Tara Leigh Grove & Neal Devins, *Congress's (Limited) Power to Represent Itself in Court*, 99 Cornell L. Rev. 571, 593 (2014) (stating that Congress did not historically claim the power to appear as a party in courts).

Congress.¹⁴² Legislatures, however, have increasingly gained a foothold as parties in federal court, as manifested in the Court's decision in *Berger v. North Carolina Conference of the NAACP*.¹⁴³

In *Berger*, the plaintiffs sought to enjoin the use of state photo identification requirements for voting,¹⁴⁴ and state executive officials were defending the state's laws. The Speaker of the House and President *pro tempore* of the Senate sought to intervene, under a North Carolina statute authorizing them "'to intervene on behalf of the General Assembly as a party in any judicial proceeding challenging a North Carolina statute or provision of the North Carolina Constitution.'"¹⁴⁵ Federal Rule of Civil Procedure 24(a) requires an intervenor of right to show "an interest relating to ... the transaction that is the subject of the action" that may be practically impaired by the action "unless existing parties adequately represent that interest." The Fourth Circuit en banc denied intervention, saying that the legislature faced a "heightened presumption" that executive official representation was adequate.¹⁴⁶

The Supreme Court granted review of the denial of intervention to the legislature, and reversed the Fourth Circuit.¹⁴⁷ States, the Court said, have an interest in the continued enforceability of their own laws.¹⁴⁸ Although enforcement officials are usually the proper defendants in

---

[142] U.S. CONST. art. I, § 9, cl. 3; U.S. CONST. art. I § 10, cl. 1. *See* John Hart Ely, Note, *The Bounds of Legislative Specification: A Suggested Approach to the Bill of Attainder Clause*, 72 YALE L.J. 330, 343 (1962) ("A given policy can, in theory, be effectuated only be a combination of legislative enactment, judicial application, and executive implementation.... The section proscribing bills of attainder ... establishes that there are certain types of decision that are in varying degrees inappropriate for *legislative* resolution." (emphasis in original)); *id.* at 343–48 (citing authority that the attainder and ex post facto clauses were rooted in fears of legislatures' assuming executive and judicial authority). The Note particularly emphasizes legislatures' assuming judicial authority. *See id.* at 346. *See generally id.* at 331, 365–66 n.195 (discussing the similar origins of the ex post facto prohibition, and differences between the prohibitions).

[143] 597 U.S. 179 (2022). Additional examples can be found in Lumen N. Mulligan, *Self-Intervention*, 94 U. COLO. L. REV. 987, 994–96 (2023).

[144] 597 U.S. at 188. The requirements were in the state constitution and implementing legislation that was passed over the governor's veto.

[145] *See id.* at 180 (quoting N.C. GEN. STAT. ANN. § 1-72.2(b) (2017)). The Court further noted that state law provided that "both the General Assembly and the Governor constitute the State of North Carolina." N.C. GEN. STAT. ANN. § 1-72.2(a) (2017). Another provision cited by the Court was entitled "General Assembly Acting on Behalf of the State of North Carolina in Certain Actions" and stated "the General Assembly shall be deemed to be the State of North Carolina to the extent provided in G.S. 1-72.2(a) unless waived pursuant to this subsection." *See Berger*, 597 U.S. at 193.

[146] *See id.* at 195 (citing *Berger*, 999 F.3d 915, 927, 932–34 (4th Cir. 2021)).

[147] *Id.* at 200.

[148] *Id.* at 184 (citing Maine v. Taylor, 477 U.S. 131, 136 (1986)).

cases challenging state law, states are not bound by federal separation of powers principles, and "[w]ithin wide constitutional bounds, States are free to structure themselves as they wish."[149] The legislature and the executive may have different views, and the state may designate different officials to reflect those views.[150] "Appropriate respect for these realities suggests that a State's interests will be practically impaired or impeded if its duly authorized representatives are excluded from participating in federal litigation challenging state law."[151]

Justice Sotomayor dissented from allowing the legislature to intervene,[152] and some scholars have agreed with her views. A *Harvard Law Review* Note argued that the Fourth Circuit had properly applied a presumption of adequate representation by the state attorney general.[153] Professor Lumen Mulligan argued that *Berger* contravenes Rule 24 by incorrectly allowing an existing party to intervene in its own case.[154] In addition, Professors Grove and Devins have persuasively argued against congressional standing,[155] although they do not attack state legislative standing.[156]

This Part builds on these critiques and particularly addresses state legislative standing. It focuses less on Rule 24 intervention and more

---

[149] *Id.* at 183–84; *see also id.* at 191 (stating that states may "choose[] to allocate authority among different officials"); Cameron v. EMW Women's Surgical Ctr., 595 U.S. 267, 279 n.5 (2022) (indicating that the lack of an enforcement role with respect to the abortion statute at issue did not stop the state attorney general's intervention and noting state law allowing the AG's defense of a statute if other state officials were not defending it); *id.* at 1011 ("Respect for state sovereignty must also take into account the authority of a State to structure its executive branch in a way that empowers multiple officials to defend its sovereign interests in federal court."); Brianne Gorod, *Defending Executive Nondefense and the Principal-Agent Problem*, 106 Nw. U. L. Rev. 1201, 1222 (2012) (arguing that government should be allowed to speak in multiple voices, given the multiplicity of views as to constitutionality of a statute).

[150] *Berger*, 597 U.S. at 183–86.

[151] *Id.* at 191; *see generally* Ahdout & Fahey, *supra* note 67 (recommending that the federal courts show greater respect for state institutional allocations where those allocations intersect with federal law).

[152] *Id.* at 200–14.

[153] *See* Note, *Civil Procedure-Intervention-Federal Rule of Civil Procedure 24(a)*—Berger v. North Carolina State Conference of the NAACP, 136 Harv. L. Rev. 390, 397–98 (2022) (arguing for a presumption of adequate representation by state executive officials).

[154] Mulligan, *supra* note 143, at 998, 1001–12 (arguing that the Court's requiring intervention was improper, because Rule 24(a)(2) does not allow intervention by an existing party); *id.* at 1012–16 (arguing that the state is the real party in interest when the attorney general appears as a party).

[155] Grove & Devins, *supra* note 141; Grove, *supra* note 126, at 1364–65.

[156] *See* Grove, *supra* note 126, at 1330–31.

on state legislatures' not being proper parties to defend state law in federal courts.[157]

A. OVERVIEW OF ALLOWANCE OF LEGISLATURE STANDING

The critical appearance of legislatures as parties occurred in *Coleman v. Miller*.[158] In *Coleman*, the Court entertained direct review at the instance of twenty Kansas state senators whose vote against the child-labor amendment had been on the losing side when the lieutenant governor cast a vote of approval for the amendment. Chief Justice Hughes's opinion stated, "We think that these senators have a plain, direct and adequate interest in maintaining the effectiveness of their votes."[159]

Justice Frankfurter's separate opinion, joined by three other Justices, took issue with recognizing standing of state legislators. Legislators' role in making law gave them no more interest than private parties in defending state legislation.[160] And while states could determine who could sue in their own courts, they could not define the contours of the authority of the federal courts, including on direct review.[161]

---

[157] *See generally* Caleb Nelson, *Intervention*, 106 VA. L. REV. 271 (2020) (arguing that only those who are proper parties should be allowed to intervene under Rule 24); *see also* Note, *supra* note 153, at 395 (agreeing with Professor Nelson that intervenors should be proper parties); *cf.* Aaron-Andrew P. Bruhl, *One Good Plaintiff Is Not Enough*, 67 DUKE L.J 481, 481 (2017) (arguing that all parties should have to have standing). The discussion in this article is directed to legislatures' defense of general state laws rather than particular legislative prerogatives; *infra* note 171 and accompanying text.

[158] 307 U.S. 433 (1939).

[159] *Id.* at 438. For the difficulties in discerning the lineup of Justices in *Coleman*, see Raines v. Byrd, 521 U.S. 811, 822 n.5 (1997); *cf.* John Harrison, *Legislative Power, Executive Duty, and Legislative Lawsuits*, 31 J.L. & POL. 103, 110, 130 (2015) (characterizing *Coleman* as a case involving "the production of authoritative records of the law-making process, not execution of the law in the usual sense").

[160] 307 U.S. at 467.

[161] *Id.* at 462; *see also* Barnes v. Kline, 759 F.2d 21, 48 (D.C. Cir. 1985) (Bork, J., dissenting) (objecting to allowing Members of the House of Representatives to contest the President's attempted use of the pocket veto). Among Judge Bork's parade of horribles was that "all states would have standing to challenge any action by any branch of the federal government even though nothing more concrete than disagreement about constitutional powers was at stake." *Id.* at 48; *see also id.* at 47 ("States, after all, have constitutional functions and powers as surely as Congress does."); Ariz. State Legislature v. Ariz. Indep. Redistricting Comm'n, 576 U.S. 787, 854 (2015) (Scalia, J., dissenting) ("Disputes between governmental branches or departments regarding the allocation of political power do not in my view constitute 'cases' or 'controversies' committed to our resolution by Art. III, § 2, of the Constitution.").

Coleman opened the way for greater standing for both state and federal legislatures—which followed somewhat parallel paths. The Court generally has disallowed party status for individual legislators, state or federal, although they may file amicus briefs.[162] Thus, in *Raines v. Byrd*, the Court did not permit individual members of Congress to challenge the Line Item Veto Act, despite the Act's authorizing challenges by any member of Congress.[163] And in *Karcher v. May*[164] and *Virginia House of Delegates v. Bethune-Hill*,[165] the Court refused to recognize standing of individual state legislators to defend the constitutionality of state law.

When the legislature acted with broader institutional authorization to defend a statute, however, the Court has been more receptive to legislative standing. Where both Houses of Congress authorized intervention by resolutions, the Court allowed the House and Senate as intervenors to defend the legislative veto in *Immigration and Naturalization Service v. Chadha*.[166] And it allowed the Bipartisan Legal Advisory Group of the House (BLAG) to present a defense of DOMA in *United States v. Windsor*.[167] In both cases, the executive withheld relief from the private plaintiffs, although agreeing with the plaintiffs' position.[168] The Court in both cases thus found a live controversy between the government and the plaintiffs apart from the legislative parties, although at points seeming to treat them as full-fledged parties.[169]

Similarly to the result in *Chadha*, the Court has permitted state legislatures to defend certain claimed legislative prerogatives.[170] This

---

[162] *See infra* note 187.

[163] 521 U.S. 811, 815 (1997).

[164] 484 U.S. 72, 78 (1987).

[165] 139 S. Ct. 1945, 1953 (2019).

[166] 462 U.S. 919, 930 n.5, 939 (1982).

[167] 570 U.S. 744, 754 (2013).

[168] *Chadha*, 462 U.S. at 930 (indicating that the INS had appealed and remained a proper party because the Court of Appeals decision restrained it from deporting Chadha and the INS continued to withhold relief); United States v. Windsor, 570 U.S. 744, 753, 758, 761 (2013) (indicating that U.S. had sought certiorari and had not given the plaintiff the tax refund); *see* Grove & Devins, *supra* note 141, at 629 ("Notably, the Supreme Court did not conclude that the intervention of the House and Senate counsel was necessary to establish Article III jurisdiction in *Chadha*.").

[169] *See, e.g., Chadha*, 462 U.S. at 939 (indicating that Congress was a proper party to defend under the applicable review statutes and provided adversariness); *Windsor*, 570 U.S. at 761 (indicating that BLAG provided adversariness).

[170] *See, e.g.*, Ariz. State Legislature v. Ariz. Indep. Redistricting Comm'n, 576 U.S. 787, 802, 803–04 (2015) (allowing the legislature to appear to claim that a referendum could not

Article, however, is particularly concerned with treating state legislatures as proper parties to defend more general state laws, as in *Berger v. North Carolina Conference of the NAACP*[171]—analogously to the allowance of congressional standing in *Windsor*.

In this context, one may point out possible distinctions among individual legislators, the legislature, and the state. Individual legislators generally do not have standing. The legislature itself, however, may have standing if properly authorized by the legislative body. In the latter case, one might characterize the legislature as representing itself or representing the state, or both.

In *Berger*, the intervening parties were authorized "to intervene on behalf of the General Assembly" although the Court also treated them as more or less representing the state.[172] The characterization as either the "legislature" or the "state" made little practical difference in the legislature's role in the litigation. The views forwarded were those of the legislative majority. The role was analogous to that of the House in *Windsor*, where the Court seemed to treat the House as representing itself.[173]

There are a number of reasons to question treating state legislatures as proper parties to defend state laws. They are not enforcement officials; they are not proper parties due to federalism and separation-of-powers concerns; state separation-of-powers designations of their institutions do not control characterizations for federal standing; and state legislative standing presents problems similar to allowing private parties to defend state laws on behalf of the states.

---

supersede the legislature's districting role); *cf.* Moore v. Harper, 600 U.S. 1 (2023) (referring to legislative defendants); Jonathan Remy Nash, *A Functional Theory of Congressional Standing*, 114 MICH. L. REV. 339, 373 (2015) (recommending standing where executive action substantially diminishes a House or Senate majority's bargaining power).

[171] 597 U.S. 179 (2022).

[172] *Id.* at 186. Saying that the legislature represents the state may reinforce that executive officers will be bound by the decree, at least if properly brought before the court. *See supra* note 145; *see also* Mulligan, *supra* note 143, at 1022–26 (stating that a different perspective is not a ground for allowing intervention by an existing party).

[173] *See* 570 U.S. at 754 (indicating that district court "denied BLAG's motion to enter the suit as of right, on the rationale that the United States already was represented by the Department of Justice. The District Court, however, did grant intervention by BLAG as an interested party."); *id.* at 760–62 (indicating that BLAG enhanced adversariness); *cf. id.* at 803–05 (Alito, J., dissenting) (reasoning that the legislature had suffered its own injury, despite arguing that the United States was not a proper petitioner in the case given its agreement with the decision below). Perhaps if the executive had accorded the plaintiff the tax refund, the case might not have proceeded at the instance of the House. *Cf. id.* at 757–58 (noting that the government was still withholding the tax refund).

B. ENFORCEMENT OFFICIALS ARE THE PROPER PARTIES TO DEFEND STATE LAW

The *Berger* Court identified the interest of the legislative intervenors as the state's "interest in the continued enforceability of its own laws."[174] The truism that the state and the state legislature have interests in the ongoing viability of state laws, however, is not the same as saying that either the state or the legislature is a proper party in a particular suit. The traditional means for the state's interest to confer party status was by way of enforcement actions in its own courts, with direct review in the United States Supreme Court as a possibility. In addition, enforcement objects could bring actions to enjoin trespasses and enforcement actions against enforcement officials.

To bring a prosecution, an executive official must be authorized to represent the state in enforcing or administering the law. An enforcement role was also required if the official were named as a defendant in an action seeking to enjoin trespasses and enforcement actions. To be a proper defendant the defendant needed to be someone who could provide the redress in the event of a favorable decree.[175]

The Court in *Haaland v. Brackeen* recently emphasized that proper defendants are those who can provide the ordered redress. In *Haaland*, the private plaintiffs challenged as violative of equal protection the Indian Child Welfare Act's provision of adoption preferences for Indian families, seeking injunctive and declaratory relief against federal

---

[174] 597 U.S. at 191.

[175] *See id.* (noting that normally a party could not sue the state but could sue an enforcement official); *cf.* Coleman v. Miller, 307 U.S. 433, 466 (1939) (Frankfurter, J., concurring) (indicating standing of state officials to seek direct review in the Supreme Court was tied to their enforcement role); Camreta v. Greene, 563 U.S. 692, 727 (2011) (Kennedy, J., dissenting) ("[T]he proper defendant in a suit for prospective relief is the party prepared to enforce the relevant legal rule against the plaintiff."); *id.* (indicating it would be inconsistent with Article III to allow a declaratory judgment action "against Congress in response to its enactment of an unconstitutional law"). There are cases, however, in which the state's attorney general may not have an enforcement role as to a particular state statute and nevertheless may defend it. *See* 28 U.S.C. § 2403(b) (providing that when a state law "affecting the public interest is drawn in question" in any "court of the United States," and neither the State nor any state agency or officer is a party, the court must notify the state attorney general, and the State must be allowed to intervene); *see also supra* note 126. But the attorney general is generally considered a default law enforcement official for the state, and generally exercises some authority over other state officials. *See* Howard W. Wasserman & Charles W. "Rocky" Rhodes, *Solving the Procedural Puzzles of the Texas Heartbeat Act and Its Imitators: The Limits and Opportunities of Offensive Litigation*, 71 AM. U. L. REV. 1029, 1060 (2022) (indicating that the attorney general was treated as the default enforcer in *Ex parte* Young, 209 U.S. 123 (1908)); Mulligan, *supra* note 143, at 1030 (stating that state attorneys general are typically vested with authority to represent state interests in litigation).

officials. The Court held that the plaintiffs had not shown that a decree would likely redress their injuries "because state courts apply the placement preferences, and state agencies carry out the court-ordered placements."[176]

Related to a defendant's ability to provide redress is the requirement that the Court needs to be able to enter a binding decree.[177] Where enforcement or administering officials are defendants, their attempts at continued enforcement or administration of state law, after an adverse decree, would be subject to contempt sanctions. Such sanctions are not obviously available against the legislature. Rather, if a court determines that a statute is unconstitutional, a state legislature may reenact a similar statute to manifest its disagreement or to retest the holding.[178] Legislation is a form of legislative speech that the judiciary cannot suppress.[179] The courts can only exercise their restraining power to prevent enforcement.[180]

---

[176] Haaland v. Brackeen, 599 U.S. 255, 261 (2023). In the cases of legislative intervention, however, presumably there would be some binding effect on state enforcement officials.

[177] *See* Caleb Nelson, *Sovereign Immunity as a Doctrine of Personal Jurisdiction*, 115 HARV. L. REV. 1559 (2002); Bruhl, *supra* note 157, at 517 (2017) (arguing against the courts' often taking the standing of one plaintiff as sufficient, and reasoning that a judgment is specific to the parties before the court, and establishing their rights and duties); *id.* at 531 (noting problems with, *inter alia*, the scope of preclusion where some parties lack standing). At least where other proper parties are present, the Court sometimes ignores problems of proper party status for intervenors. *See, e.g.*, Trbovich v. United Mine Workers, 404 U.S. 528 (1972). Caleb Nelson has persuasively argued that intervenors should have to be proper parties. *See* Nelson, *supra* note 157; *cf.* Bruhl, *supra* note 143, at 481 (arguing that all parties should have standing).

[178] *See* New Orleans Water Works Co. v. New Orleans, 164 U.S. 471, 475 (1896) (refusing to issue an injunction against the city's continuing to pass ordinances allowing rival water works, in contravention of prior Supreme Court decisions enjoining particular rival waterworks). The Court treated the city as exercising delegated state legislative power in passing ordinances and said "a court of equity cannot properly interfere with, or in advance restrain, the discretion of a municipal body while it is in the exercise of powers that are legislative in their character." *Id.* at 481; *see also* JAMES L. HIGH, 2 THE LAW OF INJUNCTIONS § 1243 (4th ed. 1902) ("[I]t is unquestionably true that purely legislative acts such as passage of resolutions, or the adoption of ordinances by a municipal body, will not be enjoined ...."); New York v. United States, 505 U.S. 144, 177 (1992) (indicating that Congress exceeded its powers and trenched on reserved state powers by requiring the state to legislate or take title to certain toxic waste).

[179] *See* Ann Woolhandler, *Patterns of Official Immunity and Accountability*, 37 CASE W. RSRV. L. REV. 396, 407 (1987).

[180] *See* HIGH, *supra* note 178, § 1243 ("And while courts of equity will not enjoin municipal bodies from the passage of ordinances or resolutions, yet after the passage of such ordinances or resolutions the courts may and will ... prevent their enforcement ...."); *cf.* 52 U.S.C. § 10304 (providing for preclearance before changes in voting requirements can go into effect).

Perhaps one could argue that the legislature is representing and binding the "State" rather than itself.[181] Any coercive enforcement, however, would presumably occur through individual enforcement officers who could be subject to sanctions—reinforcing that it is the executive and not the legislature that is the appropriate party to defend state laws in federal courts.[182]

C. LEGISLATURES ARE NOT PROPER PARTIES DUE TO FEDERALISM AND SEPARATION-OF-POWERS CONCERNS

The reasons legislatures are not proper parties in part derive from federalism and separation of powers.[183] As noted above, it is questionable that a federal court could forbid legislatures from passing new legislation that may seek to evade or retest a prior court decision. As a matter of separation of powers and due process, moreover, few would argue that legislatures should engage in individualized enforcement actions—a norm reinforced by the prohibitions on state legislatures' enactment of ex post facto laws and bills of attainder.[184]

---

[181] The *Berger* Court did not apparently treat legislative intervention as waiving either legislative or sovereign immunities. Berger v. N.C. State Conf. of the NAACP, 597 U.S. 179, 194 (2022) (rejecting the NAACP's argument that the legislative leaders were seeking to represent an existing party—that is, the state—because the state could not be sued as a matter of sovereign immunity). An agreement by the legislature to abide by a possible future court decree commanding legislation on pain of monetary contempt sanctions against the State would be both unlikely and of questionable validity. *See* New York v. United States, 505 U.S. at 180–83 (indicating that the state would not be deemed to have consented to legislate or assume ownership of toxic waste and certain other liabilities with respect to such waste). *But cf.* Spallone v. United States. 493 U.S. 265 (1990) (indicating approval of contempt sanctions against a city for failure to pass ordinances that the city had, in a consent decree, agreed to pass). State prison-conditions suits demonstrate problems with seeking to compel state-level legislative action. *See* DOUGLAS LAYCOCK & RICHARD L. HASEN, MODERN AMERICAN REMEDIES 340–44 (5th ed. 2019) (discussing prison-reform litigation).

[182] *See* Baude & Bray, *supra* note 1, at 182 (stating that courts "may enjoin the enforcement of a statute or rule, but properly speaking the injunction runs against those who would enforce the statute or rule"). Enforcement officials would need to be individually brought before the court before being subject to contempt sanctions.

[183] *Cf.* Mulligan, *supra* note 143, at 1028–34 (arguing that legislative intervention violates state separation of powers and that state courts would not approve the legislature's giving itself an executive role).

[184] *But cf.* CARL B. SWISHER, V HISTORY OF THE SUPREME COURT OF THE UNITED STATES; THE TANEY PERIOD 1836–64, at 538 (1974) (describing state legislatures' involvement in *Prigg v. Pennsylvania*, 41 U.S. (16 Pet.) 539 (1842), to facilitate Supreme Court review of the Pennsylvania kidnapping law). Legislatures also had a role in authorizing suits in the United States Supreme Court's original jurisdiction. *See, e.g.*, Rhode Island v. Massachusetts, 37 U.S. (12 Pet.) 657, 716 (1838) (indicating that the legislature had approved the governor's appointing counsel; Pennsylvania v. Wheeling & Belmont Bridge Co., 54 U.S. (13 How.)

Some commentators have argued that legislative defense of a statute is less harmful than enforcing it;[185] certainly, a legislature's attempting to bring enforcement actions against individuals appears more prone to arbitrariness than its arguing to uphold a statute at a more general level. But Professors Grove and Devins have convincingly argued in the context of congressional standing that defending the law is an aspect of enforcement.[186] Party status, they say, "gives Congress the power to decide which cases (and which appeals) to pursue and thus the discretion to decide against which parties the law will be enforced."[187] Professor Grove notes, for example, that Congress's intervention interfered with Mr. Chadha's individual liberty in avoiding deportation.[188]

Even if questions remain as to how far Congress can give itself an executive role,[189] the Court seems to say that it is allowable for state legislatures to give themselves the executive powers involved in defending state law. The *Berger* decision reasoned that States are not subject to the same separation of powers strictures as the federal

---

518, 560 (1852) (indicating that the attorney general had filed the suit and that the legislature later passed a resolution approving pursuit of the action).

[185] *See, e.g.*, Gorod, *supra* note 149, at 1219–20 (arguing that enforcement requires the executive "to make [a] determination[] of how the law should be implemented" while defense "generally will not affect [the law's] operation at all"); *id.* at 1228 (indicating that the executive's interests differ from Congress's); *see also* Harrison, *supra* note 159, at 117, 126 (distinguishing a legislature's interest in the validity of a law as opposed to the legislature's interest in the executive's compliance and implementation); Amanda Frost, *Congress in Court*, 59 UCLA L. Rev. 914, 919 (2012) (emphasizing Congress's interests in different interpretive methodologies as a reason for allowing Congress to appear as a party).

[186] Grove & Devins, *supra* note 141, at 583, 626–27; Grove, *supra* note 126, at 1364–65 (stating that congressional standing allows it to determine not only which laws to defend but which to appeal, and may involve an unpopular opposing party); *cf. id.* at 574 (arguing that Congress lacks power to implement federal law which belongs to the executive under the Take Care Clause); *id.* at 604 (indicating that bicameralism and presentment are also violated); Neal Devins & Saikrishna B. Prakash, *The Indefensible Duty to Defend*, 112 Colum. L. Rev. 507, 513 & n.17 (2012) ("The duty to defend is typically seen as a subset of a broader duty to enforce the law.").

[187] Grove & Devins, *supra* note 141, at 626–27. Party status also gives the legislature more say in how the law should be interpreted. Grove and Devins distinguish amicus status, and they note some history of congressional amici. *See* Grove & Devins, *supra* note 141, at 586–87, 592. They also note that such briefs do not involve enforcement discretion. *Id.* at 626–27.

[188] Grove, *supra* note 126, at 1351 (noting that the interference with liberty can be substantial, as in *Chadha*); *cf.* Maine v. Taylor, 477 U.S. 131, 132 (1986) (concerning a state's successful appeal of the holding that its statute violated the Commerce Clause would lead to reinstatement of Taylor's guilty plea). On the other hand, the plaintiffs in anticipatory suits have identified themselves as potential enforcement defendants.

[189] *See* Grove, *supra* note 126, at 1330–31 (distinguishing state legislatures from Congress).

government, and proper respect for federalism means the federal courts should defer to such allocations.[190]

D. STATE SEPARATION-OF-POWERS CHARACTERIZATIONS DO NOT CONTROL FEDERAL STANDING

Standing in the federal courts, however, has ultimately remained a matter of federal law.[191] The federal courts' constitutional and statutory role is implicated in standing questions—whether states seek to narrow or widen federal standing. Thus, the federal courts have often refused to defer to state allocations of governmental power in the adjudicative context—*Berger*'s language of deference notwithstanding.

Some of the cases in which the federal courts did not defer involved states' attempts to insulate decisions of state governmental bodies from federal jurisdiction or more searching federal judicial review.[192] The Court repeatedly rejected states' characterizations as controlling the officials' status as federal court defendants. For example, in *Ex parte Young*,[193] the attorney general of Minnesota argued that he effectively was the state and therefore immune from suit—a plausible argument given that the suit against him was based on his role in bringing enforcement actions on behalf of the state in the state courts. But these arguments did not stop the Court's finding that the attorney general could be sued in the federal courts as an individual when threatening enforcement of an allegedly unconstitutional law.

The Court also rejected attempts by state administrators, such as railroad commissioners, to claim that they were entitled to be treated as immune legislators, rather than as executive officers who could be sued as individuals for their enforcement roles.[194] And the federal courts refused to honor state characterizations of their administrative tribunals as state "courts," which might have insulated the administrative decisions from review in the lower federal courts.[195]

---

[190] *See* Berger v. N.C. State Conf. of the NAACP, 597 U.S. 179, 191 (2022).

[191] *See* Coleman v. Miller, 307 U.S. 433, 462 (Frankfurter, J., dissenting); *cf.* Mulligan, *supra* note 143, at 999 (stating that federal law controls intervention in federal court).

[192] *See* Ann Woolhandler, *State Separation of Powers and the Federal Courts*, 31 Wm. & Mary Bill of Rts. J. 633, 634–35 (2023).

[193] 209 U.S. 123 (1908).

[194] Woolhandler, *supra* note 192, at 637–44.

[195] *Id.* at 644–48.

State characterizations could control in state courts, but not in federal courts.[196]

The Court has not only resisted state characterizations that would have limited federal judicial review, but also state attempts to increase federal jurisdiction and push the boundaries of cases and controversies.[197] In instances where states attempted to sue as plaintiffs in the Court's original jurisdiction, the Court historically generally limited state standing to common law interests, and rejected sovereignty and *parens patriae* claims.[198] So, too, the Supreme Court on direct review held that state officials did not, by virtue of their role in administering certain laws, become proper parties to seek review on behalf of their constituents to claim that a state law violated the Constitution, even when the state courts treated those officials as proper parties to raise the federal claims.[199]

Thus, it is no anomaly for federal courts to follow their own lights when characterizing state institutions for purposes of standing in the federal courts. While state characterizations may play an important role, the federal courts may ignore states' characterizations that depart from the federal courts' own views of governmental institutions in their relationships to the federal courts.[200]

E. PROBLEMS SIMILAR TO PRIVATE-PARTY STANDING TO DEFEND STATE LAW

The federal courts, moreover, have not deferred to state determinations that private parties could shoulder the defense of state law after state official defendants declined to seek further review.[201] Thus,

---

[196] *See, e.g., In re* Summers, 325 U.S. 561, 565 (1945) (characterizing state proceedings against an attorney as nonjudicial).

[197] *But cf.* ASARCO v. Kadish, 490 U.S. 605 (1989) (holding that defendants who were injured by a state court decree in a case in which the original plaintiffs would have lacked standing in a federal court could obtain review in the Supreme Court).

[198] *See supra* notes 31–35 and accompanying text.

[199] See *supra* notes 84–90 and accompanying text; Smith v. Indiana, 191 U.S. 138, 148–49 (1903) (holding that an assessor lacked sufficient personal interest to raise an equal protection claim on behalf of taxpayers).

[200] *See* Mulligan, *supra* note 143, at 1035 (arguing that the federal courts should apply a uniform law of intervention and may ignore unique state approaches that would give multiple representatives for the same state party).

[201] *See, e.g.,* Diamond v. Charles, 476 U.S. 54, 64 (1986) (denying standing to appeal a decision setting aside legislation restricting abortion and noting that "a private citizen lacks a judicially cognizable interest in the prosecution or nonprosecution of another" (citation omitted)).

in *Hollingsworth v. Perry*,[202] the Court held that state initiative proponents lacked standing to defend an opposite-sex-only marriage provision, despite the California supreme court's saying that initiative proponents had standing to defend the law.[203] The United States Supreme Court noted that the proponents' role was only in enacting, not enforcing the measure[204]—a problem shared with state legislatures.[205]

It may here be objected that the private parties are different from public parties—a distinction the Court itself noted in *Hollingsworth*.[206] Private parties can "pursue a purely ideological commitment" without "cognizance of resource constraints, changes in public opinion, or potential ramifications for other state priorities."[207] In effect, they lack the constraints that give rise to a considered prosecutorial discretion.[208]

But legislatures present analogous risks. True, they are elected and serve as agents of the public, thus differing from private parties. But their legislative role entails serving as more or less unfiltered conduits for political preferences, rather than exercising a more considered

---

[202] 570 U.S. 693 (2013). *But see* Ahdout & Fahey, *supra* note 67, at 51 (criticizing *Hollingsworth* for imposing a cost on state structural innovation by removing a tool for defending the state initiative in court).

[203] *Id.* at 703 (discussing certification from the Ninth Circuit); *see also* Perry v. Broan, 52 Cal. 4th 1116, 1127 (2011); *cf.* Arizonans for Off. Eng. v. Arizona, 520 U.S. 42, 65–66 (1996) (expressing doubts as to whether initiative proponents had standing to defend the measure they had sponsored); *id.* at 67 (holding the case moot because the individual plaintiff who challenged the constitutional provision had left the employ of the state).

[204] 570 U.S. at 707.

[205] As Justice Frankfurter said in *Coleman*, "The fact that these legislators are part of the ratifying mechanism while the ordinary citizen of Kansas is not, is wholly irrelevant" to the legislators' ability to bring suit. Coleman v. Miller, 307 U.S. 433, 464 (1939) (Frankfurter, J., concurring) (disagreeing with main opinion as to legislative standing); *cf.* Va. House of Delegates v. Bethune-Hill, 139 S. Ct. 1945, 1953 (2019) (in denying standing to individual legislators, stating, "This Court has never held that a judicial decision invalidating a state law as unconstitutional inflicts a discrete, cognizable injury on each organ of government that participated in the law's passage."). *But cf. id.* at 1951, 1953 (distinguishing instances where the legislature acted collectively).

[206] *See also Arizonans for Off. Eng.*, 520 U.S. at 65 (in expressing doubts as to initiative proponents' standing, distinguishing state legislators).

[207] *Hollingsworth*, 570 U.S. at 714; *cf.* Laufer v. Acheson Hotels, LLC, 50 F.4th 259 (1st Cir. 2022), *vacated as moot*, 601 U.S. 1 (2023) (presenting issue of private testers' enforcement role). This case is discussed in Rachel Bayefsky, *Public Law Litigation at the Crossroads*, 99 N.Y.U. L. Rev. Online (forthcoming 2024), Virginia Public Law & Legal Theory Paper No, 2023-64, at *20, https://ssrn.com/abstract=4565291 ("[I]t is doubtful that courts could operationalize the idea of Article II enforcement discretion to identify the kind of public-law litigation that warrants skepticism.").

[208] Woolhandler, *supra* note 192, at 656–57 (and authorities cited). This is not to suggest that executive officials always exercise a more considered discretion.

discretion. Resource constraints play little role given their ability to appropriate funds. That legislators will not personally be bound by a decree may further loosen constraints on them.

Justice Gorsuch in *Berger*, however, treated the legislature's lack of ordinary prosecutorial constraints as entailing different interests from the executive—thus making the legislature all the more appropriate as an intervenor of right. "They are not burdened by misgivings about the law's wisdom. If allowed to intervene, the legislative leaders say, they will focus on defending the law vigorously on the merits without an eye to crosscutting administrative concerns."[209] But the executive's potential filtering of the legislature's raw politics provides a reason to keep the legislature from giving itself executive power to appear in court.

Nor should it make a difference if one says that the legislature is not representing itself but the state. In either event, the legislature takes on an executive role. Consider whether a legislature's setting up its own legislator-led prosecutorial office would be any more acceptable if the office is said to represent "The State" as opposed to "The Legislature."[210]

F. CONCERNS AS TO EVASION OF REVIEW

Concerns have arisen that a lower federal court's holding that a state law violates the Constitution will be allowed to stand due to lack of an executive official who pursues Supreme Court review.[211] As an initial matter, state attorneys general generally do and should defend state statutes.[212] But if they sometimes do not, the problem may not be as bad as it seems,[213] even if one assumes the Supreme Court in

---

[209] 597 U.S. at 198. *Cf.* Mulligan, *supra* note 143, at 1022 ("A textualist approach to Rule 24 (a)(2) cannot accommodate a focus upon 'perspective' as part of an intervention as of right analysis.").

[210] Taking on the prosecutorial function would seem to run contrary to the prohibition on bills of attainder. *See supra* note 142. Even if the legislature did not commit to itself the final determination of guilt, its involvement in prosecution involves the application of the criminal law to fact as to individuals.

[211] *See* Grove & Devins, *supra* note 141, at 573 n.9 (citing authority).

[212] *See* Meltzer, *supra* note 158, at 1235 (recommending that the Department of Justice should normally enforce and defend federal statutes even if there is no absolute rule that it do so); Devins & Prakash, *supra* note 186, at 573 (although arguing against a duty to defend, anticipating that the executive would normally enforce and defend congressional statutes).

[213] *See* Devins & Prakash, *supra* note 186, at 520 (arguing that the executive has no duty to set up a case for determination of whether a law is constitutional).

some cases would reverse the lower court and uphold the state legislation at issue. Prior to 1914, states were not allowed to seek direct review when state courts held their laws unconstitutional under the federal Constitution. And in cases such as *Karcher v. May* and *Bethune-Hill*, the Supreme Court—based on individual legislators' lack of standing—forewent review of federal court decisions holding state legislation unconstitutional. State legislatures may renew contests when they deem the time propitious by passing substitute legislation.[214] And one should not forget the passive virtues. As Professor Bickel said, doctrines such as standing may help the Court avoid lending legitimacy to ill-intentioned but constitutional statutes.[215]

G. DOES IT MATTER?

One may think allowing the North Carolina legislature to intervene in *Berger* makes little difference. But as shown in the state-as-plaintiff cases, recognition of standing in governmental institutions tends toward increase.[216] The growth of legislative standing will further erode the principle that the legitimacy of federal courts' pronouncing on the legality of government action derives from the necessity of deciding cases and controversies.[217]

---

[214] Frost, *supra* note 185, at 921 (in arguing in favor of allowing congressional standing, noting that Congress can pass new laws but that can be difficult).

[215] BICKEL, *supra* note 38, at 174; *id.* at 30–31 ("Not only is the Supreme Court capable of generating consent for hotly controverted legislative or executive measures; it has the subtler power of adding a certain impetus to measures that the majority enacts rather tentatively."); *id.* at 129 (declaring a statute constitutional "may entrench and solidify measures that may have been tentative in the conception or that are on the verge of abandonment in the execution"); *id.* at 131 ("Today's declaration of constitutionality will not only tip today's political balance but may add impetus to the next generation's choice of one policy over another.").

[216] *Cf.* Nelson, *supra* note 157.

[217] Judge Bork elaborated on the problem of treating the exercise of governmental power as a general basis for standing:

> The first problem with this court's doctrine of congressional standing is that, on the terms of its own rationale, the concept is uncontrollable. Congress is not alone in having governmental powers created or contemplated by the Constitution. This means that the vindication-of-constitutional-powers rationale must confer standing upon the President and the judiciary to sue other branches just as much as it does upon Congress. "Congressional standing" is merely a subset of "governmental standing." This rationale would also confer standing upon states or their legislators, executives, or judges to sue various branches of the federal government. Indeed, no reason appears why the power or duty being vindicated must derive from the Constitution. One would think a legal interest created by statute or regulation

Conclusion

Political polarization and the degraded tenor of popular and academic discourse are putting pressure on the Supreme Court's legitimacy.[218] Thus, this is an especially inopportune time for the Court to appear to be willing to depart from its traditional judicial functions.

To be sure, it is understandable that the Court opted to reach to find standing for the state plaintiffs in *Biden v. Nebraska*. The administration's use of the HEROES Act to implement its loan forgiveness program appeared to be a clear case of overreach by the executive branch that trenched on one of Congress's core powers: its control of the public purse.[219] What is more, plausible accusations were levied that the loan forgiveness plan was designed to elude judicial review.[220] And no other plausible plaintiff had come forward: MOHELA remained on the sidelines, and the claims of injury advanced by the individual plaintiffs were highly attenuated.[221]

To a significant degree, the Court is the architect of its own predicament. The expansive, nebulous concept of state standing articulated in *Massachusetts v EPA* and other leading precedents invited state attorneys general to push the envelope.[222] It is no surprise that state actors, including politically ambitious state attorneys general, have been swift to respond to the incentives created by the Court's state standing doctrine. But what the Court did, it can undo, building on its decisions this past Term in *United States v. Texas* and *Haaland v.*

---

would suffice to confer standing upon an agency or official who thought that interest had been invaded.

Barnes v. Kline, 759 F.2d 21, 44 (D.C. Cir. 1985) (Bork, J., dissenting) (disapproving of allowing members of Congress to contest the President's attempted use of the pocket veto).

[218] *Cf.* Richard H. Fallon, Jr., Law and Legitimacy in the Supreme Court 174 (2018) ("[T]he foundations of constitutional legitimacy, and of legal and moral legitimacy in constitutional adjudication by the Supreme Court, are easily misunderstood" and "should not be idealized, nor taken for granted.").

[219] *See* Biden v. Nebraska, 143 S. Ct. 2355, 2375 (2023) (characterizing "control of the purse" as "[a]mong Congress's most important authorities").

[220] *See supra* note 58 and accompanying text.

[221] *See supra* notes 58–63 and accompanying text.

[222] *See* Seth Davis, *The New Public Standing*, 71 Stan. L. Rev. 1229, 1232 (2019) (arguing that the Court's decision in *Massachusetts v. EPA* "all but announced state governments as the new public interest litigants").

Brackeen. It is within the Court's power to get the federal courts and other components of government back in their respective lanes, thereby promoting more effective government and reducing perceptions the Court is willing to allow the federal courts to be turned into a political battleground.

ARMAND DERFNER

CAN OUR DEMOCRACY SURVIVE THIS SUPREME COURT?

Introduction

When the Supreme Court dispatched *Roe v. Wade* in June 2022, the opinions doing so were replete with the message that it was time to return the abortion debate "to the people and their elected representatives."[1] That phrase is presumably intended to convey a partnership—a unity of purpose between "the people" and "their elected representatives"—but that is often wishful thinking, and the Supreme Court is busy making it more so.

Of course, responsible representation does not mean just following constituents' preferences. Still, a gap between the people and their elected representatives has been increasingly widened by state voting

---

Armand Derfner is the Distinguished Scholar in Constitutional Law at the Charleston School of Law.

Author's note: I am grateful to Justin Driver for fruitful exchanges of ideas at various stages of this Article. I appreciate the assistance I have received from Gabriel Mangold, Charleston School of Law, Class of 2024, and Kedar Veeraswamy, Williams College, Class of 2024.

I have had the good fortune over many years to work with and learn from outstanding lawyers, scholars, and ordinary citizens in the great enterprise of securing and protecting the right to vote—for everyone. This Article is dedicated to the memory of those who are no longer here.

[1] Dobbs v. Jackson Women's Health Org., 597 U.S. 215, 259, 292, 302 (2022) (op. of Alito, J.); *id.* at 347 (Kavanaugh, J., concurring).

and election laws. This has been abetted by the Supreme Court, which, in the time of Chief Justice Roberts, has repeatedly sided with the "elected representatives" against "the people." In the process, voters' protections we thought were safely housed in the Constitution and the laws of Congress have been wiped away.

It is a political-science truism that electorates are "political artifacts" that can be constructed, within limits, "to a size and composition deemed desirable by those in power."[2] "In other words, although voters theoretically choose their representatives, in real life it often seems like the representatives are choosing their voters." If so, the cases discussed in this Article have freed state legislators to become more aggressive in picking and choosing their voters.

That the Roberts Court has made voters unwelcome is widely acknowledged by friends and critics alike. One supporter of the Court's approach calls it "a 20-year string of Supreme Court cases emphasizing that the political process, not the federal courts, remains the principal place to advance most election law issues."[3] But if the problem is the political process itself, isn't the Court telling the voters to make bricks without straw? And if the voters can't do that, and the courts won't help, aren't the voters on their way to becoming mere ornaments?

The Roberts Court has now been in charge of the right to vote for nearly two decades, long enough to shrink the right drastically, but short enough to make us wonder how it could happen so fast. Like it or not, the cases discussed here are the measure of our democracy today.

This Article is divided into several parts. Part I reminds us that it wasn't always this way. This Part chronicles the vibrant period in the middle of the last century when the Supreme Court led the way in creating a robust federal right to vote—a right that, despite some serious intervening backward steps, was still largely intact when the Roberts Court began.

Part II, the heart of this Article, surveys the major voting cases of the Roberts Court over these past two decades, ranging from the blockbuster cases (concerning the Voting Rights Act, campaign finance,

---

[2] Stanley Kelley, Richard Ayres & William G. Bowen, *Registration and Voting: Putting First Things First*, 61 AM. POL. SCI. REV. 359, 375 (1967).

[3] Derek T. Muller, Brnovich v. DNC: *Election Litigation Migrates from Federal Courts to the Political Process*, 2021 CATO SUP. CT. REV. 217.

and gerrymandering) to the lower-profile but important decisions upholding state voter-suppression laws and rebuffing minority voters' claims of race discrimination. This is not just a collection of separate cases, but a stockade of decisions representing virtually the entirety of the right to vote today. Some of this discussion calls out the Court's too-often distressing workmanship, which includes inventing doctrine, doctoring quotations, reading words out of federal statutes, manipulating rules of evidence and appellate procedure, and more.

Part III examines whether the distance between the people and their elected representatives matters to our system of government. Surveying the aftermath of the Supreme Court's 2022 abortion decision, this Part looks at how state abortion laws have been affected by divergent choices of state legislatures and referendum voters.

The Conclusion worries that the Supreme Court may not just be making bad law but threatening our unexpectedly fragile democracy.

I. Recognizing a Right to Vote

It wasn't always like this, and it was worse before it got better.

When I started law school in 1960, my Constitutional Law casebook contained no subject headings or index entries about voting or elections, and almost no cases.[4] That was hardly surprising, since at that time American citizens' only right to vote was mostly limited to what the states chose to provide.[5] The federal Constitution and laws created essentially no right to vote except for the landmark Nineteenth Amendment (women's suffrage), a few laws against stealing congressional elections, and the Fifteenth Amendment's useless ban on race discrimination in voting—"useless" because Supreme Court decisions had turned it into a bulwark for, not against, Jim Crow disfranchisement.[6]

Yet, in a few short years between the late 1950s and the early 1970s, the three branches of our national government swiftly and steadily

---

[4] *See* Paul Freund et al., Constitutional Law: Cases and Other Problems (1960).

[5] Minor v. Happersett, 88 U.S. 162 (1875) (holding that states can deny women the right to vote and that the right to vote is not an attribute of citizenship); Pope v. Williams, 193 U.S. 621 (1904) (holding that state voting rules are essentially beyond federal scrutiny). The Supreme Court also upheld the poll tax in *Breedlove v. Suttles*, 302 U.S. 277 (1937), and the literacy test in *Lassiter v. Northampton Cnty. Bd. of Elections*, 360 U.S. 45 (1959).

[6] Orville Vernon Burton & Armand Derfner, Justice Deferred: Race and the Supreme Court 87–88, 95–96, 100–03 (2021).

fashioned a comprehensive federal right to vote—with both constitutional and statutory dimensions and with protections both for voters in general and for minority voters in particular. The new rights were enshrined in a half-dozen congressional statutes,[7] three constitutional amendments,[8] and a long string of Supreme Court decisions.[9]

Predictably, the road began with race. In 1957 and 1960, Congress enacted the first federal civil rights laws in nearly a century, which authorized Department of Justice suits against intransigent voting registrars. When state tactics stymied the first suits, three Supreme Court decisions in early 1960 swiftly swept the barriers aside, including overruling a pernicious nineteenth-century precedent that stood in the way.[10]

Later in 1960, the Supreme Court also began breaking new ground in constitutional protection for African American voters. As racial segregation came under increased attack in the 1950s, Jim Crow lawmakers manufactured new devices to maintain lily-white elections, devices that appeared impregnable at the time, even if they seem almost comical in retrospect. Alabama changed the town boundaries of Tuskegee from a traditional square into "an uncouth, 28-sided figure" and thus removed all but four of the town's 400 Black residents (potential voters if they were ever allowed to register).[11] Louisiana mandated that ballots contain each candidate's race, to guarantee that, if African Americans had to be allowed to vote and run for office, at least White voters would know who *not* to vote for.[12]

---

[7] Civil Rights Act of 1957, Pub. L. No. 85-315, 71 Stat. 634; Civil Rights Act of 1960, Pub. L. No. 86-449, 74 Stat. 86; Civil Rights Act of 1964 (Title I), Pub. L. No. 88-352, 78 Stat. 241; Voting Rights Act of 1965, Pub. L. No. 89-110, 79 Stat. 437, *as amended by* Voting Rights Act Amendments of 1970, Pub. L. No. 91-285, 84 Stat. 314. There were further amendments to the Voting Rights Act in 1975 and 1982. Act of Aug. 6, 1975, Pub. L. No. 94-73, 89 Stat. 400; Act of June 29, 1982, Pub. L. No. 97-205, 96 Stat. 134.

[8] U.S. CONST. amends. XXIII (extending the right to vote for President to residents of Washington, D.C.); XXIV (prohibiting poll taxes in federal elections); XXVI (barring age discrimination in voting and lowering the voting age to eighteen).

[9] *See infra* notes 10–24 (collecting cases). Many of the cases are also collected in Armand Derfner, *Racial Discrimination and the Right to Vote*, 26 VAND. L. Rev. 523, 545–83 (1973).

[10] United States v. Raines, 362 U.S. 17 (1960); United States v. Thomas, 361 U.S. 950 (1960); United States v. Thomas, 362 U.S. 58 (1960); United States v. Alabama, 362 U.S. 602 (1960). *Raines* overruled *United States v. Reese*, 92 U.S. 214 (1876).

[11] Gomillion v. Lightfoot, 364 U.S. 339, 340 (1960).

[12] Anderson v. Martin, 375 U.S. 399 (1964).

Before the 1960s, the Supreme Court had never held any scheme to disfranchise Black voters unconstitutional, except for the notorious "grandfather clause"[13] and "white-only primary."[14] But by then, times and the Court had changed. The Alabama law was struck down under the Fifteenth Amendment in *Gomillion v. Lightfoot*,[15] and the Louisiana law under the Fourteenth Amendment in *Anderson v. Martin*.[16]

The Supreme Court's rejection of Tuskegee's "gerrymandered" town boundaries in *Gomillion* led to a revolutionary new doctrine. That came in *Baker v. Carr*, which held that voters, without regard to race, could challenge malapportioned (mathematically unequal) election districts under the Fourteenth Amendment's Equal Protection Clause—the Court's first case recognizing a voting discrimination claim *not* based on race.[17] Within two years, the Court advanced to adopting the rule of one person, one vote.[18]

Having applied the Equal Protection Clause to a nonracial voting issue, the Court took a giant step with the Clause in another case not involving race, *Carrington v. Rash*.[19] There, the Court held that the Equal Protection Clause was violated by a Texas law treating on-base military personnel as nonresidents ineligible to vote. That was the first Supreme Court decision ever to strike down a state voter-eligibility law that did not involve race. It was soon followed by cases striking down other categorical eligibility requirements, like poll taxes, property ownership, and taxpayer status.[20] Some of these cases described the right to vote as "fundamental" and said restrictions were invalid unless supported by a "compelling state interest."[21]

---

[13] Guinn v. United States, 238 U.S. 347 (1915); Myers v. Anderson, 238 U.S. 368 (1915); Lane v. Wilson, 307 U.S. 268 (1939).

[14] Nixon v. Herndon, 273 U.S. 536 (1927); Nixon v. Condon, 286 U.S. 7 (1932); Smith v. Allwright, 321 U.S. 649 (1944); Terry v. Adams, 345 U.S. 461 (1953). In one other case, the Supreme Court summarily affirmed, without opinion, a three-judge court decision striking down an Alabama provision as intentional discrimination against African American registrants. Schnell v. Davis, 336 U.S. 933 (1949).

[15] 364 U.S. 339, 340 (1960) (describing the new town boundary's shape as "uncouth").

[16] 375 U.S. 399 (1964).

[17] 369 U.S. 186 (1962).

[18] Reynolds v. Sims, 377 U.S. 533 (1964).

[19] 380 U.S. 89 (1965).

[20] *See* Harper v. Va. State Bd. of Elections, 383 U.S. 663 (1966); Kramer v. Union Free Sch. Dist., 395 U.S. 621 (1969).

[21] *See* Williams v. Rhodes, 393 U.S. 23 (1968).

Meanwhile, Congress was moving again. A voting protection measure was included as Title I of the landmark Civil Rights Act of 1964, but it was soon overtaken by dramatic events in Selma, Alabama, which led to the Voting Rights Act of 1965.[22] That Act, using an objective formula, identified states with the grossest records of persistent disfranchisement (which unsurprisingly turned out to be the former Confederate states). In those states, the Act suspended all literacy tests and, in a procedure called "preclearance," blocked discriminatory changes in voting rules. The Supreme Court quickly affirmed Congress's far-reaching work, holding the Act constitutional in *South Carolina v. Katzenbach*,[23] and then giving the broadest interpretation to the Act's suspension of literacy tests[24] and its blocking of discriminatory new voting changes.[25] The Court said its broad interpretations were necessary to further Congress's "laudable goal" of making "the guarantees of the Fifteenth Amendment finally a reality for all citizens."[26]

In those years, Congress and the states also joined in constitutional amendments expanding the right to vote. The Twenty-Third Amendment afforded Washington, D.C., residents the vote in presidential elections. The Twenty-Fourth Amendment ended the poll tax in federal elections (shortly before the Supreme Court ended the poll tax in all elections). And the Twenty-Sixth Amendment gave eighteen-year-olds the vote in all elections. When Virginia tried to skirt the Twenty-Fourth Amendment by adopting a transparent poll-tax substitute, the Supreme Court quickly shut it down in *Harman v. Forssenius*.[27]

The momentum continued for a time after the end of the Warren Court in 1969. In 1972, the Supreme Court took a major step which built on Congress's enactment in 1970 of a maximum thirty-day residence and registration period for presidential elections. In *Dunn v. Blumstein*, the Court struck down Tennessee's one-year residence rule (and, by implication, early registration deadlines), saying that any restriction exceeding the registrar's processing needs (typically

---

[22] Civil Rights Act of 1964 (Title I), Pub. L. No. 88-352, 78 Stat. 241; Voting Rights Act of 1965, Pub. L. No. 89-110, 79 Stat. 437.

[23] South Carolina v. Katzenbach, 383 U.S. 301 (1966).

[24] Gaston Cnty. v. United States, 395 U.S. 285 (1969).

[25] Allen v. State Bd. of Elections, 393 U.S. 544 (1969).

[26] *Id.* at 556.

[27] 380 U.S. 528 (1965).

thirty days) violated the "fundamental" right to vote protected by the Equal Protection Clause.[28] This ruling affected state laws throughout the Nation.[29]

It was only ten years from *Baker v. Carr* to *Dunn v. Blumstein*, and in that short time, a powerful federal right to vote, unrelated to race, had been fashioned. In the same period, the race-based right to vote—always recognized in theory since ratification of the Fifteenth Amendment in 1870—had been fleshed out in detail in both constitutional and statutory dimensions.

As it turned out, *Dunn v. Blumstein* marked the end of rapid growth for the right to vote. President Nixon's third and fourth Supreme Court justices, Lewis F. Powell and William H. Rehnquist, had been appointed but had not yet started sitting when *Dunn* was argued, so they did not participate in the decision. Their arrival spelled the beginning of the real Nixon-Burger Court and largely, though not entirely, stalled the federal right to vote.

Under Chief Justices Burger and Rehnquist, the next three decades saw mixed results in defining the federal right to vote. The Supreme Court weakened the right to vote under the Equal Protection Clause and the Fifteenth Amendment by requiring proof of discriminatory purpose[30] and weakened the Voting Rights Act by limiting the preclearance requirement to only those voting changes that made discrimination worse.[31]

Around the same time, the Supreme Court broke new ground by applying the First Amendment to voting in two ways. In *Buckley v. Valeo*,[32] the Court held that spending money in political campaigns is a form of speech protected by the First Amendment. And in *Anderson*

---

[28] 405 U.S. 330, 336 (1972) ("By denying some citizens the right to vote, [durational residence] laws deprive them of 'a fundamental political right.'" (quoting Reynolds v. Sims, 377 U.S. 533, 562 (1964))).

[29] ALEXANDER KEYSSAR, THE RIGHT TO VOTE 276–77 (2000).

[30] City of Mobile v. Bolden, 446 U.S. 55 (1980). The Court mitigated that requirement somewhat by emphasizing that discriminatory purpose could be proved by circumstantial evidence. *See* Village of Arlington Heights v. Metro. Hous. Dev. Corp., 429 U.S. 252 (1977).

[31] The Court limited its new rule to changes that had a discriminatory effect. Beer v. United States, 425 U.S. 130 (1976). A later ruling weakened the Act further by applying this "non-retrogression rule" to changes with a discriminatory purpose. Reno v. Bossier Parish Sch. Bd., 528 U.S. 320 (2000).

[32] 424 U.S. 1 (1976).

v. *Celebrezze*,[33] it held that the voter's right to vote is protected (albeit subject to regulation) by the free-speech and free-association guarantees of the First Amendment and, as to the states, the Fourteenth Amendment.

During the same period, Congress stepped in with major laws to strengthen the right to vote. In a 1982 amendment to Section 2 of the Voting Rights Act, Congress prohibited voting rules that have a discriminatory *result* even without proof of discriminatory purpose.[34] This was designed to fill the gap created by the Supreme Court's new discriminatory *purpose* rule for Equal Protection Clause cases. Then, in 1993, Congress moved to spur registration and voting by enacting the National Voter Registration Act, which directed states to make voter registration available at motor vehicle offices.[35]

In the last decade of the twentieth century, the Supreme Court saw the change that would alter history for the Court and the Nation: Justice Thurgood Marshall retired and was succeeded by Justice Clarence Thomas. It changed a middle-of-the-road Court into one with five solidly conservative justices.

The new majority's work included major voting decisions. In a series of cases, it held that White voters could challenge redistricting plans under the Equal Protection Clause and that a districting plan was void if drawn along racial lines but valid if politics was predominant.[36] It undermined the Voting Rights Act with a ruling that voting changes, even if motivated by racial animus, were immune from the Act's coverage unless they were more discriminatory than the rules they replaced.[37] The most momentous decision of the new

---

[33] 460 U.S. 780 (1983).

[34] Act of June 29, 1982, Pub. L. No. 97-205, 96 Stat. 131. The "results" test was in Section 2, originally 42 U.S.C. § 1973, now 52 U.S.C. § 10301. The 1982 amendments also added and amended other provisions of the Voting Rights Act. Other Voting Rights Act amendments outlawed literacy tests nationwide and created protections for language minority voters as well as racial minority voters.

[35] Act of May 20, 1993, Pub. L. No. 103-31, 107 Stat. 77.

[36] Shaw v. Reno, 509 U.S. 630 (1993); Miller v. Johnson, 515 U.S. 900 (1995).

[37] Reno v. Bossier Parish Sch. Bd., 528 U.S. 320 (2000). The decision, flatly contrary to the statutory language, was written by Justice Scalia, whose proclaimed textualist preference was apparently overcome here by his antipathy to the Voting Rights Act. He also said the decision was necessary for consistency with *Beer v. United States*, 425 U.S. 130 (1976), but that case specifically said its rule should not apply to constitutional violations—which the *Bossier Parish* case did involve since it was about discriminatory purpose.

5-4 Court was of course *Bush v. Gore*, which elected George W. Bush President by stopping the Florida recount.[38]

That was the state of the federal right to vote when Chief Justice John G. Roberts, Jr. joined the Supreme Court in 2005. His arrival maintained the a 5-4 majority of justices who take a narrow view of the federal right to vote. That majority has retained control and become even more conservative, with a dramatic sea change in late 2020. That was when very liberal Justice Ginsburg died and was succeeded by very conservative Justice Barrett. The five-member majority is now a six-member supermajority, with no better prospects for the right to vote.[39]

The course of the right to vote in the years since Chief Justice Roberts's arrival in 2005 is the subject of the next Part of this Article.

II. THE ROBERTS COURT'S RETREAT

The federal right to vote created in the mid-twentieth century was a structure formed of both constitutional and statutory protections for both voters in general and minority voters in particular. Decisions of the Roberts Court since 2005 have taken aim at every part of that structure, and are discussed below under four headings: Voting Rights Act, First Amendment, Fourteenth Amendment, and National Voter Registration Act.

A. VOTING RIGHTS ACT

1. *Section 5*. In 2007, barely a year after the arrival of Chief Justice Roberts, a 5-4 majority blocked two school districts' modest efforts at racial integration, famously saying "the way to stop discrimination on the basis of race is to stop discriminating on the basis of race."[40] Not long afterward, these Justices showed that their concern was limited to discrimination against White people when they struck down the Nation's most potent law protecting minority voters, the Voting

---

[38] 531 U.S. 98 (2000). Thinking about that decision raises the question: Who would have been elected President in 2004 and therefore in a position to nominate replacements for the two conservatives who left the Court in late 2005?

[39] Two other changes before 2020 were also significant. In 2006, Justice O'Connor was succeeded by the far more conservative Justice Alito, who has become a leader in turning back the clock on the right to vote. The year 2019 saw the arrival of Justice Kavanaugh, who seems thus far to be significantly more conservative than his predecessor, Justice Kennedy.

[40] Parents Involved in Cmty. Schs. v. Seattle Sch. Dist. No. 1, 551 U.S. 701, 748 (2007).

Rights Act.[41] It was the first civil rights law to be held unconstitutional in 130 years.[42]

No one who knew Chief Justice Roberts's history of opposition to the Act was surprised. In 1981 to 1982, Roberts was special assistant to Attorney General William French Smith, writing a stream of memoranda attacking the Voting Rights Act.[43] When Roberts became Chief Justice in September 2005, Congress, by coincidence, was beginning work on an extension of the Act. When President George W. Bush signed the bill in a Rose Garden ceremony on July 27, 2006,[44] a collision course was set.

By that time, the longtime workhorse of the Act was Section 5, the preclearance mechanism. Applying only in the states with the worst records of voting discrimination,[45] "preclearance" meant that any new voting law or rule in those "covered" states was blocked, unless the state showed that the new law was not discriminatory. Over the years, the preclearance rule had blocked more than a thousand voting changes, large and small, each one the equivalent of a court injunction.[46] Many other discriminatory changes were not even attempted. As one

---

[41] Shelby Cnty. v. Holder, 570 U.S. 529 (2013) (holding Section 4(b) of the Act unconstitutional).

[42] Sections 1 and 2 of the Civil Rights Act of 1875 were held unconstitutional in the *Civil Rights Cases*, 109 U.S. 3 (1883). Later cases included some negative constitutional rulings but none actually holding a civil rights law unconstitutional.

[43] Memorandum from John Roberts, Special Assistant to the Att'y Gen., to the Att'y Gen., Voting Rights Act: Section 2 (Dec. 22, 1981), https://www.archives.gov/files/news/john-roberts/accession-60-88-0498/030-black-binder1/folder030.pdf; Memorandum from John Roberts, Special Assistant to the Att'y Gen., to the Att'y Gen., Talking Points for White House Meeting on Voting Rights Act, at 5 (Jan. 26, 1982) https://www.archives.gov/files/news/john-roberts/accession-60-88-0498/030-black-binder1/folder030.pdf (referencing Section 5 preclearance and racial quotas in particular); *see generally* Records Pertaining to John G. Roberts, Jr., NAT'L ARCHIVES, www.archives.gov/news/john-roberts/accession-60-89-0372; *see also* ARI BERMAN, GIVE US THE BALLOT: THE MODERN STRUGGLE FOR VOTING RIGHTS IN AMERICA 147–52 (2015).

[44] The legislative background of the 2006 extension is described in Justice Ginsburg's dissent in *Shelby County v. Holder*, 570 U.S. 529, 565–66 (2013) (Ginsburg, J., dissenting).

[45] The Act's preclearance requirement in Section 5, 42 U.S.C. § 1973c (1994), was geared to the Act's suspension of literacy tests, *id.* § 1973b, and applied in states and counties that (1) used a literacy test and (2) had less than 50% voter turnout in 1964. The principal covered areas were the states of Alabama, Georgia, Louisiana, Mississippi, North Carolina (in part), South Carolina, and Virginia. Later amendments added Texas, Arizona, and counties in some other states.

[46] For a list of Section 5 objections by the Attorney General since 1965, see generally *Section 5 Objection Letters*, U.S. DEP'T OF JUST. C.R. DIV., https://www.justice.gov/crt/section-5-objection-letters.

election supervisor stated, "When they call me with crackpot ideas, I just tell them we can never get that precleared."[47]

The Act's broad language allowed it to adapt to combat new modes of disfranchisement as time passed.[48] The covered states' main mode of disfranchisement as of 1965 had been to keep African Americans from registering to vote, chiefly by sham literacy tests.[49] The Act responded to that tactic by simply outlawing literacy tests in those states, which quickly produced a million new Black voters in three years.[50] In response, the states began shifting to other methods of maintaining White political control (e.g., gerrymandering, discriminatory changes in city boundaries, etc.), commonly called methods of "vote dilution." Congress had included Section 5 in the original Act to forestall new tactics yet unknown. Two early cases by the Warren Court and the Burger Court in 1969 and 1971 affirmed that gerrymandering and other vote-dilution tactics fell within Section 5's reach.[51]

Section 5 was temporary because preclearance was a stringent remedy, but Congress extended it several times in 1970, 1975, and 1982.[52] Each extension followed hearings that showed the remedy was still necessary—not surprising in a region where strict racial disfranchisement had been the rule for generations. Each extension was upheld by the Supreme Court.[53]

Enactment of the 2006 extension followed the same pattern, but there was a new Supreme Court in town.

---

[47] Conversation with Dan Martin, Supervisor, Charleston Cnty. (S.C.) Bd. of Voter Registration and Elections (June 25, 2013). The conversation took place on the Supreme Court's front steps immediately after that day's session in which the *Shelby County* decision was announced.

[48] Section 5 required the covered states to preclear any new "voting qualification or prerequisite to voting, or standard, practice or procedure with respect to voting." 42 U.S.C. § 1973c (1994). The Supreme Court said "Congress intended to reach any state enactment which altered the election law of a covered State in even a minor way." Allen v. State Bd. of Elections, 393 U.S. 544, 566 (1969).

[49] These states had no interest in literacy but simply wanted a device to give registrars power to pick and choose voters by race. "Understanding tests" and grandfather clauses allowed White voters to bypass literacy tests, and court records showed the tests were shams. *See* South Carolina v. Katzenbach, 383 U.S. 301, 310–13 (1966) and accompanying notes.

[50] U.S. COMM'N ON C.R., POLITICAL PARTICIPATION, 222–56 (1968).

[51] *Allen*, 393 U.S. 544; Perkins v. Matthews, 400 U.S. 379 (1971).

[52] *See supra* note 7.

[53] Oregon v. Mitchell, 400 U.S. 112 (1970); City of Rome v. United States, 446 U.S. 156 (1980); Lopez v. Monterey Cnty., 525 U.S. 266 (1999).

The law was quickly challenged, but that first suit was resolved in *Northwest Austin Municipal Utility District v. Holder*[54] on a statutory issue, without deciding the constitutionality of the Act. Embedded in the opinion by Chief Justice Roberts was one small paragraph, strangely unremarked, that was to spell doom for the Voting Rights Act.

That paragraph introduced a supposed constitutional doctrine which the Court called "equal sovereignty." Such a doctrine had been argued in the original Voting Rights Act case, *South Carolina v. Katzenbach*, but had been explicitly rejected by the Supreme Court in that case. Now, in *Northwest Austin*, Chief Justice Roberts's opinion resurrected the doctrine and quoted *selected words* from the *Katzenbach* opinion that made the earlier case seem as though it supported the "equal sovereignty" doctrine, while leaving out twenty-two crucial words that showed *South Carolina v. Katzenbach* held exactly the opposite.[55]

Printed here on the left is the paragraph as it appeared in *South Carolina v. Katzenbach*, and on the right as it was rendered in *Northwest Austin*:

Katzenbach	Northwest Austin
"The doctrine of the equality of States, invoked by South Carolina, does not bar this approach, for that doctrine applies only to the terms upon which States are admitted to the Union, and not to the remedies for *local* evils which have subsequently appeared."	"The doctrine of the equality of States, . . . , does not bar . . . remedies for *local* evils which have subsequently appeared."

Nor did the rest of the *Northwest Austin* opinion provide any support for "equal sovereignty." The crucial paragraph of the opinion did cite three cases, but each one stood only for the "equal footing" doctrine recognized in *Katzenbach*, not for *Northwest Austin*'s invention.[56] Based on this misrepresentation, the 2009 Court said "equal

---

[54] 557 U.S. 193 (2009).

[55] *Compare* South Carolina v. Katzenbach, 383 U.S. 301, 328–29 (1966), *with Nw. Austin*, 557 U.S at 203.

[56] *Nw. Austin*, 557 U.S. at 203 (citing United States v. Louisiana, 363 U.S. 1 (1960); Lessee of Pollard v. Hagan, 44 U.S. (3 How.) 212, 223 (1845); Texas v. White, 74 U.S. (7 Wall.) 700, 725–26 (1869)).

sovereignty of the states" is a "fundamental principle," and that the Voting Rights Act's different treatment of different states was a "departure" that must be justified.[57]

Four years later in *Shelby County, Alabama v. Holder*,[58] the *Northwest Austin* chickens came home to roost. *Shelby County* cited *Northwest Austin* more than twenty times, repeatedly wielding the words "equal sovereignty" with a vengeance. The grievous misquotation from *South Carolina v. Katzenbach* was not repeated, but its damaging work had been done. A 5-4 opinion by Chief Justice Roberts treated "equal sovereignty" as a settled constitutional principle, supported by no authority other than *Northwest Austin* with its misbegotten heritage.

The question before the Court should have been simply whether the Voting Rights Act was an exercise of Congress's express Fifteenth Amendment power to combat race discrimination in voting. Two hundred years of constitutional law going back to *McCulloch v. Maryland* make clear that the Supreme Court cannot question Congress's exercise of an express *power*—unless Congress violates a constitutional *prohibition*:

> But where the law is not prohibited, and is really calculated to effect any of the objects intrusted to the government, to undertake here to inquire into the degree of its necessity, would be to pass the line which circumscribes the judicial department, and to tread on legislative ground. This court disclaims all pretensions to such a power.[59]

By manufacturing its new doctrine, the Supreme Court changed the question from power to prohibition. This was no small matter because it reversed every principle of constitutional law by assuming the law was invalid unless Congress could justify it. It also made the Fifteenth Amendment essentially beside the point.[60]

Reaction to the newly minted "equal sovereignty" doctrine was fierce.[61] Michael McConnell, formerly a Tenth Circuit judge appointed by President George W. Bush, stated: "This is a nice idea; it

---

[57] *Id.* at 203.

[58] 570 U.S. 529 (2013). Technically, the decision did not hold the preclearance remedy of Section 5 unconstitutional, but by striking down the Section 4(b) formula for which states are subject to preclearance, the result is the same.

[59] 17 U.S. (4 Wheat.) 316, 423 (1819).

[60] The opinion nowhere said Congress had exceeded its Fifteenth Amendment power.

[61] *See, e.g.*, Thomas Colby, *In Defense of the Equal Sovereignty Principle*, 65 DUKE L.J. 1087, 1089 nn.4–9 (2016) (listing critics).

might be on my list of desirable constitutional amendments. But it is not in the Constitution we have now."[62] Judge Richard A. Posner, appointed to the Seventh Circuit by President Ronald Reagan, agreed: "This is a principle of constitutional law of which I had never heard—for the excellent reason that . . . there is no such principle."[63] If Posner's derision had not been sufficiently clear, he added, "It floats on air."[64] Even the few scholars who said the "equal sovereignty" doctrine had some foundation were emphatic in declaring that it must give way in the face of other mandates, especially a remedial one like the Fifteenth Amendment.[65]

That was not the end of the Court's mischief. Even under the Court's novel theory of "equal sovereignty," different treatment of different states could be justified by evidence of continuing problems in the covered states.

The majority opinion in *Shelby County*, though, stated that all the evidence received by Congress was simply irrelevant because the evidence before Congress in 2005–2006 related to state tactics like gerrymandering and other vote dilution methods, rather than the literacy tests and other outright disfranchisement devices which had been the basis of the Act's coverage formula in 1965. The majority opinion treated these different facets of vote discrimination as unrelated, so it said Congress could not respond to this continuing discrimination by continuing its Fifteenth Amendment remedy.[66]

This strange notion contradicted more than four decades of Supreme Court decisions applying the Voting Rights Act to vote-dilution tactics and upholding extensions of the Act supported by the same

---

[62] *Town Hall Debate: McConnell and Rosen on the Voting Rights Act*, YAHOO NEWS, (June 25, 2013), https://news.yahoo.com/town-hall-debate-mcconnell-rosen-voting-rights-act-184607340.html.

[63] Richard A. Posner, *The Supreme Court and the Voting Rights Act: Striking Down the Law Is All About Conservatives' Imagination*, SLATE (June 26, 2013), https://slate.com/news-and-politics/2013/06/the-supreme-court-and-the-voting-rights-act-striking-down-the-law-is-all-about-conservatives-imagination.html.

[64] *Id.*

[65] James Blacksher & Lani Guinier, *Free at Last: Rejecting Equal Sovereignty and Restoring the Right to Vote*, 8 HARV. L. & POL'Y REV. 39 (2014); *see* Colby, *supra* note 61, at 1167–70; Jeffrey Schmitt, *In Defense of* Shelby County's *Principle of Equal State Sovereignty*, 68 OKLA. L. REV. 262 (2016); Andrew Belia & Bradford Clark, *The International Origins of American Federalism*, 120 COLO. L. REV. 940 (2020).

[66] Shelby Cnty. v. Holder, 570 U.S. 529, 554 (2013).

congressional findings of continuing vote dilution. This view was blind to what discrimination is. The Court imagined that acts of discrimination are discrete, separate incidents, instead of the reality: Discrimination is a continuum, selecting "whatever works" and shifting to other modes when one mode is disallowed.

Shelby County found that "the Act imposes current burdens and must be justified by current needs."[67] Congress, filled with men and women whose political life depends on understanding current needs, concluded overwhelmingly that the law was still needed to assure compliance with the Fifteenth Amendment. That conclusion should have satisfied the Supreme Court.

In the end, the Court's decision rewarded state misconduct and showed a disdain for Congress by Justices who typically claim to have great respect for the legislative branch. That disdain was nowhere better expressed than by Justice Scalia's airy dismissal of the strong congressional votes: "Do you ever expect, do you really expect Congress to vote against a re-extension of the Voting Rights Act? Do you really think any incumbent would, would vote to do that?"[68]

2. *Section 2 "Results" Test.* When the Supreme Court ended Section 5 preclearance in *Shelby County*, it said "our decision in no way affects the permanent, nationwide ban on racial discrimination in voting found in § 2."[69] Hollowing out that statement took only five years to the day, from June 25, 2013, to June 25, 2018.

On that fifth anniversary of the *Shelby County* decision, the Supreme Court, in *Abbott v. Perez*,[70] reversed a lower court finding that Texas violated Section 2 in its congressional and legislative redistricting. *Abbott* was followed by a watershed case from Arizona, *Brnovich v. Democratic National Committee*, which seemed to spell the end of Section 2 as a meaningful protection for minority voters.[71]

Brnovich involved two Arizona state laws, one that disqualified votes cast in the wrong precinct, even for countywide or statewide offices,

---

[67] *Id.* at 536, 542, 550, 556.

[68] Transcript of Oral Argument at 51, Nw. Austin Mun. Util. Dist. No. One v. Holder, 557 U.S. 193 (2009) (No. 08-322).

[69] *Shelby Cnty.*, 570 U.S. at 557.

[70] 138 S. Ct. 2305, 2330–35 (2018). The major part of this case involved reversal of the lower court finding of intentional race discrimination in the districting plan.

[71] 141 S. Ct. 2321 (2021). Part of this case also involved reversal of the lower court finding of intentional race discrimination in passage of one of the Arizona laws.

and another law that limited the categories of people who could bring a voter's completed absentee ballot to the election office. A lower court held that both laws violated Section 2, but was reversed by the Supreme Court's new 6-3 lineup, including the new Justice Barrett.

The evidence of a discriminatory result was not overwhelming, so the outcome of the case was not surprising. Justice Alito's majority opinion, however, went far beyond the issues in the case and pronounced a near post-mortem on Section 2. Almost ignoring the words "discriminatory result" in Section 2, he emphasized the many voting options afforded to Arizona voters. "Arizona law generally makes it very easy to vote," was the second sentence of the opinion, and that theme, repeated several times, was essentially enough to support Arizona's laws under Section 2.[72]

The grim forecast for Section 2 seemed to be confirmed during the 2021–2022 Term as the Court reversed or stayed state and federal court rulings in three different circuits that had granted relief based on Section 2.[73] Thus, until the end of the 2022–2023 Term, Section 2 looked like a dead letter.

"Then a shocking thing happened."[74] In *Allen v. Milligan*, the Supreme Court astounded *every* observer (including me) by striking down Alabama's congressional redistricting plan under Section 2.[75] The challengers had won a preliminary injunction below,[76] but the Supreme Court had immediately stayed the injunction,[77] and then stayed another lower court's similar ruling involving Louisiana's congressional districts.[78] The Supreme Court's stays seemed in line with the Court's hostile construction of Section 2 just a year earlier in *Brnovich v. DNC*.[79]

---

[72] *Brnovich*, 141 S. Ct. at 2330; *see also id.* at 2333, 2244.

[73] Merrill v. Milligan, 142 S. Ct. 879 (2022); Wis. Legislature v. Wis. Election Comm'n, 595 U.S. 398 (2022); Ardoin v. Robinson, 142 S. Ct. 2892 (2022).

[74] That was the lead sentence in the report of a usually austere law review. Note, *The Supreme Court 2022 Term: Voting Rights Act of 1965*, 137 Harv. L. Rev. 480 (2023).

[75] Allen v. Milligan, 599 U.S. 1 (2023).

[76] Singleton v. Merrill, 582 F. Supp. 3d 924 (N.D. Ala. 2022).

[77] *Merrill*, 142 S. Ct. 879.

[78] *Ardoin*, 142 S. Ct. 2892.

[79] 141 S. Ct. 2321 (2021).

But in *Allen v. Milligan*, Chief Justice Roberts wrote the majority opinion and was joined by Justice Kavanaugh to supply the deciding votes in a 5-4 decision invalidating Alabama's plan and giving Section 2 new life.[80] In other times, the decision would not have been a surprise. It was a close copy of the nearly forty-year-old precedent of *Thornburg v. Gingles*,[81] which interpreted the Section 2 amendment soon after its passage. *Gingles* invalidated a legislative redistricting in North Carolina and paved the way for many lower-court cases in later years that also found Section 2 violations.

Four dissenting Justices were also shocked because they thought the more recent cases had disposed of *Gingles*. Justice Alito's dissent said *Gingles* was no longer a correct interpretation of Section 2, that the correct interpretation was his opinion in *Brnovich*, and under that interpretation, Alabama had not violated Section 2.

Alabama was also in disbelief, so on remand, the state legislature drew a new plan not much different from its rejected plan. When the lower court rejected the new plan, Alabama asked the Supreme Court for a stay, which was promptly denied.[82] That finally cleared the way for a special master's plan, with a significant Black population in two districts, which will be used in the 2024 elections.[83]

What explains a decision so unexpected? To be sure, the decision represented a sound view of the law (as laid out in *Gingles*, though not *Brnovich*). But could other factors have played a part, consciously or not? The Supreme Court may not "follow[] th' iliction returns" (to quote Mr. Dooley, the fictional barkeeper-philosopher created a century ago by Finley Peter Dunne),[84] but the Justices read the newspapers. Spring 2023 was a particularly brutal season for the Supreme Court. Buffeted by controversy about decisions on abortion and guns, the Court was already at a basement-level public-approval

---

[80] 599 U.S. 1 (2023). The Court also lifted its stay in the Louisiana case, so Louisiana would have a new plan too. Ardoin v. Robinson, 143 S. Ct. 2654 (2023).

[81] 478 U.S. 30 (1986).

[82] Allen v. Milligan, 144 S. Ct. 476 (2023) (mem.); Allen v. Caster, 144 S. Ct. 476 (2023) (mem.).

[83] Singleton v. Allen, No. 2:21-CV-1291, 2023 WL 6567895 (N.D. Ala. Oct. 5, 2023) (ordering the special master's plan to be used for 2024 congressional elections).

[84] Finley Peter Dunne, *The Supreme Court's Decisions*, Mr. Dooley's Opinions 21, 26 (1906).

rating when it was hit by a series of self-inflicted ethical wounds, including acceptance—without disclosure—of very expensive gifts and, in one instance, secret payments to one Justice's wife for Court-related work.[85] All the Justices may feel the sting of public scorn, but it is the Chief Justice whose name, for good or ill, is and will forever be linked with the Court, like the "Earl Warren Court" or the "Roger Taney Court."

B. FIRST AMENDMENT—FOR WHOM?

The Roberts Court early on dealt with a pair of cases involving voting and the First Amendment. Seemingly unrelated, the cases showed a Supreme Court disparaging voters and exalting financial contributors.

1. *The Voter Suppression Case – Photo ID Law.* Voting is a classic "low-incentive" activity—so low that almost half of eligible Americans skip even presidential elections. Therefore, election rules that impose burdens, even burdens that can theoretically be surmounted by any voter, will discourage some people from voting, and some people more than others—especially those who are poor or of a minority group.[86]

Recent years have seen a sharp rise in such laws, many of which are plainly "voter suppression laws." Even if such a law affects only a limited number of voters, that limited number can affect the outcome of an election, even a presidential election. That seems to explain the appeal of such laws to many lawmakers.

Unfortunately, the main protection against unfair voter-suppression laws, the First Amendment right of free speech and free association, was riddled by the Supreme Court early in the Roberts era and is dubious protection against voter suppression.

This confrontation involved a new type of state law requiring a voter to present photographic identification—"photo ID"—at the polling place in order to vote. Election officials everywhere routinely check a voter's identity by matching the voter's sign-in signature or by identification card, piece of mail, etc. Beginning in the early 2000s,

---

[85] Emma Brown, Shawn Bobert & Jonathan O'Connell, *Legal Activist Directed Fees to Clarence Thomas's Wife, Urged 'No Mention of Ginni,'* WASH. POST (May 4, 2023), https://www.washingtonpost.com/investigations/2023/05/04/leonard-leo-clarence-ginni-thomas-conway.

[86] KEYSSAR, *supra* note 29, at 311–15. Some of the sources for this seemingly obvious proposition are cited in the notes to these pages.

however, some states began enacting laws requiring photo ID—not just any photo ID, but one from a limited list of government-issued IDs. Every state's list of permitted IDs included driver's licenses and non-driver's ID issued by the state motor vehicle agency, as well as other IDs in lists that varied from state to state.[87]

Supporters of photo ID laws typically say (1) such laws protect against voter fraud and (2) almost everyone has a driver's license or other qualifying photo ID. As it happens, both propositions are wrong.

First, as to fraud prevention: the only type of voter fraud a photo ID prevents is "in-person impersonation," that is, one person coming to the polling place and pretending to be someone else. That type of fraud virtually never happens, and it is not hard to see why. One must impersonate a specific documented registered voter, not simply wave a fake ID at a bartender. "It is done in a public place where poll officials or candidates' poll watchers may well recognize the imposter or know it is not the impersonated voter."[88] Any rational person can foresee the risk of being caught and prosecuted, which is why the rare attempts are usually from idiosyncratic individuals. Repeated observation and research indicate that, over the years and in untold millions of votes cast in state after state, the number of impersonations falls in the single digits.[89]

Second, "almost everyone has one." True enough as a proportion, but not in numbers. "Almost everyone" turns out to mean about ninety-five percent, as agreed by experts who have testified on both sides of photo ID cases. The "other" five percent is a lot of voters,

---

[87] An important impetus was a report of the Commission on Federal Election Reform (Carter-Baker Commission), which recommended a universal photo ID card for voters. The Commission also recommended an active program to ensure universal possession of the needed ID, including an eight-year phase-in period and intensive outreach efforts. COMMISSION ON FEDERAL ELECTION REFORM, BUILDING CONFIDENCE IN U.S. ELECTIONS Recommendation 2.5.1 (Sept. 2005). States adopting photo ID laws universally put them into effect immediately, belying any interest in safeguarding the right to vote.

[88] See Justice Souter's dissent, where he also highlighted the vastly overblown fears by citing the famous poem about an imaginary man: "As I was going up the stair, I met a man who wasn't there." Crawford v. Marion Cnty. Election Bd., 553 U.S. 181, 227 n.29 (2008) (Souter, J., dissenting).

[89] See Armand Derfner & J. Gerald Hebert, *Voting Is Speech*, 34 YALE L. & POL'Y REV. 471, 484 n.90 (2016). A personal experience confirmed this point for me. At a panel discussion, when I raised the issue, Ilya Shapiro, a renowned conservative scholar who was then at the Cato Institute, said such impersonation virtually never happens. He added that he still supports photo ID laws because many people *believe* it happens, so such laws will promote voter confidence. Ilya Shapiro, Panel Discussion at the University of Mississippi, Oxford, Miss. (Apr. 7, 2016).

more than 600,000 in Texas and 130,000 even in the smaller state of South Carolina.[90] Even though many of the five percent wind up going to get a photo ID, a significant number of people who are registered to vote will not do so, and they will cease to be voters.

Nevertheless, a photo ID law seems at first glance to be a sensible measure, and the negative side often takes time to catch up with first impressions. Judge Richard Posner of the Seventh Circuit has said that a photo ID law is "a type of law now widely regarded as a means of voter suppression rather than fraud prevention."[91] Unfortunately, this was a delayed recognition in 2013, six years after he wrote the court of appeals opinion upholding the Indiana law discussed below.[92]

After a photo ID law was mostly upheld in Georgia[93] and another one struck down in Missouri,[94] the photo ID law that reached the Supreme Court was from Indiana, which required a photo ID issued by the state of Indiana or the United States government.

In *Crawford v. Marion County Election Board*,[95] the challenge was based primarily on the free-speech and free-association guarantees of the First and Fourteenth Amendments.[96] Under that test, a voting regulation must meet strict scrutiny if the burden on voters is severe and must still pass a "balancing" test if not. In the balancing test, the burden on voters, "however slight," can be justified only by "precise interests" of the state that are "sufficiently weighty to justify the limitation."[97]

---

[90] Experts for the challengers and the State agreed that in South Carolina five percent of registered voters (approximately 130,000) lacked a qualifying photo ID when the law was passed. *See* South Carolina v. United States, 898 F. Supp. 2d 30, 40, 53 (D.D.C. 2012). In Texas, the challengers' experts' figure was 4.5% (approximately 608,000), and the State's expert differed by a fraction of a percentage point. Veasey v. Perry, 71 F. Supp. 3d 627, 659–64 (S.D. Tex. 2014). *See also* Charles Stewart III, *Voter ID: Who Has Them? Who Shows Them?* 66 OKLA. L. REV. 21 (2013).

[91] Richard A. Posner, *I Did Not 'Recant' on Voter ID Laws*, NEW REPUBLIC (Oct. 27, 2013), https://newrepublic.com/article/115363/richard-posner-i-did-not-recant-my-opinion-voter-id; Richard Hasen, *Why Judge Posner Changed His Mind*, ELECTION L. BLOG, (Oct. 13, 2013), https://electionlawblog.org/?p=56216.

[92] Crawford v. Marion Cnty. Election Bd., 472 F.3d 949 (7th Cir. 2007).

[93] Common Cause/Ga. v. Billups, 554 F.3d 1340 (11th Cir. 2009) (summarizing rulings on earlier versions of the law).

[94] Weinschenk v. State, 203 S.W.3d 201 (Mo. 2006).

[95] 553 U.S. 181 (2008).

[96] *See* Anderson v. Celebrezze, 460 U.S. 780 (1983); Burdick v. Takushi, 504 U.S. 428 (1992).

[97] *Crawford*, 553 U.S. at 191.

In *Crawford*, however, the Supreme Court's review turned out to be no real balancing and little or no review at all.[98] The plurality opinion did correctly identify state interests in preventing fraud and promoting voter confidence, but it failed in the other step of the analysis—confirming whether the Indiana law really advanced those interests.

The opinion began by correctly describing the Indiana law's very limited reach: "The only kind of voter fraud that [the Indiana law] addresses is in-person voter impersonation at polling places."[99] But, the opinion acknowledged, "the record contains no evidence of any such fraud actually occurring in Indiana at any time in its history."[100]

But then, having begun with a pair of accurate statements, the Court took it all back: "It remains true, however, that flagrant examples of such fraud in other parts of the country have been documented throughout this Nation's history . . . ."[101]

This statement, which effectively decided the case, was flatly wrong, as shown by the Court's own documentation. It is true, as the Court's examples showed, that flagrant examples of "fraud" have been documented, but not "such fraud" (i.e., *not* in-person voter impersonation at polling places).[102]

Specifically, *Crawford*'s footnote twelve referred to election fraud in eight states and two cities over the years, but the footnote itself cited an amicus brief which had analyzed all of those reports and found that none of the fraud reports was a confirmed instance of impersonation at the polling place—except one voter in one election in one state.[103] A folktale from the Boss Tweed days rounded out the Court's constitutional analysis.

---

[98] There was no majority opinion. Most often cited (and called the plurality opinion) is the opinion of Justice Stevens for three Justices—himself, the Chief Justice and Justice Kennedy—but Justice Scalia wrote a concurring opinion that was also for three Justices—himself and Justices Thomas and Alito.

[99] *Crawford*, 553 U.S. at 194.

[100] *Id.*

[101] *Id.* at 195.

[102] *Id.*

[103] The examples were cited in the district court opinion, Ind. Democratic Party v. Rokita, 458 F. Supp. 2d 775, 793–94 (S.D. Ind. 2006), but were refuted in the amicus brief. Brief for Brennan Center for Justice et al. as Amici Curiae in Support of Petitioners at 11–28, *Crawford*, 553 U.S. 181 (Nos. 07-21 & 07-25), 2007 WL 4102238 [hereinafter Brennan Center Brief]. As the footnote reported, the one confirmed instance of in-person impersonation involved the Washington governor's election in 2004, in which 2,812,675 votes were

Crawford's conclusion on this critical issue said nothing about the Indiana law in dispute: "There is no question about the legitimacy or importance of the State's interest in counting only the votes of eligible voters."[104] True enough, but beside the point, since that interest, undeniably important, was not advanced by this particular Indiana law.

The Court's treatment of the other important state interest—safeguarding voter confidence—was also lacking. The Court simply asserted that voter confidence is important, as of course it is, but made no attempt to demonstrate that voters lack confidence or that the Indiana law promotes voter confidence. The Court's sole source was the Carter-Baker Commission, which had already drawn a conclusion: "The electoral system cannot inspire public confidence if no safeguards exist to deter or detect fraud or to confirm the identity of voters."[105] A photo ID law could be justified only by the last five words of that quotation and, unfortunately, the Carter-Baker Report's evidence of impersonation fraud was faulty.[106] It may be hard to fault the Supreme Court for relying on a seemingly strong source, but the Court should have been aware of the weakness of the Commission's supposed examples of voter impersonation (as opposed to other types of fraud) and should not have been satisfied to rely on this single, derivative source to answer such a central question.

While overstating the State's interest, the Court undervalued the voters' interest. The Court reduced the voters' fundamental First Amendment right to a single question—whether the burden was severe—and answered that question in the negative by finding that a voter who is really determined to get a photo ID can do so.

But the magnitude of the burden on individual voters should have been only the starting point in the balancing test, not the end. For

---

cast. An investigation turned up nineteen possible instances of fraud, and after further investigation, "one person was confirmed to have committed in-person voting fraud." *Crawford*, 553 U.S. at 195 n.12.

[104] *Crawford*, 553 U.S. at 196.

[105] *Id.* at 197 (quoting the Carter-Baker Report).

[106] The Carter-Baker Report's only specific examples of fraud were in Washington state and Milwaukee. COMM'N ON FED. ELECTION REFORM, BUILDING CONFIDENCE IN U.S. ELECTIONS 4 (Sept. 2005). Both of these were addressed in the Brennan Center Brief, *supra* note 103. The Washington state example boiled down to one voter. The Milwaukee example, based on a joint state-federal investigative report, showed in-person voting fraud of types which would not be prevented by a photo ID requirement (such as felon voting and double voting), but *not* impersonation. *Id.* at 17.

one thing, a voting law must be nondiscriminatory, but the photo ID law imposed an added task only on nondrivers, while voters with driver's licenses are given a pass and required to do nothing more. Yet if a law made all voters get a separate ID for voting, without exempting drivers, surely there would be vast numbers of drivers who failed to comply and would lose their right to vote. Would such a law pass First Amendment muster?

Recognizing that voting is protected by the freedom of association also means that an important issue should have been the number of voters affected, not just the effect on any single voter.[107] Responsible organizations, public and private, rarely make significant moves without a feasibility or impact study, and the freedom of association of voters (plural) should require a state imposing a serious regulation to provide reliable data on impact to satisfy its First Amendment burden.[108] Conversely, not requiring such proof makes it too easy to pass laws that, intentionally or not, suppress the right to vote.

After the *Crawford* decision, other states started passing photo ID laws and, in some states, openly picking and choosing their voters. Texas allows federal military IDs (and state gun permit IDs) but not federal civilian IDs.[109] Ohio keeps the military preference and goes a step further by allowing state national guard IDs but not state employee IDs.[110] Idaho used to allow state-university student IDs but disallowed them after increased student political activity.[111]

Notably, the two judges who wrote the key opinions in *Crawford* soon had second thoughts. As noted above, Seventh Circuit Judge Richard Posner has described photo ID laws as a "means of voter

---

[107] Of course, assessing such "effect" means not only asking how many voters lack a qualifying photo ID when the law is passed, but also how the policy affects rates of actual voting (e.g., how many voters would still lack a qualifying photo ID after a reasonable time, how many of those would actually have voted)? Even though some of these data are uncertain, they should all be part of the calculus in measuring the impact of a law on the right to vote.

[108] The district court rejected plaintiffs' figures as unreasonably high and used its own highly speculative figure of 43,000, about 1% of Indiana's 4,000,000 registered voters. Ind. Democratic Party v. Rokita, 458 F. Supp. 2d at 803–08 (S.D. Ind. 2006). Even if that figure was almost certainly too low (the 5% figure shown by expert testimony in other states would have meant over 200,000), 43,000 is still a substantial number of voters.

[109] Tex. Elect. Code §§ 63.001, 63.0101(a) (2021). For a spreadsheet of qualifying IDs in each state as of 2014, see Veasey v. Perry, 71 F. Supp. 3d 627, 642 (S.D. Tex. 2014).

[110] Ohio Rev. Code Ann. §§ 3501.01(AA)(1)(c)–3505.18(A)(1) (2023).

[111] Idaho Code § 34-1113, *as amended by* H.B. 124, 66th Leg., Reg. Sess. (2023).

suppression rather than fraud prevention."¹¹² Justice Stevens, author of the Supreme Court's plurality opinion, also expressed regret.¹¹³ These two judges' towering reputations had given *Crawford* some undeserved weight. Despite these sadder-but-wiser reactions, *Crawford* is still there as authority for upholding voter-suppression laws.

Since the 2020 and 2022 elections, some states have gone even further in partisan picking and choosing, adopting laws patently designed to disfranchise voters in urban areas that vote Democratic. For example, after ballot drop boxes were used by many voters in 2020, a Georgia law reduced drop boxes by more than three-quarters—but only in the Atlanta-area counties.¹¹⁴ A 2023 Texas law authorized the Secretary of State to take over a county election administration—but only in Democratic-leaning Harris County (Houston).¹¹⁵

These and many other examples show that voter suppression has been on a steep rise in many states. The states that like it will be relying on that old standby justification—the need to promote voter confidence—and will be looking to the *Crawford* decision as precedent to help them pick and choose their favorite voters.

2. *Money and the First Amendment.* Two years after the First Amendment rights of voters got short shrift in the photo-ID case, the First Amendment came roaring back as a protection for corrosive money in political campaigns. The case, *Citizens United v. Federal Election Commission*,¹¹⁶ was an uncompromising endorsement of money in politics wrapped in the noble garb of the First Amendment. And concern for voter confidence in elections, so decisive in the photo-ID case two years earlier? Just swept aside.

---

¹¹² Posner, *supra* note 91.

¹¹³ Robert Barnes, *Stevens Says Supreme Court Decision on Voter ID Was Correct, but Maybe Not Right*, WASH. POST (May 15, 2016), https://www.washingtonpost.com/politics/courts_law/stevens-says-supreme-court-decision-on-voter-id-was-correct-but-maybe-not-right/2016/05/15/9683c51c-193f-11e6-9e16-2e5a123aac62_story.html.

¹¹⁴ S.B. 202, 2022 Gen. Assemb., Reg. Sess. (Ga. 2022). The law provided one drop box for every 100,000 voters in a county. This sham show of equality was fine for the 150 Georgia counties with fewer than 100,000 voters; but in the four counties comprising the Atlanta urban area, the law deprived voters of more than three-quarters of the drop boxes available in 2020, from 107 to 25.

¹¹⁵ S.B. 933, 88th Leg., Reg. Sess. (Tex. 2023). The law is "neutral" because it applies to *every* Texas county with a population of more than 3.5 million, but of course, only one of Texas's 254 counties fits that bill—Harris County.

¹¹⁶ 558 U.S. 310 (2010).

The direct question involved spending by corporations, specifically, the ban on such spending in the Bipartisan Campaign Reform Act of 2002 ("McCain-Feingold Act"),[117] but the Court's decision went far beyond that issue. Before this case, corporate political contributions had been a federal crime for a hundred years. That rule came from the Tillman Act of 1907,[118] passed in the wake of the glut of money poured into Theodore Roosevelt's presidential re-election campaign of 1904. Over the years, more campaign finance laws followed, culminating in the comprehensive Federal Election Campaign Act of 1971.[119]

The legislation was challenged on the previously unthinkable theory that spending money on elections should have constitutional protection. The result was the Supreme Court's revolutionary decision in *Buckley v. Valeo*.[120] *Buckley* held that money spent on political campaigns is a form of speech because it is spent to inform voters.[121] In other words, political money received constitutional protection not for its own sake, but to enhance *voters'* constitutional rights.

The Supreme Court found two interests that could justify Congress's curbs on the newly recognized First Amendment rights: "preventing corruption" and "preventing the appearance of corruption." The first interest is self-evident (especially as to what the Court has called "*quid pro quo*" corruption), but the Supreme Court put the second interest, "preventing the appearance of corruption," on a par with preventing corruption itself. The Court stressed "the impact of the appearance of corruption stemming from public awareness of the opportunities for abuse inherent in a regime of large individual financial contributions."[122] Applying these principles, the Court held that Congress's interest was sufficient to uphold the Act's limits on contributions to candidates and political parties but insufficient for the Act's limits on independent expenditures.

No one in *Buckley* challenged the longstanding ban on corporate and union campaign spending. When that ban was challenged a few

---

[117] Pub. L. No. 107-155, 116 Stat. 81 (codified at 52 U.S.C. §§ 30125 *et seq.*).
[118] Tillman Act of 1907, Pub. L. No. 59-35, 34 Stat. 864.
[119] Federal Election Campaign Act of 1971, Pub. L. No. 92-225, 86 Stat. 3.
[120] 424 U.S. 1 (1976).
[121] *Id.* at 15.
[122] *Id.* at 27.

years later, in *Federal Election Commission v. National Right to Work Commission,* the challenge was swiftly rejected in a unanimous opinion by Justice Rehnquist.[123] The Court now added a third basic interest in regulating political spending, this one specifically supporting the total ban on corporate contributions. The Court said this ban was justified "to ensure that substantial aggregations of wealth amassed by the special advantages which go with the corporate form of organization should not be converted into political 'war chests' which could be used to incur political debts from legislators who are aided by the contributions."[124] In addition, the Court again put the danger of corruption's appearance on par with actual corruption: "[We reaffirm] the importance of preventing both the actual corruption threatened by large financial contributions and the eroding of public confidence in the electoral process through the appearance of corruption. These interests directly implicate 'the integrity of our electoral process.'"[125]

That case was decided in the 1980s. The Supreme Court upheld laws banning corporate contributions again in the 1990s and early 2000s.[126] As before, the Court recognized that corporate contributions posed a special risk to election integrity and public confidence: "the corrosive and distorting effect of massive corporate aggregations of [corporate] wealth."[127]

There the law stood while the Supreme Court still included Chief Justice Rehnquist and Justice O'Connor, both of whom voted to uphold some campaign finance restrictions.[128] Since their departures and their replacements by Chief Justice Roberts and Justice Alito, the Supreme Court has *never* affirmed a campaign finance restriction. Instead, rulings striking restrictions down are a near-annual ritual, with performances in 2006 and 2007 and 2008 and 2010 and 2011 and 2012 and 2014 and 2019 and 2022.[129]

---

[123] 459 U.S. 197 (1982).

[124] *Id.* at 207–08.

[125] *Id.* at 208.

[126] Austin v. Mich. Chamber of Com., 494 U.S. 652 (1990) (concerning a state law); McConnell v. Fed. Election Comm'n, 540 U.S. 93 (2003) (concerning a federal law).

[127] *Austin,* 494 U.S at 660; *McConnell,* 540 U.S. at 205.

[128] Both voted for the law in *National Right to Work Commission.* Chief Justice Rehnquist also voted to uphold the law in *Austin,* while Justice O'Connor voted for the law in *McConnell.*

[129] *See* Randall v. Sorrell, 548 U.S. 230 (2006); Fed. Election Comm'n v. Wis. Right to Life, Inc., 551 U.S. 449 (2007); Davis v. Fed. Election Comm'n, 554 U.S. 724 (2008); Citizens United v. Fed. Election Comm'n, 558 U.S. 310 (2010); Ariz. Free Enter. Club's Freedom

Citizens United v. Federal Election Commission was the most breathtaking of the new Court's run of campaign finance cases. A 5-4 majority swept aside the hundred-year-old restriction on corporate campaign spending and put corporations on a fully equal footing with live human beings (and ahead of voters, who get only one vote each). The "corrosive and distorting effect of immense aggregations" of corporate wealth, so recently and repeatedly thought by the Supreme Court to be a grave threat to the electoral process, was now derided as government censorship that interferes with the "open marketplace" of ideas.[130]

But the commodity being traded, if not deeply discounted, in the majority's "marketplace" is democracy itself. *Buckley* had said public awareness of "opportunities for abuse inherent in a regime of large individual financial contributions" made the "appearance of corruption" a serious risk that justified regulation.[131] Later cases stuck by that common-sense view. Now, however, the *Citizens United* majority opinion was a lilting hosanna to the virtues of "influence," "access," "favoritism" and elected officials' "responsiveness" to money.[132] It may seem hard to believe, but the majority used these very words and said these were all just a normal part of representative government. The message was: Get over it![133]

The opinion read less like the U.S. Reports and more like Ayn Rand. Most striking was the Court's blithe dismissal of any concern over voter confidence. Citing no basis for suddenly abandoning forty years of concern for voter confidence and election integrity, the majority simply proclaimed: "The appearance of influence or access will not cause the electorate to lose faith in our democracy."[134] This assertion was especially bizarre in light of the two-year-old precedent of *Crawford v. Marion County Election Board*. In that photo-ID

Club PAC v. Bennett, 564 U.S. 721 (2011); Am. Tradition P'ship, Inc. v. Bullock, 576 U.S. 516 (2012); McCutcheon v. Fed. Election Comm'n, 572 U.S. 185 (2014); Thompson v. Hebdon, 140 S. Ct. 348 (2019); Fed. Election Comm'n v. Cruz, 596 U.S. 289 (2022).

[130] Citizens United v. Fed. Election Comm'n, 558 U.S. at 353–54 (2010).

[131] *Buckley*, 424 U.S. at 7.

[132] 558 U.S. at 359.

[133] If such a message were explicit, it would not be unprecedented. Justice Scalia said "Get over it" in response to criticism of the Court after the 2000 election. *See, e.g.*, CBS News, *Scalia: Get Over It!*, YouTube (April 24, 2008), https://www.youtube.com/watch?v=RjaB3cxH-XE.

[134] 558 U.S. at 360.

case, with ink barely dry, the Court simply assumed—without any support—that voters would lack confidence without a photo-ID rule; here, again with no basis and in fact contrary to universal belief, the Court simply assumed that voters would *not* lack confidence. Both assumptions were equally baseless, but they determined what our Constitution *now* means.

Lacking support did not prevent the Court from offering a theory, saying "independent" expenditures would not weaken voters' faith in elections because voters would know these expenditures are "not coordinated with a candidate."[135] If this naive assertion had ever been true, reality quickly caught up with it.

Citizens United was announced in January 2010. It took little time for the gaping holes opened by that case to be filled with unimaginable amounts of political money. Much of it came through the new entities unleashed by *Citizens United.* Called "Super PACs," these groups could gather money from anyone, including corporations, and they enabled donors to give unlimited amounts.

The first major Super PAC, within weeks or months of *Citizens United*, was created by and for the 2012 presidential campaign of Mitt Romney. Like other Super PACs that soon followed, it was clearly identified as "his" Super PAC but bore an innocuous-sounding name—in this case, "Restore Our Future." "[B]y law, the campaign was barred from coordinating with 'Restore,' . . . [but] in every historical, genetic, and practical sense, [Restore] was a subsidiary of the campaign."[136] The Super PAC was run by the top aides of Romney's previous campaigns, including his chief fundraiser, and it was kicked off by a series of fundraising events starring Romney himself, to make clear to the biggest donors that "Restore" was Romney and Romney was "Restore."[137]

This new Super PAC device was instantly successful. "Restore Our Future" raised $8,000,000 in the first month and doubled that in the next two months, "in chunks ranging from $100,000 to $1,000,000."[138]

"Restore Our Future" was quickly followed by other Super PACs, each one a stand-in for a particular political candidate. It is now

---

[135] *Id.*

[136] Mark Halperin & John Heilemann, Double Down: Game Change 2012, at 225–26 (2013).

[137] *Id.* at 225.

[138] *Id.* at 226.

customary for every candidate for major public office to have his or her "own" Super PAC, with droll names like "Unite the Country" (supporting Joe Biden in the 2020 election) or "Make Us Great Again" (supporting Rick Perry in 2012 and later adapted by Donald Trump's "Make America Great Again"). Public records show the phenomenal amounts of money raised by Super PACs and the huge contributions by tiny numbers of individuals and corporations. The donors know exactly which candidate the money is for, and the candidates know exactly whom they should be grateful to—or *very* grateful to, in the case of larger donors.

For the 2022 Senate and House races, there were 2,476 Super PACs, which raised nearly three billion dollars.[139] As has been stated, with extreme understatement: "Super PACs have emphatically shifted the electoral balance of power away from everyday voters and toward wealthy donors able and willing to spend millions of dollars on the candidates who will best cater to their private interests."[140]

As to the lack of coordination with campaigns, the supposed reason why voters would not lose confidence, the same article describes the countless methods by which each campaign maintains tight control of "its" Super PAC's activities, even including explicit instructions by email—and the failure of efforts to block this supposedly forbidden coordination.[141]

Citizens United, with its uncompromising, no-balancing approach to money in politics, has carried forward in other cases. When the Montana Supreme Court upheld a state law limiting corporate campaign spending, saying there was a record of corruption in Montana related to corporate spending, the U.S. Supreme Court reversed in a two-paragraph summary reversal on the petition for certiorari with no briefing or oral argument—apparently deemed unnecessary.[142]

Even the seemingly bedrock rule allowing stiff regulation of money paid directly to candidates, so clearly upheld in *Buckley v. Valeo*, is

---

[139] *2022 Outside Spending, by Super PAC*, OPEN SECRETS, https://www.opensecrets.org/outside-spending/super_pacs.

[140] Paul Smith & Saurav Ghosh, *Recent Changes in the Economics of Voting Caused by the Arrival of Super PACS*, 48 AM. BAR ASS'N (Oct. 24, 2022), https://www.americanbar.org/groups/crsj/publications/human_rights_magazine_home/economics-of-voting/the-arrival-of-super-pacs. Needless to say, massive spending has also infected state elections, from legislative and state supreme court to local school board seats.

[141] *Id.*

[142] Am. Tradition P'ship, Inc. v. Bullock, 576 U.S. 516 (2012).

now at risk. The *Buckley* rule lasted without qualification until 2014. In that year, the Supreme Court began chipping away at the compelling interest in regulating direct contributions by striking down aggregate limits for a donor's total contributions to all candidates.[143] Apparently, *quid pro quo* corruption operates on a sliding scale.

And the rules requiring disclosure, sacrosanct until now, may also be on the chopping block. In 1958, the Supreme Court held that the Alabama NAACP could resist disclosure of its members' names because a reign of Ku Klux Klan bombings meant that releasing NAACP members' names could realistically be a death sentence.[144] In 2021, the Supreme Court demeaned that precedent by relying on it to justify confidentiality of large charitable contributors who complained about having received some annoying letters.[145]

* * *

One could draw many lessons from reading *Crawford* and *Citizens United* together, such as the accordion-like treatment of "voter confidence," but the simplest may be this question: If campaign spenders are accorded such reverence, why are the voters treated like trash?

C. EQUAL PROTECTION CLAUSE

1. *Gerrymandering.* In 2019, when the Supreme Court held in *Rucho v. Common Cause*[146] that partisan gerrymandering claims are not justiciable in federal courts, the trial record contained an object lesson of the evil involved. The legislative leader in charge of North Carolina's congressional reapportionment testified that he instructed the legislative draftsman to draw a plan for the state's thirteen congressional districts that would produce ten Republican and three Democratic seats. When asked why he called for a 10-3 plan (in a state where voters are evenly divided between the two major parties), he said it was because he did "not believe it possible to draw a map with 11 Republicans and 2 Democrats."[147]

---

[143] McCutcheon v. Fed. Election Comm'n, 572 U.S. 185 (2014).

[144] NAACP v. Alabama *ex rel.* Patterson, 357 U.S. 449 (1958).

[145] Ams. for Prosperity Found. v. Bonta, 141 S.Ct. 2373 (2021).

[146] Rucho v. Common Cause, 139 S. Ct. 2484 (2019).

[147] *Id.* at 2491. Voting results by party are described in Justice Kagan's dissent, *id.* at 2510. Note also that in both 2016 and 2020, Republicans won the presidential vote while Democrats won the governorship, all by the narrowest of margins.

Gerrymandering is the elected representatives' ultimate means of picking and choosing their voters. It flourished long before the Supreme Court came on the scene. It has bedeviled the Court in cases going back a half-century, but it was not until the Roberts Court in 2019 that gerrymandering got an explicit free pass.

Yet, even as it was declaring itself powerless to deal with gerrymandering, the Supreme Court recognized what a Frankenstein's monster it was turning loose. The Court said gerrymandering, or what it called "excessive partisanship in districting," cannot be "condone[d]," produces "unjust" results, and is "incompatible with democratic principles."[148] Ordinary people use words like "wrong" and "dishonest" or, in common parlance, "crooked." That is why elected officials rarely publicly admit to engaging in the practice, unless the admission serves a political or (since *Rucho*) judicial end.

It has been sixty years since *Baker v. Carr* began the reapportionment revolution.[149] The requirement of population equality among districts and the murkier requirement of avoiding outright racial gerrymanders still leave ample room to engage in manipulation, favoring one's political party, friends, contributors and other allies. Today's advanced technology provides megareams of data and the capacity to draw huge numbers of plans, annotated with data descriptions, at lightning speed. Indeed, the population-equality rule of *Baker v. Carr* recedes into the background because it is hard to take disputes over tiny percentage points seriously when a gerrymandering free-for-all is the main event.

Trying to regulate partisan gerrymandering is obviously a knotty problem. Over the years, the Supreme Court has ruled, or almost ruled, on the issue several times. In 1973, the Court held that considering politics in drawing districts is permissible, even inevitable. The Court said, "fair and effective representation for all citizens" is "the basic aim of legislative apportionment."[150] The plan upheld in that case aimed for a degree of fairness through "a rough approximation of the [parties'] statewide political strength."[151]

---

[148] *Id.* at 2506.

[149] Baker v. Carr, 369 U.S. 186 (1962). I use "redistricting" and "reapportionment" interchangeably here, although some limit "reapportionment" to changes in allocating seats among fixed districts, as the U.S. House of Representatives does after every census.

[150] Gaffney v. Cummings, 412 U.S. 735, 748 (1973) (quoting Reynolds v. Sims, 377 U.S. 533, 555–56 (1964)).

[151] *Id.* at 762.

Later cases involved more ignoble plans—those designed for maximum aggrandizement. A 1986 case suggested, but did not hold, that partisan gerrymandering is justiciable,[152] while cases in 2004,[153] 2006[154] and 2018[155] stopped just short of holding that they are not. In the post-2000 cases, four Justices would have held partisan gerrymandering nonjusticiable, but Justice Kennedy, concurring, said that while he did not yet see a way to adjudicate partisan gerrymandering claims, he was unwilling to foreclose such a claim for the future.[156]

Finally, in 2019, with Justice Kennedy gone, the Court ended the long speculation, holding squarely that federal courts cannot entertain claims of partisan gerrymandering. The case, *Rucho v. Common Cause*,[157] involved a Republican gerrymander in North Carolina (the 10-3 plan described earlier) and a Democratic gerrymander of Maryland's congressional districts.[158] The opinion, by the Chief Justice, while emphasizing that the Court "does not condone" gerrymandering, said partisan politics is part of the process of drawing district lines, that gerrymandering claims rest on "unstable ground outside judicial expertise," and that the Constitution "provides no standard for determining when partisan activity goes too far."[159]

The *Rucho* decision settled the partisan gerrymandering question for federal courts, but in his farewell to political gerrymandering cases, Roberts sought to reassure voters that other avenues remain for their protection, particularly state courts: "Nor does our conclusion condemn complaints about districting to echo into a void. The States, for example, are actively addressing the issue on a number of fronts."[160]

This point, however, raised more questions, because, if state courts could adjudicate partisan gerrymandering claims, didn't that undermine the Supreme Court's contrary view? The dissent made this

---

[152] Davis v. Bandemer, 478 U.S. 109 (1986)

[153] Vieth v. Jubelirer, 541 U.S. 267 (2004). For a critique of *Vieth*, see Justin Driver, *Rules, the New Standards: Partisan Gerrymandering and Judicial Manageability after* Vieth v. Jubelirer, 73 GEO. WASH. L. REV. 1166 (2005).

[154] League of United Latin Am. Citizens v. Perry, 548 U.S. 399 (2006).

[155] Gill v. Whitford, 138 S. Ct. 1916 (2018).

[156] *Vieth*, 541 U.S. at 306 (Kennedy, J., concurring).

[157] Rucho v. Common Cause, 139 S. Ct. 2484 (2019).

[158] The Maryland case decided in the same opinion was *Lamone v. Benisek*, No. 18-726, on appeal from *Benisek v. Lamone*, 348 F. Supp. 3d 493 (D. Md. 2018).

[159] *Rucho*, 139 S. Ct. at 2504.

[160] *Id.* at 2507–08.

point, to which the majority responded by pointing to the differences between the federal Constitution and the various state provisions.[161]

The Justices' debate raises the question of how widespread and effective state court review of gerrymandering may prove to be. A pair of North Carolina decisions soon showed both the potential and the perils of relying on state courts. After the U.S. Supreme Court rejected scrutiny of North Carolina's 10-3 plan, a state court lawsuit resulted in a 2022 North Carolina Supreme Court decision striking the plan down as a partisan gerrymander that violated the state constitution.[162] But later that year, North Carolina's judicial elections produced a new state supreme court majority which in 2023 vacated the previous decision and held it had no power to second-guess the state legislature's redistricting plan.[163] Thus, the 10-3 congressional delegation upheld in *Rucho*, which became a 7–7 delegation after the 2022 elections,[164] will undoubtedly revert to a lopsided delegation in the 2024 elections.

* * *

If the foregoing cases seem to free the elected representatives to gerrymander almost at will, a 2023 case came close to making it much worse, and another case to be decided in 2024 also has the possibility of making things worse.

Last year's near-miss came in *Moore v. Harper*,[165] which threatened to bar *all* state court review of gerrymanders for congressional districts, no matter what state constitutions said and no matter that state court review had been "promised" in *Rucho*. The basis for barring state court review was the quaintly named "independent state legislature" ("ISL") theory. This theory argues that state legislators have dominion over congressional districting, completely free of *state* court oversight, because Article I, Section 4 of the federal Constitution gives state legislatures that power.[166]

---

[161] *Compare id.* at 2507, *with id.* at 2524–25 (Kagan, J., dissenting).

[162] Harper v. Hall, 868 S.E.2d 499 (N.C. 2022).

[163] Harper v. Hall, 886 S.E.2d 393 (N.C. 2023).

[164] North Carolina's population growth gained it a seat after the 2020 census.

[165] 600 U.S. 1 (2023).

[166] "The Times, Places and Manner of holding Elections for Senators and Representatives, shall be prescribed in each State by the Legislature thereof; but the Congress may at any time by Law make or alter such regulations, except as to the place of choosing Senators." U.S Const. art. I, § 4, cl. 1.

The ISL reading of Article I, Section 4 is at war with the fundamental structure of American government. In every state and the national government, the lawmaking power is vested in three branches, not one or another of those branches. In *Smiley v. Holm*,[167] the Supreme Court unanimously rejected a redistricting of Minnesota's congressional seats, which had been adopted by that state's legislature but vetoed by the Governor. The Court held that the word "legislature" in Article I, Section 4 means the state's lawmaking power, not a rump part of it. Likewise in 2015, when the people of Arizona adopted a constitutional amendment transferring the reapportionment function to an independent commission, the Supreme Court upheld the amendment. In *Arizona State Legislature v. Arizona Independent Redistricting Commission*,[168] the majority opinion by Justice Ginsburg said Article I, Section 4 refers to the state's lawmaking process as designated by the state's people and its constitution.

Nevertheless, anything seemed possible in the perfervid atmosphere following the 2020 elections. When the North Carolina legislature challenged the state supreme court's 2022 decision (the one striking the 10-3 plan down), enough Justices were taken with the ISL theory to grant certiorari. Three Justices actually voted to grant an emergency stay and a fourth almost joined them.[169]

In the end, in *Moore v. Harper*, the Supreme Court soundly rejected the ISL theory in favor of our basic constitutional system which includes judicial review as an integral component. This was not as surprising as the fact that the case was decided at all. Most observers thought the case became moot in early 2023 when the North Carolina Supreme Court reversed itself and reinstated the state legislature's gerrymander, but the U.S. Supreme Court held otherwise.[170]

Laying the ISL theory to rest in *Moore v. Harper* did more than preserve a check on gerrymanders of congressional districts; it averted or at least diminished the prospect of a lawless Electoral College battle in the 2024 presidential election[171]—a real possibility because similar

---

[167] 285 U.S. 355 (1932).

[168] 576 U.S. 787 (2015). Four Justices dissented, including Chief Justice Roberts.

[169] Moore v. Harper, 142 S. Ct. 1089 (2022).

[170] The mootness issue was debated between the Court's opinion, 600 U.S. at 14–18, and Justice Thomas's dissent, *id.* at 41–57.

[171] Many commentators have traced the dreary story of ISL theory as a tool for undermining democracy. *See, e.g.*, Vikram David Amar & Akhil Reed Amar, *Eradicating Bush-League*

ISL-type language in Article II, Section 1 of the Constitution says each state's presidential electors are to be chosen "in such Manner as the Legislature thereof may direct."[172] Mischief may still come in 2024, but perhaps not the ISL.

The other case that could worsen gerrymandering is before the Supreme Court in the October 2023 Term and has probably been decided by the time this Article is published. The case is *Alexander v. South Carolina State Conference of the NAACP*,[173] an appeal by South Carolina from a decision holding that its most recent congressional redistricting plan is a classic racial gerrymander violating the constitutional rights of African American voters.[174]

This case is an application of the Supreme Court's modern "predominance" rule for racial gerrymandering: A districting plan is unconstitutional if race predominated in its design but valid if politics predominated.[175] Applied first in cases where White voters challenged plans that arguably promoted Black voters' representation, the Court in 2017 applied the rule to the opposite case, i.e., the time-honored use of gerrymandering against Black voters. In *Cooper v. Harris*, the Court struck down a plan that set a quota of Black voters to be moved to achieve population equality among districts.[176]

In the current case, South Carolina says it drew the plan to guarantee Republican voters more representation and Democratic voters less. Legislative witnesses at trial said their goal was to "pull the first red"—i.e., to make District 1 more Republican—by moving Republican voters into the district and Democratic voters out.[177]

Arguments Root and Branch: The Article II Independent-State-Legislature Notion and Related Rubbish, 2021 Sup. Ct. Rev. 1 (2022).

[172] "Each State shall appoint, in such Manner as the Legislature thereof may direct, a Number of Electors, equal to the whole Number of Senators and Representatives to which the State may be entitled in the Congress . . . ." U.S Const. art. II, § 1, cl. 2.

[173] No. 22-807, 143 S. Ct. 2456 (2023) (noting probable jurisdiction).

[174] S.C. State Conf. of NAACP v. Alexander, 649 F. Supp. 3d 177 (D.S.C. 2023).

[175] The cause of action for White voters was first recognized in *Shaw v. Reno*, 509 U.S. 630 (1993), and the rule was stated in *Miller v. Johnson*, 515 U.S. 900 (1995).

[176] 581 U.S. 285 (2017). *Cooper* built on an earlier case. Ala. Legislative Black Caucus v. Alabama, 575 U.S. 254 (2015). *Cooper v. Harris* was decided by a majority that no longer exists. The five-vote majority included Justice Ginsburg as well as Justice Thomas, who emphasized that he was deferring to the district court.

[177] Brief for Appellants at 2, 14, Alexander v. S.C. State Conf. of the NAACP, 143 S. Ct. 2456 (2023) (No. 22-807), 2023 WL 4197083. This was all *post hoc* trial testimony, with no claim that this gerrymandering motive was ever asserted or confessed during the legislative process.

But whatever the underlying goal may have been, the district court found that the plan "sort[ed voters] on the basis of race,"[178] which the Supreme Court has repeatedly condemned as unconstitutional.[179] The district court found that the legislature set a target of no more than 17% African American voters in District 1 and met that target by "bleaching" concentrations of Charleston County's African American voters out of District 1 and into neighboring District 6, which already had a large African American population and an African American member of Congress.[180]

The South Carolina district court held that Congressional District 1 was a racial gerrymander because "race was the predominant motivating factor in the General Assembly's design of Congressional District No. 1 and that traditional districting principles were subordinated to race."[181]

This is a bellwether case that will test whether *Rucho* allows not just partisan gerrymandering, but also racial gerrymandering dressed up as partisan gerrymandering—will the Supreme Court use *Rucho* to swallow up what is left of the Fifteenth Amendment?[182]

2. *Equal Protection Clause—For Which Race?* The Supreme Court's aversion to race discrimination is well-known, almost its trademark—at least it is in cases where White people allege injury. When the shoe is on the other foot, i.e., when minority plaintiffs allege injury, it's not so clear.

Two recent voting cases involving the Equal Protection Clause—*Abbott v. Perez*[183] and *Brnovich v. Democratic National Committee*[184]—tell a tale of the Supreme Court ditching minority voters' claims. Two

---

[178] *S.C. State Conf.*, 649 F. Supp. 3d at 191.

[179] *E.g.*, Cooper v. Harris, 585 U.S. 285, 335 (2017); Bush v. Vera, 517 U.S. 952, 1007–08 (1996).

[180] This tactic, well-known as "packing," has been recognized by the Supreme Court as a means of minimizing minority voters' influence by moving concentrations of such voters "into districts where they constitute an excessive majority." Thornburg v. Gingles, 478 U.S. 30, 46 n.11 (1986). The concept has been repeated in many cases, most recently in *Allen v. Milligan*, 599 U.S. 1, 43–44 (2023) (Kavanaugh, J., concurring).

[181] *S.C. State Conf.*, 649 F. Supp. 3d at 193.

[182] This case is a bellwether in another respect, as the third Supreme Court case in six years in which a lower court has made a finding of fact of purposeful racial discrimination committed against minority voters. The Supreme Court reversed the last two such findings, which are discussed in the next Part of this Article. What will the Supreme Court do now with the third such case?

[183] 138 S. Ct. 2305 (2018).

[184] 141 S. Ct. 2321, 2348–50 (2021) (addressing the Equal Protection claims in Part V of the opinion).

cases might seem a small sample for such a strong charge but the two cases share remarkable features. In each case, a lower court made a finding of fact that a state statute was enacted with a purpose to discriminate against minority voters, but in each case the finding of discrimination was reversed by the Supreme Court. In each case, the reversal was based on the Supreme Court's mishandling of the landmark *Arlington Heights* rule, aggravated by the Court's manipulation—there is no other suitable word—of basic rules of evidence and appellate procedure.

For a half century, race-discrimination claims under the Equal Protection Clause have had to be supported by proof of discriminatory intent. For that purpose, the circumstantial evidence rules of *Village of Arlington Heights v. Metropolitan Housing Development Corporation*[185] are central. Those rules call for a searching inquiry of the entirety of the process leading to adoption of a law or other governmental action, emphasizing "the legislative or administrative history," including "the specific sequence of events leading up to the challenged decision," "departures from the normal procedural sequence," and "substantive departures."[186]

The Supreme Court said this examination is designed to see if race was "a motivating factor"[187] (not requiring it to be the only factor or even a primary or dominant factor).[188] Courts rightly give great deference to legislatures and other public officials, but "when there is a proof that a discriminatory purpose has been a motivating factor in the decision, this judicial deference is no longer justified."[189]

In law, something which is deemed "fruit of the poisonous tree" remains poisonous unless steps are taken to break the connection,[190] but in *Abbott v. Perez*, Texas seemed to find a shortcut around the rule.

---

[185] 429 U.S. 252 (1977). This case followed the decision that Equal Protection claims must rest on proof of discriminatory purpose. *See* Washington v. Davis, 426 U.S. 229 (1976). The purpose rule was applied to the Fifteenth Amendment and Section 2 of the Voting Rights Act, as it then read, in *Mobile v. Bolden*, 446 U.S. 55 (1980).

[186] 429 U.S. at 267–68.

[187] *Id.* at 266.

[188] *Id.* at 265.

[189] *Id.* at 265–66.

[190] One of the most famous instances in American law involves the Iran-Contra scandal, when prosecutions of high officials were ended because they depended on testimony that came from leads obtained in questioning conducted under a grant of immunity. United States v. Oliver North, 920 F.2d 240 (D.C. Cir. 1990).

That case involved a lower court finding that several districts in a 2013 state redistricting plan were discriminatory. The disputed districts originated in a 2011 state plan that never went into effect. The 2011 plan remained the same in a 2012 court-drawn plan (drawn after limited review to cure the most obvious problems in time for elections), and again remained the same in 2013 when the state incorporated the court's 2012 plan in a new state statute. The question was whether Texas had a discriminatory intent in adopting these districts in 2013.[191]

Texas's position was that its intent in 2013 was simply to follow the 2012 court plan as the most expeditious route to resolve all litigation.[192] A three-judge district court, however, made a finding that the legislature's failure to consider whether these districts were discriminatory was evidence of discriminatory intent, and it struck the districts down.[193]

In a 5-4 decision, the Supreme Court in *Abbott v. Perez* reversed the lower court's finding of discriminatory intent. "Intent" is a question of fact, so a trial court's finding is shielded from review unless there is "plain" or "clear" error—a high bar.[194] Here, however, the Supreme Court majority bypassed that barrier by saying the lower court erroneously put the burden of proof on Texas to defend itself rather than on the challengers to make their case.[195] Allocating the burden of proof is a question of law, subject to plenary review. Therefore, if the lower court did in fact misallocate the burden of proof, this would have canceled out the district court's finding of discriminatory purpose.

---

[191] Texas's 2011 plan was denied preclearance under the Voting Rights Act, Texas v. United States, 887 F.Supp.2d 133 (D.D.C. 2012), making it unusable, so the district court in Texas drew a plan for the 2012 elections, which, by Supreme Court order, was restricted to following the state's policy choices except where constitutional problems were obvious. Perry v. Perez, 565 U.S. 388 (2012). (In 2013, the Section 5 order denying preclearance of Texas's 2011 plan was vacated when the Supreme Court ended Section 5 preclearance, but events had moved on by then.)

[192] Abbott v. Perez, 138 S. Ct. 2305, 2327 (2018).

[193] Perez v. Abbott, 274 F. Supp. 3d 624, 648–52 (W.D. Tex. 2017) (concerning congressional districts); Perez v. Abbott, 267 F. Supp. 3d 750 (W.D. Tex. 2017) (concerning state legislative districts). The district court also held that several districts violated Section 2 of the Voting Rights Act.

[194] FED. R. CIV. P. 52.

[195] *Abbott*, 138 S. Ct. at 2324–26.

But the Supreme Court majority's conclusion was unfounded, as the lower court opinions clearly show.[196] The lower court repeatedly said the plaintiffs had the burden of proof and it carried that view out carefully by rejecting plaintiffs' claims as to several districts on the specific ground that plaintiffs failed to meet their burden of proof as to intent.[197]

The Supreme Court's sole basis for saying the lower court put the burden of proof on the State was the lower court's examination of the 2013 plan's legislative history.[198] The lower court had followed the *Arlington Heights* rule which calls for looking at the legislature's actions and inactions, but the Supreme Court carefully cropped the *Arlington Heights*'s language, reducing it to the following:

> The historical background of a legislative enactment is "one evidentiary source" relevant to the question of intent. *Arlington Heights v. Metropolitan Housing Development Corp.*, 429 U.S. 252, 267. But we have never suggested that past discrimination flips the evidentiary burden on its head.[199]

Left out was the crucial part of the *Arlington Heights* formula, the directive to look at "the specific sequence of events leading up to the challenged decision."[200] By thus cropping the *Arlington Heights* quotation, the Supreme Court misrepresented the governing law of the case. Under a fair reading, the lower court's consideration of what Texas did *not* do was a requirement of *Arlington Heights*, not a misallocation of the burden of proof.

That was not the end. When a trial court makes an error of law in dealing with evidence, the remedy is to send the case back for the

---

[196] For detailed discussion on this point, see Dan Tokaji, *Denying Systemic Equality: The Last Words of the Kennedy Court*, 13 Harv. L. & Pol'y Rev. 539, 555–56 & nn.103–15 (2019).

[197] An example of the lower court's discussion of burden of proof in the state legislative districting case: "The Court concludes that the Task Force has failed to carry its burden of showing discriminatory intent to minimize, cancel out, or dilute the Latino vote in HD90." *Perez*, 267 F. Supp. 3d at 794. For other statements by the district court about the plaintiffs' burden of proof in the legislative case, see also *id.* at 765.
There are more examples in the congressional districting case: "In such a claim, the plaintiff's evidentiary burden is 'to show, either through circumstantial evidence of a district's shape and demographics or more direct evidence going to legislative purpose, that race was the predominant factor motiving the legislature's decision to place a significant number of voters within or without a particular district.'" *Perez*, 274 F. Supp. 3d at 643 (quoting Ala. Legislative Black Caucus v. Alabama, 575 U.S. 254, 266 (2015)). For other statements by the district court about the plaintiffs' burden of proof in the congressional case, *see also id.* at 652, 669, 673, 675.

[198] *Abbott*, 138 S. Ct. at 2325–26.

[199] *Id.* at 2325.

[200] Vill. of Arlington Heights v. Metro. Hous. Dev. Corp., 429 U.S. 252, 267–68 (1977).

lower court to reconsider. Appellate courts are *not* supposed to take over the fact-finding function themselves, as the Supreme Court itself has made abundantly plain.[201] Here, however, the Supreme Court did exactly what it says not to do.[202] It simply proceeded (unhampered by the plain-error rule) to make its own findings of fact that predictably gave Texas's discriminatory districts a clean bill of health.[203]

* * *

The other Equal Protection case in this category was *Brnovich v. Democratic National Committee*.[204] Most of that case involved Section 2 of the Voting Rights Act and is discussed above.[205] Part V of the majority opinion, however, addressed an Equal Protection challenge to an Arizona state law limiting the categories of people eligible to bring a completed absentee ballot to the election office.[206] The district court found no racially discriminatory purpose[207] but was reversed for plain error by the court of appeals,[208] which was then reversed by the Supreme Court.

The key issue in this part of *Brnovich* was what significance attached to racist motives of a bill's originator if they were not shared by other legislators. A notoriously bigoted legislator introduced the bill with an inflammatory racist video and bogus statistics falsely claiming there were widespread Hispanic absentee ballot delivery abuses.[209] Aided by his efforts, the bill was enacted, with no indication that other legislators who voted for the bill did so out of bias.

---

[201] *See, e.g.*, Pullman-Standard v. Swint, 456 U.S. 273 (1982).

[202] Neither case cited by the majority supports fact-finding by an appellate court, including the Supreme Court. The cases cited were *Ricci v. DeStefano*, 557 U.S. 557, 585 (2009) and *McCleskey v. Zant*, 499 U.S. 467, 497 (1991). In both those cases, the Supreme Court *accepted* the trial court's findings of fact but ruled *as a matter of law* that those facts were insufficient to support the party's claim. That is completely different from what the majority did here, which was to weigh a multitude of testimony and exhibits and decide for itself that the evidence added up to a different answer than the trial court's answer.

[203] *Abbott*, 138 S. Ct. at 2327.

[204] 141 S. Ct. 2321, 2348–50 (2021).

[205] *See supra* Section III.A.2.

[206] The absentee ballot law was H.B. 2023, enacted by Arizona in 2016. Justice Kagan, who dissented on the Section 2 issue, did not address the Equal Protection issue. *See Brnovich*, 141 S. Ct. at 2366 n.20.

[207] Democratic Nat'l Comm. v. Reagan, 329 F. Supp. 3d 824 (D. Ariz. 2018).

[208] Democratic Nat'l Comm. v. Hobbs, 948 F.3d 989 (9th Cir. 2020) (en banc).

[209] *Brnovich*, 141 S. Ct. at 2349.

The court of appeals said there was evidence that, "convinced by the false and race-based allegations of fraud, they [the other legislators] were used to serve the discriminatory purposes of Senator Shooter, Republican Chair LaFaro, and their allies."[210] Because the district court failed to consider the facts in this light, the court of appeals reversed for plain error and found there was some evidence of a discriminatory purpose. This resulted in striking the law down because the state offered no countervailing evidence under the *Arlington Heights* framework. The court of appeals used the phrase "cat's paw" (an allusion to Aesop's well-known fable) in describing the possible relationship between Senator Shooter's discriminatory purpose and enlistment of other legislators.[211]

The Supreme Court, reversing, disposed of this issue in a single paragraph beginning with a supposed rule of law:

> The "cat's paw" theory has no application to legislative bodies. The theory rests on the agency relationship that exists between an employer and a supervisor, but the legislators who vote to adopt a bill are not the agents of the bill's sponsor or proponents.[212]

This is just nonsense. The "cat's paw" analogy can apply where an employer's liability depends on an agency relationship,[213] but "cat's paw" is a common expression reflecting that people often follow the lead of another person such as a colleague without sharing—and often without knowing—the colleague's aim. This can be equally so for legislators—from U.S. Senators to town council members—who must often do so to manage the volume of bills and other paperwork they must act on. Instead of the Court's would-be rule, *Arlington Heights* makes the entire legislative process relevant in the inquiry about purpose and possible race discrimination.[214]

The bottom line was that a lower court's finding that a state law was biased against non-White voters was thrust aside for the second time in three years, on the most dubious of grounds, by a Court that is otherwise allergic to the slightest sign that a decision has been infected by race.

---

[210] *Hobbs*, 948 F.3d at 1041.

[211] *Id.* at 1040–42.

[212] *Brnovich*, 141 S. Ct. at 2350.

[213] *E.g.*, Staub v. Proctor Hosp., 562 U.S. 411 (2011), which includes a fascinating discussion of the "cat's paw" theory by Justices Scalia and Alito.

[214] Rejecting the "cat's paw" theory here could suggest that other legislators must have been complicit in voting for a bill that was born out of racism and lies.

If the Supreme Court reverses the finding of racial purpose in the South Carolina gerrymandering case discussed in the previous Section, it will be the third successive reversal of a finding of fact of race discrimination against minority voters. It will show that white supremacy is safe in the hands of these Justices.

D. NEUTERING THE NATIONAL VOTER REGISTRATION ACT

In 1993, Congress enacted the National Voter Registration Act (NVRA, also known as the "Motor Voter law").[215] The Supreme Court's first response was promising. When Arizona sought to require proof of U.S. citizenship in its registration process, the Roberts Court rejected Arizona's bid as a violation of NVRA.[216]

Six years later, the Court's response was quite different in *Husted v. A. Philip Randolph Institute*, a test of the Act's provisions for "purging" registered voters who die or move out of the jurisdiction.[217] Ohio voters alleged that a state purging procedure was overbroad and therefore violated NVRA's requirement that a purging procedure be "reasonable." The Supreme Court rejected the claim, holding that the statutory word "reasonable" (which the Court called "this supposed 'reasonableness' requirement") means nothing at all.[218]

NVRA's prime purpose was to spur voter registration, but it also promoted accurate voter rolls by authorizing but regulating careful removal ("purging") of voters who were no longer eligible.[219] Purging is useful or necessary to keep voter rolls current, but it has often been intentionally abused.[220] Even used in good faith, it risks purging

---

[215] National Voter Registration Act of 1993 (NVRA), Pub. L. No. 103-31, 107 Stat. 77 (codified as amended in scattered sections of 52 U.S.C.).

[216] Arizona v. Inter Tribal Council of Ariz., Inc., 570 U.S. 1 (2013). An early encounter with another feature of the Arizona law gave rise to the so-called *Purcell* rule. In 2006, a lower court issued an order shortly before an election, blocking part of the Arizona law (requiring ID at the polls, but not necessarily with a photo). The Supreme Court stayed the injunction in *Purcell v. Gonzalez*, 549 U.S. 1 (2006). That case has been followed many times and stands for the proposition that election changes should not be mandated by federal courts in the period before an election. The rule was used extensively in advance of the 2020 presidential election. It has been criticized for being vague, especially because it is often used in cases on the so-called "shadow docket."

[217] 138 S. Ct. 1833 (2018).

[218] *Id.* at 1848 (referring to 52 U.S.C. § 20507(a)(4)).

[219] The Act's findings and purposes are stated at 52 U.S.C. § 20501(a) and (b).

[220] The Supreme Court was familiar with the abuse of purges. In the late 1950s, when the Washington Parish, Louisiana, registrar purged 85 percent of the African American registered

still-eligible voters. This is particularly true of "non-vote purge" laws—laws that purge voters who skip several years of elections. These laws assume such voters have likely moved or died, but they can disfranchise those who simply vote infrequently.

NVRA tried to steer a middle course, barring the too-easy use of non-vote purging but still allowing the fact of not voting to play a part in keeping registration rolls current. Congress started with an overall mandate in Section 8(a)(4) of the Act: "In the administration of voter registration for elections for federal office, . . . each State shall conduct a general program that makes a reasonable effort to remove the names of ineligible voters from the lists of eligible voters by reason of . . . death . . . or change in the residence . . . ."[221] Stripped to its operative words, the mandate to the states is to make a "reasonable effort"—to do what? "To remove the names of ineligible voters"—meaning voters who have in fact moved or died.

In addition to being "reasonable," NVRA includes a number of specific prohibitions and requirements.[222] The statute also contains detailed provisions for confirming whether a voter who is identified as possibly ineligible has in fact moved or died.[223]

Notably, in contrast to the detailed procedures regulating confirmation of possible "ineligibles," NVRA is open-ended about the process of identifying those who may have become ineligible. That open-endedness was a source of dispute in the case, specifically as it affected Ohio's Supplemental Process.

Ohio, like most states, uses a basic process that begins with information from Postal Service sources and then follows NVRA's confirmation procedures.[224] In addition, however, the Ohio Secretary

---

voters after challenges by the White Citizens' Council, the Supreme Court of that day made short work of this tactic. United States v. Thomas, 361 U.S. 950 (1960); United States v. Thomas, 362 U.S. 58 (1960).

[221] 52 U.S.C. § 20507(a)(4). The words "change in the residence" and the word "move" as used in this Article, refer only to voters who move outside their voting registrar's jurisdiction (in Ohio, their county) since the Act provides that voters who move within their voting jurisdiction shall simply have their registration records changed. 52 U.S.C. § 20507(c)(1)(B)(i).

[222] A state purging program must be uniform, nondiscriminatory, and comply with the Voting Rights Act. 52 U.S.C. § 20507(b)(1). No voter may be removed for failure to vote. *Id.* § 20507(b)(2). The Help America Vote Act repeated this language, adding the word "solely." 52 U.S.C. § 21083(a)(4)(A).

[223] 52 U.S.C. § 20507(c) (titled "Voter removal programs"); 52 U.S.C. § 20507(d) (titled "Removal of names from voting rolls").

[224] OHIO REV. CODE ANN. § 3503.21(B) (2016).

of State has adopted a second procedure called the "Supplemental Process."[225] The question before the Supreme Court was whether the Supplemental Process complied with NVRA.

The Supplemental Process, used every year, identifies every Ohio registered voter who did not vote that year or the previous year.[226] They are sent a notice and then purged if they do not respond to the notice and fail to vote within the next four years. Because voting rates are so low in this country, including Ohio,[227] the Supplemental Process sweeps in many voters who have not moved or died. There is no systematic data, but available facts in this case suggest that a huge majority of those identified by the Supplemental Process—likely as many as three-quarters of them—are "false positives" (i.e., still-eligible voters).[228] With so many "false positives" at the start, the Supplemental Process inevitably ends up purging many still-eligible voters. More than 7000 such Ohioans came forward in 2016 and were allowed to vote that year by an order in the then-pending litigation.[229]

Most of the Supreme Court's debate about the Supplemental Process focused on NVRA's detailed requirements for confirming

---

[225] The version involved in this litigation was cited as "Secretary of State Directive 2015-09." *See* Ohio A. Phillip Randolph Inst. v. Husted, No. 2:16-CV-303, 2016 WL 3542450, at *1 (S.D. Ohio June 29, 2016).

[226] Those who engage in other "voter activity," such as signing a petition, are also exempt from the Supplementary Process. Husted v. A. Philip Randolph Institute, 138 S. Ct. 1833, 1840–41 (2018). The Supplemental Process is used every year, so someone who votes or engages in other "voter activity" in one year can still be subjected to the Supplemental Process two years later.

[227] For example, the Record before the Supreme Court showed that 51% of Ohio registered voters failed to vote in 2010, and 59% did not vote in 2014. *Voter Turnout in General Elections*, OHIO SEC'Y OF STATE, https://www.ohiosos.gov/elections/election-results-and-data/historical-election-comparisons/voter-turnout-in-general-elections.

[228] The Supreme Court was provided information for Cuyahoga County (Cleveland), Ohio's largest county. The Supplemental Process targeted 150,182 registered voters in that county who had no voter activity in 2009–2010 (the years involved in the Supreme Court), but only 40,627 (27%) were eventually removed. Declaration of Cameron Bell, ¶¶ 8–10, *Ohio A. Phillip Randolph Inst.*, No. 2:16-CV-303, 2018 WL 4956609 (S.D. Ohio Oct. 12, 2018) (No. 9-1). The number of false positives is in fact higher than 73% since even some of those removed were still-eligible voters. Declaration of Cameron Bell at 8-10, (April 7, 2016), *Ohio A. Phillip Randolph Inst.*, No. 2:16-CV-303, 2018 WL 4956609, (S.D. Ohio Oct. 12, 2018) (No. 9-1).

[229] The provisional ballots were allowed in that year by order in the then-pending litigation and totaled 7,515. Brief for the Petitioner at 14, *Husted*, 138 S. Ct. 1833 (2018) (No. 16-980), 2017 WL 3412011.

whether a voter has in fact moved or died, which the majority (over vigorous dissents) held Ohio had satisfied.[230]

But the most arresting feature of the majority opinion was its dismissal, with no consideration whatever, of the Supplemental Process's gross overreach in targeting large numbers of still-eligible voters just for not voting in two years. Justice Alito's response was that this was simply of no interest to the Court: "What matters for present purposes is not whether the Ohio legislature overestimated.... For us, all that matters is that no provision of the NVRA prohibits that judgment."[231] Then, referring to specific prohibitions contained in the Act, he said that as long as a plan was uniform, nondiscriminatory and complied with the Voting Rights Act, "States can use whatever plan they think best."[232]

That statement gave no consideration to NVRA's word "reasonable." If the voters removed by Ohio's program include very large numbers of still-eligible voters, as was likely the case, how can that be a "reasonable effort" to remove the names of "ineligible voters," as required by Section 8(a)(4)?

The majority opinion dealt with the inconvenient word "reasonable" by reading the word out of the statute. Pointing to the Act's specific limitations (any plan must be uniform, nondiscriminatory, and in compliance with the Voting Rights Act), the Court said the word "reasonable" meant nothing more.[233] Nothing.

The Court said it should not be deciding what is "reasonable," but that is what Congress directed. And reasonability is not an unusual standard. The U.S. Code is honeycombed with laws using the word "reasonable" that the Supreme Court has been called on to interpret[234]—not to mention the Fourth Amendment (i.e., "unreasonable searches or seizures").

It is true that voters purged by the Supplemental Process could have avoided their fate—even without voting—by simply responding

---

[230] For example, a major issue involved NVRA's failure-to-vote clause. The dissent argued that the Supplemental Process violated that clause because all the information on which the purge was based was the failure to vote—both initially and in the confirmation period. *Husted*, 138 S. Ct. at 1851–53. The majority countered, however, that the voter's failure to respond to the notice was the decisive added fact. *Id.* at 1842–45.

[231] *Id.* at 1847.

[232] *Id.*

[233] *Id.* at 1848.

[234] *E.g.*, Farrar v. Hobby, 506 U.S. 103 (1992).

to the notice they received, but voter suppression laws thrive on imposing burdens that will disfranchise voters, even if the burden is one that, as one often hears, "anyone can meet if they really want to."[235]

It is also true that the Ohio Supplemental Process might have been upheld as "reasonable" if it had been subjected to real judicial review, but the Supreme Court rejected that course and thereby defeated Congress's purpose.

III. Does It Matter?

If, indeed, the Supreme Court is increasingly freeing elected representatives from the people, does it matter? In *Dobbs v. Jackson Women's Health Organization*,[236] the case that began this Article, the Supreme Court sent the most dramatic issue of our time back to "the people and their elected representatives." What can we learn from events since then?

The decision in *Roe v. Wade*[237] froze abortion laws where they were, but in recent years, legislatures in many states, responding or claiming to respond to the people's will, enacted anti-abortion laws that were aggressively contrary to *Roe v. Wade*. Some of these were "trigger" laws that would go into effect automatically if the Supreme Court overturned *Roe*,[238] while other states jumped the gun to outlaw almost all abortions without waiting for *Roe*'s demise.[239]

These states' impatient actions were seemingly vindicated by the Supreme Court's decisions in its 2021–2022 Term, first, signaling in a Texas case that a majority of the Justices had already decided (perhaps long ago) to overrule *Roe*,[240] and then following through in

---

[235] The Record showed that in 2012 Ohio sent 1.5 million warning postcards in the Supplemental Process and 1.2 million were not returned. *Husted*, 138 S. Ct. at 1856 (Breyer, J., dissenting). Even allowing for people who had in fact died or moved, that still left a huge number of recipients who did not send the cards back.

[236] 597 U.S. 215 (2022).

[237] 410 U.S. 113 (1973).

[238] Juliana Kim, *3 More States Are Poised to Enact Abortion Trigger Bans This Week*, Nat'l Pub. Radio (Aug. 22, 2022), www.npr.org/2022/08/22/1118635642/abortion-trigger-ban-tennessee-idaho-texas.

[239] *Tracking Abortion Bans Across the Country*, N.Y. Times, https://www.nytimes.com/interactive/2022/us/abortion-laws-roe-v-wade.html.

[240] Whole Woman's Health v. Jackson, 595 U.S. 30 (2021). The Texas law, a "fetal-heartbeat" law, was plainly unconstitutional under *Roe v. Wade*.

Dobbs. Other states got ready to join the Supreme Court's anti-abortion bandwagon. Then came Kansas.

Kansas looked like a classic anti-abortion state, with the legislature and populace seemingly aligned. By happenstance, when *Dobbs* was announced, Kansas already had an abortion referendum scheduled for August 2022, just two months away. The referendum was designed to overturn a 2019 Kansas Supreme Court decision that found a right to abortion in the state constitution.[241] The ballot question was on a proposed amendment that would say the Kansas constitution "does not create or secure a right to abortion."[242]

The referendum turned out to be an icy bath for abortion opponents. The anti-abortion amendment was defeated by 180,000 votes, with a margin of 59% to 41%,[243] more than flipping the Republican margin of 56% to 42% in the 2020 presidential election.[244]

This outcome was followed by five other state abortion referendums on Election Day, November 8, 2022, all five of which voted for a right to abortion or against an anti-abortion clause.[245] That was no surprise in three of the states (i.e., California, Michigan and Vermont), but it was quite a shocker in the other two states (i.e., Kentucky and Montana). These two states, even more heavily Republican than Kansas, both rejected anti-abortion clauses by closer but still decisive five-point margins.[246]

One might have thought this small but decisive wave would have some impact on the "elected representatives," and so it did—but it was hardly a lesson in representative democracy. Instead, the elected representatives seem to have learned to make sure those pesky "people" don't get in the elected representatives' way.

---

[241] Hodes & Nauser v. Schmidt, 430 P.3d 461 (Kan. 2019).

[242] H.C.R. No. 5003, 89th Leg., Reg. Sess. (Kan. 2021).

[243] *Kansas Abortion Amendment Election Results*, N.Y. TIMES (Sept. 28, 2022), https://www.nytimes.com/interactive/2022/08/02/us/elections/results-kansas-abortion-amendment.html.

[244] *See Federal Elections 2020: Election Results for the U.S. President, the U.S. Senate and the U.S. House of Representatives*, FED. ELECTION COMM'N 7 (Oct. 2022), https://www.fec.gov/resources/cms-content/documents/federalelections2020.pdf.

[245] Tiffany Cusaac-Smith, *Abortion Rights Were on the Ballot in 5 States: Here's What Voters Decided*, USA TODAY (Nov. 9, 2022), https://www.usatoday.com/story/news/nation/2022/11/09/abortion-election-results-kentucky-california-michigan-montana-vermont/8302538001.

[246] *Kentucky Voters Reject Constitutional Amendment on Abortion*, PBS (Nov. 9, 2022), www.pbs.org/newshour/politics/kentucky-voters-reject-constitutional-amendment-on-abortion.

In North Carolina, the elected representatives learned that if they gerrymandered their own elections grotesquely enough, they could ignore any contrary views. With a 60% Republican majority in each house of the legislature, that was just enough to override the Governor's veto of a stringent anti-abortion bill.[247]

In South Carolina, one of two states where the legislature selects the judges, when the state supreme court held that the state constitution's "right of privacy" clause protected abortion rights, the General Assembly simply remade the state supreme court. Within eight months, the remade court issued a new decision rejecting abortion rights.[248] The Speaker of the House, asked about the will of the people, said the strong legislative vote "was a reflection of the will of the people."[249] When all five female Senators (three Republicans and two Democrats) wanted to test that view by a voters' referendum, they got nowhere, not surprising in light of widespread speculation that a stringent abortion ban would lose at the polls.[250]

But Ohio displayed the most brazen reaction by "elected representatives." Ohio's voters collected enough petition signatures to "initiate" a proposed new clause protecting abortion rights, which would become part of the state constitution if approved by a 50% vote at the November 2023 elections. Suddenly, after the new question had already qualified for the ballot, Ohio's elected representatives decided to put an extra roadblock in the people's way—a new rule raising the bar for constitutional amendments to *sixty percent* of the vote.

---

[247] Julia Harte, *North Carolina Legislature Overrides Veto of 12-Week Abortion Ban, Making It Law*, REUTERS (May 16, 2023), https://www.reuters.com/world/us/north-carolina-lawmakers-vote-overriding-veto-12-week-abortion-ban-2023-05-16.

[248] Planned Parenthood S. Atl. v. State, 882 S.E.2d 70 (S.C. 2023) (striking down 2021 anti-abortion law); Planned Parenthood S. Atl. v. State, 892 S.E.2d 121 (S.C. 2023) (upholding the 2023 anti-abortion law). The first decision was by a 3-2 vote. When the court's lone female justice (who voted to strike the law down) reached retirement age soon after the first decision, her male replacement voted to uphold the second law. One other justice also changed positions.

[249] Seanna Adcox, *SC High Court Temporarily Blocks "Fetal Heartbeat" Law As Lawmakers Consider Abortion Ban*, POST & COURIER (Aug. 18, 2022), https://www.postandcourier.com/columbia/sc-high-court-temporarily-halts-fetal-heartbeat-law-as-legislators-consider-abortion-ban/article_42a76b18-1e62-11ed-a390-1315b4126a25.html.

[250] The state judicial commission recommended three appellate judges, two women and one man, for the state supreme court vacancy, but both women judges suddenly and silently withdrew as soon as legislators began consideration, resulting in selection of the male nominee. *See* Jennifer Berry Hawes, *How South Carolina Ended Up with an All-Male Supreme Court*, PROPUBLICA (Apr. 28, 2023), https://www.propublica.org/article/how-south-carolina-ended-up-with-all-male-supreme-court.

Unluckily for the elected representatives, their 60% proposal was itself a state constitutional amendment so it still needed a vote of the people, but only a 50% vote at that. The legislature set this first election for mid-summer in the obvious hope that it could slip by with little notice. The hope for stealth failed, and in a high-turnout election, the 60% proposal lost by 400,000 votes.[251]

That still left the November referendum on the abortion proposal itself. On Election Day, November 7, 2023, the people put abortion rights into the Ohio constitution by more than a half million votes. The margin was 57%-43%, which means the abortion rights measure would have failed if the legislative "60% Hail Mary" had succeeded.[252]

The elected representatives have other ways to foil the people. When petitions were circulated in Missouri for an abortion rights referendum, the elected Secretary of State, tasked by statute with supervising the election, prepared ballot language that began: "Do you want the Missouri constitution to allow for dangerous, unregulated, and unrestricted abortions from conception to live birth. . . ." Missouri courts promptly shot the language down.[253]

Thus, with almost two years of learning since the end of *Roe v. Wade*, the people's elected representatives have learned more and more to run away from the people. Do the people have a remedy? One frustrated Tennessee lawmaker said, "What needs to happen is for some people to lose elections."[254]

If many elected representatives respond mainly to the fear of becoming ex-representatives, then, yes, voting laws matter. And yes, what the Supreme Court does and doesn't do about the right to vote matters.

CONCLUSION

Just over fifty years ago, I cast my first vote for President at the ripe old age of thirty-four, after being disqualified in four previous

---

[251] *Voters in Ohio Reject GOP-Backed Proposal That Would Have Made It Tougher to Protect Abortion Rights*, AP NEWS (Aug. 9, 2023), https://apnews.com/article/ohio-abortion-rights-constitutional-amendment-special-election-227cde039f8d51723612878525164f1a.

[252] *Ohio Voters Enshrine Abortion Access Constitution in Latest Statewide Win for Reproductive Rights*, AP NEWS (Nov. 7, 2023), https://apnews.com/article/ohio-abortion-amendment-election-2023-fe3e06747b616507d8ca21ea26485270.

[253] Fitz-James v. Ashcroft, 678 S.W.3d 194 (Mo. Ct. App. 2023).

[254] Kate Zernike, *Why Democracy Hasn't Settled the Abortion Question*, N.Y. TIMES (Dec. 17, 2023), https://www.nytimes.com/2023/12/17/us/where-will-abortion-rights-land.html.

elections by restrictions that no longer exist—the age twenty-one minimum, one-year residence requirements, and the like. If the current Supreme Court had been in charge, I fear those restrictions would still prevail.[255]

My close friend and classmate John Hart Ely wrote a great book called *Democracy and Distrust*.[256] It had a simple but overpowering message: the Supreme Court's primary responsibility is protecting our democracy, or, as John also put it, keeping the channels of the political process clear. That may sound strange when the Court is the unrepresentative branch of the national government, but the Court referees the ground rules for the representative branches, including the rules for choosing the members of those branches, federal and state.

I wish our Supreme Court Justices might read the book and heed the message. If the Court is telling the people to look to the political process, not the courts, it has a correlative obligation to keep the channels of the political process clear. But when the Court puts money in charge of elections, allows partisans free rein to shape representation at will, when it approves voter-suppression laws while scoffing at voter-protective laws, and when it destroys the most effective voting-rights law in American history and repeatedly shows that its supposed opposition to race discrimination is a one-way, one-race street, it turns the political process into a wasteland.

Our democracy is far more fragile than we might have imagined. Millions of our people believe, against all proof,[257] that the 2020 presidential election was stolen. Thousands of them stormed the Capitol in that belief. Countless public officials who know better are

---

[255] Even the age twenty-one rule would likely still prevail. The Twenty-Sixth Amendment was quickly ratified to prevent chaos after the Supreme Court held Congress's eighteen-year-old voting-age minimum was constitutional for federal elections, but not state elections. Oregon v. Mitchell, 400 U.S. 112, 117–18 (1970) (construing the Voting Rights Act amendments of 1970). Today's Court would most likely have struck the eighteen-year-old voting law down for both state and federal elections—so, no conflict, no fear of chaos, and probably no Twenty-Sixth Amendment.

[256] JOHN ELY, DEMOCRACY AND DISTRUST: A THEORY OF JUDICIAL REVIEW 78 (1980).

[257] SENATOR JOHN DANFORTH ET AL., LOST, NOT STOLEN: THE CONSERVATIVE CASE THAT TRUMP LOST AND BIDEN WON THE 2020 PRESIDENTIAL ELECTION (2022), https://lostnotstolen.org/wp-content/uploads/2022/07/Lost-Not-Stolen-The-Conservative-Case-that-Trump-Lost-and-Biden-Won-the-2020-Presidential-Election-July-2022.pdf. The Report's other authors are prominent Republicans (longtime Republican National Committee counsel Ben Ginsberg, former Solicitor General Ted Olson, former Senator Gordon Smith, and congressional leadership Chief of Staff David Hoppe), as well as Republican-appointed former appellate judges (Michael McConnell, J. Michael Luttig, and Thomas Griffith).

feeding that fantasy in the apparent hope of winning elections by means fair or foul.

Nations are not guaranteed to live forever. Our nation may not dissolve or disappear, but autocracy may not be far away, along with its cousin kakistocracy.

This may all sound hyperbolic, even hysterical, but did we ever expect to see a band of armed men come within an ace of overthrowing a presidential election? Or see sworn public officials—including some who ran for their lives that day—seemingly pretend it never happened? Nearly a century ago, during the Great Depression of the 1930s, the Supreme Court was perceived as a stumbling block, even a threat to the Nation's survival. During that period, the Justice Roberts of that day (Justice Owen J. Roberts) came to perceive that the Court, with his participation, was overstepping its role and undermining the Constitution.[258] He changed, and his change helped save the Supreme Court and the Nation. Justice Willis Van Devanter's retirement soon thereafter sealed the change.

What will it take to secure and protect the right to vote today?

---

[258] OWEN J. ROBERTS, THE COURT AND THE CONSTITUTION 61–62 (1951).